Learn Visual Basic®

A Computer Programming Tutorial

Visual Studio 2019 Edition

16th Edition

By
Philip Conrod & Lou Tylee

©2019 Kidware Software LLC
PO Box 701
Maple Valley, WA 98038
http://www.kidwaresoftware.com

Customer Comments For Previous Editions of This Tutorial

"I just want to thank you for the many tutorials that I have ordered from your company over the past decade. Your tutorials have been instrumental in allowing me, a secondary school teacher in Ontario, to learn what I need to know in order to conduct my own High School Computer Science Classes in Visual Basic and Visual C#. I thank you, and urge you to keep up the excellent work. It has been instrumental in helping me learn and grow as a teacher." - Alan Payne, TA, Blakelock High School, Oakville, ON

"I really enjoyed the Learn Visual Basic tutorial, especially the examples it provided."
- Bruce Chin, Amateur Developer, Toronto, Ontario

"I liked the Learn Visual Basic Tutorial because of the pacing. The tutorial is light and succinct and just enough to get one going with just the right amount of information to start off with." - Mike Martin, Teacher, Queensland, Australia

"This course is a blessing. I have learned more in these lessons than I did taking VB two years ago in college for my information science degree." - CC, New York, New York.

"I can't wait to learn all of this and start making my own applications, thank you for making such a wonderful product!" - LA, Rego Park, New York.

"Thank you for a truly great book for someone who had no prior knowledge of programming." - JJ, Inverness, Florida.

"I have read the first chapters am very impressed with the very well written notes with their clear, precise, easy-to-follow style." - CP, San Francisco, California.

"This tutorial is amazing. I have spent a lot of money on books and software but for some reason found them difficult to 'get into.' Not so with your tutorial!" - BW, London, England.

"I just want to tell you that your product is excellent. I have had more fun applying your examples and building on to them through exploration than any book could ever provide - your chapters and examples help drive the information home and make programming fun." - BC, Houston, Texas.

"It is obvious you have a teaching background. Your approach to explaining material is excellent. Your tutorial has been met with great enthusiasm at my company." - BG, Cincinnati, Ohio.

"The lessons are great!!" - MT, Johannesburg, South Africa.

"Your lessons are very specific with how to's ... I have spent over $250 on books and never found the practicality and simplicity of your explanations." - GA, Seattle, Washington.

"I appreciate your to the point approach of learning. Other authors are seemingly more concerned about showing their intelligence than they are about teaching. You've accomplished both." - GW, Cincinnati, Ohio.

"I appreciate the wealth of examples. Many times, it's very difficult to figure out how to do the simplest of tasks from some programming books. " - MT, San Diego, California.

"I learned programming with your Visual Basic series. Now, I'm working through LEARN VISUAL BASIC .NET. It is a great resource - thanks." - MH, Seattle, Washington.

"Your new tutorial is amazing. I didn't think you could improve upon your LEARN VISUAL BASIC series, but you did!" - TT, Garfield, Washington.

"I found your course materials to be very useful as it contains a lot of practical examples." -SS, New Delhi, India.

"Just working through LEARN VISUAL BASIC 6, I am currently doing a software development course and am finding it more helpful than the designated text." -KB, Sydney, Australia.

"I really love these courses. They keep me going when I'm housebound." -CO, London, England.

"I think your LEARN VISUAL BASIC 6 course is extremely well-written and laid out and would have gladly paid more than $20." - AC, Norristown, Pennsylvania.

"I have published several 'textbooks' teaching various computer skills, spent 10 years as a computer instructor at the college level, and I want to commend you on the quality of these materials." - SM, Reno, Nevada.

"I have both your VB6 and VB6 database courses and they have both been excellent tools for learning." - GO, Otaki, New Zealand.

"Thanks again for the Learn Visual Basic manual. I find it quite easy to use." - HT, Otjowarongo, Namibia.

"Your notes and lessons are more meaningful than the professional looking books by Microsoft experts." - BT, Gladstone, Missouri.

"The lessons are great!!" - MT, Johannesburg, South Africa.

"I found your course package on the internet. It is the best I ever found. " - WV, Belgium.

"Your product is superior - very excellent." - MA, Greenacres, Washington.

"Your writing in the notes has been a revelation to me. I've started to get it in a way that had eluded me in the past. " - MBW, Manchester, New Hampshire.

"The first three classes taught me more about Visual Basic than any book I have read! " - RF, Orange, New South Wales, Australia.

"I love the way this course is presented. Thanks for free access to the first few chapters - I have been stung by too many inferior courses. " - DW, Santa Margarita, California.

"Your notes contain ALL the key information I am looking for. They explain very clearly how to accomplish tasks. I took VB in college and understand more from your lessons. " - SB, Niagara Falls, Ontario, Canada.

"These notes are done really well. They are better than any of those books I spent $50 for. " - RS, Greeley, Colorado.

"I found LEARN VISUAL BASIC to be an excellent course. It's well written and easy to follow. " - MS, West Midlands, United Kingdom.

"I really appreciate the quality of this tutorial. Great job! " - AB, Hope Mills, North Carolina.

"Your courseware is well-designed and helpful. " - DA, Calcutta, India.

"Of the hundreds of Visual Basic books out there, this is the best! " - DF, Fort Worth, Texas.

"Having spent much on large Visual Basic textbooks, I found your training material to be much more user friendly and, above all, practical for application developers. " - PN, Leeds, England.

"My students declared to be the best VB tutorial they've found on the Internet. " - GF, Langley, British Columbia, Canada.

"I find LEARN VISUAL BASIC very useful for people like me who want to learn at their own pace. Thank you for all your hard work!! " - SD, Addis Ababa, Ethiopia.

"Congratulations on assembling such an excellent course. I will be recommending it to anyone who asks me about Visual Basic tutorials." - AO, Slough, Berkshire, United Kingdom.

"I've got four other books on Visual Basic, but your course is the BEST! " - SV, Scottsdale, Arizona.

"Congratulations on a wonderful self-tutoring program. " - RS, South Africa.

"I find the course of great help in my new career. " - RS, Milton Keynes, England.

"I have found your Visual Basic course to be excellent and recommend it highly. " - AS, Guthrie, Oklahoma.

"For someone who does not know programming, I am really delighted and thrilled that the notes are very easy to follow." - RC, Singapore.

"The lessons were great. Best I've seen or used." - JL, Theodore, Alabama.

"The course is well done and covers many aspects which are not easily found in other Visual Basic books." - JF, Gatineau, Quebec, Canada.

"I want to commend you for your very nice course." - CB, Bromma, Sweden.

"Just what I have been looking for. Excellently written." - VB, Chesley, Ontario, Canada.

"I'm impressed and you can quote me. I'd like to use this material at my school." - PS, Whangarei, New Zealand.

"The contents of your package are good and understandable. Congratulations from an education major." - SD, Las Vegas, Nevada.

"I am very impressed at the quality of your product." - CS, London, England.

"I like the way you wrote these lessons very much." - DP, Amsterdam, Holland.

About The Authors

Philip Conrod has authored, co-authored and edited over two dozen computer programming books over the past thirty years. Philip holds a bachelor's degree in Computer Information Systems and a Master's certificate in the Essentials of Business Development from Regis University. Philip has served in various Information Technology leadership roles in companies like Sundstrand Aerospace, Safeco Insurance, FamilyLife, Kenworth Truck Company, and PACCAR. Philip last served as the Chief Information Officer (CIO) at Darigold for over a decade before returning to teaching and writing full-time. Today, Philip serves as the President & Publisher of Kidware Software LLC which is based in Maple Valley, Washington.

Lou Tylee holds BS and MS degrees in Mechanical Engineering and a PhD in Electrical Engineering. Lou has been programming computers since 1969 when he took his first Fortran course in college. He has written software to control suspensions for high speed ground vehicles, monitor nuclear power plants, lower noise levels in commercial jetliners, compute takeoff speeds for jetliners, locate and identify air and ground traffic and to let kids count bunnies, learn how to spell and do math problems. He has written several on-line texts teaching Visual Basic, Visual C# and Java to thousands of people. He taught computer programming courses for over 15 years at the University of Washington and

currently teaches math and engineering courses at the Oregon Institute of Technology. Lou also works as a research engineer at a major Seattle aerospace firm. He is the proud father of five children, has six grandchildren and is married to an amazing woman. Lou and his family live in Seattle, Washington.

Acknowledgements

I want to thank my three wonderful daughters - Stephanie, Jessica and Chloe, who helped with various aspects of the book publishing process including software testing, book editing, creative design and many other more tedious tasks like finding errors and typos. I could not have accomplished this without all your hard work, love and support.

I also want to thank my multi-talented co-author, Lou Tylee, for doing all the real hard work necessary to develop, test, debug, and keep current all the 'beginner-friendly' applications, games and base tutorial text found in this book. Lou has tirelessly poured his heart and soul into so many previous versions of this tutorial and there are so many beginners who have benefited from his work over the years. Lou is by far one of the best application developers and tutorial writers I have ever worked with.   Thank you, Lou, for collaborating with me on this book project.

Last, but definitely not least, I want to thank my best friend Jesus, who has always been there by my side giving me wisdom and guidance. Without you, this book would have never been printed and published.

Contents

1. Introduction to the Visual Basic Environment

2. The Visual Basic Language

3. Object-Oriented Programming (OOP)

4. Exploring the Visual Basic Toolbox

5. More Exploration of the Visual Basic Toolbox

6. Windows Application Design and Distribution

7. Sequential Files, Error-Handling and Debugging

8. Graphics Techniques with Visual Basic

9. More Graphics Methods and Multimedia Effects

10. Other Windows Application Topics

11. Visual Basic Database and Web Applications

Course Description

Learn Visual Basic is an 11-week, self-paced overview of the Visual Basic programming environment. Upon completion of the course, you will:

1. Understand the benefits of using Microsoft Visual Basic as an object-oriented Windows application development tool.
2. Understand the Visual Basic event-driven programming concepts, terminology, and available controls.
3. Learn the fundamentals of designing, implementing, and distributing a wide variety of Visual Basic Windows applications.

Learn Visual Basic is presented using a combination of course notes (written in Microsoft Word format) and over 100 Visual Basic examples and applications.

Course Prerequisites

To grasp the concepts presented in **Learn Visual Basic**, you should possess a working knowledge of the Windows operating system. You should know how to use Windows Explorer to locate, copy, move and delete files. You should be familiar with the simple tasks of using menus, toolbars, resizing windows, and moving windows around.

You should have had some exposure to programming concepts. If you have never programmed a computer before, you'll have to put in a little more effort - perhaps, find a book in your local library on programming using Visual Basic, QBasic or some other dialect of the BASIC computer language. You might also consider our companion course, **Beginning Visual Basic** , which is aimed at the person who has never programmed before.

Finally, and most obvious, you need to have Microsoft Visual Basic Community Edition (part of Visual Studio Community Edition). This is a free product that can be downloaded from Microsoft.

System Requirements

Visual Studio 2019 will install and run on the following operating systems:
• Windows 10 version 1507 or higher: Home, Professional, Education, and Enterprise (LTSB is not supported)
• Windows Server 2016: Standard and Datacenter
• Windows 8.1 (with Update 2919355): Basic, Professional, and Enterprise
• Windows Server 2012 R2 (with Update 2919355): Essentials, Standard, Datacenter
• Windows 7 SP1 (with latest Windows Updates): Home Premium, Professional, Enterprise, Ultimate
• 1.8 GHz or faster processor. Dual-core or better recommended
• 2 GB of RAM; 4 GB of RAM recommended (2.5 GB minimum if running on a virtual machine)
• Hard disk space: 1GB to 40GB, depending on features installed
• Video card that supports a minimum display resolution of 720p (1280 by 720); Visual Studio will work best at a resolution of WXGA (1366 by 768) or higher

Installing and Using the Downloadable Solution Files

If you purchased this directly from our website you received an email with a special and individualized internet download link where you could download the compressed Program Solution Files.   If you purchased this book through a 3rd Party Book Store like Amazon.com, the solutions files for this tutorial are included in a compressed ZIP file that is available for download directly from our website at:

http://www.kidwaresoftware.com/lvb2019-registration.html

Complete the online web form at the webpage above with your name, shipping address, email address, the exact title of this book, date of purchase, online or physical store name, and your order confirmation number from that store. After we receive all this information we will email you a download link for the Source Code Solution Files associated with this book.

Warning: If you purchased this book "used" or "second hand" you are not licensed or entitled to download the Program Solution Files. However, you can purchase the Digital Download Version of this book at a discounted price which allows you access to the digital source code solutions files required for completing this tutorial.

Using Learn Visual Basic

The source code and multimedia files for **Learn Visual Basic** are included in one or more ZIP file(s). Use your favorite 'unzipping' application to write all files to your computer.   The course is included in the folder entitled **LearnVB**. This folder contains two other folders: **VB Notes** and **VB Code**. There's a chance when you copy the files to your computer, they will be written as '**Read-Only.**' To correct this (in **Windows Explorer** or **My Computer**), right-click the **LearnVB** folder and remove the check next to **Read only**. Make sure to choose the option to apply this change to all sub-folders and files.

The **VB Code** folder includes all applications developed during the course. The applications are further divided into **Class** folders. Each class folder contains the Visual Basic project folders. As an example, to open the Visual Basic project named Example 1-1 discussed in Class 1, you would go to this directory:

C:\LearnVB\VB Code\Class 1\Example 1-1\

How to Take the Course

Learn Visual Basic is a self-paced course. The suggested approach is to do one class a week for eleven weeks. Each week's class should require about 4 to 10 hours of your time to grasp the concepts completely. Prior to doing a particular week's work, open the class notes file for that week and print it out. Then, work through the notes at your own pace. Try to do each example as they are encountered in the notes. If you need any help, all solved examples are included in the **VB Code** folder.

After completing each week's notes, practice problems and homework exercise (sometimes, two) is given; covering many of the topics taught that in that class. Like the examples, try to work through the practice problems and homework exercise, or some variation thereof, on your own. Refer to the completed exercise in the **VB Code** folder, if necessary. This is where you will learn to be a Visual Basic programmer. You only learn how to build applications and write code by doing lots of it. The problems and exercises give you that opportunity. And, you learn coding by seeing lots of code. Programmers learn to program by seeing how other people do things. Feel free to 'borrow' code from the examples that you can adapt to your needs. I think you see my philosophy here. I don't think you can teach programming. I do, however, think you can teach people how to become programmers. This course includes numerous examples, problems, and exercises to help you toward that goal. We show you how to do lots of different things in the code examples. You will learn from the examples!

A Note on Visual Basic Naming Conventions

Controls

The accepted standard for naming controls is to assign a three letter (lower case) prefix (identifying the type of control) followed by a descriptive name you assign. Some of the prefixes are:

Control	Prefix	Example
Form	frm	frmWatch
Button	btn	btnExit, btnStart
Label	lbl	lblStart, lblEnd
Text Box	txt	txtTime, txtName
Menu	mnu	mnuExit, mnuSave
Check Box	chk	chkChoice

Event Procedures

Once a control is named, the standard for naming an event procedure associated with a control is

Private Sub ControlName_Event (**Arguments**) **Handles** ControlName.Event
.
.
End Sub

So, for a button control name **btnExample**, the event procedure for the **Click** event would be named **btnExample_Click.** And, since the earliest days of Visual Studio, if you double-click on a button control named **btnExample**, the event procedure appearing in the code window was:

```
Private Sub btnExample_Click(sender As Object, e As
EventArgs) Handles btnExample.Click

End Sub
```

This has changed with Visual Studio 2019.

In Visual Studio 2019, if you double-click on a button control named **btnExample**, the event procedure appearing in the code window is:

```
Private Sub BtnExample_Click(sender As Object, e As
EventArgs) Handles btnExample.Click

End Sub
```

Note that the first letter of the control name is automatically capitalized. The folks at Microsoft have decided that the first letter of every procedure in Visual Basic should be upper case (and there doesn't appear to be any way to turn off this "feature"). This creates a mismatch between the assigned control name (**btnExample**) and the name used in the event procedure (**BtnExample**). For our Visual Basic tutorials, we needed to decide what to do about this new convention.

Our Naming Conventions

The mismatch between control name and event procedure name would quickly go away if we simply choose to apply a new control naming convention where the first letter of every control name is an upper case letter. We did not take this route - it would require a massive paradigm shift. And, it would require extensive rewriting of all legacy code written using the standard convention. We decided to continue use of the time-tested control naming convention, a three letter lower case prefix, followed by a describing name with mixed upper and lower case letters. This standard has been around forever and will probably remain so. With this decision, we had to choose what to do about event procedure names.

First, realize that the name of the event procedure associated with a control is completely arbitrary. You can give the procedure any name you want as long as it's properly connected to the correct event procedure using the Visual Studio properties window. So, we could continue to use our old standard of naming event procedures, starting with a lower case letter. For a button control named **btnExample**, the **Click** event procedure would be

```
Private Sub btnExample_Click(sender As Object, e As
EventArgs) Handles btnExample.Click

End Sub
```

Such a convention will work in Visual Studio 2019, but comes with problems.

The first problem in using the 'old standard' is that Visual Studio will flag each so named event procedure with an error message saying: 'Naming rule violation: These words must begin with upper case characters: btnExample_Click'. Again, the code will still work, but there will be all these annoying messages.

The second problem in using the 'old standard' in Visual Studio 2019 is that when building a project, if you double-click on a control to establish an event procedure, the first letter will be automatically capitalized. Then, you have to remember to change the case of that letter for every event procedure established. This would be a headache.

We have decided to live with this new naming convention where the first letter of every event procedure is capitalized, realizing there is a mismatch between the control names and associated event procedures. So, in our tutorials, when we refer to the **Click** event procedure for a control named **btnExample**, that procedure's name in code will be **BtnExample_Click**. We recognize this is a change for programmers, but hopefully is something you can get used to. In our experience, it just took a few examples for the new convention to seem 'normal'.

Foreword By David B. Taylor

Do you remember when you learned to ride a bike? The person holding you up let go and you were on your way. The exhilaration of that accomplishment, the freedom, and empowerment were indescribable and easily recalled to this day. Completing a computer program that you designed and built, either on your own or with a team, warrants the same degree of fulfilment and jubilation.
Computer programming has a lot of parts so the better the explanation the more likely you are to succeed.

As a programmer, a long-time college professor, and as the former head of the Computer, Engineering, and Business Department, I have reviewed countless programming books for most of the popular programming languages. "Learn Visual Basic" by Philip Conrod and Lou Tylee is my favorite.

The order in which the topics are presented is very easy for students to follow. The transitions from one topic to the next are so smooth it doesn't feel like steps but just a continuously smooth flow from start to finish.

Object-oriented programming (OOP) is often difficult to explain to new programmers and most books give it no consideration until the second half of the book. The authors have made OOP clear, logical, and astonishingly easy to understand and they have successfully presented it in the third chapter...it is absolute genius. Consequently, every topic after that is much clearer and relevant to students.

The examples in the book are interesting and easy to follow. I have worked through all of them line by line and found them easy to follow and replicate. Students quickly become frustrated with examples that contain errors so the fact that these work so well is critically important to the success of every student.

Topics included in "Learn Visual Basic" are date, time, and financial calculations which are lacking in most first year programming books. I really appreciate the chapters that include business graphics for pie and bar charts and general graphics applied to multimedia.

The authors use code to access databases instead of the Visual Studio wizards. This gives the students a much better understanding of how databases work and how to program their interactions. Consequently, that also makes the eventual use of the database wizards less of a mystery and gives the student far more confidence in their application.

The useful topics in the examples and the well written explanations make this my favorite book for learning Visual Basic programming so it is with absolute confidence that I recommend this book to you.

David B. Taylor, B.S.E.T., M.A.Ed., Ed.S.
Former Professor and Department Chair
Computer, Engineering, and Business
Seminole State College
Sanford, Florida

Foreword by Alan Payne

"These lessons are a highly organized and well-indexed set of lessons in the Visual Basic programming environment. They are written for the initiated programmer - the college-prep or university student seeking to advance their Computer Science repertoire. The applications are practical, but the learning has far-reaching benefits in the student's Computer Science career. Every student at the college-prep age should be doing these programming tutorials in their summers off before attending a college or university.

While full solutions are provided, the projects are presented in an easy-to-follow set of lessons explaining the rational for the solution - the form layout, coding design and conventions, and specific code related to the problem. The learner may follow the tutorials at their own pace while focusing upon context relevant information. The finished product is the reward, but the adult student is fully engaged and enriched by the process. This kind of learning is often the focus of teacher training at the highest level. Every Computer Science teacher and self-taught learner knows what a great deal of work is required for projects to work in this manner, and with these tutorials, the work is done by an author who understands the adult need for streamlined learning. The author taught Visual Basic Programming at the University level for 15 years.

Graduated Lessons for Every Project ... Lessons, examples, problems and projects. Graduated learning. Increasing and appropriate difficulty... Great results.

With these projects, there are lessons providing a comprehensive background on the programming topics to be covered. Once understood, concepts are easily applicable to a variety of applications. Then, specific examples are drawn out so that a learner can practice with the Visual Basic form designer. Conventions relating to event-driven programming, naming controls and the scope of variables are explained. Then specific coding for the example is provided so that the user can see all the parts of the project come together for the finished product.

After the example is completed, then short problems challenge the user to repeat the process on their own, and finally, exercises provide a "summative" for the unit. By presenting lessons in this graduated manner, adult students are fully engaged and appropriately challenged to become independent thinkers who can come up with their own project ideas and design their own forms and do their own coding. Once the process is learned, then student engagement is unlimited! I have seen even adult student literacy improve dramatically when students cannot get enough of what is being presented.

Indeed, lessons encourage accelerated learning - in the sense that they provide an enriched environment to learn computer science, but they also encourage accelerating learning because students cannot put the lessons away once they start! Computer Science provides this unique opportunity to challenge students, and it is a great testament to the authors that they are successful in achieving such levels of engagement with consistency.

How independent learners use the materials. The style of presentation (lessons, examples, problems, exercises) encourages self-guided learning. Students may trust the order of presentation in order to have sufficient background information for every project. But the lessons are also highly indexed, so that students may pick and choose projects if limited by time.

Materials already condense what is available from MSDN so that students remember what they learn.

My history with the Kidware Software products.

I have used single license or shareware versions of the tutorials for over a decade to keep up my own learning as a Secondary School teacher of advanced Computer Science. As a learner who just wants to get down to business, these lessons match my learning style. I do not waste valuable time ensconced in language reference libraries for programming environments and help screens which can never be fully remembered! With every project, the pathway to learning is clear and immediate, though the topics in Computer Science remain current, relevant and challenging.

Some of the topics covered in these tutorials include:

- Data Types and Ranges
- Scope of Variables
- Naming Conventions
- Decision Making
- Looping
- Language Functions - String, Date, Numerical
- Arrays, Control Arrays
- Writing Your own Methods and Classes
- Windows Application Design and Distribution
- Sequential File Access, Error-Handling and Debugging techniques
- Graphics and Multimedia applications
- Visual Basic Database and Web Applications
- and more... it's all integrated into the tutorials.

Any further advanced topics in post-secondary computing (advanced data structures such as Lists and Linked Lists, Stacks, Queues, Binary Trees, etc...) derive directly from those listed above. Nothing is forgotten. All can be extrapolated from the lessons provided.

Quick learning curve by Contextualized Learning.

Having projects completed ahead of time encourages Contextualized Learning. Once a problem statement is understood, then the process of form-design, naming controls and coding is mastered for a given set of Visual Basic controls. Then, it is much more likely that students create their own problems and solutions from scratch. This is the pattern of learning for any language!

Meet Different State and Provincial Curriculum Expectations and More

Different states and provinces have their own curriculum requirements for Computer Science. With the Kidware Software products, you have at your disposal a series of projects which will allow you to pick and choose from among those which best suit your learning needs. Students focus upon design stages and sound problem-solving techniques from a Computer Science perspective. In doing so, they become independent problem-solvers, who will be able to meet the challenges of post-secondary Computer Science with confidence. Computer Science topics not explicitly covered in tutorials can be added at the learner's discretion. For example, recursive functions could be dealt with in a project which calculates factorials, permutations and combinations with a few text boxes and buttons on a form. Students learn to process information by collecting it in text boxes, and they learn to code command buttons. The language - whether it is Visual Basic, Visual C#, Visual C++, or Console Java, Java GUI, etc... is really up to the individual learner!

Lessons encourage your own programming extensions.

Once concepts are learned, it is difficult to NOT know what to do for your own projects.

Having developed my own projects in one language, such as Visual Basic, I know that I could easily adapt them to other languages once I have studied the Kidware Software tutorials. I do not believe there is any other reference material out there which would cause me to make the same claim! In fact, I know there is not as I have spent over a decade looking! With their programming tutorials, I have learned to teach Small Basic, Visual Basic, Visual C#, and Java!

Having used Kidware Software tutorials for the past decade, I have been successful at the expansion of my own learning of other platforms such as XNA for the Xbox, and the latest developer suites for tablets and phones.
I thank Kidware Software and its authors for continuing to stand for what is right in the teaching methodologies which not only inspire, but propel the self-guided learner through what can be an intelligible landscape of opportunities."

Alan Payne, B.A.H. , B.Ed.
Computer Science Teacher
T.A. Blakelock High School
Oakville, Ontario

1. Introduction to the Visual Basic Environment

Preview

In this first class, we will do an overview of how to build a Windows application using Visual Basic. You'll learn a new vocabulary, a new approach to programming, and ways to move around in the Visual Basic environment. Once finished, you will have written your first Visual Basic program.

Course Objectives

- Understand the benefits of using Microsoft Visual Basic as an application tool
- Understand Visual Basic event-driven programming concepts, object-oriented programming, and available controls
- Learn the fundamentals of designing, implementing, and distributing a Visual Basic Windows application
- Learn to use the Visual Basic toolbox
- Learn to create objects, modify object properties and use object methods
- Use menu and toolbar design tools
- Learn how to read and write sequential files
- Understand proper debugging and error-handling procedures
- Gain an understanding of graphic methods and simple animations
- Obtain an introduction to multimedia effects
- Learn how to print text and graphics from a Visual Basic application
- Gain skills to develop and implement an HTML-based help system
- Introduce database management using Visual Basic

What is Visual Basic?

Visual Basic is part of a grand initiative by Microsoft. With Visual Basic, you are able to quickly build Windows-based applications (the emphasis in this course), web-based applications and software for other devices, such as hand-held computers.

Windows applications built using Visual Basic feature a Graphical User Interface (GUI). Users interact with a set of visual tools (buttons, text boxes, tool bars, menu items) to make an application do its required tasks. The applications have a familiar appearance to the user. As you develop as a Visual Basic programmer, you will begin to look at Windows applications in a different light. You will recognize and understand how various elements of Word, Excel, Access and other applications work. You will develop a new vocabulary to describe the elements of Windows applications.

Visual Basic Windows applications are **event-driven**, meaning nothing happens until an application is called upon to respond to some event (button pressing, menu selection, ...). Visual Basic is governed by an event processor. As mentioned, nothing happens until an event is detected. Once an event is detected, a corresponding event procedure is located and the instructions provided by that procedure are executed. Those instructions are the actual code written by the programmer. In Visual Basic, that code is written using a version of the BASIC programming language. Once an event procedure is completed, program control is then returned to the event processor.

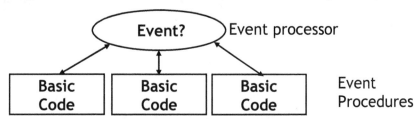

All Windows applications are event-driven. For example, nothing happens in Word until you click on a button, select a menu option, or type some text. Each of these actions is an event.

The event-driven nature of applications developed with Visual Basic makes it very easy to work with. As you develop a Visual Basic application, event procedures can be built and tested individually, saving development time. And, often event procedures are similar in their coding, allowing re-use (and lots of copy and paste).

Some Features of Visual Basic

- All new, easy-to-use, powerful Integrated Development Environment (IDE)
- Object-oriented language
- Full set of controls - you 'draw' the application
- Response to mouse and keyboard actions
- Clipboard and printer access
- Full array of mathematical, string handling, and graphics functions
- Can easily work with arrays of variables and objects
- Sequential file support
- Useful debugger and structured error-handling facilities
- Easy-to-use graphic tools
- Powerful database access tools
- Ability to develop both Windows and internet applications using similar techniques
- New common language runtime module makes distribution of applications a simple task

Visual Basic History

If you've followed programming for a while, you may know the term 'Visual Basic' has been around for over 20 years. Let's see where the current Visual Basic fits into this history. The earliest versions of Visual Basic all had version numbers. There was Visual Basic 3, Visual Basic 4, Visual Basic 5 and they stopped at Visual Basic 6. Then came Visual Basic .NET and Visual Basic .NET 2003.

The current version is Visual Basic 2019. If you are familiar with the older Visual Basic products, the new Visual Basic will look familiar, but there are many differences. And, for the most part, the differences are vast improvements over older versions. When you realize that the BASIC language has not undergone substantial changes in 20 years, you should agree it was time for a clean-up and improvement.

A few of the features of the newer Visual Basic, which, from now on, we will just refer to as Visual Basic:

- New Integrated Development Environment
- Uses Object-Oriented Programming (OOP) methods
- New controls and control properties
- Redesigned code window
- Zero-based arrays (no adjustable first dimension)
- Easier to use common dialog boxes
- Structured error-handling (no more On Error Go To)
- New menu design tools
- New techniques for working with sequential files
- All new graphics methods
- New approaches to printing from an application
- Improved support to incorporating help systems in applications
- New web forms for internet applications
- New objects for database access

To use Visual Basic 2019, you (and your students) must be using Windows 7, 8 or 10. These notes were developed using Windows 10.

A Brief Look at Object-Oriented Programming (OOP)

Since Visual Basic was first introduced in the early 1990's, a major criticism from many programmers (especially those using C and C++) was that it was not a true object-oriented language. And, with that limitation, many dismissed Visual Basic as a "toy" language. That limitation no longer exists!

Visual Basic is fully **object-oriented**. What this means is that each application we write will be made up of **objects**. Just what is an object? It can be many things: a variable, a font, a graphics region, a rectangle, a printed document. The key thing to remember is that objects represent reusable entities that are used to develop an application. This 'reusability' makes our job much easier as a programmer.

In Visual Basic, there are three terms we need to be familiar with in working with object-oriented programming: **Namespace**, **Class** and **Object**. **Objects** are what are used to build our application. We will learn about many objects throughout this course. Objects are derived (constructed) from **classes**. Think of classes as general descriptions of objects, which are then specific implementations of a class. For example, a class could be a general description of a car, where an object from that class would be a specific car, say a red 1965 Ford Mustang convertible (a nice object!). Lastly, a **namespace** is a grouping of different classes used in the Visual Basic world. One namespace might have graphics classes, while another would have math functions. We will see several namespaces in our work. And, you'll start creating your very own objects in Class 3.

The biggest advantage of the object-oriented nature of Visual Basic is that it is no longer a "toy" language. In fact, Visual Basic uses the same platform for development and deployment (incorporating the new Common Language Runtime (CLR) module) as the more esoteric languages (Visual C++ and the new Visual C#). Because of this, there should be no performance differences between applications written in Visual Basic, Visual C++, or Visual C#!

Structure of a Visual Basic Windows Application

We want to get started building our first Visual Basic Windows application. But, first we need to define some of the terminology we will be using. In Visual Basic, a Windows **application** is defined as a **solution**. A solution is made up of one or more **projects**. Projects are groups of forms and code that make up some application. In most of our work in this course, our applications (solutions) will be made up of a single project. Because of this, we will usually use the terms application, solution and project synonymously.

As mentioned, a project (application) is made up of forms and code. Pictorially, this is:

Project

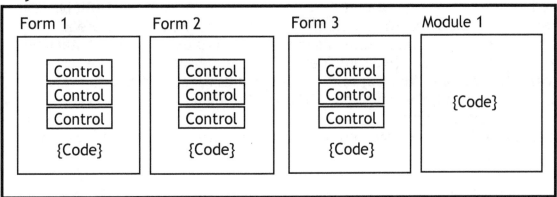

Application (Project) is made up of:

- ➢ **Forms** - Windows that you create for user interface
- ➢ **Controls** - Graphical features drawn on forms to allow user interaction (text boxes, labels, scroll bars, buttons, etc.) (Forms and Controls are **objects.**)
- ➢ **Properties** - Every characteristic of a form or control is specified by a property. Example properties include names, captions, size, color, position, and contents. Visual Basic applies default properties. You can change properties when designing the application or even when an application is executing.

- ➢ **Methods** - Built-in procedures that can be invoked to impart some action to a particular object.
- ➢ **Event Procedures** - **Code** related to some object or control. This is the code that is executed when a certain event occurs. In our applications, this code will be written in the BASIC language (covered in detail in Chapter 2 of these notes).
- ➢ **General Procedures** - **Code** not related to objects. This code must be invoked or called in the application.
- ➢ **Modules** - Collection of general procedures, variable declarations, and constant definitions used by an application.

The application displayed above has three forms and a single module. Visual Basic uses a very specific directory structure for saving all of the components for a particular application. When you save a new project (solution), you will be asked for a **Name** and **Location** (directory). A folder named **Name** will be established in the selected **Location**. That folder will be used to store all solution files, project files, form and module files (**vb** extension) and other files needed by the project. Two subfolders will be established within the Name folder: **Bin** and **Obj**. The **Obj** folder contains files used for debugging your application as it is being developed. The **Bin\Debug** folder contains your compiled application (the actual executable code or **exe** file). Later, you will see that this folder is considered the 'application path' when ancillary data, graphics and sound files are needed by an application.

In a project folder, you will see these files (and possibly more):

SolutionName.**sln**	Solution file for solution named SolutionName
ProjectName.**vbproj**	Project file – one for each project in solution
App.**config**	Project configuration file
FormName.**Designer.vb**	Form resources file – one for each form
FormName.**vb**	Form code file – one for each form

Steps in Developing a Windows Application

The Visual Basic Integrated Development Environment (IDE) makes building an application a straightforward process. There are three primary steps involved in building a Visual Basic application:

1. **Draw** the user **interface** by placing controls on a Windows form
2. **Assign properties** to controls
3. **Write code** for control events (and perhaps write other procedures)

These same steps are followed whether you are building a very simple application or one involving many controls and many lines of code.

The event-driven nature of Visual Basic applications allows you to build your application in stages and test it at each stage. You can build one procedure, or part of a procedure, at a time and try it until it works as desired. This minimizes errors and gives you, the programmer, confidence as your application takes shape.

As you progress in your programming skills, always remember to take this sequential approach to building a Visual Basic application. Build a little, test a little, modify a little and test again. You'll quickly have a completed application. This ability to quickly build something and try it makes working with Visual Basic fun – not a quality found in some programming environments! Now, we'll start Visual Basic and look at each step in the application development process.

Starting Visual Basic

We assume you have Visual Basic installed and operational on your computer. **Visual Basic** is included as a part of **Microsoft Visual Studio**. Visual Studio includes not only Visual Basic, but also Visual C++ and Visual C#. All three languages use the same development environment.

To start Visual Basic:

> ➤ Click on the **Start** button on the Windows task bar.
> ➤ Scroll down to **Visual Studio 2019**
> ➤ Click on **Visual Studio 2019**

Visual Studio will start and (among other things) a start page similar to this will appear:

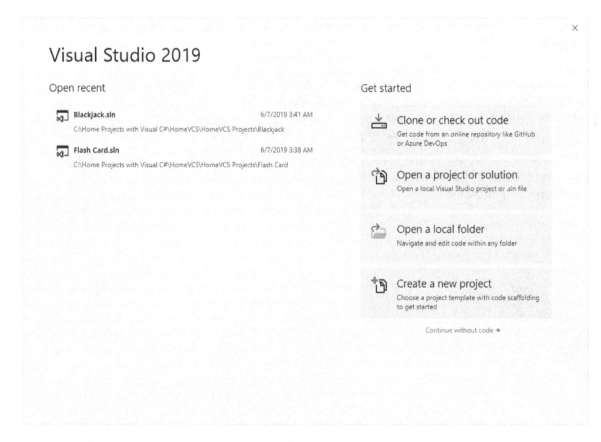

We want to start a project.

On the screen is a **New Project** link. Click that link and the following dialog box should appear:

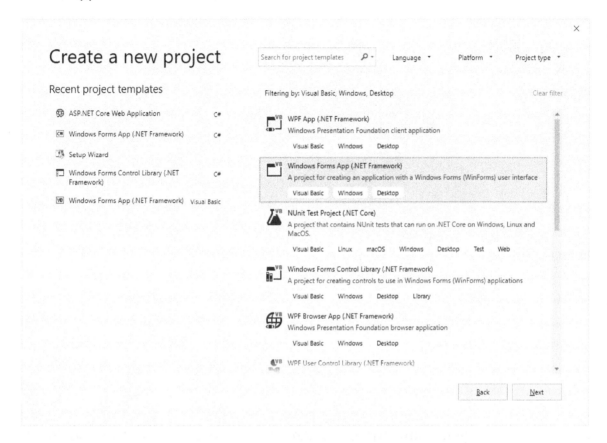

In the **Language** drop-down box, choose **Visual Basic.** In the **Platform** drop-down box, choose **Windows.** In the **Project type** drop-down box, choose **Desktop.** Then, select the **Windows Forms App** template. Click **Next.** The selected options will be saved to your IDE environment, so you don't have to reselect them each time you create a new project.

This window appears

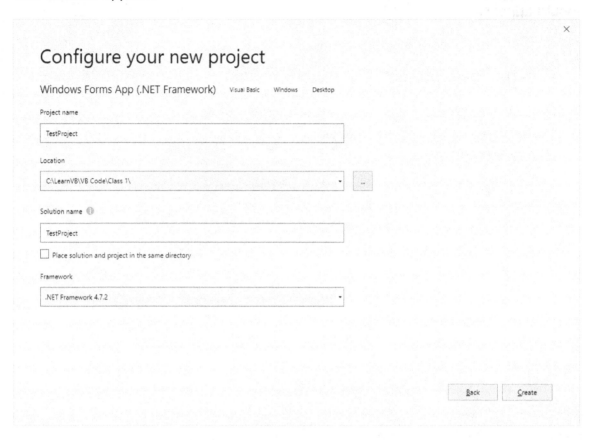

Assign a **Name** to your project (mine is named **TestProject**). **Location** should show the directory your project folder will be in. You can **Browse** to an existing location or create a new directory by checking the indicated box. For this course, we suggest saving each of your project folders in the same directory. For the course notes, all project folders are saved in the **\LearnVB\VB Code** folder, with additional folders for each individual class' projects. We suggest you save your projects in a folder you create.

Once done, click **Create** and the Visual Basic development environment will appear. Your project will consist of a single Windows form.

Visual Basic Integrated Development Environment (IDE)

The **Visual Basic IDE** is where we build and test our application via implementation of the three steps of application development (draw controls, assign properties, write code). As you progress through this course, you will learn how easy-to-use and helpful the IDE is. There are many features in the IDE and many ways to use these features. Here, we will introduce the IDE and some of its features. You must realize, however, that its true utility will become apparent as you use it yourself to build your own applications.

Several windows appear when you start Visual Basic. Each window can be viewed (made visible or active) by selecting menu options, depressing function keys or using the displayed toolbar. As you use the IDE, you will find the method you feel most comfortable with.

The title bar area shows you the name of your project. When running your project you will also see one of two words in brackets: **Running** or **Debugging**. This shows the mode Visual Basic is operating in. Visual Basic operates in three modes.

> ➢ **Design** mode - used to build application (the mode if not **Running** or **Debugging**)
> ➢ **Running** mode - used to run the application
> ➢ **Debugging** mode - application halted and debugger is available

We focus here on the **design** mode. You should, however, always be aware of what mode you are working in.

Under the title bar is the **Menu**. This menu is dynamic, changing as you try to do different things in Visual Basic. When you start working on a project, it should look like:

File   Edit   View   Project   Build   Debug   Format   Test   Analyze   Tools   Extensions   Window   Help

You will become familiar with each menu topic as you work through the course. Briefly, they are:

File	Use to open/close projects and files. Use to exit Visual Basic
Edit	Used when writing code to do the usual editing tasks of cutting, pasting, copying and deleting text
View	Provides access to most of the windows in the IDE
Project	Allows you to add/delete components to your project
Build	Controls the compiling process
Debug	Comes in handy to help track down errors in your code (works when Visual Basic is in **Debugging** mode)
Format	Used to modify appearance of your graphic interface.
Test	Allows you to compile and run your completed application (go to **Running** mode)
Analyze	Performs analytics on your code.
Tools	Allows custom configuration of the IDE. Be particularly aware of the **Options** choice under this menu item. This choice allows you to modify the IDE to meet any personal requirements.
Extensions	Allows customization of IDE
Window	Lets you change the layout of windows in the IDE
Help	Perhaps, the most important item in the Menu. Provides access to the Visual Basic on-line documentation via help contents, index or search. Get used to this item!

The View menu also allows you to choose from a myriad of toolbars available in the Visual Basic IDE. Toolbars provide quick access to many features. The **Standard** (default) toolbar appears below the menu:

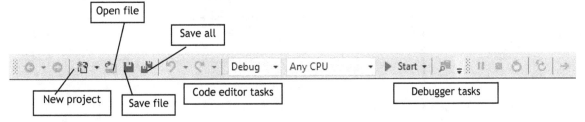

If you forget what a toolbar button does, hover your mouse cursor over the button until a descriptive tooltip appears. We will discuss most of these toolbar functions in the remainder of the IDE information.

In the middle of the Visual Basic IDE is the **Design Window**. This window is central to developing Visual Basic applications. Various items are available by selecting tabs at the top of the window. The primary use is to draw your application on a form and, later, to write code. Forms are selected using the tab named **FormName.vb [Design]**:

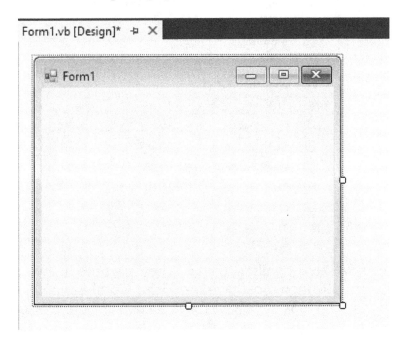

The corresponding code for a form is found using the **FormName.vb** tab. The design window will also display help topics and other information you may choose.

The **Toolbox** is the selection menu for controls used in your application. It is active when a form is shown in the design window. A view of the toolbox:

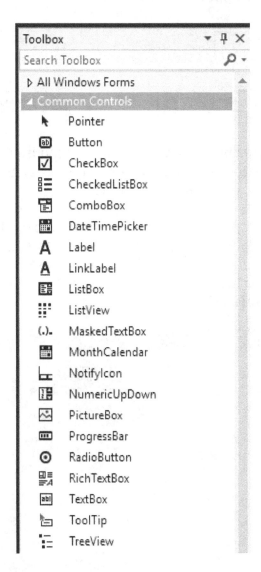

Many of these tools will look familiar to you. They are used in a wide variety of Windows applications you have used (the Visual Basic IDE even uses them!) We will soon look at how to move a control from the toolbox to a form.

The **Properties Window** is used to establish design mode (initial) property values for objects (controls). The drop-down box at the top of the window lists all objects in the current form. Two views are available: **Alphabetic** and **Categorized** (selection is made using menu bar under drop-down box). Under this box are the available properties for the active (currently selected) object. Help with any property can be obtained by highlighting the property of interest and pressing **<F1>**.

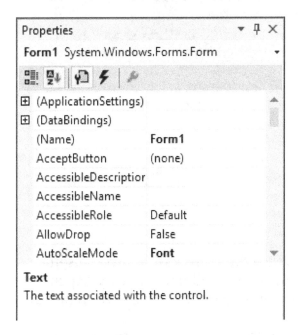

We will examine how to assign properties after placing some controls on a form.

The **Solution Explorer Window** displays a list of all forms, modules and other files making up your application. To view a form from this window, simply double-click the file name. Or, highlight the file and press **<Shift>-<F7>**. Or, you can obtain a view of the **Code** window (window containing the actual Basic coding) from the Project window, using the toolbar near the top of the window. As we mentioned, there are many ways to do things using the Visual Basic IDE.

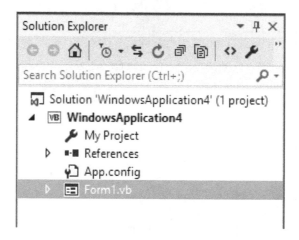

The help facilities of Visual Basic are vast and very useful. As you work more and more with Visual Basic, you will become very dependent on these facilities. The on-line help feature is web-based (use the **Help** menu).

One other very useful source for help with Visual Basic programming tasks is the Internet. Using a search engine such a Google will locate many helpful websites.

This completes our quick tour of the Visual Basic IDE. After taking a look at how to save a project, we turn our attention to building our first application using these three steps:

- Draw the user interface (place controls on the form).
- Set control properties
- Write code

Saving a Visual Basic Project

When a new project is created in Visual Basic, it is automatically saved in the location you specify. If you are making lots of changes, you might occasionally like to save your work prior to running the project. Do this by clicking the **Save All** button in the Visual Basic toolbar. Look for a button that looks like several floppy disks. (With writeable CD's so cheap, how much longer do you think people will know what a floppy disk looks like? – many new machines don't even have a floppy disk drive!)

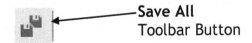 Save All
Toolbar Button

Always make sure to save your project before running it or before leaving Visual Basic.

Drawing the User Interface

The first step in developing a Visual Basic Windows application is to draw the user interface on the form. Make sure the Form appears in the Design window. There are four ways to place controls on a form:

1. Click the tool in the toolbox and hold the mouse button down. Drag the selected tool over the form. When the cursor pointer is at the desired upper left corner, release the mouse button and the default size control will appear. This is the classic "drag and drop" operation.

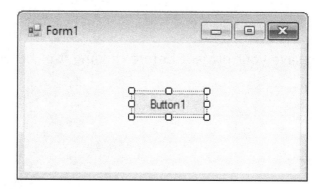

2. Double-click the tool in the toolbox and it is created with a default size on the form. You can then move it or resize it. Here is a button control placed on the form using this method:

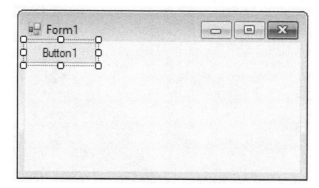

3. Click the tool in the toolbox, then move the mouse pointer to the form window. The cursor changes to a crosshair. Place the crosshair at the upper left corner of where you want the control to be and click the left mouse button. The control will appear at the clicked point. Here is a default size button placed on the form using this technique:

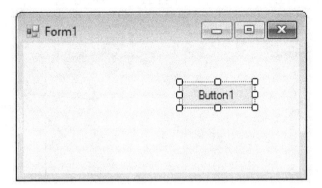

4. Click the tool in the toolbox, then move the mouse pointer to the form window. The cursor changes to a crosshair. Place the crosshair at the upper left corner of where you want the control to be, press the left mouse button and hold it down while dragging the cursor toward the lower right corner. A rectangle will be drawn. When you release the mouse button, the control is drawn in the rectangle. A big button drawn using this method:

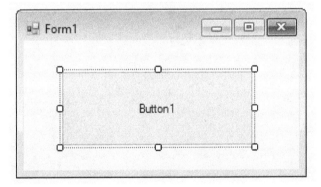

To **move** a control you have drawn, click the object in the form (a cross with arrows will appear). Now, drag the control to the new location. Release the mouse button.

To **resize** a control, click the control so that it is selected (active) and sizing handles appear. Use these handles to resize the object.

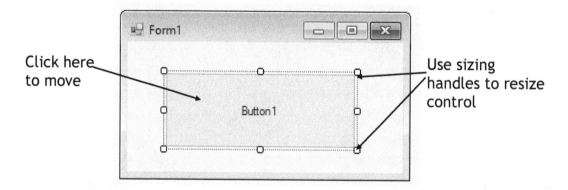

Click here
to move

Use sizing
handles to resize
control

To delete a control, select that control so it is active (sizing handles will appear). Then, press **<Delete>** on the keyboard. Or, right-click the control. A menu will appear. Choose the **Delete** option. You can change your mind immediately after deleting a control by choosing the **Undo** option under the **Edit** menu.

Example 1-1

Stopwatch Application - Drawing Controls

1. Start a new project. The idea of this project is to start a timer, then stop the timer and compute the elapsed time (in seconds).

2. Place three buttons, three labels and three text box controls on the form. Move and size the controls and form so it looks something like this:

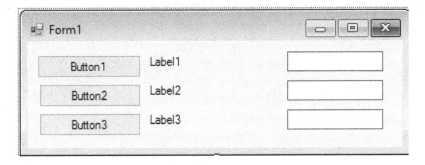

3. Save this project (saved in the **Example 1-1** folder in **LearnVB\VB Code\Class 1** folder).

Opening a Saved Visual Basic Project

Every example, problem and exercise presented in this course has an accompanying Visual Basic solution folder. This lets you see how we did things. These folders are saved in the **LearnVB\VB Code** directory, sorted by chapter number. You need to know how to open these projects. And, you need to know how to open any projects you may have saved.

Opening a previously saved Visual Basic project is a simple task. Choose the **File** menu option in the Visual Basic IDE and select **Open**, then **Project/Solution**. The **Open Project** dialog box will appear. Open the desired project folder and you see:

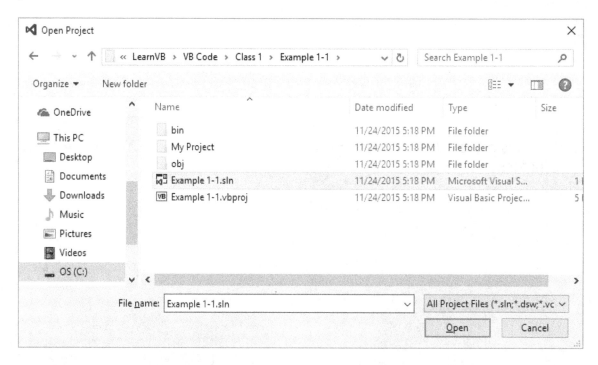

At this point, click on the **Solution** file and click **Open**. Or, double-click the **Solution** file. All the components of your project will be assembled and displayed. It's that easy!

Setting Properties of Controls at Design Time

Each form and control has **properties** assigned to it by default when you start up a new project. There are two ways to display the properties of an object. The first way is to click on the object (form or control) in the form window. Sizing handles will appear on that control. When a control has sizing handles, we say it is the **active** control. Now, click on the Properties window or the Properties window button in the tool bar. The second way is to first click on the Properties window. Then, select the object from the drop-down box at the top of the Properties window. When you do this, the selected object (control) will now be active (have sizing handles). Shown is the Properties window for the stopwatch application (for the Form object):

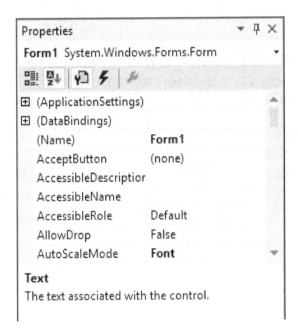

The drop-down box at the top of the Properties Window is the **Object** box. It displays the name of each object in the application as well as its type. This display shows the **Form** object. The **Properties** list is directly below this box. In this list, you can scroll through the list of properties for the selected object. You select a property by clicking on it. Properties can be changed by typing a new value or choosing from a list of predefined settings (available as a drop down list). Properties can be viewed in two ways: **Alphabetic** and **Categorized** (selected using the menu bar under the Object box). At the bottom of the Properties window is a short description of the selected property (a kind of dynamic help system).

A very important property for each control is its **Name**. The name is used by Visual Basic to refer to a particular object or control in code. A convention has been established for naming Visual Basic controls. This convention is to use a three letter (lower case) prefix (identifying the type of control) followed by a name you assign. A few of the prefixes are (we'll see more as we progress in the class):

Control	Prefix	Example
Form	frm	frmWatch
Button	btn	btnExit, btnStart
Label	lbl	lblStart, lblEnd
Text Box	txt	txtTime, txtName
Menu	mnu	mnuExit, mnuSave
Check box	chk	chkChoice

Even though the names we have used in these examples have both lower and upper case letters, Visual Basic is **case-insensitive**. Hence, the names **frmWatch** and **FRMWATCH** would be assumed to be the same name.

Control (object) names can be up to 40 characters long, must start with a letter, must contain only letters, numbers, and the underscore (_) character. Names are used in setting properties at run-time and also in establishing procedure names for control events. Use meaningful names that help you (or another programmer) understand the type and purpose of the respective controls.

Another set of important properties for each control are those that dictate position and size. There will be times you want to refer to (or change) these properties. There are four properties:

Left   Distance from left side of form to left edge of control, in pixels

Top   Distance from title bar of form to top edge of control, in pixels

Width   Width of control, in pixels

Height   Height of control, in pixels

Pictorially, these properties for a button control are:

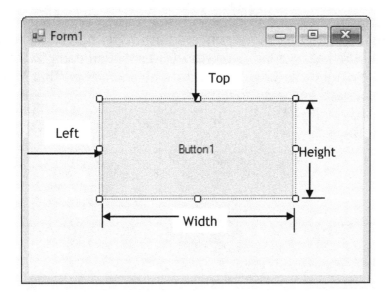

Finding these properties in the Properties window is a bit tricky. To find the **Left** and **Top** properties, expand the **Location** property. The displayed X value is the **Left** property, while Y is the **Top** property. To find the **Width** and **Height** properties, expand the **Size** property – the width and height are displayed and can be modified.

Setting Properties at Run Time

In addition to setting properties at design time, you can set or modify properties while your application is running. To do this, you must write some code. The code format is:

    ObjectName.PropertyName = NewValue

Such a format is referred to as dot notation. For example, to change the **BackColor** property of a button named **btnStart**, we'd type:

```
btnStart.BackColor = Color.Blue
```

You've just seen your first line of code in Visual Basic. Good naming conventions make it easy to understand what's going on here. The button named **btnStart** will now have a blue background. We won't learn much code in this first chapter (you'll learn a lot in Chapter 2), but you should see that the code that is used is straightforward and easy to understand.

How Names are Used in Control Events

The names you assign to controls are also used by Visual Basic to set up a framework of event-driven procedures for you to add code to. Hence, proper naming makes these procedures easier to understand.

The format for each of these procedures, or subroutines (all event procedures in Visual Basic are subroutines), is:

Private Sub ControlName_Event (**Arguments**) **Handles** ControlName.Event
.
.
End Sub

where **Arguments** provides information needed by the procedure to do its work.

Visual Basic provides the **Sub** line with its arguments and the **End Sub** statement. You provide any needed code. Don't worry about how to provide this code right now. Just notice that with proper naming convention, it is easy to identify what tasks are associated with a particular event of a particular control.

Use of Form Name Property

When setting run-time properties or accessing events for the **Form** object, the **Name** property is not used in the same manner as it is for other controls. To set properties, rather than use the name property, the keyword **Me** is used. Hence, to set a form property at run-time, use:

    Me.PropertyName = Value

The format for an **event procedure** associated with the form is:

    Private Sub FormName_Event (**Arguments**) **Handles** MyBase.Event
      .
      .
    End Sub

Note the use of the keyword **MyBase** rather than the form name in the **Handles** clause.

We also need to distinguish between the form **Name** property and the **File Name** used within Visual Basic to save the form file (which includes control descriptions and all code associated with a particular form). The Name property and File Name are two different entities. We have seen how the form Name property is used. A look at the Solution Explorer window for a sample application shows how the form File Name is used:

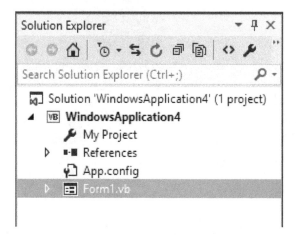

The name preceding the **vb** extension (**Form1**) is the form file name. Again, this is <u>not</u> the same as the name assigned in the Form Properties window.

To change the form file name, click the file in the Solution Explorer window to see the **File Properties** window (this is <u>not</u> the same as the Form Properties window):

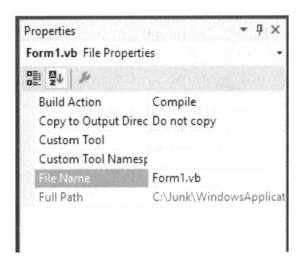

In this window, you change the File Name by simply typing another name (with the **vb** extension). Visual Basic will then automatically save the form file with this new name. This name is then used to refer to the form file. This is the name you would use if you want to load a particular form into a Visual Basic solution or project.

Example 1-2

Stopwatch Application - Setting Properties

1. Continue with Example 1-1. Set properties of the form, three buttons, three labels, and three text boxes:

   Form1:
Name	frmStopWatch
FormBorderStyle	Fixed Single
StartPosition	CenterScreen
Text	Stopwatch Application

   Button1:
Name	btnStart
Text	&Start Timing

   Button2:
Name	btnEnd
Text	&End Timing

   Button3:
Name	btnExit
Text	E&xit

   Label1:
Text	Start Time

   Label2:
Text	End Time

   Label3:
Text	Elapsed Time (sec)

TextBox1:
  Name   txtStart

TextBox2:
  Name   txtEnd

TextBox3:
  Name   txtElapsed

In the **Text** properties of the three buttons, notice the ampersand (**&**). The ampersand precedes a button's **access key**. That is, in addition to clicking on a button to invoke its event, you can also press its access key (no need for a mouse). The access key is pressed in conjunction with the **Alt** key. Hence, to invoke 'Start Timing', you can either click the button or press **<Alt>+S**. Note in the button text on the form, the access keys appear with an underscore (_).

2. Your form should now look something like this:

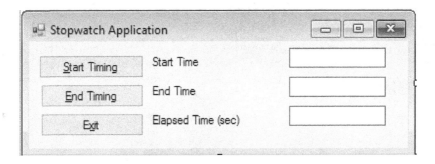

3. Save this project (**Example 1-2** folder in **LearnVB\VB Code\Class 1** folder).

Writing Code

The last step in building a Visual Basic application is to write code using the **BASIC** language. This is the most time consuming task in any Visual Basic application. It is also the most fun and most rewarding task.

As controls are added to a form, Visual Basic automatically builds a framework of all event procedures. We simply add code to the event procedures we want our application to respond to. And, if needed, we write general procedures. For those who may have never programmed before, the code in these procedures is simply a line by line list of instructions for the computer to follow. A useful feature when working with code is to put line numbers next to each line of code. To do this, select the **Tools** menu item in the IDE. Then, choose **Options**. In the left side of the window that appears, choose **Text Editor**, **Basic** and **General**. Then, choose the **Line numbers** option:

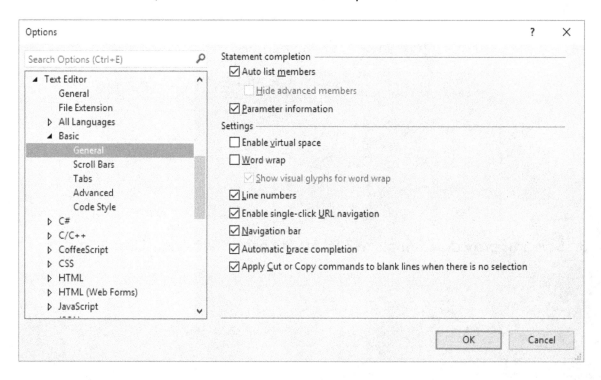

You will find the line numbers very useful as you write code. Any errors you make are identified by line number in the **Error List Window**. To view this window, choose the **View** menu option. Then select **Other Windows**, then **Error List**. The **Error List** window will appear:

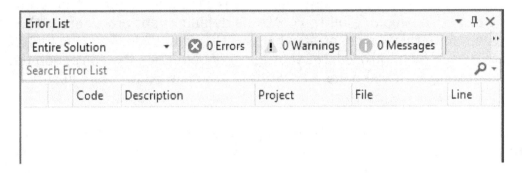

Errors are listed under **Description**. The file the error occurs in is listed under **File**. And, the line number is listed under **Line**. You will use this window a lot while writing code.

Code is placed in the **Code Window**. Typing code in the code window is just like using any word processor. You can cut, copy, paste and delete text (use the **Edit** menu or the toolbar). Learn how to access the code window using the menu (**View**), toolbar, or by pressing <**F7**> (and there are still other ways) while the form is active. Here is the Code window for the stopwatch application we are working on:

We see that our project is a **class** named **frmStopWatch**. Our application (an **object**) will be derived from this class. All code for the project will lie between the header line (**Public Class frmStopWatch**) and the footer line (**End Class**).

Working with Event Procedures

There are two ways to establish event procedures for controls - one directly from the form and one using the properties window. Let's look at both. Every control has a **default event procedure.** This is the method most often used by the control. For example, a button control's default event procedure is the Click event, since this is most often what we do to a button. To access a control's default event procedure, you simply double-click the control on the form. For example, if you double-click the button named **btnStart** in the stopwatch project, the bottom of the code window will display:

```
Private Sub BtnStart_Click(ByVal sender As Object, ByVal e
As System.EventArgs) Handles btnStart.Click

End Sub
```

Let's spend some time looking at this method - all event procedures used in Visual Basic look just like this. The time spent clarifying things now will be well worth it.

The assigned name for the event procedure is seen to be **BtnStart_Click.** Our naming convention tells us this is the procedure executed when the user clicks on the **btnStart** button (you will notice the IDE converts the first letter to upper case). The procedure has two arguments: **sender** and **e.** Sender tells the procedure what control caused the Click event to occur and e gives us some information about the event. Now, notice the **Handles** keyword:

```
Handles btnStart.Click
```

This tells us that his procedure **Handles** the **Click** event for **btnStart.** You might ask - didn't the name of the procedure (**btnStart_Click**) tell us the same thing? Isn't the Handles clause redundant? The answer is No. The name of the procedure is arbitrary (you can change it if you want and sometimes we want to). The Handles clause tells us what event has to occur for the procedure to be invoked. In fact, in later classes, we will see how to attach multiple events to a single procedure. That's why the sender argument is there - to tell us which control (in a multiple control scenario) caused the event to occur. We will learn much more about this later.

Though simple and quick, double-clicking a control to establish a control event procedure will not work if you are not interested in the default procedure. In that case, you need to use the properties window. Recall we mentioned that the properties window is not only used to establish properties, but also event procedures. To establish an event procedure using the properties window, click on the **Events** button (appears as a lightning bolt) in the properties window toolbar:

Events button

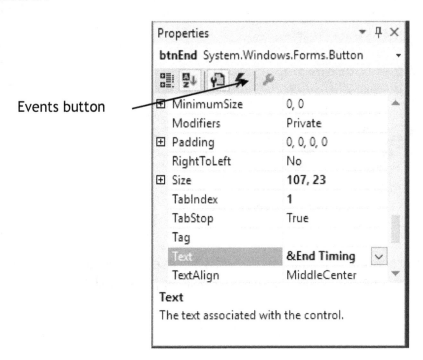

The active control's events will be listed (the default event will be highlighted):

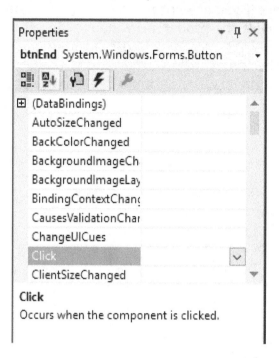

To establish an event procedure, scroll down the listed events and double-click the one of interest. The selected event procedure will appear in the code window.

There are several ways to locate a previously established method. One is to double-click the event name in the properties window, just as we did to create the method. Once you double-click the name, the code window will display the selected method. If the desired method is a default method, double-clicking the control on the form will take you to that method in the code window.

Another way to locate an event procedure is via the code window. At the top of the code window are three dropdown boxes, the **procedure list** is on the right. Selecting this box will provide a list of all methods in the code window. Find the event method of interest and select it. The selected event will appear in the code window:

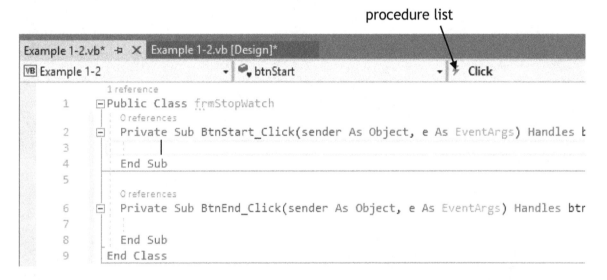

Deleting an existing event procedure can be tricky. Simply deleting the event procedure in the code window is not sufficient. When you add an event procedure to your application, Visual Basic writes a line of code to connect the procedure to your control. That line of code remains after you delete the procedure. If you delete the procedure and try to run your application, an error will occur. In the Task Window will be a message saying your application does not contain a definition for a specific event procedure. Double-click the message and Visual Basic will take you to the offending statement (the one that connects the control and the procedure). Delete that line and your code will be fixed.

The preferred way to delete a procedure is to select the desired procedure using the properties window (make sure the control of interest is the active control). Once the event is selected, right-click the event procedure name and choose **Reset** from the pop-up menu. This process deletes the event from the code window <u>and</u> deletes the line of code connecting the procedure and control.

Variables

We're now ready to write code for our application. As just seen, as controls are added to the form, Visual Basic builds a framework of event procedures. We simply add code to the event procedures we want our application to respond to. But before we do this, we need to discuss **variables**.

Variables are used by Visual Basic to hold information needed by an application. Variables must be properly named. Rules used in naming variables:

> ➢ No more than 40 characters
> ➢ They may include letters, numbers, and underscore (_)
> ➢ The first character must be a letter
> ➢ You cannot use a reserved word (keywords used by Visual Basic)

Use meaningful variable names that help you (or other programmers) understand the purpose of the information stored by the variable.

Examples of acceptable variable names:

StartingTime	Interest_Value	Letter05
JohnsAge	Number_of_Days	TimeOfDay

Visual Basic Data Types

Each variable is used to store information of a particular **type**. Visual Basic has a wide range of data types. You must always know the type of information stored in a particular variable.

Boolean variables can have one of two different values: **True** or **False** (reserved words in Visual Basic). Boolean variables are helpful in making decisions.

If a variable stores a whole number (no decimal), there are three data types available: **Short**, **Integer** or **Long**. Which type you select depends on the range of the value stored by the variable:

Data Type	Range
Short	-32,678 to 32,767
Integer	-2,147,483,648 to 2,147,483,647
Long	-9,223,372,036,854,775,808 to 9,223,372,036,854,775,807

We will almost always use the **Integer** type in our work.

If a variable stores a decimal number, there are two data types: **Single** or **Double**. The Double uses twice as much storage as Single, providing more precision and a wider range. Examples:

Data Type	Value
Single	3.14
Double	3.14159265359

Visual Basic is a popular language for performing string manipulations. These manipulations are performed on variables of type **String**. A string variable is just that - a string (list) of various characters. In Visual Basic, string variable values are enclosed in quotes. Examples of string variables:

"Visual Basic"   "012345"   "Title   Author"

Single character string variables have a special type, type **Char**, for character type. Examples of character variables:

"a"   "1"   "V"   "*"

Visual Basic also has great facilities for handling dates and times. The **Date** variable type stores both dates and times. Using different formatting techniques (we will learn these) allow us to display dates and times in any format desired.

A last data type is type **Object**. That is, we can actually define a variable to represent any Visual Basic object, like a button or form. We will see the utility of the Object type as we progress in the course.

Variable Declaration

Once we have decided on a variable name and the type of variable, we must tell our Visual Basic application what that name and type are. We say, we must **explicitly declare** the variable.

It is possible to use Visual Basic without declaring variables, but this is a dangerous practice There are many advantages to **explicitly** typing variables. Primarily, we insure all computations are properly done, mistyped variable names are easily spotted, and Visual Basic will take care of insuring consistency in variable names. Because of these advantages, and because it is good programming practice, we will <u>always</u> explicitly type variables.

To **explicitly** type a variable, you must first determine its **scope**. Scope identifies how widely disseminated we want the variable value to be. We will use four levels of scope:

> ➤ Procedure level
> ➤ Procedure level, static
> ➤ Form and module level
> ➤ Global level

The value of **procedure** level variables are only available within a procedure. Such variables are declared within a procedure using the **Dim** statement:

```
Dim MyInt As Integer
Dim MyDouble As Double
Dim MyString As String, YourString As String
```

Procedure level variables declared in this manner do not retain their value once a procedure terminates.

To make a procedure level variable retain its value upon exiting the procedure, replace the Dim keyword with **Static:**

```
Static MyInt As Integer
   Static MyDouble As Double
```

Form (**module**) level variables retain their value and are available to all procedures within that form (module). Form (module) level variables are declared in the code window right after the header line:

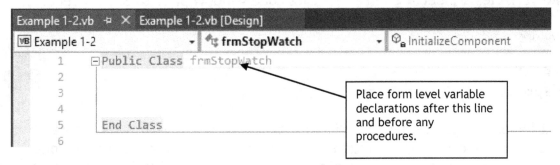

The **Dim** keyword is used to declare form (module) level variables:

```
Dim MyInt As Integer
Dim MyDate As Date
```

Global level variables retain their value and are available to all forms, modules and procedures within an application. Such variables can only be declared in a code module – a separate project component (discussed in Chapter 5). Global level variables are declared in a module's code window prior to any procedure. (It is advisable to keep all global variables in one module.) Use the **Public** keyword:

```
Public MyInt As Integer
Public MyDate As Date
```

What happens if you declare a variable with the same name in two or more places? More local variables **shadow** (are accessed in preference to) less local variables. For example, if a variable MyInt is defined as Public in a module and declared local in a routine MyRoutine, while in MyRoutine, the local value of MyInt is accessed. Outside MyRoutine, the global value of MyInt is accessed.

Example of Variable Scope:

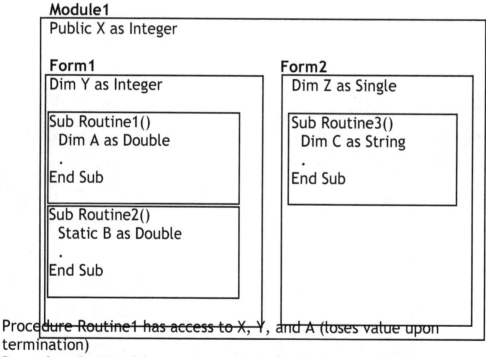

Procedure Routine1 has access to X, Y, and A (loses value upon termination)
Procedure Routine2 has access to X, Y, and B (retains value)
Procedure Routine3 has access to X, Z, and C (loses value)

Arrays

Visual Basic has powerful facilities for handling arrays, which provide a way to store a large number of variables under the same name. Each variable, called an element, in an array must have the same data type, and they are distinguished from each other by an array index. In this class, we work with one-dimensional arrays, although multi-dimensional arrays are possible.

Arrays are declared in a manner identical to that used for regular variables. For example, to declare an integer array named **'Item'**, with dimension **9**, at the procedure level, we use:

```
Dim Item(9) As Integer
```

If we want the array variables to retain their value upon leaving a procedure, we use the keyword **Static**:

```
Static Item(9) As Integer
```

At the **form** or **module** level, in the proper region of the Code window, use:

```
Dim Item(9) As Integer
```

And, at the **global** level, in a code module, use:

```
Public Item(9) As Integer
```

The index on an array variable begins at 0 and ends at the dimensioned value. Hence, the **Item** array in the above examples has **ten** elements, ranging from Item(0) to Item(9). You use array variables just like any other variable - just remember to include its name and its index. Many times, the 0 index is ignored and we just start with item 1. But sometimes (especially when working with Visual Basic controls) the 0th element cannot be ignored. You will see examples of both 0-based and 1-based arrays in the course examples.

It is also possible to have arrays of controls. For example, to have 20 button types available use:

```
Dim MyButtons(19) As Button
```

The utility of such a declaration will become apparent in later classes.

Constants

You can also define constants for use in Visual Basic. The format for defining a constant named **NumberOfUses** with a value **200** is:

```
Const NumberOfUses As Integer = 200
```

The scope of user-defined constants is established the same way a variables' scope is. That is, if defined within a procedure, they are local to the procedure. If defined in the top region of a form's code window, they are global to the form. To make constants global to an application, use the format:

```
Public Const NumberOfUses As Integer = 200
```

within a code module.

If you attempt to change the value of a defined constant, your program will stop with an error message.

Variable Initialization

By default, any declared numeric variables are initialized at zero. String variables are initialized at an empty string. If desired, Visual Basic lets you initialize variables at the same time you declare them. Just insure that the type of initial value matches the variable type (i.e. don't assign a string value to an integer variable).

Examples of variable initialization:

```
Dim MyInt As Integer = 23
Dim MyString As String = "Visual Basic"
Static MyDouble As Double = 7.28474746464
Public MyDate As Date = #1/2/2001#
```

You can even initialize arrays with this technique. You must, however, delete the explicit dimension (number of elements) and let Visual Basic figure it out by counting the number of elements used to initialize the array. An example is:

```
Dim Item() As Integer = {0, 1, 2, 3, 4, 5, 6, 7, 8, 9}
```

Visual Basic will know this array has 10 elements (a dimension of 9).

Intellisense Feature

Yes, we're finally ready to start writing some code in the code window. You will see that typing code is just like using any word processor. The usual navigation and editing features are all there.

One feature that you will become comfortable with and amazed with is called **Intellisense**. As you type code, the Intellisense feature will, at times, provide assistance in completing lines of code. For example, once you type a control name and a dot (.), a drop-down list of possible properties and methods will appear. When we use functions and procedures, suggested values for arguments will be provided. Syntax errors will be identified. And, potential errors with running an application will be pointed out.

Intellisense is a very useful part of Visual Basic. You should become acquainted with its use and how to select suggested values. We tell you about now so you won't be surprised when little boxes start popping up as you type code.

Let's finally complete the stopwatch application. We'll just give you the code. Don't worry about where it comes from for now. You'll learn a lot about coding as you venture forth in this course. Just type the code as given - you should see how easy it is to understand however.

Example 1-3

Stopwatch Application - Writing Code

All that's left to do is write code for the application. We write code for every event a response is needed for. In this application, there are three such events: clicking on each of the buttons.

1. Double-click anywhere on the form to open the code window. Or, select 'View Code' from the project window. Or, press <F7> while the form is active.

2. Under the line marked **Public Class frmStopWatch** declare three form level variables:

```
Dim StartTime As Date
Dim EndTime As Date
Dim ElapsedTime As Integer
```

This establishes **StartTime**, **EndTime**, and **ElapsedTime** as variables with form level scope. At this point, the Code window should look like this:

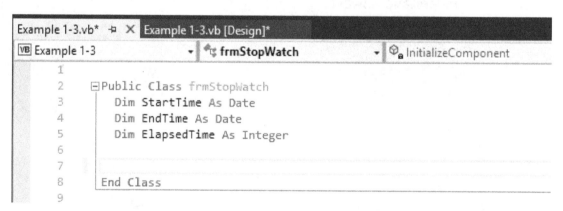

Select the **btnStart** object in the Object box of the code window. Choose **Click** from the procedure box. Or, try double-clicking the button control. Type the following code which begins the timing procedure. Note the **Sub** and **End Sub** statements are provided for you:

```
Private Sub BtnStart_Click(ByVal sender As Object, ByVal e
As System.EventArgs) Handles btnStart.Click
    'Establish and print starting time
    StartTime = Now
    txtStart.Text = Format(StartTime, "hh:mm:ss")
    txtEnd.Text = ""
    txtElapsed.Text = ""
End Sub
```

In this procedure, once the **Start Timing** button is clicked, we read the current time and print it in a text box. We also blank out the other text boxes. In the code above (and in all code in these notes), any line beginning with a single quote (') is a comment. You decide whether you want to type these lines or not. They are not needed for proper application operation.

3. Now, select the **btnEnd** object in the Object box. Choose **Click** from the procedure box. Add this code:

```
Private Sub BtnEnd_Click(ByVal sender As System.Object,
ByVal e As System.EventArgs) Handles btnEnd.Click
    'Find the ending time, compute the elapsed time
    'Put both values in text boxes
    EndTime = Now
    ElapsedTime = DateDiff(DateInterval.Second, StartTime,
EndTime)
    txtEnd.Text = Format(EndTime, "hh:mm:ss")
    txtElapsed.Text = Format(ElapsedTime, "0")
End Sub
```

Here, when the **End Timing** button is clicked, we read the current time (**End Time**), compute the elapsed time, and put both values in their corresponding text boxes.

4. Finally, select the **btnExit** object in the Object box. Choose **Click** from the procedure box. That button's Click event code:

```
Private Sub BtnExit_Click(ByVal sender As System.Object,
ByVal e As System.EventArgs) Handles btnExit.Click
    Me.Close()
End Sub
```

This routine simply closes the form (identified by the keyword Me) once the **Exit** button is clicked. Did you notice as you typed in the code, how the Intellisense feature of Visual Basic worked? Before trying to run the application, we need to take a brief, but important, interlude.

5. Run your application by clicking the **Start** button on the toolbar, or by pressing **<F5>.** Here's a short run I made (I clicked **Start Timing**, then **End Timing** 9 seconds later):

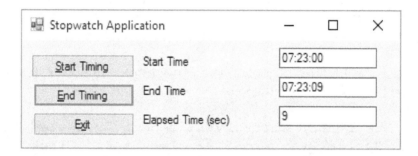

If your application doesn't run, recheck to make sure the code is typed properly. Save your application. This is saved in the **Example 1-3** folder in **LearnVB\VB Code\Class 1** folder.

6. If you have the time, some other things you may try with the **Stopwatch Application:**

   A. Try changing the form color and the fonts used in the labels, text boxes and buttons.

   B. Notice you can press the 'End Timing' button before the 'Start Timing' button. This shouldn't be so. Change the application so you can't do this. And make it such that you can't press the 'Start Timing' until 'End Timing' has been pressed. Hint: Look at the button **Enabled** property.

   C. Can you think of how you can continuously display the 'End Time' and 'Elapsed Time'? This is a little tricky because of the event-driven nature of Visual Basic. Look at the **Timer** control. By setting the **Interval** property of this control to **1000** and the **Enabled** property to **True**, it will generate its own events (the **Tick** event) every one second. Put code similar to that in the **btnEnd_Click** event in the Timer control's **Tick** event and see what happens. Also, see the exercise at the end of the class for help on this one. The Timer control will not appear on the form, but in a 'tray' below the form. This happens because the Timer control has no user interface.

Class Review

After completing this class, you should understand:

> ➢ The concept of an event-driven application
> ➢ What object-oriented programming (OOP) is about
> ➢ The parts of a Visual Basic application (form, control, property, event, ...)
> ➢ The various windows of the Visual Basic integrated development environment
> ➢ How to use the Visual Basic on-line help system
> ➢ The three steps in building a Visual Basic application
> ➢ Four ways to place controls on a form
> ➢ Methods to set properties for controls
> ➢ Proper control naming convention
> ➢ Proper variable naming and typing procedures
> ➢ The concept of variable scope
> ➢ How to properly declare a variable
> ➢ How to define a constant
> ➢ How to add code and declarations using the code window
> ➢ Ways to use the Intellisense feature when typing code

Practice Problems 1*

Problem 1-1. Beep Problem. Build an application with a single button. When the button is clicked, make the computer beep. To hear a beep, use this function:

System.Media.SystemSounds.Beep.Play()

Problem 1-2. Text Problem. Build an application with a single button. When the button is clicked, change the button's **Text** property. This allows a button to be used for multiple purposes. If you want to change the button caption back when you click again, you'll need an **If** statement. We'll discuss this statement in the next class, but, if you're adventurous, look in on-line help to try it.

Problem 1-3. Enabled Problem. Build an application with two buttons. When you click one button, make it disabled (**Enabled** = **False**) and make the other button enabled (**Enabled** = **True**).

Problem 1-4. Date Problem. Build an application with a button. When the button is clicked, have the computer display the current date in a label control.

---

*Note: Practice Problems are given after each class to give you practice in writing code for your Visual Basic applications. These are meant to be quick and, hopefully, short exercises. The Visual Basic environment makes it easy to build and test quick applications – in fact, programmers develop such examples all the time to test some idea they might have. Use your imagination in working the problems – modify them in any way you want. You learn programming by doing programming! The more you program, the better programmer you will become. Our solutions to the **Practice Problems** are provided as an addenda to these notes.

Exercise 1*

Calendar/Time Display

Design a window that displays the current month, day, and year. Also, display the current time, updating it every second (look into the **Timer** control). Make the window look something like a calendar page. Play with control properties to make it pretty.

---

*Note: After completing each class' notes, a homework exercise (and, sometimes, more) is given, covering many of the topics taught. Try to work through the homework exercise on your own. This is how programming is learned – solving a particular problem. For reference, solutions to all **Exercises** are provided as an addenda to these notes. In our solutions, you may occasionally see something you don't recognize. When this happens, use the on-line help system or Internet searches to learn what's going on. This is another helpful skill – understanding other people's applications and code.

2. The Visual Basic Language

Review and Preview

In the first class, we found there were three primary steps involved in developing a Windows application using Visual Basic:

1. Draw the user interface
2. Assign properties to controls
3. Write code for events

In this class, we are primarily concerned with Step 3, writing code. We will become more familiar with moving around in the Code window and learn some of the elements of the BASIC language.

A Brief History of BASIC

The BASIC language was developed in the early 1960's at Dartmouth College as a device for teaching programming to "ordinary" people. There is a reason it's called BASIC:

  B (eginner's)
  A (All-Purpose)
  S (Symbolic)
  I (Instruction)
  C (Code)

When timesharing systems were introduced in the 1960's, BASIC was the language of choice. Many of the first computer simulation games (Star Trek, for example) were written in timeshare BASIC.

In the mid-1970's, two college students decided that the new Altair microcomputer needed a BASIC language interpreter. They sold their product on cassette tape for a cost of $350. You may have heard of these entrepreneurs: Bill Gates and Paul Allen!

Every BASIC written since then has been based on that early version. Examples include: GW-Basic, QBasic, QuickBasic. All the toy computers of the early 80's (anyone remember TI99/4A, Commodore 64, Timex, Atari 400?) used BASIC for programming.

Visual Basic (allowing development of Windows applications) was first introduced in 1991. The latest (and last) version of Visual Basic is Version 6.0, which was released in 1997.

The new Visual Basic still uses the BASIC language to write code. Visual Basic provides a long overdue enhancement to the language with many new features. In addition, many archaic features than have been around since Bill and Paul's earliest efforts have finally been retired. This chapter provides an overview of the BASIC language used in the Visual Basic environment. If you've ever used another programming language (or some version of BASIC), you will see equivalent structures in the language of Visual Basic.

Visual Basic Statements and Expressions

The simplest (and most common) statement in Visual Basic is the **assignment** statement. It consists of a variable name, followed by the assignment operator (=), followed by some sort of **expression**. The expression on the right hand side is evaluated, then the variable (or property) on the left hand side of the assignment operator is **replaced** by that value of the expression.

Examples:

```
StartTime = Now
lblExplorer.Text = "Captain Spaulding"
BitCount = ByteCount * 8
Energy = Mass * LIGHTSPEED ^ 2
NetWorth = Assets - Liabilities
```

The assignment statement stores information.

Statements normally take up a single line with no terminator. Statements can be **stacked** by using a colon (:) to separate them. Example:

```
StartTime = Now : EndTime = StartTime + 10
```

The above code is the same as if the second statement followed the first statement. Be careful stacking statements, especially with If/End If structures (we'll learn about these soon). You may not get the response you desire. The only place we tend to use stacking is for quick initialization of like variables.

If a statement is very long, it may be continued to the next line using the **continuation** character, an underscore (_). Example:

```
Months = Math.Log(Final * IntRate / Deposit + 1) _
/ Math.Log(1 + IntRate)
```

We don't use continuation statements very much in these notes or in our examples. Be aware that long lines of code in the notes many times wrap around to the next line (due to page margins). Visual Basic 2010 supports what is called "implicit line continuation" which eliminates the need for the underscore character in many situations. We suggest consulting the Microsoft website if you want to use implicit line continuation. There are many rules for its use.

Comment statements begin with the keyword **Rem** or a single quote ('). For example:

```
Rem This is a remark
' This is also a remark
x = 2 * y ' another way to write a remark or comment
```

You, as a programmer, should decide how much to comment your code. Consider such factors as reuse, your audience, and the legacy of your code. In our notes and examples, we try to insert comment statements when necessary to explain some detail.

Strict Type Checking

In each assignment statement, it is important that the type of data on both sides of the operator (=) is the same. That is, if the variable on the left side of the operator is an **Integer**, the result of the expression on the right side should be **Integer**.

Visual Basic (by default) will try to do any conversions for you. Sometimes, however, it 'guesses' incorrectly and may provide incorrect or undesired results. To insure consistency of data types in assignment statements, Visual Basic offers, as an option, **strict type checking**. What this means is that your program will not run unless each side of an assignment operator has the same type of data. With strict type checking, the Intellisense feature of the Code window will identify where there are type inconsistencies and provide suggestions on how to correct the situation.

Strict type checking will force you to write good code and eliminate many potential errors. Because of this, all examples for the remainder of this course will use strict type checking. To turn on strict type checking, we place a single line of code at the top of each application:

```
Option Strict On
```

This line will go right before the header line for the project (at the top of the code window).

Remember, <u>every</u> application should have the above line at the top of the code window. So, as a rule, every new application's code window should immediately be changed to appear like this:

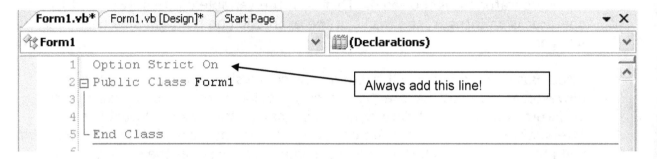

This will enforce both checking across the assignment operator, a very good programming practice.

As an alternate, choose the **Tools** menu, then **Options**. Under **Projects and Solutions**, select **VB Defaults** and make sure **Option Strict** is **On**:

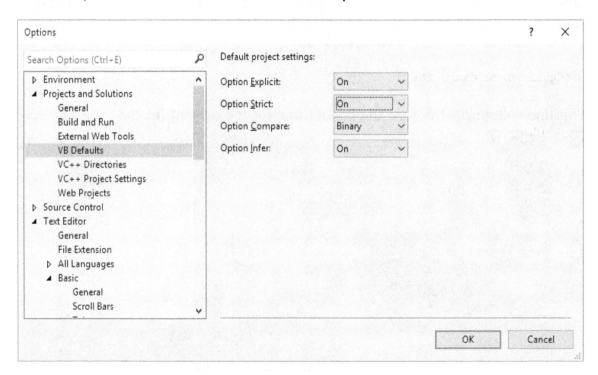

With this option on, the project will require strict type checking.

Strict type checking also means we need ways to convert one data type to another. Visual Basic offers a wealth of functions that perform these conversions. Some of these functions are:

CBool(*Expression*)	Converts a numerical *Expression* to a **Boolean** data type (if *Expression* is nonzero, the result is True, otherwise the result is False)
CChar(*Expression*)	Converts any valid single character string to a **Char** data type
CDate(*Expression*)	Converts any valid date or time *Expression* to a **Date** data type
CDbl(*Expression*)	Converts a numerical *Expression* to a **Double** data type
CInt(*Expression*)	Converts a numerical *Expression* to an **Integer** data type (any fractional parts are rounded)
CLng(*Expression*)	Converts a numerical *Expression* to a **Long** data type (any fractional parts are rounded)
CShort(*Expression*)	Converts a numerical *Expression* to a **Short** data type (any fractional parts are rounded)
CSng(*Expression*)	Converts a numerical *Expression* to a **Single** data type
CType(*Expression*, *Type*)	Converts the *Expression* to the specified *Type*

We will use many of these conversion functions as we write code for our applications and examples. The Intellisense feature of the code window will usually direct us to the function we need.

Visual Basic Arithmetic Operators

Operators modify values of variables. The simplest **operators** carry out **arithmetic** operations. There are seven **arithmetic operators** in Visual Basic.

Addition is done using the plus (+) sign and **subtraction** is done using the minus (-) sign. Simple examples are:

Operation	Example	Result
Addition	7 + 2	9
Addition	3.4 + 8.1	11.5
Subtraction	6 - 4	2
Subtraction	11.1 - 7.6	3.5

Multiplication is done using the asterisk (*) and **division** is done using the slash (/). Simple examples are:

Operation	Example	Result
Multiplication	8 * 4	32
Multiplication	2.3 * 12.2	28.06
Division	12 / 2	6
Division	45.26 / 6.2	7.3

The next operator is the **exponentiation** operator, represented by a carat symbol (^) or sometimes called a 'hat.' Some examples:

Example	Result
5 ^ 2	25
2.6 ^ 4	45.6976
3.7 ^ 3.1	57.733162065075

Notice exponentiation is not limited to whole numbers (do you know how to multiply 3.7 times itself 3.1 times?).

The other arithmetic operators are concerned with dividing integer numbers. The **integer division** operator is a backslash character (\). This works just like normal division except only integer (whole number) answers are possible - any fraction from the division is ignored. Conversely, the **modulus operator**, represented by the keyword **Mod**, divides two whole numbers, ignores the main part of the answer, and just gives you the remainder! It may not be obvious now, but the modulus operator is used a lot in computer programming. Examples of both of these operators are:

Operation	Example	Division Result	Operation Result
Integer division	7 \ 2	3.5	3
Integer division	23.2 \ 10	2.32	2
Integer division	25.2 \ 3.6	7.0	7
Modulus	7 Mod 4	1 Remainder 3	3
Modulus	14 Mod 3	4 Remainder 2	2
Modulus	25 Mod 5	5 Remainder 0	0

The mathematical operators have the following **precedence** indicating the order they are evaluated without specific groupings:

1. Exponentiation (^)
2. Multiplication (*) and division (/)
3. Integer division (\)
4. Modulus (Mod)
5. Addition (+) and subtraction (-)

If multiplications and divisions or additions and subtractions are in the same expression, they are performed in left-to-right order. **Parentheses** around expressions are used to force some desired precedence.

Comparison and Logical Operators

There are six **comparison** operators in Visual Basic used to compare the value of two expressions (the expressions must be of the same data type). These are the basis for making decisions:

Operator	Comparison
>	Greater than
<	Less than
>=	Greater than or equal to
<=	Less than or equal to
=	Equal to
<>	Not equal to

It should be obvious that the result of a comparison operation is a Boolean value (**True** or **False**). **Examples:**

A = 9.6, B = 8.1, A > B returns True
A = 14, B = 14, A < B returns False
A = 14, B = 14, A >= B returns True
A = 7, B = 11, A <= B returns True
A = "Visual", B="Visual", A = B returns True
A = "Basic", B = "Basic", A <> B returns False

Logical operators operate on Boolean data types, providing a Boolean result. They are also used in decision making. We will use three **logical** operators

Operator	Operation
Not	Logical Not
And	Logical And
Or	Logical Or

The **Not** operator simply negates a Boolean value. It is very useful for 'toggling' Boolean variables. Examples:

If A = True, then **Not**(A) = False
If A = False, then **Not**(A) = True

The **And** operator checks to see if two different Boolean data types are both True. If both are True, the operator returns a True. Otherwise, it returns a False value. Examples:

> A = True, B = True, then A **And** B = True
> A = True, B = False, then A **And** B = False
> A = False, B = True, then A **And** B = False
> A = False, B = False, then A **And** B = False

The **Or** operator checks to see if either of two Boolean data types is True. If either is True, the operator returns a True. Otherwise, it returns a False value. Examples:

> A = True, B = True, then A **Or** B = True
> A = True, B = False, then A **Or** B = True
> A = False, B = True, then A **Or** B = True
> A = False, B = False, then A **Or** B = False

Logical operators follow arithmetic operators in precedence. Use of these operators will become obvious as we delve further into coding.

Concatenation Operators

To **concatentate** two string data types (tie them together), use the **&** symbol or the **+** symbol, the string concatenation operators:

```
lblTime.Text = "The current time is" & Format(Now,
"hh:mm")
txtSample.Text = "Hook this " + "to this"
```

Be aware that I use both concatenation operators (primarily the + sign) in these notes – I'm not very consistent (an old habit that's hard to break).

Visual Basic offers other concatenation operators that perform an operation on a variable and assign the resulting value back to the variable. Hence, the operation

```
A = A + 1
```

Can be written using the addition concatenation operator (+=) as:

```
A += 1
```

This says A is incremented by 1.

Other concatenation operators and their symbols are:

Operator Name	Operator Symbol	Operator Task
String	A &= B	A = A & B
String	A += B	A = A + B
Addition	A += B	A = A + B
Subtraction	A -= B	A = A - B
Multiplication	A *= B	A = A * B
Division	A /= B	A = A / B
Integer Division	A \= B	A = A \ B
Exponentiation	A ^= B	A = A ^ B

Notice both &= and += can be used as the string concatenator.

Visual Basic Functions

Visual Basic offers a rich assortment of built-in **functions** that compute or provide various quantities. The on-line help utility will give you information on any or all of these functions and their use. The general form of a function is:

ReturnedValue = FunctionName(Arguments)

where **Arguments** represents a comma-delimited list of information needed by **FunctionName** to perform its computation. Once the arguments are supplied to the function it returns a value (**ReturnedValue**) for use in an application.

Some example functions are:

Function	Returned Value
Asc	ASCII or ANSI code of a character
Chr	Character corresponding to a given ASCII or ANSI code
Format	Date or number converted to a text string
Instr	Locates a substring in another string
Len	Number of characters in a text string
Mid	Selected portion of a text string
Now	Current time and date
Str	Number converted to a text string
Timer	Number of seconds elapsed since midnight
Trim	Removes leading and trailing spaces from string
Val	Numeric value of a given text string

String Functions

Visual Basic offers a powerful set of functions to work with string type variables, which are very important in Visual Basic. The **Text** property of the label control and the text box control are string types. You will find you are constantly converting string types to numeric data types to do some math and then converting back to strings to display the information.

To convert a string type to a numeric value, use the **Val** function. As an example, to convert the Text property of a text box control named txtExample to a number, use:

```
Val(txtExample.Text)
```

This result can then be used with the various mathematical operators. The returned data type is **Double**. If you need the returned value to be some other data type, use one of the conversion functions seen earlier.

There are two ways to convert a numeric variable to a string. The **Str** function does the conversion with no regard for how the result is displayed. This bit of code can be used to display the numeric variable MyNumber in a text box control:

```
MyNumber = 3.14159
txtExample.Text = Str(MyNumber)
```

If you need to control the number of decimal points (or other display features), the **Format** function is used. This function has two arguments, the first is the number, the second a string specifying how to display the number (use on-line help to see how these display specifiers work). As an example, to display MyNumber with no more than two decimal points, use:

```
MyNumber = 3.14159
txtExample.Text = Format(MyNumber, "#.##")
```

In the display string ("#.##"), the pound signs represent place holders.

Many times, you need to extract substrings from string variables. The **Mid** function lets you extract a specified number of characters from anywhere in the string (you specify the string, the starting position and the number of characters to extract). This example extracts 6 characters from the string variable, starting at character 3:

```
MyString = "Visual Basic **** is fun!"
MidString = Mid(MyString, 3, 6)
```

The **MidString** variable is equal to **"sual B"**

Perhaps, you just want a far left portion of a string. Use the **Mid** function with a starting position of 1. This example extracts the 3 left-most characters from a string:

```
MyString = "Visual Basic **** is fun!"
LeftString = Mid(MyString, 1, 3)
```

The **LeftString** variable is equal to **"Vis"**

Getting the far right portion of a string with the **Mid** function is just a bit trickier. First, we need to introduce the **Len** function, which tells us the number of characters in (or length of) a string variable. For our example,

```
MyString = "Visual Basic **** is fun!"
LenString = Len(MyString)
```

LenString will have a value of **25**. Now, if we want the 6 far right characters in the string example, we use:

```
MyString = "Visual Basic **** is fun!"
RightString = Mid(MyString, Len(MyString) - 6 + 1, 6)
```

The **RightString** variable is equal to **"s fun!"** Note that without the **+ 1** in the second argument, we would start one character too far to the left.

The **Mid** function can also be used to replace substrings in string variables, working in a reverse manner. Again, just specify the string, the starting position and number of characters to replace, but use the Mid function on the left side of the assignment operator. With our example, try:

```
MyString = "Visual Basic **** is fun!"
Mid(MyString, 14, 4) = "####"
```

After this replacement, **MyString** will now have a value of:

```
MyString = "Visual Basic #### is fun!"
```

To locate a substring within a string variable, use the **Instr** function. Three arguments are used: starting position in String1 (optional), **String1** (the variable), **String2** (the substring to find). The function will work left-to-right and return the location of the first character of the substring (it will return 0 if the substring is not found). For our example:

```
MyString = "Visual Basic **** is fun!"
Location = Instr(3, MyString, "sic")
```

This says find the substring **"sic"** in **MyString**, starting at character **3** (if this argument is omitted, 1 is assumed). The returned **Location** will have a value of **10**.

Related to the **Instr** function is the **InstrRev** function. This function also identifies substrings using identical arguments, but works right-to-left, or in reverse. So, with our example string:

```
MyString = "Visual Basic **** is fun!"
Location = InstrRev(MyString, "is")
```

This says find the substring **"is"** in **MyString**, starting at the right and working left. The returned **Location** will have a value of **19**. Note if we use Instr instead, the returned **Location** would be **2**.

Many times, you want to convert letters to upper case or vice versa. Visual Basic provides two functions for this purpose: **UCase** and **LCase**. The UCase function will convert all letters in a string variable to upper case, while the LCase function will convert all letters to lower case. Any non-alphabetic characters are ignored in the conversion. And, if a letter is already in the desired case, it is left unmodified. For our example (modified a bit):

```
MyString = "Visual Basic **** in 2015 is fun!"
A = UCase(MyString)
B = LCase(A)
```

The first conversion using **UCase** will result in:

```
A = "VISUAL BASIC **** IN 2015 IS FUN!"
```

And the second conversion using **LCase** will yield:

```
B = "visual basic **** in 2015 is fun!"
```

Another useful pair of functions are the **Asc** and **Chr** functions. These work with individual characters. Every 'typeable' character has a numeric representation called an ASCII (pronounced "askey") code. The Asc function returns the ASCII code for an individual character. For example:

```
Asc("A")
```

returns the ASCII code for the upper case A (65, by the way). The Chr function returns the character represented by an ASCII code. For example:

```
Chr(48)
```

returns the character represented by an ASCII value of 48 (a "1"). The Asc and Chr functions are used often in determining what a user is typing.

String Class Methods

With the newer versions of Visual Basic, string type variables are not actually variables, but **objects** derived from the **String class**. This causes a bit of a problem for Visual Basic programmers. The string functions discussed in the previous section have been used for years by Visual Basic programmers working with strings. Now, that strings are objects, a new set of string properties and methods are available for working with strings.

These new string methods essentially replicate the functionality of the previously seen string functions. So, the question is which set of string functions/methods should be used? In these notes, we have chosen to use the "old functions" since these are most familiar to the Visual Basic programmer. In this section, we will present the equivalent "new methods" for you to study. It is up to you to decide which set of string functions/methods you are more comfortable using.

To convert a string type to a numeric value, use one of the conversion functions seen in the Strict Type Checking section. As an example, to convert the Text property of a text box control named txtExample to an **Integer** type, use:

```
CInt(txtExample.Text)
```

This result can then be used with the various mathematical operators. You need to be careful that the string you are converting to a number is a valid representation of a number. If it is not, an error will occur.

The **ToString** method can be used to convert a numeric variable to a string. This bit of code can be used to display the numeric variable **MyNumber** in a text box control:

```
MyNumber = 3.14159
txtExample.Text = MyNumber.ToString()
```

To control the number of decimals (or other features), use an argument in the ToString method. As an example, to display MyNumber with no more than two decimal places, use:

```
MyNumber = 3.14159
txtExample.Text = MyNumber.ToString("#.##")
```

See on-line help for further formatting information.

To determine the number of characters in (or length of) a string variable, we use the **Length** property. Using **MyString** as example:

```
MyString = "Visual Basic **** is fun!"
LenString = MyString.Length
```

LenString will have a value of **25**. The location of characters in the string object is zero-based. That is, the individual characters for this string start at character 0 and end at character 25. Note this is different from the results using the "old" Visual Basic string functions where characters started at 1.

Many times, you need to extract single characters from string variables. To do this, you specify the array index of the desired character in the string. Recall, characters in a string object start at character 0 and extend to the length of the string minus 1. To determine the character (**MyChar**) at position **n** in a string **MyString**, use:

```
MyChar = MyString(n)
```

For example:

```
MyString = "Visual Basic **** is fun!"
MyChar = MyString(7)
```

will return the **Char** type variable 'B' in **MyChar**.

You can extract substrings of characters. The **Substring** method is used for this task. You specify the string, the starting position and the number of characters to extract. This example starts at character 2 and extracts 6 characters:

```
MyString = "Visual Basic **** is fun!"
MidString = MyString.Substring(2, 6)
```

The **MidString** variable is equal to **"sual B"**

Perhaps, you just want a far left portion of a string. Use the **Substring** method with a starting position of 0. This example extracts the 3 left-most characters from a string:

```
MyString = "Visual Basic **** is fun!"
LeftString = MyString.Substring(0, 3)
```

The **LeftString** variable is equal to **"Vis"**

Getting the far right portion of a string with the **Substring** method requires a bit of math using the **Length** property. If you want r characters from the right side of a string **MyString**, use:

```
MyString.Substring(MyString.Length - r, r)
```

To get 6 characters at the end of our example, you would use:

```
MyString = "Visual Basic **** is fun!"
RightString = MyString.Substring(MyString.Length - 6, 6)
```

The **RightString** variable is equal to **"s fun!"**

To locate a substring within a string variable, use the **IndexOf** method. Three pieces of information are needed: **String1** (the variable), **String2** (the substring to find), and a starting position in **String1** (optional). The method will work left-to-right and return the location of the first character of the substring (it will return -1 if the substring is not found). For our example:

```
MyString = "Visual Basic **** is fun!"
Location = MyString.IndexOf("sic", 2)
```

This says find the substring **"sic"** in **MyString**, starting at character **2**. The returned **Location** will have a value of **9**. If the starting location argument is omitted, 0 is assumed.

Related to the **IndexOf** method is the **LastIndexOf** method. This method also identifies substrings using identical arguments, but works right-to-left, or in reverse. So, with our example string:

```
MyString = "Visual Basic **** is fun!"
Location = MyString.LastIndexOf("is")
```

This says find the substring **"is"** in **MyString**, starting at the right and working left. The returned **Location** will have a value of **18**. Note if we used **IndexOf** (without a starting location), the returned **location** would be **1**.

Many times, you want to convert letters to upper case or vice versa. Visual Basic provides two methods for this purpose: **ToUpper** and **ToLower**. The ToUpper method will convert all letters in a string variable to upper case, while the ToLower method will convert all letters to lower case. Any non-alphabetic characters are ignored in the conversion. And, if a letter is already in the desired case, it is left unmodified. For our example (modified a bit):

```
MyString = "Read Learn Visual Basic **** in 2019!"
A = MyString.ToUpper()
B = MyString.ToLower()
```

The first conversion using **ToUpper** will result in:

```
A = "READ LEARN VISUAL BASIC **** IN 2019!"
```

And the second conversion using **ToLower** will yield:

```
B = "read learn visual basic **** in 2019!"
```

To remove leading and trailing spaces from a string, use the **Trim** method. Its use is obvious:

```
MyString = "    Visual Basic **** is fun!        "
MyString = MyString.Trim()
```

After this, **MyString** = **"Visual Basic **** is fun!"** – the spaces at the beginning and end are removed.

There are many more string methods and properties. Study them as need and use the string methods/functions you feel more comfortable with.

Dates and Times

Working with dates and times in computer applications is a common task. In Class 1, in Example 1-3, Problem 1-4 and Exercise 1, we used the **Date** data type without much discussion. This particular data type is used to specify and determine dates, times and the difference betweens dates and times.

The **Date** data type is used to hold a date <u>and</u> a time. And, even though that's the case, you're usually only interested in the date <u>or</u> the time. To initialize a Date variable (**MyDate**) to a specific date, use:

```
Dim MyDate As Date
MyDate = New Date(Year, Month, Day)
```

where **Year** is the desired year (**Integer** type), **Month** the desired month (**Integer** type), and **Day** the desired day (**Integer** type). The month 'numbers' run from 1 (January) to 12 (December), not 0 to 11. As an example, if you use:

```
MyDate = New Date(1950, 7, 19)
```

then, display the result (after converting it to a string) in some control using:

```
CStr(MyDate)
```

you would get:

7/19/1950 12:00:00 AM

This is my birthday, by the way. The time is set to a default value since only a date was specified.

Other **Date** formats are available using the **Format** function. You will see some of them in further examples, problems and exercises in this course, or consult the on-line help facilities of Visual Basic. Some examples using **MyDate** are:

```
Format(MyDate, "D") ' returns Wednesday, July 19, 1950
Format(MyDate, "d") ' returns 7/19/1950
Format(MyDate, "T") ' returns 12:00:00 AM
Format(MyDate, "t") ' returns 12:00 AM
```

Individual parts of a **Date** object can be retrieved. Examples include:

```
MyDate.Month    ' returns 7
MyDate.Day    ' returns 19
MyDate.DayOfWeek    ' returns 3
```

Notice the **DayOfWeek** property yields a value from 0 (Sunday) to 6 (Saturday), so the 3 above represents a Wednesday.

Visual Basic also allows you to retrieve the current date and time using the **Date** data type. To place the current date in a variable use the **Today** function:

```
Dim MyToday As Date
MyToday = Today
```

The variable **MyToday** will hold today's date with the default time. To place the current date <u>and</u> time in a variable, use the **Now** function:

```
MyToday = Now
```

Doing that at this moment, I get:

```
CStr(MyToday)   ' returns 2/2/2005 12:51:55 PM
```

Many times, you want to know the difference between two dates and/or times, that is, determine some time span. The Visual Basic **DateDiff** function does just that – it allows you to find the difference between any two **Date** variables. The syntax is simple. To compute the difference between two **Date** variables (**Date1** and **Date2**), use:

```
DateDiff(DateInterval, Date1, Date2)
```

This function returns the computed difference (**Date2 - Date1**), using an interval specified by the **DateInterval** argument. Typical values for this argument are:

```
DateInterval.Year   DateInterval.Month
DateInterval.Day   DateInterval.Hour
DateInterval.Minute   DateInterval.Second
```

Note we used this in the Stopwatch application in Class 1.

As an example, let's use today's date (**MyToday**) and the example date (**MyDate**, my birthday) to see how long I've been alive.:

```
DateDiff(DateInterval.Year, MyDate, MyToday) ' returns 55
DateDiff(DateInterval.Month, MyDate, MyToday) ' returns
655
DateDiff(DateInterval.Day, MyDate, MyToday) ' returns
19922
DateDiff(DateInterval.Hour, MyDate, MyToday) ' returns
478144
```

The tells me I've been alive 55 years or 655 months or 19,922 days or 478,144 hours. Looks like I should be getting ready to celebrate my 20,000 days birthday!!

We have only introduced the **Date** data type. You will find it very useful as you progress in your programming studies. Do some research on your own to determine how best to use dates and times in applications you build.

Important: Recall Visual Basic is an object-oriented language. The **Date** type is the first object we have encountered (besides the button, label and text box objects used in Class 1). We will see many more in this course. Note to get a Date type, we followed two steps. We first declared a variable (object) to be from the **Date class** using the standard **Dim** statement:

```
Dim MyDate As Date
```

We then constructed the **Date object** using the **New** keyword and a **constructor** statement:

```
MyDate = New Date(Year, Month, Day)
```

Once constructed, we see the date has **properties** (Day, Month, Year) and **methods**. These new terms will become very familiar as you progress in these notes.

Random Number Object

In writing games and learning software, we use a random number generator to introduce unpredictability. This insures different results each time you try a program. Visual Basic has a few ways to generate random numbers. We will use one of them – a random generator of integers. The generator uses the Visual Basic **Random** object.

To use the Random object (named **MyRandom** here), it is first declared and constructed using:

```
Dim MyRandom As New Random()
```

This statement is placed with the variable declaration statements. Note to obtain this object, we **declared** it and **constructed** it in a single statement (unlike the two step procedure used to obtain a **Date** object).

Once created, when you need a random integer value, use the **Next** method of this Random object:

```
MyRandom.Next(Limit)
```

This statement generates a random integer value that is greater than or equal to 0 and less than **Limit**. Note it is less than limit, not equal to. For example, the method:

```
MyRandom.Next(5)
```

will generate random integers from 0 to 4. The possible values will be 0, 1, 2, 3 and 4.

As other examples, to roll a six-sided die, the number of spots would be computed using:

```
NumberSpots = MyRandom.Next(6) + 1
```

To randomly choose a number between 100 and 200, use:

```
Number = MyRandom.Next(101) + 100
```

Math Functions

A last set of functions we need are mathematical functions (yes, programming involves math!) Visual Basic provides a set of functions that perform tasks such as square roots, trigonometric relationships, and exponential functions.

Each of the Visual Basic math functions comes from the **Math** class of the .NET framework (an object-oriented programming concept). All this means is that each function name must be preceded by **Math.** (say Math-dot) to work properly. The functions and the returned values are:

Math Function	Value Returned
Math.Abs	Returns the absolute value of a specified number
Math.Acos	Returns a Double value containing the angle whose cosine is the specified number
Math.Asin	Returns a Double value containing the angle whose sine is the specified number
Math.Atan	Returns a Double value containing the angle whose tangent is the specified number
Math.Cos	Returns a Double value containing the cosine of the specified angle
Math.E	A constant, the natural logarithm base
Math.Exp	Returns a Double value containing e (the base of natural logarithms) raised to the specified power
Math.Log	Returns a Double value containing the natural logarithm of a specified number
Math.Log10	Returns a Double value containing the base 10 logarithm of a specified number
Math.Max	Returns the largert of two numbers
Math.Min	Returns the smaller of two numbers
Math.PI	A constant that specifies the ratio of the circumference of a circle to its diameter
Math.Round	Returns the number nearest the specified value
Math.Sign	Returns an Integer value indicating the sign of a number
Math.Sin	Returns a Double value containing the sine of the specified angle
Math.Sqrt	Returns a Double value specifying the square root of a number
Math.Tan	Returns a Double value containing the tangent of an angle

Examples:

Math.Abs(-5.4) returns the absolute value of -5.4 (returns 5.4)

Math.Cos(2.3) returns the cosine of an angle of 2.3 radians

Math.Max(7, 10) returns the larger of the two numbers (returns 10)

Math.Sign(-3) returns the sign on -3 (returns a -1)

Math.Sqrt(4.5) returns the square root of 4.5

Example 2-1

Savings Account

1. Start a new project. The idea of this project is to determine how much you save by making monthly deposits into a savings account. For those interested, the mathematical formula used is:

$$F = D \ [\ (1 + I)^M - 1] \ / \ I$$

where

> F - Final amount
> D - Monthly deposit amount
> I - Monthly interest rate
> M - Number of months

2. Place 4 labels, 4 text boxes, and 2 buttons on the form. It should look something like this:

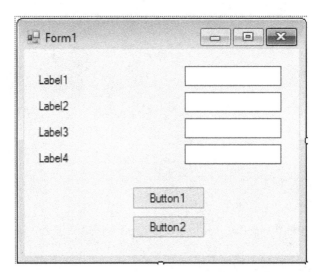

3. Set the properties of the form and each object.

Form1:
Name	frmSavings
FormBorderStyle	Fixed Single
Starting Position	CenterScreen
Text	Savings Account

Label1:
Text	Monthly Deposit

Label2:
Text	Yearly Interest

Label3:
Text	Number of Months

Label4:
Text	Final Balance

TextBox1:
Name	txtDeposit

TextBox2:
Name	txtInterest

TextBox3:
Name	txtMonths

TextBox4:
Name	txtFinal
BackColor	White
ReadOnly	True

Button1:

       Name   btnCalculate

       Text   &Calculate

Button2:

       Name   btnExit

       Text   E&xit

Now, your form should look like this:

4. Type this line in the top of the code window:

```
Option Strict On
```

5. Declare four variables under the **Public Class frmSavings** line in the Code window. This gives them form level scope, making them available to all the form procedures:

```
Dim Deposit As Double
Dim Interest As Double
Dim Months As Double
Dim Final As Double
```

At this point, the Code window should look like this:

```
Example 2-1.vb*  ⇥ ✕  Example 2-1.vb [Design]*
VB Example 2-1              ▾  ⁕ frmSavings              ▾  ⊕ InitializeComponent
   1        Option Strict On
   2      ⊟Public Class frmSavings
   3          Dim Deposit As Double
   4          Dim Interest As Double
   5          Dim Months As Double
   6          Dim Final As Double
   7
   8
   9        End Class
  10
```

6. Write code for the **btnCalculate** button **Click** event (remember to select the **btnCalculate** object from the object box and the **Click** event from the event box):

```
Private Sub BtnCalculate_Click(ByVal sender As
System.Object, ByVal e As System.EventArgs) Handles
btncalculate.Click
    Dim IntRate As Double
    'read values from text boxes
    Deposit = Val(txtDeposit.Text)
    Interest = Val(txtInterest.Text)
    IntRate = Interest / 1200
    Months = Val(txtMonths.Text)
    'compute final value and put in text box
    Final = Deposit * ((1 + IntRate) ^ Months - 1) / IntRate
    txtFinal.Text = Format(Final, "0.00")
End Sub
```

This code reads the three input values (monthly deposit, interest rate, number of months) from the text boxes, converts those string variables to numbers using the **Val** function, converts the yearly interest percentage to monthly interest (**IntRate**), computes the final balance using the provided formula, and puts that result in a text box (after converting it back to a string variable).

7. Now, write code for the **BtnExit** button **Click** event.

```
Private Sub BtnExit_Click(ByVal sender As System.Object,
ByVal e As System.EventArgs) Handles btnExit.Click
    Me.Close()
End Sub
```

8. Play with the program. Make sure it works properly. Here's a run I made:

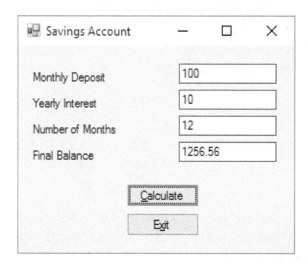

Save the project (**Example 2-1** folder in the **LearnVB\VB Code\Class 2** folder).

Tab Stops and Tab Order

When you run Example 2-1, you should have noticed the cursor didn't necessarily start out at the top text box where you enter the Monthly Deposit. And, if you try to move from text box to text box using the **<Tab>** key, there seems to be no predictable order in how the cursor moves. To enter values, you have to make sure you first click in the text box. To make this process more orderly, we need to understand two properties of controls: **TabStop** and **TabIndex**.

When interacting with a Windows application, we can work with a single control at a time. That is, we can click on a single button or type in a single text box. We can't be doing two things at once. The control we are working with is known as the **active** control or we say the control has **focus**. In our savings account example, when the cursor is in a particular text box, we say that text box has focus. In a properly designed application, focus is shifted from one control to another (in a predictable, orderly fashion) using the **<Tab>** key.

To define an orderly Tab response, we do two things. First, for each control you want accessible via the **<Tab>** key, make sure its **TabStop** property is **True**. All non-accessible controls should have the TabStop property set to False. Second, the order in which the controls will be accessed (given focus) is set by the **TabIndex** property. The control with the lowest TabIndex property will be the first control with focus. Higher subsequent TabIndex properties will be followed with each touch of the **<Tab>** key. The process can be reversed using **<Tab>** in combination with the **<Shift>** key. Once the highest TabIndex property is found, the Tab process restarts at the lowest value.

There are two ways to set **TabIndex** values. You can set the property of each control using the Properties window. This is tedious especially when new controls are introduced to the form. The Visual Basic IDE offers a great tool for setting the TabIndex property of all controls. To show how to use this tool requires a little example.

Start a new project in Visual Basic. Add two text boxes and two buttons to the form. Make your form look something like this:

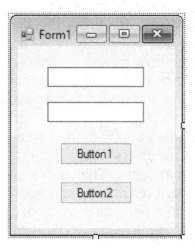

(By the way, this is something you can easily do with Visual Basic – set up quick examples to try different things.) By default, each control will have a TabStop of True and some value of TabIndex. Run the application. Yes, I know there is no code, but that's OK. Press the **<Tab>** key and watch the focus move from control to control. Stop the application. Set Button2's **TabStop** property to **False**. Rerun the application and notice (as expected) that button is now excluded from the tab sequence.

Now, we'll change the **TabIndex** properties. With the form selected (has resizing handles), choose the **View** menu option, and choose **Tab Order**. You should see this:

The little blue number on each control is its corresponding **TabIndex** property. To set (or reset) these values, simply click on each control in the sequence you want the Tab ordering to occur in. If you click on a control with a **False TabStop** property, the index value will be ignored in the Tab sequence. Reset the sequence and run the project again. Notice how easily the Tab sequence is modified. To turn off the tab order display, return to the **View** menu and choose **TabOrder** again (make sure the form is active while doing this or that menu item does not appear in the **View** menu).

Example 2-2

Savings Account – Setting Tabs

1. We will modify our savings account example so it has orderly Tab sequencing. We want the focus to start in the text box requesting Monthly Deposit. Next in sequence will be the text boxes for Interest and Number of Months. We will delete the Tab stop for the Final Deposit box, since we can't type a number there. Next the focus should move to the Calculate button (when this button has focus, if you press **<Enter>** on the keyboard, it is the same as if you clicked on the button). We'll finally delete the tab stop for the Exit key to avoid accidental stopping of the program.

2. Open Example 2-1. Add these two property changes:

    txtFinal Text Box control:
    TabStop   False

    btnExit Button control:
    TabStop   False

3. Select the form and view the **Tab Order**. Set the values as shown (only the values for controls with tab stops are used; others are ignored):

4. Now run the project and notice the nicer orderly flow as the Tab key is pressed. Save the project (**Example 2-2** folder in the **LearnVB\VB Code\Class 2** folder).

Improving a Visual Basic Application

In the previous section, we noted a weakness in the savings application (unpredictable tab ordering) and fixed the problem, improving the performance of our application. This is something you, as a programmer, will do a lot of. You will build an application and while running it and testing it, will uncover weaknesses that need to be eliminated. These weaknesses could be actual errors in the application or just things that, if eliminated, make your application easier to use.

You will find, as you progress as a programmer, that you will spend much of your time improving your applications. You will always find ways to add features to an application and to make it more appealing to your user base. You should never be satisfied with your first solution to a problem. There will always be room for improvement. And Visual Basic provides a perfect platform for adding improvements to an application. You can easily add features and test them to see if the desired performance enhancements are attained.

If you run the savings application a few more times, you can identify further weaknesses:

> ➢ For example, what happens if you input a zero interest? The program will show a final balance of **NaN** (not a number) because the formula that computes the final value will not work with zero interest.
> ➢ Notice you can type any characters you want in the text boxes when you should just be limited to numbers and a single decimal point – any other characters will cause the program to work incorrectly.
> ➢ As a convenience, it would be nice that when you hit the **<Enter>** key after typing a number, the focus would move to the next control.

We can (and will) address each of these points as we improve the savings application. But, to do so, requires learning more BASIC coding. We'll address the zero interest problem first. To solve this problem, we need to be able to make a decision. If the interest is zero, we'll do one computation. If it's not zero, we'll user another. One mechanism for making decisions with Visual Basic is the **If** statement.

Visual Basic Decisions - If Statements

The concept of an **If** statement for making a decision is very simple. We check to see if a particular condition is True. If so, we take a certain action. If not, we do something else. **If** statements are also called **branching** statements. **Branching** statements are used to cause certain actions within a program if a certain condition is met.

The simplest branching statement is the single line **If/Then** statement:

    If Condition **Then** [Do This]

In this statement, if **Condition** (some expression with a Boolean result) is **True**, then whatever single statement follow the Then keyword will be executed. If Condition is False, nothing is done and program execution continues following this line of code. **Example:**

```
If (Balance - Check) < 0 Then Trouble = True
```

Here, if and only if Balance - Check is less than zero, the Trouble variable is set to True.

Single line **If/Then** statements are not considered to be 'structured programming.' They are sloppy programming practice. But, having said this, you will see that this author (and others) uses them (a bad habit I'm trying to phase out).

The structured approach to decisions is the **If/Then/End If** blocks which allow multiple statements to be processed for a decision:

    If Condition **Then**
        [process this code]
    End If

Here, if **Condition** is **True**, the code bounded by the If/End If is executed. If Condition is False, nothing happens and code execution continues after the End If statement.

Example:

```
If Balance - Check < 0 Then
   Trouble = True
   lblBalance.ForeColor = Color.Red
End If
```

In this case, if Balance - Check is less than zero, two lines of information are processed: Trouble is set to True and the balance is displayed in red. Notice the indentation of the code between the **If** and **End If** lines. The Visual Basic Intellisense feature will automatically do this indentation. It makes understanding (and debugging) your code much easier. You can adjust the amount of indentation using the **Options** choice under the **Tools** menu. You will also notice that the Intellisense feature of the IDE will add an **End If** statement for you as soon as you type the **If/Then** line.

What if you want to do one thing if a condition is True and another if it is False? Use an **If/Then/Else/End If** block:

If Condition **Then**
    [process this code]
Else
    [process this code]
End If

In this block, if Condition is True, the code between the If and Else lines is executed. If Condition is False, the code between the Else and End If statements is processed.

Example:

```
If Balance - Check < 0 Then
   Trouble = True
   lblBalance.ForeColor = Color.Red
Else
   Trouble = False
   lblBalance.ForeColor = Color.Black
End If
```

Here, the same two lines are executed if you are overdrawn (Balance - Check < 0), but if you are not overdrawn (**Else**), the Trouble flag is turned off and your balance is in the black.

Finally, we can test multiple conditions by adding the **ElseIf** statement:

If Condition1 **Then**
    [process this code]
ElseIf Condition2 **Then**
    [process this code]
ElseIf Condition3 **Then**
    [process this code]
Else
    [process this code]
End If

In this block, if Condition1 is True, the code between the If and first ElseIf line is executed. If Condition1 is False, Condition2 is checked. If Condition2 is True, the indicated code is executed. If Condition2 is not true, Condition3 is checked. Each subsequent condition in the structure is checked until a True condition is found, a Else statement is reached or the End If is reached.

Example:

```
If Balance - Check < 0 Then
  Trouble = True
  lblBalance.ForeColor = Color.Red
ElseIf Balance - Check = 0 Then
  Trouble = False
  lblBalance.ForeColor = Color.Yellow
Else
  Trouble = False
  lblBalance.ForeColor = Color.Black
End If
```

Now, one more condition is added. If your Balance equals the Check amount (**ElseIf** Balance - Check = 0), you're still not in trouble and the balance is displayed in yellow.

In using branching statements, make sure you consider all viable possibilities in the If/Else/End If structure. Also, be aware that each If and ElseIf in a block is tested sequentially. The first time an If test is met, the code associated with that condition is executed and the If block is exited. If a later condition is also True, it will never be considered.

Select Case - Another Way to Branch

In addition to If/Then/Else type statements, the **Select Case** format can be used when there are multiple selection possibilities. Select Case is used to make decisions based on the value of a single variable. The structure is:

Select Case Variable
Case [variable has this value]
   [process this code]
Case [variable has this value]
   [process this code]
Case [variable has this value]
   [process this code]
Case Else
   [process this code]
End Select

The way this works is that the value of **Variable** is examined. Each **Case** statement is then sequentially examined until the value matches one of the specified cases. Once found, the corresponding code is executed. If no case match is found, the code in the Case Else segment (if there) is executed.

As an example, say we've written this code using the **If** statement:

```
If Age = 5 Then
  Category = "Five Year Old"
ElseIf Age >= 13 and Age <= 19 Then
  Category = "Teenager"
ElseIf (Age >= 20 and Age <= 35) Or Age = 50 Or (Age >= 60
and Age <= 65) Then
  Category = "Special Adult"
ElseIf Age > 65 Then
  Category = "Senior Citizen"
Else
  Category = "Everyone Else"
End If
```

This will work, but it is ugly code and difficult to maintain.

The corresponding code with **Select Case** is much 'cleaner':

```
Select Case Age
Case 5
  Category = "Five Year Old"
Case 13 To 19
  Category = "Teenager"
Case 20 To 35, 50, 60 To 65
  Category = "Special Adult"
Case Is > 65
  Category = "Senior Citizen"
Case Else
  Category = "Everyone Else"
End Select
```

Notice there are several formats for the **Case** statement. Consult on-line help for discussions of these formats.

Like the If structure, the Select Case searches down each Case until it finds the first 'match.' Then, that code is executed. Only one Case for each Select Case can be executed. There is no possibility of a 'global' Select Case that would execute multiple Case statements. Make sure each Select Case you use accurately reflects the decision you are trying to implement.

Key Trapping

Recall in the savings example, there is nothing to prevent the user from typing in meaningless characters (for example, letters) into the text boxes expecting numerical data. We want to keep this from happening. Whenever getting input from a user using a text box control, we want to limit the available keys they can press. This process of intercepting and eliminating unacceptable keystrokes is called **key trapping**.

Key trapping is done in the **KeyPress** event procedure of a text box control. Such a procedure has the form (for a text box named **txtText**):

```
Private Sub TxtText_KeyPress(ByVal sender As Object, ByVal
e As System.Windows.Forms.KeyPressEventArgs) Handles
txtText.KeyPress
    .
    .
    .
End Sub
```

What happens in this procedure is that every time a key is pressed in the corresponding text box, the **KeyPressEventArgs** class passes the key that has been pressed into the procedure via the **Char** type **e.KeyChar** property. Recall the **Char** type is used to represent a single character. We can thus examine this key. If it is an acceptable key, we set the **e.Handled** property to **False**. This tells Visual Basic that this procedure has not been handled and the KeyPress should be allowed. If an unacceptable key is detected, we set **e.Handled** to **True**. This 'tricks' Visual Basic into thinking the KeyPress event has already been handled and the pressed key is ignored.

We need someone way of distinguishing what keys are pressed. The usual alphabetic, numeric and character keys are fairly simple to detect. To help detect other keys, known as control keys, Visual Basic has predefined values in the **ControlChars** module. Some values for these keys we will use:

Value	Definition
ControlChars.Back	Backspace
ControlChars.Cr	Carriage return (<Enter> key)
ControlChars.NullChar	Null character
ControlChars.Quote	Double quote
ControlChars.Tab	Tab

As an example, let's build a key trapping routine for our savings application example. We'll work with the **txtDeposit** control, knowing the KeyPress events for the other text box controls will be similar. There are several ways to build a key trapping routine. I suggest a Select Case structure that, based on different values of **e.KeyChar**, takes different steps. If e.KeyChar represents a number, a decimal point or a backspace key (always include backspace or the user won't be able to edit the text box properly), we will allow the keypress (e.Handled = False). Otherwise, we will set e.Handled = True to ignore the keypress. The code to do this is:

```
Select Case e.KeyChar
  Case CChar("0") To CChar("9"), CChar("."),
ControlChars.Back
   'Acceptable keystrokes
    e.Handled = False
  Case Else
    e.Handled = True
End Select
```

Note the use of the **CChar** function to convert single characters to Char type variables, the same type as e.KeyChar. And, note ControlChars.Back is not on a separate line in the code window, it is just displayed that way here due to page margins.

Note, the above code does not eliminate one of the earlier identified problems. That is, there is nothing to keep the user from typing multiple decimal points. To solve this, we let the 'decimal point' have its own case:

```
Case CChar(".")
  If InStr(txtInterest.Text, ".") = 0 Then
  'No decimal point yet
    e.Handled = False
  Else
    e.Handled = True
  End If
```

In this new case, if there is no decimal point (determined using the **Instr** function), the keypress is allowed. If a decimal point is already there (Instr returns a nonzero value), the keypress is disallowed.

Control Focus

Earlier we saw that, in a running application, only one control can have user interaction at any one time. We say that control has **focus**. A text box with the cursor has focus – if the user begins typing, the typed characters go in that text box. If a button control has focus, that button can be 'clicked' by simply pressing the **<Enter>** key.

We also saw that the **<Tab>** key could be used to move from control to control, shifting the focus. Many times, you might like to move focus from one control to another in code, or programmatically. For example, in our savings example, once the user types in a Deposit Amount, it would be nice if focus would be moved to the Interest text box if the user presses **<Enter>**. We can do that with another 'Case' in our KeyPress event.

To programmatically assign focus to a control, apply the Focus() method to the control using this dot-notation:

ControlName.**Focus**()

The **Case** to do this in our **txtDeposit** text box key trapping routine would be:

```
Case ControlChars.Cr
   'enter key - move to next box
   txtInterest.Focus()
   e.Handled = False
```

Here, if the <Enter> key is pressed (ControlChars.Cr), focus is shifted to the txtInterest text box control. We'll now put this code with our earlier code to add complete key trapping capabilities to our savings application.

Example 2-3

Savings Account - Key Trapping

1. We modify the Savings Account example to handle a zero interest value and to implement key trapping in the three text box **KeyPress** events. The key trapping implemented will only allow numbers, a single decimal point and the backspace. If **<Enter>** is pressed, focus is passed to the next control.

2. Modify the **btnCalculate Click** event code to accommodate a zero interest input. Note if Interest is zero, the final value is just the deposited amount times the number of months. The modified routine is (new code shaded):

```
Private Sub BtnCalculate_Click(ByVal sender As
System.Object, ByVal e As System.EventArgs) Handles
btnCalculate.Click
    Dim IntRate As Double
    'read values from text boxes
    Deposit = Val(txtDeposit.Text)
    Interest = Val(txtInterest.Text)
    IntRate = Interest / 1200
    Months = Val(txtMonths.Text)
    'compute final value and put in text box
    If Interest = 0 Then
      'zero interest case
      Final = Deposit * Months
    Else
      Final = Deposit * ((1 + IntRate) ^ Months - 1) /
IntRate
    End If
    txtFinal.Text = Format(Final, "0.00")
  End Sub
```

(In some of the statements above, the word processor may cause a line break where there really shouldn't be one. In all code in these notes, always look for such things.)

3. Add the following code to **TxtDeposit** text box **KeyPress** event:

```
Private Sub txtDeposit_KeyPress(ByVal sender As Object,
ByVal e As System.Windows.Forms.KeyPressEventArgs) Handles
txtDeposit.KeyPress
    'only allow numbers, a single decimal point, backspace
or enter
    Select Case e.KeyChar
      Case CChar("0") To CChar("9"), ControlChars.Back
        'acceptable keystrokes
        e.Handled = False
      Case ControlChars.Cr
        'enter key - move to next box
        txtInterest.Focus()
        e.Handled = False
      Case CChar(".")
        'check for existence of decimal point
        If InStr(txtDeposit.Text, ".") = 0 Then
          e.Handled = False
        Else
          e.Handled = True
        End If
      Case Else
        e.Handled = True
    End Select
  End Sub
```

This code limits keystrokes to numbers, a single decimal point, the backspace key and moves focus to the **txtInterest** control if <Enter> is hit.

4. Add the following code to **txtInterest** text box **KeyPress** event (nearly same as above – use cut and paste – differences involve control names and where focus moves after **<Enter>**):

```
Private Sub TxtInterest_KeyPress(ByVal sender As Object,
ByVal e As System.Windows.Forms.KeyPressEventArgs) Handles
txtInterest.KeyPress
    'only allow numbers, a single decimal point, backspace
or enter
    Select Case e.KeyChar
      Case CChar("0") To CChar("9"), ControlChars.Back
        'acceptable keystrokes
        e.Handled = False
      Case ControlChars.Cr
        'enter key - move to next box
        txtMonths.Focus()
        e.Handled = False
      Case CChar(".")
        'check for existence of decimal point
        If InStr(txtInterest.Text, ".") = 0 Then
          e.Handled = False
        Else
          e.Handled = True
        End If
      Case Else
        e.Handled = True
    End Select
End Sub
```

This code limits keystrokes to numbers, a single decimal point, the backspace key and moves focus to the **txtMonth** control if **<Enter>** is hit.

5. Add the following code to **txtMonths** text box **KeyPress** event (nearly same as above – use cut and paste – differences involve control names, no decimal points allowed and where focus moves after **<Enter>**):

```
Private Sub TxtMonths_KeyPress(ByVal sender As Object,
ByVal e As System.Windows.Forms.KeyPressEventArgs) Handles
txtMonths.KeyPress
    'only allow numbers, backspace  or enter
    Select Case e.KeyChar
      Case CChar("0") To CChar("9"), ControlChars.Back
        'acceptable keystrokes
        e.Handled = False
      Case ControlChars.Cr
        'enter key - move to calculate button
        btnCalculate.Focus()
        e.Handled = False
      Case Else
        e.Handled = True
    End Select
End Sub
```

This code limits keystrokes to numbers, the backspace key and moves focus to the **btnCalculate** control if **<Enter>** is hit. Notice we don't allow decimal points here – you can't enter a fractional month!

6. Rerun the application and test the key trapping performance. Here's I case I ran to test the zero interest possibility:

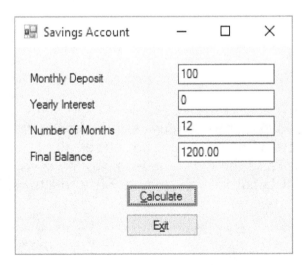

Save the application (**Example 2-3** folder in the **LearnVB\VB Code\Class 2** folder).

Visual Basic Looping

Many applications require repetition of certain code segments. For example, you may want to roll a die (simulated die of course) until it shows a six. Or, you might generate financial results until a certain sum of returns has been achieved. This idea of repeating code is called iteration or **looping**.

In Visual Basic looping is done with the **Do/Loop** format:

```
Do
    [process this code]
Loop
```

In this structure, all code between the **Do** (starts the loop) and the **Loop** statement is repeated until the loop is exited. This brings up a very important point – if you use a loop, make sure you can get out of the loop!! It is especially important in the event-driven environment of Visual Basic. As long as your code is operating in some loop, no events can be processed. The **Exit Do** statement will get you out of a loop and transfer program control to the statement following the **Loop** statement. Of course, you need logic in a loop to decide when an Exit Do is appropriate.

Another way to exit a loop is to test conditions prior to or following execution of the code in loop. This is achieved using **Until** and **While** statements. These statements can be used with the Do statement or the Loop statement. Let's look at examples of all possible combinations.

A **Do While/Loop** structure:

```
Do While Condition
    [process this code]
Loop
```

In this structure, the loop is repeated 'as long as' the Boolean expression Condition is True. Note a Do While/Loop structure will not execute even once if the While condition is False the first time through. If we do enter the loop, it is assumed at some point Condition will become False to allow exiting.

Example:

```
Counter = 1
Do While Counter <= 1000
   Counter += 1
Loop
```

This loop repeats as long as (**While**) the variable Counter is less than or equal to 1000.

A **Do Until/Loop** structure:

Do Until Condition
      [process this code]
Loop

In this structure, the loop is repeated 'until' the Boolean expression Condition is True. Note a Do Until/Loop structure will not be entered if the Until condition is already True on the first encounter. However, once the loop is entered, it is assumed at some point Condition will become True to allow exiting.

Example:

```
Roll = 0
Counter = 0
Do Until Counter = 10
   'Roll a simulated die
   Roll += 1
   If MyRandom.Next(6) + 1 = 6 Then
     Counter += 1
   End If
Loop
```

This loop repeats **Until** the Counter variable equals 10. The Counter variable is incremented each time a simulated die rolls a 6. The Roll variable tells you how many rolls of the die were needed.

A **Do/Loop While** structure:

Do
    [process this code]
Loop While Condition

This loop repeats 'as long as' the Boolean expression Condition is True. The loop is always executed at least once. Somewhere in the loop, Condition must be changed to False to allow exiting.

Example:

```
Sum = 0
Do
   Sum += 3
Loop While Sum <= 50
```

In this example, we increment a sum by 3 until that sum exceeds 50 (or **While** the sum is less than or equal to 50).

A **Do/Loop Until** structure:

```
Do
    [process this code]
Loop Until Condition
```

This loop repeats until the Boolean expression Condition is True. The loop is always executed at least once. Somewhere in the loop, Condition must be become True for proper exiting.

Example:

```
Sum = 0
Counter = 0
Do
   'Roll a simulated die
   Sum += MyRandom.Next(6) + 1
   Counter += 1
Loop Until Sum > 30
```

This loop rolls a simulated die **Until** the Sum of the rolls exceeds 30. It also keeps track of the number of rolls (Counter) needed to achieve this sum.

Again, make sure you can always get out of a loop! Infinite loops are never nice. If you get into one, try **Ctrl+Break**. That sometimes works - other times the only way out is rebooting your machine!

Visual Basic Counting

With Do/Loop structures, we usually didn't know, ahead of time, how many times we execute a loop or iterate. If you know how many times you need to iterate on some code, you want to use Visual Basic **counting**. Counting is useful for adding items to a list or perhaps summing a known number of values to find an average.

Visual Basic counting is accomplished using the **For/Next** loop:

```
For Variable = Start To End [Step Increment]
    [process this code]
Next Variable
```

In this loop, **Variable** is the counter (doesn't necessarily need to be a whole number). The first time through the loop, Variable is initialized at **Start**. Each time the corresponding **Next** statement is reached, Variable is incremented by an amount **Increment**. If the **Step** value is omitted, a default increment value of one is used. Negative increments are also possible. The counting repeats until Variable equals or exceeds the final value **End**.

Example:

```
For Degrees = 0 To 360 Step 10
  'convert to radians
  R = Degrees * Math.PI / 180
  A = Math.Sin(R)
  B = Math.Cos(R)
  C = Math.Tan(R)
Next Degrees
```

In this example, we compute trigonometric functions for angles from 0 to 360 degrees in increments (steps) of 10 degrees. . Notice that the Intellisense feature of the IDE will add a **Next** statement for you as soon as you type the **For** line. I suggest always appending the variable name to the Next statement as soon as it appears. This is not necessary (the variable name in the Next statement is optional), but good programming practice to make your code clearer.

Another Example:

```
For Countdown = 10 to 0 Step -1
   lblTimeRemaining.Text = Format(Countdown, "0") +
"Seconds"
Next Countdown
```

NASA called and asked us to format a label control to countdown from 10 to 0. The loop above accomplishes the task.

And, another Example:

```
Dim MyValues(100) as Double
Sum = 0
For I = 1 to 100
   Sum += MyValues(I)
Next I
Average = Sum / 100
```

This code finds the average value of 100 numbers stored in the array MyValues. It first sums each of the values in a **For/Next** loop. That sum is then divided by the number of terms (100) to yield the average.

You may exit a For/Next loop early using an **Exit For** statement. This will transfer program control to the statement following the **Next** statement.

Example 2-4

Savings Account - Decisions

As built, our savings account application is useful, but we can add more capability. For example, what if we know how much money we need in a number of months and the interest our deposits can earn. It would be nice if the program could calculate the needed month deposit. Or, what if we want to know how long it will take us to reach a goal, knowing how much we can deposit each month and the related interest. Here, we modify the Savings Account project to allow entering any three values and computing the fourth.

1. First, add a third button that will clear all of the text boxes. Assign the following properties:

   Button3:
        Name   btnClear
        Text   C&lear

The form should look something like this when you're done:

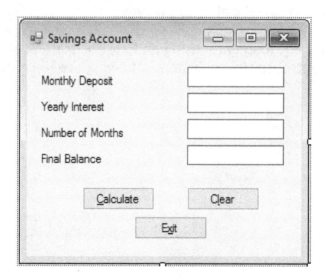

2. Code the **btnClear** button **Click** event:

```
Private Sub BtnClear_Click(ByVal sender As System.Object,
ByVal e As System.EventArgs) Handles btnClear.Click
    'blank out text boxes
    txtDeposit.Text = ""
    txtInterest.Text = ""
    txtMonths.Text = ""
    txtFinal.Text = ""
    txtDeposit.Focus()
End Sub
```

This code simply blanks out the four text boxes when the **Clear** button is clicked. It then redirects focus to the txtDeposit text box.

3. We now need the capability to enter information into the Final Balance text box. Related to this:

   ➢ Change the **ReadOnly** property of the **txtFinal** text box to False
   ➢ Change **TabStop** to **True**
   ➢ Reset the **Tab Order** so, the txtFinal text box is included
   ➢ Modify the **txtMonths KeyPress** event so focus is transferred to the **txtFinal** text box when **<Enter>** is pressed

4. Code the **KeyPress** event for the **txtFinal** object:

```
Private Sub TxtFinal_KeyPress(ByVal sender As Object,
ByVal e As System.Windows.Forms.KeyPressEventArgs) Handles
txtFinal.KeyPress
    'only allow numbers, a single decimal point, backspace
or enter
    Select Case e.KeyChar
      Case CChar("0") To CChar("9"), ControlChars.Back
        'acceptable keystrokes
        e.Handled = False
      Case ControlChars.Cr
        'enter key - move to calculate button
        btnCalculate.Focus()
        e.Handled = False
      Case CChar(".")
        'check for existence of decimal point
        If InStr(txtFinal.Text, ".") = 0 Then
          e.Handled = False
        Else
          e.Handled = True
        End If
      Case Else
        e.Handled = True
    End Select
  End Sub
```

Recall, we need this code because we can now enter information into the Final Value text box. It is very similar to the other KeyPress events. This code limits keystrokes to numbers, a single decimal point, the backspace key and moves focus to the **btnCalculate** control if **<Enter>** is hit.

5. The modified code for the **Click** event of the **btnCalculate** button is (new code is shaded):

```
Private Sub BtnCalculate_Click(ByVal sender As
System.Object, ByVal e As System.EventArgs) Handles
btnCalculate.Click
    Dim IntRate As Double
    Dim FinalCompute As Double, IntChange As Double,
IntDirection As Integer
    'Read values from text boxes
    Deposit = Val(txtDeposit.Text)
    Interest = Val(txtInterest.Text)
    IntRate = Interest / 1200
    Months = Val(txtMonths.Text)
    Final = Val(txtFinal.Text)
    'Determine which box is blank
    'Compute that missing value and put in text box
    If Trim(txtDeposit.Text) = "" Then
        'Deposit missing
        If Interest = 0 Then
            Deposit = Final / Months
        Else
            Deposit = Final / (((1 + IntRate) ^ Months - 1) /
IntRate)
        End If
        txtDeposit.Text = Format(Deposit, "0.00")
    ElseIf Trim(txtInterest.Text) = "" Then
        'Interest missing - requires iterative solution
        'IntChange is how much we change interest each step
        'IntDirection is direction (+ or -) we change interest
        Interest = 0
        IntChange = 1
        IntDirection = 1
        Do
            Interest += IntDirection * IntChange
            IntRate = Interest / 1200
            FinalCompute = Deposit * ((1 + IntRate) ^ Months -
1) / IntRate
            If IntDirection = 1 Then
                If FinalCompute > Final Then
                    IntDirection = -1
                    IntChange /= 10
                End If
            Else
                If FinalCompute < Final Then
                    IntDirection = 1
                    IntChange /= 10
```

```
            End If
         End If
      Loop Until Math.Abs(FinalCompute - Final) < 0.005
      txtInterest.Text = Format(Interest, "0.00")
   ElseIf Trim(txtMonths.Text) = "" Then
      'Months missing
      If Interest = 0 Then
        Months = Final / Deposit
      Else
        Months = Math.Log(Final * IntRate / Deposit + 1) /
Math.Log(1 + IntRate)
      End If
      txtMonths.Text = Format(Months, "0.00")
   ElseIf Trim(txtFinal.Text) = "" Then
         'Final value missing
         If Interest = 0 Then
           Final = Deposit * Months
         Else
           Final = Deposit * ((1 + IntRate) ^ Months - 1) /
IntRate
         End If
         txtFinal.Text = Format(Final, "0.00")
      End If
  End Sub
```

In this code. we first read the text information from all four text boxes and based on which one is blank (the **Trim** function strips off leading and trailing blanks), compute the missing information and display it in the corresponding text box.

Let's look at the math involved in solving for missing information. Recall the equation given in Example 2-1:

$$F = D\,[\,(1 + I)^M - 1\,]\,/\,I$$

where F is the final amount, D the deposit, I the monthly interest, and M the number of months. This is the equation we've been using to solve for **Final** and we still use it here if the **Final** box is empty, unless the interest is zero. For zero interest, we use:

$$F = DM, \text{ if interest is zero}$$

See if you can find these equations in the code.

If the **Deposit** box is empty, we can easily solve the equation for D (the needed quantity):

$$D = F/ \{[(1 + I)^M - 1] / I\}$$

If the interest is zero, this equation will not work. In that case, we use:

$$D = F/M, \text{ if interest is zero}$$

You should be able to find these equations in the code above.

Solving for missing **Months** information requires knowledge of logarithms. I'll just give you the equation:

$$M = \log (FI / D + 1) / \log (1 + I)$$

In this Visual Basic, the logarithm (log) function is one of the math functions, **Math.Log**. Like the other cases, we need a separate equation for zero interest:

$$M = F/D, \text{ if interest is zero}$$

Again, see if you can find these equations in the code.

If the **Interest** value is missing, we need to resort to a widely used method for solving equations - we'll guess! But, we'll use a structured guessing method. Here's what we'll do. We'll start with a zero interest and increase it by one percent until the computed final amount is larger than the displayed final amount. At that point, we know the interest is too high so, we decrease the interest by a smaller amount (0.1 percent) until the computed final amount is less than the displayed final amount, meaning the interest is too low. We start increasing the interest again (this time by 0.01 percent). We'll repeat this process until the computed final amount is with 1 cent of the displayed amount. This kind of process is called **iteration** and is used often in computer programs. You should be able to see each step in the code - a good example of a Do loop.

Don't be intimidated by the code in this example. I'll admit there's a lot of it! Upon study, though, you should see that it is just a straightforward list of instructions for the computer to follow based on input from the user.

6. Test and save your application (**Example 2-4** folder in the **LearnVB\VB Code\Class 2** folder). Here's a run I made (note the **Clear** button):

Try clearing each box one at a time and recalculating the missing value - then relax!.

Class Review

After completing this class, you should understand:

➤ Visual Basic statements and reasons for strict type checking
➤ The BASIC assignment operator, mathematics operators, comparison and logic operators and concatenation operators
➤ The wide variety of built-in Visual Basic functions, especially string function, the random number generator, and mathematics functions
➤ How to set tabs and assign tab order to controls
➤ The **If/Then/Else If/Else/End If** structure used for branching and decisions
➤ The **Select Case/End Select** decision structure
➤ How key trapping can be used to eliminate unwanted keystrokes from text box controls
➤ The concept of control focus and how to assign focus in code
➤ How the **Do/Loop** structure is used in conjunction with the **While** and **Until** statements
➤ How the **For/Next** loop is used for counting

Practice Problems 2

Problem 2-1. Random Number Problem. Build an application where each time a button is clicked, a random number from 1 to 100 is displayed.

Problem 2-2. Price Problem. The neighborhood children built a lemonade stand. The hotter it is, the more they can charge. Build an application that produces the selling price, based on temperature:

Temperature	Price
<50	Don't bother
50 – 60	20 Cents
61 – 70	25 Cents
71 – 80	30 Cents
81 – 85	40 Cents
86 – 90	50 Cents
91 – 95	55 Cents
96 – 100	65 Cents
>100	75 Cents

Problem 2-3. Odd Integers Problem. Build an application that adds consecutive odd integers (starting with one) until the sum exceeds a target value. Display the sum and how many integers were added.

Problem 2-4. Pennies Problem. Here's an old problem. Today, I'll give you a penny. Tomorrow, I'll give you two pennies. I'll keep doubling the amount I'll give you for 30 days. How much will you have at the end of the month (better use a **Long** integer type to keep track)?

Problem 2-5. Code Problem. Build an application with a text box and two buttons. Type a word or words in the text box. Click one of the buttons. Subtract one from the ASCII code of each character in the typed word(s), then redisplay it. This is a simple encoding technique. When you click the other button, reverse the process to decode the word.

Exercise 2-1

Computing a Mean and Standard Deviation

Develop an application that allows the user to input a sequence of numbers. When done inputting the numbers, the program should compute the mean of that sequence and the standard deviation. If N numbers are input, with the ith number represented by x_i, the formula for the mean ($\bar{x}$) is:

$$\bar{x} = \left(\sum_{i=1}^{N} x_i\right)/ N$$

and to compute the standard deviation (s), take the square root of this equation:

$$s^2 = \left[N\sum_{i=1}^{N} x_i^2 - \left(\sum_{i=1}^{N} x_i\right)^2\right]/[N(N-1)]$$

The Greek sigmas in the above equations simply indicate that you add up all the corresponding elements next to the sigma. If the standard deviation equation scares you, just write code to find the average value – you should have no trouble with that one.

Exercise 2-2

Flash Card Addition Problems

Write an application that generates random addition problems. Provide some kind of feedback and scoring system as the problems are answered.

3. Object Oriented Programming (OOP)

Review and Preview

Visual Basic is object-oriented, where objects are reusable entities of code. In the first two chapters, we have used several "built-in" objects: button controls, label controls, text box controls, Date object and Random objects. Having these reusable objects available makes our programming life much simpler, reducing the need to write and rewrite code.

In this class, we learn the terminology of object-oriented programming (OOP), learn to create our own objects and learn to extend existing objects to customize them for our use (the idea of inheritance).

Introduction to Object-Oriented Programming (OOP)

We say Visual Basic is an **object-oriented** language. In the first two classes, we have used some of the built-in objects included with Visual Basic. We have used button objects, text box objects and label objects. We see that objects have **properties** (Name, Text, BackColor) and **methods** (Focus, PerformClick). We have used date objects and random number objects where we were introduced to the ideas of **declaring** an object and **constructing** an object.

We have seen that objects are just things that have attributes (properties) with possible actions (methods). As you progress in your programming education, you may want to include your own objects in applications you build. But, it's tough to decide when you need (if ever) an object. A general rule is that you might want to consider using an object when you are working with some entity that fits the structure of having properties and methods and has some **re-use potential**.

The big advantage to objects (as seen with the ones we've used already) is that they can be used over and over again. This re-use can be multiple copies (**instances**) of a single object within a particular application or can be the re-use of a particular object in several different applications (like the controls of Visual Basic).

The most common object is some entity with several describing features (**properties**). Such objects in other languages are called **structured variables**. One could be a line object using the end points, line thickness and line color as properties. Or, a person could be an object, with name, address, phone number as properties.

You could extend these simple objects (properties only) by adding **methods**. Methods allow an object to do something. With our simple line object example, we could add methods to draw a line, erase a line, color a line, and dot a line. In the person object example, we could have methods to sort, search or print the person objects.

I realize this explanation of when to use your own objects is rather vague. And, it has to be. Only through experience can you decide when you might need an object. As we progress through the remainder of this course, we will use more and more objects. This will show you how objects can be employed in Visual Basic. And, don't feel bad if you never use a custom object. The great power of Visual Basic is that you can do many things just using the built-in objects! In this class, we'll look at how to add an object to a Visual Basic application, discussing properties, constructors and methods. And we'll look at how to modify an existing object (a Visual Basic control) to meet some custom needs.

A word of warning – we are jumping a bit ahead presenting OOP material early in this course. Some of the material introduced here (such as functions and argument lists) is covered more deeply later in the course. If anything is unclear, do a little research on our own if you need further explanation – or just accept what we say for now and it should become clearer as you progress in your programming education.

Objects in Visual Basic

Let's review some of the vocabulary of object-oriented programming. These are terms you've seen before in working with the built-in objects of Visual Basic. A **class** provides a general description of an **object**. All objects are created from this class description. The first step in creating an object is adding a class to a Visual Basic project. Every application we build in this course is a class itself. Note the top line of every application has the keyword **Class**.

The **class** provides a framework for describing three primary components:

> ➢ **Properties** – attributes describing the objects
> ➢ **Constructors** – procedures that initialize the object
> ➢ **Methods** – procedures describing things an object can do

Once a class is defined, an object can be declared or **instantiated** from the class. This simply means we use the class description to create a copy of the object we can work with. Once the instance is created, we **construct** the finished object for our use.

One last important term to define, related to OOP, is **inheritance**. This is a capability that allows one object to 'borrow' properties and methods from another object. This prevents the classic 'reinventing the wheel' situation. Inheritance is one of the most powerful features of OOP. In this chapter, we will see how to use inheritance in a simple example and how we can create our own control that inherits from an existing control.

Adding a Class to a Visual Basic Project

The first step in creating our own object is to define the class from which the object will be created. This step (and all following steps) is best illustrated by example. In the example here, we will be creating **Widget** objects that have two properties: a **color** and a **size**. Start a new project in Visual Basic – name the project **WidgetClass**. Place a text box control on the form. Set these properties:

Form1:

Name	frmWidget
FormBorderStyle	Fixed Single
Starting Position	CenterScreen
Text	Widget Class Example

TextBox1:

Name	txtWidget
Font Size	10
Multiline	True
ScrollBars	Vertical

Use **WidgetExample.vb** to save the form file. Your finished form should resemble this:

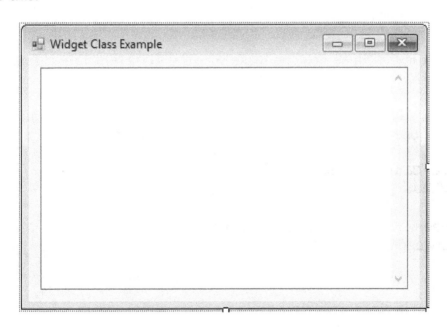

We need to add a class to this project to allow the definition of our **Widget** objects. We could add the class in the existing form file. However, doing so would defeat a primary advantage of objects, that being re-use. Hence, we will create a separate file to hold our class. To do this, go to **Solution Explorer**, right-click the project name (**WidgetClass**), choose **Add**, then **Class**. The following window will appear:

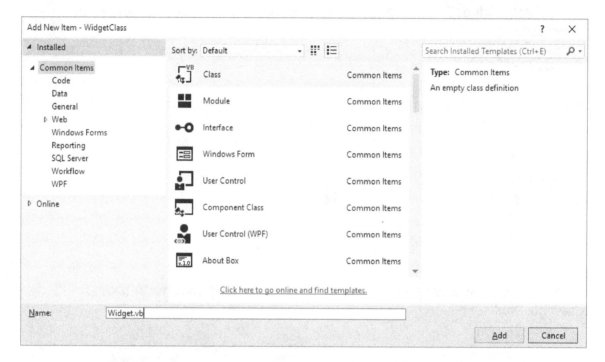

Type **Widget** in the **Name** box and make sure the **Class** template is selected. Click **Add** to open the newly created class file.

A file named **Widget.vb** will now be seen in the Solution Explorer window and that file will open. Two lines should be in this nearly empty file:

```
Public Class Widget
End Class
```

All code needed to define properties, constructors and methods for this class will be between these two lines.

Declaring and Constructing an Object

We now have a class we can use to create Widget objects. Yes, it's a very simple class, but it will work. There are two steps in creating an object from a class – **declare** the object, then **construct** the object. Note these are the same steps we've used with the built-in Visual Basic objects.

Return to the example project. The **Widget** object will be created in the **WidgetExample.vb** file (the file describing **frmWidget**). Open that file and double-click the form to navigate to its **Load** procedure in the code window:

```
Private Sub FrmWidget_Load(ByVal sender As System.Object,
ByVal e As System.EventArgs) Handles MyBase.Load

End Sub
```

All the code we write in this example will be in this **frmWidget_Load** procedure.

To declare a **Widget** object named **MyWidget**, type this line of code in this procedure:

```
Dim MyWidget As Widget
```

Note as soon as you type the keyword **As**, the Intellisense feature pops up suggesting possible object types. Notice **Widget** is one of the selections! This is due to the existence of the Widget class in the project.

Now, to construct this object, type this line of code:

```
MyWidget = New Widget()
```

This line just says "give me a new widget." Our Widget object is now complete, ready for use. There's not much we can do with it obviously – it has no properties or methods, but it does exist! You may wonder how we can construct a Widget object if we have not defined a constructor. The line above uses the **default** constructor automatically included with every class. The default constructor simply creates an object with no defined properties.

Adding Properties to a Class

There are two ways to define properties within a class description: creating direct **public variables** or creating **property procedures**. We look at the first way here. Our Widget class will have two properties: **WidgetColor** (a String variable) and **WidgetSize** (an integer variable). Class properties can be any type of variable or object – yes, properties can actually be other objects!

To define these properties in our class, return to the **Widget.vb** file and add the shaded lines to the file:

```
Public Class Widget
  Public WidgetColor As String
  Public WidgetSize As Integer
End Class
```

The keyword **Public** is used so the properties are available outside the class when the object is created.

Now, return to the **WidgetExample.vb** file so we can provide some definition to these properties in our instance of the object. In the **frmWidget_Load** procedure, add this shaded code to define and display the properties in the text box control:

```
Private Sub FrmWidget_Load(ByVal sender As System.Object,
ByVal e As System.EventArgs) Handles MyBase.Load
  Dim MyWidget As Widget
  MyWidget = New Widget()
  MyWidget.WidgetColor = "red"
  MyWidget.WidgetSize = 15
  txtWidget.Text = "Color is " + MyWidget.WidgetColor
  txtWidget.Text += ControlChars.CrLf + "Size is" +
Str(MyWidget.WidgetSize) 'adds line feed and new text to
text box
End Sub
```

Note, to refer to an object property, you use the same format (dot notation) used with controls:

ObjectName.PropertyName

You should have also seen that when typing in the properties, the Intellisense feature again recognized the existence of your Widget class, providing a drop-down list of available properties.

Run the example project. You should see this:

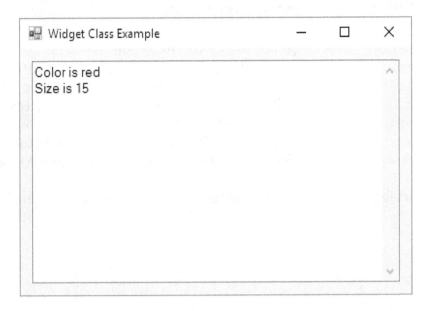

We've created and defined our first object! There's nothing to keep you from creating as many widgets as you want. Make sure your work is saved as we take a sidebar.

How Visual Basic Puts Controls on a Form

A thought may have come to you by now. You might be asking, if controls are objects, why don't we ever write code to declare and construct controls, including definition of all their properties? The answer is that we do write such code; well, actually, the Visual Basic development environment writes it for us. When we move a control from the toolbox onto a form and establish properties using the Properties window, code mimicking all these steps is written for us. All of this code resides in a hidden area of our project. Let's take a look.

Start a new project and put a single button control on the form. Here's my form:

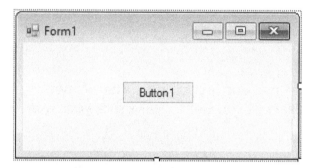

Now, go to the **Solution Explorer** window and click on the **Show All Files** button to display all files in the project. Expand the element next to **Form1.vb**:

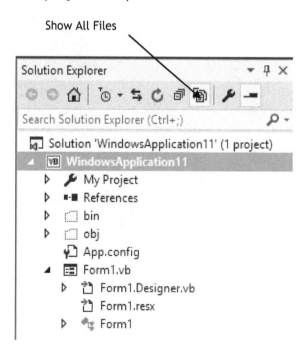

Open the **Form1.Designer.vb** file. This is the file where Visual Basic writes the code to create the form.

Let's see how the single button is declared and constructed, then positioned on the form. Near the bottom of the file is this line:

```
Friend WithEvents Button1 As System.Windows.Forms.Button
```

This line is equivalent to a **Dim** statement declaring **Button1** to be a member of the **Button** class. The line also tells Visual Basic that the object will have events.

Another place in the code shows these lines:

```
Me.Button1 = New System.Windows.Forms.Button
Me.SuspendLayout()
'
'Button1
'
Me.Button1.Location = New System.Drawing.Point(96, 40)
Me.Button1.Name = "Button1"
Me.Button1.Size = New System.Drawing.Size(75, 23)
Me.Button1.TabIndex = 0
Me.Button1.Text = "Button1"
Me.Button1.UseVisualStyleBackColor = True
```

The first line constructs **Button1** (note the **New** keyword). It then sets several properties (including **Location** and **Size**). The button control is placed on the form using this line of code (under the **Form1** section):

```
Me.Controls.Add(Me.Button1)
```

We see to add a control to the form, we need to follow four steps: (1) declare the control, (2) construct the control, (3) set control properties, and (4) add control to form. If there are events, we would also need to connect event handlers. For now, we'll let the IDE handle these tasks – later, in Chapter 10, we'll see how to add controls using code. Now, back to our Widget example. Open that example.

Another Way to Add Properties to a Class

We mentioned there are two ways to add properties to a class. We will look at the second method, creating **property procedures**, here. The rationale behind this second method is to allow validation and/or modification of properties, giving you complete control over the property.

For each property to be established using a procedure, first determine the property name (**Name**) and type (**Type**). Then type this line inside the boundaries of your Class:

```
Public Property Name As Type
```

When you press <**Enter**> at the end of this line, you will see:

```
Public Property Name() As Type
  Get

    End Get
    Set(ByVal Value As Type)

    End Set
End Property
```

There are two halves in this procedure: **Get** to determine the current property value and **Set** to establish a new property value. A local variable is used to hold the property value.

The use of this procedure is best illustrated with example. For our **Widget** class, the **WidgetColor** property can be established using:

```
Dim wColor As String
Public Property WidgetColor() As String
  Get
    Return wColor
  End Get
  Set(ByVal Value As String)
    wColor = Value
  End Set
End Property
```

In this snippet, **wColor** is a local variable representing the Widget color. This code mimics the use of public variable for properties, offering no advantage to directly reading and writing the property value. The real advantage to using procedures rather than public variables is that property values can be validated and modified. Let see how to do a validation.

Validating Class Properties

Validation of class properties is done in the **Set** procedure (the **Get** procedure can be used to modify properties before returning values). In this procedure, we can examine the value provided by the user and see if it meets the validation criteria (in range, positive, non-zero, etc.).

For our **Widget** example, let's assume there are only three color possibilities: red, white, or blue and that the size must be between 5 and 40. Return to the example and open the code window for **Widget.vb**. Delete the two lines declaring the public property variables. Type these lines after the Class header line:

```
Dim wColor As String
Dim wSize As Integer
Public Property WidgetColor() As String
  Get
    Return wColor
  End Get
  Set(ByVal Value As String)
    Select Case UCase(Value)
      Case "RED", "WHITE", "BLUE"
        wColor = Value
      Case Else
        MessageBox.Show("Bad widget color!")
    End Select
  End Set
End Property
Public Property WidgetSize() As Integer
  Get
    Return wSize
  End Get
  Set(ByVal Value As Integer)
    If (Value >= 5 And Value <= 40) Then
      wSize = Value
    Else
      MessageBox.Show("Bad widget size!")
    End If
  End Set
End Property
```

Notice how the validation works - a message box (we'll learn about them in the next chapter) will appear if a bad value is selected.

Return to the **WidgetExample.vb** code and make the shaded change (use a bad color):

```
Private Sub frmWidget_Load(ByVal sender As System.Object,
ByVal e As System.EventArgs) Handles MyBase.Load
  Dim MyWidget As Widget
  MyWidget = New Widget()
  MyWidget.WidgetColor = "green"
  MyWidget.WidgetSize = 15
  txtWidget.Text = "Color is " + MyWidget.WidgetColor
  txtWidget.Text += ControlChars.CrLf + "Size is" +
Str(MyWidget.WidgetSize)
End Sub
```

Rerun the application and this message box announcing a bad color property should appear:

Reset the color property to a proper value, change the size property to a bad value and make sure its validation also works.

We suggest that, except in very simple classes, you always use the procedure approach to setting and reading properties. This approach, though a little more complicated, allows the most flexibility in your application. Using the procedure approach, you can also make properties read-only and write-only. Consult the Visual Basic on-line help system for information on doing this.

Adding Constructors to a Class

Once an object is declared, it must be created using a **constructor**. A constructor is a procedure (named **New**) that provides a way to initialize an object. Each class has a default constructor. This is the constructor we have been using with our simple example. The default constructor simply creates the object with no properties at all.

Constructors are usually used to establish some set of default properties. A constructor that does that is:

```
Public Sub New()
  [Set properties here]
End Sub
```

This code is usually placed near the top of the Class description.

One way to establish initial properties for our **Widget** class is:

```
Public Sub New()
  wColor = "red"
  wSize = 12
End Sub
```

This will work, but the properties would not be checked in the validation code just written. To validate initial properties, use this code instead:

```
Public Sub New()
  Me.WidgetColor = "red"
  Me.WidgetSize = 12
End Sub
```

Where the keyword **Me** refers to the current object. Type the above code in the **Widget** class example. Then, return to the **WidgetExample.vb** code, delete the two lines setting the color and size, and then rerun the application. You should see (in the text box) that the color is now red and the size is 12.

You can also defined **overloaded constructors**. Such constructors still have the name **New**, but have different argument lists, providing the potential for multiple ways to initialize an object. We will see overloaded constructors with the built-in Visual Basic objects. In our Widget example, say we wanted to allow the user to specify the initial color and size at the same time the object is created. A constructor that does this task is (passing the color and size as arguments, information needed by the constructor):

```
Public Sub New(ByVal c As String, ByVal s As Integer)
  Me.WidgetColor = c
  Me.WidgetSize = s
End Sub
```

Type the above code below the default constructor, **New()**, in the **Widget.vb** code.

Return to the **WidgetExample.vb** code and modify the constructor line so it looks like the shaded line:

```
Private Sub FrmWidget_Load(ByVal sender As System.Object,
ByVal e As System.EventArgs) Handles MyBase.Load
  Dim MyWidget As Widget
  MyWidget = New Widget("blue", 22)
  txtWidget.Text = "Color is " + MyWidget.WidgetColor
  txtWidget.Text += ControlChars.CrLf + "Size is" +
Str(MyWidget.WidgetSize)
End Sub
```

Notice when you type the new constructor it appears as one of two overloaded choices in the editor Intellisense window. This code now uses the new overloaded constructor, setting the color to blue and the size to 22. Run the application to make sure it works.

A class can have any number of constructors. The only limitation is that no two constructors can have matching argument lists (same number and type of arguments).

Adding Methods to a Class

Class **methods** allow objects to perform certain tasks. Methods are written as Visual Basic functions. Like constructors, a class can have overloaded methods.

To add a method to a class description, first select a name and a type of information the method will return (if there is any returned value). The framework for a method named **MyMethod** that returns a **Type** value is:

```
Public Function MyMethod() As Type

End Function
```

This code is usually placed following the property procedures in a class description.

In our **Widget** example, say we want a method that describes the color and size of the widget. Such a method would look like this:

```
Public Function DescribeWidget() As String
   Return ("My widget is colored " + wColor +
ControlChars.CrLf + "My widget size is" + Str(wSize))
End Function
```

Type the above code near the end of the **Widget.vb** file in our example.

To use an object's method in code, use the following syntax:

ObjectName.MethodName(Arguments)

In this syntax, **ObjectName** is the name of the object, **MethodName** the name of the method and **Arguments** is a comma-delimited list of any arguments needed by the method.

To try the **DescribeWidget** method in our example, return to the
WidgetExample.vb code and modify the shaded line as shown:

```
Private Sub FrmWidget_Load(ByVal sender As System.Object,
ByVal e As System.EventArgs) Handles MyBase.Load
  Dim MyWidget As Widget
  MyWidget = New Widget("blue", 22)
  txtWidget.Text = MyWidget.DescribeWidget
End Sub
```

In this code, we now use the method to describe widget color and size. Note the
method has been added to the Intellisense menu. Run the application to check
that the method works as expected. The form should appear as:

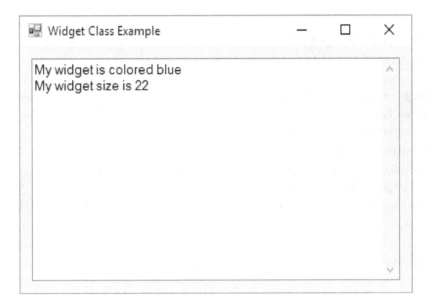

Let's try another method. This method (**CompareWidget**, in **Widget.vb**) compares a widget's size to a standard widget (which has size 20):

```
Public Function CompareWidget() As String
  Dim Diff As Integer
  Diff = wSize - 20
  If Diff > 0 Then
    Return ("My widget is" + Str(Diff) + " units larger
than a standard widget.")
  Else
    Return ("My widget is" + Str(Math.Abs(Diff)) + " units
smaller than a standard widget.")
  End If
End Function
```

Type the **CompareWidget** method into **Widget.vb**, then modify **WidgetExample.vb** as (shaded line is new):

```
Private Sub FrmWidget_Load(ByVal sender As System.Object,
ByVal e As System.EventArgs) Handles MyBase.Load
  Dim MyWidget As Widget
  MyWidget = New Widget("blue", 22)
  txtWidget.Text = MyWidget.DescribeWidget
  txtWidget.Text += ControlChars.CrLf +
MyWidget.CompareWidget
End Sub
```

Run the application to see this new output:

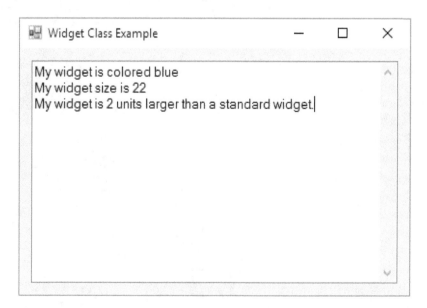

Methods can also have arguments and overload other methods. Suppose in our example, we want to input the size of a widget (**s**, an integer type) we would like to compare our widget to. This method does the job:

```
Public Function CompareWidget(ByVal s As Integer) As
String
  Dim Diff As Integer
  Diff = wSize - s
  If Diff > 0 Then
    Return ("My widget is" + Str(Diff) + " units larger
than your widget.")
  Else
    Return ("My widget is" + Str(Math.Abs(Diff)) + " units
smaller than your widget.")
  End If
End Function
```

Note this method has the same name as our previous method (**CompareWidget**), but the different argument list differentiates this overloaded version from the previous version.

Type the overloaded version of **CompareWidget** into the **Widget.vb** class code. Then, modify the **WidgetExample.vb** code to use this method (shaded line is new):

```
Private Sub FrmWidget_Load(ByVal sender As System.Object,
ByVal e As System.EventArgs) Handles MyBase.Load
  Dim MyWidget As Widget
  MyWidget = New Widget("blue", 22)
  txtWidget.Text = MyWidget.DescribeWidget
  txtWidget.Text += ControlChars.CrLf +
MyWidget.CompareWidget
  txtWidget.Text += ControlChars.CrLf +
MyWidget.CompareWidget(15)
End Sub
```

Note when adding **CompareWidget** to the code, the Intellisense feature presents the two overloaded versions. Run the modified application and you should see:

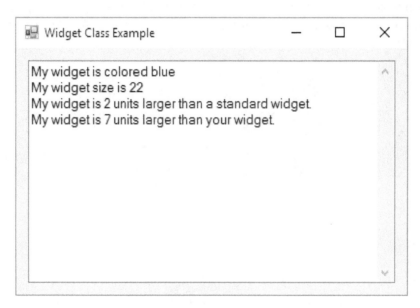

Inheritance

The people you built the Widget class for are so happy with it, they've decided they now want to develop an 'armed' widget. This new widget will be just like the old widget (have a color and size), but will also have arms. This means this new class (**ArmedWidget**) will have one additional property – the number of arms.

To build the **ArmedWidget** class, we could start from scratch – develop a class with three properties, a method that describes the armed widget and a method that compares the armed widget. Or, we could take advantage of a very powerful concept in object-oriented programming, **inheritance**. Inheritance is the idea that you can base one class on another existing class, adding properties and/or methods as needed. This saves lots of work.

Let's see how inheritance works with our widget. Return to the **WidgetClass** project we've been using. Add another class to the project, naming it **ArmedWidget**. Use this code for the class:

```
Public Class ArmedWidget
   Inherits Widget
   Dim nArms as Integer
   Public Property WidgetArms() As Integer
     Get
       Return nArms
     End Get
     Set(ByVal Value As Integer)
       nArms = Value
     End Set
   End Property
End Class
```

The key line here is:

Inherits Widget

This makes all the properties and methods of the Widget class available to our new class (**ArmedWidget**). The remaining code simply adds the unvalidated property **WidgetArms**. We could, of course, add validation to this property if desired.

Now, return to the **WidgetExample.vb** code file. We will modify the code to create and define an **ArmedWidget** object. The modifications are shaded:

```
Private Sub FrmWidget_Load(ByVal sender As System.Object,
ByVal e As System.EventArgs) Handles MyBase.Load
  Dim MyWidget As Widget
  MyWidget = New Widget("blue", 22)
  txtWidget.Text = MyWidget.DescribeWidget
  txtWidget.Text += ControlChars.CrLf +
MyWidget.CompareWidget
  txtWidget.Text += ControlChars.CrLf +
MyWidget.CompareWidget(15)
  Dim MyArmedWidget As ArmedWidget
  MyArmedWidget = New ArmedWidget()
  MyArmedWidget.WidgetColor = "white"
  MyArmedWidget.WidgetSize = 33
  MyArmedWidget.WidgetArms = 11
  txtWidget.Text += ControlChars.CrLf + ControlChars.CrLf
+ MyArmedWidget.DescribeWidget
  txtWidget.Text += ControlChars.CrLf + "My armed widget
has" + Str(MyArmedWidget.WidgetArms) + " arms."
  txtWidget.Text += ControlChars.CrLf +
MyArmedWidget.CompareWidget
  txtWidget.Text += ControlChars.CrLf +
MyArmedWidget.CompareWidget(15)
End Sub
```

Notice that when you type this new code, the Intellisense feature recognizes the inherited properties and methods of the new class.

Run the application and view the form to see:

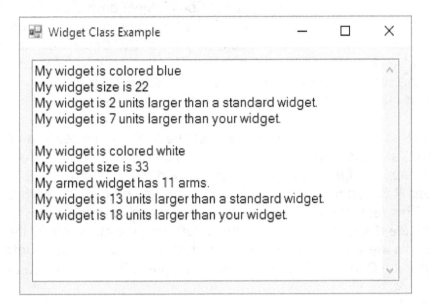

You see the descriptions of both the old 'standard' widget and the new, improved 'armed' widget.

You may have noticed a couple of drawbacks to this inherited class. First, the method used to describe the widget (**DescribeWidget**) only provides color and size information. We added an extra line of code to define the number of arms. It would be nice if this information could be part of the **DescribeWidget** method. That process is called **overriding** methods. Second, we need to know how to use the constructors developed for the **Widget** class in our new **ArmedWidget** class. Let's attack both drawbacks.

If your new class is to use a method that has the same name (and same argument list) as a method in the base class (the class you inherit from), two things must happen. First, the base class method must be **overridable**. This simply means it is defined using the **Overridable** keyword in its original definition. This requires a little thinking ahead when defining a class. That is, you must decide if any method might be redefined by a class inheriting the base class. Then, to use an overridable method in the new class, you redefine the method using the **Overrides** keyword. An example will make this clear.

Return to the **Widget.vb** class file. We will make the **DescribeWidget** function overridable. Add the shaded keyword to its definition:

```
Public Overridable Function DescribeWidget() As String
   Return ("My widget is colored " + wColor +
ControlChars.CrLf + "My widget size is" + Str(wSize))
End Function
```

Now, go to the **ArmedWidget.vb** file and add this method to the class definition:

```
Public Overrides Function DescribeWidget() As String
   Return ("My armed widget is colored " + Me.WidgetColor +
ControlChars.CrLf + "My armed widget size is" +
Str(Me.WidgetSize) + " and has" + Str(nArms) + " arms.")
End Function
```

Some comments about this function. This now adds a method **DescribeWidget** to the **ArmedWidget** class, allowing the number of arms to be included in the description. It **overrides** the method in the Widget class. Since nArms is a local variable in the class, it can be referred to by its name. The color property is not local to the ArmedWidget class. Note, to refer to properties inherited from the base class, you use the syntax:

`Me.PropertyName`

Hence, in this example, we use:

`Me.WidgetColor` and `Me.WidgetSize`

to refer to the inherited color and size properties, respectively.

Now, rerun the application and the output window should display:

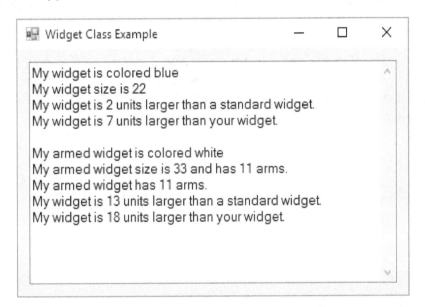

The armed widget description now includes the number of arms (making the line of code following the **DescribeWidget** method invocation redundant). Any method in the base class can be overridden using the same approach followed here.

Before leaving this example, let's see how constructors in base classes can be used in the new class. Any base class constructor can be called using this syntax:

```
MyBase.New()
```

Where there may or not be an argument list. Recall the default constructor in the **Widget** class created a red widget that was 12 units in size. To use this constructor in the **ArmedWidget** class (while at the same time, setting the number of arms to 4), add this constructor to that class code file:

```
Public Sub New()
  MyBase.New()
  Me.WidgetArms = 4
End Sub
```

This constructor will first invoke the Widget constructor, then add the new property value.

Now, return to the **WidgetExample.vb** code and delete the three lines defining properties for the ArmedWidget and the line printing out the number of arms (since that information is now in the **DescribeWidget** method). Run the modified application and note in the output window:

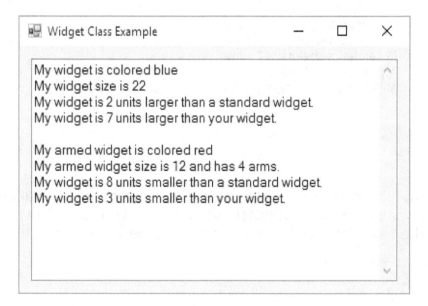

As expected, the new default armed widget is red, size 12, and has 4 arms.

We're done playing with our widget example. The information you've learned should help when you want to implement custom objects in your applications. The final version of our WidgetClass example is saved in the **WidgetClass** folder in the **LearnVB\VB Code\Class 3** folder.

Let's leave our 'make-believe' widget world and do a real-world OOP example. We'll modify the savings account example we did in Class 2 using a **Savings** object.

<u>Example 3-1</u>

Savings Account

In Example 2-4, we completed a Savings Account calculator that would compute one of these values: monthly deposit, yearly interest, number of months or final amount, given the other three values. In this example, we will do the same computations, using OOP, rather than the 'sequential' process followed in Example 2-4.

Load the finished project in Example 2-4. Add a **Savings** class file (**Savings.vb**) from which to create Savings objects. The class will have four public properties: **Deposit**, **Interest**, **Months**, and **Final**, all **Double** types. The class will have four methods:

ComputeFinal	Computes **Final** (a **Double** type), given **Deposit**, **Interest** and **Months**
ComputeDeposit	Computes **Deposit** (a **Double** type), given **Interest**, **Months** and **Final**
ComputeInterest	Computes **Interest** (a **Double** Type), given **Deposit**, **Months** and **Final**
ComputeMonths	Computes **Months** (a **Double** type), given **Deposit**, **Interest** and **Final**

The code is:

```
Public Class Savings
  Public Deposit As Double
  Public Interest As Double
  Public Months As Double
  Public Final As Double
  Private IntRate As Double

  Public Function ComputeFinal() As Double
    'Final missing
    IntRate = Me.Interest / 1200.0
    If Me.Interest = 0 Then
      'zero interest case
      Return (Me.Deposit * Me.Months)
    Else
      Return (Me.Deposit * ((1 + IntRate) ^ Me.Months - 1)
/ IntRate)
    End If
  End Function

  Public Function ComputeDeposit() As Double
    'Deposit missing
    IntRate = Me.Interest / 1200.0
    If Me.Interest = 0 Then
      Return (Me.Final / Me.Months)
    Else
      Return (Me.Final / (((1 + IntRate) ^ Me.Months - 1)
/ IntRate))
    End If
  End Function

  Public Function ComputeInterest() As Double
    'Interest missing - requires iterative solution
    'IntChange is how much we change interest each step
    'IntDirection is direction (+ or -) we change interest
    Dim Interest As Double = 0
    Dim IntChange As Double = 1
    Dim IntDirection As Integer = 1
    Dim FinalCompute As Double
    Do
      Interest += IntDirection * IntChange
      IntRate = Interest / 1200
      FinalCompute = Me.Deposit * ((1 + IntRate) ^
Me.Months - 1) / IntRate
        If IntDirection = 1 Then
          If FinalCompute > Me.Final Then
```

```
                IntDirection = -1
                IntChange /= 10
            End If
        Else
            If FinalCompute < Me.Final Then
                IntDirection = 1
                IntChange /= 10
            End If
        End If
        Loop Until Math.Abs(FinalCompute - Me.Final) < 0.005
        Return (Interest)
    End Function

    Public Function ComputeMonths() As Double
        'Months missing
        IntRate = Me.Interest / 1200.0
        If Me.Interest = 0 Then
            Return (Me.Final / Me.Deposit)
        Else
            Return (Math.Log(Me.Final * IntRate / Me.Deposit +
1) / Math.Log(1 + IntRate))
        End If
    End Function
End Class
```

1. Return to the Savings account form. Modify the code in the **btnCalculate** button **Click** event to use the newly formed class (all new code):

```
Private Sub Btncalculate_Click(ByVal sender As
System.Object, ByVal e As System.EventArgs) Handles
btnCalculate.Click
    ' create and construct Savings object
    Dim SavingsAccount As Savings
    SavingsAccount = New Savings()
    'Read properties from text boxes
    SavingsAccount.Deposit = Val(txtDeposit.Text)
    SavingsAccount.Interest = Val(txtInterest.Text)
    SavingsAccount.Months = Val(txtMonths.Text)
    SavingsAccount.Final = Val(txtFinal.Text)
    'Determine which box is blank
    'Compute that missing value and put in text box
    If Trim(txtDeposit.Text) = "" Then
      txtDeposit.Text =
Format(SavingsAccount.ComputeDeposit, "0.00")
    ElseIf Trim(txtInterest.Text) = "" Then
      txtInterest.Text =
Format(SavingsAccount.ComputeInterest, "0.00")
    ElseIf Trim(txtMonths.Text) = "" Then
      txtMonths.Text = Format(SavingsAccount.ComputeMonths,
"0.00")
    ElseIf Trim(txtFinal.Text) = "" Then
      txtFinal.Text = Format(SavingsAccount.ComputeFinal,
"0.00")
    End If
  End Sub
```

This code creates a **SavingsAccount** object from the **Savings** class. It then reads the property values (monthly deposit, interest rate, number of months, final amount) from the text boxes, establishes the object properties, determines which text box is empty and computes the missing information using the corresponding method and puts that result in a text box.

Compare this OOP code with the more 'sequential' code used in Example 2-4, where we established variables (Deposit, Interest, Months, Final) and computed the missing value using formulas within the event procedure. The two approaches are not that different. The advantage to the OOP approach is that the Savings class can be re-used in other applications and it would be very simple to model other savings account objects within this application.

2. Delete the form level variable declarations – these variables have been replaced by the object properties.

3. Play with the program. Make sure it works properly. Here's a run I made:

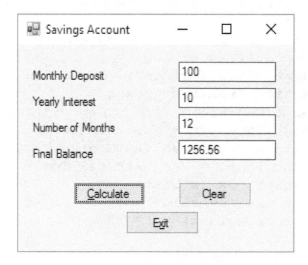

Save the project (**Example 3-1** folder in the **LearnVB\VB Code\Class 3** folder). Try eliminating the values one at a time to make sure the computations are correct.

Inheriting from Visual Basic Controls

We saw in the Widget example that we could create new, enhanced widgets from an existing widget class. We can do the same with the existing Visual Basic controls. That is, we can design our own controls, based on the standard controls, with custom features. (Actually, you can design controls that aren't based on existing controls, but that's beyond the scope of this discussion.)

Inheriting from existing controls allows us to:

> ➢ Establish new default values for properties.
> ➢ Introduce new properties.
> ➢ Establish commonly used event procedures or methods.

As an example, note whenever a text box is used for numeric input (like the **Savings Account** example), we need to validate the key strokes to make sure only numeric input is provided. Wouldn't it be nice to have a text box control with this validation "built-in?" To demonstrate inheritance from Visual Basic controls, we will build just this control – a **numeric text box**.

Our numeric text box control will be built in several stages to demonstrate each step. Once done, we will have a control that anyone can add to their Visual Basic toolbox and use in their applications. The specifications for our numeric text box are:

> ➢ Yellow background color
> ➢ Blue foreground color
> ➢ Size 10, Arial font
> ➢ Allows numeric digits (0-9)
> ➢ Allows a backspace
> ➢ Allows a single decimal point (optional)
> ➢ Allows a negative sign (optional)
> ➢ Ignores all other keystrokes

Note some specifications address setting and defining properties while others (keystroke validation) require establishing a common control event procedure. Let's start with setting properties.

Building a Custom Control

As a start, we'll build a text box control with the desired background color (Yellow), foreground color (Blue), and font (Size 10, Arial). Start a new Visual Basic project. In the **New Project** window, choose **Visual Basic, Windows, Desktop**. Select **Windows Forms Control Library**, then click **Next**.

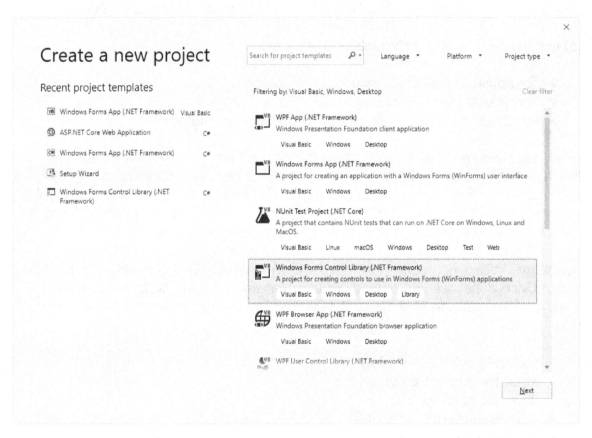

Name the project **NumericTextBox** (put the project in a folder of your choice – here we use **LearnVCS\VCS Code\Class 3**):

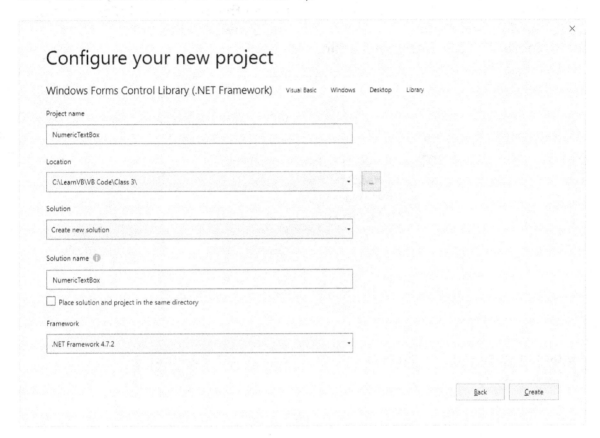

Click **Create.**

By default, when you create a new Windows Control Library project, a new blank user control, and associated code, will be created as a starting point and saved as a file named **UserControl1.vb**. Rename this file **NumericTextBox.vb**. Go to the **Solution Explorer** window, click the **Show All Files** button and delete the **NumericTextBox.Designer.vb** file.

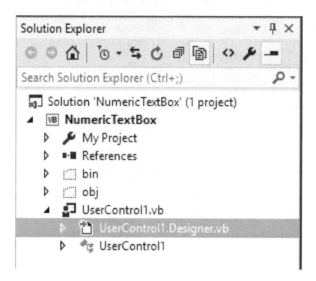

We do not need this file since our control has no separate interface (it uses the TextBox interface).

Open the code window in the **NumericTextBox.vb** file and add the shaded line:

```
Public Class NumericTextBox
   Inherits System.Windows.Forms.TextBox

End Class
```

This says we are creating a class named **NumericTextBox** that inherits from the **TextBox** control. Since there is no other code, this new control will act and behave just like a normal text box. Nothing will change until we add properties and methods of our own.

We want our numeric text box to have a default background color of yellow, a default foreground color of blue and a default font of size 10, Arial. These default properties are established in the default constructor for the control. Modify the **NumericTextBox** class code with the shaded lines to implement such a constructor:

```
Public Class NumericTextBox
   Inherits System.Windows.Forms.TextBox
   Public Sub New()
     Me.BackColor = Color.Yellow
     Me.ForeColor = Color.Blue
     Me.Font = New Font("Arial", 10)
   End Sub
End Class
```

Let's create the control and try it out. First, save the project in a desired location. Select **Build** from the Visual Basic menu, and click **Build NumericTextBox**. If you made no errors, a **DLL** (dynamic link library) for the new control will be found in the **Bin\Release** folder (or **Bin\Debug** folder) for the **NumericTextBox** project. The file will be named **NumericTextBox.dll**. If you'd like, check to see that it truly is there.

To try out the new control, start a <u>new</u> Windows application (make sure you have saved the **NumericTextBox** project). We need to add the **NumericTextBox** control to the toolbox. To do this, follow these steps:

> ➢ Choose **Tools** from the menu.
> ➢ Select **Choose Toolbox Items**.
> ➢ When the **Choose Toolbox Items** window appears, click the **.NET Framework Components** tab.
> ➢ Click the **Browse** button. Navigate to the directory (the **Bin\Release** or **Bin\Debug** folder of the **NumericTextBox** project) containing the **NumericTextBox.dll** file. Select that file.

At this point, you should see:

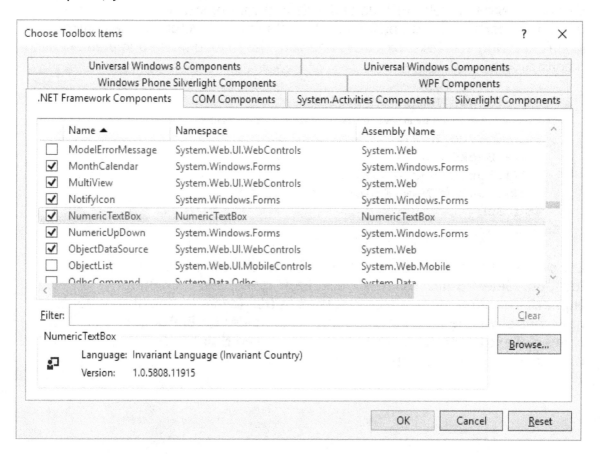

Make sure there is a check mark next to the **NumericTextBox** control, and click **OK**.

Scroll down on the toolbox and you should now see (in the **General** tab):

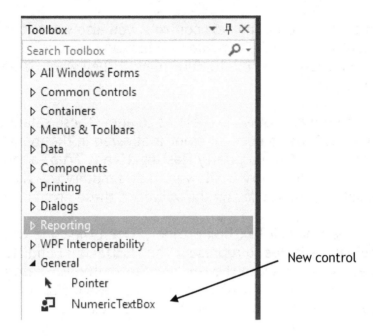

New control

Give it a try. Place the **NumericTextBox** control on your form and you should see (after making the control a bit wider and setting the **Text** property to something):

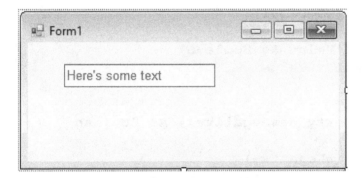

Note the default colors and font are apparent. Save this Windows project – we will be returning to it.

Adding New Properties to a Control

Many times, when creating new controls, you also want to define new properties for the control. To make the **NumericTextBox** control as general as possible, we want the user to be able to determine if they want decimal inputs and/or negative inputs.

We will define two Boolean properties to allow these selections. If the property **HasDecimal** is **True**, a decimal point is allowed in the input; if **False**, no decimal point is allowed. If the property **HasNegative** is **True**, a minus sign is allowed; if **False**, no minus sign entry is allowed. Let's modify the **NumericTextBox** class to allow setting and retrieving the values of these properties.

Return to the **NumericTextBox** project. Open the code window. Define two local Boolean variables to represent the **HasDecimal** and **HasNegative** properties. And, establish the **Get** and **Set** methods. I used **wDecimal** to represent HasDecimal and **wNegative** to represent HasNegative. Add this code at the top of the class to get/set the properties:

```
Dim wDecimal As Boolean
Dim wNegative As Boolean
Public Property HasDecimal() As Boolean
  Get
    Return (wDecimal)
  End Get
  Set(ByVal Value As Boolean)
    wDecimal = Value
  End Set
End Property
Public Property HasNegative() As Boolean
  Get
    Return (wNegative)
  End Get
  Set(ByVal Value As Boolean)
    wNegative = Value
  End Set
End Property
```

We also need to initialize the two new properties in the constructor code (add the two shaded lines):

```
Public Sub New()
  Me.BackColor = Color.Blue
  Me.ForeColor = Color.Yellow
  Me.Font = New Font("Arial", 14)
  Me.HasDecimal = True
  Me.HasNegative = False
End Sub
```

You could rebuild the control at this point and try it, but you won't notice any difference in behavior. Why? Well, for one thing, we aren't doing anything with the two new properties (**HasDecimal** and **HasNegative**). We use them next when writing the code that limits acceptable keystrokes. And, if we add the new control to a form and go to the properties window, the two new properties don't even appear! Let's fix that.

To add new properties to the property window for a new control, you first decide on what **category** the properties should be listed under (for most of this course, we have used an alphabetical, rather than categorized, view of properties). The choices for category are:

Appearance
Behavior
Configurations
Data
Design
Focus
Layout
Misc
Window Style

Then, preface the property declaration line with this code:

<System.ComponentModel.Category("category")>

With this addition, the new properties will appear in the properties window for the new control.

Modify the property declaration lines in the **NumericTextBox** class code as follows (shaded code is new):

```
<System.ComponentModel.Category("Behavior")> Public
Property HasDecimal() As Boolean

<System.ComponentModel.Category("Behavior")> Public
Property HasNegative() As Boolean
```

Rebuild the control (select **Build** from menu, then **Build NumericTextBox**).

Return to the Windows application where you added the **NumericTextBox** control to a form to look at default properties. Look in the properties window for the **NumericTextBox** and you should now see the two new properties and their default values displayed:

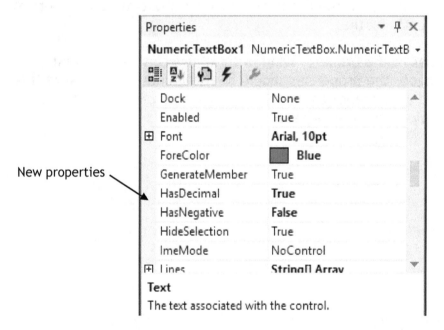

Now, let's write some code that uses these new properties while limiting allowable keystrokes.

Adding Control Event Procedures and Methods

The major impetus for building this new control is to limit keystrokes to only those that can be used for numeric inputs: numbers, decimal (optional based on **HasDecimal** property), negative sign (optional based on **HasNegative** property) and backspace (needed for proper editing).

As in previous work with text boxes to limit keystrokes, we use the **KeyPress** event procedure. To add an event procedure to an inherited control, simply type the procedure making sure you match the argument list of the base control (the one you inherit from). In the **Handles** clause, use the keyword **MyBase** to refer to the control.

The code for our numeric text box is essentially the same code used in each text box in the Savings Account example. Type this code in the **NumericTextBox** class (you must type each line as listed). Note the proper arguments and the **Handles MyBase.KeyPress** clause in the header line.

```
Private Sub NumericTextBox_KeyPress(ByVal sender As
Object, ByVal e As System.Windows.Forms.KeyPressEventArgs)
Handles MyBase.KeyPress
  'check pressed key
  Select Case e.KeyChar
    Case CChar("0") To CChar("9"), ControlChars.Back
      'allow numbers or backspace
      e.Handled = False
    Case CChar(".")
      'allow decimal if HasDecimal is True
      If (HasDecimal) Then
        'check if decimal already there
        If InStr(Me.Text, ".") = 0 Then
          e.Handled = False
        Else
          e.Handled = True
        End If
      Else
        e.Handled = True
      End If
    Case CChar("-")
      'allow single negative sign in first position only if
HasNegative is True
      If (HasNegative) Then
        If InStr(Me.Text, "-") = 0 And Me.SelectionStart =
0 Then
          e.Handled = False
        Else
          e.Handled = True
```

```
                End If
            Else
                e.Handled = True
            End If
        Case Else
            'no other keys allowed
            e.Handled = True
    End Select
End Sub
```

Let's go through this code step-by-step to understand just what's going on. The first line overrides the **KeyPress** procedure of the standard TextBox control. We then examine **e.KeyChar** (the pressed key) to see if it is acceptable (e.Handled = False) or not acceptable (e.Handled = True). Checking for a number or backspace is straightforward. Note in checking for a decimal point, we check two conditions – first, we make sure HasDecimal is True; second, we make sure there is not a decimal point there already. Similarly, in checking for a negative sign, we make sure HasNegative is True and make sure we are typing the first character in the text box.

Rebuild the **NumericTextBox** control. Then, return to the Windows application with the NumericTextBox on the form. Run the application and test the performance of the code. By default, you should only be able to type a positive (no negative sign) decimal number. Here's one I did:

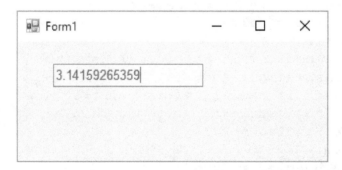

Note you can't type anything but numbers and a single decimal point.

Now, stop the application, change **HasDecimal** to **False** and **HasNegative** to **True**. Now, you should only be able to type integer values (no decimal) with or without a negative sign. Here's one I did:

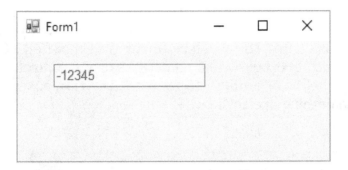

In this example, we have added an event procedure to our control. You can also override existing control methods using the **Overrides** keyword. Consult the Visual Basic literature for the steps involved.

This completes our look at inheriting from existing controls. The final result is saved in the **NumericTextBox** folder in the **LearnVB\VB Code\Class 3** folder. With these new found skills, you can probably think of several ways you might modify existing Visual Basic controls to fit your needs.

Example 3-2

Savings Account (Revisited)

1. Let's modify the Savings Account example (Example 3-1) to use the new numeric text box control to show how things are simplified. Open Example 3-1. Replace each text box with a numeric text box control. Change the **Font** on each label to **Arial**, **Size 10** to match the text boxes. The form should look something like this:

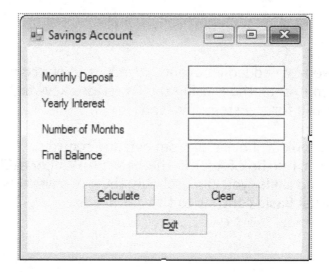

2. Set the properties of the new controls.

   NumericTextBox1:
       Name   txtDeposit

   NumericTextBox2:
       Name   txtInterest

   NumericTextBox3:
       Name   txtMonths
       HasDecimal   False

   NumericTextBox4:
       Name   txtFinal

3. Re-establish proper tab ordering among the controls. Eliminate the **KeyPress** event procedures for each of the text box controls. They are no longer needed.

4. That's all the needed changes. Play with the program. Make sure it works properly. Here's a run I made:

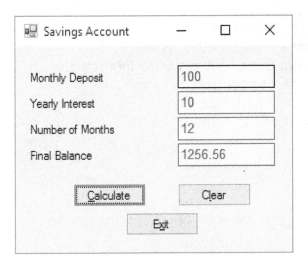

Save the project (**Example 3-2** folder in the **LearnVB\VB Code\Class 3** folder). To open this project from the class folder, the **NumericTextBox** project must be built and the resulting **dll** file located in the **LearnVB\VB Code\Class 3\NumericTextBox\Bin\Release** folder or the **LearnVB\VB Code\Class 3\NumericTextBox\Bin\Debug** folder.

One bit of functionality we've lost is the detection of pressing the <Enter> key which would move the focus from one control to the other. See if you can add this functionality. You need some way to determine which control is next in line for focus.

Class Review

After completing this class, you should understand:

- ➤ Creating classes and objects.
- ➤ Setting and validating object properties.
- ➤ Creating class methods.
- ➤ Creating object constructors.
- ➤ How inheritance is used with classes.
- ➤ Extending Visual Basic controls using inheritance
- ➤ Adding properties to controls
- ➤ Overriding control methods.
- ➤ Adding new controls to toolbox.

Practice Problems 3

Problem 3-1. Mortgage Problem. The two lines of Visual Basic code that compute the monthly payment on a mortgage are:

```
Multiplier = (1 + Interest / (12 * 100)) ^ (Years * 12)
Payment = Loan * Interest * Multiplier / (12 * 100 *
(Multiplier - 1))
```

where:

Loan	Loan amount
Interest	Yearly interest percentage
Years	Number of years of payments
Multiplier	Interest multiplier
Payment	Computed monthly payment

(The 12 * 100 value in these equations converts yearly interest to a monthly rate.) Use this code to build a class that computes the monthly payment, given the other three variables. Also, compute the total of payments over the life of the mortgage.

Problem 3-2. Accelerated Mortgage Problem. Rather than make monthly payments on a mortgage, say you make a specified number of payments spread evenly throughout the year (for example, bi-weekly payments). The two lines of Visual Basic code that compute the periodic payment on such an "accelerated mortgage" are:

```
Multiplier = (1 + Interest / (NumberPayments * 100)) ^
(Years * NumberPayments)
Payment = Loan * Interest * Multiplier / (NumberPayments *
100 * (Multiplier - 1))
```

where:

Loan	Loan amount
Interest	Yearly interest percentage
Years	Number of years of payments
NumberPayments	Number of payments each year
Multiplier	Interest multiplier
Payment	Computed monthly payment

Modify Problem 3-1 to allow computation of such an accelerated mortgage. Have your new mortgage class inherit from the class developed in Problem 3-1. Use this class to compute the periodic payment, given the other four variables. Also, compute the total of payments over the life of the mortgage.

Problem 3-3. Flashing Label Problem. Create a label control that looks like a text box (3D border, white background) with the option of flashing its **Text** property.

Exercise 3

Mailing List

Build an application that accepts a person's name, address, city, state and zip for use in a mailing list. Use a class to describe each person and develop a new text control that can accept just letters, just numbers or both.

4. Exploring the Visual Basic Toolbox

Review and Preview

We have now learned the three steps in developing a Windows application, have been introduced to the Basic language and seen some object-oriented programming concepts. In this class, we begin a journey where we look at each tool in the Visual Basic toolbox. We will revisit some tools we already know and learn a lot of new tools. Examples of how to use each control will be presented.

Function Overloading

As we delve further into Visual Basic, we will begin to use many of its built-in functions and methods for dialog boxes, drawing graphics, and other tasks. Before using these functions and methods (we will use **MessageBox** methods soon), you need be aware of an object-oriented concept known as **overloading**. We were briefly introduced to this idea in the last chapter.

Overloading lets a function vary its behavior based on its input arguments. Visual Basic will have multiple functions with the same name, but with different argument lists. The different argument lists may have different numbers of arguments and different types of arguments.

What are the implications of overloading? What this means to us is that when using a Visual Basic function, there will be several different ways to use that function. In these notes, we will show you a few ways, but not all. You are encouraged to use on-line help to investigate all ways to use a function.

Another implication is that, when typing code for a function, the Intellisense feature of the Visual Basic IDE will appear with a drop-down list of all implementations of a particular function. As you type in your implementation, Intellisense adjusts to the particular form of the function it "thinks" you are using. Suggestions are made for possible arguments – it's like magic! Sometimes, Intellisense guesses right, sometimes not. You must insure the implementation is the one you desire. If, after typing in a function use, Intellisense does not recognize it as proper usage, it will be flagged with an error indication (underlined) and you are given some direction for correcting the error.

Overloading is a powerful feature of Visual Basic. You will quickly become accustomed to using multiple definitions of functions and how Intellisense interacts with you, the programmer.

MessageBox Dialog

One of the most often used functions in Visual Basic is the **MessageBox** object. This object lets you display messages to your user and receive feedback for further information. It can be used to display error messages, describe potential problems or just to show the result of some computation. The **MessageBox** object is versatile, with the ability to display any message, an optional icon, and a selected set of Button buttons. The user responds by clicking a button in the message box

You've seen message boxes if you've ever used a Windows application. Think of all the examples you've seen. For example, message boxes are used to ask you if you wish to save a file before exiting and to warn you if a disk drive is not ready. For example, if while writing these notes in Microsoft Word, I attempt to exit, I see this message box:

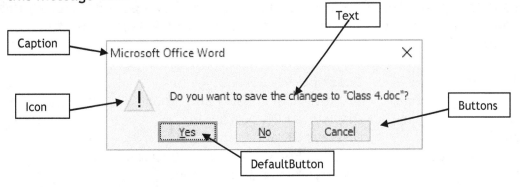

In this message box, the different parts that you control have been labeled. You will see how you can format a message box any way you desire.

To use the **MessageBox** object, you decide what the **Text** of the message should be, what **Caption** you desire, what **Icon** and **Buttons** are appropriate, and which **DefaultButton** you want. To display the message box in code, you use the MessageBox **Show** method.

The MessageBox is **overloaded** with several ways to implement the **Show** method. Some of the more common ways are:

```
MessageBox.Show(Text)
MessageBox.Show(Text, Caption)
MessageBox.Show(Text, Caption, Buttons)
MessageBox.Show(Text, Caption, Buttons, Icon)
MessageBox.Show(Text, Caption, Buttons, Icon,
DefaultButton)
```

In these implementations, if **DefaultButton** is omitted, the first button is default. If **Icon** is omitted, no icon is displayed. If **Buttons** is omitted, an 'OK' button is displayed. And, if **Caption** is omitted, no caption is displayed.

You decide what you want for the message box **Text** and **Caption** information (string data types). The other arguments are defined by Visual Basic predefined constants. The **Buttons** constants are defined by the **MessageBoxButtons** constants:

Member	Description
AbortRetryIgnore	Displays Abort, Retry and Ignore buttons
OK	Displays an OK button
OKCancel	Displays OK and Cancel buttons
RetryCancel	Displays Retry and Cancel buttons
YesNo	Displays Yes and No buttons
YesNoCancel	Displays Yes, No and Cancel buttons

The syntax for specifying a choice of buttons is the usual dot-notation:

MessageBoxButtons.Member

So, to display an OK and Cancel button, the constant is:

```
MessageBoxButtons.OKCancel
```

You don't have to remember this, however. When typing the code, the Intellisense feature will provide a drop-down list of button choices when you reach that argument! Again, like magic! This will happen for all the arguments in the MessageBox object.

The displayed Icon is established by the **MessageBoxIcon** constants:

Member	Description
IconAsterisk	Displays an information icon
IconInformation	Displays an information icon
IconError	Displays an error icon (white X in red circle)
IconHand	Displays an error icon
IconNone	Display no icon
IconStop	Displays an error icon
IconExclamation	Displays an exclamation point icon
IconWarning	Displays an exclamation point icon
IconQuestion	Displays a question mark icon

To specify an icon, the syntax is:

MessageBoxIcon.Member

Note there are eight different members of the **MessageBoxIcon** constants, but only four icons (information, error, exclamation, question) available. This is because the current Windows operating system only offers four icons. Future implementations may offer more.

When a message box is displayed, one of the displayed buttons will have focus or be the default button. If the user presses <Enter>, this button is selected. You specify which button is default using the **MessageBoxDefaultButton** constants:

Member	Description
Button1	First button in message box is default
Button2	Second button in message box is default
Button3	Third button in message box is default

To specify a default button, the syntax is:

MessageBoxDefaultButton.Member

The specified default button is relative to the displayed buttons, left to right. So, if you have Yes, No and Cancel buttons displayed and the second button is selected as default, the No button will have focus (be default).

When you invoke the Show method of the MessageBox object, the method returns a value from the **DialogResult** constants. The available members are:

Member	Description
Abort	The Abort button was selected
Cancel	The Cancel button was selected
Ignore	The Ignore button was selected
No	The No button was selected
OK	The OK button was selected
Retry	The Retry button was selected
Yes	The Yes button was selected

MessageBox **Example**:

This little code snippet (the first line is very long):

```
If MessageBox.Show("This is an example of a message box",
"Message Box Example", MessageBoxButtons.OKCancel,
MessageBoxIcon.Information,
MessageBoxDefaultButton.Button1) = DialogResult.OK Then
   'everything is OK
Else
   'cancel was pressed
End If
```

displays this message box:

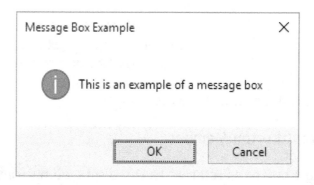

Of course, you would need to add code for the different tasks depending on whether OK or Cancel is clicked by the user.

Another MessageBox **Example**:

Many times, you just want to display a quick message to the user with no need for feedback (just an OK button). This code does the job:

```
MessageBox.Show("Quick message for you.", "Hey You!")
```

The resulting message box:

Notice there is no icon and the OK button (default if no button specified) is shown. Also, notice in the code, there is no need to read the returned value – we know what it is! You will find a lot of uses for this simple form of the message box (with perhaps some kind of icon) as you progress in Visual Basic.

We now start our study of the Visual Basic toolbox, looking at important properties, methods and events for many controls. We start this study with the most important 'control,' the form.

Form Object

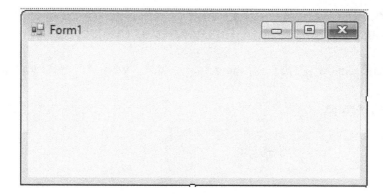

The **Form** is the object where the user interface is drawn. It is central to the development of Visual Basic applications. The form is known as a **container** object, since it 'holds' other controls. One implication of this distinction is that controls placed on the form will share **BackColor**, **ForeColor** and **Font** properties. To change this, select the desired control (after it is placed on the form) and change the desired properties. Another feature of a container control is that when its Enabled property is False, all controls in the container are disabled. Likewise, when the container control Visible property is False, all controls in the container are not visible.

Here, we present some of the more widely used **Properties**, **Methods** and **Events** for the form. Recall **properties** described the appearance and value of a control, **methods** are actions you can impose on controls and **events** occur when something is done to the control (usually by a user). This is not an exhaustive list – consult on-line help for such a list. You may not recognize all of these terms now. They will be clearer as you progress in the course. The same is true for the remaining controls presented in this chapter.

Form **Properties:**

Name	Gets or sets the name of the form (three letter prefix for form name is **frm**).
AcceptButton	Gets or sets the button on the form that is clicked when the user presses the <Enter> key.
BackColor	Get or sets the form background color.
CancelButton	Gets or sets the button control that is clicked when the user presses the <Esc> key.
ControlBox	Gets or sets a value indicating whether a control box is displayed in the caption bar of the form.

Form **Properties** (continued)

Enabled	If False, all controls on form are disabled.
Font	Gets or sets font name, style, size.
ForeColor	Gets or sets color of text or graphics.
FormBorderStyle	Sets the form border to be fixed or sizeable.
Height	Height of form in pixels.
Help	Gets or sets a value indicating whether a Help button should be displayed in the caption box of the form.
Icon	Gets or sets the icon for the form.
Left	Distance from left of screen to left edge of form, in pixels.
MaximizeButton	Gets or sets a value indicating whether the maximize button is displayed in the caption bar of the form.
MinimizeButton	Gets or sets a value indicating whether the minimize button is displayed in the caption bar of the form.
StartPosition	Gets or sets the starting position of the form when the application is running.
Text	Gets or sets the form window title.
Top	Distance from top of screen to top edge of form, in pixels.
Width	Width of form in pixels.

Form **Methods:**

Close	Closes the form.
Focus	Sets focus to the form.
Hide	Hides the form.
Refresh	Forces the form to immediately repaint itself.
Show	Makes the form display by setting the Visible property to True.

The normal syntax for invoking a method is to type the control name, a dot, then the method name. For form methods, the name to use is **Me**. This is a Visual Basic keyword used to refer to a form. Hence, to close a form, use:

```
Me.Close()
```

Form **Events**:

Activated	Occurs when the form is activated in code or by the user.
Click	Occurs when the form is clicked by the user.
FormClosing	Occurs when the form is closing.
DoubleClick	Occurs when the form is double clicked.
Load	Occurs before a form is displayed for the first time.
Paint	Occurs when the form is redrawn.

To access a form event in the Code window, select **(FormName Events)**.

Typical use of **Form** object (for each control in this, and following chapters, we will provide information for how that control is typically used):

> ➤ Set the **Name** and **Text** properties
> ➤ Set the **StartPosition** property (in this course, this property will almost always be set to **CenterScreen**)
> ➤ Set the **FormBorderStyle** to some value. In this course, we will mostly use **FixedSingle** forms. You can have resizable forms in Visual Basic (and there are useful properties that help with this task), but we will not use resizable forms in this course.
> ➤ Write any needed initialization code in the form's **Load** event. To access this event in the Code window, double-click the form or select the **(FormName Events)** object, then the **Load** event.

Button Control

In Toolbox:

On Form (Default Properties):

We've seen the **Button** control before. It is probably the most widely used Visual Basic control. It is used to begin, interrupt, or end a particular process. Here, we provide some of the more widely used properties, methods and events for the button control.

Button **Properties:**

Name	Gets or sets the name of the button (three letter prefix for button name is **btn**).
BackColor	Get or sets the button background color.
Enabled	If False, button is visible, but cannot accept clicks.
Font	Gets or sets font name, style, size.
ForeColor	Gets or sets color of text or graphics.
Image	Gets or sets the image that is displayed on a button control.
Text	Gets or sets string displayed on button.
TextAlign	Gets or sets the alignment of the text on the button control.

Button **Methods:**

Focus	Sets focus to the button.
PerformClick	Generates a Click event for a button.

Button **Events:**

Click	Event triggered when button is selected either by clicking on it or by pressing the access key.

Typical use of **Button** control:

> ➢ Set the **Name** and **Text** property.
> ➢ Write code in the button's **Click** event.
> ➢ You may also want to change the **Font**, **Backcolor** and **Forecolor** properties.

Label Control

In Toolbox:

A Label

On Form (Default Properties):

Label1

A **Label** control is used to display text that a user can't edit directly. We've seen, though, in previous examples, that the text of a label box can be changed at run-time in response to events.

Label **Properties:**

Name	Gets or sets the name of the label (three letter prefix for label name is **lbl**).
AutoSize	Gets or sets a value indicating whether the label is automatically resized to display its entire contents.
BackColor	Get or sets the label background color.
BorderStyle	Gets or sets the border style for the label.
Font	Gets or sets font name, style, size.
ForeColor	Gets or sets color of text or graphics.
Text	Gets or sets string displayed on label.
TextAlign	Gets or sets the alignment of text in the label.

Note, by default, the label control has no resizing handles. To resize the label, set AutoSize to False.

Label **Methods:**

Refresh	Forces an update of the label control contents.

Label **Events:**

Click	Event triggered when user clicks on a label.
DblClick	Event triggered when user double-clicks on a label.

Typical use of **Label** control for static, unchanging display:

> ➤ Set the **Name** (though not really necessary for static display) and **Text** property.
> ➤ You may also want to change the **Font**, **Backcolor** and **Forecolor** properties.

Typical use of **Label** control for changing display:

> ➤ Set the **Name** property. Initialize **Text** to desired string.
> ➤ Set **AutoSize** to **False**, resize control and select desired value for **TextAlign**.
> ➤ Assign **Text** property (String type) in code where needed.
> ➤ You may also want to change the **Font**, **Backcolor** and **Forecolor** properties.

TextBox Control

In Toolbox:

On Form (Default Properties):

A **TextBox** control is used to display information entered at design time, by a user at run-time, or assigned within code. The displayed text may be edited.

TextBox **Properties:**

Name	Gets or sets the name of the text box (three letter prefix for text box name is **txt**).
AutoSize	Gets or sets a value indicating whether the height of the text box automatically adjusts when the font assigned to the control is changed.
BackColor	Get or sets the text box background color.
BorderStyle	Gets or sets the border style for the text box.
Font	Gets or sets font name, style, size.
ForeColor	Gets or sets color of text or graphics.
HideSelection	Gets or sets a value indicating whether the selected text in the text box control remains highlighted when the control loses focus.
Lines	Gets or sets the lines of text in a text box control.
MaxLength	Gets or sets the maximum number of characters the user can type into the text box control.
MultiLine	Gets or sets a value indicating whether this is a multiline text box control.
PasswordChar	Gets or sets the character used to mask characters of a password in a single-line TextBox control.
ReadOnly	Gets or sets a value indicating whether text in the text box is read-only.
ScrollBars	Gets or sets which scroll bars should appear in a multiline TextBox control.

TextBox **Properties** (continued)

SelectedText	Gets or sets a value indicating the currently selected text in the control.
SelectionLength	Gets or sets the number of characters selected in the text box.
SelectionStart	Gets or sets the starting point of text selected in the text box.
Tag	Stores a string expression.
Text	Gets or sets the current text in the text box.
TextAlign	Gets or sets the alignment of text in the text box.
TextLength	Gets length of text in text box.

TextBox **Methods:**

AppendText	Appends text to the current text of text box.
Clear	Clears all text in text box.
Copy	Copies selected text to clipboard.
Cut	Moves selected text to clipboard.
Focus	Places the cursor in a specified text box.
Paste	Replaces the current selection in the text box with the contents of the Clipboard.
SelectAll	Selects all text in text box.
Undo	Undoes the last edit operation in the text box.

TextBox **Events:**

Click	Occurs when the user clicks the text box.
Enter	Occurs when the control receives focus.
KeyDown	Occurs when a key is pressed down while the control has focus.
KeyPress	Occurs when a key is pressed while the control has focus - used for key trapping.
Leave	Triggered when the user leaves the text box. This is a good place to examine the contents of a text box after editing.
TextChanged	Occurs when the Text property value has changed.

Typical use of **TextBox** control as display control:

> ➢ Set the **Name** property. Initialize **Text** property to desired string.
> ➢ Set **ReadOnly** property to **True**.
> ➢ If displaying more than one line, set **MultiLine** property to **True**.
> ➢ Assign **Text** property in code where needed.
> ➢ You may also want to change the **Font**, **Backcolor** and **Forecolor** properties.

Typical use of **TextBox** control as input device:

> ➢ Set the **Name** property. Initialize **Text** property to desired string.
> ➢ If it is possible to input multiple lines, set **MultiLine** property to **True**.
> ➢ In code, give **Focus** to control when needed. Provide key trapping code in **KeyPress** event. Read **Text** property when **Leave** event occurs.
> ➢ You may also want to change the **Font**, **Backcolor** and **Forecolor** properties.

Use of the TextBox control should be minimized if possible. Whenever you give a user the option to type something, it makes your job as a programmer more difficult. You need to validate the information they type to make sure it will work with your code (recall the **Savings Account** example in the last class, where we need key trapping to insure only numbers were being entered). There are many controls in Visual Basic that are 'point and click,' that is, the user can make a choice simply by clicking with the mouse. We'll look at such controls through the course. Whenever these 'point and click' controls can be used to replace a text box, do it!

Example 4-1

Password Validation

1. Start a new project. The idea of this project is to ask the user to input a password. If correct, a message box appears to validate the user. If incorrect, other options are provided.

2. Place a two buttons, a label box, and a text box on your form so it looks something like this:

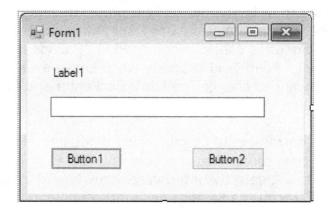

3. Set the properties of the form and each object (we do the buttons first so their names are available for the form properties).

   Button1:
Name	btnValid
Text	&Validate

   Button2:
Name	btnExit
Text	E&xit

   Form1:
Name	frmPassword
AcceptButton	btnValid
CancelButton	btnExit
FormBorderStyle	FixedSingle
StartPosition	CenterScreen
Text	Password Validation

Label1:

AutoSize	False
BorderStyle	Fixed3D
Font Size	10
Font Style	Bold
Text	Please Enter Your Password:

TextBox1:

Name	txtPassword
Font Size	14
PasswordChar	*
Tag	[Whatever you choose as a password]

Your form should now look like this:

4. Use the following code in the **btnValid Click** event.

```
Private Sub BtnValid_Click(ByVal sender As System.Object,
ByVal e As System.EventArgs) Handles btnValid.Click
    'This procedure checks the input password
    Dim Response As DialogResult
    If txtPassword.Text = CStr(txtPassword.Tag) Then
      'If correct, display message box
      MessageBox.Show("You've passed security!", "Access
Granted", MessageBoxButtons.OK, MessageBoxIcon.Exclamation)
    Else
      'If incorrect, give option to try again
      Response = MessageBox.Show("Incorrect password",
"Access Denied", MessageBoxButtons.RetryCancel,
MessageBoxIcon.Error)
      If Response = Windows.Forms.DialogResult.Retry Then
        txtPassword.SelectionStart = 0
        txtPassword.SelectionLength = Len(txtPassword.Text)
      Else
        Me.Close()
      End If
    End If
    txtPassword.Focus()
  End Sub
```

This code checks the input password to see if it matches the stored value. If so, it prints an acceptance message. If incorrect, it displays a message box to that effect and asks the user if they want to try again. If Yes (Retry), another try is granted. If No (Cancel), the program is ended. Notice the use of **SelectionLength** and **SelectionStart** to highlight an incorrect entry. This allows the user to type right over the incorrect response.

5. Use the following code in the **frmPassword Load** event (double-click the form to reach this event).

```
Private Sub FrmPassword_Load(ByVal sender As
System.Object, ByVal e As System.EventArgs) Handles
MyBase.Load
    'make sure focus starts in text box
    txtPassword.Focus()
  End Sub
```

6. Use the following code in the **btnExit Click** event.

```
Private Sub BtnExit_Click(ByVal sender As System.Object,
ByVal e As System.EventArgs) Handles btnExit.Click
   Me.Close()
End Sub
```

7. Try running the program. Here's a run I made (notice the echo character):

Try both options. Input the correct password (note it is case sensitive) to see:

Input the incorrect password to see:

Save your project (saved in **Example 4-1** folder in the **LearnVB\VB Code\Class 4** folder).

If you have time, define a constant, TRYMAX = 3, and modify the code to allow the user to have just TRYMAX attempts to get the correct password. After the final try, inform the user you are logging him/her off. You'll also need a variable that counts the number of tries (make it a **Static** variable).

CheckBox Control

In Toolbox:

On Form (Default Properties):

As mentioned earlier, Visual Basic features many 'point and click' controls that let the user make a choice simply by clicking with the mouse. These controls are attractive, familiar and minimize the possibility of errors in your application. We will see many such controls. The first, the **CheckBox** control, is examined here.

The **CheckBox** control provides a way to make choices from a list of potential candidates. Some, all, or none of the choices in a group may be selected. Check boxes are used in all Windows applications (even the Visual Basic IDE). Examples of their use would be to turn options on and off in an application or to select from a 'shopping' list.

CheckBox **Properties:**

Name	Gets or sets the name of the check box (three letter prefix for check box name is **chk**).
AutoSize	Gets or sets a value indicating whether the check box is automatically resized to display its entire contents.
BackColor	Get or sets the check box background color.
Checked	Gets or sets a value indicating whether the check box is in the checked state.
Font	Gets or sets font name, style, size.
ForeColor	Gets or sets color of text or graphics.
Text	Gets or sets string displayed next to check box.
TextAlign	Gets or sets the alignment of text of the check box.

CheckBox **Methods:**

Focus	Moves focus to this check box.

CheckBox **Events**:

CheckedChanged	Occurs when the value of the Checked property changes, whether in code or when a check box is clicked.
Click	Triggered when a check box is clicked. **Checked** property is automatically changed by Visual Basic.

When a check box is clicked, if there is no check mark there (Checked = False), Visual Basic will place a check there and change the Checked property to True. If clicked and a check mark is there (Checked = True), then the check mark will disappear and the Checked property will be changed to False. The check box can also be configured to have three states: checked, unchecked or indeterminate. Consult on-line help if you require such behavior.

Typical use of **CheckBox** control:

> ➤ Set the **Name** and **Text** property. Initialize the **Checked** property.
> ➤ Monitor **Click** or **CheckChanged** event to determine when button is clicked. At any time, read **Checked** property to determine check box state.
> ➤ You may also want to change the **Font**, **Backcolor** and **Forecolor** properties.

RadioButton Control

In Toolbox:

On Form (Default Properties):

RadioButton controls provide the capability to make a "mutually exclusive" choice among a group of potential candidate choices. This simply means, radio buttons work as a group, only one of which can be selected. Radio buttons are seen in all Windows applications. They are called radio buttons because they work like a tuner on a car radio – you can only listen to one station at a time! Examples for radio button groups would be twelve buttons for selection of a month in a year, a group of buttons to let you select a color or buttons to select the difficulty in a game.

A first point to consider is how do you define a 'group' of radio buttons that work together? Any radio buttons placed on the form will act as a group. That is, if any radio button on a form is 'selected', all other buttons will be automatically 'unselected.' What if you need to make two independent choices; that is, you need two independent groups of radio buttons? To do this requires one of two grouping controls in Visual Basic: the **GroupBox** control or the **Panel** control. Radio buttons placed on either of these controls are independent from other radio buttons. We will discuss the grouping controls after the RadioButton control. For now, we'll just be concerned with how to develop and use a single group of radio buttons.

RadioButton **Properties:**

Name	Gets or sets the name of the radio button (three letter prefix for radio button name is **rdo**).
AutoSize	Gets or sets a value indicating whether the radio button is automatically resized to display its entire contents.
BackColor	Get or sets the radio button background color.
Checked	Gets or sets a value indicating whether the radio button is checked.
Font	Gets or sets font name, style, size.
ForeColor	Gets or sets color of text or graphics.
TextAlign	Gets or sets the alignment of text of the radio button.

RadioButton **Methods:**

Focus	Moves focus to this radio button.
PerformClick	Generates a Click event for the button, simulating a click by a user.

RadioButton **Events:**

CheckedChanged	Occurs when the value of the Checked property changes, whether in code or when a radio button is clicked.
Click	Triggered when a button is clicked. **Checked** property is automatically changed by Visual Basic.

When a radio button is clicked, it's Checked property is automatically set to True by Visual Basic. And, all other radio buttons in that button's group will have a Checked property of False. Only one button in the group can be checked.

Typical use of **RadioButton** control:

- ➢ Establish a group of radio buttons.
- ➢ For each button in the group, set the **Name** (give each button a similar name to identify them with the group) and **Text** property. You might also change the **Font, BackColor** and **Forecolor** properties.
- ➢ Initialize the **Checked** property of one button to **True**.
- ➢ Monitor the **Click** or **CheckChanged** event of each radio button in the group to determine when a button is clicked. The 'last clicked' button in the group will always have a **Checked** property of **True.**

GroupBox Control

In Toolbox:

On Form (Default Properties):

We've seen that both radio buttons and check boxes usually work as a group. Many times, there are logical groupings of controls. For example, you may have a scroll device setting the value of a displayed number. The **GroupBox** control provides a convenient way of grouping related controls in a Visual Basic application. And, in the case of radio buttons, group boxes affect how such buttons operate.

To place controls in a group box, you first draw the GroupBox control on the form. Then, the associated controls must be placed in the group box. This allows you to move the group box and controls together. There are several ways to place controls in a group box:

> ➢ Place controls directly in the group box using any of the usual methods.
> ➢ Draw controls outside the group box and drag them in.
> ➢ Copy and paste controls into the group box (prior to the paste operation, make sure the group box is selected).

To insure controls are properly placed in a group box, try moving it and make sure the associated controls move with it. To remove a control from the group box, simple drag it out of the control.

Like the Form object, the group box is a **container** control, since it 'holds' other controls. Hence, controls placed in a group box will share **BackColor**, **ForeColor** and **Font** properties. To change this, select the desired control (after it is placed on the group box) and change the desired properties. Another feature of a group box control is that when its Enabled property is False, all controls in the group box are disabled. Likewise, when the group box control Visible property is False, all controls in the group box are not visible.

As mentioned, group boxes affect how radio buttons work. Radio buttons within a GroupBox control work as a **group**, independently of radio buttons in other GroupBox controls. Radio buttons on the form, and not in group boxes, work as another independent group. That is, the form is itself a group box by default. We'll see this in the next example.

GroupBox **Properties**:

Name	Gets or sets the name of the group box (three letter prefix for group box name is **grp**).
BackColor	Get or sets the group box background color.
Enabled	Gets or sets a value indicating whether the group box is enabled. If False, all controls in the group box are disabled.
Font	Gets or sets font name, style, size.
ForeColor	Gets or sets color of text.
Text	Gets or sets string displayed in title region of group box.
Visible	If False, hides the group box (and all its controls).

The GroupBox control has some methods and events, but these are rarely used. We are more concerned with the methods and events associated with the controls in the group box.

Typical use of **GroupBox** control:

> ➤ Set **Name** and **Text** property (perhaps changing **Font**, **BackColor** and **ForeColor** properties).
> ➤ Place desired controls in group box. Monitor events of controls in group box using usual techniques.

Panel Control

In Toolbox:

On Form (Default Properties):

The **Panel** control is another Visual Basic grouping control. It is nearly identical to the **GroupBox** control in behavior. The Panel control lacks a Text property (titling information), but has optional scrolling capabilities. Controls are placed in a Panel control in the same manner they are placed in the GroupBox. And, radio buttons in the Panel control act as an independent group. Panel controls can also be used to display graphics (lines, curves, shapes, animations). We will look at those capabilities in later chapters.

Panel **Properties:**

Name	Gets or sets the name of the panel (three letter prefix for panel name is **pnl**).
AutoScroll	Gets or sets a value indicating whether the panel will allow the user to scroll to any controls placed outside of its visible boundaries.
BackColor	Get or sets the panel background color.
BorderStyle	Get or set the panel border style.
Enabled	Gets or sets a value indicating whether the panel is enabled. If False, all controls in the panel are disabled.
Visible	If False, hides the panel (and all its controls).

Like the GroupBox control, the Panel control has some methods and events, but these are rarely used (we will see a few Panel events in later graphics chapters). We usually only are concerned with the methods and events associated with the controls in the panel.

Typical use of **Panel** control:

> ➢ Set **Name** property.
> ➢ Place desired controls in panel control.
> ➢ Monitor events of controls in panel using usual techniques.

Handling Multiple Events in a Single Event Procedure

In the few applications we've built in this course, each event procedure handles a single event. Now that we are grouping controls like check boxes and radio buttons, it would be nice if a single procedure could handle multiple events. For example, if we have 4 radio buttons in a group, when one button is clicked, it would be preferable to have a single procedure where we decide which button was clicked, as opposed to having to monitor 4 separate event procedures. Let's see how to do this.

We use the radio button example to illustrate. Assume we have four radio buttons (**RadioButton1, RadioButton2, RadioButton3, RadioButton4**). The form for the **CheckedChanged** event procedure for **RadioButton1** is:

```
Private Sub RadioButton1_CheckedChanged(ByVal sender As
System.Object, ByVal e As System.EventArgs) Handles
RadioButton1.CheckedChanged
     .
     .
End Sub
```

The name assigned to this procedure by Visual Basic (**RadioButton1_CheckedChanged**) is <u>arbitrary</u>. We could change it to anything we want and it would still handle the **CheckedChanged** event for **RadioButton1**. Why, you ask?

The important clause in the procedure structure is the **Handles** statement:

```
Handles RadioButton1.CheckedChanged
```

This clause assigns the **RadioButton1.CheckedChanged** event to this particular procedure. This clause cannot be changed. We can assign additional events to this procedure by appending other control events to the **Handles** clause. For example, if we want this procedure to also handle the **CheckedChanged** event for **RadioButton2**, we can change the clause to:

```
Handles RadioButton1.CheckedChanged,
RadioButton2.CheckedChanged
```

Then if either of these two radio buttons is clicked (changing the Checked property), the procedure named **RadioButton1_CheckedChanged** will be invoked.

The **Handles** clause allows us to attach any event of any control to any procedure we want! It is best to append like events of like controls. It is possible to process dissimilar events of dissimilar controls with a single event procedure, but you need to be careful.

Let's complete the example we've been doing and add the remaining two radio buttons (**RadioButton3** and **RadioButton4**) to the event procedure. While we're at it, we'll rename the event procedure (new name is **MyButtons_CheckedChanged**) to clear up any possible misunderstanding of the name. The code that does this is:

```
Private Sub MyButtons_CheckedChanged(ByVal sender As
System.Object, ByVal e As System.EventArgs) Handles
RadioButton1.CheckedChanged, RadioButton2.CheckedChanged,
RadioButton3.CheckedChanged, RadioButton4.CheckedChanged
    .
    .
    .
End Sub
```

If we have a single procedure responding to events from multiple controls, how do we determine which particular event from which particular control invoked the procedure. In our example with a single procedure handling the CheckedChanged event for 4 radio buttons, how do we know which of the 4 buttons was clicked to enter the procedure? The **sender** argument of the event procedure provides the answer.

Each event procedure has a **sender** argument (the first argument of two) which identifies the control whose event caused the procedure to be invoked. With a little BASIC coding, we can identify the **Name** property (or any other needed property) of the sending control. For our radio button example, that code is:

```
Dim rdoExample As RadioButton
Dim ButtonName As String
'Determine which button was clicked
rdoExample = CType(sender, RadioButton)
ButtonName = rdoExample.Name
```

In this code, we define a variable (**rdoExample**) to be the type of the control attached to the procedure (a **RadioButton** in this case). Then, we assign this variable to **sender** (after converting sender to the proper control type). Once this variable is established, we can determine any property we want. In the above example, we find the radio button's **Name** property. With this information, we now know which particular button was clicked and we can process any code associated with clicking on this radio button.

Control Arrays

When using controls that work in groups, like check boxes and radio buttons, it is sometimes desirable to have some way to quickly process every control in that group. A concept of use in this case is that of a **control array**.

In the Chapter 2, we learned about variable arrays – variables referred by name and index to allow quick processing of large amounts of data. The same idea applies here. We can define an array of controls, using the same statements used to declare a variable array. For example, to declare an array of 20 buttons, use:

```
Dim MyButtons(20) As Button
```

Actually, there are 21 buttons since indices start at 0 and go to 20. This array declaration is placed according to desired scope, just like variables. For form level scope, place the statement at the top of the form code. For procedure level scope, place it in the respective procedure. Once the array has been declared, each element of the 'control array' can be referred to by its name (**MyButton**) and index. An example will clarify the advantage of such an approach.

Say we have 10 check boxes (chkBox01, chkBox02, chkBox03, chkBox04, chkBox05, chkBox06, chkBox07, chkBox08, chkBox09, chkBox10) on a form and we need to examine each check box's Checked property. If that property is True, we need to process 30 lines of additional code. For one check box, that code would be:

```
If chkBox01.Checked Then
   [do these 30 lines of code]
End If
```

We would need to repeat this 9 more times (for the nine remaining check boxes), yielding a total of 32 x 10 = 320 lines of code. And, if we needed to add a few lines to the code being processed, we would need to add these lines in 10 different places – a real maintenance headache. Let's try using an array of check boxes to minimize this headache.

Here's the solution. Define an array of 10 check box controls and assign the array values to existing controls:

```
Dim MyCheck(10) As CheckBox
MyCheck(1)  = chkBox01
MyCheck(2)  = chkBox02
MyCheck(3)  = chkBox03
MyCheck(4)  = chkBox04
MyCheck(5)  = chkBox05
MyCheck(6)  = chkBox06
MyCheck(7)  = chkBox07
MyCheck(8)  = chkBox08
MyCheck(9)  = chkBox09
MyCheck(10) = chkBox10
```

Again, make sure the declaration statement is properly located for proper scope. Having made these assignments, the code for examining the Checked property of each has been reduced to these few lines:

```
Dim I As Integer
      .
      .
For I = 1 To 10
  If MyCheck(I).Checked Then
    [do these 30 lines of code]
  End If
Next I
```

The 320 lines of code have been reduced to about 45 (including all the declarations) and code maintenance is now much easier.

Obviously, it is not necessary to use control arrays, but they do have their advantages. You will start to see such arrays in the course examples and problems, so you should understand their use.

Example 4-2

Pizza Order

1. Start a new project. We'll build a form where a pizza order can be entered by simply clicking on check boxes and radio buttons. The pizza we build will be described by a Pizza class. Since this is the first example built using classes and objects, study it carefully to understand how OOP is used.

2. Draw three group boxes. In the first, draw three radio buttons, in the second, draw two radio buttons, and in the third, draw six check boxes. Draw two radio buttons on the form. Add two buttons. Make things look something like this.

3. Set the properties of the form and each control.

     Form1:
          Name   frmPizza
          FormBorderStyle   FixedSingle
          StartPosition   CenterScreen
          Text   Pizza Order

     GroupBox1:
          Text   Size

     GroupBox2:
          Text   Crust Type

     GroupBox3
          Text   Toppings

     RadioButton1:
          Name   rdoSmall
          Checked   True
          Text   Small

     RadioButton2:
          Name   rdoMedium
          Text   Medium

     RadioButton3:
          Name   rdoLarge
          Text   Large

     RadioButton4:
          Name   rdoThin
          Checked   True
          Text   Thin Crust

     RadioButton5:
          Name   rdoThick
          Text   Thick Crust

RadioButton6:

Name	rdoIn
Checked	True
Text	Eat In

RadioButton7:

Name	rdoOut
Text	Take Out

CheckBox1:

Name	chkCheese
Text	Extra Cheese

CheckBox2:

Name	chkMushrooms
Text	Mushrooms

CheckBox3:

Name	chkOlives
Text	Black Olives

CheckBox4:

Name	chkOnions
Text	Onions

CheckBox5:

Name	chkPeppers
Text	Green Peppers

CheckBox6:

Name	chkTomatoes
Text	Tomatoes

Button1:

Name	btnBuild
Text	&Build Pizza

Button2:

Name	btnExit
Text	E&xit

The form should look like this now:

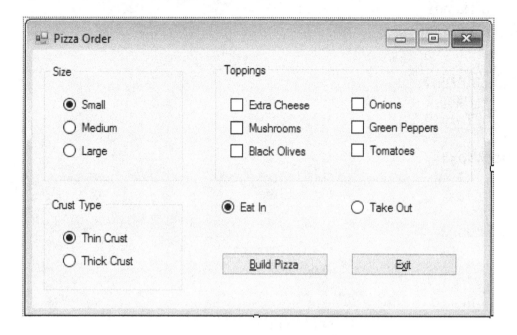

4. Add a class to your project named **Pizza.vb**. Use this code for the class:

```
Public Class Pizza
  Public PizzaSize As String
  Public PizzaCrust As String
  Public PizzaWhere As String
  Public PizzaTopping(6) As String

  Public Sub New()
    Me.PizzaSize = "Small"
    Me.PizzaCrust = "Thin Crust"
    Me.PizzaWhere = "Eat In"
    Me.PizzaTopping(1) = ""
    Me.PizzaTopping(2) = ""
    Me.PizzaTopping(3) = ""
    Me.PizzaTopping(4) = ""
    Me.PizzaTopping(5) = ""
    Me.PizzaTopping(6) = ""
  End Sub

  Public Function DescribePizza() As String
    Dim s As String
    'This procedure builds a string that describes the
pizza
    Dim I As Integer
    s = Me.PizzaWhere + ControlChars.Cr
    s += Me.PizzaSize + " Pizza" + ControlChars.Cr
    s += Me.PizzaCrust + ControlChars.Cr
    'Check each topping using the array we set up
    For I = 1 To 6
      If Me.PizzaTopping(I) <> "" Then
        s += Me.PizzaTopping(I) + ControlChars.Cr
      End If
    Next I
    Return (s)
  End Function
End Class
```

The Pizza class has several properties: **PizzaSize**, **PizzaCrust**, **PizzaWhere** and **PizzaTopping** (an array). A method **DescribePizza** forms a string variable that describes the pizza. In this method, a string is established by concatenating the pizza size, crust type, and eating location (recall **ControlChars.Cr** is a constant representing a 'carriage return' that puts each piece of ordering information on a separate line). Next, the code cycles through the six toppings and adds any non-blank information to the string.

5. Return to the form code window. Form level scope variable declarations:

```
Dim MyPizza As Pizza
Dim Topping(6) As CheckBox
Dim Loading As Boolean = True
```

This makes the **MyPizza** object global to the form. The array of check box controls will help us determine which toppings are selected. As mentioned in the notes, it is common to use 'control arrays' when working with check boxes and radio buttons. The **Loading** variable is used often in Visual Basic to avoid triggering event procedures while the form is being created.

6. Use this code in the **Form Load** procedure. This constructs the initial pizza object.

```
Private Sub FrmPizza_Load(ByVal sender As System.Object,
ByVal e As System.EventArgs) Handles MyBase.Load
    MyPizza = New Pizza()
    'Define an array of topping check boxes
    Topping(1) = chkCheese
    Topping(2) = chkMushrooms
    Topping(3) = chkOlives
    Topping(4) = chkOnions
    Topping(5) = chkPeppers
    Topping(6) = chkTomatoes
    Loading = False
End Sub
```

Here, the MyPizza object is constructed.. The Topping variables are set to their respective check boxes. The Loading variable is set to False once this procedure is executed.

7. Use this code to define single **CheckedChanged** events for each of the three groups of radio buttons:

```
Private Sub RdoSize_CheckedChanged(ByVal sender As
System.Object, ByVal e As System.EventArgs) Handles
rdoSmall.CheckedChanged, rdoMedium.CheckedChanged,
rdoLarge.CheckedChanged
    If Loading Then Exit Sub
    Dim rdoSize As RadioButton
    'Determine which button was clicked and change size
    rdoSize = CType(sender, RadioButton)
    MyPizza.PizzaSize = rdoSize.Text
End Sub

Private Sub RdoCrust_CheckedChanged(ByVal sender As
Object, ByVal e As System.EventArgs) Handles
rdoThin.CheckedChanged, rdoThick.CheckedChanged
    If Loading Then Exit Sub
    Dim rdoCrust As RadioButton
    'Determine which button was clicked and change crust
    rdoCrust = CType(sender, RadioButton)
    MyPizza.PizzaCrust = rdoCrust.Text
End Sub

Private Sub RdoWhere_CheckedChanged(ByVal sender As
Object, ByVal e As System.EventArgs) Handles
rdoIn.CheckedChanged, rdoOut.CheckedChanged
    If Loading Then Exit Sub
    Dim rdoWhere As RadioButton
    'Determine which button was clicked and change where
    rdoWhere = CType(sender, RadioButton)
    MyPizza.PizzaWhere = rdoWhere.Text
End Sub
```

In each of these routines, when a radio button's Checked property changes, the value of the corresponding button's Text is loaded into the respective pizza object property. Note if Loading is True, none of these procedures is executed. This is needed because, when the form is being built by Visual Basic, the Pizza object does not exist yet and an error would occur when attempting to set a property.

4-44   Learn Visual Basic

8. Use this code in the **btnBuild Click** event.

```
Private Sub BtnBuild_Click(ByVal sender As System.Object,
ByVal e As System.EventArgs) Handles btnBuild.Click
    'This procedure builds a message box that displays your
pizza type
    'Identify selected toppings
    Dim I As Integer
    For I = 1 To 6
      If Topping(I).Checked Then
        MyPizza.PizzaTopping(I) = Topping(I).Text
      Else
        MyPizza.PizzaTopping(I) = ""
      End If
    Next I
    MessageBox.Show(MyPizza.DescribePizza, "Your Pizza",
MessageBoxButtons.OK)
    End Sub
```

This cycles through the six topping check boxes (defined by our Topping array) and sets the MyPizza object properties. The code then displays the pizza order in a message box (using the object DescribePizza method).

9. Use this code in the **btnExit Click** event.

```
Private Sub BtnExit_Click(ByVal sender As Object, ByVal e
As System.EventArgs) Handles btnExit.Click
    Me.Close()
    End Sub
```

10. Get the application working. Notice how the different selection buttons work in their individual groups. Here's some choices in my run:

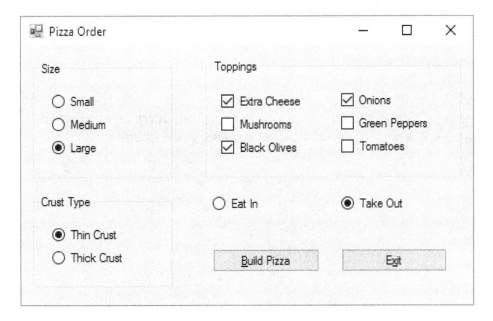

Then, when I click **Build Pizza**, I see:

Save your project (saved in **Example 4-2** folder in the **LearnVB\VB Code\Class 4** folder).

If you have time, try these modifications:

A. Add a new program button that resets the order form to the initial default values. You'll have to reinitialize the pizza object, reset all check boxes to unchecked, and reset all three radio button groups to their default values.

B. Modify the Pizza class code so that if no toppings are selected, the message "Cheese Only" appears on the order form. You'll need to figure out a way to see if no check boxes were checked.

ListBox Control

In Toolbox:

On Form (Default Properties):

Check boxes are useful controls for selecting items from a list. But, what if your list has 100 items? Do you want 100 check boxes? No, but fortunately, there is a tool that solves this problem. A **ListBox** control displays a list of items (with as many items as you like) from which the user can select one or more items. If the number of items exceeds the number that can be displayed, a scroll bar is automatically added. Both single item and multiple item selections are supported.

ListBox **Properties:**

Name	Gets or sets the name of the list box (three letter prefix for list box name is **lst**).
BackColor	Get or sets the list box background color.
Font	Gets or sets font name, style, size.
ForeColor	Gets or sets color of text.
Items	Gets the Items object of the list box.
SelectedIndex	Gets or sets the zero-based index of the currently selected item in a list box.
SelectedIndices	Zero-based array of indices of all currently selected items in the list box.
SelectedItem	Gets or sets the currently selected item in the list box.
SelectedItems	SelectedItems object of the list box.
SelectionMode	Gets or sets the method in which items are selected in list box (allows single or multiple selections).

ListBox **Properties** (continued)

Sorted	Gets or sets a value indicating whether the items in list box are sorted alphabetically.
Text	Text of currently selected item in list box.
TopIndex	Gets or sets the index of the first visible item in list box.

ListBox **Methods:**

ClearSelected	Unselects all items in the list box.
FindString	Finds the first item in the list box that starts with the specified string.
GetSelected	Returns a value indicating whether the specified item is selected.
SetSelected	Selects or clears the selection for the specified item in a list box.

ListBox **Events:**

SelectedIndexChanged	Occurs when the SelectedIndex property has changed.

Some further discussion is needed to use the list box **Items** object, **SelectedItems** object and **SelectionMode** property. The Items object has its own properties to specify the items in the list box. It also has its own methods for adding and deleting items in the list box. Two properties of use: **Item** is a zero-based array of the items in the list and **Count** is the number of items in the list. Hence, the first item in a list box named **lstExample** is:

```
lstExample.Items.Item(0)
```

The last item in the list is:

```
lstExample.Items.Item(lstExample.Items.Count - 1)
```

The minus one is needed because of the zero-based array.

To add an item to a list box, use the **Add** method, to delete an item, use the **Remove** or **RemoveAt** method and to clear a list box use the **Clear** method. For our example list box, the respective commands are:

Add Item:	`lstExample.Items.Add`(ItemToAdd)
Delete Item:	`lstExample.Items.Remove`(ItemToRemove)
	`lstExample.Items.RemoveAt`(IndexofItemToRemove)
Clear list box:	`lstExample.Items.Clear`

List boxes normally list string data types, though other types are possible. Note, when removing items, that indices for subsequent items in the list change following a removal.

In a similar fashion, the **SelectedItems** object has its own properties to specify the currently selected items in the list box Of particular use is **Count** which tells you how many items are selected. This value, in conjunction with the SelectedIndices array, identifies the set of selected items.

The **SelectionMode** property specifies whether you want single item selection or multiple selections. When the property is **SelectionMode.One**, you can select only one item (works like a group of option buttons). When the SelectionMode property is set to **SelectionMode.MultiExtended**, pressing <Shift> and clicking the mouse or pressing <Shift>and one of the arrow keys extends the selection from the previously selected item to the current item. Pressing <Ctrl>and clicking the mouse selects or deselects an item in the list. When the property is set to **SelectionMode.MultiSimple**, a mouse click or pressing the spacebar selects or deselects an item in the list.

The **CheckedListBox** is a nearly identical control in Visual Basic. The only difference is, with the CheckedListBox, a check mark appears before selected items. Other than that, performance is identical to the ListBox control.

Typical use of **ListBox** control:

- ➢ Set **Name** property, **SelectionMode** property and populate **Items** object (usually in **Form_Load** procedure).
- ➢ Monitor **SelectedIndexChanged** event for individual selections.
- ➢ Use **SelectedIndex** and **SelectIndices** properties to determine selected items.

ComboBox Control

In Toolbox:

On Form (Default Properties):

The **ListBox** control is equivalent to a group of check boxes (allowing multiple selections in a long list of items). The equivalent control for a long list of radio buttons is the **ComboBox** control. The ComboBox allows the selection of a single item from a list. And, in some cases, the user can type in an alternate response.

ComboBox **Properties:**

ComboBox properties are nearly identical to those of the ListBox, with the deletion of the **SelectionMode** property and the addition of a **DropDownStyle** property.

Name	Gets or sets the name of the combo box (three letter prefix for combo box name is **cbo**).
BackColor	Get or sets the combo box background color.
DropDownStyle	Specifies one of three combo box styles.
Font	Gets or sets font name, style, size.
ForeColor	Gets or sets color of text.
Items	Gets the Items object of the combo box.
MaxDropDownItems	Maximum number of items to show in dropdown portion.
SelectedIndex	Gets or sets the zero-based index of the currently selected item in list box portion.
SelectedItem	Gets or sets the currently selected item in the list box portion.
SelectedText	Gets or sets the text that is selected in the editable portion of combo box.
Sorted	Gets or sets a value indicating whether the items in list box portion are sorted alphabetically.
Text	String value displayed in combo box.

ComboBox **Events:**

KeyPress	Occurs when a key is pressed while the combo box has focus.
SelectedIndexChanged	Occurs when the SelectedIndex property has changed.

The **Items** object for the ComboBox control is identical to that of the ListBox control. You add and remove items in the same manner and values are read with the same properties.

The **DropDownStyle** property has three different values. The values and their description are:

Value	Description
DropDown	Text portion is editable; drop-down list portion.
DropDownList	Text portion is not editable; drop-down list portion.
Simple	The text portion is editable. The list portion is always visible. With this value, you'll want to resize the control to set the list box portion height.

Typical use of **ComboBox** control:

➢ Set **Name** property, **DropDownStyle** property and populate **Items** object (usually in form **Load** procedure).
➢ Monitor **SelectedIndexChanged** event for individual selections.
➢ Read **SelectedText** property to identify choice.

Example 4-3

Flight Planner

1. Start a new project. In this example, you select a destination city, a seat location, and a meal preference for airline passengers

2. Place a list box, two combo boxes, three labels and two buttons on the form. The form should appear similar to this:

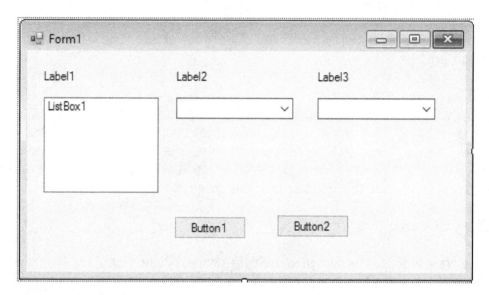

3. Set the form and object properties:

Form1:
Name	frmFlight
FormBorderStyle	FixedSingle
StartPosition	CenterScreen
Text	Flight Planner

Label1:
Text	Destination City

Label2:
Text	Seat Location

Label3:
Text	Meal Preference

ListBox1:

Name	lstCities
Sorted	True

ComboBox1:

Name	cboSeat
DropDownStyle	DropdownList

ComboBox2:

Name	cboMeal
DropDownStyle	Simple

(You'll want to resize this control after setting properties).

Button1:

Name	btnAssign
Text	&Assign

Button2:

Name	btnExit
Text	E&xit

Now, the form should look like this:

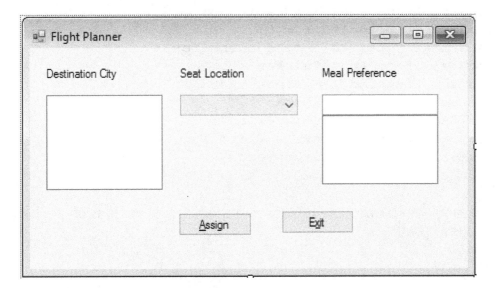

4. Use this code in the **Form Load** procedure:

```
Private Sub FrmFlight_Load(ByVal sender As System.Object,
ByVal e As System.EventArgs) Handles MyBase.Load
    'Add city names to list box
    lstCities.Items.Clear()
    lstCities.Items.Add("San Diego")
    lstCities.Items.Add("Los Angeles")
    lstCities.Items.Add("Orange County")
    lstCities.Items.Add("Ontario")
    lstCities.Items.Add("Bakersfield")
    lstCities.Items.Add("Oakland")
    lstCities.Items.Add("Sacramento")
    lstCities.Items.Add("San Jose")
    lstCities.Items.Add("San Francisco")
    lstCities.Items.Add("Eureka")
    lstCities.Items.Add("Eugene")
    lstCities.Items.Add("Portland")
    lstCities.Items.Add("Spokane")
    lstCities.Items.Add("Seattle")
    lstCities.SelectedIndex = 0
    'Add seat types to first combo box
    cboSeat.Items.Add("Aisle")
    cboSeat.Items.Add("Middle")
    cboSeat.Items.Add("Window")
    cboSeat.SelectedIndex = 0
    'Add meal types to second combo box
    cboMeal.Items.Add("Chicken")
    cboMeal.Items.Add("Mystery Meat")
    cboMeal.Items.Add("Kosher")
    cboMeal.Items.Add("Vegetarian")
    cboMeal.Items.Add("Fruit Plate")
    cboMeal.Text = "No Preference"
End Sub
```

This code simply initializes the list box and the list box portions of the two combo boxes.

5. Use this code in the **btnAssign Click** event:

```
Private Sub BtnAssign_Click(ByVal sender As System.Object,
ByVal e As System.EventArgs) Handles btnAssign.Click
    'Build message box that gives your assignment
    Dim Message As String
    Message = "Destination: " + lstCities.Text +
ControlChars.Cr
    Message += "Seat Location: " + cboSeat.Text +
ControlChars.Cr
    Message += "Meal: " + cboMeal.Text + ControlChars.Cr
    MessageBox.Show(Message, "Your Assignment",
MessageBoxButtons.OK, MessageBoxIcon.Information)
    End Sub
```

When the **Assign** button is clicked, this code forms a message box message by concatenating the selected city (from the list box **lstCities**), seat choice (from **cboSeat**), and the meal preference (from **cboMeal**).

6. Use this code in the **btnExit Click** event:

```
Private Sub BtnExit_Click(ByVal sender As System.Object,
ByVal e As System.EventArgs) Handles btnExit.Click
    Me.Close()
    End Sub
```

7. Run the application. Here's my screen with choices I made:

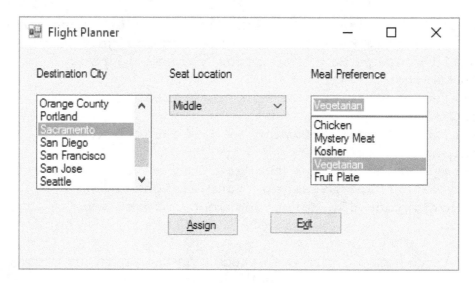

And, after clicking **Assign**, I see:

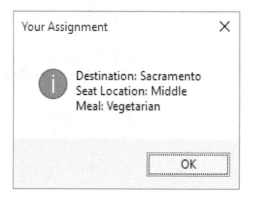

Save the project (saved in **Example 4-3** folder in **LearnVB\VB Code\Class 4** folder).

Can you modify this application to include a Passenger class from which to create Passenger objects?

Class Review

After completing this class, you should understand:

> ➢ How to use the MessageBox dialog assigning messages, icons and buttons
> ➢ Useful properties, events, and methods for the form, button, text box, label, check box, and radio button controls
> ➢ Where the above listed controls can and should be used
> ➢ How GroupBox and Panel controls are used to group controls, particularly radio buttons
> ➢ How several events can be handled by a single event procedure
> ➢ The concept of 'control arrays' and how to use them
> ➢ How to use list box and combo box controls

Practice Problems 4

Problem 4-1. Message Box Problem. Build an application that lets you see what various message boxes look like. Allow selection of icon, buttons displayed, default button, and input message. Provide feedback on button clicked on displayed message box.

Problem 4-2. Tray Problem. Here's a sheet of cardboard (**L** units long and **W** units wide). A square cut **X** units long is made in each corner:

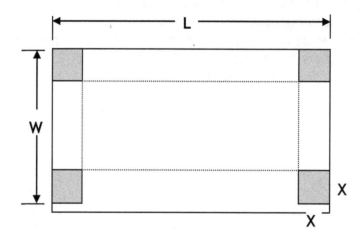

If you cut out the four shaded corners and fold the resulting sides up along the dotted lines, a tray is formed. Build an application that lets a user input the length (L) and width (W). Have the application decide what value X should be such that the tray has the largest volume possible. Use the NumericTextBox class developed in Chapter 3 for input.

Problem 4-3. List Box Problem. Build an application with two list boxes. Select items from one box. Click a button to move selected items to the other list box. If you then double-click an item in the second list box, have it return to the first box.

Problem 4-4. Combo Box Problem. Build an application with a Simple style combo box. Populate with some kind of information. If the user decides to type in their own selection (that is, they don't choose one of the listed items), add that new item to the list box portion of the combo box.

Exercise 4

Customer Database Input Screen

A new sports store wants you to develop an input screen for its customer database. The required input information is:

1. Name
2. Age
3. City of Residence
4. Sex (Male or Female)
5. Activities (Running, Walking, Biking, Swimming, Skiing and/or In-Line Skating)
6. Athletic Level (Extreme, Advanced, Intermediate, or Beginner)

Set up the screen so that only the Name and Age (use text boxes) and, perhaps, City (use a combo box) need to be typed; all other inputs should be set with check boxes and radio buttons. When a screen of information is complete, display the summarized profile in a message box. Use object-oriented programming to describe the customer. This profile message box should resemble this:

5. More Exploration of the Visual Basic Toolbox

Review and Preview

In this class, we continue looking at tools in the Visual Basic toolbox. We will look at some input tools, scroll bars, picture boxes and controls that allow direct interaction with drives, directories, and files. In the examples, you should start trying to do as much of the building and programming of the applications you can with minimal reference to the notes. This will help you build your programming skills.

Control Z Order

As you build Windows applications using Visual Basic, you will notice that whenever controls occupy the same space on a form, one control is on top of the other. The relative location of controls on a form is established by what is called the **Z Order**.

As each control is placed on the form, it is assigned a Z Order value. Controls placed last will lie over controls placed earlier. While designing an application, the Z Order can be changed by right-clicking the control of interest. A menu will appear. Selecting **BringToFront** will bring that control 'in front' of all other controls. Conversely, selecting **SendToBack** will send that control 'behind' all other controls.

A control's Z Order can also be changed in code. Why would you want to do this? Perhaps, you have two controls on the form in exactly the same location, one that should be accessible for one particular operation and the other accessible for another operation. To place one control in front of the other, you need to change the Z Order. The **BringToFront** and **SendToBack** methods accomplish this task. For a control named ControlExample, the code to accomplish this is:

```
ControlName.BringToFront()
```

Or

```
ControlName.SendToBack()
```

Now, let's continue our look at the Visual Basic toolbox, looking first at more controls that allow 'point and click' selections.

NumericUpDown Control

In Toolbox:

On Form (Default Properties):

The **NumericUpDown** control is used to obtain a numeric input. It looks like a text box control with two small arrows. Clicking the arrows changes the displayed value, which ranges from a specified minimum to a specified maximum. The user can even type in a value, if desired. Such controls are useful for supplying a date in a month or are used as volume controls in some Windows multimedia applications.

NumericUpDown **Properties:**

Name	Gets or sets the name of the numeric updown (three letter prefix for numeric updown name is **nud**).
BackColor	Get or sets the numeric updown background color.
BorderStyle	Gets or sets the border style for the updown control.
Font	Gets or sets font name, style, size.
ForeColor	Gets or sets color of text or graphics.
Increment	Gets or sets the value to increment or decrement the updown control when the up or down buttons are clicked.
Maximum	Gets or sets the maximum value for the updown control.
Minimum	Gets or sets the minimum value for the updown control.
ReadOnly	Gets or sets a value indicating whether the text may be changed by the use of the up or down buttons only.
TextAlign	Gets or sets the alignment of text in the numeric updown.
Value	Gets or sets the value assigned to the updown control.

NumericUpDown **Methods**:

DownButton	Decrements the value of the updown control.
UpButton	Increments the value of the updown control.

NumericUpDown **Events**:

Leave	Occurs when the updown control loses focus.
ValueChanged	Occurs when the Value property has been changed in some way.

The **Value** property can be changed by clicking either of the arrows or, optionally by typing a value. If using the arrows, the value will always lie between **Minimum** and **Maximum**. If the user can type in a value, you have no control over what value is typed. However, once the control loses focus, the typed value will be compared to Minimum and Maximum and any adjustments made. Hence, if you allow typed values, only check the Value property in the **Leave** event.

Typical use of **NumericUpDown** control:

➤ Set the **Name, Minimum** and **Maximum** properties. Initialize **Value** property. Decide on value for **ReadOnly.**
➤ Monitor **ValueChanged** (or **Leave**) event for changes in Value.
➤ You may also want to change the **Font, Backcolor** and **Forecolor** properties.

DomainUpDown Control

In Toolbox:

On Form (Default Properties):

The **DomainUpDown** control is similar in appearance to the NumericUpDown control. The difference is that the DomainUpDown control displays a list of string items (rather than numbers) as potential choices. It is much like a single line ComboBox control with no dropdown list. You will see it shares many of the properties of the ComboBox. The DomainUpDown control is usually reserved for relatively small lists. Examples of use are selecting a state in the United States for an address book, selecting a month for a calendar input or selecting a name from a short list.

DomainUpDown **Properties:**

Name	Gets or sets the name of the domain updown (three letter prefix for domain updown name is **dud**).
BackColor	Get or sets the domain updown background color.
Font	Gets or sets font name, style, size.
ForeColor	Gets or sets color of text.
Items	Gets the Items object of the domain updown.
ReadOnly	Gets or sets a value indicating whether the text may be changed by the use of the up or down buttons only.
SelectedIndex	Gets or sets the zero-based index of the currently selected item.
SelectedItem	Gets or sets the selected item based on the index value of the selected item.
Sorted	Gets or sets a value indicating whether items are sorted alphabetically.

Text	Gets or sets the text displayed in the updown control.
TextAlign	Gets or sets the alignment of the text in the updown control.
Wrap	Gets or sets a value indicating whether the list of items continues to the first or last item if the user continues past the end of the list.

DomainUpDown **Methods:**

| DownButton | Displays the next item in the control. |
| UpButton | Displays the previous item in the control. |

DomainUpDown **Events:**

KeyPress	Occurs when a key is pressed while the domain updown has focus.
Leave	Occurs when the control loses focus.
SelectedItemChanged	Occurs when the SelectedItem property has changed.
TextChanged	Occurs when the Text property has changed.

Like the ListBox and ComboBox controls, the Items object provides details on what is in the control and how to add/delete information from the control. The first item in a updown control named **dudExample** is:

```
dudExample.Items.Item(0)
```

The last item in the list is:

```
dudExample.Items.Item(dudExample.Items.Count - 1)
```

To add an item to the control, use the **Add** method, to delete an item, use the **Remove** or **RemoveAt** method and to clear it use the **Clear** method. For our example:

Add Item:	`dudExample.Items.Add`(StringToAdd)
Delete Item:	`dudExample.Items.Remove`(ItemToRemove)
	`DudExample.Items.RemoveAt`(IndexOfItemToRemove)
Clear list box:	`dudExample.Items.Clear`

Typical use of **DomainUpDown** control:

> ➢ Set **Name** property, decide whether **ReadOnly** should be True and populate **Items** object (usually in form **Load** procedure).
> ➢ Monitor **SelectedItemChanged** (or **TextChanged**) event for individual selections.
> ➢ Read **Text** property to identify choice.
> ➢ As usual, you may also want to change the **Font**, **Backcolor** and **Forecolor** properties.

Example 5-1

Date Input Device

1. Start a new project. In this project, we'll use a NumericUpDown control, in conjunction with a DomainUpDown control, to select a month and day of the year.

2. Place a NumericUpDown control, a DomainUpDown control and a Label control on the form. The form should resemble this:

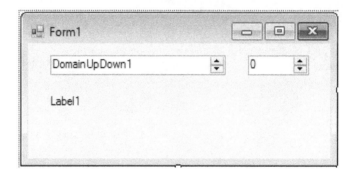

3. Set these properties:

    Form1:
    <table>
    <tr><td>Name</td><td>frmDate</td></tr>
    <tr><td>FormBorderStyle</td><td>FixedSingle</td></tr>
    <tr><td>StartPosition</td><td>CenterScreen</td></tr>
    <tr><td>Text</td><td>Date Input</td></tr>
    </table>

    DomainUpDown1:
    <table>
    <tr><td>Name</td><td>dudMonth</td></tr>
    <tr><td>BackColor</td><td>White</td></tr>
    <tr><td>Font Size</td><td>14</td></tr>
    <tr><td>ReadOnly</td><td>True</td></tr>
    <tr><td>Text</td><td>December</td></tr>
    <tr><td>Wrap</td><td>True</td></tr>
    </table>

NumericUpDown1:

Name	nudDay
BackColor	White
Font Size	14
Maximum	31
Minimum	1
ReadOnly	True
TextAlign	Center
Value	1

Label1:

Name	lblDate
Font Size	12
Text	[Blank]

When done, the form should look like this:

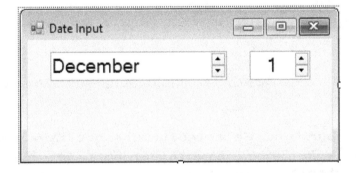

The label control cannot be seen.

4. Use this code in the **frmDate Load** procedure to populate the control with the month names:

```
Private Sub FrmDate_Load(ByVal sender As System.Object,
ByVal e As System.EventArgs) Handles MyBase.Load
    dudMonth.Items.Add("January")
    dudMonth.Items.Add("February")
    dudMonth.Items.Add("March")
    dudMonth.Items.Add("April")
    dudMonth.Items.Add("May")
    dudMonth.Items.Add("June")
    dudMonth.Items.Add("July")
    dudMonth.Items.Add("August")
    dudMonth.Items.Add("September")
    dudMonth.Items.Add("October")
    dudMonth.Items.Add("November")
    dudMonth.Items.Add("December")
    dudMonth.SelectedIndex = 0
    lblDate.Text = dudMonth.Text + Str(nudDay.Value)
End Sub
```

5. Use this code in the **dudMonth SelectedItemChanged** event to update date if month changes:

```
Private Sub DudMonth_SelectedItemChanged(ByVal sender As
Object, ByVal e As System.EventArgs) Handles
dudMonth.SelectedItemChanged
    lblDate.Text = dudMonth.Text + Str(nudDay.Value)
End Sub
```

6. Use this code in the **nudDay ValueChanged** event to update date if day changes:

```
Private Sub NudDay_ValueChanged(ByVal sender As Object,
ByVal e As System.EventArgs) Handles nudDay.ValueChanged
    lblDate.Text = dudMonth.Text + Str(nudDay.Value)
End Sub
```

7. Run the program. Here's some selections I made:

Scroll through the month names. Notice how the **Wrap** property allows the list to return to January after December. Scroll through the day values, noticing how the displayed date changes. Save the project (saved in **Example 5-1** folder in the **LearnVB\VB Code\Class 5** folder).

Do you notice that you could enter April 31 as a date, even though it's not a legal value? Can you think of how to modify this example to make sure you don't exceed the number of days in any particular month? And, how would you handle February – you need to know if it's a leap year.

Horizontal and Vertical ScrollBar Controls

Horizontal ScrollBar In Toolbox:

Horizontal ScrollBar On Form (Default Properties):

Vertical ScrollBar In Toolbox:

Vertical ScrollBar On Form (Default Properties):

The NumericUpDown control is useful for relatively small ranges of numeric input. It wouldn't work well for large number ranges – you'd spend a lot of time clicking those little arrows. For large ranges of numbers, we use horizontal (**HScrollBar**) and vertical (**VScrollBar**) scroll bar controls. Scroll bars are widely used in Windows applications. Scroll bars provide an intuitive way to move through a list of information and make great input devices. Here, we use a scroll bar to obtain a whole number (**Integer** data type).

Both type of scroll bars are comprised of three areas that can be clicked, or dragged, to change the scroll bar value. Those areas are:

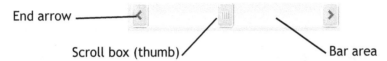

Clicking an **end arrow** increments the **scroll box** a small amount, clicking the **bar area** increments the scroll box a large amount, and dragging the scroll box (thumb) provides continuous motion. Using the properties of scroll bars, we can completely specify how one works. The scroll box position is the only output information from a scroll bar.

ScrollBar **Properties** (apply to both horizontal and vertical controls):

Name	Gets or sets the name of the scroll bar (three letter prefix for horizontal scroll bar is **hsb**, for vertical scroll bar **vsb**).
LargeChange	Increment added to or subtracted from the scroll bar Value property when the bar area is clicked.
Maximum	The maximum value of the horizontal scroll bar at the far right and the maximum value of the vertical scroll bar at the bottom.
Minimum	The minimum value of the horizontal scroll bar at the left and the vertical scroll bar at the top
SmallChange	The increment added to or subtracted from the scroll bar Value property when either of the scroll arrows is clicked.
Value	The current position of the scroll box (thumb) within the scroll bar. If you set this in code, Visual Basic moves the scroll box to the proper position.

Location of properties for **horizontal** scroll bar:

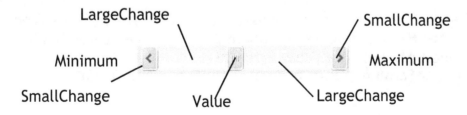

Location of properties for **vertical** scroll bar:

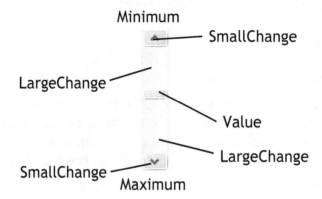

A couple of important notes about scroll bar properties:

1. Notice the vertical scroll bar has its Minimum at the top and its Maximum at the bottom. This may be counter-intuitive in some applications. That is, users may expect things to 'go up' as they increase. You can give this appearance of going up by defining another variable that varies 'negatively' with the scroll bar Value property.

2. If you ever change the **Value, Minimum,** or **Maximum** properties in code, make sure Value is at all times between Minimum and Maximum or the program will stop with an error message.

ScrollBar **Events:**

Scroll	Occurs when the scroll box has been moved by either a mouse or keyboard action.
ValueChanged	Occurs whenever the scroll bar **Value** property changes, either in code or via a mouse action.

Typical use of **HScrollBar** and **VScrollBar** controls:

➤ Decide whether horizontal or vertical scroll bar fits your needs best.
➤ Set the **Name, Minimum, Maximum, SmallChange, LargeChange** properties. Initialize **Value** property.
➤ Monitor **Scroll** or **ValueChanged** event for changes in Value.

A Note on the **Maximum** Property:

If **LargeChange** is not equal to one, the **Maximum** value cannot be achieved by clicking the end arrows, the bar area or moving the scroll box. It can only be achieved by setting the **Value** property in code. The maximum achievable **Value,** via mouse operations, is given by the relation:

$$\text{Achievable Maximum} = \text{Maximum} - \text{LargeChange} + 1$$

What does this mean? To meet an "achievable maximum," you need to set the scroll bar Maximum property using this equation:

$$\text{Maximum} = \text{Achievable Maximum} + \text{LargeChange} - 1$$

For example, if you want a scroll bar to be able to reach 100 (with a LargeChange property of 10), you need to set **Maximum** to **109**, not 100! Very strange, I'll admit ...

TrackBar Control

In Toolbox:

On Form (Default Properties):

The **TrackBar** control is similar to the scroll bar control with a different interface. It is used to establish numeric input (usually a fairly small range). It can be oriented either horizontally or vertically.

TrackBar **Properties**:

Name	Gets or sets the name of the track bar (three letter prefix is **trk**).
LargeChange	Increment added to or subtracted from the track bar Value property when the user clicks the track bar or presses the <**PageUp**> or <**PageDn**> keys.
Maximum	The maximum value of the horizontal track bar at the far right and the maximum value of the vertical track bar at the top (this is different than the scroll bar).
Minimum	The minimum value of the horizontal track bar at the left and the vertical track bar at the bottom.
Orientation	Specifies a vertical or horizontal orientation for the control
SmallChange	The increment added to or subtracted from the track bar Value property when user presses left or right cursor control keys (horizontal orientation); when user presses up or down cursor control keys (vertical orientation).
TickFrequency	Determines how many tick marks appear on the track bar.
TickStyle	Determines how and where ticks appear.
Value	The current position of the pointer within the track bar. If you set this in code, Visual Basic moves the pointer to the proper position.

A couple of important notes about track bar properties:

1. Notice the vertical track bar has its Maximum at the top. This is different than the vertical scroll bar control.

2. If you ever change the **Value**, **Minimum**, or **Maximum** properties in code, make sure Value is at all times between Minimum and Maximum or the program will stop with an error message.

3. The track bar **Maximum** property can be achieved in code or via mouse operations. It does not exhibit the odd behavior noted with the scroll bar control.

TrackBar **Events:**

Scroll	Occurs when the track bar pointer has been moved by either a mouse or keyboard action.
ValueChanged	Occurs whenever the track bar **Value** property changes, either in code or via a mouse action.

Typical use of **TrackBar** control:

➢ Decide whether horizontal or vertical track bar fits your needs best.
➢ Set the **Name, Minimum, Maximum, SmallChange, LargeChange** properties. Initialize **Value** property.
➢ Monitor **Scroll** or **ValueChanged** event for changes in Value.

Example 5-2

Temperature Conversion

Start a new project. In this project, we convert temperatures in degrees Fahrenheit (set using a horizontal scroll bar) to degrees Celsius. The formula for converting Fahrenheit (F) to Celsius (C) is:

$$C = (F - 32) * 5 / 9$$

Temperatures will be adjusted and displayed in tenths of degrees.

1. Place a horizontal scroll bar, two labels and two text boxes on the form. Place two more label controls (right behind each other, with **AutoSize** set to **False** so they can be resized) behind the scroll bar (we'll use these for special effects). It should resemble this:

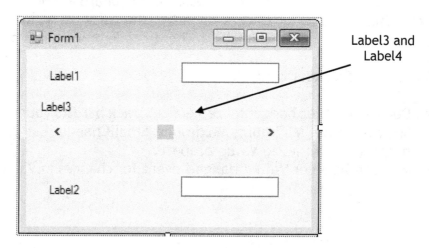

2. Set the properties of the form and each control:

Form1:

Name	frmTemp
FormBorderStyle	FixedSingle
StartPosition	CenterScreen
Text	Temperature Conversion

Label1:

Font	Microsoft Sans Serif, Bold, Size 10
Text	Fahrenheit

TextBox1:

Name	txtTempF
BackColor	White
Font	Microsoft Sans Serif, Bold, Size 10
ReadOnly	True
TabStop	False
Text	32.0
TextAlign	Center

Label2:

Font	Microsoft Sans Serif, Bold, Size 10
Text	Celsius

TextBox2:

Name	txtTempC
BackColor	White
Font	Microsoft Sans Serif, Bold, Size 10
ReadOnly	True
TabStop	False
Text	0.0
TextAlign	Center

Label3:
Name	lblBlue
AutoSize	False
BackColor	Blue

Label4:
Name	lblRed
AutoSize	False
BackColor	Red

HScrollBar1:
Name	hsbTemp
LargeChange	10
Maximum	1209
Minimum	-600
SmallChange	1
Value	320

Note the scroll bar properties (Value, Minimum, Maximum, SmallChange, LargeChange) are in tenths of degrees. The initial temperatures are initialized at 32.0 F (Value = 320 tenths of degrees) and 0.0 C, known values.

We want an "achievable maximum" of 120.0 degrees or a value of 1200. Why, then, is Maximum = 1209 and not 1200? Recall the formula for the actual Maximum to use is:

Maximum = Achievable Maximum + LargeChange – 1

Or, using our numbers:

Maximum = 1200 + 10 – 1 = 1209

When done, the form should look like this:

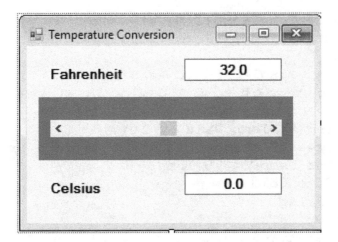

3. Form level scope declarations:

```
Dim IsHot As Boolean
```

4. Use this code in the **hsbTemp Scroll** event.

```
Private Sub HsbTemp_Scroll(ByVal sender As System.Object,
ByVal e As System.Windows.Forms.ScrollEventArgs) Handles
hsbTemp.Scroll
    Dim TempF As Single, TempC As Single
    'Read F and convert to C - divide by 10 needed since
Value is tenths of degrees
    TempF = CSng(hsbTemp.Value / 10)
    'check to see if changed from hot to cold or vice versa
    If IsHot And TempF < 70 Then
      'changed to cold
      IsHot = False
      lblBlue.BringToFront()
      hsbTemp.BringToFront()
    ElseIf Not (IsHot) And TempF >= 70 Then
      'changed to hot
      IsHot = True
      lblRed.BringToFront()
      hsbTemp.BringToFront()
    End If
    txtTempF.Text = Format(TempF, "0.0")
    TempC = (TempF - 32) * 5 / 9
    txtTempC.Text = Format(TempC, "0.0")
  End Sub
```

This code determines the scroll bar Value as it changes, takes that value as Fahrenheit temperature, computes Celsius temperature, and displays both values. A blue label is used for cold temperatures, a red label for warm temperatures.

5. Give the program a try. Make sure it provides correct information at obvious points. For example, 32.0 F better always be the same as 0.0 C! What happens around 70 F? Here's a run I made:

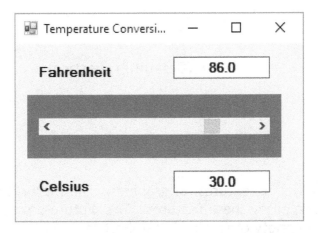

Save the project (saved in **Example 5-2** folder in the **LearnVB\VB Code\Class 5** folder).

Can you find a point where Fahrenheit temperature equals Celsius temperature? If you don't know this off the top of your head, it's obvious you've never lived in extremely cold climates. I've actually witnessed one of those bank temperature signs flashing degrees F and degrees C and seeing the same number! Ever wonder why body temperature is that odd figure of 98.6 degrees F? Can your new application give you some insight to an answer to this question?

PictureBox Control

In Toolbox:

On Form (Default Properties):

Visual Basic has powerful features for graphics. The **PictureBox** control is a primary tool for exploiting these features. The picture box control can display graphics files (in a variety of formats), can host many graphics functions and can be used for detailed animations. Here, we concentrate on using the control to display a graphics file.

PictureBox **Properties:**

Name	Gets or sets the name of the picture box (three letter prefix for picture box name is **pic**).
BackColor	Get or sets the picture box background color.
BorderStyle	Indicates the border style for the picture box.
Height	Height of picture box in pixels.
Image	Establishes the graphics file to display in the picture box.
Left	Distance from left edge of form to left edge of picture box, in pixels.
SizeMode	Indicates how the image is displayed.
Top	Distance bottom of form title bar area to top edge of picture box, in pixels.
Width	Width of picture box in pixels.

PictureBox **Events:**

Click	Triggered when a picture box is clicked.

The **Image** property specifies the graphics file to display. It can be established in design mode or at run-time. Five types of graphics files can be viewed in a picture box:

File Type	Description
Bitmap	An image represented by pixels and stored as a collection of bits in which each bit corresponds to one pixel. This is the format commonly used by scanners and paintbrush programs. Bitmap filenames have a **.bmp** extension.
Icon	A special type of bitmap file of maximum 32 x 32 size. Icon filenames have an **.ico** extension. We'll create icon files in Class 6
Metafile	A file that stores an image as a collection of graphical objects (lines, circles, polygons) rather than pixels. Metafiles preserve an image more accurately than bitmaps when resized. Many graphics files available for download from the internet are metafiles. Metafile filenames have a **.wmf** extension.
JPEG	JPEG (Joint Photographic Experts Group) is a compressed bitmap format which supports 8 and 24 bit color. It is popular on the Internet and is a common format for digital cameras. JPEG filenames have a **.jpg** extension.
GIF	GIF (Graphic Interchange Format) is a compressed bitmap format originally developed by CompuServe. It supports up to 256 colors and is also popular on the Internet. GIF filenames have a **.gif** extension.

Setting the Image property in design mode requires a few steps. Let's do an example to illustrate the process. Start a new project and put a picture box control on the form. Mine looks like this:

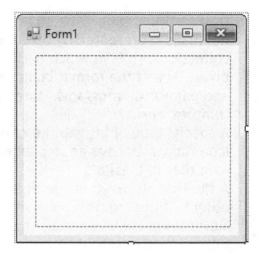

Graphics files used at design-time are saved as program **Resources**. Once these resources are established, they can be used to set the **Image** property. The process to follow is to display the **Properties** window for the picture box control and select the **Image** property. An ellipsis (...) will appear. Click the ellipsis. A **Select Resource** window will appear. Make sure the **Project resource file** radio button is selected and click the button marked **Import** - a file open window will appear.

Move (as shown) to the **\LearnVB\VB Code\Class 5\Example 5-3** folder and you will see some sample files listed:

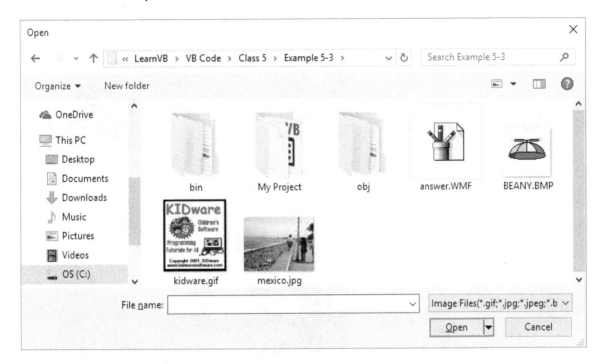

We have included one of each file type. There is a bitmap picture of a beany (**beany.bmp**), a metafile of an answering machine (**answer.wmf**), a copy of the KIDware logo (**kidware.gif**) and a picture from my Mexico vacation (**mexico.jpg**). Notice there is no icon file (ico extension). By default, icon files are not displayed. To see the icon file (a CD-ROM), click the drop-down box next to **Files of type** and choose **All Files**. All files (including the **ico** file and even non-graphics files will be displayed). Hence, if you need an icon file in a picture box, you must take an extra step to select it. Select all five graphics files and click **Open**.

You should now see the **Select Resource** window, with all five files now added to the program resources. Individual images are selected using this window:

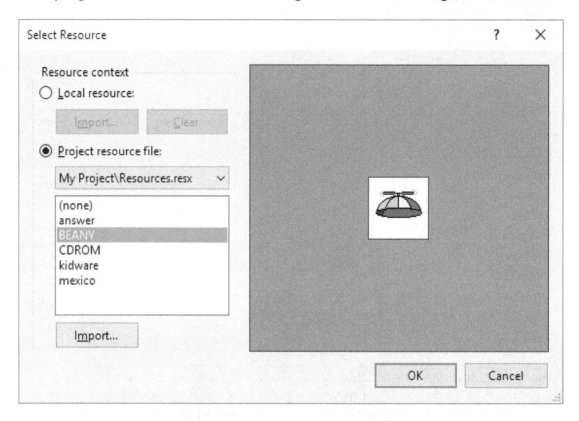

Select the beany graphic (a bitmap) and click the **OK** button.

It will be displayed in the picture box on our form:

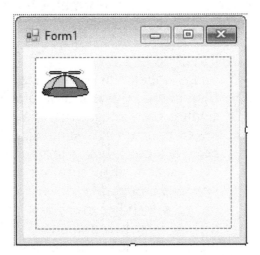

To set the **Image** property at run-time, you use the **FromFile** method associated with the **Image** object. As an example, to load the file **c:\sample\myfile.bmp** into a picture box name **picExample**, the proper code is:

```
picExample.Image = Image.FromFile("c:\sample\myfile.bmp")
```

The argument in the **Image.From** method must be a legal, complete path and file name, or your program will stop with an error message.

To clear an image from a picture box control at run-time, simply set the corresponding Image property to **Nothing** (a Basic keyword). This disassociates the Image property from the last loaded image. For our example, the code is:

```
picExample.Image = Nothing
```

The **SizeMode** property dictates how a particular image will be displayed. There are five possible values for this property: **Normal**, **CenterImage**, **StretchImage**, **AutoSize**, **Zoom**. The effect of each value is:

SizeMode	Effect
Normal	Image appears in original size. If picture box is larger than image, there will be blank space. If picture box is smaller than image, the image will be cropped.
CenterImage	Image appears in original size, centered in picture box. If picture box is larger than image, there will be blank space. If picture box is smaller than image, image is cropped.
StretchImage	Image will 'fill' picture box. If image is smaller than picture box, it will expand. If image is larger than picture box, it will scale down. Bitmap and icon files do not scale nicely. Metafiles, JPEG and GIF files do scale nicely.
AutoSize	Reverse of StretchImage - picture box will change its dimensions to match the original size of the image. Be forewarned – metafiles are usually very large!
Zoom	Similar to StretchImage. The image will adjust to fit within the picture box, however its actual height to width ratio is maintained.

Notice picture box dimensions remain fixed for **Normal**, **CenterImage**, **StretchImage**, and **Zoom SizeMode** values. With **AutoSize**, the picture box will grow in size. This may cause problems at run-time if your form is not large enough to 'contain' the picture box.

Typical use of **PictureBox** control for displaying images:

  ➢ Set the **Name** and **SizeMode** property (most often, **StretchImage**).
  ➢ Set **Image** property, either in design mode or at run-time, remembering icon files are not automatically displayed.

OpenFileDialog Control

In Toolbox:

Below Form (Default Properties):

Note that to set the **Image** property of the picture box control, you need the path and filename for the image file. How can you get this from a user? One possibility would be to use a text box control, asking the user to type in the desired information? This is just asking for trouble. Even the simplest of paths is difficult to type, remembering drive names, proper folder names, file names and extensions, and where all the slashes go. And then you, the programmer, must verify that the information typed contains a valid path and valid file name.

I think you see that asking a user to type a path and file name is a bad idea. We want a 'point and click' type interface to get a file name. Every Windows application provides such an interface for opening files. [Click on the **Open File** toolbar button in Visual Basic and an 'Open File' dialog box will appear.] Visual Basic lets us use this same interface in our applications via the **OpenFileDialog** control. This control is one of a suite of dialog controls we can add to our applications. There are also dialog controls to save files, change fonts, change colors, and perform printing operations. We'll look at other dialog controls as we work through the course.

What we learn here is not just limited to opening image files for the picture box control. There are many times in application development where we will need a file name from a user. Applications often require data files, initialization files, configuration files, sound files and other graphic files. The **OpenFileDialog** control will also be useful in these cases.

OpenFileDialog **Properties:**

Name	Gets or sets the name of the open file dialog (I usually name this control **dlgOpen**).
AddExtension	Gets or sets a value indicating whether the dialog box automatically adds an extension to a file name if the user omits the extension.
CheckFileExists	Gets or sets a value indicating whether the dialog box displays a warning if the user specifies a file name that does not exist.
CheckPathExists	Gets or sets a value indicating whether the dialog box displays a warning if the user specifies a path that does not exist.
DefaultExt	Gets or sets the default file extension.
FileName	Gets or sets a string containing the file name selected in the file dialog box.
Filter	Gets or sets the current file name filter string, which determines the choices that appear in "Files of type" box.
FilterIndex	Gets or sets the index of the filter currently selected in the file dialog box.
InitialDirectory	Gets or sets the initial directory displayed by the file dialog box.
Title	Gets or sets the file dialog box title.

OpenFileDialog **Methods:**

ShowDialog	Displays the dialog box. Returned value indicates which button was clicked by user (**OK** or **Cancel**).

To use the **OpenFileDialog** control, we add it to our application the same as any control. Since the OpenFileDialog control has no immediate user interface (you control when it appears), the control does not appear on the form at design time. Such Visual Basic controls (the **Timer** control seen briefly back in Chapter 1 was a similar control) appear in a 'tray' below the form in the IDE Design window. Once added, we set a few properties. Then, we write code to make the dialog box appear when desired. The user then makes selections and closes the dialog box. At this point, we use the provided information for our tasks.

The **ShowDialog** method is used to display the **OpenFileDialog** control. For a control named **dlgOpen**, the appropriate code is:

```
dlgOpen.ShowDialog()
```

And the displayed dialog box is:

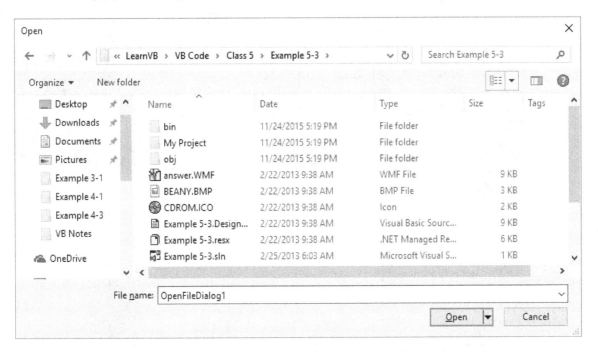

The user selects a file using the dialog control (or types a name in the **File name** box). The file type is selected form the **Files of type** box (values here set with the **Filter** property). Once selected, the **Open** button is clicked. **Cancel** can be clicked to cancel the open operation. The ShowDialog method returns the clicked button. It returns **DialogResult.OK** if Open is clicked and returns **DialogResult.Cancel** if Cancel is clicked. The nice thing about this control is that it can validate the file name before it is returned to the application. The **FileName** property contains the complete path to the selected file.

Typical use of **OpenFileDialog** control:

> ➤ Set the **Name, Filter**, and **Title** properties.
> ➤ Use **ShowDialog** method to display dialog box.
> ➤ Read **FileName** property to determine selected file

Example 5-3

Picture Box Playground

1. Start a new project. In this project, we will use a **OpenFileDialog** control to select image files. The selected file will be displayed in five different picture box controls (one for each setting of the **SizeMode** property).

2. Place five labels on a form. Place a picture box control under each of the labels. Place another label, a text box and a button control under these controls. Finally, place the OpenFileDialog control in the 'tray' under the form. The form (which will be rather large) should look like this:

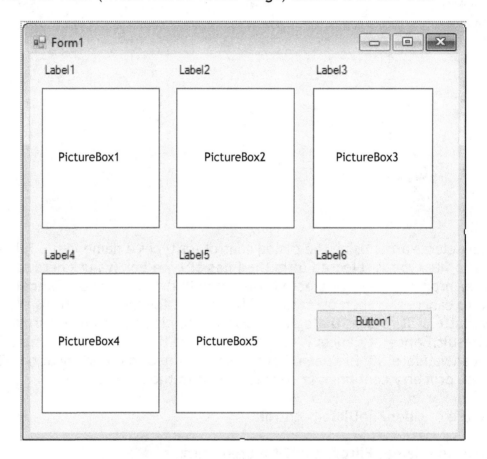

Other controls in tray:

🔲 OpenFileDialog1

3. Set the properties of the form and each control:

Form1:
Name	frmPlayground
Text	Picture Box Playground

Label1:
Text	Normal:

Label2:
Text	CenterImage:

Label3:
Text	AutoSize:

Label4:
Text	StretchImage:

Label5:
Text	Zoom:

PictureBox1:
Name	picNormal
BackColor	White
BorderStyle	FixedSingle
SizeMode	Normal

PictureBox2:
Name	picCenter
BackColor	White
BorderStyle	FixedSingle
SizeMode	CenterImage

PictureBox3:
Name	picAuto
BackColor	White
BorderStyle	FixedSingle
SizeMode	AutoSize

PictureBox4:
    Name   picStretch
    BackColor   White
    BorderStyle   FixedSingle
    SizeMode   StretchImage

PictureBox5:
    Name   picZoom
    BackColor   White
    BorderStyle   FixedSingle
    SizeMode   Zoom

Label6:
    Text   Size:

TextBox1:
    Name   txtSize
    TextAlign   Center

Button1:
    Name   btnImage
    Text   &Select Image

OpenFileDialog1:
    Name   dlgOpen
    Filter   Bitmaps (*.bmp)|*.bmp|Icons
                         (*.ico)|*.ico|Metafiles (*.wmf)|*.wmf|JPEG
                         (*.jpg)|*.jpg|GIF (*.gif)|*.gif
                         [Type this line carefully! – consult on-line help as
                         reference]
    Title   Open Image File

When done, the form should look like this:

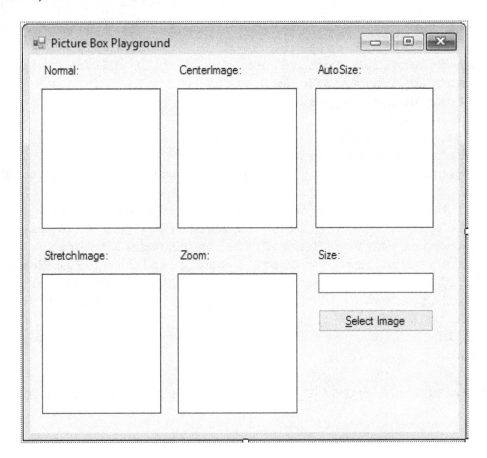

4. Form level scope declarations:

```
Dim WSave As Integer, HSave As Integer
```

5. Use this code in the **frmPlayground Load** event to initialize positions and save size:

```
Private Sub FrmPlayground_Load(ByVal sender As Object,
ByVal e As System.EventArgs) Handles MyBase.Load
    'start form in upper left corner
    Me.Left = 0
    Me.Top = 0
    'save form width/height for initialization
    WSave = Me.Width
    HSave = Me.Height
End Sub
```

6. Use this code in the **btnImage Click** event:

```
Private Sub BtnImage_Click(ByVal sender As System.Object,
ByVal e As System.EventArgs) Handles btnImage.Click
    'reset autosize picture box and form to initial size
    picAuto.Width = picNormal.Width
    picAuto.Height = picNormal.Height
    Me.Width = WSave
    Me.Height = HSave
    'display open dialog box
    If dlgOpen.ShowDialog = Windows.Forms.DialogResult.OK
Then
        picNormal.Image = Image.FromFile(dlgOpen.FileName)
        picCenter.Image = Image.FromFile(dlgOpen.FileName)
        picAuto.Image = Image.FromFile(dlgOpen.FileName)
        picStretch.Image = Image.FromFile(dlgOpen.FileName)
        picZoom.Image = Image.FromFile(dlgOpen.FileName)
        txtSize.Text = Str(picAuto.Width) + " pixels x" +
Str(picAuto.Height) + " pixels"
    End If
  End Sub
```

This code reads the selected file and displays it in each of the picture box controls.

7. Save the application (saved in **Example 5-3** folder in the **LearnVB\VB Code\Class 5** folder). Run the application and open different types of image files (we've included one of each type in the project folder). Here's a beany:

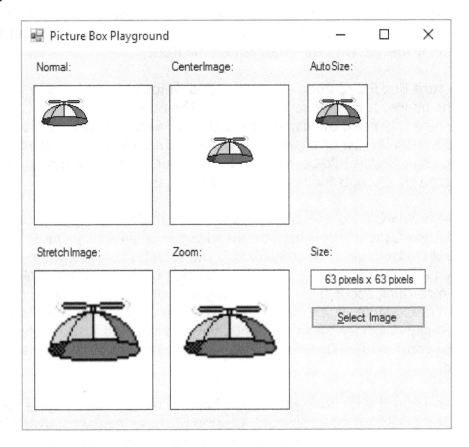

Notice how the different SizeMode properties affect the display. Images in the AutoSize mode may be very large requiring resizing of the form.

Legacy Controls

Visual Basic provides a wealth of useful controls in its toolbox. Compared to previous incarnations of Visual Basic, there are many new, improved tools. Visual Basic has also eliminated some controls that existed in Visual Basic. For the most part, elimination of these **legacy controls** is a good thing. But there are three controls we wish they had not eliminated.

In the **Picture Box Playground** example just developed, every time we want to change the image, it is necessary to bring up the open file dialog box. What would be nice is to have the capability of the dialog box built into the form providing a clickable list of image files. As each file name was clicked, the corresponding image would be displayed in each of the picture boxes. Visual Basic offered three controls that allowed this capability.

The **DriveListBox** Control was a dropdown box that allowed selection of drives. The **DirListBox** Control was a list box allowing folder selection. And, the **FileLIstBox** control was a list box allowing file selection. Using these three controls on a form allowed a 'built-in' replication of the open file dialog box. And, the nice thing about these controls is you could use as many (or as few) as you like. For example, if you just wanted to present your user a selection of files in a single directory they could not change, you could just use the FileListBox control. The **OpenFileDialog** control does not allow such a limitation.

So, are we just left with our 'wishing and hoping' these controls were back? Unfortunately, no. Visual Basic still has some of these legacy controls (as part of the **Microsoft.Visual Basic.Compatibility.VB6** namespace), but they must be added to the toolbox. To do this, click the **Tools** menu item and select **Choose Toolbox Items**. When the dialog box appears, select **.NET Framework Components**. Place check marks next to: **DriveListBox**, **DirListBox** and **FileListBox**. Click **OK** and the controls will appear in the toolbox and become available for use (on-line help is available for documentation).

You may see other legacy controls in the Customize Toolbox dialog box. You can decide if you need any other such controls. Be aware, however, that using legacy controls could be dangerous. Microsoft may decide to drop support for such controls at any time. Our hope is that controls similar to the drive, directory and file list tools are added with the next version of Visual Basic - their utility calls out for their inclusion.

DriveListBox Controls

In Toolbox:

 DriveListBox

On Form (Default Properties):

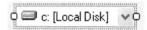

The **DriveListBox** control allows a user to select a valid disk drive at run-time. It displays the available drives in a drop-down combo box. No code is needed to load a drive list box with valid drives; Visual Basic does this for us. We use the box to get the current drive identification.

DriveListBox **Properties:**

Name	Gets or sets the name of the drive list box (three letter prefix for drive list box name is **drv**).
BackColor	Get or sets the drive list box background color.
Drive	Contains the name of the currently selected drive.
DropDownStyle	Gets or sets a value specifying the style of the drive list box.
Font	Gets or sets font name, style, size.
ForeColor	Gets or sets color of text.

DriveListBox **Events:**

SelectedValueChanged	Triggered whenever the user or program changes the drive selection.

This control is always used in conjunction with the DirListBox and FileListBox controls – we rarely look at the **Drive** property.

Typical use of **DriveListBox** control:

➢ Set the **Name** property.
➢ Use **SelectedValueChanged** event to update displayed directories.

DirListBox Control

In Toolbox:

 DirListBox

On Form (Default Properties):

The **DirListBox** control displays an ordered, hierarchical list of the user's disk directories and subdirectories. The directory structure is displayed in a list box. Like, the drive list box, little coding is needed to use the directory list box - Visual Basic does most of the work for us.

DirListBox **Properties:**

Name	Gets or sets the name of the directory list box (three letter prefix for directory list box name is **dir**).
BackColor	Get or sets the directory list box background color.
BorderStyle	Establishes the border for directory list box.
Font	Gets or sets font name, style, size.
ForeColor	Gets or sets color of text.
Path	Gets or sets the current directory path.

DirListBox **Events:**

Change	Triggered when the directory selection is changed.

Typical use of **DirListBox** control:

> ➤ Set the **Name** property.
> ➤ Use **Change** event to update displayed files.
> ➤ Read **Path** property for current path.

FileListBox Control

In Toolbox:

 FileListBox

On Form (Default Properties):

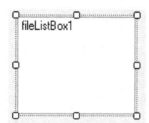

The **FileListBox** control locates and lists files in the directory specified by its **Path** property at run-time. You may select the types of files you want to display in the file list box. You will notice most of its properties are very similar to those of the list box control.

FileListBox **Properties:**

Name	Gets or sets the name of the file list box (three letter prefix for file list box name is **fil**).
BackColor	Get or sets the file list box background color.
FileName	Contains the currently selected file name.
Font	Gets or sets font name, style, size.
ForeColor	Gets or sets color of text.
Items	Gets the Items object of the file list box.
Path	Contains the current path directory.
Pattern	Contains a string that determines which files will be displayed. It supports the use of * and ? wildcard characters. For example, using *.dat only displays files with the .dat extension.
SelectedIndex	Gets or sets the zero-based index of the currently selected item in a list box.
SelectionMode	Gets or sets the method in which items are selected in file list box (allows single or multiple selections).

FileListBox **Events:**

   SelectedIndexChanged   Occurs when the SelectedIndex property
                                                    has changed.

If needed, the number of items in the list is provided by the **Items.Count**
property. The individual items in the list are found by examining elements of
the **Items.Item** zero-based array.

Typical use of **FileListBox** control:

  ➢ Set **Name** and Pattern properties.
  ➢ Monitor **SelectedIndexChanged** event for individual selections.
  ➢ Use **Path** and **FileName** properties to form complete path to selected file.

Synchronizing the Drive, Directory, and File List Box Controls

The drive, directory and file list boxes are controls that can be used independently of each other. As such, there are no common properties or linking mechanisms. When used with each other to obtain a file name, their operation must be synchronized to insure the displayed information is always consistent.

When the drive selection is changed (drive list box **SelectedValueChanged** event), you need to update the directory list box path. For example, if the drive list box is named **drvExample** and the directory list box is **dirExample**, use the code:

```
dirExample.Path = drvExample.Drive
```

When the directory selection is changed (directory list box **Change** event), you must update the names displayed in the file list box. With a file list box named **filExample**, this code is:

```
filExample.Path = dirExample.Path
```

Once all of the selections have been made and you want the file name, you need to form a text string that specifies the complete path to the file. This string concatenates the **Path** and **FileName** information from the file list box. This should be an easy task, except for one problem. The problem involves the backslash (\) character. If you are at the root directory of your drive, the path name ends with a backslash. If you are not at the root directory, there is no backslash at the end of the path name and you have to add one before tacking on the file name.

Example code for concatenating the available information into a proper file name (**YourFile**):

```
Dim YourFile As String

If Mid(filExample.Path, Len(filExample.Path), 1) = "\"
Then
   YourFile = filExample.Path + filExample.FileName
Else
   YourFile = filExample.Path + "\" + filExample.FileName
End If
```

The **Mid()** statement checks the last character in the Path property to see if it is a backslash. Note we only have to use properties of the file list box. The drive and directory box properties are only used to create changes in the file list box via code.

<u>Example 5-4</u>

Image Viewer

1. Start a new project. In this application, we search our computer's file structure for graphics files and display the results of our search in a picture box control.

2. First, place a group box control on the form. In this group box, place a drive list box, directory list box, file list box, a text box and three labels. Make sure you have added the three legacy list box controls to your toolbox using instructions provided earlier. Add a second group box. In that group box, place a picture box control and four radio buttons. The form should look like this:

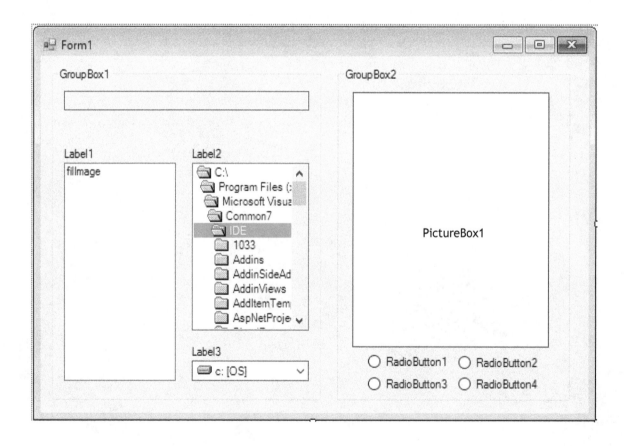

3. Set properties of the form and each control.

Form1:

Name	frmImage
FormBorderStyle	FixedSingle
StartPosition	CenterScreen
Text	Image Viewer

GroupBox1:

Name	grpFile
BackColor	Red
Text	[Blank]

TextBox1:

Name	txtImage
BackColor	Yellow
Multiline	True

Label1:

ForeColor	Yellow
Text	Files:

Label2:

ForeColor	Yellow
Text	Directories:

Label3:

ForeColor	Yellow
Text	Drives:

FileListBox1:

Name	filImage
Pattern	*.bmp;*.ico;*.wmf;*.gif;*jpg
	[type this line with <u>no</u> spaces]

DirLIstBox1:

Name	dirImage

DriveListBox1:

Name	drvImage

GroupBox2:
    Name   grpImage
    BackColor   Blue
    Text   [Blank]

PictureBox1:
    Name   picImage
    BackColor   White
    BorderStyle   FixedSingle

RadioButton1:
    Name   rdoNormal
    ForeColor   Yellow
    Text   Normal

RadioButton2:
    Name   rdoCenter
    ForeColor   Yellow
    Text   Center

RadioButton3:
    Name   rdoStretch
    ForeColor   Yellow
    Text   Stretch

RadioButton4:
    Name   rdoZoom
    ForeColor   Yellow
    Text   Zoom

My finished form is this:

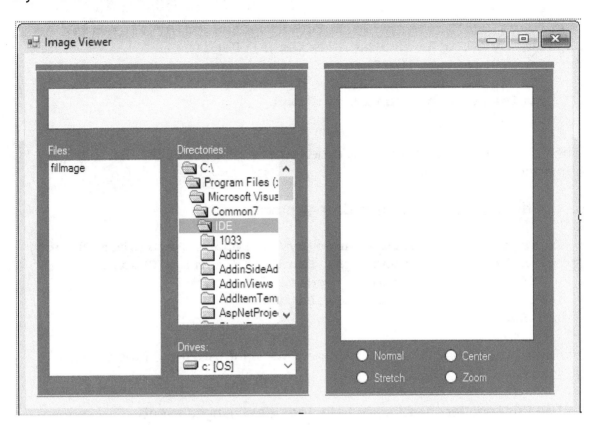

4. Use this code in the **frmImage Load** procedure (initializes Stretch size mode):

```
Private Sub FrmImage_Load(ByVal sender As System.Object,
ByVal e As System.EventArgs) Handles MyBase.Load
    'initialize stretch mode
    rdoStretch.PerformClick()
End Sub
```

5. Use this code in the **drvImage SelectedValueChanged** procedure.

```
Private Sub DrvImage_SelectedValueChanged(ByVal sender As
Object, ByVal e As System.EventArgs) Handles
drvImage.SelectedValueChanged
    'If drive changes, update directory
    dirImage.Path = drvImage.Drive
End Sub
```

When a new drive is selected, this code forces the directory list box to display directories on that drive.

6. Use this code in the **dirImage Change** procedure.

```
Private Sub DirImage_Change(ByVal sender As System.Object,
ByVal e As System.EventArgs) Handles dirImage.Change
    'If directory changes, update file path
    filImage.Path = dirImage.Path
End Sub
```

Likewise, when a new directory is chosen, we want to see the files on that directory.

7. Use this code for the **filImage SelectedIndexChanged** event.

```
Private Sub FilImage_SelectedIndexChanged(ByVal sender As
System.Object, ByVal e As System.EventArgs) Handles
filImage.SelectedIndexChanged
    'Get complete path to file name and open graphics
    Dim ImageName As String
    If Mid(filImage.Path, Len(filImage.Path), 1) = "\" Then
      ImageName = filImage.Path + filImage.FileName
    Else
      ImageName = filImage.Path + "\" + filImage.FileName
    End If
    txtImage.Text = ImageName
    picImage.Image = Image.FromFile(ImageName)
End Sub
```

This code forms the file name (**ImageName**) by concatenating the directory path with the file name. It then displays the complete name and loads the image into the picture box.

8. Lastly, code the four radio button **CheckedChanged** events to change the display size mode:

```
Private Sub RdoNormal_CheckedChanged(ByVal sender As
System.Object, ByVal e As System.EventArgs) Handles
rdoNormal.CheckedChanged
    picImage.SizeMode = PictureBoxSizeMode.Normal
End Sub


Private Sub RdoCenter_CheckedChanged(ByVal sender As
System.Object, ByVal e As System.EventArgs) Handles
rdoCenter.CheckedChanged
    picImage.SizeMode = PictureBoxSizeMode.CenterImage
End Sub


Private Sub RdoStretch_CheckedChanged(ByVal sender As
System.Object, ByVal e As System.EventArgs) Handles
rdoStretch.CheckedChanged
    picImage.SizeMode = PictureBoxSizeMode.StretchImage
End Sub


Private Sub RdoZoom_CheckedChanged(ByVal sender As
System.Object, ByVal e As System.EventArgs) Handles
rdoZoom.CheckedChanged
    picImage.SizeMode = PictureBoxSizeMode.Zoom
End Sub
```

9. Save your project (saved in **Example 5-4** folder in **LearnVB\VB Code\Class 5** folder). Run and try the application. Find bitmaps, icons, metafiles, gif files, and JPEGs (an example of each is included in the **Example 5-3** project folder). Here's how the form should look when displaying the example JPEG file (a photo from my Mexican vacation) in **Stretch** mode:

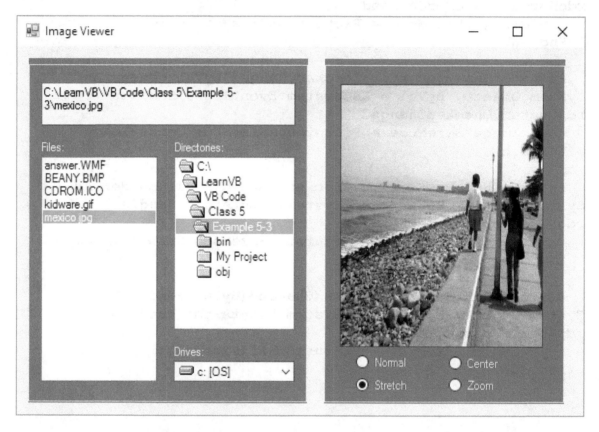

Note the picture is distorted a bit. Click the **Zoom** mode and you'll see the height to width ratio is correct.

Class Review

After completing this class, you should understand:

> ➢ The concept of Z Order for a control
> ➢ Useful properties, events, methods and typical uses for the numeric updown and domain updown controls
> ➢ Properties, events, methods, and uses for the horizontal and vertical scroll bar controls
> ➢ The five types of graphics files that can be displayed by the picture box control
> ➢ How the picture box SizeMode property affects Image display
> ➢ How to load image files at both design time and run time
> ➢ How to use the file open common dialog box to obtain file names for opening files
> ➢ How the legacy drive, directory, and file list controls work and when they could be used

Practice Problems 5

Problem 5-1. Tic-Tac-Toe Problem. Build a simple Tic-Tac-Toe game. Use 'skinny' label controls for the grid and picture box controls for markers (use different pictures to distinguish players). Click the image controls to add the markers. Can you write logic to detect a win?

Problem 5-2. Number Guess Problem. Build a game where the user guesses a number between 1 and 100. Use a scroll bar for entering the guess and change the extreme limits (**Minimum** and **Maximum** properties) with each guess to help the user adjust their guess.

Problem 5-3. File Times Problem. Using the drive, directory and file list controls, write an application that lists all files in a directory. For every file, find what time the file was created (use the **FileDateTime()** function to get time details). Determine the most popular hours of the day for creating files.

Exercise 5

Student Database Input Screen

You did so well with last chapter's assignment that, now, a school wants you to develop the beginning structure of an input screen for its students. The required input information is:

1. Student Name
2. Student Grade (1 through 6)
3. Student Sex (Male or Female)
4. Student Date of Birth (Month, Day, Year)
5. Student Picture (Assume they can be loaded as jpeg files)

Set up the screen so that only the Name needs to be typed; all other inputs should be set with option buttons, scroll bars, and common dialog boxes. When a screen of information is complete, display the summarized profile in a message box. Use an object to describe the student. This profile message box should resemble this:

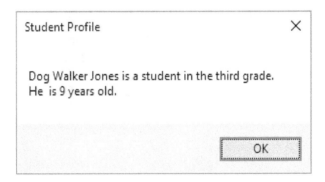

Note the student's age must be computed from the input birth date - watch out for pitfalls in doing the computation. The student's picture does not appear in the profile, only on the input screen.

6. Windows Application Design and Distribution

Review and Preview

We've finished looking at many of the Visual Basic controls and have been introduced to most of the BASIC language features. In this class, we learn how to enhance our application design using multiple forms, general procedures and menus. And, we learn how to distribute the finished product to our user base.

Application Design Considerations

Before beginning the actual process of building your application by drawing the Visual Basic interface, setting the control properties, and writing the BASIC code, many things should be considered to make your application useful. A first consideration should be to determine what processes and functions you want your application to perform. What are the inputs and outputs? Develop a framework or flow chart of all your application's processes.

Decide what controls you need. Do the built-in Visual Basic controls and functions meet your needs? Do you need to develop some controls or functions of your own? You can design and build your own controls using Visual Basic, but that topic is beyond the scope of this course. The skills gained in this course, however, will be invaluable if you want to tackle such a task.

Design your user interface. What do you want your form to look like? Consider appearance and ease of use. Make the interface consistent with other Windows applications. Familiarity is good in program design.

Write your code. Make your code readable and traceable - future code modifiers (including yourself) will thank you. Consider developing reusable code - classes and objects with utility outside your current development. This will save you time in future developments.

Make your code 'user-friendly.' Make operation of your application obvious to the user. Step the user through its use. Try to anticipate all possible ways a user can mess up in using your application. It's fairly easy to write an application that works properly when the user does everything correctly. It's difficult to write an application that can handle all the possible wrong things a user can do and still not bomb out.

Debug your code completely before distributing it. There's nothing worse than having a user call you to point out flaws in your application. A good way to find all the bugs is to let several people try the code - a mini beta-testing program.

Multiple Form Visual Basic Applications

All applications developed so far in this class use a single form. Many Visual Basic applications use **multiple forms**. The **About** window associated with most applications is a common example of using a second form in an application. We need to learn how to manage multiple forms in our projects. There are four major considerations in using multiple forms:

1. Adding forms to a project
2. Deciding which form appears when the project begins
3. How to make forms appear and disappear using code
4. Transferring information from one form to another

We will consider each of these points.

To add a new, blank form to an application, click the **Add New Item** button on the toolbar and select **Add Windows Form** or select **Add Windows Form** under the **Projects** menu. A dialog box will appear asking you to name the new form. Choose a name and click **Open**. The newly added form will be listed in the **Solution Explorer** window. To have the new form appear in the Design window, highlights its name and click the **View Designer** button in the Solution Explorer toolbar. Or, just double-click its name in the Solution Explorer. Each form is designed using exactly the same procedure we always use: draw the controls, assign properties, and write code.

It is also possible to add an existing form to an application. You can use such a form, as is, or modify it for the new application. To add an existing form to a project, choose the **Project** menu item and select **Add Existing Item**. Browse the directories until the desired form file is located. Select it and click **Open**.

If you want to delete a form from a project, simply right-click the form name in the Solution Explorer window. A menu will appear. Select **Delete**. Make sure you really want to delete the form – you will not be asked if you know what you're doing!

Display of the different forms is handled by code you write. You need to decide when and how you want particular forms to be displayed. The user always interacts with the 'active' form.

The first decision to make is to determine which form will be the **startup form**. This is the form that appears when your application first begins. Up to now, we have always set the startup form to be the one, single form in our project. Now, we must choose among multiple forms. To do this, in **Solution Explorer**, right-click the project name and choose **Properties**. The **Project** property page opens with the **Application** properties displayed. Choose the form you want as the startup form from the **Startup form:** drop-down list.

Startup Form

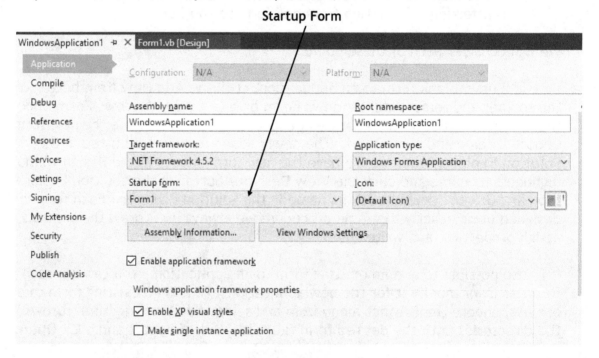

The startup form automatically loads when your application is run. Any other form in the project will not display itself by default. When you want another form to appear, you write code to load and display it (using the **Show** or **ShowDialog** methods). Similarly, when you want a form to disappear, you write code to unload or hide it (using **Close** and **Hide** methods).

There are two ways to display a form (here, named **frmExample**). It can then be displayed as a modal form:

```
frmExample.ShowDialog() `Modal display
```

or as a modeless form:

```
frmExample.Show()
```

In **modal** display, no other open window in the application may be accessed as long as the modal window is open (works like a message box). In **modeless** display, any other open application window may be clicked and made active. Modeless forms are harder to program, because users can access them in an unpredictable order.

To make a form disappear, we can use the **Close** method (removes form from memory) or the **Hide** method (sets the **Visible** property to **False**). To close the current form, use:

```
Me.Close()
```

To hide the form, use:

```
Me.Hide()
```

One alternative to multiple form applications is the use of the **tab control**, which allows 'stacked' panels of controls. You've seen tabbed controls in many of the applications you work with. We discuss this control briefly in Class 10.

Adding a Module

The last consideration in a multiple form application is to decide how (if needed) to transfer information from one form to another. Properties of any control on any form are easily accessed using a 'double-dot' notation. That is, if you need to know the **PropertyName** of **ControlName** on **FormName**, use:

```
FormName.ControlName.PropertyName
```

Forms cannot directly pass variable information to each other. That transfer can only occur via a **code module**. A code module is essentially a form without any interface. It is just a code window. And the primary purpose of the code module is to declare variables global to an application and to provide any code that should be accessible from each form in an application.

A code module is added to an application in the same manner as a form. Click the **Add New** button on the toolbar and select **Add Module** or select **Add Module** under the **Projects** menu. A dialog box will appear asking you to name the new module. Choose a name and click **Add**. The newly added module will be listed in the **Solution Explorer** window. To have the new module appear in the Design window, highlight the module name and click the **View Code** button in the Solution Explorer toolbar. Or, just double-click its name in the Solution Explorer. A blank module looks like this:

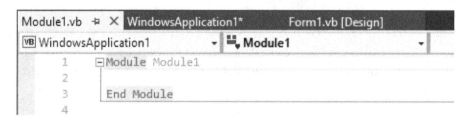

All code is placed in the module between the **Module** line and the **End Module** line. Variables with application level scope are declared using the **Public** keyword. Similarly, any procedures or functions (discussed after the next example) placed in the module are prefaced with the keyword **Public**. That makes such procedures available to any form in the application.

Visual Basic Multiple Document Interface (MDI)

In the previous section, we looked at using multiple forms in a Visual Basic application. Visual Basic actually provides a system for maintaining multiple-form applications, known as the **Multiple Document Interface** (**MDI**). MDI allows you to maintain multiple forms within a single container form. Examples of MDI applications are Word, Excel, the Windows Explorer program and, yes, the Visual Basic IDE.

An MDI application allows the user to display many forms at the same time. The container window is called the **parent** form, while the individual forms within the parent are the **child** forms. Both parent and child forms are modeless, meaning you can leave one window to move to another. An application can have only one parent form. Creating an MDI application is a two-step process. You first create the MDI form and define its menu structure. Next, you design each of the application's child forms.

At **run-time**, the parent and child forms take on special characteristics and abilities. Some of these are:

> ➤ At run-time all child forms are displayed within the parent form's internal area. The user can move and size child forms like any other form, but they must stay in this internal area.
> ➤ When a child is minimized, its icon appears on the MDI parent form instead of the user's desktop. When the parent form is minimized, a single icon represents the entire application. When restored, all forms are redisplayed as they were.
> ➤ When a child form is maximized, its title is combined with the parent form's title and displayed in the parent title bar.
> ➤ You can display child forms automatically when forms are loaded or load child forms as hidden.
> ➤ The active child form's menus (if any) are displayed on the parent form's menu bar, not the child form.
> ➤ New child forms can be created at run-time.
> ➤ You can easily determine the active child form.

Multi-document interfaces offer another way to maintain multiple form applications. We will not discuss MDI applications here, but the information you learn in this course will make them easy to understand.

Example 6-1

Shopping Cart

1. Start a new project. We will build a multi-form application that provides a good start for a simple 'on-line' commerce system. One form will be used to enter a mailing address and add items to a shopping cart. Other forms will display a mailing label and display the current contents of the shopping cart. Products will be described by simple objects. We will also use a code module to declare global variables (application level scope). We'll build each form and module individually.

2. Add a class to the project named **Product.vb**. Use this code (properties only and a constructor):

```
Public Class Product
  Public Description As String
  Public Cost As Double
  Public NumberOrdered As Integer
  Public Sub New(ByVal d As String, ByVal c As Double)
    Me.Description = d
    Me.Cost = c
    Me.NumberOrdered = 0
  End Sub
End Class
```

3. Add a module to the application. Place these lines of code in the module:

```
Public Address As String
'we have ten products in a zero-based array
Public Const NumberProducts As Integer = 10
Public MyProduct(NumberProducts - 1) As Product
```

Here, you can see what information will be transferred from one form to another in the application. Note the declaration of a **Public** constant (**NumberProducts**).

Order Form:

1. Return to the form in the newly started project. This will be the order form.
    Place a label, two text boxes, a domain updown control and five button
    controls on the form so they look something like this:

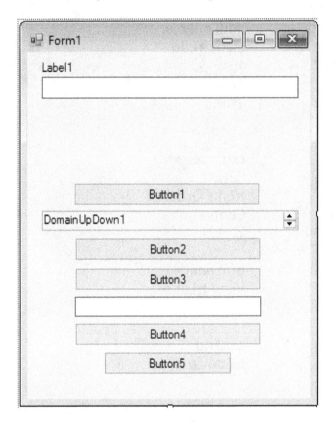

2. Set the properties of the form and controls:

    Form1:
    >
    > | | |
    > |---|---|
    > | Name | frmEdit |
    > | FormBorderStyle | FixedSingle |
    > | StartPosition | CenterForm |
    > | Text | Order Form |

    Label1:
    >
    > | | |
    > |---|---|
    > | Font | Microsoft Sans Serif, Bold, Size 10 |
    > | Text | Order Address |

TextBox1:

Name	txtOrder
Font Size	10
MultiLine	True

DomainUpDown1:

Name	dudOrder
BackColor	Light Yellow
Font Size	10
Text	True
Wrap	True

TextBox2:

Name	txtOrdered
TabStop	False
Text	Items Ordered: 0
TextAlign	Center

Button1:

Name	btnLabel
Text	View &Label

Button2:

Name	btnAdd
Text	&Add to Order

Button3:

Name	btnView
Text	&View Order

Button4:

Name	btnNew
Text	&New Order

Button5:

Name	btnExit
Text	E&xit

This first form should look something like this when you're done:

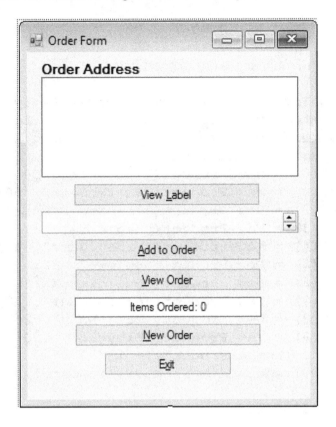

We'll now add code to this form.

4. Form level scope variable declarations:

```
Dim ItemsOrdered As Integer
```

5. Use this code in **frmOrder Load** procedure:

```
Private Sub FrmOrder_Load(ByVal sender As System.Object,
ByVal e As System.EventArgs) Handles MyBase.Load
    Dim I As Integer
    'define products and cost
    MyProduct(0) = New Product("Tricycle", 50)
    MyProduct(1) = New Product("Skateboard", 60)
    MyProduct(2) = New Product("In-Line Skates", 100)
    MyProduct(3) = New Product("Magic Set", 15)
    MyProduct(4) = New Product("Video Game", 45)
    MyProduct(5) = New Product("Helmet", 25)
    MyProduct(6) = New Product("Building Kit", 35)
    MyProduct(7) = New Product("Artist Set", 40)
    MyProduct(8) = New Product("Doll Baby", 25)
    MyProduct(9) = New Product("Bicycle", 150)
    For I = 0 To NumberProducts - 1
      dudOrder.Items.Add(MyProduct(I).Description)
    Next
    dudOrder.SelectedIndex = 0
  End Sub
```

This code initializes the available products.

6. Use this code in the **btnAdd Click** procedure:

```
Private Sub BtnAdd_Click(ByVal sender As System.Object,
ByVal e As System.EventArgs) Handles btnAdd.Click
    'increment selected product by one
    'products are base 0 array
    MyProduct(dudOrder.SelectedIndex).NumberOrdered += 1
    ItemsOrdered += 1
    txtOrdered.Text = "Items Ordered:" + Str(ItemsOrdered)
  End Sub
```

This code adds a selected item to the shopping cart.

7. Use this code in the **btnLabel Click** procedure:

```
Private Sub BtnLabel_Click(ByVal sender As System.Object,
ByVal e As System.EventArgs) Handles btnLabel.Click
    'establish address and show label form
    If txtOrder.Text = "" Then
      MessageBox.Show("Address is blank.", "Error",
MessageBoxButtons.OK, MessageBoxIcon.Error)
      txtOrder.Focus()
      Exit Sub
    End If
    Address = txtOrder.Text
    frmLabel.ShowDialog()
  End Sub
```

This code displays the mailing label.

8. Use this code in the **btnNew Click** procedure:

```
Private Sub BtnNew_Click(ByVal sender As System.Object,
ByVal e As System.EventArgs) Handles btnNew.Click
    Dim I As Integer
    'clear form
    txtOrder.Text = ""
    ItemsOrdered = 0
    txtOrdered.Text = "Items Ordered: 0"
    For I = 0 To NumberProducts - 1
      MyProduct(I).NumberOrdered = 0
    Next I
    dudOrder.SelectedIndex = 0
  End Sub
```

This code clears the form for a new order.

9. Use this code in the **btnView Click** procedure:

```
Private Sub BtnView_Click(ByVal sender As System.Object,
ByVal e As System.EventArgs) Handles btnView.Click
    If ItemsOrdered = 0 Then
      MessageBox.Show("No items have been ordered.",
"Error", MessageBoxButtons.OK, MessageBoxIcon.Error)
      Exit Sub
    End If
    frmView.ShowDialog()
End Sub
```

This code brings up the window that displays the shopping cart.

10. Use this code in the **btnExit Click** procedure which stops the application:

```
Private Sub BtnExit_Click(ByVal sender As System.Object,
ByVal e As System.EventArgs) Handles btnExit.Click
    Me.Close()
End Sub
```

Shopping Cart Form:

1. We now build the form that will display the shopping cart. Add a new form to the application. Make sure this form is displayed. Add a list box control, a text box and a button control. The form should look like this:

2. Set the properties of the form and controls:

Form2:
Name	frmView
FormBorderStyle	FixedSingle
StartPosition	CenterForm
Text	View Order

ListBox1:
Name	lstProducts
Font Size	10

TextBox1:
Name	txtCost
BackColor	Light Yellow
Font	Microsoft Sans Serif, Bold, Size 10
Text	Total Cost

Button1:
    Name   btnClose
    Text   &Close

When done, this is my form:

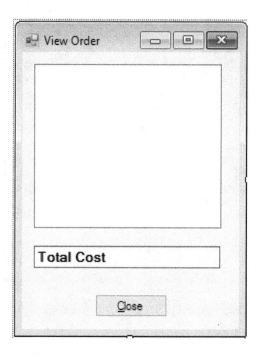

3. Add this code to the **frmView Load** event:

```
Private Sub FrmView_Load(ByVal sender As System.Object,
ByVal e As System.EventArgs) Handles MyBase.Load
    Dim I As Integer
    Dim TotalCost As Single
    'load in ordered items
    TotalCost = 0
    For I = 0 To NumberProducts - 1
      If MyProduct(I).NumberOrdered <> 0 Then

lstProducts.Items.Add(Str(MyProduct(I).NumberOrdered) + " "
+ MyProduct(I).Description)
        TotalCost += MyProduct(I).NumberOrdered *
MyProduct(I).Cost
      End If
    Next
    txtCost.Text = Format(TotalCost, "0.00")
  End Sub
```

This code uses the MyProduct object information to list the items ordered in the list box control.

4. Add this code to the **btnClose Click** event:

```
Private Sub BtnClose_Click(ByVal sender As System.Object,
ByVal e As System.EventArgs) Handles btnClose.Click
    Me.Close()
  End Sub
```

Mailing Label Form:

1. Add another form to the application. This will display a mailing label. Add a text box and button control to this new form. It should look like this:

2. Set these properties:

   Form3:
Name	frmLabel
FormBorderStyle	FixedSingle
StartPosition	CenterForm
Text	Mailing Label

   TextBox1:
Name	txtLabel
Font Size	10
MultiLine	True

   Button1:
Name	btnOK
Text	&OK

My finished mailing label form looks like this:

3. Add this code to the **frmLabel Load** procedure:

```
Private Sub FrmLabel_Load(ByVal sender As System.Object,
ByVal e As System.EventArgs) Handles MyBase.Load
    Dim LF As String
    LF = CStr(ControlChars.CrLf)
    'form label
    txtLabel.Text = "My Company" + LF + "My Address" + LF +
"My City, State, Zip" + LF + LF + LF
    txtLabel.Text += Address
    txtLabel.SelectionLength = 0
End Sub
```

This code puts a return address and customer's mailing address on a label.

4. Add this code to the **btnOK Click** event to close the form:

```
Private Sub BtnOK_Click(ByVal sender As System.Object,
ByVal e As System.EventArgs) Handles btnOK.Click
    Me.Close()
End Sub
```

5. The application is, at long last, complete. Run it. Notice how the shopping cart works and how the different forms work together. Here's a run I made, first entering an order:

With such an order, the shopping cart appears as (click **View Order**):

And, the mailing label is (click **View Label**):

As mentioned, this is a start to an e-commerce type system. If you're interested in such projects, you can expand this to meet your needs. Save the project (saved in **Example 6-1** folder in the **LearnVB\VB Code\Class 6** folder).

Using General Procedures in Applications

So far in this class, the only procedures we have studied are the event procedures associated with the various controls. Most applications have tasks not related to controls that require some code to perform these tasks. Such tasks are usually coded in a general **Sub** procedure (essentially the same as a subroutine in other languages).

Using general procedures can help divide a complex application into more manageable units of code. This helps meet the earlier stated goals of readability and reusability. As you build applications, it will be obvious where such a procedure is needed. Look for areas in your application where code is repeated in different places. It would be best (shorter code and easier maintenance) to put this repeated code in a procedure. And, look for places in your application where you want to do some long, detailed task – this is another great use for a general procedure. It makes your code much easier to follow.

The form for a general procedure named **MyProcedure** is:

> **Private Sub** MyProcedure(**Arguments**)   'Definition header
>   .
>   .
> **End Sub**

The definition header names the **Sub** procedure and defines any arguments needed by the procedure. Each procedure definition is prefaced by a keyword of **Private** or **Public**. Private procedures are only available in the form they are defined in. Public procedures (defined in code modules) can be accessed from any form in a multiple form application.

Arguments are a comma-delimited list of variables passed to and, perhaps, returned from the procedure. If there are arguments, we need to take care in how they are declared in the header statement. In particular, we need to be concerned with:

> Number of arguments
> Order of arguments
> Type of arguments
> How each argument is passed

We will address each point separately.

The **number** of arguments is dictated by how many variables the procedure needs to do its job. You need a variable for each piece of input information and a variable for each piece of output information. You then place these variables in a particular **order** for the argument list.

Each variable in the argument list will be a particular **data type**. This must be known for each variable. Finally, each variable is either providing input information (the value will not change in the procedure) or receiving output information (the value may change in the procedure). If the variable is input information, we say it is passed to the procedure by **value**. If the variable is output information, we say it is passed by **reference**.

Variables passed by **value** (the default option in Visual Basic) have the same value after the procedure is called. They are declared in the argument list using:

ByVal VariableName **As** Type

Variables passed by **reference** (if the value of the variable is changed, that change will be seen in the 'calling' procedure) are declared using:

ByRef VariableName **As** Type

With either declaration, the variable **VariableName** is treated as a local (procedure level) variable in the procedure.

(With the introduction of Visual Studio 2012, the **ByVal** keyword is no longer automatically inserted by the Visual Basic editor, but it is implied – we always include it to make clear our intentions).

Arrays work a little differently in argument lists. Even when passed by value, if an element of an array is changed, that change will be reflected in the calling routine. It is as if it is passed by reference. Why? It has to do with how arrays are stored. To declare an array as an argument, use:

   ByVal **ArrayName()** As Type

The parentheses indicate an array is being passed.

Once you have defined a procedure and typed the appropriate code (we'll see how to do this is just a bit), how do you invoke or '**call**' the procedure? There are two ways to do this. A procedure named MyProcedure can be called using:

   Call MyProcedure(Arguments**)**

or you can leave off the **Call** keyword and use:

   MyProcedure(Arguments**)**

I prefer the first method for calling a procedure, however, you will see both methods in the course examples. When calling a procedure, make sure the calling arguments meet the requirements of: proper number of arguments, proper order of arguments, and proper type of arguments.

An example should make things clearer. Assume you are a carpet layer and always need the perimeter and area for a rectangle. We'll build a procedure that helps you with the computations. We need, for inputs, the length and width of the rectangle. The output information will be the perimeter and area. Here is the procedure that does the job:

```
Private Sub RectangleInfo(ByVal Length As Double, ByVal
Width As Double, ByRef Perimeter As Double, ByRef Area As
Double)
   Perimeter = 2 * (Length + Width)
   Area = Length * Width
End Sub
```

The procedure is named **RectangleInfo**. It has four arguments, all of type **Double**. The first two arguments are **Length** and **Width**, passed by **value**. The other arguments are **Perimeter** and **Area**, passed by **reference**, since the computed values will be used by the calling procedure. This code segment will call our procedure:

```
Dim L As Double, W As Double, P As Double, A As Double
   .

   .
L = 6.2
W = 2.3
Call RectangleInfo(L, W, P, A)
```

Once this code is executed, the variable P will have the perimeter of a rectangle of length 6.2 and width 2.3. The variable A will have the area of the same rectangle. Notice there is no reason for the variables in the calling argument sequence to have the same names assigned in the procedure declaration. The location of each variable in the calling sequence defines which variable is which (that's why order of arguments is important).

You will find lots of uses for general procedures, but how do you get one into a Visual Basic application? Let's do it. Once you have completed definition of your procedure (decided on arguments and code), open the code window for the form (or module) where the procedure will be. Begin typing the header statement 'outside' of any existing procedure, i.e. before an existing **Sub** header line or after an existing **End Sub** line. Once your header line is complete, press **<Enter>** and the IDE will add an **End Sub** line for you.

When typing the header line, you need to preface each procedure declaration with either **Private** or **Public**. Procedures in forms must be Private (only accessible from within that form). In a code module, you have the choice of Public or Private. If a module procedure is Public, it can be called from any other procedure in any other form or module in your application, assuming it has multiple forms or modules. If a module procedure is Private, it can only be called from the module it is defined in. Here is a code window with a framework for the rectangle example (note it is below the existing **Form Load** procedure):

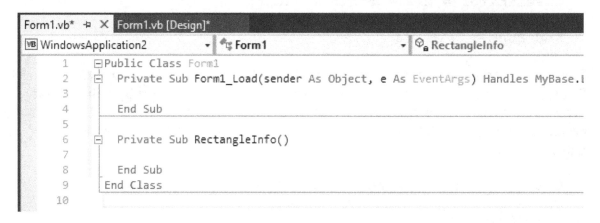

You must also define arguments (if any) in the header line. I usually leave the argument list blank when I first type the header. I did this in the example above. Then, I go back and fill in the arguments, naming and typing them. A warning: as you type variables in the argument list, if you leave off the keywords **ByVal** or **ByRef**, the IDE will, by default, add ByVal to each variable. This is okay if you truly want to pass variables by value. If, however, you desire to pass a variable by reference (its value may change), then you need to make sure it is prefaced by the ByRef keyword.

Once the header line is complete, you write the code for the procedure. Obviously, this code goes between the header line and End Sub line.

Example 6-2

Circle Geometry

1. Start a new project. This will be a simple application that illustrates use of a Public procedure in a code module. The procedure will compute the area and circumference of a circle, given its diameter.

2. Add a module to the application. Type this procedure in the module:

```
Public Sub CircleGeometry(ByVal Diameter As Double, ByRef
Circumference As Double, ByRef Area As Double)
    Circumference = Math.PI * Diameter
    Area = Math.PI * Diameter ^ 2 / 4
End Sub
```

Notice the variable Diameter is input and the Circumference and Area are output parameters (declared ByRef).

3. Return to the application form and add three labels, three text boxes and a button control. Make your form look similar to this:

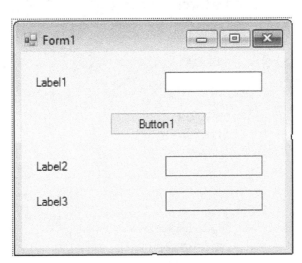

4. Set the properties of the form and controls:

Form1:

Name	frmCircle
FormBorderStyle	FixedSingle
StartPosition	CenterForm
Text	Circle Geometry

Label1:

Text	Enter Diameter

Label2:

Text	Computed Circumference

Label3:

Text	Computed Area

TextBox1:

Name	txtDiameter

TextBox2:

Name	txtCircumference
BackColor	Light Yellow
ReadOnly	True
TextAlign	Center

TextBox3:

Name	txtArea
BackColor	Light Yellow
ReadOnly	True
TextAlign	Center

Button1:

Name	btnCompute
Text	&Compute

The finished form appears as:

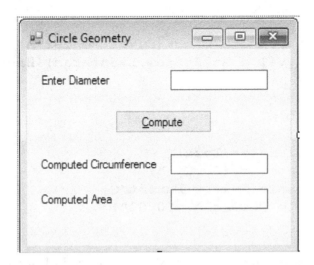

5. Use this code in the **txtDiameter KeyPress** event for key trapping:

```
Private Sub TxtDiameter_KeyPress(ByVal sender As Object,
ByVal e As System.Windows.Forms.KeyPressEventArgs) Handles
txtDiameter.KeyPress
    'only allow numbers, a single decimal point, backspace
or enter
    Select Case e.KeyChar
      Case CChar("0") To CChar("9"), ControlChars.Back
        'acceptable keystrokes
        e.Handled = False
      Case ControlChars.Cr
        'enter key - click on compute button
        btnCompute.PerformClick()
        e.Handled = False
      Case CChar(".")
        'check for existence of decimal point
        If InStr(txtDiameter.Text, ".") = 0 Then
          e.Handled = False
        Else
          e.Handled = True
        End If
      Case Else
        e.Handled = True
    End Select
End Sub
```

6. Use this code in the **btnCompute Click** to compute the values using the general procedure in the code module:

```
Private Sub BtnCompute_Click(ByVal sender As
System.Object, ByVal e As System.EventArgs) Handles
btnCompute.Click
    Dim C As Double
    Dim A As Double
    Dim D As Double
    D = Val(txtDiameter.Text)
    Call CircleGeometry(D, C, A)
    txtCircumference.Text = Format(C, "0.00")
    txtArea.Text = Format(A, "0.00")
End Sub
```

7. Save the application (saved in **Example 6-2** folder in **LearnVB\VB Code\Class 6** folder). Run the application and try some different diameters. Here's my try:

Go to the code module and change the **ByRef** keyword next to **Area** to **ByVal**. Rerun the application and notice the computed Area is always zero since ByVal does not return the computed value back to the calling procedure. Make sure you change ByVal back to ByRef before you leave this example.

Using General Functions in Applications

Related to general procedures in Visual Basic are general **functions**. A function is usually simpler than a procedure, performing a specific task and returning a single value. If, in your applications, you find you are continually using the same sequence of steps to compute a certain parameter, consider using a function. We've seen some built-in functions such as the **MsgBox** and the **Format** function.

The form for a general function named **MyFunction** is:

 Private Function MyFunction(**Arguments**) **As** Type 'Definition header
  .
  .
 Return(ReturnedValue)
 End Function

The definition header names the **Function**, specifies its **Type** (the type of the returned value) and defines any input **Arguments** passed to the function. Rules for using arguments for functions are identical to those outlined for procedures. All arguments to a function should be passed **by value**, since they should all be input information. The scope of a function can be **Private** (for forms) or **Public** (for modules). And, somewhere in the function, the returned value must be computed. This value is returned to the calling routine as the argument in the **Return** function.

To use a general function, simply refer to it, by name, in code (with appropriate arguments). Wherever it is used, it will be replaced by the computed value. A function can be used to return a value:

 RtnValue = **MyFunction**(Arguments)

or in an expression:

 ThisNumber = 7 * **MyFunction**(Arguments) / AnotherNumber

Let's build a quick example that converts Fahrenheit temperatures to Celsius (remember the example in Class 4?) Here's such a function:

```
Private Function DegFToDegC(ByVal TempF As Double) As
Double
  Dim TempC As Double
  TempC = (TempF - 32) * 5 / 9
  Return(TempC)
End Sub
```

The function is named **DegFToDegC**. It has a single argument, **TempF**, of type **Double**. It returns a **Double** data type. This code segment converts 45.7 degrees Fahrenheit to the corresponding Celsius value:

```
Dim T As Double
    .
    .
T = DegFToDegC(45.7)
```

To put a function in a Visual Basic application, you follow the same steps used to insert a procedure. Open the code window for the form (or module) where the function will be. Begin typing the header statement 'outside' of any existing procedure or function. Once your header line is complete, press **<Enter>** and the IDE will add an **End Function** line for you. At this point, define the arguments and returned value type. Then, write the code for the function. In the code, make sure to include the **Return()** line that establishes the returned value.

Example 6-3

Average Value

1. Start a new project. This will be an application where a user inputs a list of numbers. Once complete, the average value of the input numbers is computed using a general function. This example illustrates the use of arrays in argument lists.

2. On the form, add a label, two text boxes, three button controls and a listbox control. Make your form look similar to this:

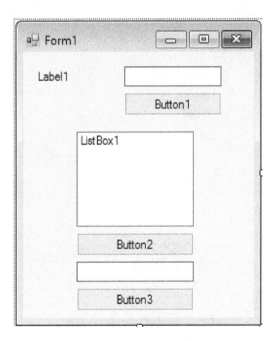

3. Set the properties of the form and controls:

Form1:
    Name   frmAverage
    FormBorderStyle   FixedSingle
    StartPosition   CenterForm
    Text   Average Value

Label1:
    Text   Enter Number

TextBox1:
    Name   txtValue

TextBox2:
    Name   txtAverage
    BackColor   White
    ReadOnly   True
    TextAlign   Center

ListBox1:
    Name   lstValue

Button1:
    Name   btnAccept
    Text   Add to &List

Button2:
    Name   btnClear
    Text   &Clear List

Button3:
    Name   btnCompute
    Text   Compute &Average

The finished form appears as:

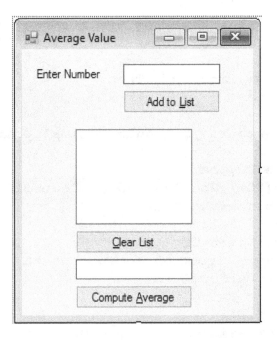

4. Here is the code for a function that computes an average. The numbers it averages are in the 1-based array **Values**. There are **NumberValues** elements in the array:

```
Private Function Average(ByVal NumberValues As Integer,
ByVal Values() As Double) As Double
    'Uses a 1-based array
    Dim I As Integer
    Dim Sum As Double
    Sum = 0
    For I = 1 To NumberValues
      Sum += Values(I)
    Next I
    Return (Sum / NumberValues)
  End Function
```

Notice how the array (Values) is passed into the function

5. Use this code in the **txtValue KeyPress** event for key trapping:

```
Private Sub TxtValue_KeyPress(ByVal sender As Object,
ByVal e As System.Windows.Forms.KeyPressEventArgs) Handles
txtValue.KeyPress
    If Val(txtValue.Text) = 0 Then
      Exit Sub
    End If
    'only allow numbers, a single decimal point, backspace
or enter
    Select Case e.KeyChar
      Case CChar("0") To CChar("9"), ControlChars.Back
        'acceptable keystrokes
        e.Handled = False
      Case ControlChars.Cr
        'enter key - click on accept button
        btnAccept.PerformClick()
        e.Handled = False
      Case CChar(".")
        'check for existence of decimal point
        If InStr(txtValue.Text, ".") = 0 Then
          e.Handled = False
        Else
          e.Handled = True
        End If
      Case Else
        e.Handled = True
    End Select
  End Sub
```

6. Use this code in the **btnClear Click** event – it clears the list box for another average:

```
Private Sub BtnClear_Click(ByVal sender As System.Object,
ByVal e As System.EventArgs) Handles btnClear.Click
    'resets form for another average
    lstValue.Items.Clear()
    txtAverage.Text = ""
    txtValue.Text = ""
    txtValue.Focus()
  End Sub
```

7. Use this code for the **btnAccept Click** event:

```
Private Sub BtnAccept_Click(ByVal sender As System.Object,
ByVal e As System.EventArgs) Handles btnAccept.Click
    'accept typed value
    If lstValue.Items.Count = 100 Then
      MessageBox.Show("Maximum of 100 items has been
reached.", "Error", MessageBoxButtons.OK,
MessageBoxIcon.Error)
      Exit Sub
    End If
    lstValue.Items.Add(txtValue.Text)
    txtValue.Text = ""
    txtValue.Focus()
End Sub
```

This adds the value to the list box.

8. Use this code for the **btnCompute Click** event:

```
Private Sub BtnCompute_Click(ByVal sender As
System.Object, ByVal e As System.EventArgs) Handles
btnCompute.Click
    Dim MyValues(100) As Double
    Dim MyAverage As Double
    Dim I As Integer
    If lstValue.Items.Count <> 0 Then
      'load values in array and compute average
      For I = 1 To lstValue.Items.Count
        'myvalues is 1-based, item is 0-based
        MyValues(I) = Val(lstValue.Items.Item(I - 1))
      Next I
      MyAverage = Average(lstValue.Items.Count, MyValues)
      txtAverage.Text = Format(MyAverage, "0.00")
    End If
    txtValue.Focus()
End Sub
```

This takes the values from the list box and finds the average value.

9. Save the application (saved in **Example 6-3** folder in **LearnVB\VB Code\Class 6** folder). Run the application and try different values. This averaging function might come in handy for some task you may have. Here's a run I made averaging the first 10 integers:

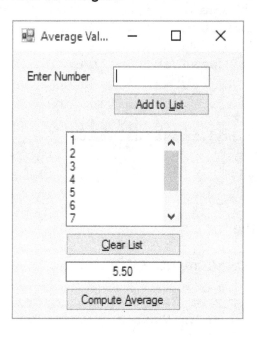

MenuStrip Control

In Toolbox:

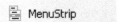

Below Form (Default Properties):

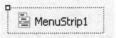

As the applications you build become more and more detailed, with more features for the user, you will need some way to organize those features. A **menu** provides such organization. Menus are a part of most applications. They provide ways to navigate within an application and access desired features. Menus are easily incorporated into Visual Basic programs using the **MenuStrip** control.

The **MenuStrip** control has many features. It provides a quick and easy way to add menus, menu items and submenu elements to your Visual Basic application. And it also has an editor to make any changes, deletions or additions you need. Modifications to the menu structure are also possible at run-time.

A good way to think about elements of a menu structure is to consider them as a hierarchical list of button-type controls that only appear when pulled down from the menu. Each element in the menu structure is an object of type **ToolStripMenuItem**. When you click on a menu item, some action is taken. Like buttons, menu items are named, have properties and a **Click** event. The best way to learn to use the MenuStrip control is to build an example menu. The menu structure we will build is:

File	Edit	Format
New	Cut	Bold
Open	Copy	Italic
Save	Paste	Underline
———		Size
Exit		10
		15
		20

The underscored characters in this structure are access keys, just like those on button controls. The level of indentation indicates position of a menu item within the hierarchy. For example, **New** is a sub-element of the **File** menu. The line under **Save** in the **File** menu is a separator bar (separates menu items).

With this structure, at run-time, the menu would display:

   F̲ile   E̲dit   F̲ormat

The sub-menus appear when one of these 'top' level menu items is selected. Note the **Size** sub-menu under **Format** has another level of hierarchy. It is good practice to not use more than two levels in menus. Each menu element will have a **Click** event associated with it.

When designing your menus, follow formats used by standard Windows applications. For example, if your application works with files, the first heading should be **File** and the last element in the sub-menu under **File** should be **Exit**. If your application uses editing features (cutting, pasting, copying), there should be an **Edit** heading. Use the same access and shortcut keys (keys that let you immediately invoke the menu item without navigating the menu structure) you see in other applications. By doing this, you insure your user will be comfortable with your application. Of course, there will be times your application has unique features that do not fit a 'standard' menu item. In such cases, choose headings that accurately describe such unique features.

We're ready to use the **MenuStrip** control. For this little example, we'll start a new project with a blank form. Drag the **MenuStrip** control to the form. The control will be placed in the 'tray' area below the form. Set a single property for the menu control – **Name** it **mnuMain**. Click on the form and make sure its **MainMenuStrip** property now reads **mnuMain**. If it doesn't, make the change. This property sets which MenuStrip control is used by the form to establish its menu structure.

Now, select the menu control (make it the active control) and your form will display the first menu element:

In the displayed box, type the first main heading (**&File** in this case). This establishes the first property (**Text**) for the menu element. Once done typing this heading, you can move to the properties window and set any other properties. What I usually do, though, is type all the **Text** properties, building the menu structure. Then, I return to each item and assign properties. You choose which method you like best: set properties as you go or build structure, then set properties. We'll talk more about properties after building the menu structure.

After typing the first heading, the form will look like this:

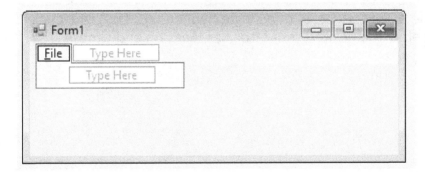

At this point, the menu control will let you type either the first sub-menu heading under the File heading or move to the next heading. If you press **<Enter>** after typing an entry, the cursor will stay within the menu structure (go to a sub-heading).

Type the first sub-menu heading of **&New**:

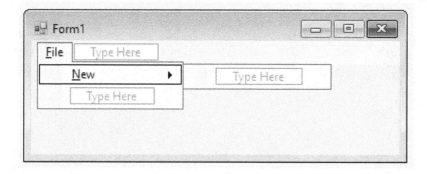

The menu control suggests locations for the next heading.

I think you see how the MenuStrip control works. It's really easy. Just type headings (**Text** properties) where they belong in the menu hierarchy. At any time, you can click on an "already entered" value to change it. Or, a right-click on any element allows adding or deleting elements. Once you've built a few menu structures, you will see how easy and intuitive this control is to use. The best hint I can give is just click where you want to type and magical boxes will appear. Click on the form or any other control to stop menu editing.

Separator bars are used in menu structures to delineate like groups of menu items. There are two ways to enter a 'separator bar' in a menu. First, you can simply type a **Text** property of a single hyphen (-). Or, right-click on the element below the desired separator bar location and choose **Insert Separator**.

After typing the remaining elements of our example menu (with just the captions), the form will look like this:

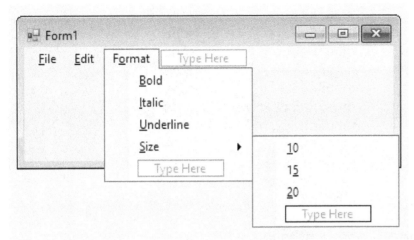

Our menu framework is built, but we must still set properties. Each element in the menu structure has several properties that must be established:

Property	Description
Name	Each menu item must have a name, even separator bars! The prefix **mnu** is used to name menu items. Sub-menu item names usually refer back to main menu headings. For example, if the menu item **New** is under the main heading **File** (name **mnuFile**) menu, use the name **mnuFileNew**
Checked	If True, a check mark appears next to the menu item.
Enabled	If True, the menu item can be selected. If False, the menu item is grayed and cannot be selected.
Shortcut	Used to assign shortcut keystrokes to any item in a menu structure. The shortcut keystroke will appear to the right of the menu item.
Text	Caption appearing on menu item, including assignment of any access keys (these captions are what the user sees).
Visible	Controls whether the menu item appears in the structure.

We've set the **Text** properties already. At this point, you need to go back and select each menu item and set desired properties. To do this, make the appropriate menu item active by clicking on it. Once active, move to the properties window (I press <F4>) and assign whatever properties you want. Do this for each menu item. Yes, I realize there's a lot to do, but then a menu structure does a lot for your application.

For our example menu structure, I used these properties:

Text	Name	Shortcut
&File	mnuFile	None
&New	mnuFileNew	None
&Open	mnuFileOpen	None
&Save	mnuFileSave	None
-	mnuFileBar	None
E&xit	mnuFileExit	None
&Edit	mnuEdit	None
Cu&t	mnuEditCut	CtrlX
&Copy	mnuEditCopy	CtrlC
&Paste	mnuEditPaste	CtrlV
F&ormat	mnuFmt	None
&Bold	mnuFmtBold	CtrlB
&Italic	mnuFmtItalic	CtrlI
&Underline	mnuFmtUnderline	CtrlU
&Size	mnuFmtSize	None
&10	mnuFmtSize10	None
1&5	mnuFmtSize15	None
&20	mnuFmtSize20	None

In particular, notice how the naming convention makes it easy to identify the purpose of each menu item. Notice, too, we have to name the separator bar. And, open the menu structure to see how the shortcut keys are listed.

I also assigned a **Checked** property of **True** to the **10** element under the **Size** sub-menu. This indicates the size of the default font in the application using this structure. Be aware you need to control when this checkmark appears and disappears. It does not work like the check in the check box control. That is, it will not automatically appear when a menu item is clicked.

You might think we're finally done, but we're not. We still need to write code for each menu item's **Click** event. Yes, even more work is needed. The Click event procedure for a menu item is found in the same manner any other event procedure is located. Select the menu item in the object box and the Click event in the procedure box. The event framework will appear and code can be entered. Alternately, double-click the desired menu item and the event procedure will appear.

ContextMenuStrip Control

In Toolbox:

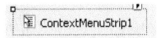

Below Form (Default Properties):

ContextMenuStrip1

There is another type of menu you can add to an application – a context menu. This is a menu that appears when you right-click a control. It lets you customize features for a particular control. Perhaps, you want to allow a user to change a color or font. The **ContextMenuStrip** control makes it easy to add such menus to any control. There are two simple steps: design the menu and assign it to the control.

For each context menu you need, you add a ContextMenuStrip control to your application and set the **Name** property. The context menu control appears in the tray area below the form since there is no user interface. The menu is then designed using exactly the same steps followed for the main menu control. Select the ContextMenuStrip control and the structure will appear on the form. Fill in the desired headings. The difference here is that you are only designing a single menu listing (with sub-headings).

Once your menu is designed, assigning **Name** (still use **mnu** prefix), **Text**, **Checked** and other properties, and writing code for the **Click** events, you assign it to the control by setting the control's **ContextMenuStrip** property. Run the application, right-click the control and the menu appears. It's that simple! Be aware that some controls (for example, the text box) have default context menus. Setting the ContextMenuStrip property for such a control will override the default menu with your custom menu.

Font Object

Each Visual Basic control with a **Text** property (or some other 'text-related' property) also has a **Font** property, allowing us to select how the text will appear. Changing the font at design time is a simple task. You simply click **Font** in the properties window and click the ellipsis (...) that appears. A **Font** dialog box appears allowing you to make selections determining font name, font style (bold, italic, underline) and font size.

With the introduction of menus to an application, we might want to let our user change the font for a particular control at run-time. To do this, we introduce the idea of the **Font** object. The Font object (part of the **Drawing** namespace) is simply the structure used by Visual Basic to define all characteristics of a particular font (name, size, effects).

To change a font at run-time, we assign the **Font** property of the corresponding control to a **New** instance of a Font object using the **Font** constructor from the **Drawing** namespace. The syntax is:

ControlName.**Font** = **New Drawing.Font**(FontName, FontSize, FontStyle)

In this line of code, **FontName** is a string variable defining the name of the font and **FontSize** is an integer value defining the font size in points. These are the same values you choose using the Font dialog at design-time.

The **FontStyle** argument is a Visual Basic constant defining the style of the font. It has five possible values:

Value	Description
Regular	Regular text
Bold	Bold text
Italic	Italic text
Strikeout	Text with a line through the middle
Underline	Underlined text

The basic (no effects) font is defined by **Drawing.FontStyle.Regular**. To add any effects, use the corresponding constant. If the font has more than one effect, combine them using a logical 'Or.' For example, if you want an underlined, bold font, the **FontStyle** argument in the Font constructor would be:

```
Drawing.FontStyle.Underline Or Drawing.FontStyle.Bold
```

Let's look at a couple of examples. To change a button control (**btnExample**) font to Arial, Bold, Size 24, use:

```
btnExample.Font = New Drawing.Font("Arial", 24,
Drawing.FontStyle.Bold)
```

or, to change the font in a text box (**txtExample**) to Courier New, Italic, Underline, Size 12, use:

```
txtExample.Font = New Drawing.Font("Courier New", 12,
Drawing.FontStyle.Italic Or Drawing.FontStyle.Underline)
```

You can also define a variable to be of type **Font**. Declare the variable according to the usual scope considerations. Then, assign a font to that variable for use in other controls:

```
Dim MyFont as Font
      .
      .
MyFont = New Drawing.Font("Courier New", 12,
Drawing.FontStyle.Regular)
ThisControl.Font = MyFont
ThatControl.Font = MyFont
```

Note this is the usual OOP code – declare the object as a member of the class (**Font** in this case), then construct the object using the **New** keyword.

When you declare an object with a **Dim** statement and then assign it a value (creating the object), you should dispose of the object when you are done with it. This conserves system resources. To dispose of the font object created above, use its **Dispose** method:

```
MyFont.Dispose()
```

FontDialog Control

In Toolbox:

Below Form (Default Properties):

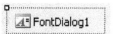

Remember the Font dialog box that appears when you set a control Font property at design-time? That same dialog box is available for use in your Visual Basic applications whenever you want to allow the user to change fonts. The **FontDialog** control provides display of the Font dialog box, allowing the user to choose font and font color.

FontDialog **Properties:**

Name	Gets or sets the name of the font dialog (I usually name this control **dlgFont**).
Color	Indicates selected font color.
Font	Indicates selected font.
MaxSize	Maximum font size (in points) user can select.
MinSize	Maximum font size (in points) user can select.
ShowColor	Indicates whether dialog box displays Color choice (default value is False).
ShowEffects	Indicates where the dialog box allows the user to specify strikethrough and underline.

FontDialog **Methods:**

ShowDialog	Displays the dialog box. Returned value indicates which button was clicked by user (**OK** or **Cancel**).

To use the **FontDialog** control, we add it to our application the same as any control. It will appear in the tray below the form. Once added, we set a few properties. Then, we write code to make the dialog box appear when desired. The user then makes selections and closes the dialog box. At this point, we use the provided information for our tasks.

The **ShowDialog** method is used to display the **FontDialog** control. For a control named **dlgFont**, the appropriate code is:

```
dlgFont.ShowDialog()
```

And the displayed dialog box is:

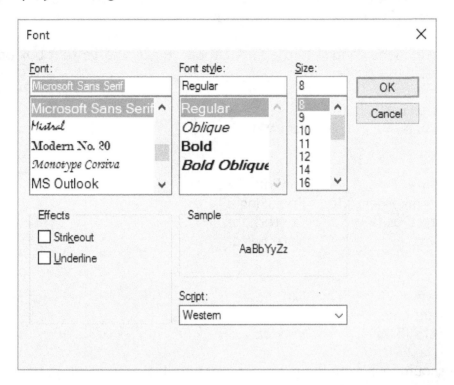

The user selects a font by making relevant choices. Once complete, the **OK** button is clicked. At this point, the **Font** property is available for use (as is **Color**, if available). **Cancel** can be clicked to cancel the font change. The ShowDialog method returns the clicked button. It returns **DialogResult.OK** if OK is clicked and returns **DialogResult.Cancel** if Cancel is clicked.

Typical use of **FontDialog** control:

➢ Set the **Name** property. Decide if **Color** should be a choice.
➢ Use **ShowDialog** method to display dialog box.
➢ Use **Font** property (and perhaps **Color**) to change control **Font** (and perhaps **ForeColor**) property.

Example 6-4

Note Editor

1. Start a new project. We will use this application the rest of this class. We will build a note editor with a menu structure that allows us to control the appearance of the text in the editor box.

2. Add a main menu control to the application. Place a large text box on a form. Set these properties:

    MenuStrip1:
Name	mnuMain

    Form1:
Name	frmEdit
FormBorderStyle	FixedSingle
StartPosition	CenterForm
Text	Note Editor

    Text1:
Name	txtEdit
MultiLine	True
ScrollBars	Vertical

    The form should look something like this with controls (no menu yet):

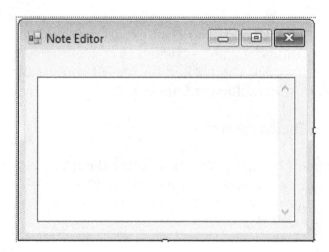

Other controls in tray:

 mnuMain

3. We want to add this menu structure to the Note Editor:

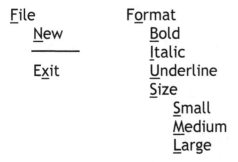

File   Format
  New   Bold
  ————   Italic
  Exit   Underline
                  Size
                    Small
                    Medium
                    Large

Note the identified access keys. Use the MenuStrip control to enter this structure and the following Text, Name, and Shortcut properties for each item:

Text	Name	Shortcut
&File	mnuFile	[None]
&New	mnuFileNew	[None]
-	mnuFileBar	[None]
E&xit	mnuFileExit	[None]
F&ormat	mnuFmt	[None]
& Bold	mnuFmt Bold	CtrlB
&Italic	mnuFmtItalic	CtrlI
&Underline	mnuFmtUnderline	CtrlU
&Size	mnuFmtSize	[None]
&Small	mnuFmtSizeSmall	CtrlS
&Medium	mnuFmtSizeMedium	CtrlM
&Large	mnuFmtSizeLarge	CtrlL

The **Checked** property of the **Small** item (Name **mnuFmtSizeSmall**) under the **Size** sub-menu should also be **True** to indicate the initial font size. When done, look through your menu structure in design mode to make sure it looks correct.

With a menu, the form will appear like:

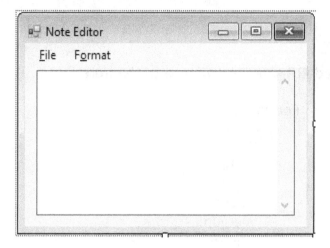

4. Declare a variable and a constant with form level scope:

```
Dim FontSize As Integer = 8
Const FontName As String = "MS Sans Serif"
```

5. Add a general procedure called **ChangeFont**, with no arguments. This generates the **Font** object for the text box based on user menu choices:

```
Private Sub ChangeFont()
   'Put together font based on menu selections
   Dim NewFont As FontStyle
   NewFont = Drawing.FontStyle.Regular
   If mnuFmtBold.Checked Then
     NewFont = NewFont Or Drawing.FontStyle.Bold
   End If
   If mnuFmtItalic.Checked Then
     NewFont = NewFont Or Drawing.FontStyle.Italic
   End If
   If mnuFmtUnderline.Checked Then
     NewFont = NewFont Or Drawing.FontStyle.Underline
   End If
   txtEdit.Font = New Drawing.Font(FontName, FontSize,
NewFont)
   End Sub
```

6. Each menu item that performs an action requires code for its **Click** event. The only menu items that do <u>not</u> have events are the menu and sub-menu headings, namely File, Format, and Size. All others need code. Use the following code for each menu item **Click** event. (This may look like a lot of typing, but you should be able to use a lot of cut and paste.)

If **mnuFileNew** is clicked, the program checks to see if the user really wants a new file and, if so (the default response), clears out the text box:

```
Private Sub MnuFileNew_Click(ByVal sender As
System.Object, ByVal e As System.EventArgs) Handles
mnuFileNew.Click
    'If user wants new file, clear out text
    If MessageBox.Show("Are you sure you want to start a new
file?", "New File", MessageBoxButtons.YesNo,
MessageBoxIcon.Question) = Windows.Forms.DialogResult.Yes
Then
        txtEdit.Text = ""
    End If
End Sub
```

If **mnuFileExit** is clicked, the program checks to see if the user really wants to exit. If not (the default response), the user is returned to the program:

```
Private Sub MnuFileExit_Click(ByVal sender As
System.Object, ByVal e As System.EventArgs) Handles
mnuFileExit.Click
    'Make sure user really wants to exit
    If MessageBox.Show("Are you sure you want to exit the
note editor?", "Exit Editor", MessageBoxButtons.YesNo,
MessageBoxIcon.Question, MessageBoxDefaultButton.Button2) =
Windows.Forms.DialogResult.No Then
        Exit Sub
    Else
        Me.Close()
    End If
End Sub
```

If **mnuFmtBold** is clicked, the program toggles the current bold status:

```
Private Sub MnuFmtBold_Click(ByVal sender As
System.Object, ByVal e As System.EventArgs) Handles
mnuFmtBold.Click
    'Toggle bold font status
    mnuFmtBold.Checked = Not (mnuFmtBold.Checked)
    Call ChangeFont()
End Sub
```

If **mnuFmtItalic** is clicked, the program toggles the current italic status:

```
Private Sub MnuFmtItalic_Click(ByVal sender As
System.Object, ByVal e As System.EventArgs) Handles
mnuFmtItalic.Click
    'Toggle italic font status
    mnuFmtItalic.Checked = Not (mnuFmtItalic.Checked)
    Call ChangeFont()
End Sub
```

If **mnuFmtUnderline** is clicked, the program toggles the current underline status:

```
Private Sub MnuFmtUnderline_Click(ByVal sender As
System.Object, ByVal e As System.EventArgs) Handles
mnuFmtUnderline.Click
    'Toggle underline font status
    mnuFmtUnderline.Checked = Not (mnuFmtUnderline.Checked)
    Call ChangeFont()
End Sub
```

If either of the three size sub-menus is clicked (we use one procedure for all three Click events), indicate the appropriate check mark location and change the font size:

```
Private Sub FontSize_Change(ByVal sender As System.Object,
ByVal e As System.EventArgs) Handles mnuFmtSizeSmall.Click,
mnuFmtSizeMedium.Click, mnuFmtSizeLarge.Click
    Dim SizeClick As ToolStripMenuItem
    'determine which size was clicked
    SizeClick = CType(sender, ToolStripMenuItem)
    mnuFmtSizeSmall.Checked = False
    mnuFmtSizeMedium.Checked = False
    mnuFmtSizeLarge.Checked = False
    Select Case SizeClick.Text
      Case "&Small"
        FontSize = 8
        mnuFmtSizeSmall.Checked = True
      Case "&Medium"
        FontSize = 12
        mnuFmtSizeMedium.Checked = True
      Case "&Large"
        FontSize = 18
        mnuFmtSizeLarge.Checked = True
    End Select
    Call ChangeFont()
End Sub
```

7. Save your application (saved in **Example 6-4** folder in **LearnVB\VB Code\Class 6** folder). We will use it again in Class 7 where we'll learn how to save and open text files created with the Note Editor. Test out all the options. Notice how the toggling of the check marks works. Try the shortcut keys. Here's some text I wrote – note the appearance of the scroll bar since the text exceeds the size allotted to the text box:

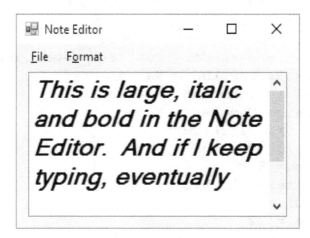

Notice whatever formatting is selected is applied to all text in the control. You cannot selectively format text in a text box control. In Class 10, we look at another control, the rich text control that does allow selective formatting.

Distribution of a Visual Basic Windows Application

I bet you're ready to show your friends and colleagues some of the applications you have built using Visual Basic. Just give them a copy of all your project files, ask them to buy and install Visual Basic and learn how to open and run a project. Then, have them open your project and run the application. I think you'll agree this is asking a lot of your friends, colleagues, and, ultimately, your user base. We need to know how to run an application **without** Visual Basic.

To run an application without Visual Basic, you need to create an **executable** version of the application. So, how is an executable created? A little secret ... Visual Basic builds an executable version of an application every time we run the application! In every project folder is a sub-folder named **Bin\Debug**. The executable file is in that folder. Open the Bin\Debug folder for any project you have built and you'll see a file with your project name of type **Application**. For example, using Windows Explorer to open the Bin\Debug folder for Example 6-4 shows:

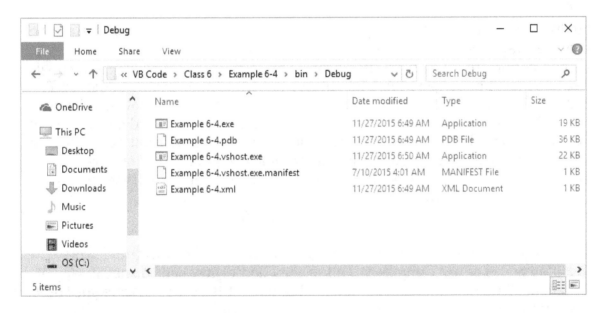

The file named **Example 6-4.exe** (of size 19 KB) is the executable version of the application. If I make sure Visual Basic is not running and double-click this file, the following appears:

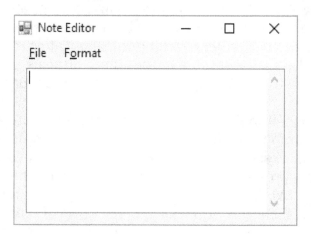

Voila! The Note Editor application is running outside of the Visual Basic IDE!

So distributing a Visual Basic application is as simple as giving your user a copy of the executable file, having them place it in a folder on their computer and double-clicking the file to run it? Maybe. This worked on my computer (and will work on yours) because I have a very important set of files known as the **.NET Framework** installed (they are installed when Visual Basic is installed). Every Visual Basic application needs the .NET Framework to be installed on the hosting computer. The .NET Framework is central to Microsoft's .NET initiative. It is an attempt to solve the problem of first determining what language (and version) an application was developed in and making sure the proper run-time files were installed. The .NET Framework supports all Visual Studio languages, so it is the only runtime software need by Visual Studio applications.

The next question is: how do you know if your user has the .NET Framework installed on his or her computer? And, if they don't, how can you get it installed? These are difficult questions. For now, it is best to assume your user does not have the .NET Framework on their computer.

So, in addition to our application's executable file, we also need to give a potential user the Microsoft .NET Framework files and inform them how to install and register these files on their computer. Things are getting complicated. Further complications for application distribution are inclusion and installation of ancillary data files, graphics files and configuration files. Fortunately, Visual Basic offers help in distributing, or **deploying**, applications.

Visual Basic uses **Setup Wizard** for deploying applications. **Setup Wizard** will identify all files needed by your application and bundle these files into a **Setup** program. You distribute this program to your user base (usually on a CD-ROM). Your user then runs the resulting **Setup** program. This program will:

> ➢ Install the application (and all needed files) on the user's computer.
> ➢ Add an entry to the user's **Start/Programs** menu to allow execution of your application.
> ➢ Add an icon to the user's desktop to allow execution of your application.

We'll soon look at use of Setup Wizard to build a deployment package for a Visual Basic application. First, let's quickly look at the topic of icons.

Application Icons

Notice there is an icon file that looks like a little, blank Windows form associated with the application executable. And, notice that whenever you design a form in the Visual Basic IDE (and run it), a small icon appears in the upper left hand corner of the form. Icons are used in several places in Visual Basic applications: to represent files in Windows Explorer, to represent programs in the Programs menu, to represent programs on the desktop and to identify an application removal tool. Icons are used throughout applications. The default icons are ugly! We need the capability to change them.

Changing the icon connected to a form is simple. The idea is to assign a unique icon to indicate the form's function. To assign an icon, click on the form's **Icon** property in the properties window. Click on the ellipsis (...) and a window that allows selection of icon files will appear. The icon file you load must have the **.ico** filename extension and format.

A different icon can be assigned to the application. This will be the icon that appears next to the executable file's name in Windows Explorer, in the Programs menu and on the desktop. To choose this icon, first make sure the project file is highlighted in the **Solution Explorer** window of the IDE. Choose the **View** menu item and select **Property Pages**. Select the **Application** page and this window will appear:

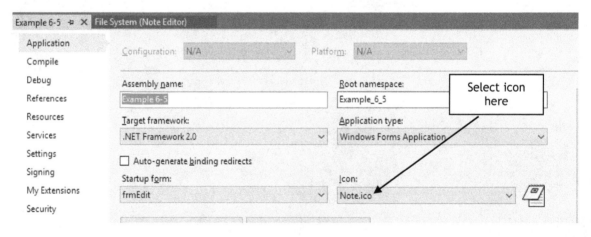

The icon is selected in the **Icon** drop-down box. You can either choose an icon already listed or click the ellipsis (...) that allows you to select an icon using a dialog box. Once you choose an icon, two things will happen. The icon will appear on the property pages and the icon file will be added to your project's folder. This will be seen in the Solution Explorer window.

The Internet and other sources offer a wealth of icon files from which you can choose an icon to assign to your form(s) and applications. But, it's also fun to design your own icon to add that personal touch.

It is possible to create your own icon using Visual Studio. To create an icon for a particular project, in **Solution Explorer**, right-click the project name, choose **Add**, then **New Item**. This window will appear:

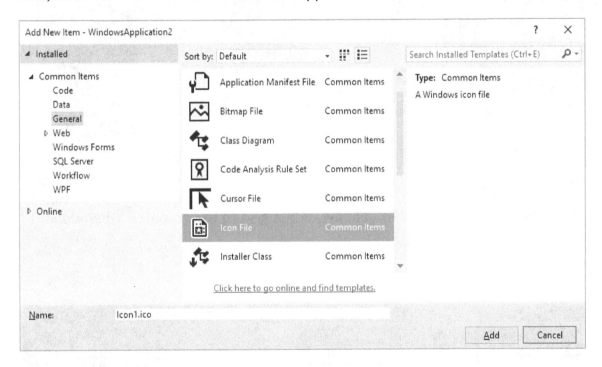

As shown, expand **Common Items** and choose **General**. Then, pick **Icon File**. Name your icon and click **Add**.

A generic icon will open:

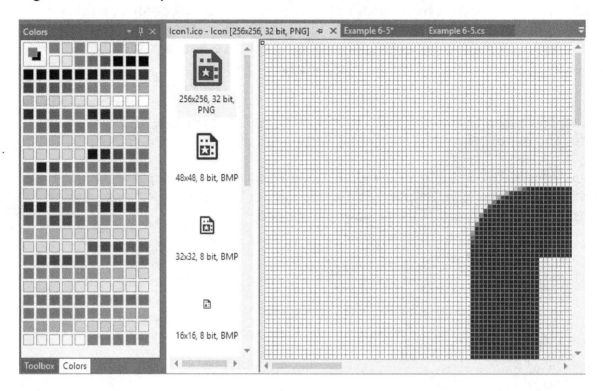

The icon is very large. Let's make a few changes to make it visible and editable. First, resize the image to 32 x 32 pixels. Then, use the magnifying tool to make the image as large as possible. Finally, add a grid to the graphic. When done, I see:

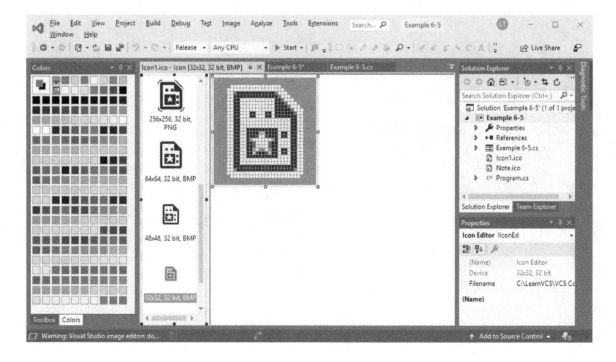

At this point, we can add any detail we need by setting pixels to particular colors. Consult on-line help for the exact steps needed. Once done, the icon will be saved in your project file and can be used by your project. The icon file (**Icon1.ico** in this case) is also listed in **Solution Explorer**:

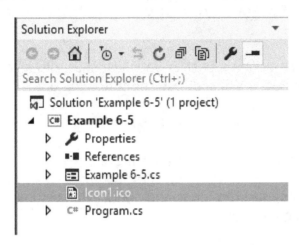

Setup Wizard

As mentioned earlier, to allow someone else to install and run your Visual Basic application requires more than just a simple transfer of the executable file. Visual Basic provides **Setup Wizard** that simplifies this task of application **deployment**.

Note: **Setup Wizard** must be a part of your Visual Studio installation. To download and install **Setup Wizard**, use the following link:

Download Setup Wizard

Setup Wizard will build a **Setup** program that lets the user install the application (and other needed files) on their computer. At the same time, **Program** menu entries, desktop icons and application removal programs are placed on the user's computer.

The best way to illustrate use of **Setup Wizard** is through an example. In these notes, we will build a Setup program for our **Note Editor** example. Follow the example closely to see all steps involved. All results of this example will be found in the **Example 6-5** and **Note Editor** folders of the **LearnVB\VB Code\Class 6** folder. Let's start.

Open the **Note Editor** project (**Example 6-4**). Attach an icon to the **Titles** form (one possible icon, **NOTE.ICO**, is included in the project folder). The form should look like this with its new icon:

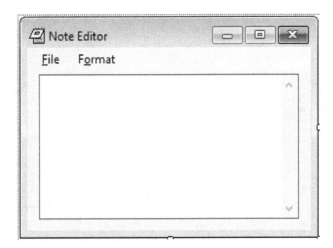

Assign this same icon to the application using the steps mentioned earlier:

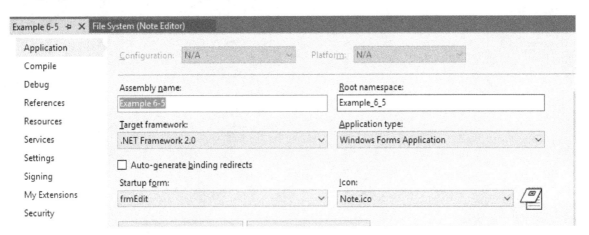

Setup Wizard is a separate project you add to your application solution. Choose the **File** menu option, then **New** then **Project**. In the window that appears, select **Setup Wizard** and click **Next**:

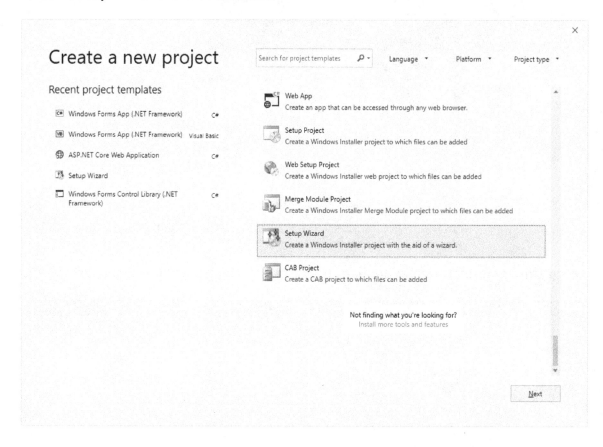

This window appears:

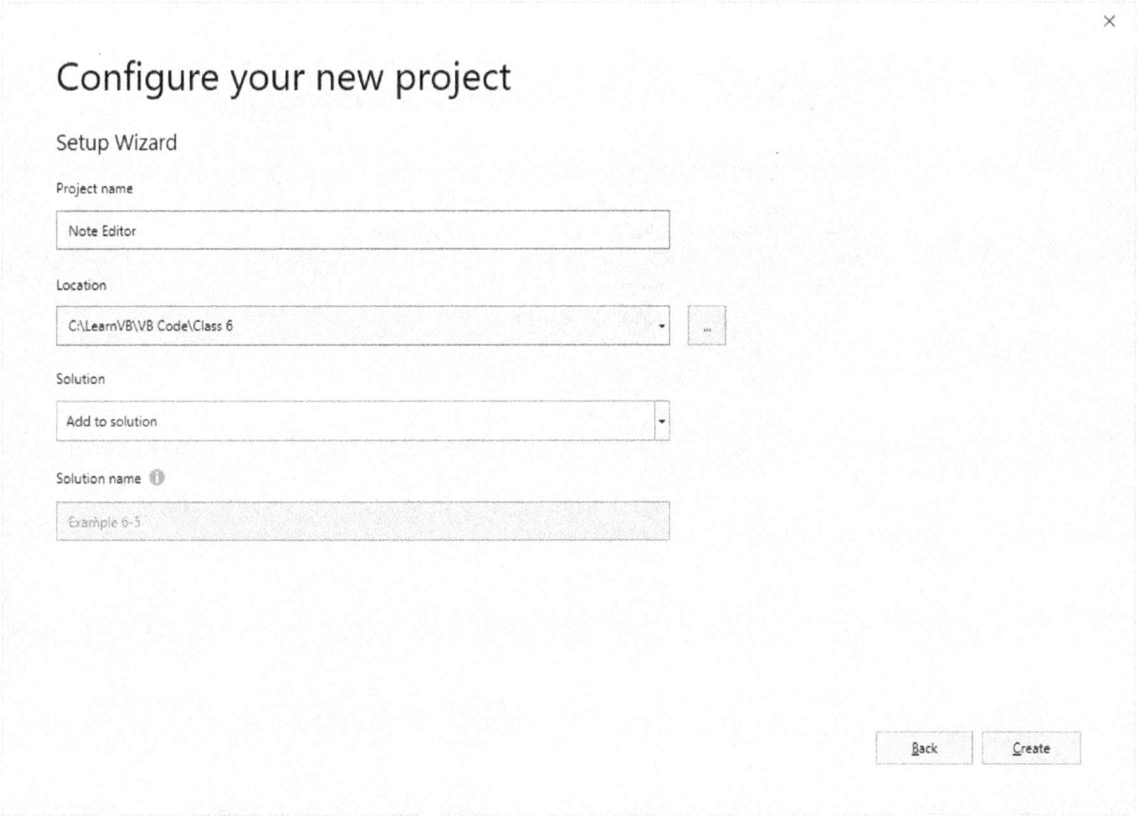

Under **Solution**, choose **Add to Solution.** **Name** the project **Note Editor** and click **Create.** Notice I have put the project folder in the **LearnVCS\VCS Code\Class 6** folder.

The **Setup Wizard** will begin with Step 1 of 5.

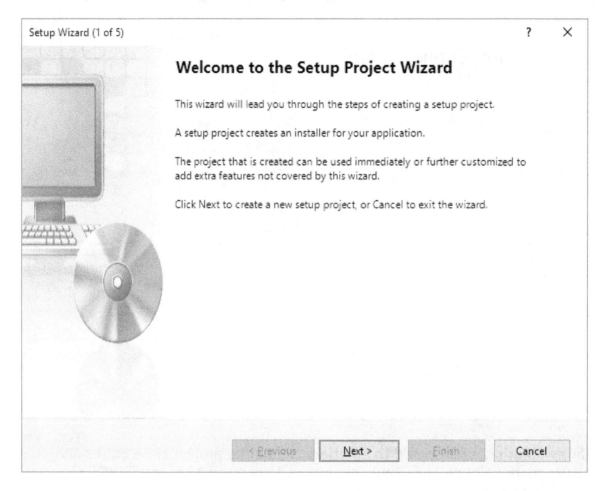

Continue from step to step, providing the requested information. Here, just click **Next**.

Step 2.

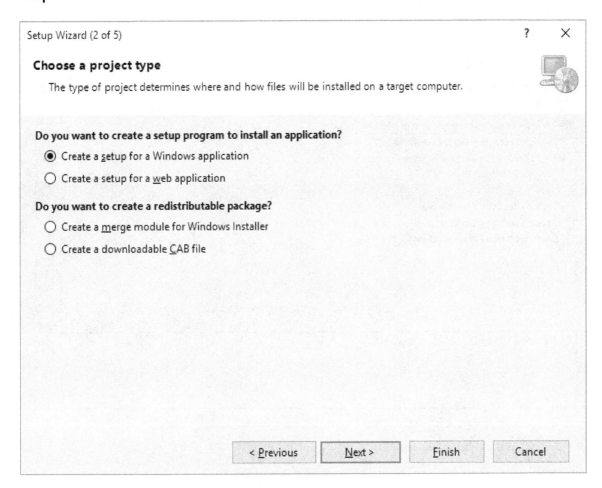

Choose **Create a setup for a Windows application.** Click **Next.**

Step 3.

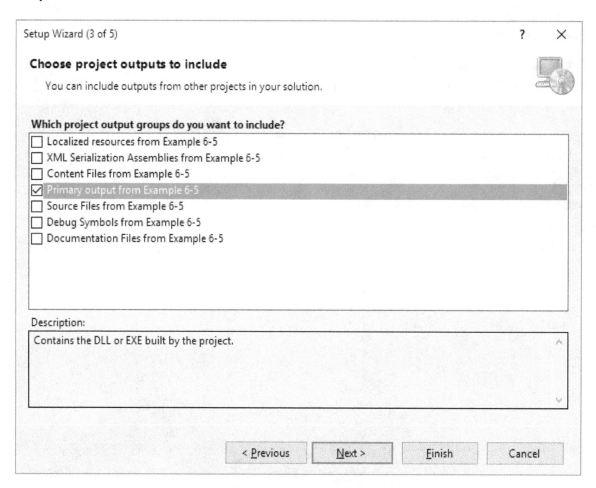

Here you choose the files to install. The main one is the executable file (known here as the **primary output file**). Place a check next to **Primary ouput from Example 6-5** and click **Next.**

Step 4.

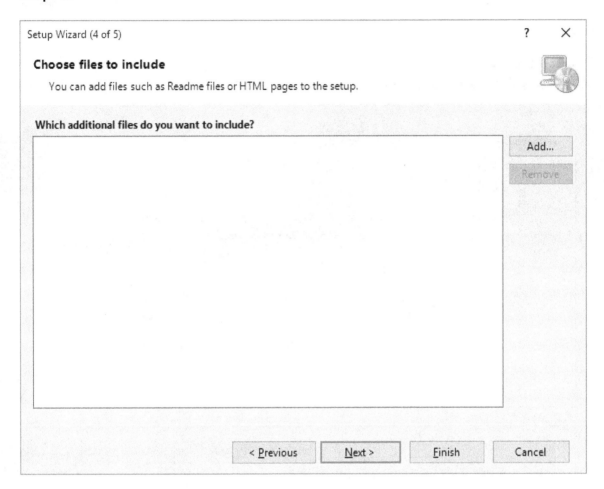

Here you can also additional files with your deployment package. You could specify ReadMe files, configuration files, help files, data files, sound files, graphic files or any other files your application needs. Our simple application needs no such files, so we just move to the next step. If you did need to add a file, click the **Add Files** button to select the desired file.

Move to the next step (click **Next**).

Step 5.

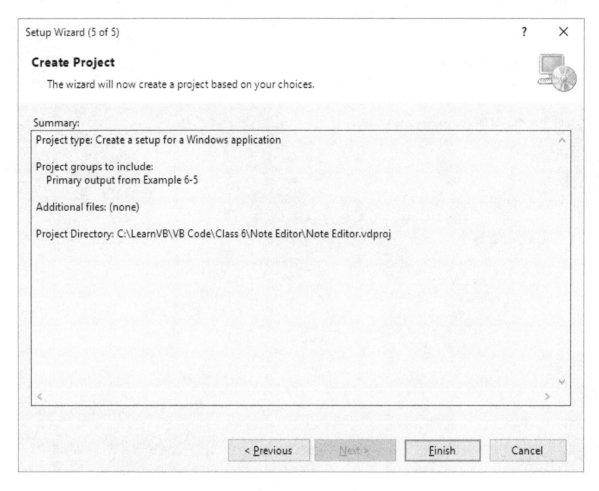

Click **Finish** to see the resulting **File System**:

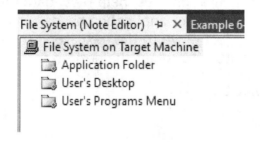

We also want shortcuts to start the program both on the **Desktop** and the **Programs Menu.** First, we do the **Desktop** shortcut. To do this, open the **Application Folder** to see:

Right-click **Primary output from ...** and choose **Create Shortcut to Primary output ....** Cut the resulting shortcut from the **Application Folder** and paste it into the **User's Desktop** folder:

Rename the shortcut **Note Editor** to yield

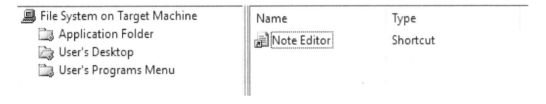

Lastly, we want to change the icon associated with the shortcut. This is a little tricky. The steps are:

> ➢ Highlight the shortcut and choose the **Icon** property in the Properties window
> ➢ Choose **Browse.**
> ➢ When the **Icon** dialog box appears, click **Browse.** You will see

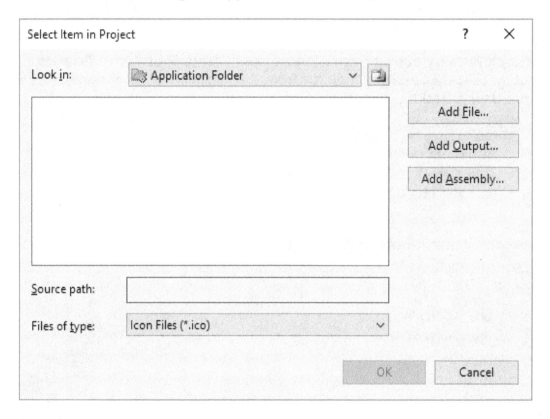

As shown, look in the **Application Folder** and click **Add File.**

> ➤ Locate and select the icon file (there is one in the **LearnVB\VB Code\Class 6\Example 6-5** folder), then click **OK**. The **Icon** window will appear:

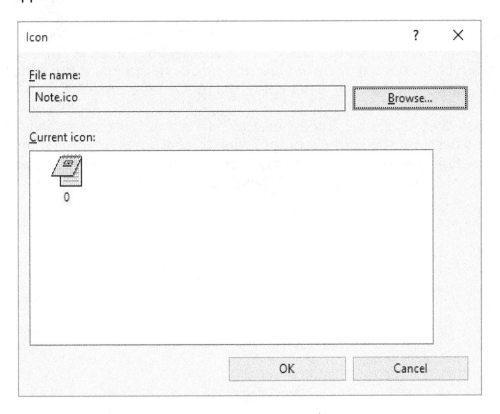

Select the desired icon and click **OK.**

Next, follow nearly identical steps to put a shortcut in the **User's Programs Menu** folder. The **Setup Wizard** has completed its job.

Debug Versus Release Configurations

When you create an executable (run your application) in Visual Basic, it is created using the default **debug configuration**. We have been using this configuration for every application studied thus far. You use the debug configuration while designing, testing and debugging your application. An application built in debug mode has lots of symbolic references included for debug purposes and the code is not optimized for best performance.

When you have fully tested your application, are sure it is error free and ready for deployment, we suggest switching to **release configuration**. To do this, select the **Build** menu option and choose **Configuration Manager** (this option is only available when a setup project is being used. This window will appear:

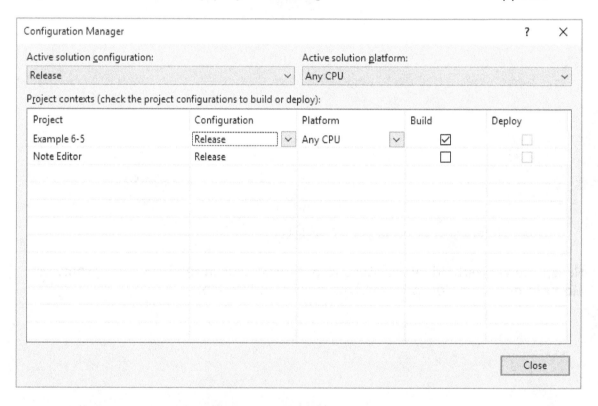

Under **Active solution configuration**, choose **Release**. Click **Close**. Next, in the **Solution Explorer**, right click the project name (not the setup project) and choose **Build**.

The **release** configuration of an application is fully optimized and contains no symbolic debugging information. Such an application will usually be smaller in size, have the fastest speed and provide the best performance. This is the configuration that should be part of a deployment package. If you ever need to make significant changes to a project, you probably want to change back to **Debug** configuration while testing your changes.

Building the Setup Program

Now, let's build the **Setup** program. In the Solution Explorer window, right-click the **Note Editor** project and choose **Build** from the menu. After a short time, the **Setup** program and an msi (Microsoft Installer) file will be written. They will be located in the executable folder of the **Note Editor** project folder (**LearnVB\VB Code\Class 6\Note Editor\Release**). The **Setup** program is small. A look at the resulting directory shows:

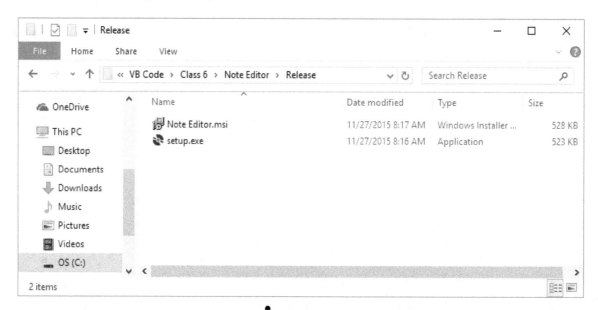

Use some media (zip disk, CD-ROM or downloaded files) to distribute these files your user base. Provide the user with the simple instruction to run the **Setup.exe** program and installation will occur.

Installing a Visual Basic Application

To install the program, simply run the **Setup.exe** program. These are the same brief instructions you need to provide a user. Users have become very familiar with installing software and running Setup type programs. Let's try the example just created and see what a nice installation interface is provided. Double-click the **Setup.exe** program and this introduction window should appear:

Click **Next** and you will be asked where you want the application installed.

After a few clicks, installation is complete and you will see:

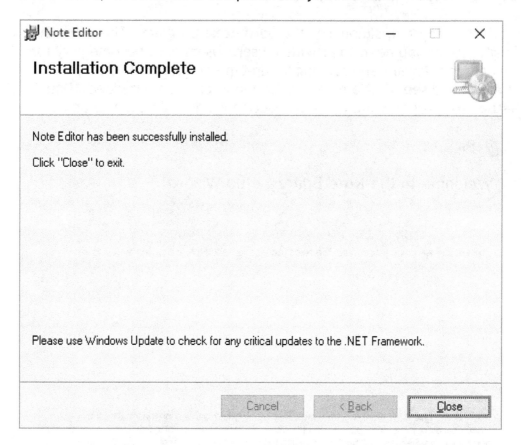

After installing, look on your desktop. There should be an icon named **Note Editor**. Double-click that icon and the program will run. Similarly, the program can be accessed by clicking **Start** on your taskbar, then choosing **All Apps**. Click the **Note Editor** entry and the program runs. I think you'll agree the installer does a nice job.

Class Review

After completing this class, you should understand:

- ➤ How to work with multiple forms and modules in a Visual Basic application
- ➤ How to use general procedures and functions in a Visual Basic application
- ➤ How to insert a menu structure into a Visual Basic application using the MenuStrip control
- ➤ How to use the ContextMenuStrip control to add menus to controls
- ➤ The concept of a Font object and use of the FontDialog control
- ➤ How to design an icon using Image Editor and how to assign an icon to a Visual Basic application
- ➤ Use of the Setup Wizard to create a deployment package (Setup program) for a Visual Basic application

Practice Problems 6

Problem 6-1. Note Editor About Box Problem. Most applications have a **Help** menu heading. When you click on this heading, at the bottom of the menu is an **About** item. Choosing this item causes a dialog box to appear that provides the user with copyright and other application information. Prepare such an About box for the Note Editor we built in this chapter (Example 6-4). Implement the About box in the application.

Problem 6-2. Normal Numbers Problem. There are other ways to generate random numbers in Visual Basic. One is the **NextDouble** method (associated with the **Random** object) that returns a double type number between 0 and 1. These numbers produce what is known as a uniform distribution. This means all numbers come up with equal probabilities. Statisticians often need a 'bell-shaped curve' to do their work. This curve is what is used in schools when they 'grade on a curve.' Such a 'probability distribution' is spread about a mean with some values very likely (near the mean) and some not very likely (far from the mean). Such distributions (called normal distributions) have a specified mean and a specified standard deviation (measure of how far spread out possible values are). One way to simulate a single 'normally distributed' number, using the 'uniformly distributed' random number generator, is to sum twelve random numbers (from the **NextDouble** method) and subtract six from the sum. That value is approximately 'normal' with a mean of zero and a standard deviation of one. See if such an approximation really works by first writing a general method that computes a single 'normally distributed number.' Then, write general methods to compute the mean (average) and standard deviation of an array of values (the equations are found back in Exercise 2-1). See if the described approximation is good by computing a large number of 'normally approximate' numbers.

Problem 6-3. Context Menu Problem. Build an application with a single button control. When you click on the button, have a font dialog box appear, allowing you to change the font and color of the displayed text. When you right-click the button, have a context menu appear allowing you to change the background color of the button.

Exercise 6

US/World Capitals Quiz

Develop an application that quizzes a user on states and capitals in the United States and/or capitals of world countries. Or, if desired, quiz a user on any matching pairs of items - for example, words and meanings, books and authors, or inventions and inventors. Use a menu structure that allows the user to decide whether they want to name states (countries) or capitals and whether they want multiple choice or type-in answers. Thoroughly test your application. Design an icon for your program using the Paint program or some other program. Create an executable file. Create a **Setup** program using the Setup Wizard. Try installing and removing the program from your computer. Or, give it to someone else and let him or her enjoy your nifty little program.

7. Sequential Files, Error-Handling and Debugging

Review and Preview

In this class, we expand our Visual Basic knowledge from past classes and examine a few new topics. We first study reading and writing sequential disk files. We then look at handling errors in programs, using both run-time error trapping and debugging techniques.

Sequential Files

In many applications, it is helpful to have the capability to read and write information to a disk file. This information could be some computed data or perhaps information needed by your Visual Basic project. Visual Basic supports several file formats. We will look at the most common format: **sequential files**.

A sequential file is a line-by-line list of data that can be viewed with any text editor. Sequential access easily works with files that have lines with mixed information of different lengths. Hence, sequential files can include both variables and text data. When using sequential files, it is helpful, but not necessary, to know the order data was written to the file to allow easy retrieval.

The ability to read and generate sequential files is a very powerful capability of Visual Basic. This single capability is the genesis of many applications I've developed. Let's examine a few possible applications where we could use such files. One possibility is to use sequential files to provide initialization information for a project. Such a file is called a **configuration** or **initialization file** and almost all applications use such files. Here is the idea:

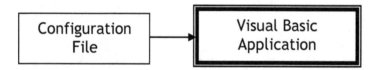

In this diagram, the configuration file (a sequential file) contains information that can be used to initialize different parameters (control properties, variable values) within the Visual Basic application. The file is opened when the application begins, the file values are read and the various parameters established.

Similarly, when we exit an application, we could have it write out current parameter values to an output configuration file:

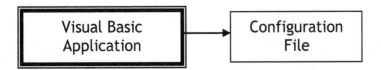

This output file could then become an input file the next time the application is executed. We will look at how to implement such a configuration file in a Visual Basic application.

Many data-intensive, or not-so intensive, Windows applications provide file export capabilities. For example, you can save data from a Microsoft Excel spreadsheet to an external file. The usual format for such an exported data file is a **CSV** (comma separated variables) sequential file. You can write a Visual Basic application that reads this exported file and performs some kind of analysis or further processing of the data:

In the above example, the results of the Visual Basic program could be displayed using Windows controls (text boxes, list boxes, picture boxes) or the program could also write another sequential file that could be used by some other application (say Microsoft Access or Microsoft Word). This task is actually more common than you might think. Many applications support exporting data. And, many applications support importing data from other sources. A big problem is that the output file from one application might not be an acceptable input file to another application. Visual Basic to the rescue:

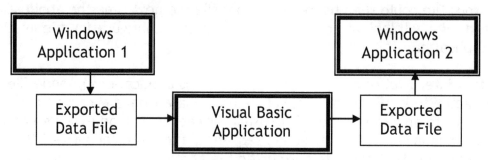

In this diagram, Application 1 writes an exported data file that is read by the Visual Basic application. This application writes a data file in an input format required by Application 2.

You will find that you can use Visual Basic to read a sequential file in any format and, likewise, write a file in any format. As we said, the ability to read and generate sequential files is a very powerful capability of Visual Basic.

Sequential File Output (Variables)

We will first look at **writing** values of **variables** to sequential files. The initial step in accessing any sequential file (either for input or output) is to open the file using the **FileOpen** function. The syntax for opening a sequential file for output is:

```
FileOpen(N, FileName, OpenMode.Output)
```

where **FileName** is the name of the file to open and **N** is an integer file number. The filename must be a complete path to the file. You must insure if opening multiple files that no two files share the same file number. A useful function in helping with this task is the **FreeFile** function. It will generate a unique file identifier number. The syntax for using this function to open a file is:

```
Dim FileNumber As Integer
        .
FileNumber = FreeFile()
FileOpen(FileNumber, FileName, OpenMode.Output)
```

As you type the **FileOpen** function line, the Intellisense feature of the IDE will help you fill in the arguments.

A word of warning - when you open a file using the **FileOpen** function and **Output** mode, if the file already exists, it will be erased immediately! So, make sure you really want to overwrite the file. Using the **SaveFileDialog** control (discussed in this chapter) can prevent accidental overwriting. Just be careful. You can append to an existing sequential file by opening it using the **Append** mode. That syntax is:

```
FileOpen(N, FileName, OpenMode.Append)
```

If the file to append doesn't exist or can't be found, it will be created as an empty file.

When done writing to a sequential file, it must be closed using the **FileClose** function:

```
FileClose(N)
```

where N is the same file number used to open the file. Once a file is closed, it is saved on the disk under the path and filename used to open the file.

Information (variables or text) is written to a sequential file in an appended fashion. Separate BASIC statements are required for each appending. There are four different ways to write variables to a sequential file. You choose which method you want based on your particular application.

The first method uses the **Write** statement. For a file opened using file number N, the syntax is:

   Write(N, VariableList)

where **VariableList** is a comma-delimited list of variable names. This statement will append the specified variables to the current line in the sequential file. If you only use **Write** for output, everything will be written in one very long line.

The output variables will be delimited by commas. Other appearance characteristics of data written with the **Write** function depend on variable type. Numeric data types appear as is (no special formatting) and string data will be enclosed in quotes ("). Boolean values are written as either #TRUE# or #FALSE#. Date data is written in universal date format, surrounded by # signs. An example date for April 12, 2001 is #2001-04-12#.

Example using **Write** function:

```
Dim A As Integer, B As String, C As Single, D As Date
Dim E As Boolean, F As Double
    .
    .
    .
FileOpen(1, "c:\junk\TestOut.txt", OpenMode.Output)
Write(1, A, B, C)
Write(1, D)
Write(1, E, F)
FileClose(1)
```

After this code runs, the file **c:\junk\TestOut.txt** will have a single line with all six variables, each separated by a comma. The string variable (B) will be enclosed in quotes, while the date variable (D) and Boolean variable (E) will be surrounded by pound signs.

A second method for writing variables is the **WriteLine** function:

WriteLine(N, VariableList)

This function works identically to the **Write** function with the exception that a 'carriage return' is added, placing the variables on a single line in the file. By omitting the variable list, WriteLine can be used to add blank lines to sequential files. Variables written to file using WriteLine will still be comma-delimited with the special formatting provide to string, date and Boolean variables.

Example using **WriteLine** function:

```
Dim A As Integer, B As String, C As Single, D As Date
Dim E As Boolean, F As Double
     .
     .
FileOpen(1, "c:\junk\TestOut.txt", OpenMode.Output)
WriteLine(1, A, B, C)
WriteLine(1, D)
WriteLine(1, E, F)
FileClose(1)
```

After this code runs, the file **c:\junk\TestOut.txt** will have three lines. The first will have variables A, B (in quotes) and C. The second line will have D (in pound signs). The final line will have E (in pound signs) and F.

The **Write** and **WriteLine** functions provide very specific, non-flexible formatting for variables written to a sequential file. This formatting is an excellent choice for application configuration files and for exporting files to other applications like Excel. This format is the CSV (comma-separated variables) used by many Windows applications. If, however, a file in this specific format does not fit your needs, there are two other functions that can be tailored to any needs: **Print** and **PrintLine**.

A third way to write variables to a sequential file is the **Print** function. Its syntax (for a file opened with number N) is identical to that of Write and WriteLine:

    Print(N, VariableList)

where **VariableList** is still a comma-delimited list of output variables. What is different here is how variables written to a file are formatted. This statement will append the specified variables to the current line in the sequential file. And, like Write, if you only use **Print** for output, everything will be written in one very long line.

The output variables will be delimited by tab characters, meaning variable amounts of space will appear between variables written to the file. And, no special characters surround string, date or Boolean variables.. Boolean variables are written as True or False. Dates are written in short format - April 12, 2001 is written as 4/12/2001. Be careful using the **Print** function with string, date and Boolean variables. The lack of formatting characters makes it difficult to read them back in.

Example using **Print** function:

```
Dim A As Integer, B As String, C As Single, D As Date
Dim E As Boolean, F As Double
    .
    .
FileOpen(1, "c:\junk\TestOut.txt", OpenMode.Output)
Print(1, A, B, C)
Print(1, D)
Print(1, E, F)
FileClose(1)
```

After this code runs, the file **c:\junk\TestOut.txt** will have a single line with all six variables, each separated by varying amounts of space. There will be no quotes or pound signs anywhere in the line to delimit strings, dates and Boolean values from the accompanying numeric values.

The final way to write variables to a sequential file is **PrintLine**, the companion to **Print**. Its syntax is:

PrintLine(N, VariableList)

This function works identically to the **Print** function with the exception that a 'carriage return' is added, placing the variables on a single line in the file. It can be used to insert blank lines by omitting the variable list. Variables written to file using PrintLine will still be tab-delimited with no special formatting for string, date and Boolean variables.

Example using **PrintLine** function:

```
Dim A As Integer, B As String, C As Single, D As Date
Dim E As Boolean, F As Double
    .
    .
FileOpen(1, "c:\junk\TestOut.txt", OpenMode.Output)
PrintLine(1, A, B, C)
PrintLine(1, D)
PrintLine(1, E, F)
FileClose(1)
```

After this code runs, the file **c:\junk\TestOut.txt** will have three lines. The first will have variables A, B (no quotes) and C. The second line will have D (no pound signs). The final line will have E (no pound signs) and F.

Of all these functions for writing variables to a file, I prefer **WriteLine** and **PrintLine**. I like having information on separate lines. WriteLine is rigid about formatting – that rigidity is good for some files (configuration files, for example). PrintLine can be used to write data in any format you want. If you want dollar signs between variables you can do it:

```
PrintLine(1, A, "$", B, "$", C)
```

And, if you need quotes around a string variable, just add them:

```
PrintLine(1, A, Chr(34) + B + Chr(34), C)
```

PrintLine offers infinite flexibility in how data is written to a file. If you need this flexibility, it is the function to use.

Application Path

We have seen in the **FileOpen** statement that a path to the file to be opened is needed. Many times, the file we want to open (for either writing or reading) is located in the same directory as the application (the project). But, how do we know what directory that is? Visual Basic maintains a parameter that has the location of an application's executable file. That path is a string data type defined by:

```
Application.StartupPath
```

When a user installs an application on their own machine (using a Setup program like that developed in Class 6), this same parameter will hold the executable location.

As an example, to use this parameter to open a file (for writing) named **TestOut.txt** and store it in the current application directory, we would use the statement:

```
FileOpen(1, Application.StartupPath + "\TestOut.txt",
OpenMode.Output)
```

Note an additional backslash (\) must be appended to the path, before adding the file name. We will use the **Application.StartupPath** parameter whenever we need to open or save files within the application directory (data files or initialization files are examples).

Example 7-1

Writing Variables to Sequential Files

1. Start a new project. We will build a simple application that writes data to sequential files using each of the four methods for doing such writing. The **Application.StartupPath** parameter will be used to save the file. Add a label control to the form in your new project.

2. Set the properties of the form and each control:

   Form1:

Name	frmWrite
FormBorderStyle	FixedSingle
StartPosition	CenterScreen
Text	Sequential File Output

   Label1:

Name	lblPath
AutoSize	False
BackColor	White
Text	[Blank]

The form should look something like this:

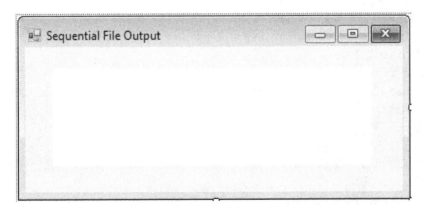

3. Use this code in the **frmWrite Load** event:

```
Private Sub FrmWrite_Load(ByVal sender As System.Object,
ByVal e As System.EventArgs) Handles MyBase.Load
    Dim V1 As Integer, V2 As String, V3 As Single, V4 As
Integer
    Dim V5 As Boolean, V6 As Double, V7 As Date
    lblPath.Text = "Path is: " + Application.StartupPath
    V1 = 5
    V2 = "Visual Basic 2019"
    V3 = 1.23
    V4 = -4
    V5 = True
    V6 = 3.14159265359
    V7 = CDate("11/13/15")
    'Write function
    FileOpen(1, Application.StartupPath + "\test1.txt",
OpenMode.Output)
    Write(1, V1, V2, V3)
    Write(1, V4, V5)
    Write(1, V6, V7)
    FileClose(1)
    'Writeline function
    FileOpen(1, Application.StartupPath + "\test2.txt",
OpenMode.Output)
    WriteLine(1, V1, V2, V3)
    WriteLine(1, V4, V5)
    WriteLine(1, V6, V7)
    FileClose(1)
    'Print function
    FileOpen(1, Application.StartupPath + "\test3.txt",
OpenMode.Output)
    Print(1, V1, V2, V3)
    Print(1, V4, V5)
    Print(1, V6, V7)
    FileClose(1)
    'Printline function
    FileOpen(1, Application.StartupPath + "\test4.txt",
OpenMode.Output)
    PrintLine(1, V1, V2, V3)
    PrintLine(1, V4, V5)
    PrintLine(1, V6, V7)
    FileClose(1)
End Sub
```

This code writes seven variables of different types to four different sequential files (using the four different writing functions).

4. Save the application (saved in **Example 7-1** folder in **LearnVB\VB Code\Class 7** folder) and run it. Four files will be written to the folder containing the Example 7-1 executable file. That folder will be displayed in the label control. Here is where my files are:

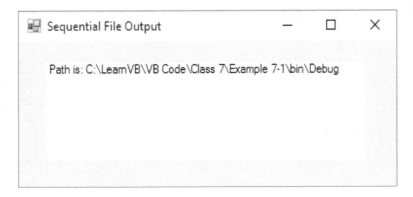

In that folder will be four files: test1.txt (written using **Write** function), test2.txt (written using **WriteLine** function), test3.txt (written using **Print** function), and test4.txt (written using **PrintLine** function). Open each file using Windows Notepad and notice how each file is different. Pay particular attention to how variables of different types are represented. My files look like this:

test1.txt (uses Write)

```
5,"Visual Basic 2019",1.23,-4,#TRUE#,3.14159265359,#2015-11-13#,
```

test2.txt (uses WriteLine)

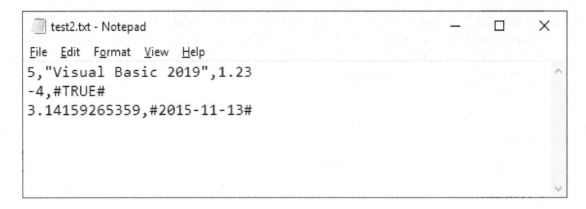

test3.txt (uses Print)

A very long line – I had to reduce the screen dump size to fit it on the page!

test4.txt (uses PrintLine)

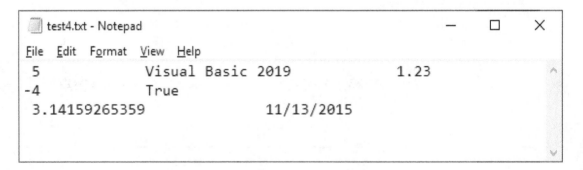

Sequential File Input (Variables)

To **read variables** from a sequential file, we essentially reverse the write procedure. First, open the file using **OpenMode.Input**:

```
FileOpen(N, FileName, OpenMode.Input)
```

where **N** is an integer file number and **FileName** is a complete path to the file. N must be a unique number (no other file open with the same value). As discussed earlier, the function **FreeFile** can insure the uniqueness.

If the file you are trying to open does not exist, an error will occur. Later in this class, we will learn how to deal with such errors. For now, we'll assume the file exists or you could use the **OpenFileDialog** control to insure the file exists before trying to open it.

When all values have been read from the sequential file, it is closed using:

```
FileClose(N)
```

Variables are read from a sequential file in the same order they were written. Hence, to read in variables from a sequential file, you need to know:

> ➤ How many variables are in the file
> ➤ The order the variables were written to the file
> ➤ The type of each variable in the file

If you developed the structure of the sequential file (say for a configuration file), you obviously know all of this information. And, if it is a file you generated from another source (Excel, Access), the information should be known. If the file is from an unknown source, you may have to do a little detective work. Open the file in a text editor and look at the data. See if you can figure out what is in the file.

Many times, you may know the order and type of variables in a sequential file, but the number of variables may vary. For example, you may export monthly sales data from an Excel spreadsheet. One month may have 30 lines, the next 31 lines, and February would have 28 or 29. In such a case, you can read from the file until you reach an end-of-file condition. This is checked using:

```
EOF(N)
```

where N is the file number. EOF is initialized at False when the file is opened. EOF becomes True once the end-of-file is reached.

Variables are read from a sequential file using the **Input** function. The syntax for a file opened as number **N** is:

```
Input(N, Variable)
```

where **Variable** is the variable being read. Note Input only reads in one variable at a time. So, if a file has 100 variables, no matter where how they are formatted in the file (on a single line, on multiple lines), you will need 100 Input statements in your code!

The **Input** statement can read numeric, date and Boolean type variables from Visual Basic-generated files written with the Write, WriteLine, Print, or PrintLine functions. Input will run into problems reading string variables written using Print and PrintLine. The lack of delimiting quotes causes problems. If you need to use Print or PrintLine for string variables, we suggest appending quotes to such variables. If you can't do this (your application won't allow it), there are still ways to read in string variables not in quotes. See the **Parsing Lines** section that follows in these notes.

Example using **Input** function:

```
Dim A As Integer, B As String, C As Single, D As Date
Dim E As Boolean, F As Double
    .
    .
    .
FileOpen(1, "c:\junk\TestOut.txt", OpenMode.Input)
Input(1, A)
Input(1, B)
Input(1, C)
Input(1, D)
Input(1, E)
Input(1, F)
FileClose(1)
```

This code opens the file **c:\junk\TestOut.txt** and sequentially reads six variables. The only variable it may have difficulty reading is C, the string variable.

Example 7-2

Reading Variables from Sequential Files

1. Start a new project. We will build an application that opens and reads in each of the four data files written in Example 7-1. As a first step, copy those four files into the **Bin\Debug** folder in your new project's folder (you may have to create the folder first). We want these files to be in our application path, so we can use the **Application.StartupPath** parameter to open them.

2. Add a list control, four radio buttons and a button control to the form so it looks like this:

3. Set the properties of the form and each control:

Form1:
      Name   frmRead
      FormBorderStyle   FixedSingle
      StartPosition   CenterScreen
      Text   Sequential File Input

ListBox1:
      Name   lstInput

RadioButton1:

Name	rdoWrite
Checked	True
Text	Write

RadioButton2:

Name	rdoWriteLine
Text	Write

RadioButton3:

Name	rdoPrint
Text	Print

RadioButton4:

Name	rdoPrintLine
Text	PrintLine

Button1:

Name	btnRead
Text	&Read Data

The form should look something like this:

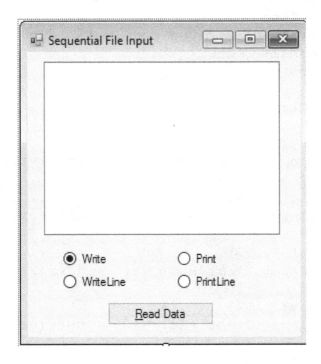

4. Use this code in the **btnRead Click** event:

```
Private Sub BtnRead_Click(ByVal sender As System.Object,
ByVal e As System.EventArgs) Handles btnRead.Click
    Dim V1 As Integer, V2 As String, V3 As Single, V4 As
Integer
    Dim V5 As Boolean, V6 As Double, V7 As Date
    Dim I As Integer
    lstInput.Items.Clear()
    If rdoWrite.Checked Then
      FileOpen(1, Application.StartupPath + "\test1.txt",
OpenMode.Input)
    ElseIf rdoWriteLine.Checked Then
      FileOpen(1, Application.StartupPath + "\test2.txt",
OpenMode.Input)
    ElseIf rdoPrint.Checked Then
      FileOpen(1, Application.StartupPath + "\test3.txt",
OpenMode.Input)
    ElseIf rdoPrintLine.Checked Then
      FileOpen(1, Application.StartupPath + "\test4.txt",
OpenMode.Input)
    End If
    For I = 1 To 7
      If EOF(1) Then
        lstInput.Items.Add("No more data!")
        FileClose(1)
        Exit Sub
      Else
        Select Case I
          Case 1
            Input(1, V1)
            lstInput.Items.Add("V1=" + CStr(V1))
          Case 2
            Input(1, V2)
            lstInput.Items.Add("V2=" + CStr(V2))
          Case 3
            Input(1, V3)
            lstInput.Items.Add("V3=" + CStr(V3))
          Case 4
            Input(1, V4)
            lstInput.Items.Add("V4=" + CStr(V4))
          Case 5
            Input(1, V5)
            lstInput.Items.Add("V5=" + CStr(V5))
          Case 6
            Input(1, V6)
            lstInput.Items.Add("V6=" + CStr(V6))
```

```
          Case 7
            Input(1, V7)
            lstInput.Items.Add("V7=" + CStr(V7))
        End Select
      End If
   Next I
   lstInput.Items.Add("File successfully read.")
   FileClose(1)
 End Sub
```

This code checks which radio button is selected and opens/reads the appropriate file. We check the EOF condition before each **Input** statement in case we run into trouble. Admittedly, this is very ugly, clunky code, but it works to demonstrate what we need to show.

5. Save the application (saved in **Example 7-2** folder **in LearnVB\VB Code\Class 7** folder). Run the application, trying to open the four files written with the specified writing functions. We will look at each case so you can understand what's going on. It's important you recognize problems that may arise.

Recall each file has seven variables of different types:

```
   V1 = 5 ' Integer type
   V2 = "Visual Basic 2019" ` String type
   V3 = 1.23 ` Single type
   V4 = -4 ' Integer type
   V5 = True ' Boolean type
   V6 = 3.14159265359 ' Double type
   V7 = CDate("11/13/15") ' Date type
```

Write and WriteLine:

You will have no problem reading in this data from files written with **Write** and **WriteLine**. Try it! You should see this:

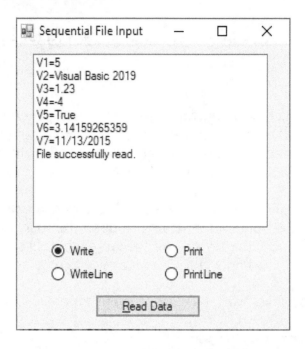

The specific formatting provided by the Write functions gives this precise performance. The Print and PrintLine files are a different story.

Print:

When you try to read the file written with **Print** (click that radio button prior to clicking **Read Data**), you will see:

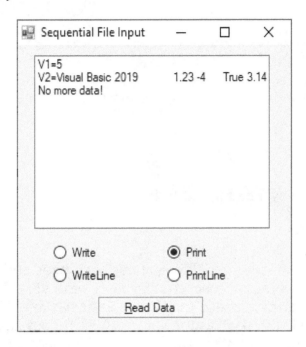

V1 is read correctly, but then the program expects a string variable. Without delimiting quotes, the program assumes everything remaining on the single line file (look back at Example 7-1 to see this line) is the string variable V2. After this, there is no data left, so the end-of-file is reached. The other five variables are not seen!

Try editing the file (**test3.txt**), putting quotes around Visual Basic 2019 (the string variable) and running the program again. You should see this error message:

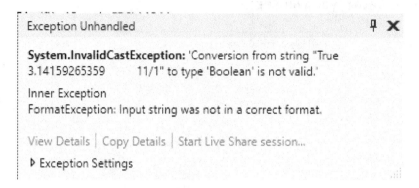

and this line in code will be highlighted:

```
Input(1, V5)
```

The problem with the string variable (V2) has been fixed and V3 and V4 are also read correctly. Trouble is encountered trying to read V5, a Boolean variable. You can see in the error message that Visual Basic has read "True 3.14159265359   11/12/2015" as the value of V5! It does not recognize this as a Boolean variable and hence stops the program. The only way to correct this problem is to start a new line (containing V6 and V7), leaving V5 at the end of this line by itself. Try it if you like. Otherwise, we cannot read the file written using the Print function. We can read it and get variable values, though. We just have to use different techniques – see the **Parsing Lines** section that follows this example.

PrintLine:

When you try to read the file written with **PrintLine** (click that radio button prior to clicking **Read Data**), you will see:

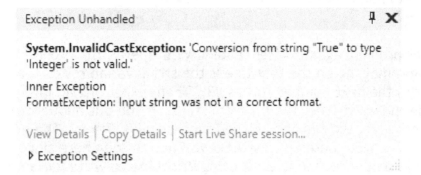

Exception Unhandled   ⊸ ✕

System.InvalidCastException: 'Conversion from string "True" to type 'Integer' is not valid.'

Inner Exception
FormatException: Input string was not in a correct format.

View Details | Copy Details | Start Live Share session...
▷ Exception Settings

and this line in code will be highlighted:

```
Input(1, V4)
```

Somehow it seems to be trying to read the fifth variable, a Boolean type, into V4. What's up? Here's the file we are trying to read:

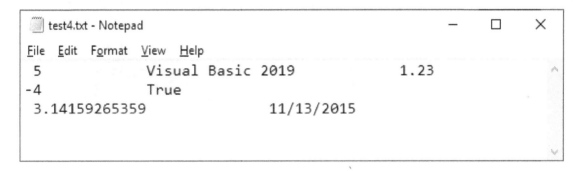

test4.txt - Notepad

File Edit Format View Help

```
 5            Visual Basic 2019          1.23
-4            True
 3.14159265359              11/13/2015
```

Using debugging tools (we'll learn how to use these later in this chapter) our application reads:

```
V1 = 5
V2 = "Visual Basic 2019      1.23"
V3 = -4
```

The quotes problem again! After reading V1 properly, the program thinks everything remaining on the first line is the string variable V2. It reads (incorrectly) the next number (-4) as V3. Then, expecting an integer number and seeing the word True, the program stops. If you put quotes around Visual Basic in **test4.txt**, the file can be read successfully. Try it. The problem with the Boolean variable noted in **test3.txt** will not be seen here since True is the last variable on the second line. If using **PrintLine** to write variables, it is best to write one variable on each line. You can usually read such files in successfully.

Parsing Data Lines

We saw that variables written to sequential files using the **Print** function (and sometimes the **PrintLine** function) may not always be read properly with the **Input** statement. One possible correction for this problem is to restructure the file so it can be read. But, many times this is not possible. If the file is coming from a source you have no control over, you need to work with what you are given. But, there's still hope. You can do anything with Visual Basic!

The approach we take is called **parsing** a line. We read in a single line as a long string. Then, we successively remove substrings from this longer line that represent each variable. To do this, we still need to know how many variables are in a line, their types and their location in the line. The location can be specified by some kind of delimiter (a quote, a space, a slash) or by an exact position within the line. All of this can be done with the Visual Basic string functions. Though here we are concerned with lines read from a sequential file, note these techniques can be applied to any string data type in Visual Basic.

The first thing we need to do is open the file with the lines to be parsed and read in each line as a string. The file is opened in **Input** mode using the **FileOpen** function. To read an entire line from a file opened as number N, use the **LineInput** function:

```
MyLine = LineInput(N)
```

where **MyLine** will be the line represented as a **string** data type. It is this line that we parse into the individual variables. Any carriage return and/or line feed characters will be stripped from **MyLine** by the **LineInput** function (these can cause trouble when parsing).

Once we have the line (**MyLine**) to parse, what we do with it depends on what we know. The basic idea is to determine the bounding character positions of each variable within the line. If the first position is **FP** and the last position is **LP**, the substring representation of this variable (**VariableString**) can be found using the Visual Basic **Mid** function:

```
VariableString = Mid(MyLine, FP, LP - FP + 1)
```

Recall this says return the substring in MyLine that starts at position FP and is LP - FP + 1 characters long.

Once we have extracted **VariableString**, we must convert it to the proper data type. Use the standard conversion functions to do this task. The **Val** function can be used to convert numeric variables. Be aware that **Val** returns a **Double** data type, so further conversion may be needed.

So, how do you determine the starting and ending positions for a variable in a line? The easiest case is when you are told by those providing the file what 'columns' bound certain data. This is common in engineering data files. Otherwise, you must know what 'delimits' variables. You can search for these delimiters using the **Instr** and **InstrRev** functions. A common delimiter is just a lot of space between each variable (you may still have trouble with strings containing spaces unless there are surrounding quotes). Other delimiters include slashes, commas, pound signs and even exclamation points. The power of Visual Basic allows you to locate any delimiters and extract the needed information. In the example that follows, we will parse the line in our example **test3.txt** file using space as a delimiter.

As variables are extracted from the input data line, we typically shorten the line (excluding the extracted substring) before looking for the next variable. The Visual Basic **Len, Mid** and **Trim** functions help in this regard. If **LP** was the last position of the substring removed from left side of **MyLine**, we shorten this line using:

```
MyLine = Trim(Mid(MyLine, LP + 1, Len(MyLine) - LP))
```

This removes the first LP characters from the left side of MyLine. The Trim function removes any leading and/or trailing spaces and MyLine is replaced by the shortened line. Notice by shortening the string in this manner, the first position for finding each extracted substring will always be 1 (**FP** = 1).

Example 7-3

Parsing Data Lines

1. Start a new project. We will build an application that opens and reads in the single line data file written with the Print function in Example 7-1. We will then parse that line to extract all the variables. As a first step, copy the **test3.txt** file into the **Bin\Debug** folder in your new project's folder (you may have to create the folder first). We want the file to be in our application path, so we can use the **Application.StartupPath** parameter to open it.

2. Add a list control and a button control to the form so it looks like this:

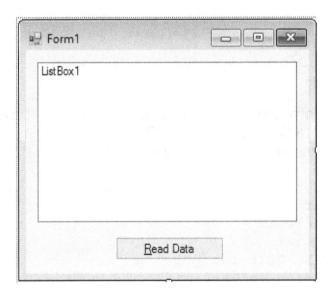

3. Set the properties of the form and each control:

Form1:
Name	frmParse
FormBorderStyle	FixedSingle
StartPosition	CenterScreen
Text	Parsing Lines

ListBox1:
Name	lstInput

Button1:
Name	btnRead
Text	&Read Data

The form should look something like this:

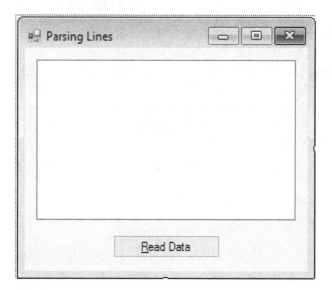

4. Use this general procedure named **GetVariable**. In this procedure, a **Delimiter** and data line (**L**) are input. The extracted string variable (**V**) and shortened data line are computed and returned.

```
Private Sub GetVariable(ByVal Delimit As String, ByRef L
As String, ByRef V As String)
    Dim LD As Integer
    'Find delimiter
    Ld = InStr(L, Delimit) - 1
    'extract string value
    V = Mid(L, 1, LD)
    'shorten line
    L = Trim(Mid(L, LD + 1, Len(L) - LD))
End Sub
```

5. Use this code in the **btnRead Click** event:

```
Private Sub BtnRead_Click(ByVal sender As System.Object,
ByVal e As System.EventArgs) Handles btnRead.Click
    Dim V1 As Integer, V2 As String, V3 As Single, V4 As
Integer
    Dim V5 As Boolean, V6 As Double, V7 As Date
    Dim MyLine As String, VariableString As String
    lstInput.Items.Clear()
    FileOpen(1, Application.StartupPath + "\test3.txt",
OpenMode.Input)
    'read in the line
    MyLine = LineInput(1)
    FileClose(1)
    'strip off leading and trailing spaces
    MyLine = Trim(MyLine)
    'find V1, an integer
    Call GetVariable(" ", MyLine, VariableString)
    V1 = CInt(Val(VariableString))
    lstInput.Items.Add("V1=" + CStr(V1))
    'find V2, a string - look for two spaces to identify
    Call GetVariable("  ", MyLine, VariableString)
    V2 = Trim(VariableString)
    lstInput.Items.Add("V2=" + CStr(V2))
    'find V3, a single type
    Call GetVariable(" ", MyLine, VariableString)
    V3 = CSng(Val(VariableString))
    lstInput.Items.Add("V3=" + CStr(V3))
    'find V4, an integer type
    Call GetVariable(" ", MyLine, VariableString)
    V4 = CInt(Val(VariableString))
    lstInput.Items.Add("V4=" + CStr(V4))
    'find V5, a Boolean type
    Call GetVariable(" ", MyLine, VariableString)
    V5 = CBool(VariableString)
    lstInput.Items.Add("V5=" + CStr(V5))
    'find V6, a double type
    Call GetVariable(" ", MyLine, VariableString)
    V6 = Val(VariableString)
    lstInput.Items.Add("V6=" + CStr(V6))
    'find V7, a date type, the last variable
    V7 = CDate(MyLine)
    lstInput.Items.Add("V7=" + CStr(V7))
    lstInput.Items.Add("File successfully read.")
End Sub
```

This code opens the file and reads the single line as a string data type. It then extracts each variable from that line. It primarily uses space as delimiters, with a little trick to extract the string variable (V2).

6. Save the application (saved in **Example 7-3** folder **in LearnVB\VB Code\Class 7** folder). Run the application. The seven variables should all display correctly in the list box:

Don't get the idea that this code worked the first time I tried it. It required several iterations. Fortunately, Visual Basic is a great platform for 'playing around.' The way I approach such problems is to look at the data and make up ad hoc rules that seem to work. Then, I keep using that code until it breaks. I then fix it and try again.

Here's the line we parsed:

In this example, I used space as a delimiter. The only trick was looking for more than a single space to delimit the string variable (**V2 = Visual Basic 2019**). Had I only looked for a single space, I would have obtained **V2 = Visual** and errors for the remaining variables. This again points out the nicety of having string variables surrounded by quotes (they make great delimiters), if at all possible.

Building Data Lines

The same Visual Basic string functions used to parse, or break up, a line of data can also be used to build a line of data that can then be used in a control such as a text box control or written to a sequential file. The primary application for such lines is to write precisely formatted data files. It allows left justification, centering and right justification of values. It also allows positioning data in any 'column' desired.

The usual approach to building data lines is to first choose the maximum number of characters that will be in each line. This length is usually established by the width of a displaying control or the width of a printed page (we'll look at this in Chapter 9). Once this maximum width is selected, each line is initialized as a blank line of that length. The Visual Basic **Space** function does this initialization. If you want a data line (**MyLine**) with **N** blank characters, use:

```
MyLine = Space(N)
```

Once the blank line is established, the spaces are filled in using the **Mid** function. Recall Mid can be used to extract substrings and to replace substrings. Here, we use the latter purpose, replacing substrings. Assume we have a substring **MySubString** we want to place at location **LP** in **MyLine**. Simply use:

```
Mid(MyLine, LP, Len(MySubString)) = MySubString
```

This particular replacement left justifies the substring. When doing these replacements, always make sure you are within the bounding length of MyLine.

So, to build a line of variable data, we decide what variables we want in each line and where we want to position them. We then successively convert each variable to a string (usually using **Format**) and place it in the line using the **Mid** function. When a line is complete, if it is for a sequential file, it is printed to the file using the **PrintLine** function:

```
PrintLine(N, MyLine)
```

where N is the number assigned to the file when it was opened. Don't use the **WriteLine** function or your neatly prepared data line will have quotes on both ends!

We don't have to use the newly constructed line in a data file. It could also be added to the **Text** property of any control. In such a case, if you want the new line on its own separate line, be sure to append the proper line feed character.

We saw how to left justify a substring in a data line. We can also center justify and right justify. To right justify **MySubString** in **MyLine** at location **RP**, use:

```
Mid(MyLine, RP + 1 - Len(MySubString), Len(MySubString)) =
MySubString
```

And to center **MySubString** in **MyLine**, use:

```
Mid(MyLine, CInt(0.5 * (Len(MyLine) - Len(MySubString))) +
1, Len(MySubString)) = MySubString
```

Of course, to center justify a substring, the substring must be shorter than the line it is being centered in. To see how both of these replacements work, just go through an example and you'll see the logic.

Most of what is presented here works best with fixed width fonts (each character is the same width). I usually use **Courier New**. You will have to experiment if using proportional fonts to obtain desired results.

Example 7-4

Building Data Lines

1. Start a new project. We will build an application that lets a user enter a minimum and maximum circle diameter. The program then computes perimeter and area for twenty circles between those two input values. We will use the **CircleGeometry** procedure developed in Example 6-2 for the computations. The computed results are displayed in tabular form.

2. Place two labels, three text box controls and a button control on your form so it looks like this:

3. Set the properties of the form and each control:

Form1:

Name	frmCircle
FormBorderStyle	FixedSingle
StartPosition	CenterScreen
Text	Circle Geometries

Label1:

Text	Minimum Diameter

TextBox1:

Name	txtMinimum

Label2:

Text	Maximum Diameter

TextBox2:

Name	txtMaximum

Button1:

Name	btnCompute
Text	&Compute Geometries

TextBox3:

Name	txtOutput
BackColor	White
Font	Courier New, Size 8
MultiLine	True
ReadOnly	True
ScrollBars	Vertical

The finished form should look something like this:

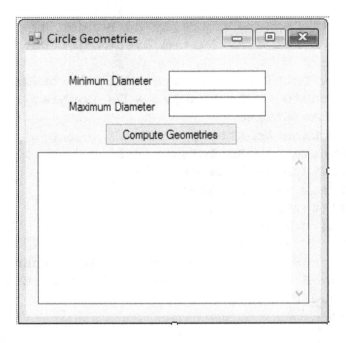

I set the width of the big text box so that it would hold 36 characters across. How? At design time, set the **Text** property to something 36 characters wide and increase the text box width until it fits!

4. Add the **CircleGeometries** general function from Example 6-2:

```
Private Sub CircleGeometry(ByVal Diameter As Double, ByRef
Circumference As Double, ByRef Area As Double)
    Circumference = Math.PI * Diameter
    Area = Math.PI * Diameter ^2 / 4
End Sub
```

5. Use this code in the **btnCompute Click** event:

```
   Private Sub BtnCompute_Click(ByVal sender As
System.Object, ByVal e As System.EventArgs) Handles
btnCompute.Click
     Dim DMin As Double, DMax As Double, Delta As Double
     Dim D As Double, C As Double, A As Double
     Dim MyLine As String
     Dim MySubString As String
     Const NumberValues As Integer = 20
     Const LineWidth As Integer = 36
     'read min/max and increment
     DMin = Val(txtMinimum.Text)
     DMax = Val(txtMaximum.Text)
     If DMin >= DMax Then
       MessageBox.Show("Maximum must be less than minimum.",
"Error", MessageBoxButtons.OK, MessageBoxIcon.Error)
       txtMinimum.Focus()
       Exit Sub
     End If
     Delta = (DMax - DMin) / NumberValues
     'center header
     MyLine = Space(LineWidth)
     MySubString = "Circle Geometries"
     Mid(MyLine, CInt(0.5 * (Len(MyLine) - Len(MySubString))
+ 1), Len(MySubString)) = MySubString
     txtOutput.Text = MyLine + ControlChars.CrLf
     txtOutput.Text += "Diameter      Perimeter        Area" +
ControlChars.CrLf
     For D = DMin To DMax Step Delta
       Call CircleGeometry(D, C, A)
       'right justify three values with two decimals
       MyLine = Space(LineWidth)
       MySubString = Format(D, "0.00")
       Mid(MyLine, 9 - Len(MySubString), Len(MySubString)) =
MySubString
       MySubString = Format(C, "0.00")
       Mid(MyLine, 23 - Len(MySubString), Len(MySubString)) =
MySubString
       MySubString = Format(A, "0.00")
       Mid(MyLine, 37 - Len(MySubString), Len(MySubString)) =
MySubString
       txtOutput.Text += MyLine + ControlChars.CrLf
     Next D
     txtMinimum.Focus()
   End Sub
```

This code reads the input and determines the diameter range. It writes some header information and then, for each diameter, computes and prints geometries. Values are right justified.

6. Save the application (saved in **Example 7-4** folder **in LearnVB\VB Code\Class 7** folder). Run the application. When I used 30 and 70 for minimum and maximum diameters, respectively, I obtain this neatly formatted table of results:

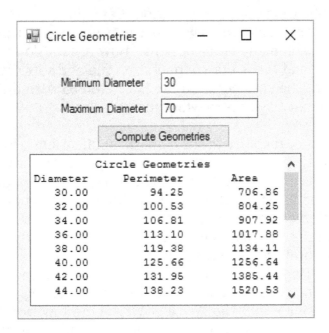

Configuration Files

In the introduction to this chapter, we discussed one possible application for a sequential file - an **initialization** or **configuration file**. These files are used to save user selected options from one execution of an application to the next. With such files, the user avoids the headache of re-establishing desired values each time an application is run.

Every Windows application uses configuration files. For example, Microsoft Word remembers your favorite page settings, what font you like to use, what toolbars you want displayed, and many other options. How does it do this? When you start Word, it opens and reads the configuration file and sets your choices. When you exit Word, the configuration file is written back to disk, making note of any changes you may have made while running Word.

You can add the same capability to Visual Basic applications. How do you decide what your configuration file will contain and how it will be formatted? That is completely up to you, the application designer. Typical information stored in a **configuration** file includes: current dates and times, check box settings, radio button settings, selected colors, font name, font style, font size, and selected menu options. You decide what is important in your application. You develop variables to save information and read and write these variables from and to the sequential configuration file. There is usually one variable (numeric, string, date, Boolean) for each option being saved. It is strongly suggested that data be written to the file using either the **Write** or **WriteLine** function. We have seen that the rigid formatting used by these functions minimizes errors when reading values back from a file.

Once you've decided on values to save and the format of your file, how do you proceed? A first step is to create an initial file using a text editor. If the number of variables being saved is relatively short, I suggest putting one variable on each line of the file. Save your configuration file in the same folder your application's executable will be written to (the **Bin\Debug** folder of your project in Visual Basic). Configuration files will always be kept in the application path. And, the usual three letter file extension for a configuration file is **ini** (for initialization). When creating a **Setup** program for an application using a configuration file, you need to include the file in **Step 4** of the **Setup Wizard** (refer to those steps in Chapter 6).

Once you have developed the configuration file, you need to write code to fit this framework:

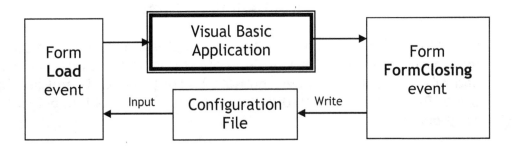

When your application begins (Form **Load** event), open (**FileOpen** function) and read (**Input** function) the configuration file and use the variables to establish the respective options. Establishing options involves things like setting Font objects, establishing colors, simulating click events on check boxes and radio buttons, and setting properties.

When your application ends (Form **FormClosing** event), examine all options to be saved, establish respective variables to represent these options, and open (**FileOpen** function) and write (**WriteLine** function, usually) the configuration file. We write the configuration file in the Form FormClosing event for two reasons. Usually an application will have an Exit button or an Exit option in the menu structure. The code to exit an application is usually:

```
Me.Close()
```

This statement will activate the Form **FormClosing** event. Also, most Windows applications have a little box with an **X** in the upper right hand corner of the form that can be used to stop an application. In fact, in most applications we have built in this class, we need to use this box to stop things. When this 'X box' is clicked, any exit routine you have coded is **ignored** and the program immediately transfers to the Form **FormClosing** event.

Example 7-5

Configuration Files

1. We will modify the Note Editor built in Chapter 6 to save four pieces of information in a configuration file: bold status, italic status, underline status and selected font size. Open the **Note Editor** project. Use either **Example 6-4** or **Problem 6-1**, if you did that problem. I use Problem 6-1 (it includes an About form).

2. Use this code in the **frmEdit Load** event procedure:

```
Private Sub FrmEdit_Load(ByVal sender As System.Object,
ByVal e As System.EventArgs) Handles MyBase.Load
    Dim I As Integer
    'Open configuration file and set font values
    FileOpen(1, Application.StartupPath + "\note.ini",
OpenMode.Input)
    Input(1, mnuFmtBold.Checked)
    Input(1, mnuFmtItalic.Checked)
    Input(1, mnuFmtUnderline.Checked)
    Input(1, I)
    Select Case I
      Case 1
        mnuFmtSizeSmall.PerformClick()
      Case 2
        mnuFmtSizeMedium.PerformClick()
      Case 3
        mnuFmtSizeLarge.PerformClick()
    End Select
    FileClose(1)
    Call ChangeFont()
  End Sub
```

In this code, the configuration file (named **note.ini**) is opened. We read three Boolean values that establish whether checks should be next to bold, italic and underline, respectively, in the menu structure. Then, an integer is read and used to set font size (1-small, 2-medium, 3-large). Note use of the **PerformClick** function to simulate clicking on the corresponding menu option.

3. Use this code in the **FrmEdit FormClosing** event procedure:

```
Private Sub frmEdit_FormClosing(ByVal sender As Object,
ByVal e As System.Windows.Forms.FormClosingEventArgs)
Handles Me.FormClosing
    'Open configuration file and write font values
    FileOpen(1, Application.StartupPath + "\note.ini",
OpenMode.Output)
    WriteLine(1, mnuFmtBold.Checked)
    WriteLine(1, mnuFmtItalic.Checked)
    WriteLine(1, mnuFmtUnderline.Checked)
    If mnuFmtSizeSmall.Checked Then
      WriteLine(1, 1)
    ElseIf mnuFmtSizeMedium.Checked Then
      WriteLine(1, 2)
    Else
      WriteLine(1, 3)
    End If
    FileClose(1)
  End Sub
```

This code does the 'inverse' of the procedure followed in the frmEdit Load event. The configuration file is opened for output. Three Boolean variables representing current status of the bold, italic, and underline check marks are written to the file. Then, an integer representing the selected font size is written prior to closing and saving the file.

4. Save the application (saved in **Example 7-5** folder **in LearnVB\VB Code\Class 7** folder). Run the application. You will see this error message:

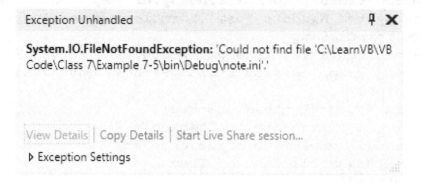

Exception Unhandled   ⟁ ✕

System.IO.FileNotFoundException: 'Could not find file 'C:\LearnVB\VB Code\Class 7\Example 7-5\bin\Debug\note.ini'.'

View Details | Copy Details | Start Live Share session...
▷ Exception Settings

and this line of code is highlighted:

```
FileOpen(1, Application.StartupPath + "\note.ini",
OpenMode.Input)
```

This message is telling us that the configuration file cannot be found. Of course, it can't – we forgot to create it! If you are using configuration files, you must always create an initial version. Open a text editor (**Notepad** will work) and type these four lines:

```
#FALSE#
#FALSE#
#FALSE#
1
```

This says that bold, italic and underline options will be unchecked (False) and the font size will be small (represented by the 1). Save this four line file as **note.ini** in the application directory (the **Bin\Debug** folder within your project folder). Try running it again and things should be fine. Try changing any of the saved options and exit the program. Run it again and you should see the selected options are still there. Any text typed will have disappeared. We'll solve the 'disappearing text' problem next when we look at how to save text in a sequential file.

Writing and Reading Text Using Sequential Files

In many applications, we would like to be able to save text information and retrieve it for later reference. This information could be a **text file** created by an application or the contents of a Visual Basic **text box** control. . Writing and reading text using sequential files involves some functions we have already seen and a couple of new ones.

To **write** a sequential text file, we follow the simple procedure: open the file (**Output** mode), write the file, close the file. If the file is a line-by-line text file, each line of the file is written to disk using a single **PrintLine** statement:

```
PrintLine(N, MyLine)
```

where **MyLine** is the current line (a text string) and **N** the integer assigned to the file when it was opened. This assumes you have somehow generated the string **MyLine**. How you generate this data depends on your particular application. The **PrintLine** statement should be in a loop that encompasses all lines of the file. You must know the number of lines in your file, beforehand. A typical code segment to accomplish this task is:

```
FileOpen(1, "c:\MyFolder\MyFile.txt", OpenMode.Output)
For I = 1 To NumberLines
.. 'need code here to generate string data MyLine
..PrintLine(1, MyLine)
Next I
FileClose(1)
```

This code writes **NumberLines** text lines to the sequential file **c:\MyFolder\Myfile.txt**.

If we want to write the contents of the **Text** property of a text box named **txtExample** to a file named **c:\MyFolder\Myfile.txt**, we only need three lines of code:

```
FileOpen(1, "c:\MyFolder\MyFile.txt", OpenMode.Output)
Print(1, txtExample.Text)
FileClose(1)
```

The text is now saved in the file for later retrieval.

To **read** the contents of a previously-saved text file, we follow similar steps to the writing process: open the file (**Input** mode), read the file, close the file. If the file is a text file, we read each individual line with the **LineInput** function:

```
MyLine = LineInput(N)
```

This line is usually placed in a **Do/Loop** structure that is repeated until all lines of the file are read in. The **EOF**() function can be used to detect an end-of-file condition, if you don't know, beforehand, how many lines are in the file. A typical code segment to accomplish this task is:

```
FileOpen(1, "c:\MyFolder\MyFile.txt", OpenMode.Input)
Do Until EOF(1)
..MyLine = LineInput(1)
   'probably need code here to do something with MyLine
Loop
FileClose(1)
```

This code reads text lines from the sequential file **c:\MyFolder\Myfile.txt** until the end-of-file is reached. You could put a counter in the loop to count lines if you like.

To place the contents of a sequential file into a text box control, we use a new function, **InputString**. Syntax for using this function is:

ReturnedString = **InputString**(N, NumberCharacters)

In this expression, **N** is the number used to open the file. **NumberCharacters** is the number of characters we read from the file and return in the variable **ReturnedString**. In this case, we want **all** the characters from the opened file. The length-of-file function (LOF) provides this information. Its syntax is:

NumberCharacters = **LOF**(N)

For a file opened with **N**, this returns the number of characters in the file (**NumberCharacters**). The returned value is of type **Long**, where the **InputString** function is expecting an **Integer** argument, so conversion is needed.

So, to place the contents of a previously saved sequential file into the **Text** property of a text box control named **txtExample**, we need these three lines of code:

```
FileOpen(1, "c:\MyFolder\MyFile.txt", OpenMode.Input)
TxtExample.Text = InputString(1, CInt(LOF(1)))
FileClose(1)
```

SaveFileDialog Control

In Toolbox:

Below Form (Default Properties):

As mentioned earlier, when a sequential file is opened in **Output** mode, if the file being opened already exists, it is first erased. This is fine for files like configuration files. We want to overwrite these files. But, for other files, this might not be desirable behavior. Hence, prior to overwriting a sequential file, we want to make sure it is acceptable. Using the **SaveFileDialog** control to obtain filenames will provide this "safety factor." This control insures that any path selected for saving a file exists and that if an existing file is selected, the user has agreed to overwriting that file.

SaveFileDialog **Properties:**

Name	Gets or sets the name of the save file dialog (I usually name this control **dlgSave**).
AddExtension	Indicates whether the dialog box automatically adds an extension to a file name if the user omits the extension.
CheckFileExists	Indicates whether the whether the dialog box displays a warning if the user specifies a file name that does not exist. Useful if you want the user to save to an existing file.
CheckPathExists	Indicates whether the dialog box displays a warning if the user specifies a path that does not exist.
CreatePrompt	Indicates whether the dialog box prompts the user for permission to create a file if the user specifies a file that does not exist.
DefaultExt	Gets or sets the default file extension.
FileName	Gets or sets a string containing the file name selected in the file dialog box.
Filter	Gets or sets the current file name filter string, which determines the choices that appear in "Files of type" box.

SaveFileDialog **Properties** (continued)

FilterIndex	Gets or sets the index of the filter currently selected in the file dialog box.
InitialDirectory	Gets or sets the initial directory displayed by the file dialog box.
OverwritePrompt	Indicates whether the dialog box displays a warning if the user specifies a file name that already exists. Default value is True.
Title	Gets or sets the file dialog box title.

SaveFileDialog **Methods:**

ShowDialog	Displays the dialog box. Returned value indicates which button was clicked by user (**OK** or **Cancel**).

The **SaveFileDialog** control will appear in the tray area of the design window. The **ShowDialog** method is used to display the **SaveFileDialog** control. For a control named **dlgSave**, the appropriate code is:

```
dlgSave.ShowDialog()
```

And the displayed dialog box is:

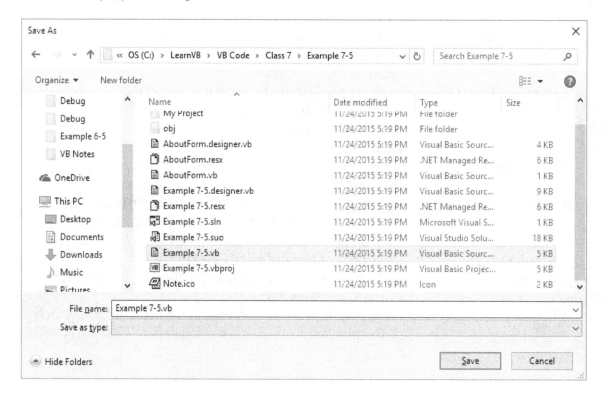

The user types a name in the File name box (or selects a file using the dialog control). The file type is selected form the **Files of type** box (values here set with the **Filter** property). Once selected, the **Save** button is clicked. **Cancel** can be clicked to cancel the save operation. If the user selects an existing file and clicks **Save**, the following dialog will appear:

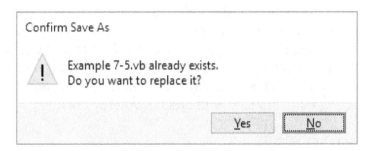

This is the aforementioned protection against inadvertently overwriting an existing file.

The ShowDialog method returns the clicked button. It returns **DialogResult.OK** if Save is clicked and returns **DialogResult.Cancel** if Cancel is clicked. The **FileName** property contains the complete path to the selected file.

Typical use of **SaveFileDialog** control:

➤ Set the **Name, DefaultExt, Filter**, and **Title** properties.
➤ Use **ShowDialog** method to display dialog box.
➤ Read **FileName** property to determine selected file

Example 7-6

Note Editor - Reading and Saving Text Files

1. We'll now add the capability to read in and save the contents of the text box in the Note Editor application we modified in Example 7-5. Load that application (saved in the **Example 7-5** folder in **LearnVB\VB Code\Class 7** folder). If you started a new project folder for this modification, make sure to copy the configuration file (**note.ini**) to the **Bin\Debug** folder in the project folder (you may have to create the folder first). Add OpenFileDialog and SaveFileDialog controls to the project's startup form.

2. Set these properties:

   OpenFileDialog1:
Name	dlgOpen
Filter	Text Files (*.txt)|*.txt
Title	Open File

   SaveFileDialog1:
Name	dlgSave
DefaultExt	txt
FileName	[Blank]
Filter	Text Files (*.txt)|*.txt
Title	Save File

3. Modify the **File** menu in your application, such that **Open** and **Save** options are included. To do this, click on the **File** option, right-click the separator bar and choose **Insert New**. A blank item will appear above the separator bar. Repeat the insert process to add another item. Type the **Text** properties. The File menu should now read:

File
    New
    Open
    Save
    ——————
    Exit

Properties for these new menu items should be:

Text	Name
&Open	mnuFileOpen
&Save	mnuFileSave

4. The two new menu options need code. Use this code in the **mnuFileOpen Click** event:

```
Private Sub MnuFileOpen_Click(ByVal sender As
System.Object, ByVal e As System.EventArgs) Handles
mnuFileOpen.Click
    If dlgOpen.ShowDialog() = DialogResult.OK Then
        FileOpen(1, dlgOpen.FileName, OpenMode.Input)
        txtEdit.Text = InputString(1, CInt(LOF(1)))
        FileClose(1)
        txtEdit.SelectionLength = 0
    End If
End Sub
```

5. And for the **mnuFileSave Click** procedure, use this code:

```
Private Sub MnuFileSave_Click(ByVal sender As
System.Object, ByVal e As System.EventArgs) Handles
mnuFileSave.Click
    If dlgSave.ShowDialog() = DialogResult.OK Then
       FileOpen(1, dlgSave.FileName, OpenMode.Output)
       Print(1, txtEdit.Text)
       FileClose(1)
    End If
End Sub
```

6. Save your application (saved in **Example 7-6** folder in the **LearnVB\VB Code\Class 7** folder). Run it and test the **Open** and **Save** functions. Note you have to save a file before you can open one.

Note, too, that after opening a file, text is displayed based on current format settings. It would be nice to save formatting information along with the text. You could do this by saving an additional file with the format settings (bold, italic, underline status and font size). Then, when opening the text file, open the accompanying format file and set the saved format. Note this is much like having a configuration file for each saved text file. See if you can make these modifications. In Class 10, we will see another text control (the rich text box) that saves formatting at the same time it saves the text.

Another thing you could try: Modify the message box that appears when you try to **Exit**. Make it ask if you wish to save your file before exiting - provide **Yes**, **No**, **Cancel** buttons. Program the code corresponding to each possible response. Use calls to existing procedures, if possible.

StreamWriter Object

The techniques studied here to write and read information to and from sequential files are 'classic' Visual Basic techniques. It's the way things have been done for years and works fine. Visual Basic includes a similar, more object-oriented approach to sequential files. For completeness, we look at this approach. We leave it to you, the reader, to decide which approach works best for you.

To write information to a sequential file, we use the **StreamWriter** object, which is part of the **System.IO** namespace. To open a file (**FileName**) for output, use:

```
Dim OutputFile As System.IO.StreamWriter
OutputFile = New System.IO.StreamWriter(FileName)
```

where **FileName** is the name (a **String**) of the file to open and **OutputFile** is the returned **StreamWriter** object used to write information to disk. To append information to an existing file, use this overloaded version of the constructor:

```
OutputFile = New System.IO.StreamWriter(FileName, True)
```

The second argument (**True**) specifies you want to add information.

When done writing to the file, it is closed using the **Close** method:

```
OutputFile.Close()
```

Once a file is closed, it is saved on the disk under the path and filename used to open the file.

Information (variables or text) is written to a sequential file in an appended fashion. Separate Visual Basic statements are required for each appending. There are two different ways to write variables to a sequential file. You choose which method you want based on your particular application.

The first method uses the **Write** method. For a file opened as **OutputFile**, the syntax is to print a variable named **MyVariable** is:

```
OutputFile.Write(MyVariable)
```

This statement will append the specified variable to the current line in the sequential file. If you only use **Write** for output, everything will be written in one very long line. And, if no other characters (**delimiters**) are entered to separate variables, they will all be concatenated together. (Note this **Write** method is equivalent to the **Print** function used in the 'classic' approach.)

Example using **Write** method:

```
Dim A As Integer = -5
Dim B As String = "Visual Basic"
Dim C As Double = 3.14159265359
Dim D As Boolean = False
Dim E As Date = CDate("11/13/2015")
Dim OutputFile As System.IO.StreamWriter
OutputFile = New
System.IO.StreamWriter("c:\junk\TestOut.txt")
OutputFile.Write(A)
OutputFile.Write(B)
OutputFile.Write(C)
OutputFile.Write(D)
OutputFile.Write(e)
OutputFile.Close()
```

After this code runs, the file **c:\junk\TestOut.txt** will have a single line with all five variables (a, b, c, d, e) concatenated together:

The other way to write variables to a sequential file is **WriteLine**, the companion to **Write**. Its syntax is:

```
OutputFile.WriteLine(MyVariable)
```

This method works identically to the **Write** method with the exception that a 'carriage return' is added, moving down a line in the file once the write is complete. It can be used to insert blank lines by omitting the variable. (Note this **WriteLine** method is equivalent to the **PrintLine** function used in the 'classic' approach.)

Example using **WriteLine** method:

```
Dim A As Integer = -5
Dim B As String = "Visual Basic"
Dim C As Double = 3.14159265359
Dim D As Boolean = False
Dim E As Date = CDate("11/13/2015")
Dim OutputFile As System.IO.StreamWriter
OutputFile = New
System.IO.StreamWriter("c:\junk\TestOut.txt")
OutputFile.WriteLine(A)
OutputFile.WriteLine(B)
OutputFile.WriteLine(C)
OutputFile.WriteLine(D)
OutputFile.WriteLine(E)
OutputFile.Close()
```

After this code runs, the file **c:\junk\TestOut.txt** will have five lines, each of the variables (a, b, c, d, e) on a separate line:

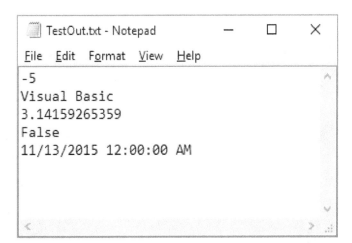

To **write** a sequential text file, we follow the simple procedure: open the file for output, write the file, close the file. If the file is a line-by-line text file, each line of the file is written to disk using a single **Write** or **WriteLine** statement. Use **Write** if a line already has a new line character appended to it. Use **WriteLine** if there is no such character. So, to write **MyLine** to **OutputFile**, use either:

```
OutputFile.Write(MyLine)
```

or

```
OutputFile.WriteLine(MyLine)
```

If we want to write the contents of the **Text** property of a text box named **txtExample** to a file named **c:\MyFolder\MyFile.txt**, we only need four lines of code:

```
Dim OutputFile As System.IO.StreamWriter
OutputFile = New
System.IO.StreamWriter("c:\MyFolder\MyFile.txt")
OutputFile.Write(txtExample.Text)
OutputFile.Close()
```

The text is now saved in the file for later retrieval.

StreamReader Object

To **read variables** from a sequential file, we essentially reverse the write procedure. First, open the file using a **StreamReader:**

```
Dim InputFile As System.IO.StreamReader
InputFile = New System.IO.StreamReader(FileName)
```

where **InputFile** is the returned file object and **FileName** is a valid path to the file.

When all values have been read from the sequential file, it is closed using:

```
InputFile.Close()
```

Recall, variables are read from a sequential file in the same order they were written. Hence, to read in variables from a sequential file, you need to know:

> How many variables are in the file
> The order the variables were written to the file
> The type of each variable in the file

Variables are read from a sequential file using the **ReadLine** method. The syntax for our example file is:

```
MyVariableString = InputFile.ReadLine()
```

where **MyVariableString** is the **String** representation of the variable being read. To retrieve the variable value from this string, we need to convert the string to the proper type. Conversions for **Integer**, **Double**, **Boolean** and **Date** variables are:

```
MyIntegerVariable = CInt(MyVariableString)
MyDoubleVariable = CDbl(MyVariableString)
MyBooleanVariable = CBool(MyVariableString)
MyDateVariable = CDate(MyVariableString)
```

Example using **ReadLine** method:

```
Dim A As Integer
Dim B As String
Dim C As Double
Dim D As Boolean
Dim E As Date
Dim InputFile As System.IO.StreamReader
InputFile = New
System.IO.StreamReader("c:\junk\TestOut.txt")
A = CInt(InputFile.ReadLine())
B = InputFile.ReadLine()
C = CDbl(InputFile.ReadLine())
D = CBool(InputFile.ReadLine())
E = CDate(InputFile.ReadLine())
InputFile.Close()
```

This code opens the file **TestOut.txt** (in the **c:\junk** folder) and sequentially reads five variables. Notice how the **ReadLine** method is used directly in the conversions. Also notice, the string variable **B** (obviously) requires no conversion.

To **read** the contents of a previously-saved text file, we follow similar steps to the writing process: open the file (**StreamReader** object), read the file, close the file. If the file is a text file, we read each individual line with the **ReadLine** method:

```
MyLine = InputFile.ReadLine()
```

The **Peek** method can be used to detect an end-of-file condition, if you don't know, beforehand, how many lines are in the file. A typical code segment to accomplish this task is:

```
Dim InputFile As System.IO.StreamReader
InputFile = New System.IO.StreamReader(myFile)
Do
  MyLine = InputFile.ReadLine()
  ' do something with the line of text
While (InputFile.Peek() <> -1)
```

This code reads text lines from the sequential file **MyFile** until the end-of-file is reached. You could put a counter in the loop to count lines if you like.

To place the contents of a sequential file into a text box control, we use a new method, **ReadToEnd**. This method reads a text file until the end is reached. So, to place the contents of a previously saved sequential file (**c:\MyFolder\MyFile.txt**) into the **Text** property of a text box control named **txtExample**, we need these four lines of code:

```
Dim InputFile As System.IO.StreamReader
InputFile = New
System.IO.StreamReader("c:\junk\testout.txt")
txtExample.Text = InputFile.ReadToEnd()
InputFile.Close()
```

This completes our review of the **StreamWriter** and **StreamReader** objects. You decide which you prefer. I personally prefer the 'classic' method approach to Write and WriteLine with the specific variable formatting. This avoids the conversion of strings to variable types as needed with the **StreamReader**.

Error Handling

No matter how hard we try, **errors** do creep into our applications. These errors can be grouped into three categories:

1. **Syntax** errors
2. **Run-time** errors
3. **Logic** errors

Syntax errors occur when you mistype a command, leave out an expected phrase or argument, or omit needed punctuation. Visual Basic and the Intellisense feature detects these errors as they occur and even provides help in correcting them. You cannot run a Visual Basic program until all syntax errors have been corrected. The **Task** window in the Visual Basic IDE lists all syntax errors and identifies the line they occur in. To help locate syntax errors, it is advisable to turn on the line number option in the code window. To do this, select the **Tools** menu item in the IDE. Then, choose **Options**. In the left side of the window that appears, choose **Text Editor** (and perhaps **Basic**). Then, choose the **Line Numbers** option.

Run-time errors are usually beyond your program's control. Examples include: when a variable takes on an unexpected value (divide by zero), when a drive door is left open, or when a file is not found. We saw examples of run-time errors in building some of our sequential file examples. In Example 7-2, we encountered end-of-file problems and invalid data type errors. In Example 7-5, we encountered a missing file error when trying to read a configuration file. Visual Basic lets us trap such errors and make attempts to correct them. Doing so precludes our program from unceremoniously stopping. User's do not like programs that stop unexpectedly!

Logic errors are the most difficult to find. With logic errors, the program will usually run, but will produce incorrect or unexpected results. The Visual Basic debugger is an aid in detecting logic errors.

Some ways to minimize errors are:

> ➢ Always use **Option Strict** in your code.
> ➢ Design your application carefully. More design time means less debugging time.
> ➢ Use comments where applicable to help you remember what you were trying to do.
> ➢ Use consistent and meaningful naming conventions for your variables, controls, objects, and procedures.

Run-Time Error Trapping and Handling

Run-time errors (also called **exceptions**) are trappable. That is, Visual Basic recognizes an error has occurred and enables you to trap it and take corrective action (handle the error). As mentioned, if an error occurs and is not trapped, your program will usually end in a rather unceremonious manner. Most run-time errors occur when your application is working with files, either trying to open, read, write or save a file. Other common run-time errors are divide by zero, overflow (exceeding a data type's range) and improper data types.

Visual Basic uses a structured approach to trapping and handling errors. The structure is referred to as a **Try/Catch/Finally** block. And the annotated syntax for using this block is:

Try
  'here is code you try where some kind of error may occur
    .
    .
Catch *Exception* **AS** *Type*
  'if error described by *Exception* of *Type* occurs, process this code
    .
    .
Catch
  'if any other error occurs, process this code
    .
    .
Finally
  'Execute this code whether error occurred or not
  'this block is optional
    .
    .
End Try

The above code works from the top, down. It 'tries' the code between **Try** and the first **Catch** statement. If no error is encountered, any code in the **Finally** block will be executed and the program will continue after the **End Try** statement. If an error (exception) occurs, the program will look to find, if any, the first **Catch** statement (you can have multiple Catch statements) that matches the exception that occurred. If one is found, the code in that respective block is executed (code to help clear up the error – the error handling), then the code in the **Finally** block, then program execution continues after **End Try**. If an error occurs that doesn't match a particular exception, the code in the 'generic' **Catch** block is executed, followed by the code in the **Finally** block. And, program execution continues after the **End Try** statement.

This structure can be used to trap and handle any **Type** of exception defined in the Visual Basic **Exception** class. There are hundreds of possible exceptions related to data access, input and output functions, graphics functions, data types and numerical computations. Here is a list of example exception types (their names are descriptive of the corresponding error condition):

```
ArgumentException              ArgumentNullException
ArgumentOutOfRangeException     ArithmeticException
ArrayTypeMismatchException      DivideByZeroException
DllNotFoundException            Exception
FormatException                 IndexOutOfRangeException
IO.DirectoryNotFoundException   IO.EndOfStreamException
IO.FileNotFoundException        IO.IOException
OutOfMemoryException            OverflowException
```

Let's take a closer look at the **Catch** block. When you define a Catch block, you specify a name for the exception and define the exception type you want to catch. For example, if want to catch a **DivideByZeroException**, we use:

```
Catch MyException As DivideByZeroException
    'Code to execute if divide by zero occurs
```

If in the **Try** block, a divide by zero occurs, the code following this **Catch** statement will be executed. You would probably put a message box here to tell the user what happened and provide him or her with options of how to fix the problem. To help with the messaging capability, the variable you define as the exception (**MyException**, in this case) has a **Message** property you can use.

A **Try/End Try** loop may be exited using the **Exit Try** statement. Be aware any code in the **Finally** block will still be executed even if an Exit Try is encountered. Once the Finally code is executed, program execution continues after the End Try statement.

Example of **Try/End Try** block to catch an end-of-file error:

```
Try
   'Code to open file
Catch EOFError As IO.EndOfStreamException
   MessageBox.Show(EOFError.Message)
Finally
   'Code to close file (even if error occurred)
End Try
```

Example of a **generic** error trapping routine:

```
Try
   'Code to try
Catch MyException As Exception
   MessageBox.Show(MyException.Message)
Finally
   'Code to execute before leaving block
End Try
```

We've only taken a brief look at the structured run-time error handling capabilities of Visual Basic. It is difficult to be more specific without knowing just what an application's purpose is. You need to know what type of errors you are looking for and what corrective actions should be taken if these errors are encountered. As you build and run your own applications, you will encounter run-time errors. These errors may be due to errors in your code. If so, fix them. But, they may also be errors that arise due to some invalid inputs from your user, because a file does not meet certain specifications or because a disk drive is not ready. You need to use error handling to keep such errors from shutting down your application, leaving your user in a frustrated state.

Example 7-7

Note Editor - Error Trapping

1. Many times, users may delete files (including configuration files) not knowing what they're doing. In this example, we modify the Note Editor application (again) so that if the configuration file cannot be found, the program will still run. We use error trapping to catch the 'file not found' exception. If the file can't be found, we'll establish values for the four missing format variables and continue Load Example 7-6 (saved in the **Example 7-6** folder in **LearnVB\VB Code\Class 7** folder). Make sure the **note.ini** file is not in your project's **Bin\Debug** folder. We want to see if our program works without it.

2. Modify the **frmEdit Load** event to enable error trapping (new code is shaded):

```
Private Sub FrmEdit_Load(ByVal sender As System.Object,
ByVal e As System.EventArgs) Handles MyBase.Load
   Dim I As Integer
   Try
      'Open configuration file and set font values
      FileOpen(1, Application.StartupPath + "\note.ini",
OpenMode.Input)
      Input(1, mnuFmtBold.Checked)
      Input(1, mnuFmtItalic.Checked)
      Input(1, mnuFmtUnderline.Checked)
      Input(1, I)
      Select Case I
        Case 1
          mnuFmtSizeSmall.PerformClick()
        Case 2
          mnuFmtSizeMedium.PerformClick()
        Case 3
          mnuFmtSizeLarge.PerformClick()
      End Select
   Catch IOExcept As IO.FileNotFoundException
      MessageBox.Show("Configuration file not found.",
"Default Reset")
      mnuFmtBold.Checked = False
      mnuFmtItalic.Checked = False
      mnuFmtUnderline.Checked = False
      mnuFmtSizeSmall.PerformClick()
   Finally
      FileClose(1)
   End Try
   Call ChangeFont()
End Sub
```

In this code, if the file is not found, the **Catch** block establishes values for the bold, italic and underline status (all False) and a font size (small). This allows the program to run to completion.

3. Save your application (saved in **Example 7-7** folder in the **LearnVB\VB Code\Class 7** folder). Run it and you should see this:

If you don't get this message and the program runs, stop the application and delete the **note.ini** file from the project's folder **Bin\Debug** folder. Then, run again and you should see the above message box generated in the Catch block.

Choose some formatting features, stop the application and run it again. The error message box will not be seen – why? The reason you don't see the error message again is that when you exited the program, it wrote the **note.ini** file in the proper folder. The neat thing about such code is that we fixed a problem without the user even knowing there was a problem.

Debugging Visual Basic Programs

We now consider the search for, and elimination of, **logic errors**. These are errors that don't prevent an application from running, but cause incorrect or unexpected results. Logic errors are sometimes difficult to find; they may be very subtle. Visual Basic provides an excellent set of **debugging** tools to aid in this search.

A typical logic error could involve an **If/End If** structure. Look at this example:

```
If A > 5 And B < 4 Then
..'do this code
ElseIf A = 6 Then
  'do this code
End If
```

In this example, if A = 6 and B =2, the **ElseIf** statement (which you wanted executed if A = 6) will never be seen. In this case, swap the two **If** clauses to get the desired behavior. Or, another possible source of a logic error:

```
FileOpen(1, dlgOpen.FileName, OpenMode.Output)
Input(1, MyVariable)
```

In this little 'snippet,' a file the user selected using an file open dialog control is opened and the first variable read. It looks okay, but what if the user selected a file that really wasn't meant to be used by your application. This would be a classic case of GIGO (garbage in – garbage out).

Debugging code is an art, not a science. There are no prescribed processes that you can follow to eliminate all logic errors in your program. The usual approach is to eliminate them as they are discovered.

What we'll do here is present the debugging tools available in the Visual Basic environment and describe their use with an example. You, as the program designer, should select the debugging approach and tools you feel most comfortable with. The more you use the debugger, the more you will learn about it. Fortunately, the simpler tools will accomplish the tasks for most debugging applications.

The interface between your application and the debugging tools is via several different windows in the Visual Basic IDE: the **Output window**, the **Locals** window, the **Breakpoints** window, the **Watch** window, and the **Auto** window. These windows can be accessed from the **View** and **Debug** menus (the Output window can also be accessed by pressing **Ctrl+G**). Or, they can be selected from the dropdown button on the **Debug Toolbar** (accessed using the **Toolbars** option under the **View** menu):

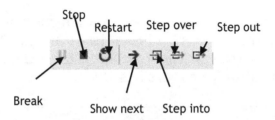

We will examine buttons on this toolbar as we continue. This toolbar can be customized with more features using the **Options** button. Consult on-line help for the procedure to do this.

All debugging using the debug windows is done when your application is in **debugging** (or **break**) mode. Recall the application mode is always displayed in the title bar of Visual Basic. You usually enter debugging mode by setting **breakpoints** (we'll look at this in a bit), pressing the **Break** button on the toolbar or when your program encounters an untrapped run-time error, the program usually goes into debugging mode.

Once in debugging mode, the debug windows and other tools can be used to:

> ➢ Determine values of variables
> ➢ Set breakpoints
> ➢ Set watch variables and expressions
> ➢ Manually control the application
> ➢ Determine which procedures have been called
> ➢ Change the values of variables and properties

The best way to learn proper debugging is do an example. We'll build that example now, then learn how to use the Visual Basic debugger.

Example 7-8

Debugging Example

1. This example simply has a form with two button controls used to execute some code. You can either build it or just load it from the course notes (saved in **Example 7-8** folder in **LearnVB\VB Code\Class 7** folder).

2. If you choose to build, start a new application and put two button controls on the form. **Name** the buttons **btnProcedure1** and **btnProcedure2**. Set the buttons' **Text** properties to **Run Procedure &1** and **Run Procedure &2**, respectively. My little form looks like this:

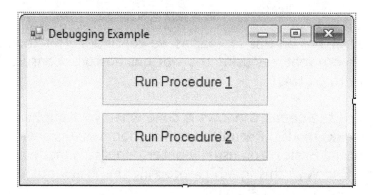

3. The application has two variables with form level scope:

```
Dim XCount As Integer, YSum As Integer
```

XCount keeps track of the number of times each of two counter variables is incremented. **YSum** sums all computed Y values.

4. The two form level variables are initialized in the **frmDebug Load** event:

```
Private Sub FrmDebug_Load(ByVal sender As System.Object,
ByVal e As System.EventArgs) Handles MyBase.Load
    XCount = 0
    YSum = 0
End Sub
```

5. The first button's **Name** property is **btnProcedure1**. The code for its **Click** event is:

```
Private Sub BtnProcedure1_Click(ByVal sender As
System.Object, ByVal e As System.EventArgs) Handles
btnProcedure1.Click
    Dim X1 As Integer, Y1 As Integer
    X1 = -1
    Do
      X1 += 1
      Y1 = Fcn(X1)
      XCount += 1
      YSum += Y1
    Loop Until X1 = 20
  End Sub
```

This code uses a **Do/Loop** structure to increment the counter variable **X1** from 0 to 20. For each X1, a corresponding **Y1** is computed using the general function **Fcn**. In each cycle of the Do/Loop, the form level variables **XCount** and **YSum** are adjusted accordingly.

6. The general function (**Fcn**) used by this procedure is:

```
Private Function Fcn(ByVal X As Integer) As Integer
   Dim Value As Double
   Value = 0.1 * X ^ 2
   Return (CInt(Value))
End Function
```

This code just computes an 'integer parabola.' No need to know what that means. Just recognize, given an X value, it computes and returns a Y.

7. The **Click** event for the second button (**Name btnProcedure2**) is:

```
Private Sub BtnProcedure2_Click(ByVal sender As
System.Object, ByVal e As System.EventArgs) Handles
btnProcedure2.Click
    Dim X2 As Integer, Y2 As Integer
    For X2 = -10 To 10
      Y2 = 5 * Fcn(X2)
      XCount += 1
      YSum += Y2
    Next X2
End Sub
```

This code is similar to that for the other button. It uses a **For/Next** structure to increment the counter variable **X2** from -10 to 10. For each X2, a corresponding **Y2** is computed using the same general function **Fcn**. In each cycle of the For/Next loop, the form level variables **XCount** and **YSum** are adjusted accordingly.

8. Save and run the application (as mentioned, saved in **Example 7-8** folder in **LearnVB\VB Code\Class 7** folder). Notice not much happens if you click either button. Admittedly, this code doesn't do much, especially without any output, but it makes a good example for looking at debugger use. So, get ready to try debugging.

Using the Debugging Tools

There are several **debugging tools** available for use in Visual Basic. Access to these tools is provided via both menu options and buttons on the **Standard** and **Debug** toolbars. Some of the tools we will examine are:

> ➢ **Breakpoints** which let us stop our application.
> ➢ **Locals, Watch** and **Autos windows** which let us examine variable values.
> ➢ **Call stack** which let us determine how we got to a certain point in code.
> ➢ **Step into**, **step over** and **step out** which provide manual execution of our code.

These tools work in conjunction with the various debugger windows.

Writing to the Output Window:

There is even a simpler debugging tool than any of those mentioned above. You can write directly to the **output** window while an application is running. Sometimes, this is all the debugging you may need. A few carefully placed write statements can sometimes clear up all logic errors, especially in small applications. To write to the output window, use the **WriteLine** method of the **Debug** object:

Debug.WriteLine(StringData)

This will write the string information **StringData** as a line in the output window. Hence, the output window can be used as a kind of scratch pad for your application. Any information written here is just for your use. Your users will never see it. You also must maintain the output window. Nothing is ever deleted. To manually clear the window, right-click it and select **Clear All**.

Debug.WriteLine Example:

1. Modify the **btnProcedure1 Click** event in Example 7-8 by including the shaded line:

```
Private Sub BtnProcedure1_Click(ByVal sender As
System.Object, ByVal e As System.EventArgs) Handles
btnProcedure1.Click
    Dim X1 As Integer, Y1 As Integer
    X1 = -1
    Do
      X1 += 1
      Y1 = Fcn(X1)
      Debug.WriteLine(Str(X1) + Str(Y1))
      XCount += 1
      YSum += Y1
    Loop Until X1 = 20
  End Sub
```

Run the application. Click the **Run Procedure 1** button.

2. Examine the output window. To view the output window, select the **Debug** menu option, then **Windows**. Select **Output** from the next submenu. You should see this:

```
Output                                                    ▼ ↧ X
Show output from:  Debug                              ▼  ⦿       ''
 'Example 7-8.vshost.exe' (CLR v2.0.50727: Example 7-8.vshost.exe)▲
  0 0
  1 0
  2 0
  3 1
  4 2
  5 2
  6 4
  7 5
  8 6
  9 8
 10 10
 11 12
 12 14
 13 17
 14 20
 15 22
 16 26
 17 29
 18 32
 19 36
 20 40
The thread 0x1568 has exited with code 0 (0x0).
The thread 0x83c has exited with code 0 (0x0).
 |                                                            ▼
```

Note how, at each iteration of the loop, the program prints the value of X1 and Y1. You can use this information to make sure X1 is incrementing correctly, ending at the proper value and that Y1 values look acceptable. You can get a lot of information using Debug.WriteLine. If needed, you can add additional text information (treat as strings) in the WriteLine argument to provide specific details on what is printed (variable names, procedure names, etc.).

3. Before leaving this example, delete the **Debug.WriteLine** statement.

Breakpoints:

In the above example, the program ran to completion before we could look at the output window. In many applications, we want to stop the application while it is running, examine variables and then continue running. This can be done with **breakpoints.** A breakpoint marks a line in code where you want to stop (temporarily) program execution, that is force the program into **debugging** mode. One way to set a breakpoint is to put the cursor in the line of code you want to break at and press **<F9>**. Or, a simpler way is to click next to the desired line of code in the vertical shaded bar at the left of the code window:

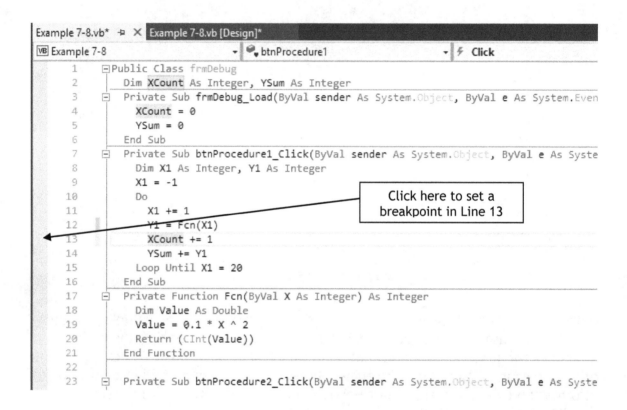

```
Example 7-8.vb*  ⊟  ✕  Example 7-8.vb [Design]*
VB Example 7-8                        ▼ • btnProcedure1              ▼ ⚡ Click
     1    ⊟Public Class frmDebug
     2        Dim XCount As Integer, YSum As Integer
     3    ⊟    Private Sub frmDebug_Load(ByVal sender As System.Object, ByVal e As System.Even
     4          XCount = 0
     5          YSum = 0
     6        End Sub
     7    ⊟    Private Sub btnProcedure1_Click(ByVal sender As System.Object, ByVal e As Syste
     8          Dim X1 As Integer, Y1 As Integer
     9          X1 = -1
    10          Do
    11            X1 += 1
    12            Y1 = Fcn(X1)
    13            XCount += 1
    14            YSum += Y1
    15          Loop Until X1 = 20
    16        End Sub
    17    ⊟    Private Function Fcn(ByVal X As Integer) As Integer
    18          Dim Value As Double
    19          Value = 0.1 * X ^ 2
    20          Return (CInt(Value))
    21        End Function
    22
    23    ⊟    Private Sub btnProcedure2_Click(ByVal sender As System.Object, ByVal e As Syste
```

Click here to set a breakpoint in Line 13

Once set, a large red dot marks the line along with shading:

```
Example 7-8.vb* ⇥ ✕  Example 7-8.vb [Design]*
[VB] Example 7-8                        ▼  ⬢, btnProcedure1              ▼  ⚡ Click
    1      ⊟Public Class frmDebug
    2          Dim XCount As Integer, YSum As Integer
    3      ⊟  Private Sub frmDebug_Load(ByVal sender As System.Object, ByVal e As System.Event
    4            XCount = 0
    5            YSum = 0
    6          End Sub
    7      ⊟  Private Sub btnProcedure1_Click(ByVal sender As System.Object, ByVal e As System.
    8            Dim X1 As Integer, Y1 As Integer
    9            X1 = -1
   10            Do
   11               X1 += 1
   12               Y1 = Fcn(X1)
●  13               XCount += 1
   14               YSum += Y1
   15            Loop Until X1 = 20
   16          End Sub
   17      ⊟  Private Function Fcn(ByVal X As Integer) As Integer
   18            Dim Value As Double
   19            Value = 0.1 * X ^ 2
   20            Return (CInt(Value))
   21          End Function
   22
   23      ⊟  Private Sub btnProcedure2_Click(ByVal sender As System.Object, ByVal e As System.
   24            Dim X2 As Integer, Y2 As Integer
```

To remove a breakpoint, repeat the above process. Pressing **<F9>** or clicking the line at the left will 'toggle' the breakpoint. If you need to clear all breakpoints in an application, select the **Debug** menu item and the **Delete All Breakpoints** option. Breakpoints can be added/deleted at **design** time or in **debugging** mode.

When you run your application, Visual Basic will stop when it reaches lines with breakpoints and allow you to check variables and expressions. To continue program operation after a breakpoint, press **<F5>**, click the **Continue** button on the toolbar, or choose **Continue** from the **Debug** menu.

Breakpoint Example:

1. Set a breakpoint on the **XCount += 1** line in the **btnProcedure1 Click** event (as demonstrated above). Run the program and click the **Run Procedure 1** button. The program will stop at the desired line (it will be highlighted). Hold the cursor over **X1** two lines above this line and you should see:

```
 7     ⊟    Private Sub btnProcedure1_Click(ByVal sender As System.Object, By\
 8             Dim X1 As Integer, Y1 As Integer
 9             X1 = -1
10             Do
11                 X1 += 1
12                 Y1 ⬤ X1 0 ⏏
13                 XCount += 1
14                 YSum += Y1
15             Loop Until X1 = 20
16           End Sub
```

Notice a tooltip appears displaying the current value of this variable (**X1 0**). You can move the cursor onto any variable in this procedure to see its value. If you check values on lines prior to the line with the breakpoint, you will be given the current value. If you check values on lines at or after the breakpoint, you will get their last computed value.

2. Continue running the program (click the **Continue** button or press **<F5>**). The program will again stop at this line, but **X1** will now be equal to **1**. Check it. Continue running the program, examining **X1** and **Y1** (and **XCount** and **YSum** too).

3. Try other breakpoints in the application if you have time. Once done, make sure you clear all the breakpoints you used.

Viewing Variables in the Locals Window:

In the breakpoint example, we used tooltips to examine variable values. We could see variable values, no matter what their scope. The **locals** window can also be used to view variables, but only those with procedure level scope. As execution switches from procedure to procedure, the contents of the local window change to reflect only the variables applicable to the current procedure. The locals window can be viewed using the **Locals** button on the debug toolbar or select the **Debug** menu option, choose **Windows**, then **Locals**.

Locals Window Example:

1. Set breakpoints on the **XCount += 1** lines in both the **btnProcedure1 Click** event and the **btnProcedure2 Click** event. Run the program and click the **Run Procedure 1** button. The program will stop at the desired line. View the locals window and you should see:

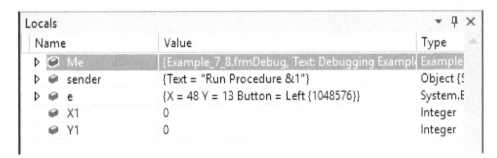

Name	Value	Type
▷ Me	{Example_7_8.frmDebug, Text: Debugging Exampl	Example
▷ sender	{Text = "Run Procedure &1"}	Object {
▷ e	{X = 48 Y = 13 Button = Left {1048576}}	System.E
X1	0	Integer
Y1	0	Integer

All the variables local to the this procedure are seen. Continue running the application (click **Continue** button or press **<F5>**), watching X1 and Y1 change with each loop execution.

2. Eventually, the application form will reappear. When it does, click the **Run Procedure 2** button. The program will stop at the desired line in that procedure and you will see:

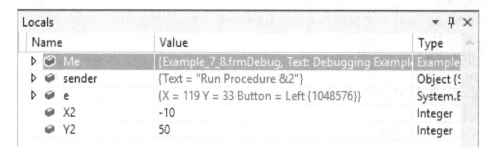

which are initial values for the local variables (X2 and Y2) in this procedure. Continue running, watching the values change. Stop the example whenever you want. Remove the breakpoint in the **btnProcedure2 Click** event.

Viewing Variables in the Watch Window:

Watch windows can also be used to examine variables. They can maintain values for both local and form level variables. And, you can even change the values of variables in the watch window (be careful if you do this; strange things can happen). The watch window can only be accessed in **debugging** mode. At that time, you simply right-click on any variables you want to add to the watch window and select the **Add Watch** option. A watch window can be viewed using the **Watch** button on the debug toolbar or select the **Debug** menu option, choose **Windows**, then **Watch,** then one of four available watch windows.

Watch Window Example:

1. Make sure there is still a breakpoint on the `XCount += 1` line in the **btnProcedure1 Click** event. Run the program and click the **Run Procedure 1** button. The program will stop at the desired line. Open a watch window. Right-click on the **XCount** variable and select **Add Watch.** Do the same for the **YSum** variable. You should now see:

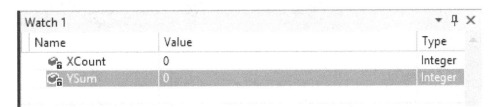

The current value of **XCount** and **YSum** are seen. They are both zero. Continue running the application (click **Continue** button or press **<F5>**), watching XCount and YSum change with each loop execution.

2. When the form reappears, click **Run Procedure 2.** Then, click **Run Procedure 1** again. The program will again stop at the marked line. The values of XCount and YSum should have changed significantly with the new values added when the btnProcedure2 Click event was executed.

The two watch variables can be deleted by right-clicking the variable name in the watch window and selecting **Delete Watch.** Again, you can only do this in **debugging** mode.

Viewing Variables in the Autos Window:

The **autos window** combines features of the locals and watch windows. This window displays values of all local and form level variables for the current procedure. As program control moves from one procedure to another, the autos window adapts to the new variable set. The autos window can only be accessed in **debugging** mode. The auto window can be selecting the **Debug** menu option, choose **Windows**, then **Autos**.

Autos Window Example:

1. Set breakpoints on the **XCount += 1** lines in both the **btnProcedure1 Click** event and the **btnProcedure2 Click** event. Run the program and click the **Run Procedure 1** button. The program will stop at the desired line. View the autos window and you should see:

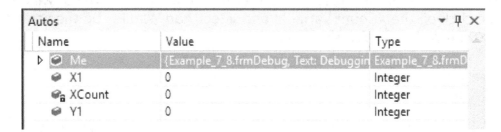

All the variables used in this procedure (local and form level scope) are seen. Continue running the application (click **Continue** button or press **<F5>**), watching the values change with each loop execution.

2. Eventually, the application form will reappear. When it does, click the **Run Procedure 2** button. The program will stop at the desired line in that procedure and you will see:

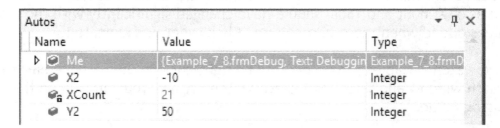

which are current values for the local and form level scope variables in this procedure. Continue running, watching the values change. Stop the example whenever you want. Remove all breakpoints.

Call Stack Window:

General functions and procedures can be called from many places in an application. That's the idea of using a general function or procedure! If an error occurs in such a function or procedure, it is helpful to know which procedure was calling it. While in debugging mode, the **Call Stack** window will provide will display all active procedures, that is those that have not been exited. The call stack window provides a road map of how you got to the point you are in the code. The call stack window can be viewed using the **Call Stack** button on the debug toolbar or select the **Debug** menu option, choose **Windows**, then **Call Stack**.

Call Stack Window Example:

1. Set a breakpoint on the `Value = 0.1 * X ^ 2` line in the general function procedure (**Fcn**). Run the application. Click **Run Procedure 1**. The program will break at the marked line. Open the call stack window and you will see:

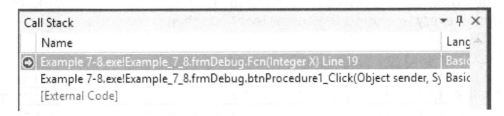

These lines tell us we are in the **Fcn** procedure and it was called by the **btnProcedure1_Click** procedure on a form named **frmDebug**. This would be very useful information if there were an error occurring in the function.

2. Keep running the application until the form appears again. Click **Run Procedure 2** and view the call stack window. You should now be able to see the function has been called by **btnProcedure2_Click**.

Single Stepping (Step Into) An Application:

A powerful feature of the Visual Basic debugger is the ability to manually control execution of the code in your application. The **Step Into** option lets you execute your program one line at a time. It lets you watch how variables change (in the locals window) or how your form changes, one step at a time.

Once in debugging mode (at a breakpoint), you can use **Step Into** by pressing **<F11>**, choosing the **Step Into** option in the **Debug** menu, or by clicking the **Step Into** button on the toolbar:

You may choose to step through several lines at a time by using **Run To Cursor** option. With this option, click on a line below your current point of execution. Right-click that line and select **Run to Cursor** from the menu.. The program will run through every line up to the cursor location, then stop.

Step Into Example:

1. Set a breakpoint at the `For X2 = - 10 To 10` line in the **btnProcedure2 Click** event. Run the application. Click **Run Procedure 2**. The program will stop and the marked line will be highlighted in the code window:

```
22
23    Private Sub btnProcedure2_Click(ByVal sender As System.Object, ByVal e As Syste
24        Dim X2 As Integer, Y2 As Integer
25        For X2 = -10 To 10
26            Y2 = 5 * Fcn(X2)
27            XCount += 1
28            YSum += Y2
29        Next X2
30
31    End Sub
```

2. Open the locals window and use the **Step Into** button to single step through the program. It's fun to see the program logic being followed. Notice how the contents of the locals window change as program control moves from the **btnProcedure2 Click** event to the general function **Fcn**. When you are in the btnProcedure2 Click procedure, values for **X2** and **Y2** are listed. When in the function, values for **X** and **Value** are given.

3. At some point, put the cursor on the **End Sub** line in the **btnProcedure2 Click** event. Try the **Run To Cursor** option (right-click while on the code line). The procedure will finish its **For/Next** loop without stopping again. Now, press **<F5>** to continue and the form will reappear.

Procedure Stepping (Step Over):

Did you notice in the example just studied that, after a while, it became annoying to have to single step through the function evaluation at every step of the For/Next loop? While single stepping your program, if you come to a procedure or function call that you know operates properly, you can perform **procedure stepping**. This simply executes the entire procedure at once, treating as a single line of code, rather than one step at a time.

To move through a procedure in this manner, while in debugging mode, press **<F10>**, choose **Step Over** from the **Debug** menu, or press the **Step Over** button on the toolbar:

Step Over Example:

1. Run the previous example. Single step through it a couple of times.

2. One time through, when you are at the line calling the **Fcn** function, press the **Step Over** button. Notice how the program did not single step through the function as it did previously.

Function Exit (Step Out):

While stepping through your program, if you wish to complete the execution of a procedure (or function) you are in, without stepping through it line-by-line, choose the **Step Out** option. The procedure will be completed and you will be returned to the procedure accessing that function.

To perform this step out, press **Shift+<F11>**, choose **Step Out** from the **Debug** menu, or press the **Step Out** button on the toolbar

Step Out Example:

1. Run the previous example. Single step through it a couple of times. Also, try stepping over the function.

2. At some point, while single stepping through the function, press the **Step Out** button. Notice how control is immediately returned to the calling procedure (**btnProcedure2 Click** event).

3. At some point, while in the **btnProcedure2 Click** event, press the **Step Out** button. The procedure will be completed and the application form will reappear with the two button controls displayed.

Debugging Strategies

We've looked at each debugging tool briefly. Be aware this is a cursory introduction. Use the on-line help to delve into the details of each tool described. In particular, you might like to look at the **immediate window** and the **breakpoints** window. In the immediate window, you can type any legal BASIC construct. You can print variable values, change values and run little snippets of code. In the breakpoints window, you can see a summary of all breakpoints and even add counters which keep track of how many times a breakpoint has been reached.

Only through lots of use and practice can you become a proficient debugger. You'll get this practice, too. Every time your application encounters a run-time error, you will enter debugging mode where you can start using your new found debugging skills.

There are some common sense guidelines to follow when debugging. My first suggestion is: keep it **simple**. Many times, you only have one or two bad lines of code. And you, knowing your code best, can usually quickly narrow down the areas with bad lines. Don't set up some elaborate debugging procedure if you haven't tried a simple approach to find your error(s) first. Many times, just a few intelligently-placed **Debug.WriteLine** statements or a few examinations of the watch and locals windows can solve your problem.

A tried and true approach to debugging can be called **Divide and Conquer**. If you're not sure where your error is, guess somewhere in the middle of your application code. Set a breakpoint there. If the error hasn't shown up by then, you know it's in the second half of your code. If it has shown up, it's in the first half. Repeat this division process until you've narrowed your search.

And, of course, the best debugging strategy is to be careful when you first design and write your application to minimize searching for errors later.

Class Review

After completing this class, you should understand:

> ➢ How to read and write sequential files (and the difference between using Write, WriteLine, Print and PrintLine functions)
> ➢ How to parse and build a text string
> ➢ How to use configuration files in an application
> ➢ How to use the FileSaveDialog control to save files
> ➢ How to use the StreamWriter and StreamReader objects
> ➢ How to implement run-time error trapping and handling in a Visual Basic procedure
> ➢ How to use the various capabilities of the Visual Basic debugger to find and eliminate logic errors

Practice Problems 7

Problem 7-1. Option Saving Problem. Load **Problem 4-1** (in the **LearnVB\VB Code\Class 4** folder), the practice problem used to examine sample message boxes. Modify this program to allow saving of the user inputs when application ends. Use a text file to save the information. When the application begins, it should reflect this set of saved inputs.

Problem 7-2. Text File Problem. Build an application that lets you look through your computer directories for text files (.txt extension) and view those files in a text box. The image viewer (Example 5-4) built in Class 5 is a good starting point.

Problem 7-3. Data File Problem. In the **LearnVB\VB Code\Class 7\Problem 7-3** folder is a file entitled **MAR95.DAT**. Open this file using the Windows Notepad. The first several lines of the file are:

```
144
"4/27/95","Detroit          ",2,3,0,"Opening Night  "
"4/28/95","Detroit          ",2,8,2,"               "
"4/29/95","Detroit          ",2,11,1,"               "
"4/30/95","Detroit          ",2,1,10,"               "
"5/1/95","Texas             ",1,4,1,"               "
"5/2/95","Texas             ",1,15,3,"               "
"5/3/95","Texas             ",1,5,1,"               "
"5/5/95","California        ",1,0,10,"               "
"5/6/95","California        ",1,5,7,"               "
"5/7/95","California        ",1,3,2,"               "
```

This file chronicles the strike-shortened 1995 season of the Seattle Mariners baseball team, their most exciting year up until 2001. (Our apologies to foreign readers who don't understand the game of baseball!) The first line tells how many lines are in the file. Each subsequent line represents a single game. There are six variables on each line:

Variable Number	Variable Type	Description
1	String	Date of Game
2	String	Opponent
3	Integer	(1-Away game, 2-Home game)
4	Integer	Mariners runs
5	Integer	Opponent runs
6	String	Comment

Write an application that reads this file, determines which team won each game and outputs to another file (a comma-separated, or **csv**, file) the game number and current Mariners winning or losing streak (consecutive wins or losses). Use positive integers for wins, negative integers for losses.

As an example, the corresponding output file for the lines displayed above would be:

    1,1 (a win)
    2,2 (a win)
    3,3 (a win)
    4,-1 (a loss)
    5,1 (a win)
    6,2 (a win)
    7,3 (a win)
    8,-1 (a loss)
    9,-2 (a loss)
    10,1 (a win)

There will be 144 lines in this output file. Load the resulting file in Excel and obtain a bar chart for the output data.

Problem 7-4. Debugging Problem. Load the **Problem 7-4** project in the **LearnVB\VB Code\Class 7\Problem 7-4** folder. It's the temperature conversion example from Class 4 with some errors introduced. Run the application. It shouldn't run. Debug the program and get it running correctly.

Exercise 7-1

Information Tracking

Design and develop an application that allows the user to enter (on a daily basis) some piece of information that is to be saved for future review and reference. Examples could be stock price, weight, or high temperature for the day. The input screen should display the current date and an input box for the desired information. All values should be saved on disk for future retrieval and update. A scroll bar should be available for reviewing all previously-stored values.

Exercise 7-2

'Recent Files' Menu Option

Under the File menu on nearly every application (that opens files) is a list of the four most recently-used files (usually right above the Exit option). Modify your information tracker to implement such a feature. This is not trivial -- there are lots of things to consider. For example, you'll need a file to store the last four file names. You need to open that file and initialize the corresponding menu entries when you run the application -- you need to rewrite that file when you exit the application. You need logic to re-order file names when a new file is opened or saved. You need logic to establish new menu items as new files are used. You'll need additional error-trapping in the open procedure, in case a file selected from the menu no longer exists. Like I said, a lot to consider here.

8. Graphics Techniques with Visual Basic

Review and Preview

In Chapter 5, we looked at using the picture box control to display graphics files. In this chapter, we extend our graphics programming skills to learn how to perform simple animations, build little games, draw lines, rectangles and ellipses and do some basic plotting of lines, bars and pie segments. Most of the examples in this class will be relatively short. We show you how to do many graphics tasks. You can expand the examples to fit your needs.

Simple Animation

One of the more fun things to do with Visual Basic programs is to create animated graphics. We'll look at a few simple **animation** techniques here. In Chapter 9, we look at even more detailed animations.

One of the simplest animation effects is achieved by **toggling** between two **images**. For example, you may have a picture of a stoplight with a red light. By quickly changing this picture to one with a green light, we achieve a dynamic effect - animation. Other two image animations could be open and closed file drawers, open and closed mail or smiling and frowning faces. The **Picture Box** control is used to achieve this animated effect.

The idea here is simple. A picture box control displays some picture (set via the **Image** property). Some event, for example clicking on the picture box or clicking on a button control, occurs. When this event occurs, we want to change or toggle the **Image** property to another picture.

In Chapter 5, we saw that one way to change the Image property of a picture box control at run-time was via the **FromFile** method of the **Image** object. You need to provide this method with a complete path to the graphics file to load into the picture box. Once given this path, the **FromFile** method loads the image from the specified disk file. In a simple animation, accessing a disk file each time the picture is toggled can cause problems. First, for detailed graphics files, the toggling effect may be slowed as the file is loaded. Second, you must insure the graphics file being accessed exists in the specified directory. Finally, if you plan to distribute your application, you need to remember to include any graphics files with the deployment package. Let's simplify this process a bit.

A better approach to simple animation is to include, in your project, an additional picture box control for each picture in the animation sequence (here, just two pictures). Set the **Image** property (at design time) of these controls to the pictures in the sequence. Set the **Visible** property of these controls to **False** so they are not seen at run-time. You will still have the visible picture box displaying the animation. Upon detection of the toggling event, simply set the **Image** property of this displaying picture box to the **Image** property of the appropriate 'hidden' picture box. With this approach, toggling is quick and no disk files are accessed. The graphics in the sequence are 'attached' to the form and do not have to be included as separate files with any deployment package.

The BASIC code for 'two-state' simple animation is straightforward. Define a form level scope variable (**PictureNumber**) that keeps track of the currently displayed picture (either a 1 or 2).

```
Dim PictureNumber As Integer
```

Then, in the toggling event procedure use this code (**picDisplay** is the displaying picture box control, **picChoice1** is a hidden picture box with one graphic, **picChoice2** is another hidden picture box with the 'toggled' graphic):

```
If PictureNumber = 1 Then
  picDisplay.Image = picChoice2.Image
  PictureNumber = 2
Else
  picDisplay.Image = picChoice1.Image
  PictureNumber = 1
End If
```

One question you may be asking is where do I get the graphics for toggling pictures? Search web sites and find graphics files available for purchase. You've probably seen the CD-ROM sets with 100,000 graphics! Also, look for icons and bitmaps installed on your computer by other applications.

Example 8-1

Simple Animation

1. Start a new application. We'll build a simple animation example. Place three picture box controls on the form. The form should look like this:

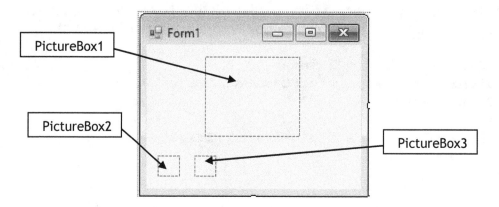

2. Set the following properties:

Form1:

Name	frmSimple
FormBorderStyle	SingleFixed
StartPosition	CenterScreen
Text	Simple Animation

PictureBox1:

Name	picDisplay
Image	image0.gif (found in **Example 8-1** folder of **LearnVB\VB Code\Class 8** folder)
SizeMode	StretchImage
Visible	True

PictureBox2:

Name	picChoice1
Image	image0.gif (found in **Example 8-1** folder of **LearnVB\VB Code\Class 8** folder)
SizeMode	StretchImage
Visible	False

PictureBox3:

Name	picChoice2
Image	image1.gif (found in **Example 8-1** folder of **LearnVB\VB Code\Class 8** folder)
SizeMode	StretchImage
Visible	False

When done, my form looks like this:

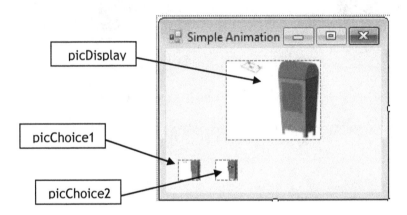

picDisplay is our display box, while the other picture box controls (**picChoice1** and **picChoice2**) store the images we toggle.

3. Use this form level scope declaration that declares and initializes **PictureNumber**:

```
Dim PictureNumber As Integer = 1
```

4. Use the following code in the **picDisplay Click** procedure:

```
Private Sub PicDisplay_Click(ByVal sender As
System.Object, ByVal e As System.EventArgs) Handles
picDisplay.Click
    If PictureNumber = 1 Then
      picDisplay.Image = picChoice2.Image
      PictureNumber = 2
    Else
      picDisplay.Image = picChoice1.Image
      PictureNumber = 1
    End If
End Sub
```

5. Save and run the application (saved in **Example 8-1** folder in **LearnVB\VB Code\Class 8** folder). Click the graphic and watch the letter go in the mailbox. Here's the sequence:

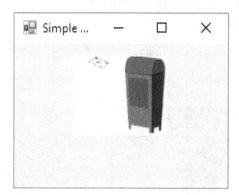
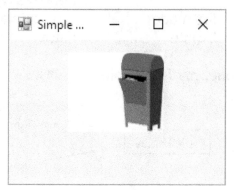

Timer Control

In Toolbox:

⏱ Timer

Below Form (Default Properties):

⏱ Timer1

If want to expand simple animation to more than two graphics, the first step is to add additional pictures to the sequence. But, then how do we cycle through the pictures? We could ask a user to keep clicking on a button or picture to see all the pictures. That's one solution, but perhaps not a desirable one. What would be nice is to have the pictures cycle without user interaction. To do this, we need to have the capability to generate events without user interaction.

The Visual Basic **Timer** control (looked at very briefly way back in Class 1) provides this capability of generating events. The timer control is very easy to implement and provides useful functionality beyond simple animation tasks. Other control events can be detected while the timer control processes events in the background. This multi-tasking allows more than one thing to be happening in your application.

Timer **Properties:**

Name	Gets or sets the name of the timer control (three letter prefix is **tim**).
Enabled	Used to turn the timer on and off. When True, timer control continues to operate until the Enabled property is set to False.
Interval	Number of milliseconds (there are 1000 milliseconds in one second) between each invocation of the timer control's **Tick** event.

Timer **Events:**

Tick	Event procedure invoked every **Interval** milliseconds while timer control's **Enabled** property is **True**.

To use the **Timer** control, we add it to our application the same as any control. There is no user interface, so it will appear in the tray area below the form in the design window. You write code in the timer control's **Tick** event. This is the code you want to repeat every **Interval** milliseconds. In the animation-sequencing example, this is where you would change the picture box **Image** property.

The timer control's **Enabled** property is **False** at design time. You 'turn on' a timer in code by changing this property to **True**. Usually, you will have some control that toggles the timer control's **Enabled** property. That is, you might have a button that turns a timer on and off. The logical **Not** operator is very useful for this toggling operation. If you have a timer control named **timExample**, this line of code will turn it on (set Enabled to True) if it is off (Enabled is False). It will do the reverse if the timer is already on:

```
timExample.Enabled = Not(timExample.Enabled)
```

It is best to start and end applications with the timer controls off (**Enabled** set to **False**).

Applications can (and many times do) have multiple timer controls. You need separate timer controls if you have events that occur with different regularity (different **Interval** values). Timer controls are used for two primary purposes. First, you use timer controls to periodically repeat some code segment. This is what we need to expand our animation example. Second, you can use a timer control to implement some 'wait time' established by the **Interval** property. In this case, you simply start the timer and when the Interval is reached, have the **Tick** event turn its corresponding timer off.

Typical use of **Timer** control:

> ➤ Set the **Name** property and **Interval** property.
> ➤ Write code in **Tick** event.
> ➤ At some point in your application, set **Enabled** to **True** to start timer. Also, have capability to reset **Enabled** to **False**, when desired.

Example 8-2

Timer Control

1. Start a new application. We want an application that generates a beep every second. Place a single button control on the form. Add a Timer control. Set the following properties:

    Form1:
Name	frmTimer
FormBorderStyle	SingleFixed
StartPosition	CenterScreen
Text	Timer Example

    Button1:
Name	btnBeep
Text	&Start Beeping

    Timer1:
Name	timBeep
Interval	1000

When done, my form looks like this:

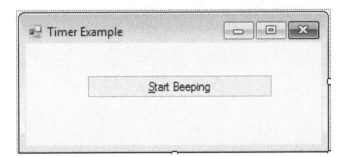

Other controls in tray:

⏱ timBeep

2. Use this code in the **btnBeep Click** event (this code toggles the timer and button text):

```
Private Sub BtnBeep_Click(ByVal sender As System.Object,
ByVal e As System.EventArgs) Handles btnBeep.Click
    'toggle timer and button text
    timBeep.Enabled = Not (timBeep.Enabled)
    If timBeep.Enabled Then
      btnBeep.Text = "&Stop Beeping"
    Else
      btnBeep.Text = "&Start Beeping"
    End If
End Sub
```

3. Use the following code in the **timBeep Tick** procedure to make the beep:

```
Private Sub TimBeep_Tick(ByVal sender As System.Object,
ByVal e As System.EventArgs) Handles timBeep.Tick
    Beep()
End Sub
```

4. Save and run the application (saved in **Example 8-2** folder in **LearnVB\VB Code\Class 8** folder). Start and stop the beeping until you get tired of hearing it. If you don't hear a beep, it's probably because your computer has no internal speaker. The beep sound does not usually play through sound cards.

Basic Animation

We return to the question of how to do animation with more than two pictures. More detailed animations are obtained by rotating through several pictures - each a slight change in the previous picture. This is the principle motion pictures are based on. In a movie, pictures flash by us at 24 frames per second and our eyes are tricked into believing things are smoothly moving.

Basic animation is done in a Visual Basic application by adding hidden picture controls for each picture in the animation sequence. A timer control changes the display - with each **Tick** event, a new picture is seen. Once the end of the sequence is reached, you can 'loop' back to the first picture and repeat or you can simply stop. To achieve this effect in code, we have a form level scope variable that keeps track of the currently displayed **PictureNumber**:

```
Dim PictureNumber As Integer
```

You need to initialize this at some point, either in this declaration or when you start the timer.

Assume we have **N** pictures to cycle through. We will have N hidden picture controls with the respective animation pictures. If **picDisplay** is the displaying picture box control and **picChoice1** through **picChoiceN** are the hidden picture boxes, the code in the timer control's Tick event is:

```
Select Case PictureNumber
  Case 1
    picDisplay.Image = picChoice1.Image
  Case 2
    picDisplay.Image = picChoice2.Image
  Case 3
    picDisplay.Image = picChoice3.Image
    .
   'there will be a Case for each picture up to N
    .
End Select
PictureNumber += 1
```

You would need to check when **PictureNumber** exceeds **N**. When it does, you can stop the sequence (set timer control's **Enabled** property to **False**). Or, you can reset **PictureNumber** to **1** to repeat the animation sequence.

More elaborate effects can be achieved by moving an image while, at the same time, changing the displayed picture. Effects such as a little guy walking across the screen are easily achieved. Appearance of control movement is achieved by incrementing or decrementing the **Left** and **Top** properties. For example, to move our picture box (**picDisplay**) 20 pixels to the right at the same time we update the picture, we use:

```
picDisplay.Left += 20
```

The techniques shown here work fine for animation sequences with fewer than 10 pictures or so. With more pictures, you need to use more sophisticated tools. Consult Visual Basic on-line help for information about the **ImageList** control. It is helpful with animations.

Example 8-3

Basic Animation

1. Start a new application. We'll build an animation example that uses the timer control to display a spinning earth! Place seven picture box controls and a button control on the form. Add a timer control. The form should look like this::

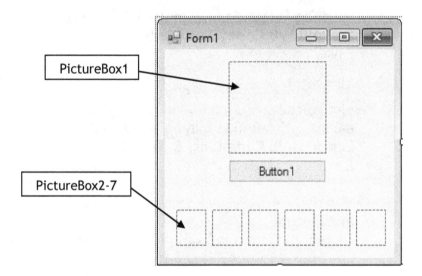

Other controls in tray:

⏱ Timer1

2. Set the following properties:

Form1:

Name	frmAnimation
FormBorderStyle	SingleFixed
StartPosition	CenterScreen
Text	Animation Example

PictureBox1:
    Name   picDisplay
    Image   earth0.gif (found in **Example 8-3** folder of **LearnVB\VB Code\Class 8** folder)
    SizeMode   StretchImage
    Visible   True

PictureBox2:
    Name   picChoice1
    Image   earth0.gif (found in **Example 8-3** folder of **LearnVB\VB Code\Class 8** folder)
    Visible   False

PictureBox3:
    Name   picChoice2
    Image   earth1.gif (found in **Example 8-3** folder of **LearnVB\VB Code\Class 8** folder)
    Visible   False

PictureBox4:
    Name   picChoice3
    Image   earth2.gif (found in **Example 8-3** folder of **LearnVB\VB Code\Class 8** folder)
    Visible   False

PictureBox5:
    Name   picChoice4
    Image   earth3.gif (found in **Example 8-3** folder of **LearnVB\VB Code\Class 8** folder)
    Visible   False

PictureBox6:
    Name   picChoice5
    Image   earth4.gif (found in **Example 8-3** folder of **LearnVB\VB Code\Class 8** folder)
    Visible   False

PictureBox7:
    Name   picChoice6
    Image   earth5.gif (found in **Example 8-3** folder of **LearnVB\VB Code\Class 8** folder)
    Visible   False

Button1:

Name	btnTimer
Text	Start/Stop

Timer1:

Name	timAnimation
Interval	500

When done, my form looks like this:

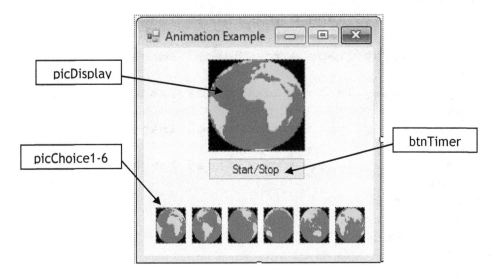

picDisplay is our display box, while the other picture box controls (**picChoice1**, **picChoice2**, **picChoice3**, **picChoice4**, **picChoice5** and **picChoice6**) store the images we cycle through.

3. Use this form level scope declaration that declares and initializes **PictureNumber:**

```
Dim PictureNumber As Integer = 1
```

4. Use the following code in the **btnTimer Click** procedure to toggle the timer:

```
Private Sub BtnTimer_Click(ByVal sender As System.Object,
ByVal e As System.EventArgs) Handles btnTimer.Click
    timAnimation.Enabled = Not (timAnimation.Enabled)
End Sub
```

5. Use this code in the **timAnimation Tick** event to cycle through the different pictures (I choose to repeat the sequence when the end is reached):

```
Private Sub TimAnimation_Tick(ByVal sender As
System.Object, ByVal e As System.EventArgs) Handles
timAnimation.Tick
    Select Case PictureNumber
      Case 1
        picDisplay.Image = picChoice1.Image
      Case 2
        picDisplay.Image = picChoice2.Image
      Case 3
        picDisplay.Image = picChoice3.Image
      Case 4
        picDisplay.Image = picChoice4.Image
      Case 5
        picDisplay.Image = picChoice5.Image
      Case 6
        picDisplay.Image = picChoice6.Image
    End Select
    PictureNumber += 1
    If PictureNumber > 6 Then
      PictureNumber = 1
    End If
End Sub
```

6. Save and run the application (saved in **Example 8-3** folder in **LearnVB\VB Code\Class 8** folder). Start and stop the timer control and watch the earth spin! Here's my spinning earth::

Add this line of code after the `PictureNumber += 1` line in the timer **Tick** event:

```
picDisplay.Left += 10
```

This will make the picture move to the right at the same time it is spinning. Make your form fairly wide. Run the application again and watch the earth 'walk off' the right side of the form. Can you think of logic that makes it scroll around to the left side after it disappears? Just study the geometry of the situation (**Left** and **Width** properties).

Random Numbers (Revisited) and Games

A fun thing to do with Visual Basic is to create **games**. You can write games that you play against the computer or against another opponent. Graphics and animations play a big part in most games. And, each time we play a game, we want the response to be different. It would be boring playing a game like Solitaire if the same cards were dealt each time you played. Here, we review the random number object introduced back in Chapter 2.

To introduce chaos and randomness into games, we use **random numbers**. Random numbers are used to have the computer roll a die, spin a roulette wheel, deal a deck of cards, and draw bingo numbers. Visual Basic develops random numbers using a built-in **random number generator**.

The random number generator we use in Visual Basic must be declared and constructed. The statement to do this (assuming the object is named **MyRandom**):

```
Dim MyRandom As New Random()
```

This statement is placed with the variable declaration statements.

Once constructed, when you need a random integer value, use the **Next** method of this Random object:

```
MyRandom.Next(Limit)
```

This statement generates a random integer value that is greater than or equal to 0 and less than **Limit**. Note it is less than limit, not equal to. For example, the method:

```
MyRandom.Next(5)
```

will generate random numbers from 0 to 4. The possible values will be 0, 1, 2, 3 and 4.

Random Object **Examples:**

To roll a six-sided die, the number of spots would be computed using:

```
NumberSpots = MyRandom.Next (6) + 1
```

To randomly choose a card from a deck of 52 cards (indexed from 1 to 52), use:

```
CardValue = MyRandom.Next(52) + 1
```

To pick a number from 0 to 100, use:

```
Number = MyRandom.Next(101)
```

Let's use our new animation skills and random numbers to build a little game.

Example 8-4

One-Buttoned Bandit

1. Start a new application. In this example, we will build a computer version of a slot machine. We'll use random numbers and timers to display three random pictures. Certain combinations of pictures win you points. You'll need seven picture box controls (three for display, four for hiding pictures), a panel control, two label controls, two button controls and two timer controls. The form should look like this:

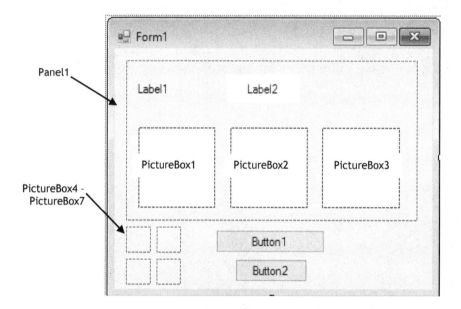

Other controls in tray:

2. Set the following properties:

Form1:

Name	frmBandit
AcceptButton	btnSpin
FormBorderStyle	FixedSingle
StartPosition	CenterScreen
Text	One-Buttoned Bandit

Panel1:

Name	pnlBandit
BackColor	Blue

Label1:

AutoSize	False
BackColor	Blue
Font	Microsoft Sans Serif, Bold, Italic, Size 14
ForeColor	Yellow
Text	Bankroll
TextAlign	MiddleLeft

Label2:

Name	lblBank
AutoSize	False
BackColor	White
BorderStyle	Fixed3D
Font	Microsoft Sans Serif, Bold, Size 14
Text	100
TextAlign	MiddleCenter

PictureBox1:

Name	picBandit1
BackColor	White
BorderStyle	Fixed3D
SizeMode	StretchImage

PictureBox2:

Name	picBandit2
BackColor	White
BorderStyle	Fixed3D
SizeMode	StretchImage

PictureBox3:

Name	picBandit3
BackColor	White
BorderStyle	Fixed3D
SizeMode	StretchImage

PictureBox4:

Name	picChoice1
Image	arrow.gif (in **Example 8-4** folder in **LearnVB\VB Code\Class 8** folder)
SizeMode	StretchImage
Visible	False

PictureBox5:

Name	picChoice2
Image	ball.gif (in **Example 8-4** folder in **LearnVB\VB Code\Class 8** folder)
SizeMode	StretchImage
Visible	False

PictureBox6:

Name	picChoice3
Image	bullseye.gif (in **Example 8-4** folder in **LearnVB\VB Code\Class 8** folder)
SizeMode	StretchImage
Visible	False

PictureBox7:

Name	picChoice4
Image	jackpot.gif (in **Example 8-4** folder in **LearnVB\VB Code\Class 8** folder)
SizeMode	StretchImage
Visible	False

Button1:

Name	btnSpin
Text	&Spin It

Button2:

Name	btnExit
Text	E&xit

Timer1:

Name	timSpin
Enabled	False
Interval	100

Timer2:

Name	timDone
Enabled	False
Interval	2000

When done, the form should look something like this:

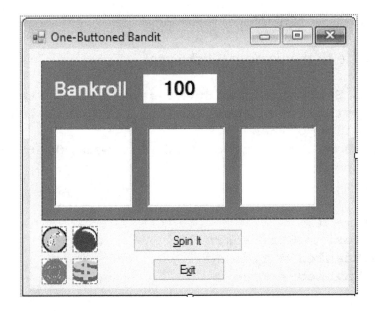

A few words on what we're doing. We will randomly fill the three large picture boxes by choosing from the four choices in the non-visible picture boxes. One timer (**timSpin**) will be used to flash pictures (every 0.1 seconds) in the boxes. One timer (**timDone**) will be used to time the entire process (lasts 2.0 seconds).

3. Use this code for form level scope declarations (**Bankroll** is your winnings):

```
Dim Bankroll As Integer
Dim MyRandom As New Random()
```

4. Use this code in the **frmBandit Load** procedure.

```
Private Sub FrmBandit_Load(ByVal sender As System.Object,
ByVal e As System.EventArgs) Handles MyBase.Load
    Bankroll = CInt(Val(lblBank.Text))
End Sub
```

Here, we initialize your bankroll.

5. Attach this code to the **btnSpin_Click** event.

```
Private Sub BtnSpin_Click(ByVal sender As System.Object,
ByVal e As System.EventArgs) Handles btnSpin.Click
    If Bankroll = 0 Then
      MessageBox.Show("Out of Cash!", "Game Over",
MessageBoxButtons.OK)
      Me.Close()
    End If
    Bankroll -= 1
    lblBank.Text = Str(Bankroll)
    timSpin.Enabled = True
    timDone.Enabled = True
  End Sub
```

Here, we first check to see if you're out of cash. If so, the game ends. If not, you are charged 1 point and the timers are turned on.

6. This is the code for the **timSpin Tick** event.

```
Private Sub TimSpin_Tick(ByVal sender As System.Object,
ByVal e As System.EventArgs) Handles timSpin.Tick
    picBandit1.Image = ShowImage(MyRandom.Next(4) + 1)
    picBandit2.Image = ShowImage(MyRandom.Next(4) + 1)
    picBandit3.Image = ShowImage(MyRandom.Next(4) + 1)
End Sub
```

which uses this **ShowImage** general function:

```
Private Function ShowImage(ByVal PictureNumber As Integer)
As Image
    Select Case PictureNumber
      Case 1
        Return (picChoice1.Image)
      Case 2
        Return (picChoice2.Image)
      Case 3
        Return (picChoice3.Image)
      Case 4
        Return (picChoice4.Image)
      Case Else
        Return (Nothing)
    End Select
End Function
```

Every 0.1 seconds (100 milliseconds), the three visible picture boxes are filled with a random image. This gives the effect of the spinning slot machine.

7. And, the code for the **timDone Tick** event. This event is triggered after the bandit spins for 2 seconds (2000 milliseconds).

```
  Private Sub TimDone_Tick(ByVal sender As System.Object,
ByVal e As System.EventArgs) Handles timDone.Tick
    Dim P1 As Integer, P2 As Integer, P3 As Integer
    Dim Winnings As Integer
    Const FACE As Integer = 4
    timSpin.Enabled = False
    timDone.Enabled = False
    'pick final pictures and see if it's a winner
    P1 = MyRandom.Next(4) + 1
    P2 = MyRandom.Next(4) + 1
    P3 = MyRandom.Next(4) + 1
    picBandit1.Image = ShowImage(P1)
    picBandit2.Image = ShowImage(P2)
    picBandit3.Image = ShowImage(P3)
    If P1 = FACE Then
      Winnings = 1
      If P2 = FACE Then
        Winnings = 3
        If P3 = FACE Then
          Winnings = 10
        End If
      End If
    ElseIf P1 = P2 Then
      Winnings = 2
      If P2 = P3 Then Winnings = 4
    End If
    Bankroll = Bankroll + Winnings
    lblBank.Text = Str(Bankroll)
  End Sub
```

First, the timers are turned off. Final pictures are displayed in each position. Then, the pictures are checked to see if you won anything.

8. Use this code in the **btnExit Click** event.

```
    Private Sub BtnExit_Click(ByVal sender As System.Object,
ByVal e As System.EventArgs) Handles btnExit.Click
    MessageBox.Show("You ended up with" + Str(Bankroll) + "
points.", "Game Over", MessageBoxButtons.OK)
    Me.Close()
    End Sub
```

When you exit, your final earnings are displayed in a message box.

9. Save and run the application (saved in **Example 8-4** folder in **LearnVB\VB Code\Class 8** folder). See if you can become wealthy. Here's what I got after a few spins:

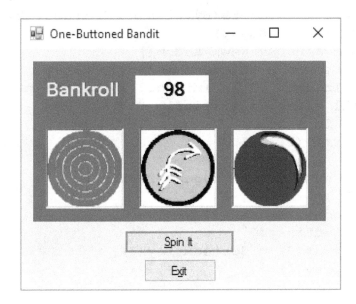

I'm quitting before I lose too much! If you have time, try these things.

   A. Rather than display the three final pictures almost simultaneously, see if you can stop each picture from spinning at a different time. You'll need a few more **Timer** controls.

   B. Do something flashy when you win something!!

   C. See if you can figure out the logic I used to specify winning. See if you can show the one-buttoned bandit returns 95.3 percent of all the 'money' put in the machine. (Hint: there are 64 possible combinations of pictures, each one equally likely.) This is higher than what Vegas machines return. But, with truly random operation, Vegas is guaranteed their return. They can't lose!

Randomly Sorting Integers

In many games, we have the need to randomly sort a sequence of integers. For example, to shuffle a deck of cards, we sort the integers from 1 to 52. To randomly sort the state names in a states/capitals game, we would randomize the values from 1 to 50.

Randomly sorting N integers is a common task. Here is a procedure that does that task. Calling arguments for the procedure are **N** (the largest integer to be sorted) and an array, **SortedArray**, dimensioned to N elements. After calling the routine **SortIntegers**, the N randomly sorted integers are returned in SortedArray. Note the procedure randomizes the integers from 1 to N, not 0 to N - the zeroth array element is ignored.

```
Private Sub SortIntegers(ByVal N As Integer, ByVal
SortedArray() As Integer)
  Dim RandomValue As New Random()
  'Randomly sorts N integers in SortedArray
  Dim I As Integer, J As Integer, T As Integer
  'Order all elements initially
  For I = 1 To N
    SortedArray(I) = I
  Next I
  'J is the number of integers remaining
  For J = N To 2 Step -1
    I = RandomValue.Next(J) + 1
    T = SortedArray(J)
    SortedArray(J) = SortedArray(I)
    SortedArray(I) = T
  Next J
End Sub
```

Look at the code, one number is pulled from the original sorted array and put at the bottom of the array. Then a number is pulled from the remaining unsorted values and put at the 'new' bottom. This selection continues until all the numbers have been sorted. This routine has been called a 'one card shuffle' because it's like shuffling a deck of cards by pulling one card out of the deck at a time and laying it aside in a pile.

This procedure has a wide range of applications. We'll use it in Exercise 8-1 to play Blackjack. I've used it to randomize the letters of the alphabet, scramble words in spelling games, randomize answers in multiple choice tests, and even playback compact disc songs in random order (yes, you can build a CD player with Visual Basic).

Example 8-5

Random Integers

1. Start a new application. We want an application that randomly sorts a selected number of integers. Add a list box control, a numeric updown control and a button control to the form. The form should look like this:

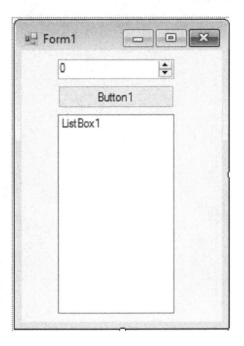

2. Set the following properties:

Form1:

Name	frmRandom
FormBorderStyle	SingleFixed
StartPosition	CenterScreen
Text	Random Sort

NumericUpDown1:

Name	nudValue
Maximum	100
Minimum	2
TextAlign	Right
Value	2

Button1:

Name	btnSort
Text	&Sort Integers

ListBox1:

Name	lstValues

When done, my form looks like this:

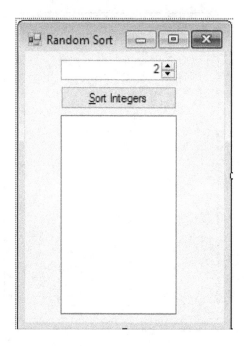

3. Include the **SortIntegers** procedure:

```
Private Sub SortIntegers(ByVal N As Integer, ByVal
SortedArray() As Integer)
    Dim RandomValue As New Random()
    'Randomly sorts N integers and puts results in
SortedArray
    Dim I As Integer, J As Integer, T As Integer
    'Order all elements initially
    For I = 1 To N
      SortedArray(I) = I
    Next I
    'J is the number of integers remaining
    For J = N To 2 Step -1
      I = RandomValue.Next(J) + 1
      T = SortedArray(J)
      SortedArray(J) = SortedArray(I)
      SortedArray(I) = T
    Next J
  End Sub
```

4. Use this code in the **btnSort Click** event procedure:

```
Private Sub BtnSort_Click(ByVal sender As System.Object,
ByVal e As System.EventArgs) Handles btnSort.Click
    Dim ArraySize As Integer
    ArraySize = CInt(nudValue.Value)
    Dim IntegerArray(ArraySize) As Integer, I As Integer
    'Clear list box
    lstValues.Items.Clear()
    'sort  integers
    Call SortIntegers(ArraySize, IntegerArray)
    'display sorted integers
    For I = 1 To ArraySize
      lstValues.Items.Add(Str(IntegerArray(I)))
    Next I
  End Sub
```

This code reads the value of the updown control establishes the array dimension and calls **SortIntegers**. The sorted values are displayed in the list box control.

5. Save and run the application (saved in **Example 8-5** folder in **LearnVB\VB Code\Class 8** folder). Try sorting different numbers of integers. Here's a couple of runs I did sorting 10 integers:

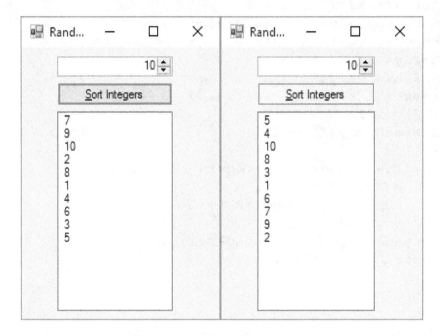

Notice you get different results every time you do a sort.

Graphics Methods

We now know how to display graphics files (pictures) in Visual Basic applications and how to do basic animations. Visual Basic also offers a wealth of **graphics methods** that let us draw lines, rectangles, ellipses, pie shapes and polygons. With these methods, you can draw anything! These methods are provided by the **GDI+** (graphical device interface), an improved version of previous interfaces.

The graphics methods examined in this chapter are part of the Visual Basic **Drawing** namespace. The methods are applied to **Graphics** objects. Using graphics objects is a little detailed, but worth the time to learn. There is a new vocabulary with many new objects to study. We'll cover every step. The basic approach to drawing with graphics objects will always be:

> ➢ Create a **Graphics** object
> ➢ Create **Pen** objects and **Brush** objects
> ➢ Draw to Graphics object using drawing methods
> ➢ Dispose of Pen and Brush objects when done with them
> ➢ Dispose of Graphics object when done with it

The process is like drawing on paper. You get your paper (graphics object) and your pens and brushes. You do all your drawing and coloring and then put your supplies away!

All the drawing methods we study are **overloaded** functions. Recall this means there are many ways to invoke a function, using different numbers and types of arguments. For each drawing method, we will look at one or two implementations of that particular method. You are encouraged to examine other implementations using the Visual Basic on-line help facilities.

In this chapter, we will learn about **Graphics** objects, **Pen** objects, **Brush** objects and the use of **colors**. We'll learn how to draw **lines**, draw and fill **rectangles**, draw and fill **ellipses** and draw **pie** segments. We'll use these skills to build basic plotting packages and, in Chapter 9, a simple paintbrush program. Let's get started.

Graphics Object

As mentioned, graphics methods (drawing functions) are applied to graphics objects. **Graphics objects** provide the "surface" for drawing methods and can be created using many of the Visual Basic controls. The usual controls for graphics methods are the **form**, the **picture box** control, and the **panel** control. In this course, we will primarily use the panel control for drawing. It provides a nicely "contained" drawing area.

There are two steps involved in creating a **graphics object**. We first declare the object (in the **Drawing** namespace) using the standard **Dim** statement:

```
Dim MyGraphics as Drawing.Graphics
```

Placement of this statement depends on scope. Place it in a procedure for procedure level scope. Place it with other form level declarations for form level scope. Once declared, the object is created using the **CreateGraphics** method:

```
MyGraphics = HostControlName.CreateGraphics()
```

where **HostControlName** is the name of the control hosting the graphics object [the form (**Me**), any other control (**Name** property)].

Once a graphics object is created, all graphics methods are applied to this object. Hence, to apply a drawing method named **DrawingMethod** to the **MyGraphics** object, use:

MyGraphics.**DrawingMethod** (**Arguments**)

where **Arguments** are any needed arguments.

There are two important drawing methods we introduce now. First, after all of your hard work drawing in a graphics object, there are times you will want to erase or clear the object. This is done with the **Clear** method:

```
MyGraphics.Clear(Color)
```

This statement will clear a graphics object and fill it with the specified **Color**. We will look at colors next. The usual color argument for clearing a graphics object is the background color of the host control, or:

```
MyGraphics.Clear(HostControlName.BackColor)
```

Once you are done drawing to an object and need it no longer, it should be properly disposed to clear up system resources. The syntax for disposing of our example graphics object uses the **Dispose** method:

```
MyGraphics.Dispose()
```

All graphics methods use the **client coordinates** of the hosting control:

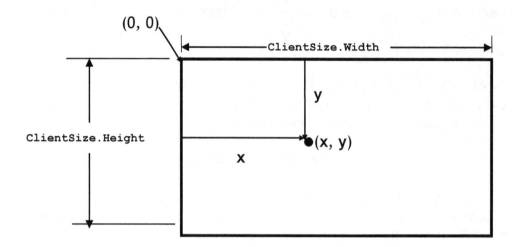

The client dimensions, **ClientSize.Width** and **ClientSize.Height** represent the "graphics" region of the control hosting the graphics object. Due to border space, they are <u>not</u> the same as the **Width** and **Height** properties. ClientSize.Width is less than Width and ClientSize.Height is less than Height. For example, you won't be able to draw in the title bar region of a form object.

Points in client coordinates will be referred to by a Cartesian pair, **(x, y)**. In the diagram, note the **x** (horizontal) coordinate runs from left to right, starting at **0** and extending to **ClientSize.Width - 1**. The **y** (vertical) coordinate goes from top to bottom, starting at **0** and ending at **ClientSize.Height - 1**. All measurements are integers and in units of **pixels**. Later, we will see how we can use any coordinate system we want.

Colors

Colors play a big part in Visual Basic applications. We have seen colors in designing some of our previous applications. At design time, we have selected background colors (**BackColor** property) and foreground colors (**ForeColor** property) for different controls. Such choices are made by selecting the desired property in the properties window. Once selected, a palette of customizable colors appears for you to choose from.

Most of the graphics methods we study will use **pen** and **brush** objects (we'll look at these objects soon). Both pen objects and brush objects have **Color** arguments that specify just what color they draw or paint in. Unlike control color properties, these colors cannot be selected at design time. They must be defined in code. How do we do this? There are two approaches we will take: (1) use built-in colors and (2) create a color.

The colors built into Visual Basic are specified by the **Color** structure (from the **Drawing** namespace). A color is specified using:

```
Drawing.Color.ColorName
```

where **ColorName** is a reserved color name. There are many, many color names (I counted 141). To see a list, consult on-line help for the **Color** structure and click **Members**. There are colors like **BlanchedAlmond**, **Linen**, **NavajoWhite**, **PeachPuff** and **SpringGreen**. You don't have to remember these names. Whenever you type the word **Drawing.Color**, followed by a dot (.), in the code window, the Intellisense feature of the IDE will pop up with a list of color selections. Just choose from the list to complete the color specification. You will have to remember the difference between BlanchedAlmond and Linen though! Personally, as my lovely wife will attest, I can only distinguish a few colors (I'm a blue, red, yellow kind of guy).

If for some reason, the selection provided by the **Color** structure does not fit your needs, there is a method that allows you to create over 16 million different colors. The method (**FromArgb**) works with the **Color** structure. The syntax to specify a color is:

```
Drawing.Color.FromArgb(Red, Green, Blue)
```

where **Red**, **Green**, and **Blue** are integer measures of intensity of the corresponding primary colors. These measures can range from 0 (least intensity) to 255 (greatest intensity). For example, `Drawing.Color.FromArgb(255, 255, 0)` will produce yellow. Sorry, but I can't tell you what values to use to create **PeachPuff**.

It is easy to specify colors for graphics methods using the **Color** structure. Any time you need a color, just use one of the built-in colors or the **FromArgb** method. These techniques to represent color are not limited to just providing colors for graphics methods. They can be used anywhere Visual Basic requires a color; for example, **Backcolor** and **Forecolor** properties can also be set (at run-time) using these techniques. For example, to change your form background color to **PeachPuff**, use:

```
Me.BackColor = Drawing.Color.PeachPuff
```

If you want to allow your users the capability of changing colors at run-time, the **ColorDialog** control, examined next, is a very useful tool.

ColorDialog Control

In Toolbox:

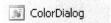

Below Form (Default Properties):

The **ColorDialog** control is a pre-configured dialog box that allows the user to select a color from a palette and to add custom colors to that palette. It is the same dialog box that you see in other Windows applications. The selected color can be used to set control properties or select colors needed by graphics objects and methods.

ColorDialog **Properties:**

Name	Gets or sets the name of the color dialog (I usually name this control **dlgColor**).
AllowFullOpen	Gets or sets a value indicating whether the user can use the dialog box to define custom colors.
AnyColor	Gets or sets a value indicating whether the dialog box displays all available colors in the set of basic colors.
Color	Indicates selected color.
CustomColors	Gets or sets the set of custom colors shown in the dialog box.
FullOpen	Gets or sets a value indicating whether the controls used to create custom colors are visible when the dialog box is opened.
SolidColorOnly	Gets or sets a value indicating whether the dialog box will restrict users to selecting solid colors only.

ColorDialog **Methods:**

ShowDialog	Displays the dialog box. Returned value indicates which button was clicked by user (**OK** or **Cancel**).

To use the **ColorDialog** control, we add it to our application the same as any control. It will appear in the tray below the form. Once added, we set a few properties. Then, we write code to make the dialog box appear when desired. The user then makes selections and closes the dialog box. At this point, we use the selected **Color** property for our tasks.

The **ShowDialog** method is used to display the **ColorDialog** control. For a control named **dlgColor**, the appropriate code is:

```
dlgColor.ShowDialog()
```

And the displayed dialog box is:

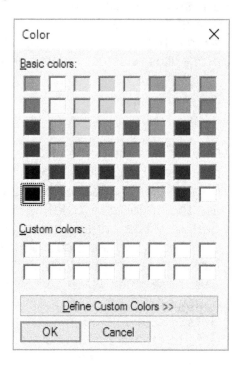

The user selects a color by making relevant choices. Once complete, the **OK** button is clicked. At this point, the **Color** property is available for use. **Cancel** can be clicked to cancel the color change. The ShowDialog method returns the clicked button. It returns **DialogResult.OK** if OK is clicked and returns **DialogResult.Cancel** if Cancel is clicked.

Typical use of **ColorDialog** control:

> ➢ Set the **Name** property (perhaps change defaults concerning what color options are displayed).
> ➢ Use **ShowDialog** method to display dialog box.
> ➢ Use **Color** property in appropriate place in code.

Pen Object

As mentioned, many of the graphics methods we study require a **Pen** object. This virtual pen is just like the pen you use to write and draw. You can choose color, width and style of the pen. You can use pens built-in to Visual Basic or create your own pen.

In many cases, the pen objects built into Visual Basic are sufficient. The **Pens** class will draw a line **1** pixel wide in a color you choose (Intellisense will present the list to choose from). If the selected color is **ColorName** (one of the 141 built-in color names), the syntax to refer to such a pen is:

```
Drawing.Pens.ColorName
```

To create your own **Pen** object (in **Drawing** namespace), you first declare the pen using:

```
Dim MyPen As Drawing.Pen
```

The pen is then created using the **Pen** constructor:

```
MyPen = New Drawing.Pen(Color, Width)
```

where **Color** is the color your new pen will draw in and **Width** is the integer width of the line (in pixels) drawn. This pen will draw a solid line. The **Color** argument can be one of the built-in colors or one generated with the **FromArgb** function. Using some of the overloaded versions of the pen constructor allow you to create pens that can draw dashed and other line styles. Consult on-line help for details.

Once created, you can change the color and width at any time using the **Color** and **Width** properties of the pen object. The syntax is:

```
MyPen.Color = NewColor
MyPen.Width = NewWidth
```

Here, **NewColor** is a newly specified color and **NewWidth** is a new integer pen width.

When done drawing with a pen object, it should be disposed using the **Dispose** method:

```
MyPen.Dispose()
```

DrawLine Method

The first graphics (drawing) method we learn is **DrawLine**. This method is used to connect two Cartesian points with a straight-line segment. It operates on a previously created graphics object. If that object is **MyGraphics** and we wish to connect the point (**x1**, **y1**) with (**x2**, **y2**) using a pen object **MyPen**, the syntax is:

```
MyGraphics.DrawLine(MyPen, x1, y1, x2, y2)
```

Each coordinate value is an integer type. As mentioned, all graphics methods (including **DrawLine**) are overloaded functions. There are other implementations of DrawLine in Visual Basic. This is just one of them.

Using a black pen with a line width of 1 (**Drawing.Pens.Black**), the **DrawLine** method with these points is:

```
MyGraphics.DrawLine(Drawing.Pens.Black, x1, y1, x2, y2)
```

This produces on a form (**MyGraphics** object):

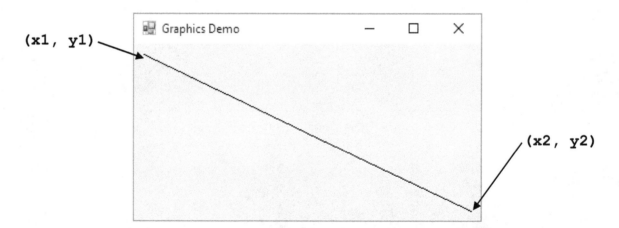

For every line segment you need to draw, you will need a separate **DrawLine** statement. Of course, you can choose to change pen color or pen width at any time you wish.

Graphics Methods (Revisited)

Before continuing, let's build and look at a little example to demonstrate a couple of (perhaps unexpected) features of graphics methods in Visual Basic. Start a new project. Place a single button control (**Text** property of **Draw Line**) in the middle of the form. We won't be concerned with proper naming conventions here. We're just playing around. When we click the button, we want to draw a blue line on the form from the upper left corner to the lower right corner. When we click the button again, we want the line to disappear.

This code (the **Button1 Click** event procedure) accomplishes that task:

```
Private Sub Button1_Click(ByVal sender As System.Object,
ByVal e As System.EventArgs) Handles Button1.Click
  Dim MyGraphics As Drawing.Graphics
  'toggle button text property
  If Button1.Text = "Draw Line" Then
    Button1.Text = "Clear Line"
    LineThere = True
  Else
    Button1.Text = "Draw Line"
    LineThere = False
  End If
  MyGraphics = Me.CreateGraphics
  If LineThere = True Then
    MyGraphics.DrawLine(Drawing.Pens.Blue, 0, 0,
Me.ClientSize.Width - 1, Me.ClientSize.Height - 1)
  Else
    MyGraphics.Clear(Me.BackColor)
  End If
  MyGraphics.Dispose()
End Sub
```

Add this code to the little example. Also, you must define and initialize one variable (**LineThere**) as having form level scope:

```
Dim LineThere As Boolean = False
```

This variable is True when a line has been drawn and False when there is no line. It is initially False, since there will be no line when the application begins.

Since this is the first graphics code we've seen, let's look at it closely. It first 'toggles' the button's **Text** property and establishes a value for **LineThere**. It then creates the **Graphics** object **MyGraphics** using the form (**Me**) as the host control. If checks the status of **LineThere** to determine if we're drawing a line or clearing the line. If drawing (**LineThere** = **True**), a blue pen draws a line. If clearing, the graphics object is cleared to the form's background color. Before leaving the procedure, the object is disposed.

Run this little application and click the button one time. You should see something like this (your results will vary assuming your form is a different size):

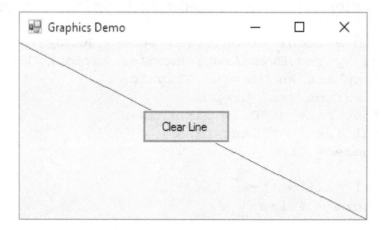

The first feature to see here is that the line appears <u>behind</u> the button control. Graphics objects are created and maintained (as a **bitmap** graphic) in their own "layer" of the hosting control. In a form, this layer lies behind the "layer" with all the controls. When you clear the graphics object, it clears this back layer. It won't clear any objects placed on the form. Click the button a few times to see how this works.

To see the second feature of graphics methods, make sure a line appears on the form and reduce the form to an icon by clicking the **Minimize** button (the one with an underscore character) in the upper right-hand corner of the form. Then, restore the form to the screen by clicking the form entry on your task bar. Here's what you should see:

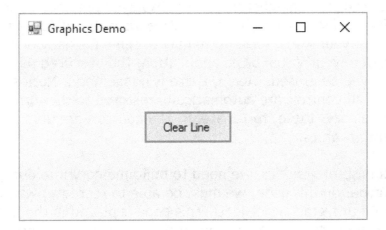

The button control is still there, but the line we carefully drew has disappeared! What happened? We'll answer that question next.

Persistent Graphics

Why did the line disappear in our little example when the form went away for a bit? Visual Basic graphics objects have <u>no</u> memory. They only display what has been last drawn on them. If you reduce your form to an icon and restore it, the graphics object cannot remember what was displayed previously – it will be cleared. Similarly, if you switch from an active Visual Basic application to some other application, your Visual Basic form may become partially or fully obscured. When you return to your Visual Basic application, the obscured part of any graphics object will be erased. Again, there is no memory. Notice in both these cases, however, all controls are automatically restored to the form. Your application remembers these, fortunately! The controls are persistent. We also want **persistent graphics**.

To maintain persistent graphics, we need to build memory into our graphics objects using code. In this code, we must be able to recreate, when needed, the current state of a graphics object. This code is placed in the host control's **Paint** event. This event is called whenever an obscured object becomes unobscured. The **Paint** event will be called for each object when a form is first activated and when a form is restored from an icon or whenever an obscured object is viewable again.

Maintaining persistent graphics does require a bit of work on your part. You need to always know what is in your graphics objects and how to recreate the objects, when needed. This usually involves developing some program variables that describe how to recreate the graphics object. And, you usually need to develop some ad hoc rules for recreation. As you build your first few **Paint** events, you will begin to develop your own ways for maintaining persistent graphics. At certain times, you'll need to force a "repaint" of your form or control. To do this, for an object named **ObjectName** use:

```
ObjectName_Paint(Nothing, Nothing)
```

That is, you simply call the **Paint** event for the object you want to repaint. Use the keyword **Nothing** for both arguments. These arguments are not used in any Paint events we create, hence are disregarded. One hint: always check for the actual name assigned to a **Paint** event procedure by Visual Basic. You want to make sure you call the correct event.

Let's see how to maintain persistent graphics in our little example. First, move all the graphics statements out of the **Button1 Click** event procedure into the **Form1 Paint** event. The **Paint** event will be:

```
Private Sub Form1_Paint(ByVal sender As Object, ByVal e As
System.Windows.Forms.PaintEventArgs) Handles MyBase.Paint
   Dim MyGraphics As Drawing.Graphics
   MyGraphics = Me.CreateGraphics
   If LineThere = True Then
     MyGraphics.DrawLine(Drawing.Pens.Blue, 0, 0,
Me.ClientSize.Width - 1, Me.ClientSize.Height - 1)
   Else
     MyGraphics.Clear(Me.BackColor)
   End If
   MyGraphics.Dispose()
End Sub
```

With this code, the line will be drawn when **LineThere** is **True**, else the graphics object will be cleared. The resulting **Button1 Click** event will now be:

```
Private Sub Button1_Click(ByVal sender As System.Object,
ByVal e As System.EventArgs) Handles Button1.Click
   'toggle button text property
   If Button1.Text = "Draw Line" Then
     Button1.Text = "Clear Line"
     LineThere = True
   Else
     Button1.Text = "Draw Line"
     LineThere = False
   End If
   Form1_Paint(Nothing, Nothing)
End Sub
```

We've added the shaded line to force a paint of the form each time the button is clicked. A common mistake is to forget to add this line. If something is drawing like you think it should, you'll probably need to add a 'forced' paint of the graphics object.

Run the application with these changes in place. Try drawing and clearing the line. The graphics should be persistent, meaning the line will be there when it's supposed to and not there when it's not supposed to be there. The last incarnation of this little graphics example is saved in the **GraphicsDemo** folder in the **LearnVB\VB Code\Class 8** folder.

So, to use persistent graphics, you need to do a little work. Once you've done that work, make sure you truly have persistent graphics. Perform checks similar to those we did for our little example here. The Visual Basic environment makes doing these checks very easy. It's simple to make changes and immediately see the effects of those changes. A particular place to check is to make sure the initial loading of graphics objects display correctly. Sometimes, Paint events cause incorrect results the first time they are invoked.

And, though, including **Paint** events in a Visual Basic application require extra coding, it also has the advantage of centralizing all graphics operations in one procedure. This usually helps to simplify the tasks of code modification and maintenance. I've found that the persistent graphics problem makes me look more deeply at my code. In the end, I write better code. I believe you'll find the same is true with your applications.

Example 8-6

Drawing Lines

1. Start a new application. In this application, we will draw random line segments in a panel control using **DrawLine**. Add a panel control and two button controls to the form. The form should look like this:

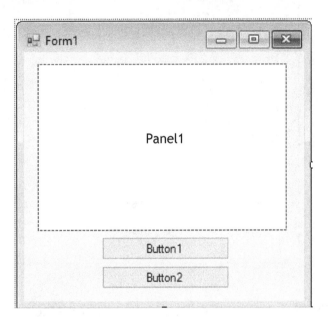

2. Set the following properties:

Form1:

Name	frmLine
FormBorderStyle	SingleFixed
StartPosition	CenterScreen
Text	Drawing Lines

Panel1:

Name	pnlDraw
BackColor	White
BorderStyle	Fixed3D

Button1:

Name	btnDraw
Text	&Draw Lines

Button2:
   Name   btnClear
   Text   &Clear Lines

When done, my form looks like this:

3. We define an **EndPoint** class (**EndPoint.vb**) to keep track of each line segment drawn:

```
Public Class EndPoint
   Public X As Integer
   Public Y As Integer
End Class
```

4. Return to the form code window. Form level scope declarations:

```
Dim NumberPoints As Integer = 0
Dim LineEnds(50) As EndPoint
Dim MyRandom As New Random()
Const MaxPoints As Integer = 50
```

7. Use this code in the **pnlDraw Paint** event. This code draws the line segments defined by array of **LineEnds** objects:

```
Private Sub PnlDraw_Paint(ByVal sender As System.Object,
ByVal e As System.Windows.Forms.PaintEventArgs) Handles
pnlDraw.Paint
    'create graphics object and connect points in x, y
arrays
    Dim I As Integer
    Dim MyGraphics As Drawing.Graphics
    Dim MyPen As Drawing.Pen
    MyGraphics = pnlDraw.CreateGraphics
    MyPen = New Drawing.Pen(Drawing.Color.Blue, 3)
    If NumberPoints <> 0 Then
      For I = 2 To NumberPoints
        MyGraphics.DrawLine(MyPen, LineEnds(I - 1).X,
LineEnds(I - 1).Y, LineEnds(I).X, LineEnds(I).Y)
      Next I
    Else
      MyGraphics.Clear(pnlDraw.BackColor)
    End If
    MyPen.Dispose()
    MyGraphics.Dispose()
  End Sub
```

8. Save and run the application (saved in **Example 8-6** folder in **LearnVB\VB Code\Class 8** folder). Try drawing (click **Draw Lines** several times) and clearing random line segments. Note that the graphics are persistent. Try obscuring the form to prove this. Here's some segments I drew:

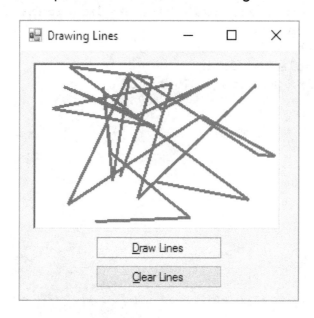

Rectangle Structure

We now begin looking at two-dimensional graphics methods. These include methods for drawing rectangles, ellipses and pie segments. Each of these methods uses a bounding rectangle within a graphics object to specify the drawing area. This rectangle is specified by a **Rectangle** structure (from the **Drawing** namespace). A structure is similar to an object; it has properties and methods. One difference between a structure and an object is you don't have to dispose of any structure you create.

Rectangle Structure **Properties:**

Bottom	Gets the y-coordinate of the lower-right corner of the rectangle
Height	Gets or sets the width of the rectangle
Left	Gets the x-coordinate of the upper-left corner of the rectangle
Right	Gets the x-coordinate of the lower-right corner of the rectangle
Top	Gets the y-coordinate of the upper-left corner of the rectangular
Width	Gets or sets the height of the rectangle
X	Gets or sets the x-coordinate of the upper-left corner of the rectangle
Y	Gets or sets the y-coordinate of the upper-left corner of the rectangle

All of the relative measurements (**Bottom**, **Left**, **Right**, **Top**, **X**, **Y**) are relative to the graphics object. A diagram shows everything:

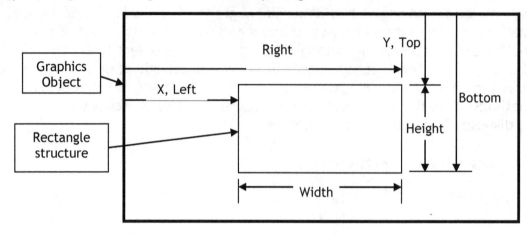

Only X, Y, Width and Height can be changed at run-time.

There are two steps involved in creating a **rectangle structure**. We first declare the structure (in the **Drawing** namespace) using the standard **Dim** statement:

```
Dim MyRectangle as Drawing.Rectangle
```

Placement of this statement depends on scope. Place it in a procedure for procedure level scope. Place it with other form level declarations for form level scope. Once declared, the structure is created using the **Rectangle** constructor:

```
MyRectangle = New Drawing.Rectangle(Left, Top, Width,
Height)
```

where **Left**, **Top**, **Width** and **Height** are the desired integer measurements (in pixels).

You can move and resize the rectangle in code, by changing any of four properties:

```
MyRectangle.X = NewX
MyRectangle.Y = NewY
MyRectangle.Width = NewWidth
MyRectangle.Height = NewHeight
```

where **NewX**, **NewY**, **NewWidth**, and **NewHeight** represent new values for the respective properties.

DrawRectangle Method

The **DrawRectangle** method will draw a rectangle in a **rectangle structure** within a **graphic object**. To draw a rectangle, you first create the graphics object. Then you create the rectangle structure using the just-defined constructor. Assuming you have created a graphics object named **MyGraphics** and a rectangle structure named **MyRectangle**, the syntax to draw a rectangle with pen object **MyPen** is:

```
MyGraphics.DrawRectangle(MyPen, MyRectangle)
```

Using a black pen with a line width of 1 (**Drawing.Pens.Black**), the code to draw a rectangle that takes up 80 percent of the width and height of the client area of a form-hosted graphics object is:

```
Dim MyGraphics As Drawing.Graphics
Dim MyRectangle As Drawing.Rectangle
MyGraphics = Me.CreateGraphics
MyRectangle = New Drawing.Rectangle(CInt(0.1 *
Me.ClientSize.Width), CInt(0.1 * Me.ClientSize.Height),
CInt(0.8 * Me.ClientSize.Width), CInt(0.8 *
Me.ClientSize.Height))
MyGraphics.DrawRectangle(Drawing.Pens.Black, MyRectangle)
MyGraphics.Dispose()
```

This code produces this rectangle:

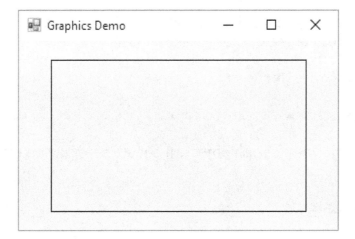

Brush Object

The rectangle we just drew is pretty boring. It would be nice to have the capability to fill it with a color and/or pattern. Filling of regions in Visual Basic is done with a **Brush** object. Like the Pen object, a brush is just like a brush you use to paint – just pick a color. You can use brushes built-in to Visual Basic or create your own brush. In this chapter, we only look at solid color brushes. Advanced brush effects are studied in Chapter 9

In most cases, the brush objects built into Visual Basic are sufficient. The **Brushes** class provides brush objects that paint using one of the 141 built-in color names we've seen before. The syntax to refer to such a brush is:

```
Drawing.Brushes.ColorName
```

To create your own **Brush** object (from the **Drawing** namespace), you first declare the brush using:

```
Dim MyBrush As Drawing.Brush
```

The solid color brush is then created using the **SolidBrush** constructor:

```
MyBrush = New Drawing.SolidBrush(Color)
```

where **Color** is the color your new brush will paint with. This color argument can be one of the built-in colors or one generated with the **FromArgb** function.

Once created, you can change the color of a brush any time using the **Color** property of the brush object. The syntax is:

```
MyBrush.Color = NewColor
```

where **NewColor** is a newly specified color.

When done painting with a brush object, it should be disposed using the **Dispose** method:

```
MyBrush.Dispose()
```

FillRectangle Method

The **FillRectangle** method will draw a filled rectangle in a **rectangle structure** within a **graphic object**. To fill a rectangle, you first create the graphics object. Then you create the rectangle structure using the rectangle constructor. Assuming you have created a graphics object named **MyGraphics** and a rectangle structure named **MyRectangle**, the syntax to fill a rectangle with brush object **MyBrush** is:

```
MyGraphics.FillRectangle(MyBrush, MyRectangle)
```

Using a red solid brush (**Drawing.Brushes.Red**), the code to fill a rectangle that takes up 80 percent of the width and height of the client area of a form-hosted graphics object is:

```
Dim MyGraphics As Drawing.Graphics
Dim MyRectangle As Drawing.Rectangle
MyGraphics = Me.CreateGraphics
MyRectangle = New Drawing.Rectangle(CInt(0.1 *
Me.ClientSize.Width), CInt(0.1 * Me.ClientSize.Height),
CInt(0.8 * Me.ClientSize.Width), CInt(0.8 *
Me.ClientSize.Height))
MyGraphics.FillRectangle(Drawing.Brushes.Red, MyRectangle)
MyGraphics.Dispose()
```

This code produces this rectangle:

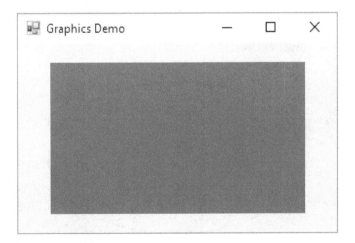

Notice the FillRectangle method fills the entire region with the selected color. If you had previously used DrawRectangle to form a border region, the fill will blot out that border. If you want a bordered, filled region, do the **fill** operation **first**, **then** the **draw** operation.

DrawEllipse Method

Ellipses can be drawn in Visual Basic using methods nearly identical to the rectangle methods. The **DrawEllipse** method will draw an ellipse in a **rectangle structure** within a **graphic object**. To draw an ellipse, you first create the graphics object. Then you create the rectangle structure using the constructor. Assuming you have created a graphics object named **MyGraphics** and a rectangle structure named **MyRectangle**, the syntax to draw an ellipse with pen object **MyPen** is:

```
MyGraphics.DrawEllipse(MyPen, MyRectangle)
```

Using a black pen with a line width of 1 (**Drawing.Pens.Black**), the code to draw an ellipse that takes up 80 percent of the width and height of the client area of a form-hosted graphics object is:

```
Dim MyGraphics As Drawing.Graphics
Dim MyRectangle As Drawing.Rectangle
MyGraphics = Me.CreateGraphics
MyRectangle = New Drawing.Rectangle(CInt(0.1 *
Me.ClientSize.Width), CInt(0.1 * Me.ClientSize.Height),
CInt(0.8 * Me.ClientSize.Width), CInt(0.8 *
Me.ClientSize.Height))
MyGraphics.DrawEllipse(Drawing.Pens.Black, MyRectangle)
MyGraphics.Dispose()
```

This code produces this ellipse:

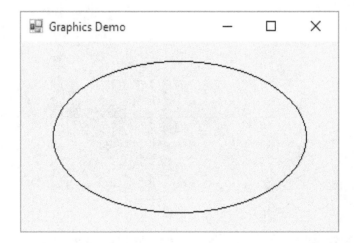

FillEllipse Method

The **FillEllipse** method will draw a filled ellipse in a **rectangle structure** within a **graphic object**. To fill an ellipse, you first create the graphics object. Then you create the rectangle structure. Assuming you have created a graphics object named **MyGraphics** and a rectangle structure named **MyRectangle**, the syntax to fill an ellipse with brush object **MyBrush** is:

```
MyGraphics.FillEllipse(MyBrush, MyRectangle)
```

Using a green solid brush (**Drawing.Brushes.Green**), the code to fill an ellipse that takes up 80 percent of the width and height of the client area of a form-hosted graphics object is:

```
Dim MyGraphics As Drawing.Graphics
Dim MyRectangle As Drawing.Rectangle
MyGraphics = Me.CreateGraphics
MyRectangle = New Drawing.Rectangle(CInt(0.1 *
Me.ClientSize.Width), CInt(0.1 * Me.ClientSize.Height),
CInt(0.8 * Me.ClientSize.Width), CInt(0.8 *
Me.ClientSize.Height))
MyGraphics.FillEllipse(Drawing.Brushes.Green, MyRectangle)
MyGraphics.Dispose()
```

This code produces this ellipse:

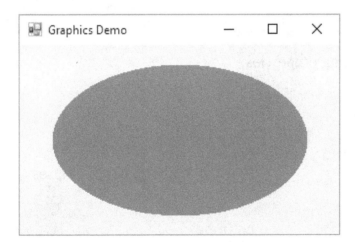

Like the rectangle methods, notice the fill operation erases any border that may have been there after a draw operation. For a bordered, filled ellipse, do the fill, then the draw.

Example 8-7

Drawing Rectangles and Ellipses

1. Start a new application. In this application, we will draw and fill random rectangles or ellipses in a panel control. The rectangles or ellipses will be filled with random colors. Add a panel control, two radio buttons and three button controls to the form. The form should look like this:

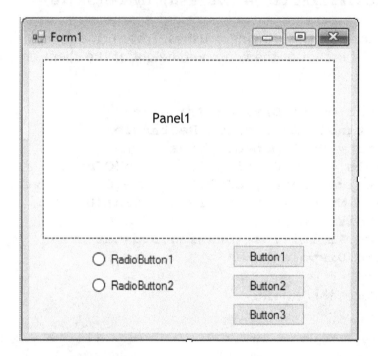

2. Set the following properties:

Form1:

Name	frmDrawing
FormBorderStyle	SingleFixed
StartPosition	CenterScreen
Text	Drawing Rectangles and Ellipses

Panel1:

Name	pnlDraw
BackColor	White
BorderStyle	Fixed3D

RadioButton1:

Name	rdoRectangle
Checked	True
Text	&Rectangle

RadioButton2:

Name	rdoEllipse
Text	&Ellipse

Button1:

Name	btnDraw
Text	&Draw

Button2:

Name	btnFill
Enabled	False
Text	&Fill

Button3:

Name	btnClear
Enabled	False
Text	&Clear

When done, my form looks like this:

3. Form level scope declarations:

```
Dim MyRectangle As Drawing.Rectangle
Dim IsDrawn As Boolean = False
Dim IsFilled As Boolean = False
Dim FillRed As Integer, FillGreen As Integer, FillBlue As
Integer
Dim MyRandom As New Random()
```

4. Use this code in the **btnDraw Click** event procedure:

```
Private Sub BtnDraw_Click(ByVal sender As System.Object,
ByVal e As System.EventArgs) Handles btnDraw.Click
    Dim W As Integer, H As Integer
    Dim L As Integer, T As Integer
    'generate new random rectangle structure
    'rectangle is centered, taking up 20 to 90 percent of
each dimension
    W = CInt(pnlDraw.ClientSize.Width * (MyRandom.Next(71) +
20) / 100)
    H = CInt(pnlDraw.ClientSize.Height * (MyRandom.Next(71)
+ 20) / 100)
    L = CInt(0.5 * (pnlDraw.ClientSize.Width - W))
    T = CInt(0.5 * (pnlDraw.ClientSize.Height - H))
    MyRectangle = New Drawing.Rectangle(L, T, W, H)
    IsDrawn = True
    IsFilled = False
    btnDraw.Enabled = False
    btnFill.Enabled = True
    btnClear.Enabled = True
    pnlDraw_Paint(Nothing, Nothing)
End Sub
```

This code establishes a new rectangle structure for the rectangle or ellipse.

5. Use this code in the **btnFill Click** event procedure:

```
Private Sub BtnFill_Click(ByVal sender As System.Object,
ByVal e As System.EventArgs) Handles btnFill.Click
    'fill rectangle or ellipse with brush
    IsFilled = True
    btnDraw.Enabled = False
    'pick colors at random
    FillRed = MyRandom.Next(255)
    FillGreen = MyRandom.Next(255)
    FillBlue = MyRandom.Next(255)
    pnlDraw_Paint(Nothing, Nothing)
End Sub
```

Here, random colors are picked and the existing rectangle or ellipse is filled.

6. Use this code in **btnClear Click** event – this clears the graphics object and allows another rectangle or ellipse to be drawn:

```
Private Sub BtnClear_Click(ByVal sender As System.Object,
ByVal e As System.EventArgs) Handles btnClear.Click
    'clear region
    IsDrawn = False
    IsFilled = False
    btnDraw.Enabled = True
    btnFill.Enabled = False
    btnClear.Enabled = False
    pnlDraw_Paint(Nothing, Nothing)
End Sub
```

7. Use this code in the **pnlDraw Paint** event. This code draws/fills the rectangle or ellipse if it is in the panel control:

```
Private Sub PnlDraw_Paint(ByVal sender As System.Object,
ByVal e As System.Windows.Forms.PaintEventArgs) Handles
pnlDraw.Paint
    Dim MyGraphics As Drawing.Graphics
    Dim MyPen As Drawing.Pen
    Dim MyBrush As Drawing.Brush
    MyGraphics = pnlDraw.CreateGraphics
    MyGraphics.Clear(pnlDraw.BackColor)
    'draw/fill rectangle or ellipse
    'fill before draw to keep border
    If IsFilled Then
      'paint with brush of random color
      MyBrush = New
Drawing.SolidBrush(Drawing.Color.FromArgb(FillRed,
FillGreen, FillBlue))
      If rdoRectangle.Checked Then
        MyGraphics.FillRectangle(MyBrush, MyRectangle)
      Else
        MyGraphics.FillEllipse(MyBrush, MyRectangle)
      End If
      MyBrush.Dispose()
    End If
      If IsDrawn Then
        'draw with pen 3 pixels wide
      MyPen = New Drawing.Pen(Drawing.Color.Black, 3)
      If rdoRectangle.Checked Then
        MyGraphics.DrawRectangle(MyPen, MyRectangle)
      Else
        MyGraphics.DrawEllipse(MyPen, MyRectangle)
      End If
      MyPen.Dispose()
    End If
      MyGraphics.Dispose()
  End Sub
```

8. Lastly, if either radio button is clicked, we clear the drawing region so a new shape can be drawn. The corresponding **rdoShape_CheckedChanged** event procedure (handles both radio buttons) is:

```
Private Sub RdoShape_CheckedChanged(ByVal sender As
System.Object, ByVal e As System.EventArgs) Handles
rdoRectangle.CheckedChanged, rdoEllipse.CheckedChanged
    'shape changes - clear drawing area
    btnClear_Click(Nothing, Nothing)
End Sub
```

9. Save and run the application (saved in **Example 8-7** folder in **LearnVB\VB Code\Class 8** folder). Try drawing and filling rectangles. Notice how the random colors work. Notice how the button controls are enabled and disabled at different points. Note that the graphics are persistent. Here's a rectangle I drew:

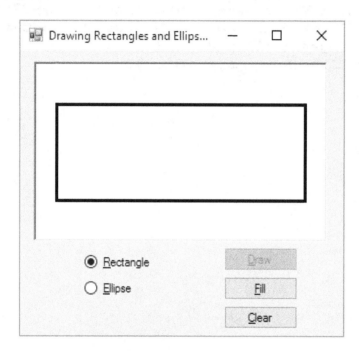

Now, its' filled:

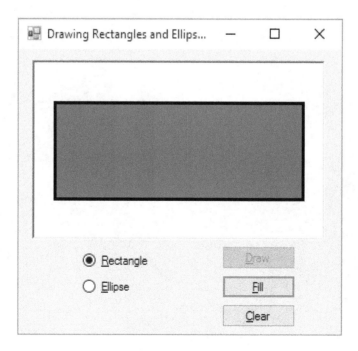

Here's an elliptical border:

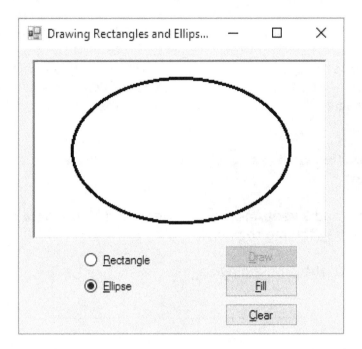

and its filled counterpart:

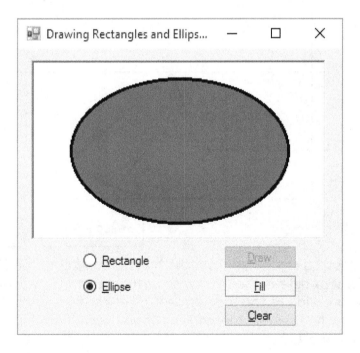

DrawPie Method

The **DrawPie** method will draw a segment of an ellipse (a slice of pie) in a **rectangle structure** within a **graphic object**. To draw a pie segment, you first create the graphics object. Then you create the rectangle structure. Assuming you have created a graphics object named **MyGraphics** and a rectangle structure named **MyRectangle**, the syntax to draw a pie segment with pen object **MyPen** is:

```
MyGraphics.DrawPie(Pen, MyRectangle, StartAngle,
SweepAngle)
```

where **StartAngle** and **SweepAngle** are angles (both **single** data types, measured in **degrees**) bounding the pie segment.

A diagram indicates these bounding angles:

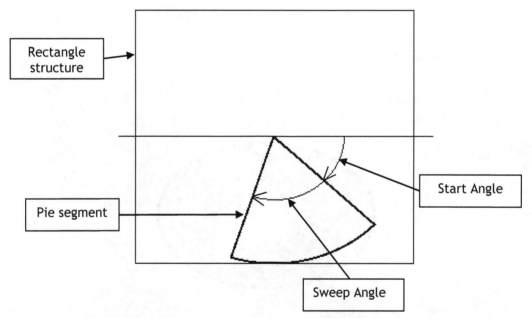

StartAngle is measured clockwise from the horizontal axis to the first side of the pie segment. **SweepAngle** is the clockwise angle starting at StartAngle and ending at the second side of the pie segment. Notice if StartAngle = 0 and SweepAngle = 360, the DrawPie method draws the same figure as DrawEllipse (you get the whole pie!).

Using a black pen with a line width of 1 (**Drawing.Pens.Black**), the code to draw a pie segment (**StartAngle** = **120**, **SweepAngle** = **80**) within a rectangle structure that takes up 80 percent of the width and height of the client area of a form-hosted graphics object is:

```
Dim MyGraphics As Drawing.Graphics
Dim MyRectangle As Drawing.Rectangle
MyGraphics = Me.CreateGraphics
MyRectangle = New Drawing.Rectangle(0.1 *
Me.ClientSize.Width, 0.1 * Me.ClientSize.Height, 0.8 *
Me.ClientSize.Width, 0.8 * Me.ClientSize.Height)
MyGraphics.DrawPie(Drawing.Pens.Black, MyRectangle, 120,
80)
MyGraphics.Dispose()
```

This code produces this pie segment:

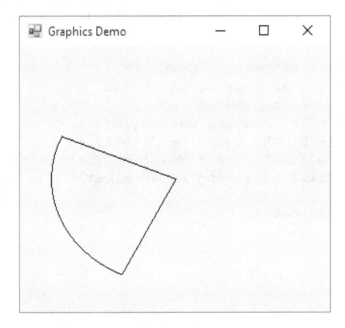

FillPie Method

The **FillPie** method will fill a segment of an ellipse (a slice of pie) in a **rectangle structure** within a **graphic object**. To fill a pie segment, you first create the graphics object. Then you create the rectangle structure. Assuming you have created a graphics object named **MyGraphics** and a rectangle structure named **MyRectangle**, the syntax to fill a pie segment with brush object **MyBrush** is:

```
MyGraphics.FillPie(MyBrush, MyRectangle, StartAngle,
SweepAngle)
```

where **StartAngle** and **SweepAngle** are the segment bounding angles (both **single** data types, measured in **degrees,** in a clockwise direction).

Using a dark blue solid brush (**Drawing.Brushes.DarkBlue**), the code to fill a pie segment (**StartAngle** = **120**, **SweepAngle** = **80**) within a rectangle structure that takes up 80 percent of the width and height of the client area of a form-hosted graphics object is:

```
Dim MyGraphics As Drawing.Graphics
Dim MyRectangle As Drawing.Rectangle
MyGraphics = Me.CreateGraphics
MyRectangle = New Drawing.Rectangle(0.1 *
Me.ClientSize.Width, 0.1 * Me.ClientSize.Height, 0.8 *
Me.ClientSize.Width, 0.8 * Me.ClientSize.Height)
MyGraphics.FillPie(Drawing.Brushes.DarkBlue, MyRectangle,
120, 80)
MyGraphics.Dispose()
```

This code produces this pie segment:

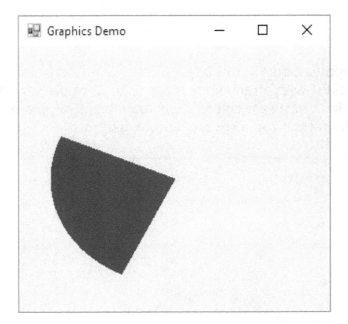

Like the rectangle and ellipse methods, notice the fill operation erases any border that may have been there after a draw operation. For a bordered, filled pie segment, do the fill, then the draw.

Example 8-8

Drawing Pie Segments

1. Start a new application. In this application, we will draw an ellipse (in panel control) and fill it with a random number (2 to 6) of pie segments. Each segment will be a different color. Add a panel control and two button controls to the form. The form should look like this:

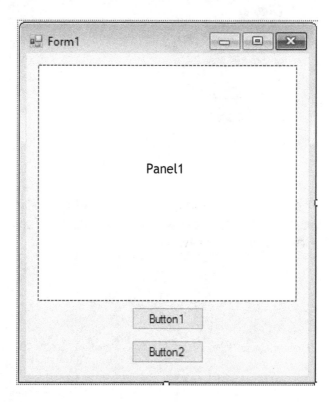

2. Set the following properties:

Form1:

Name	frmPie
FormBorderStyle	SingleFixed
StartPosition	CenterScreen
Text	Drawing Pie Segments

Panel1:

Name	pnlDraw
BackColor	White
BorderStyle	Fixed3D

Button1:

Name	btnDraw
Text	&Draw/Fill

Button2:

Name	btnClear
Enabled	False
Text	&Clear

When done, my form looks like this:

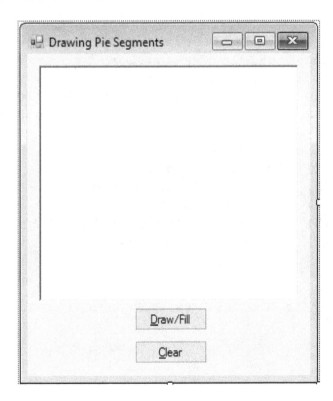

3. Add the **PieSlice** class (**PieSlice.vb**) to store information about each slice. Also, allows construction of a slice knowing the sweep angle and color:

```
Public Class PieSlice
   Public SweepAngle As Single
   Public SliceColor As Drawing.Color
   Public Sub New(ByVal a As Single, ByVal c As
Drawing.Color)
     Me.SweepAngle = a
     Me.SliceColor = c
   End Sub
End Class
```

4. Return to the form code window. Form level scope declarations:

```
Dim MyRectangle As Drawing.Rectangle
Dim NumberSlices As Integer
Dim Slices(6) As PieSlice
Dim MyColors(6) As Drawing.Color
Dim IsDrawn As Boolean = False
Dim MyRandom As New Random()
```

5. Use this code in **frmPie Load** to define the rectangle structure and set colors for the pie segments:

```
Private Sub FrmPie_Load(ByVal sender As Object, ByVal e As
System.EventArgs) Handles MyBase.Load
    'set up rectangle and colors
    MyRectangle = New Drawing.Rectangle(20, 20,
pnlDraw.ClientSize.Width - 40, pnlDraw.ClientSize.Height -
40)
    MyColors(1) = Drawing.Color.Red
    MyColors(2) = Drawing.Color.Green
    MyColors(3) = Drawing.Color.Yellow
    MyColors(4) = Drawing.Color.Blue
    MyColors(5) = Drawing.Color.Magenta
    MyColors(6) = Drawing.Color.Cyan
   End Sub
```

6. Use this code in the **btnDraw Click** event procedure:

```
Private Sub BtnDraw_Click(ByVal sender As System.Object,
ByVal e As System.EventArgs) Handles btnDraw.Click
    'new pie - get number of slices (2-6), sweep angles and
draw it
    Dim N As Integer
    Dim DegreesRemaining As Single
    'draw bounding ellipse
    'choose 2 to 6 slices at random
    NumberSlices = MyRandom.Next(5) + 2
    DegreesRemaining = 360
    'for each slice choose a sweep angle
    For N = 1 To NumberSlices
      If N < NumberSlices Then
         Slices(N) = New
PieSlice(MyRandom.Next(CInt(DegreesRemaining - 1)) + 1,
MyColors(N))
      Else
         Slices(N) = New PieSlice(DegreesRemaining,
MyColors(N))
      End If
      DegreesRemaining -= Slices(N).SweepAngle
    Next N
    IsDrawn = True
    btnDraw.Enabled = False
    btnClear.Enabled = True
    pnlDraw_Paint(Nothing, Nothing)
  End Sub
```

This code establishes the pie segments and draws them.

7. Use this code in **btnClear Click** event – this clears the graphics object and allows another pie to be drawn:

```
Private Sub BtnClear_Click(ByVal sender As System.Object,
ByVal e As System.EventArgs) Handles btnClear.Click
    'clear region
    IsDrawn = False
    btnDraw.Enabled = True
    btnClear.Enabled = False
    pnlDraw_Paint(Nothing, Nothing)
End Sub
```

8. Use this code in the **pnlDraw Paint** event. This code draws/fills an ellipse with pie segments if it is in the panel control:

```
Private Sub PnlDraw_Paint(ByVal sender As System.Object,
ByVal e As System.Windows.Forms.PaintEventArgs) Handles
pnlDraw.Paint
    Dim MyGraphics As Drawing.Graphics
    Dim MyBrush As Drawing.Brush
    Dim N As Integer, StartAngle As Single
    MyGraphics = pnlDraw.CreateGraphics
    If IsDrawn Then
      'draw pie
      StartAngle = 0
      'for each slice fill and draw
      For N = 1 To NumberSlices
        MyBrush = New
Drawing.SolidBrush(Slices(N).SliceColor)
        MyGraphics.FillPie(MyBrush, MyRectangle, StartAngle,
Slices(N).SweepAngle)
        MyGraphics.DrawPie(Drawing.Pens.Black, MyRectangle,
StartAngle, Slices(N).SweepAngle)
        StartAngle += Slices(N).SweepAngle
        MyBrush.Dispose()
      Next N
      'draw bounding ellipse
      MyGraphics.DrawEllipse(Drawing.Pens.Black,
MyRectangle)
    Else
      'clear pie
      MyGraphics.Clear(pnlDraw.BackColor)
    End If
    MyGraphics.Dispose()
End Sub
```

9. Save and run the application (saved in **Example 8-8** folder in **LearnVB\VB Code\Class 8** folder). Click **Draw/Fill Pie** to draw a segmented pie. Try several – each will be different. Note that the graphics are persistent. Here's a run I made:

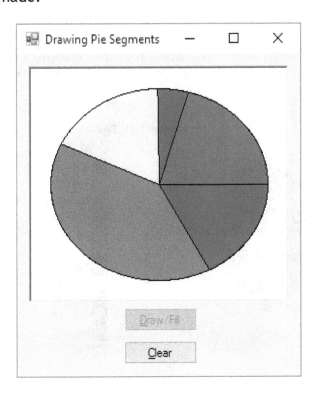

Pie Charts

The example just discussed suggests an immediate application for graphics capabilities – drawing **pie charts**. Pie charts are used to compare values of like information or to show what makes up a particular quantity. For example, a pie chart could illustrate what categories your monthly expenses fit into. Or, here is a pie chart with 12 segments illustrating monthly rainfall (in inches) for my hometown of Seattle (the segments for the winter months are very big!):

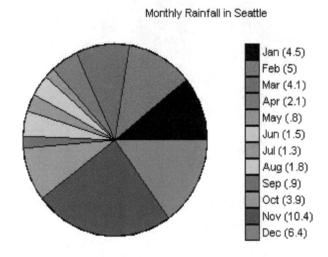

This chart was created with Visual Basic, by the way.

The steps for drawing a pie chart are straightforward. Assume you have N pieces of data (monthly rainfall, categorized expenditures, seasonal air traffic, or various income sources). Follow these steps to create a pie chart using the Visual Basic graphics methods:

> Generate **N** pieces of data to be plotted. Store this data in an array **Y(N)** (a 1-based array).
> Sum the N elements of the Y array to obtain a total value.
> Divide each Y element by the computed total to obtain the proportional contributions of each.
> Multiply each proportion by 360 degrees – the resulting values will be the **SweepAngle** arguments in the **DrawPie** and **FillPie** functions.
> Draw each pie segment (pick a unique, identifying color) using **FillPie** and **DrawPie** (fill then draw to maintain border). Initialize the **StartAngle** at zero. After drawing each segment, the next **StartAngle** will be the previous value incremented by the current **SweepAngle**.

The following code is a general class (**PieChart**) that draws a pie chart in a panel control. It uses another class (**PieSlice**, from Example 8-8) which is used to define each slice. You should be able to identify each of the steps listed above. The constructor has as arguments: **N**, the number of pie segments and **Y**, the array of data (**Double** data type) and **C**, an array of pie segment colors. Once constructed, the **Draw** method is used to draw the pie chart in **P**, the panel hosting the chart.

```
Public Class PieChart
  Dim Slice(1) As PieSlice
  Public Sub New(ByVal N As Integer, ByVal Y() As Double,
ByVal C() As Drawing.Color)
    'builds slices for pie chart
    'N - number of pie segments
    'Y - array of points (Double type) to chart (lower
index is 1, upper index is N)
    'C - color of pie segments
    Dim Sum As Double
    Dim I As Integer
    ReDim Slice(N)
    'find sum of values
    Sum = 0
    For I = 1 To N
      Sum += Y(I)
    Next I
    'for each slice assign sweep angle and color
    For I = 1 To N
      Slice(I) = New PieSlice(CSng(360 * Y(I) / Sum),
C(I))
    Next I
```

```
    End Sub
    Public Function Draw(ByVal P As Panel)
      'Draws a pie chart on panel P
      Dim I As Integer
      Dim PieChart As Drawing.Graphics
      Dim MyBrush As Drawing.Brush
      Dim MyRectangle As Drawing.Rectangle
      Dim StartAngle As Single
      'start drawing - use circle centered in narrowest
dimension of plot area
      If P.ClientSize.Height < P.ClientSize.Width Then
        MyRectangle = New Drawing.Rectangle(CInt(0.5 *
P.ClientSize.Width - 0.45 * P.ClientSize.Height),
CInt(0.05 * P.ClientSize.Height), CInt(0.9 *
P.ClientSize.Height), CInt(0.9 * P.ClientSize.Height))
      Else
        MyRectangle = New Drawing.Rectangle(CInt(0.5 *
P.ClientSize.Width - 0.45 * P.ClientSize.Width), CInt(0.5
* P.ClientSize.Height - 0.45 * P.ClientSize.Width),
CInt(0.9 * P.ClientSize.Width), CInt(0.9 *
P.ClientSize.Width))
      End If
      PieChart = P.CreateGraphics
      PieChart.Clear(P.BackColor)
      StartAngle = 0
      'for each slice compute sweep angle, fill and draw
      For I = 1 To Slice.Length - 1 'array length is one
longer than number of slices
        MyBrush = New
Drawing.SolidBrush(Slice(I).SliceColor)
        PieChart.FillPie(MyBrush, MyRectangle, StartAngle,
Slice(I).SweepAngle)
        PieChart.DrawPie(Drawing.Pens.Black, MyRectangle,
StartAngle, Slice(I).SweepAngle)
        StartAngle += Slice(I).SweepAngle
        MyBrush.Dispose()
      Next I
      PieChart.DrawEllipse(Drawing.Pens.Black, MyRectangle)
      PieChart.Dispose()
      Return (0)
    End Function
End Class
Public Class PieSlice
  Public SweepAngle As Single
  Public SliceColor As Drawing.Color
  Public Sub New(ByVal a As Single, ByVal c As
Drawing.Color)
```

```
        Me.SweepAngle = a
        Me.SliceColor = c
    End Sub
End Class
```

To use the **PieChart** class in your application, first add the class to your project. Then determine the number of slices (**N**), the array of values (**Y**) and an array of colors (**C**). Of course, you can name these variables anything you'd like. The pie chart is then constructed using:

```
Dim MyPieChart As PieChart
MyPieChart = New PieChart(N, Y, C)
```

To draw this chart on a panel control (**MyPanel**), use the **Draw** method:

```
MyPieChart.Draw(MyPanel)
```

Line Charts and Bar Charts

In addition to pie charts, two other useful data display tools are **line charts** and **bar charts**. Line charts are used to plot Cartesian pairs of data (x, y) generated using some function. They are useful for seeing trends in data. As an example, you could plot your weight while following a diet and exercise regime. And, here is a line chart (created with Visual Basic) of yearly attendance at the Seattle Mariners baseball games:

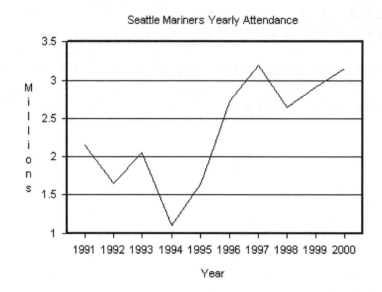

You can see there was increased interest in the team after the 1995 year (that's the exciting year we've alluded to in some of our problems – for example, see Problem 8-4 at the end of this chapter).

The Visual Basic **DrawLine** function can be used to create line charts. The steps for generating such a chart are simple:

> ➢ Generate **N** Cartesian pairs of data to be plotted. Store the horizontal values in an array **X(N)**, the corresponding vertical values in an array **Y(N)** (both 1-based arrays).
> ➢ Loop through all N points, connecting consecutive points using the **DrawLine** function.

Bar charts plot values as horizontal or vertical bars (referenced to some base value, many times zero). They can also be used to see trends and to compare values, like pie charts. Here's a vertical bar chart (drawn with Visual Basic methods) of the same attendance data in the line chart above (the base value is 1 million):

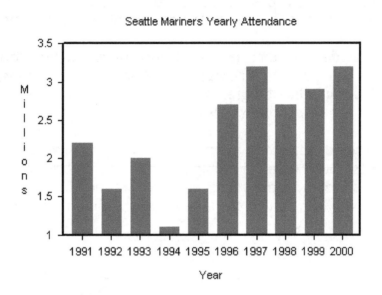

The increase in attendance after 1995 is very pronounced. And, here's a bar chart (base value of zero) of Seattle's monthly rainfall (again, note how big the 'winter' bars are):

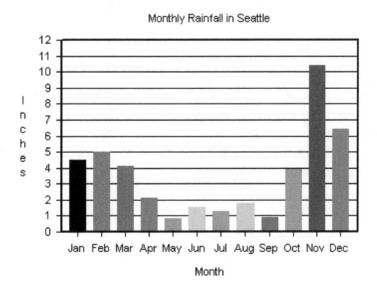

Yes, this, too, was created with Visual Basic.

The **FillRectangle** graphics method can be used for bar charts. The steps for generating a vertical bar chart:

> ➢ Generate **N** pieces of data to be plotted. Store this data in an array **Y(N)** (a 1-based array).
> ➢ Determine the width of each bar, using width of the graphics object as a guide. I usually allow some space between each bar.
> ➢ Select a base value (the value at the bottom of the bar). This is often zero.
> ➢ For each bar, determine horizontal position based on bar width and current bar being drawn. Draw each bar (pick a unique, identifying color, if desired) using **FillRectangle**. The bar height begins at the base value and ends at the respective **Y** value.

At this point, we could write code to implement general procedures for drawing line and bar charts. But, there's a problem. And, that problem relates to the **client coordinates** used by the graphics objects. Let me illustrate. Say we wanted to draw a very simple line chart described by the four Cartesian points given by:

x = 0, y = 2
x = 2, y = 7
x = 5, y = 11
x = 6, y = 13

In this plot, the horizontal axis value (x) begins at 0 and reaches a maximum of 6. The vertical axis value (y) has a minimum value of 2, a maximum of 13. And, y increases in an upward direction.

Recall, the client coordinates of the graphics object has an origin of **(0, 0)** at the upper left corner. The maximum x value is **ClientSize.Width - 1**, the maximum y value is **ClientSize.Height -1** and y increases in a downward direction. Hence, to plot our data, we need to first compute where each (x, y) pair in our 'user-coordinates' fits within the dimensions of the graphics object specified by the **ClientSize.Width** and **ClientSize.Height** properties. This is a straightforward coordinate conversion computation.

Coordinate Conversions

Drawing in the graphics object is done in **client coordinates** (measured in pixels, an integer type). Data for plotting line and bar charts is usually in some physically meaningful units (inches, degrees, dollars) we'll call **user coordinates**. In order to draw a line or bar chart, we need to be able to convert from user coordinates to client coordinates. We will do each axis (horizontal and vertical) separately.

The horizontal (**Xclient** axis) in **client coordinates** is **ClientSize.Width** pixels wide. The far left pixel is at **Xclient = 0** and the far right is at **Xclient = ClientSize.Width - 1**. Xclient increases from left to right:

0	Xclient	ClientSize.Width - 1

Assume the horizontal data (**Xuser** axis) in our user coordinates runs from a minimum, **Xmin**, at the left to a maximum, **Xmax,** at the right. Thus, the first pixel on the horizontal axis of our user coordinates will be Xmin and the last will be Xmax:

Xmin	Xuser	Xmax

With these two depictions, we can compute the **Xclient** value corresponding to a given **Xuser** value using simple **proportions**, dividing the distance from some point on the axis to the minimum value by the total distance. The process is also called **linear interpolation**. These proportions show:

$$\frac{\text{Xuser - Xmin}}{\text{Xmax - Xmin}} = \frac{\text{Xclient - 0}}{\text{ClientSize.Width} - 1 - 0}$$

Solving this for **Xclient** yields the desired conversion from a user value on the horizontal axis (**Xuser**) to a client value for plotting:

Xclient = (Xuser - Xmin)(ClientSize.Width - 1)/(Xmax - Xmin)

You can see this is correct at each extreme value. When **Xuser = Xmin**, **Xclient = 0**. When **Xuser = Xmax**, **Xclient = ClientSize.Width - 1**.

Now, we find the corresponding conversion for the vertical axis. We'll place the two axes side-by-side for easy comparison:

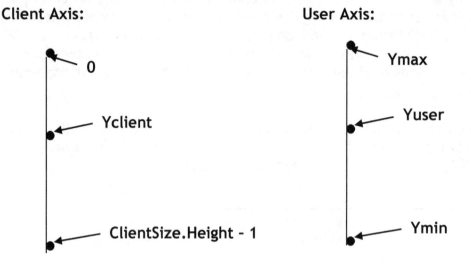

The vertical (**Yclient** axis) in **client coordinates** is **ClientSize.Height** pixels high. The topmost pixel is at **Yclient = 0** and the bottom is at **Yclient = ClientSize.Height - 1**. YClient increases from top to bottom. The vertical data (**Yuser** axis) in our user coordinates, runs from a minimum, **Ymin**, at the bottom, to a maximum, **Ymax**, at the top. Thus, the top pixel on the vertical axis of our user coordinates will be **Ymax** and the bottom will be **Ymin** (note our user axis increases up, rather than down).

With these two depictions, we can compute the **Yclient** value corresponding to a given **Yuser** value using linear interpolation. The computations show:

$$\frac{\text{Yuser - Ymin}}{\text{Ymax - Ymin}} = \frac{\text{Yclient - (ClientSize.Height - 1)}}{0 - (\text{ClientSize.Height} - 1)}$$

Solving this for **Yclient** yields the desired conversion from a user value on the vertical axis (**Yuser**) to a client value for plotting (this requires a bit algebra, but it's straightforward):

Yclient = (Ymax - Yuser)(ClientSize.Height - 1)/(Ymax - Ymin)

Again, check the extremes. When **Yuser = Ymin**, **Yclient = ClientSize.Height - 1**. When **Yuser = Ymax**, **Yclient = 0**. It looks good.

Whenever we need to plot real, physical data in a graphics object, we will need coordinate conversions. In these notes, we use two general functions to do the conversions. First, for the horizontal axis, we use **XuserToXclient**. This function has four input arguments: **P** the panel control hosting the graphics object, the **Xuser** value, the minimum user value, **Xmin**, and the maximum value, **Xmax**. All values are of **Double** data type. The function returns the client coordinate (an **Integer** type):

```
Private Function XUserToXClient(ByVal P As Panel, ByVal
Xuser As Double, ByVal Xmin As Double, ByVal Xmax As
Double) As Integer
   Return (CInt((P.ClientSize.Width - 1) * (Xuser - Xmin) /
(Xmax - Xmin)))
End Function
```

For the vertical axis, we use **YuserToYclient**. This function has four input arguments: **P** the panel control hosting the graphics object, the **Yuser** value, the minimum user value, **Ymin**, and the maximum value, **Ymax**. All values are of **Double** data type. The function returns the client coordinate (an **Integer** type):

```
Private Function YuserToYclient(ByVal P As Panel, ByVal
Yuser As Double, ByVal Ymin As Double, ByVal Ymax As
Double) As Integer
   Return (CInt(P.ClientSize.Height - 1) * (Ymax - Yuser) /
(Ymax - Ymin))
End Function
```

With the ability to transform coordinates, we can now develop general-purpose line and bar chart classes, similar to that developed for the pie chart. The modified steps to create a line chart are:

➢ Generate **N** Cartesian pairs of data to be plotted. Store the horizontal values in an array **X(N)**, the corresponding vertical values in an array **Y(N)** (both 1-based arrays).
➢ Loop through all N points to determine the minimum and maximum X and Y values.
➢ Again, loop through all N points. For each point, convert the X and Y values to client coordinates, then connect the current point with the previous point using the **DrawLine** function.

The following code is a general class (**LineChart**) that draws a line chart in a panel control. It incorporates the two coordinate conversion functions. You should be able to identify each of the steps listed above (most involve finding the minimum and maximum values). The constructor has as arguments: **P**, the panel hosting the chart, **N**, the number of points to plot, **X**, the array of horizontal values, and **Y** the array of vertical values. The **X** and **Y** arrays are of type **Double**. Once constructed, the **Draw** method is used to draw the line chart in **P** using the line color **C**.

```
Public Class LineChart
   Public XClient(1) As Integer, YClient(1) As Integer
   Public Sub New(ByVal P As Panel, ByVal N As Integer,
ByVal X() As Double, ByVal Y() As Double)
     'Constructs a  line chart - pairs of (x,y) coordinates
     'N - number of points to plot
     'X - array of x points (lower index is 1, upper index
is N)
     'Y - array of y points (lower index is 1, upper index
is N)
     Dim I As Integer
     Dim Xmin As Double, Xmax As Double
     Dim Ymin As Double, Ymax As Double
     'Need at least 2 points to plot
     If N < 2 Then
       Exit Sub
     End If
     ReDim XClient(N), YClient(N)
     'find minimums and maximums
     Xmin = X(1) : Xmax = X(1)
     Ymin = Y(1) : Ymax = Y(1)
     For I = 2 To N
       If X(I) < Xmin Then Xmin = X(I)
       If X(I) > Xmax Then Xmax = X(I)
       If Y(I) < Ymin Then Ymin = Y(I)
       If Y(I) > Ymax Then Ymax = Y(I)
     Next I
     'Extend Y values a bit so lines are not right on
borders
     Ymin = CSng((1 - 0.05 * Math.Sign(Ymin)) * Ymin)
     Ymax = CSng((1 + 0.05 * Math.Sign(Ymax)) * Ymax)
     For I = 1 To N
       'determine client coordinates
       XClient(I) = XUserToXClient(P, X(I), Xmin, Xmax)
       YClient(I) = YuserToYclient(P, Y(I), Ymin, Ymax)
     Next I
   End Sub
```

```
    Public Function Draw(ByVal P As Panel C As
Drawing.Color)
        'Draws a  line chart in P
        'N - number of points to plot
        'XClient - array of x points (lower index is 1, upper
index is N)
        'YClient - array of y points (lower index is 1, upper
index is N)
        'C - color of line
        Dim I As Integer
        Dim LineChart As Drawing.Graphics
        Dim MyPen As Drawing.Pen
        LineChart = P.CreateGraphics
        MyPen = New Drawing.Pen(C)
        LineChart.Clear(P.BackColor)
        For I = 1 To XClient.Length - 2 ' length has one more
point than needed
            'plot in client coordinates
            LineChart.DrawLine(MyPen, XClient(I), YClient(I),
XClient(I + 1), YClient(I + 1))
        Next I
        LineChart.Dispose()
        MyPen.Dispose()
        Return (0)
    End Function
    Private Function XUserToXClient(ByVal P As Panel, ByVal
Xuser As Double, ByVal Xmin As Double, ByVal Xmax As
Double) As Integer
        Return (CInt((P.ClientSize.Width - 1) * (Xuser - Xmin)
/ (Xmax - Xmin)))
    End Function
    Private Function YuserToYclient(ByVal P As Panel, ByVal
Yuser As Double, ByVal Ymin As Double, ByVal Ymax As
Double) As Integer
        Return (CInt(P.ClientSize.Height - 1) * (Ymax - Yuser)
/ (Ymax - Ymin))
    End Function
End Class
```

To use the **LineChart** class in your application, first add the class to your project. Then determine the number of points (**N**), the arrays of points (**X** and **Y**) and a line color (**C**). Of course, you can name these variables anything you'd like. The line chart is then constructed for use in a panel control named **MyPanel** using:

```
Dim MyLineChart As LineChart
MyLineChart = New LineChart(MyPanel, N, X, Y)
```

To draw this chart on the panel control using color **C**, use the **Draw** method:

```
MyLineChart.Draw(MyPanel,C)
```

The modified steps to create a bar chart are:

➢ Generate **N** pieces of data to be plotted. Store this data in an array **Y(N)** (a 1-based array).
➢ Determine the width of each bar, using width of the graphics object as a guide. I usually allow some space between each bar.
➢ Loop through all N points to determine the minimum and maximum Y value.
➢ Select a base value (the value at the bottom of the bar). This is often zero. Convert the base value to client coordinates.
➢ For each bar, determine horizontal position based on bar width and current bar being drawn. Draw each bar (pick a unique, identifying color, if desired) using **FillRectangle**. The bar height begins at the base value and ends at the respective **Y** value (converted to client coordinates.

The following code is a general class (**BarChart**) that draws a bar chart in a panel control. It incorporates the vertical coordinate conversion function. You should be able to identify each of the steps listed above (most involve finding the minimum and maximum values). The constructor has as arguments: **P**, the panel hosting the chart, **N**, the number of bars to draw, **Y** the array of values (type **Double**), and **B** the base value (type **Double**). Once constructed, the **Draw** method is used to draw the bar chart in **P** with **C** the bar color array. This routine uses a version of **FillRectangle** that does not use the rectangle structure. It simply defines the rectangle using the usual Left, Top, Width and Height properties. Also, note different coding is needed depending whether the bar value is higher or lower than the base value (i.e., whether the bar goes up or down).

```
Public Class BarChart
   Public YClient(1) As Integer
   Public BClient As Integer
   Public Sub New(ByVal P As Panel, ByVal N As Integer,
ByVal Y() As Double, ByVal B As Double)
      'Constructs a vertical bar chart
      'P - panel control to draw plot
      'N - number of points to plot
      'Y - array of points to chart (lower index is 1, upper
index is N)
      'B - base value (lower limit of bar drawn)
      Dim Ymin As Double, Ymax As Double
      Dim I As Integer
      ReDim YClient(N)
      'find minimums and maximums
      Ymin = Y(1) : Ymax = Y(1)
      If N > 1 Then
        For I = 2 To N
          If Y(I) < Ymin Then Ymin = Y(I)
          If Y(I) > Ymax Then Ymax = Y(I)
        Next I
      End If
      'Extend Y values a bit so bars are not right on
borders
      Ymin = CSng((1 - 0.05 * Math.Sign(Ymin)) * Ymin)
      Ymax = CSng((1 + 0.05 * Math.Sign(Ymax)) * Ymax)
      BClient = YuserToYclient(P, B, Ymin, Ymax)
      For I = 1 To N
        'determine client values
        YClient(I) = YuserToYclient(P, Y(I), Ymin, Ymax)
      Next I
   End Sub
   Public Function Draw(ByVal P As Panel, ByVal C() As
Drawing.Color)
```

```
'Draws a vertical bar chart on P
'P - panel control to draw plot
'N - number of points to plot
'YClient - array of points to chart (lower index is 1,
upper index is N)
'C - color of bars
'BClient - base value (lower limit of bar drawn)
Dim I As Integer
Dim BarChart As Drawing.Graphics
Dim MyBrush As Drawing.Brush
Dim BarWidth As Integer
BarChart = P.CreateGraphics
BarChart.Clear(P.BackColor)
'Find bar width in client coordinates
'use half bar-width as margins between bars
BarWidth = CInt(2 * (P.ClientSize.Width - 1) / (3 *
(YClient.Length - 1) + 1))
For I = 1 To YClient.Length - 1 ' array has one more
element than bars
    MyBrush = New Drawing.SolidBrush(C(I))
    'draw bars
    If BClient > YClient(I) Then
        BarChart.FillRectangle(MyBrush, CSng((1.5 * I - 1)
* BarWidth), YClient(I), BarWidth, BClient - YClient(I))
    Else
        BarChart.FillRectangle(MyBrush, CSng((1.5 * I - 1)
* BarWidth), BClient, BarWidth, YClient(I) - BClient)
    End If
    MyBrush.Dispose()
Next I
'line at base
BarChart.DrawLine(Pens.Black, 0, BClient,
P.ClientSize.Width - 1, BClient)
BarChart.Dispose()
Return (0)
End Function
Private Function YuserToYclient(ByVal P As Panel, ByVal
Yuser As Double, ByVal Ymin As Double, ByVal Ymax As
Double) As Integer
    Return (CInt(P.ClientSize.Height - 1) * (Ymax - Yuser)
/ (Ymax - Ymin))
End Function
End Class
```

To use the **BarChart** class in your application, first add the class to your project. Then determine the number of points (**N**), the array of points (**Y**), a base value (**B**) and a bar color array (**C**). Of course, you can name these variables anything you'd like. The bar chart is then constructed for use in a panel control named **MyPanel** using:

```
Dim MyBarChart As BarChart
MyBarChart = New BarChart(MyPanel, N, Y, B)
```

To draw this chart on the panel control using color array **C**, use the **Draw** method:

```
MyBarChart.Draw(MyPanel, C)
```

Example 8-9

Line, Bar and Pie Charts

1. Start a new application. Here, we'll use the classes we developed to plot line, bar and pie charts. The data for the plots will be random.

2. Put a panel control and main menu strip control (**Name mnuMainPlot**) on a form. Set up this simple menu structure:

Plot
    Line Chart
    Bar Chart
    Spiral Chart
    Pie Chart
    ——————

    Exit

Properties for these menu items should be:

Text	Name	Shortcut
&Plot	mnuPlot	[None]
&Line Chart	mnuPlotLine	CtrlL
&Bar Chart	mnuPlotBar	CtrlB
&Spiral Chart	mnuPlotSpiral	CtrlS
&Pie Chart	mnuPlotPie	CtrlP
-	mnuPlotSep	[None]
E&xit	mnuPlotExit	[None]

Other properties should be:

Form1:

Name	frmPlot
FormBorderStyle	Fixed Single
MainMenuStrip	mnuMainPlot
StartPosition	CenterScreen
Text	Plotting Examples

Panel1:

Name	pnlPlot
BackColor	White

The form should resemble this (menu is opened):

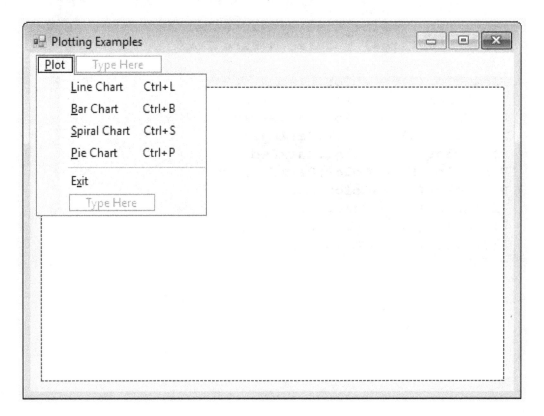

Other controls in tray:

mnuMainPlot

3. Form level scope declarations:

```
Dim WhichPlot As Integer = 0
'data arrays
Dim X(200) As Double, Y(200) As Double, YD(200) As Double
'color array
Dim PlotColor(10) As Drawing.Color
'information to construct line charts (whichplot=1, 2)
Dim Alpha As Double, Beta As Double, LineColor As
Drawing.Color
'information to construct bar chart (whichplot=3)
Dim NumberBars As Integer
'information for pie chart (whichplot=4)
Dim NumberSlices As Integer
Dim MyRandom As New Random()
```

4. Use this code in the **frmPlot Load** procedure. This sets colors to use:

```
Private Sub FrmPlot_Load(ByVal sender As Object, ByVal e
As System.EventArgs) Handles MyBase.Load
    'colors to use
    PlotColor(1) = Color.Black
    PlotColor(2) = Color.DarkBlue
    PlotColor(3) = Color.DarkGreen
    PlotColor(4) = Color.DarkCyan
    PlotColor(5) = Color.DarkRed
    PlotColor(6) = Color.DarkMagenta
    PlotColor(7) = Color.Brown
    PlotColor(8) = Color.Blue
    PlotColor(9) = Color.Gray
    PlotColor(10) = Color.Red
End Sub
```

5. Add this code to the **mnuPlotLine Click** procedure (handles both
   mnuPlotLine and **mnuPlotSpiral Click** events). This code generates random
   data to plot using the **LineChart** class:

```
Private Sub MnuPlotLine_Click(ByVal sender As
System.Object, ByVal e As System.EventArgs) Handles
mnuPlotLine.Click, mnuPlotSpiral.Click
    Dim ItemClicked As ToolStripMenuItem
    ItemClicked = CType(sender, ToolStripMenuItem)
    'clear checks
    mnuPlotLine.Checked = False
    mnuPlotSpiral.Checked = False
    mnuPlotBar.Checked = False
    mnuPlotPie.Checked = False
    'check item selected
    ItemClicked.Checked = True
    'Create a sinusoid with 200 points
    Dim I As Integer
    Alpha = (100 - MyRandom.Next(200)) / 1000
    Beta = MyRandom.Next(1000) / 100 + 5
    For I = 1 To 200
      X(I) = I
      Y(I) = CDbl(Math.Exp(-Alpha * I) * Math.Sin(Math.PI *
I / Beta))
      YD(I) = CDbl(Math.Exp(-Alpha * I) * (Math.PI *
Math.Cos(Math.PI * I / Beta) / Beta - Alpha *
Math.Sin(Math.PI * I / Beta)))
    Next I
    'choose random color
    LineColor = PlotColor(MyRandom.Next(10) + 1)
    'Draw plots
    If mnuPlotLine.Checked Then
      WhichPlot = 1
    Else
      WhichPlot = 2
    End If
    pnlPlot_Paint(Nothing, Nothing)
  End Sub
```

6. Add this code to the **mnuPlotBar Click**. This code generates random data to plot using the **BarChart** class:

```
    Private Sub MnuPlotBar_Click(ByVal sender As
System.Object, ByVal e As System.EventArgs) Handles
mnuPlotBar.Click
        'generate 5-10 bars with values from -10 to 10 and draw
bar chart
        Dim I As Integer
        'check item selected
        mnuPlotLine.Checked = False
        mnuPlotSpiral.Checked = False
        mnuPlotBar.Checked = True
        mnuPlotPie.Checked = False
        NumberBars = MyRandom.Next(6) + 5
        For I = 1 To NumberBars
           Y(I) = MyRandom.Next(2000) / 100 - 10
        Next I
        WhichPlot = 3
        pnlPlot_Paint(Nothing, Nothing)
    End Sub
```

7. Add this code to the **mnuPlotPie Click**. This code generates random data to plot using the **PieChart** class:

```
    Private Sub MnuPlotPie_Click(ByVal sender As
System.Object, ByVal e As System.EventArgs) Handles
mnuPlotPie.Click
        'Generate 3 to 10 slices at random with values from 1 to
5
        Dim I As Integer
        'check item selected
        mnuPlotLine.Checked = False
        mnuPlotSpiral.Checked = False
        mnuPlotBar.Checked = False
        mnuPlotPie.Checked = True
        NumberSlices = MyRandom.Next(8) + 3
        For I = 1 To NumberSlices
           Y(I) = MyRandom.Next(5000) / 100 + 1
        Next I
        WhichPlot = 4
        pnlPlot_Paint(Nothing, Nothing)
    End Sub
```

8. Use this code in the **pnlPlot Paint** event. This code draws the plot based on user selection:

```
Private Sub PnlPlot_Paint(ByVal sender As Object, ByVal e
As System.Windows.Forms.PaintEventArgs) Handles
pnlPlot.Paint
    Select Case WhichPlot
      Case 0
        Exit Sub
      Case 1
        'line chart (x/y)
        Dim MyLineChart As LineChart
        MyLineChart = New LineChart(pnlPlot, 200, X, Y)
        MyLineChart.Draw(pnlPlot, LineColor)
      Case 2
        'spiral chart
        Dim MySpiralChart As LineChart
        MySpiralChart = New LineChart(pnlPlot, 200, Y, YD)
        MySpiralChart.Draw(pnlPlot, LineColor)
      Case 3
        'bar chart
        Dim MyBarChart As BarChart
        MyBarChart = New BarChart(pnlPlot, NumberBars, Y, 0)
        MyBarChart.Draw(pnlPlot, PlotColor)
      Case 4
        'pie chart
        Dim MyPieChart As PieChart
        MyPieChart = New PieChart(NumberSlices, Y,
PlotColor)
        MyPieChart.Draw(pnlPlot)
    End Select
  End Sub
```

9. Add this code to the **mnuPlotExit Clik** event procedure:

```
Private Sub MnuPlotExit_Click(ByVal sender As
System.Object, ByVal e As System.EventArgs) Handles
mnuPlotExit.Click
    Me.Close()
End Sub
```

10. Make sure to create the **LineChart (LineChart.vb)**, **BarChart (BarChart.vb)**, and **PieChart (PieChart.vb)** classes and add them to your project.

11. Finally, save and run the application (saved in **Example 8-9** folder in **LearnVB\VB Code\Class 8** folder). Run it and try all the plotting options. Each time you draw any plot it will be different because of the randomness programmed in. Here's an example of each plot type:

Line Chart:

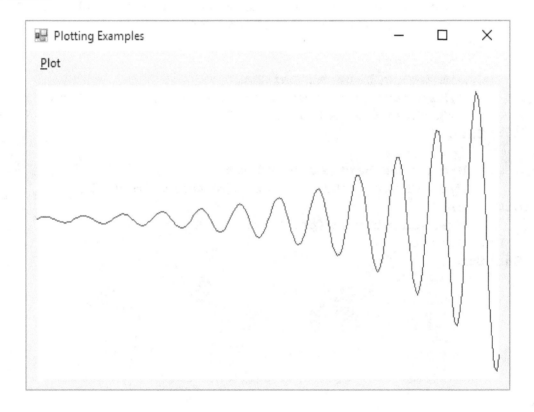

Spiral Chart:

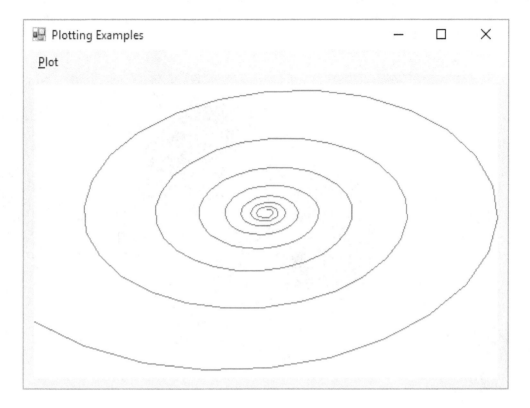

Bar Chart:

Pie Chart:

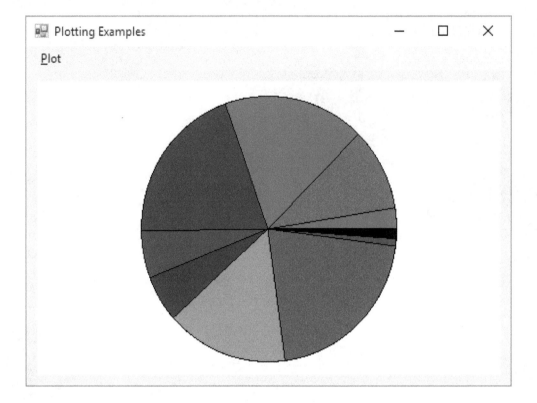

You're ready to tackle any plotting job now.

These routines just call out for enhancements. Some things you might try:

A. Draw grid lines on the plots. Use dotted or dashed lines at regular intervals.

B. Modify the line and chart classes to allow plotting more than one function. Use colors or different line styles to differentiate the lines and bars. Add a legend defining each plot.

C. Label the plot axes. Put titling information on the axes and the plot. Consult the **DrawString** function described in Chapter 9.

Class Review

After completing this class, you should understand:

- How to do simple animation with the picture box control
- How the timer control works – its properties and the Tick event
- The basics of simple games using the random number generator
- The graphics methods and objects that allow drawing directly to the graphics object
- Ways to specify colors with the graphics methods, for setting properties and use of the ColorDialog control
- The concept of persistent graphics and use of the Paint event
- The difference between client coordinates and user coordinates and conversion from one to the other
- How to draw simple line charts, bar charts and pie charts.

Practice Problems 8

Problem 8-1. Find the Burger Game. Build a game where a burger (a burger graphic is included in the **LearnVB\VB Code\Class 8\Problem 8-1** folder) is hidden behind one of three picture boxes. You click on the boxes trying to find the burger. Add a way to shuffle the boxes prior to guessing.

Problem 8-2. Dice Rolling Problem. Build an application that rolls two dice and displays the results (graphics of the six die faces are included in the **LearnVB\VB Code\Class 8\Problem 8-2** folder). Have each die 'stop rolling' at different times.

Problem 8-3. RGB Colors Problem. Build an application with three scroll bars and a label control. Use the scroll bars to adjust the red, green and blue contributions to the **FromArgb** function of the Color structure. Let the background color of the label control be set by those contributions.

Problem 8-4. Plotting Problem. Build an application that opens the output file created in Practice Problem 7-3 (the Mariners win streak file – saved as **MAR95.CSV** in the **LearnVB\VB Code\Class 7\Problem 7-3\Bin\Debug** folder) and plots the information as a bar chart in a panel control. You'll want to first copy the **CSV** file into the **Bin\Debug folder** of this new application.

Problem 8-5. Pie Chart Problem. Build an application where the user can enter a list of numbers and build a pie chart from that list.

Exercise 8-1

Blackjack

Develop an application that simulates the playing of the card game Blackjack. The idea of Blackjack is to score higher than a Dealer's hand without exceeding twenty-one. Cards count their value, except face cards (jacks, queens, kings) count for ten, and aces count for either one or eleven (your pick). If you beat the Dealer, you get 10 points. If you get Blackjack (21 with just two cards) and beat the Dealer, you get 15 points. This is not a trivial application to build.

The game starts by giving two cards (from a standard 52 card deck) to the Dealer (one face down) and two cards to the player. The player decides whether to Hit (get another card) or Stay. The player can choose as many extra cards as desired. If the player exceeds 21 before staying, it is a loss (-10 points). If the player does not exceed 21, it becomes the dealer's turn. The Dealer adds cards until 16 is exceeded. When this occurs, if the dealer also exceeds 21 or if his total is less than the player's, he loses. If the dealer total is greater than the player total (and under 21), the dealer wins. If the dealer and player have the same total, it is a Push (no points added or subtracted). There are lots of other things you can do in Blackjack, but these simple rules should suffice here. The cards should be reshuffled whenever there are fewer than fifteen (or so) cards remaining in the deck.

Exercise 8-2

Information Tracking Plotting

Add plotting capabilities to the information tracker you developed in Class 7. Plot whatever information you stored versus the date. Use a line or bar chart.

9. More Graphics Methods and Multimedia Effects

Review and Preview

In the last class, we learned a lot about graphics methods in Visual Basic. Yet, everything we drew was static; there was no user interaction. In this chapter, we extend our graphics methods knowledge by learning how to detect mouse events. An example paintbrush program is built. We look at new brush objects and how to 'draw' text. We then are introduced to concepts needed for multimedia (game) programming – animation, collision detection, and sounds. Like Chapter 8, we will build lots of relatively short examples to demonstrate concepts. You'll learn to modify the examples for your needs.

Mouse Events

In Chapter 8, we learned about the graphics object, the rectangle structure and many drawing methods. We learned how to draw lines, rectangles, ellipses and pie segments. We learned how to incorporate these drawing elements into procedures for line charts, bar charts and pie charts. Everything drawn with these elements was static; there was no user interaction. We set the parameters in code and drew our shapes or plots. We (the users) just sat there and watched pretty things appear.

In this chapter, the user becomes involved. To provide user interaction with an application, we can use the mouse as an interface for drawing graphics with Visual Basic. To do this, we need to understand **mouse events**. Mouse events are similar to control events. Certain event procedures are invoked when certain mouse actions are detected. Here, we see how to use mouse events for drawing on forms and panel controls.

We've used the mouse to click on controls in past applications. For example, we've written code for many button control **Click** events. To use the mouse for drawing purposes, however, a simple click event is not sufficient. We need to know not only that a control was clicked, but also need to know where it was clicked to provide a point to draw to. The mouse event that provides this information is the **MouseDown** event. The **MouseDown** event procedure is triggered whenever a mouse button is pressed while the mouse cursor is over a control. The form of this procedure is:

```
Private Sub ControlName_MouseDown(ByVal sender As Object,
ByVal e As System.Windows.Forms.MouseEventArgs) Handles
ControlName.MouseDown
   .
   .
End Sub
```

The arguments are:

sender	Control clicked to invoke procedure
e	Event handler revealing which button was clicked and the coordinate of mouse cursor when button was pressed.

We are interested in three properties of the event handler **e**:

e.Button	Mouse button pressed. Possible values are: **MouseButtons.Left**, **MouseButtons.Center**, **MouseButtons.Right**
e.X	X coordinate of mouse cursor when mouse was clicked
e.Y	Y coordinate of mouse cursor when mouse was clicked

In drawing applications, the **MouseDown** event is used to initialize a drawing process. The point clicked is used to start drawing a line and the button clicked is often used to select line color.

Another common task for drawing with the mouse is moving the mouse while holding down a mouse button. The mouse event that provides this information is the **MouseMove** event. The **MouseMove** event is continuously triggered whenever the mouse is being moved over a control. The form of this procedure is:

```
Private Sub ControlName_MouseMove(ByVal sender As Object,
ByVal e As System.Windows.Forms.MouseEventArgs) Handles
ControlName.MouseMove
        .
        .
        .
End Sub
```

Its arguments are identical to those of the **MouseDown** event:

sender	Control clicked to invoke procedure
e	Event handler revealing which button is pressed and the current coordinate of mouse.

Properties for the event handler **e** are the same:

e.Button	Mouse button pressed (if any). Possible values are: **MouseButtons.Left**, **MouseButtons.Center**, **MouseButtons.Right**, **MouseButtons.None**
e.X	X coordinate of mouse cursor
e.Y	Y coordinate of mouse cursor

In drawing processes, the **MouseMove** event is used to detect the continuation of a previously started line. If drawing is continuing, the current point is connected to the previous point using the current pen.

Lastly, we would like to be able to detect the release of a mouse button. The **MouseUp** event is the opposite of the **MouseDown** event. It is triggered whenever a previously pressed mouse button is released. The procedure outline is:

```
Private Sub ControlName_MouseUp(ByVal sender As Object,
ByVal e As System.Windows.Forms.MouseEventArgs) Handles
ControlName.MouseUp
    .
    .
    .
End Sub
```

The arguments are:

sender	Control invoking procedure
e	Event handler revealing which button was released and the coordinate of mouse cursor when button was released.

We are interested in three properties of the event handler **e**:

e.Button	Mouse button released. Possible values are: **MouseButtons.Left**, **MouseButtons.Center**, **MouseButtons.Right**
e.X	X coordinate of mouse cursor when button was released
e.Y	Y coordinate of mouse cursor when button was released

In a drawing program, the **MouseUp** event signifies the halting of the current drawing process. We'll find the **MouseDown**, **MouseMove** and **MouseUp** events are integral parts of any Visual Basic drawing program. We use them now (in conjunction with the **DrawLine** method) to build a paintbrush program called the **Blackboard**.

Example 9-1

Blackboard

1. Start a new application. Here, we will build a blackboard we can scribble on with the mouse (using colored 'chalk'). The left and right mouse buttons will draw with different (selectable) colors. Place a large panel control and two label controls on a form. Place a group box with 8 small label controls in it. The form should resemble this:

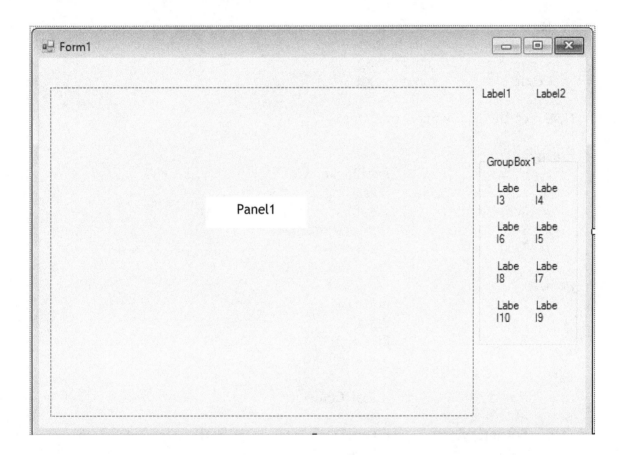

2. Add a main menu strip control (**Name mnuBlackboard**). Set up a simple menu structure for your application. The menu should be:

File
   New
   ─────
   Exit

Properties for these menu items should be:

Text	Name
&File	mnuFile
&New	mnuFileNew
-	mnuFileSep
E&xit	mnuFileExit

3. Now, set the following properties:

Form1:

Name	frmBlackboard
FormBorderStyle	FixedSingle
MainMenuStrip	mnuBlackboard
StartPosition	CenterScreen
Text	Blackboard

Panel1:

Name	pnlDraw
BackColor	Black
BorderStyle	Fixed3D

Label1:

Name	lblLeftColor
AutoSize	False
BorderStyle	Fixed3D
Text	[Blank]

Label2:

Name	lblRightColor
AutoSize	False
BorderStyle	Fixed3D
Text	[Blank]

GroupBox1:

Name	grpColors
Font Size	10
Text	Colors

Label3:

Name	lblGray
AutoSize	False
BorderStyle	Fixed3D
Text	[Blank]

Label4:

Name	lblBlue
AutoSize	False
BorderStyle	Fixed3D
Text	[Blank]

Label5:

Name	lblGreen
AutoSize	False
BorderStyle	Fixed3D
Text	[Blank]

Label6:

Name	lblCyan
AutoSize	False
BorderStyle	Fixed3D
Text	[Blank]

Label7:

Name	lblRed
AutoSize	False
BorderStyle	Fixed3D
Text	[Blank]

Label8:

Name	lblMagenta
AutoSize	False
BorderStyle	Fixed3D
Text	[Blank]

Label9:

Name	lblYellow
AutoSize	False
BorderStyle	Fixed3D
Text	[Blank]

Label10:

Name	lblWhite
AutoSize	False
BorderStyle	Fixed3D
Text	[Blank]

The finished form (menu opened) should look something like this:

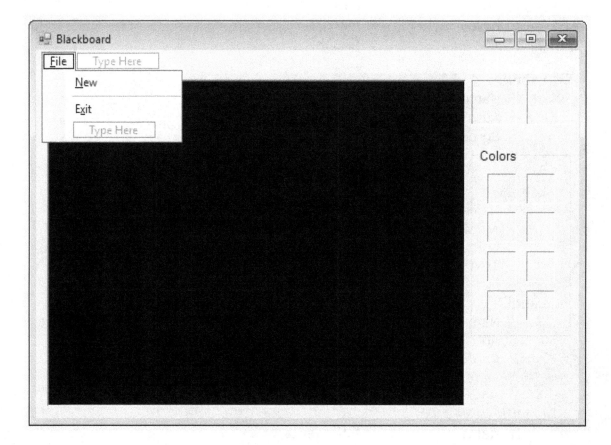

Other controls in tray:

mnuBlackboard

4. Form level scope declarations code:

```
Dim Blackboard As Drawing.Graphics
Dim MyPen As Drawing.Pen
Dim DrawingOn As Boolean = False
Dim XPrevious As Integer, YPrevious As Integer
Dim LeftColor As Drawing.Color, RightColor As
Drawing.Color
```

These are used to do drawing. **DrawingOn** indicates if drawing process is active.

5. Use this code in each indicated procedure.

Use this code in the **frmBlackboard Load** procedure to set up selection and drawing colors and form drawing objects:

```
Private Sub FrmBlackboard_Load(ByVal sender As
System.Object, ByVal e As System.EventArgs) Handles
MyBase.Load
    'establish color choices
    lblGray.BackColor = Drawing.Color.Gray
    lblBlue.BackColor = Drawing.Color.Blue
    lblGreen.BackColor = Drawing.Color.LightGreen
    lblCyan.BackColor = Drawing.Color.Cyan
    lblRed.BackColor = Drawing.Color.Red
    lblMagenta.BackColor = Drawing.Color.Magenta
    lblYellow.BackColor = Drawing.Color.Yellow
    lblWhite.BackColor = Drawing.Color.White
    'set up graphics object and drawing pen
    LeftColor = Drawing.Color.Gray
    lblLeftColor.BackColor = LeftColor
    RightColor = Drawing.Color.White
    lblRightColor.BackColor = RightColor
    'create objects
    Blackboard = pnlDraw.CreateGraphics
    MyPen = New Drawing.Pen(LeftColor)
End Sub
```

Code for **mnuFileNew Click** event where we check to see if the drawing should be erased.

```
    Private Sub MnuFileNew_Click(ByVal sender As
System.Object, ByVal e As System.EventArgs) Handles
mnuFileNew.Click
        'Make sure user wants to start over
        If MessageBox.Show("Are you sure you want to start a new
drawing?", "New Drawing", MessageBoxButtons.YesNo,
MessageBoxIcon.Question) = Windows.Forms.DialogResult.Yes
Then
            Blackboard.Clear(Drawing.Color.Black)
        End If
    End Sub
```

In **mnuFileExit Click**, make sure the user really wants to stop the application.

```
    Private Sub MnuFileExit_Click(ByVal sender As
System.Object, ByVal e As System.EventArgs) Handles
mnuFileExit.Click
        'Make sure user wants to quit
        If MessageBox.Show("Are you sure you want to exit the
Blackboard?", "Exit Blackboard", MessageBoxButtons.YesNo,
MessageBoxIcon.Error, MessageBoxDefaultButton.Button2) =
Windows.Forms.DialogResult.Yes Then
            Me.Close()
        Else
            Exit Sub
        End If
    End Sub
```

In the **frmBlackboard FormClosing** event, dispose of the graphics objects.

```
    Private Sub FrmBlackboard_FormClosing(ByVal sender As
Object, ByVal e As
System.Windows.Forms.FormClosingEventArgs) Handles
Me.FormClosing
        'dispose graphics objects
        Blackboard.Dispose()
        MyPen.Dispose()
    End Sub
```

Code for **lblColor MouseDown** event to select color (handles clicking on any of eight color choice label controls).

```
    Private Sub LblColor_MouseDown(ByVal sender As Object,
ByVal e As System.Windows.Forms.MouseEventArgs) Handles
lblGray.MouseDown, lblBlue.MouseDown, lblGreen.MouseDown,
lblCyan.MouseDown, lblRed.MouseDown, lblMagenta.MouseDown,
lblYellow.MouseDown, lblWhite.MouseDown
        Dim ColorClicked As Label
        ColorClicked = CType(sender, Label)
        'Make audible tone and set drawing color
        Beep()
        If e.Button = Windows.Forms.MouseButtons.Left Then
          LeftColor = ColorClicked.BackColor
          lblLeftColor.BackColor = LeftColor
        ElseIf e.Button = Windows.Forms.MouseButtons.Right Then
          RightColor = ColorClicked.BackColor
          lblRightColor.BackColor = RightColor
        End If
    End Sub
```

When a mouse button is clicked (left or right button), drawing is initialized at the mouse cursor location with the respective color in the **pnlDraw MouseDown** event.

```
    Private Sub PnlDraw_MouseDown(ByVal sender As Object,
ByVal e As System.Windows.Forms.MouseEventArgs) Handles
pnlDraw.MouseDown
        'if left button or right button clicked, set color and
start drawing process
        If e.Button = Windows.Forms.MouseButtons.Left Or
e.Button = Windows.Forms.MouseButtons.Right Then
          DrawingOn = True
          XPrevious = e.X
          YPrevious = e.Y
          If e.Button = Windows.Forms.MouseButtons.Left Then
            MyPen.Color = LeftColor
          Else
            MyPen.Color = RightColor
          End If
        End If
    End Sub
```

While mouse is being moved and **DrawingOn** is **True**, draw lines in current color in **pnlDraw MouseMove** event.

```
    Private Sub PnlDraw_MouseMove(ByVal sender As Object,
ByVal e As System.Windows.Forms.MouseEventArgs) Handles
pnlDraw.MouseMove
    'if drawing, connect previous point with new point
    If DrawingOn Then
      Blackboard.DrawLine(MyPen, XPrevious, YPrevious, e.X,
e.Y)
      XPrevious = e.X
      YPrevious = e.Y
    End If
  End Sub
```

When a mouse button is released, stop drawing current line in the **pnlDraw MouseUp** event.

```
    Private Sub PnlDraw_MouseUp(ByVal sender As Object, ByVal
e As System.Windows.Forms.MouseEventArgs) Handles
pnlDraw.MouseUp
    'if left or button released,connect last point and turn
drawing off
    If DrawingOn And (e.Button =
Windows.Forms.MouseButtons.Left Or e.Button =
Windows.Forms.MouseButtons.Right) Then
      Blackboard.DrawLine(MyPen, XPrevious, YPrevious, e.X,
e.Y)
      DrawingOn = False
    End If
  End Sub
```

6. Run the application. Try drawing. The left mouse button draws with one color and the right button draws with another. The current drawing colors are displayed at the top right corner of the form. To change a color, left or right click on the desired color in the **Colors** group box. Fun, huh? Here's one of my sketches:

Save the application (saved in **Example 9-1** folder in **LearnVB\VB Code\Class 9** folder). This is a neat application, but there's a problem. Draw a little something and then reduce the application to an icon. When the form is restored, your masterpiece is gone! The graphics here are not persistent. In Chapter 8, we used the panel control's **Paint** event to insure persistence. In this application, it would be difficult to always know what is displayed in the panel control. We would have to somehow store every point and every color used in the picture. Then, in the **Paint** event, every drawing step taken by the user would need to be reproduced. This is a difficult problem. We need another solution. We'll look at a potential solution next.

Persistent Graphics, Revisited (Image and Bitmap Objects)

In most of the graphics examples we studied in Chapter 8, we were able to recreate the contents of a graphics object in the **Paint** event. This allowed easy restoration of whatever was in the graphics object when the form was reactivated. In the **Blackboard** example, the user can draw anything they want in any color they want. This makes it difficult to recreate their drawing.

If we expect our graphics object to have complex graphics that are difficult to recreate in a **Paint** event, we take a different approach. The approach involves creating another type of graphics object, one that will always have a current copy of what is drawn. This copy will be maintained in a **bitmap object** using the **BackgroundImage** property of the host control (form, picture box or panel control, for example). The **BackgroundImage** property is just what it says - it sets or gets the image stored in the background of a control, a perfect choice for our Blackboard and other graphics examples. This **bitmap object** gives our graphics object some **memory**.

The idea here is based on the fact that the **BackgroundImage** property of an object is persistent. For example, if you set the **BackgroundImage** property of a control at design time, that image is persistent. You don't have to redraw it in a **Paint** event. There are three basic steps involved in creating a **graphics object** with **memory**. First, as always, declare the graphics object:

```
Dim MyGraphics As Drawing.Graphics
```

Second, create a blank **bitmap** object for the **BackgroundImage** property of the host control for **MyGraphics**. If that control is named **MyObject** (usually a panel control), the **Bitmap** constructor is:

```
MyObject.BackgroundImage = New
Drawing.Bitmap(MyObject.ClientSize.Width,
MyObject.ClientSize.Height, PixelFormat)
```

Let's look at this constructor.

The first two arguments define the bitmap as having the same dimensions (**Width** and **Height** properties of the client rectangle) as the host control.

The final argument specifies what format is used to maintain the graphics object. There are many possible values for **PixelFormat**, each of the form `Drawing.Imaging.PixelFormat.FormatValue` where:

FormatValue	Description
Format16bppArgb1555	The pixel format is 16 bits per pixel. The color information specifies 32,768 shades of color, of which 5 bits are red, 5 bits are green, 5 bits are blue, and 1 bit is alpha.
Format16bppGrayScale	The pixel format is 16 bits per pixel. The color information specifies 65536 shades of gray.
Format16bppRgb555	The pixel format is 16 bits per pixel. The color information specifies 32768 shades of color of which 5 bits are red, 5 bits are green and 5 bits are blue.
Format16bppRgb565	The pixel format is 16 bits per pixel. The color information specifies 32,768 shades of color, of which 5 bits are red, 6 bits are green, and 5 bits are blue.
Format24bppRgb	The pixel format is 24 bits per pixel. The color information specifies 16,777,216 shades of color, of which 8 bits are red, 8 bits are green, and 8 bits are blue.
Format32bppArgb	The pixel format is 32 bits per pixel. The color information specifies 16,777,216 shades of color, of which 8 bits are red, 8 bits are green, and 8 bits are blue. The 8 additional bits are alpha bits.
Format32bppPArgb	The pixel format is 32 bits per pixel. The color information specifies 16,777,216 shades of color, of which 8 bits are red, 8 bits are green, and 8 bits are blue. The 8 additional bits are premultiplied alpha bits.

For our work, we will select a 'medium resolution' value of **Format24bppRgb**. You can try other formats if you like.

Finally, we create the graphics object using the new bitmap object:

```
MyGraphics =
Drawing.Graphics.FromImage(MyObject.BackgroundImage)
```

Anything drawn to this graphics object will be remembered and easily restored (without a **Paint** event) when needed. To provide this memory, after every drawing operation to the object, the host object needs to be refreshed (copies last drawn information to the **BackgroundImage**). The syntax for this is:

```
MyObject.Refresh()
```

A side benefit of using such a graphics object is the ability to save and then, at some time, reload images. To **save** the image (a bitmap), use:

```
MyObject.BackgroundImage.Save(FileName,
Drawing.Imaging.ImageFormat.Bmp)
```

where **FileName** is a complete path to the saved file (use a save file dialog control to obtain the name).

Then, to load (or **open**) a previously saved file into the host control (**MyObject**) of the graphics object, use:

```
MyObject.BackgroundImage = Image.FromFile(FileName)
```

where **FileName** is the saved file path. An open file dialog control can be used to obtain the file name. Once the **BackgroundImage** is set, you need to reconstruct the graphics object using:

```
MyGraphics =
Drawing.Graphics.FromImage(MyObject.BackgroundImage)
```

A good question to ask at this point is why don't we always provide memory (persistent graphics) for our graphics objects? With these new techniques, we don't need to write code in a **Paint** event, where we always have to remember what is displayed in our graphics objects. The reasons we don't do this are **speed** and **resources**. Maintaining a bitmap object in memory consumes resources and slows the drawing process significantly. The more complex the object, the slower things become. You will notice the loss of speed when we modify the **Blackboard** example. You, the programmer, need to decide when to provide persistence to your graphics objects.

Example 9-2

Blackboard (Revisited)

1. Here, we will modify the **Blackboard** example so the graphics are persistent. That way, you'll never lose your masterpiece! The modifications are simple. Load **Example 9-1**.

2. We need to change how the panel graphics object is constructed. This is done in the **frmBlackboard Load** event (the new and/or modified code is shaded):

```
Private Sub FrmBlackboard_Load(ByVal sender As
System.Object, ByVal e As System.EventArgs) Handles
MyBase.Load
    'establish color choices
    lblGray.BackColor = Drawing.Color.Gray
    lblBlue.BackColor = Drawing.Color.Blue
    lblGreen.BackColor = Drawing.Color.LightGreen
    lblCyan.BackColor = Drawing.Color.Cyan
    lblRed.BackColor = Drawing.Color.Red
    lblMagenta.BackColor = Drawing.Color.Magenta
    lblYellow.BackColor = Drawing.Color.Yellow
    lblWhite.BackColor = Drawing.Color.White
    'set up graphics object and drawing pen
    LeftColor = Drawing.Color.Gray
    lblLeftColor.BackColor = LeftColor
    RightColor = Drawing.Color.White
    lblRightColor.BackColor = RightColor
    'create objects
    pnlDraw.BackgroundImage = New
Drawing.Bitmap(pnlDraw.ClientSize.Width,
pnlDraw.ClientSize.Height,
Drawing.Imaging.PixelFormat.Format24bppRgb)
    Blackboard =
Drawing.Graphics.FromImage(pnlDraw.BackgroundImage)
    MyPen = New Drawing.Pen(LeftColor)
    End Sub
```

3. We need to generate a blank bitmap when a new file is requested. The code needed to do this is in the **mnuFileNew Click** event (new code is shaded):

```
Private Sub MnuFileNew_Click(ByVal sender As
System.Object, ByVal e As System.EventArgs) Handles
mnuFileNew.Click
    'Make sure user wants to start over
    If MessageBox.Show("Are you sure you want to start a new
drawing?", "New Drawing", MessageBoxButtons.YesNo,
MessageBoxIcon.Question) = Windows.Forms.DialogResult.Yes
Then
        pnlDraw.BackgroundImage = New
Drawing.Bitmap(pnlDraw.ClientSize.Width,
pnlDraw.ClientSize.Height,
Drawing.Imaging.PixelFormat.Format24bppRgb)
        Blackboard =
Drawing.Graphics.FromImage(pnlDraw.BackgroundImage)
    End If
End Sub
```

4. Then, we need to **Refresh** the object after each drawing method. A **Refresh** is needed in the **pnlDraw MouseMove** and **pnlDraw MouseUp** events (added code is shaded):

```
Private Sub PnlDraw_MouseMove(ByVal sender As Object,
ByVal e As System.Windows.Forms.MouseEventArgs) Handles
pnlDraw.MouseMove
    'if drawing, connect previous point with new point
    If DrawingOn Then
        Blackboard.DrawLine(MyPen, XPrevious, YPrevious, e.X,
e.Y)
        XPrevious = e.X
        YPrevious = e.Y
        pnlDraw.Refresh()
    End If
End Sub
```

```
Private Sub PnlDraw_MouseUp(ByVal sender As Object, ByVal
e As System.Windows.Forms.MouseEventArgs) Handles
pnlDraw.MouseUp
    'if left or button released,connect last point and turn
drawing off
    If DrawingOn And (e.Button =
Windows.Forms.MouseButtons.Left Or e.Button =
Windows.Forms.MouseButtons.Right) Then
        Blackboard.DrawLine(MyPen, XPrevious, YPrevious, e.X,
e.Y)
        pnlDraw.Refresh()
        DrawingOn = False
    End If
End Sub
```

That's all there is to change. Save (saved in **Example 9-2** folder in **LearnVB\VB Code\Class 9** folder) and run the application. Try drawing. Once you have a few lines (with different colors) on the blackboard, reduce the program to an icon. Restore the application. Your picture is still there! The graphics are persistent. But, you should also note the drawing process is slower and the lines appear more jagged. This performance degradation is due to the resources needed to maintain the bitmap object.

A challenge for those who like challenges – add **Open** and **Save** options that allow you to load and save pictures you draw (you'll get a chance to do this in Problem 9-1).

More Graphics Methods

In Chapter 8, we learned about the graphics object, the rectangle structure and many drawing methods. We learned how to draw lines, rectangles, ellipses and pie segments. We learned how to incorporate these drawing elements into procedures for line charts, bar charts and pie charts. The GDI+ in Visual Basic is vast and offers many graphics methods.

Here, we look a few more graphics methods to use in our applications. We learn how to draw connected line segments, polygons and filled polygons. We study connected curves, closed curves and filled closed curves. And, we learn about non-solid brush objects and how to add text to a graphics object.

The steps for drawing here are exactly the same as those followed in Chapter 8:

> ➢ Create a **Graphics** object
> ➢ Create **Pen** objects and **Brush** objects
> ➢ Draw to Graphics object using drawing methods
> ➢ Dispose of Pen and Brush objects when done with them
> ➢ Dispose of Graphics object when done with it

Before studying the new methods, we look at another graphics structure, the **Point** structure.

Point Structure

We will look at graphics methods that draw line and curve segments by connecting points. These methods use a concept known as a **point structure** to define each connected point. This structure (in the **Drawing** namespace) is similar to the rectangle structure studied in Chapter 8. The point structure has just two properties: **X**, the horizontal coordinate, and **Y**, the vertical coordinate.

There are two steps involved in creating a **point** structure. We first declare the structure (in the **Drawing** namespace) using the standard **Dim** statement:

```
Dim MyPoint as Drawing.Point
```

Placement of this statement depends on scope. Place it in a procedure for procedure level scope. Place it with other form level declarations for form level scope. Once declared, the structure is created using the **Point** constructor:

```
MyPoint = New Drawing.Point(X,Y)
```

where **X** and **Y** are the desired coordinates (in pixels).

You can change the structure's properties at any time in code:

```
MyPoint.X = NewX
MyPoint.Y = NewY
```

where **NewX** and **NewY** represent new values for the respective properties.

More often than not, we work with arrays of point structures. This lets us define many points for drawing purposes. To declare an array of 31 such points (indexed from 0 to 30), we use:

```
Dim MyPoints(30) As Drawing.Point
```

To change the coordinates of element 15 of this array, we use:

```
MyPoints(15).X = NewX
MyPoints(15).Y = NewY
```

DrawLines Method

I know you're already asking "didn't we look at the **DrawLines** method in Chapter 8?" No, we looked at **DrawLine**, not **DrawLines**. The DrawLine method connects two points with a line segment. The **DrawLines** method connects an array of points with a series of line segments. The connected points are specified using the **Point** structure. The method operates on a previously created graphics object (use **CreateGraphics** method with the desired control). If that object is **MyGraphics** and we are using a pen object **MyPens**, the syntax to connect an array of points **MyPoints** is:

```
MyGraphics.DrawLines(MyPen, MyPoints)
```

Let's see how to develop the array **MyPoints**.

We first need to know how many points will be in the array. The graphics methods that use point structures assume the arrays are zero-based. So, if there are **NumberPoints** in the array, it is dimensioned using:

```
Dim MyPoints(NumberPoints - 1) As Drawing.Point
```

Then, in code, specify the **X** and **Y** coordinate of each point (**Integer** values) in the array. Once all points are specified, the **DrawLines** method begins at the **0** element in the array and consecutively connects points, ending at the **NumberPoints - 1** element.

As an example, say we have 5 points to connect with line segments. First, dimension the array to **4** (5 –1 = 4 for 0-based array):

```
Dim MyPoints(4) As Drawing.Point
```

Then assign values to each set of coordinates (no specific values are applied here):

```
MyPoints(0).X = x0 : MyPoints(0).Y = y0
MyPoints(1).X = x1 : MyPoints(1).Y = y1
MyPoints(2).X = x2 : MyPoints(2).Y = y2
MyPoints(3).X = x3 : MyPoints(3).Y = y3
MyPoints(4).X = x4 : MyPoints(4).Y = y4
```

With many points, this assignment is usually in some form of loop.

Using a black pen with line width of 1 (**Drawing.Pens.Black**), the **DrawLines** method with this array (**MyPoints**) is:

```
MyGraphics.DrawLines(Drawing.Pens.Black, MyPoints)
```

This produces on a form (**MyGraphics** object):

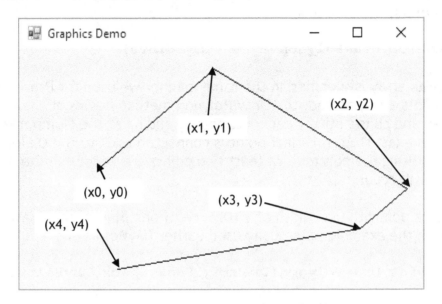

DrawLines will connect every point in the given array of points. Often, we want to use the same code to connect different numbers of points. In this case, we need to somehow change the size of the array of points. The Visual Basic **ReDim** statement is useful in this case. **ReDim** allows you to re-dimension any previously declared array to some new value. The new value cannot exceed the maximum value assigned in the original declaration. You do not provide a data type with **ReDim**, only a new dimension. For an array of points **MyPoints**, you would use:

```
ReDim MyPoints(NewDimension)
```

This assumes **MyPoints** was previously declared as type **Point** with a dimension greater than or equal to **NewDimension**.

DrawPolygon Method

The **DrawPolygon** method is similar to DrawLines. It connects a series of points (**Point** structure) with line segments, but also connects the final point with the first point, forming a closed polygon. The method assumes a graphic object has been created. For a graphics object **MyGraphics**, a pen **MyPen** and a series of points **MyPoints**, the syntax is:

```
MyGraphics.DrawPolygon(MyPen, MyPoints)
```

The **MyPoints** array is specified in the same manner we used for DrawLines. Once all points are specified, the **DrawPolygon** method begins at the **0** element in the array and consecutively connects points, ending at the **NumberPoints - 1** element. As a last step, this final point is connected back to the **0** element point, completing the polygon. At least two points are needed in the point array or an error will occur.

Using a black pen with line width of 1 (**Drawing.Pens.Black**), the **DrawPolygon** method with the example point array used earlier (**MyPoints**) is:

```
MyGraphics.DrawPolygon(Drawing.Pens.Black, MyPoints)
```

This produces on a form (**MyGraphics** object):

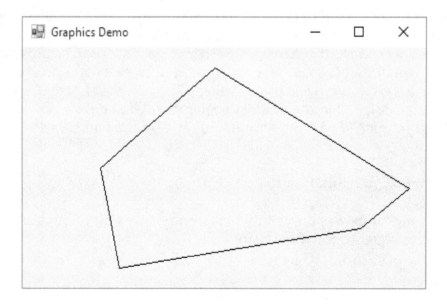

FillPolygon Method

The **FillPolygon** method will draw and fill a polygon. It connects a series of points (**Point** structure) with line segments and, like DrawPolygon, connects the final point with the first point, forming a closed polygon. That polygon is then filled using a specified **Brush** object. For a graphics object **MyGraphics**, a brush **MyBrush** and a series of points **MyPoints**, the syntax is:

```
MyGraphics.FillPolygon(MyBrush, MyPoints)
```

The **MyPoints** array is specified in the same manner as DrawLines and DrawPolygon. Once all points are specified, the **FillPolygon** method draws and fills the polygon bounded by the points. At least two points are needed in the point array or an error will occur.

Using a red solid brush (**Drawing.Brushes.Red**), the **FillPolygon** method with the example point array used earlier (**MyPoints**) is:

```
MyGraphics.FillPolygon(Drawing.Brushes.Red, MyPoints)
```

This produces on a form (**MyGraphics** object):

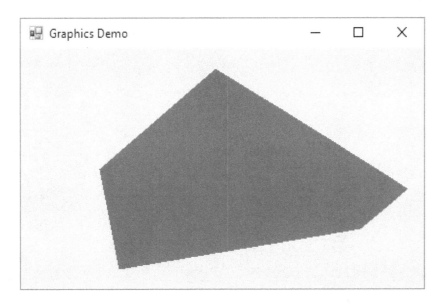

Notice the FillPolygon method fills the entire region with the selected color. If you had previously used DrawPolygon to form a border region, the fill will blot out that border. If you want a bordered, filled region, do the **fill** operation **first**, **then** the **draw** operation.

DrawCurve Method

We now look at three methods very similar to DrawLines, DrawPolygon and FillPolygon. The first is **DrawCurve.** Like DrawLines, DrawCurve connects an array of points. However, rather than connect the points with straight lines, they are connected with something called a **cardinal spline.** That's just fancy mathematics talk for a smooth curve. The connected points are specified using the **Point** structure. The method operates on a previously created graphics object (use **CreateGraphics** method with desired control). If that object is **MyGraphics** and we are using a pen object **MyPens**, the syntax to connect an array of points **MyPoints** is:

```
MyGraphics.DrawCurve(MyPen, MyPoints)
```

The **MyPoints** array is specified in the same manner we used for DrawLines and other methods. Once all points are specified, the **DrawCurve** method begins at the **0** element in the array and consecutively connects points, ending at the **NumberPoints - 1** element.

Using a black pen with line width of 1 (**Drawing.Pens.Black**), the **DrawCurve** method with a point array **MyPoints** is:

```
MyGraphics.DrawCurve(Drawing.Pens.Black, MyPoints)
```

Assuming **MyPoints** contains five points distributed on a form (**MyGraphics** object), we would see:

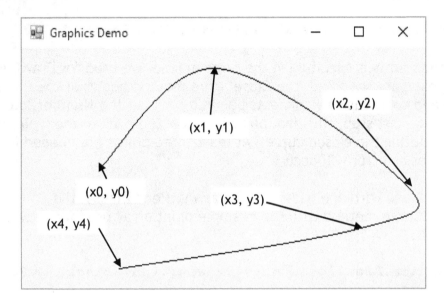

Notice the nice smooth curve that is drawn.

DrawClosedCurve Method

The **DrawClosedCurve** method is similar to DrawCurve. It connects a series of points (**Point** structure) with splines, but also connects the final point with the first point, forming a closed curve. The method assumes a graphic object has been created. For a graphics object **MyGraphics**, a pen **MyPen** and a series of points **MyPoints**, the syntax is:

```
MyGraphics.DrawClosedCurve(MyPen, MyPoints)
```

The **MyPoints** array is specified in the same manner we used for DrawCurve. Once all points are specified, the **CloseCurve** method begins at the **0** element in the array and consecutively connects points, ending at the **NumberPoints - 1** element. As a last step, this final point is connected back to the 0 element point, completing the closed curve. At least three points are needed in the point array or an error will occur.

Using a black pen with line width of 1 (**Drawing.Pens.Black**), the **DrawClosedCurve** method with the example point array used for DrawCurve (**MyPoints**) is:

```
MyGraphics.DrawClosedCurve(Drawing.Pens.Black, MyPoints)
```

This produces on a form (**MyGraphics** object):

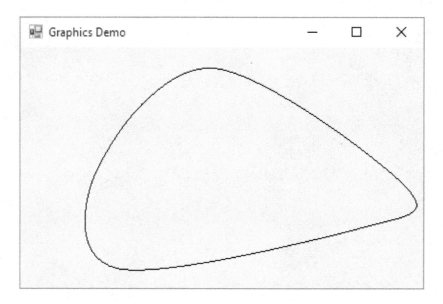

FillClosedCurve Method

The **FillClosedCurve** method will draw and fill a closed curve. It connects a series of points (**Point** structure) with splines and, like DrawClosedCurve, connects the final point with the first point, forming a closed curve. That curve is then filled using a specified **Brush** object. For a graphics object **MyGraphics**, a brush **MyBrush** and a series of points **MyPoints**, the syntax is:

```
MyGraphics.FillClosedCurve(MyBrush, MyPoints)
```

The **MyPoints** array is specified in the same manner as DrawCurve and DrawClosedCurve. Once all points are specified, the **FillClosedCurve** method draws and fills the closed curve bounded by the points. At least three points are needed in the point array or an error will occur.

Using a green solid brush (**Drawing.Brushes.Green**), the **FillClosedCurve** method with the example point array used earlier (**MyPoints**) is:

```
MyGraphics.FillClosedCurve(Drawing.Brushes.Green,
MyPoints)
```

This produces on a form (**MyGraphics** object):

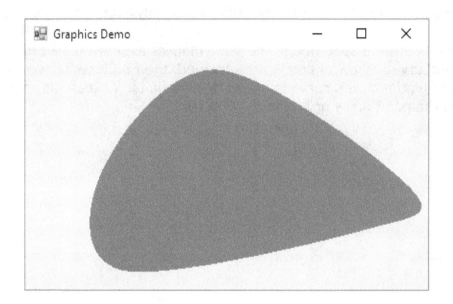

Notice the FillClosedCurve method fills the entire region with the selected color. If you had previously used DrawClosedCurve to form a border region, the fill will blot out that border. If you want a bordered, filled region, do the **fill** operation **first**, **then** the **draw** operation.

Now, let's use the **DrawLines**, **DrawPolygon**, **FillPolygon**, **DrawCurve**, **DrawClosedCurve** and **FillClosedCurve** methods, in conjunction with the **MouseDown** event, to build an example that lets a user do some interactive drawing.

Example 9-3

Drawing Lines, Polygons, Curves, Closed Curves

1. Start a new application. In this application, the user will click on a form specifying a set of points. These points will be used to draw line segments, a polygon, a filled (random color) polygon, a curve, a closed curve or a filled closed curve. Add three button controls and two radio buttons to the form. The form should look like this:

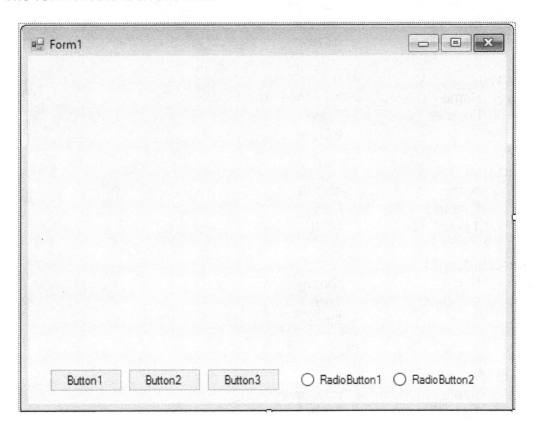

2. Set the following properties:

Form1:

Name	frmDrawing
FormBorderStyle	SingleFixed
StartPosition	CenterScreen
Text	Lines and Curves Example

Button1:

Name	btnDraw
Enabled	False
Text	&Draw

Button2:

Name	btnClose
Enabled	False
Text	&Close

Button3:

Name	btnFill
Enabled	False
Text	&Fill

RadioButton1:

Name	rdoLines
Checked	True
Text	Lines

RadioButton2:

Name	rdoCurves
Text	Curves

When done, my form looks like this:

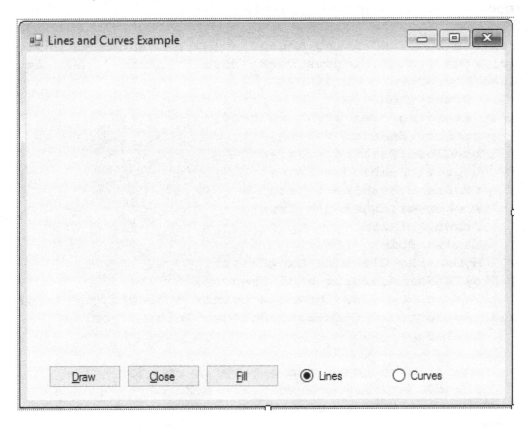

3. Form level scope declarations:

```
Dim ClickedPoint(30) As Drawing.Point, DrawingPoint(30) As
Drawing.Point
Dim MaximumPoint As Integer, LineDrawn As Boolean
Dim MyDrawing As Drawing.Graphics
Dim MyRandom As New Random()
```

4. Use this code in **frmDrawing Load** procedure:

```
Private Sub FrmDrawing_Load(ByVal sender As System.Object,
ByVal e As System.EventArgs) Handles MyBase.Load
    LineDrawn = True ' set to True to initialize properly
    MyDrawing = Me.CreateGraphics
End Sub
```

5. Use this code in the form's **MouseDown** procedure. It saves the clicked points and marks them with a red dot:

```
Private Sub FrmDrawing_MouseDown(ByVal sender As Object,
ByVal e As System.Windows.Forms.MouseEventArgs) Handles
MyBase.MouseDown
    If Drawn Then
        'starting over with new drawing
        btnDraw.Enabled = True
        btnClose.Enabled = False
        btnFill.Enabled = False
        rdoLines.Enabled = True
        rdoCurves.Enabled = True
        Drawn = False
        MaximumPoint = 0
        MyDrawing.Clear(Me.BackColor)
    ElseIf MaximumPoint > 30 Then
        MessageBox.Show("Maximum points exceeded.", "Error",
MessageBoxButtons.OK, MessageBoxIcon.Information)
        Exit Sub
    End If
    'Save clicked point and mark with red dot
    ClickedPoint(MaximumPoint).X = e.X
    ClickedPoint(MaximumPoint).Y = e.Y
    MyDrawing.FillEllipse(Drawing.Brushes.Red,
ClickedPoint(MaximumPoint).X - 1,
ClickedPoint(MaximumPoint).Y - 1, 3, 3)
    MaximumPoint += 1
End Sub
```

6. Use this code in the **btnDraw Click** event procedure:

```
Private Sub BtnDraw_Click(ByVal sender As System.Object,
ByVal e As System.EventArgs) Handles btnDraw.Click
    Dim N As Integer
    ReDim DrawingPoint(MaximumPoint - 1)
    'copy saved points into  points
    For N = 0 To MaximumPoint - 1
      DrawingPoint(N) = New Drawing.Point(ClickedPoint(N).X,
ClickedPoint(N).Y)
    Next
    'draw unless there's less than three points
    If MaximumPoint < 3 Then
      Exit Sub
    Else
      btnDraw.Enabled = False
      rdoLines.Enabled = False
      rdoCurves.Enabled = False
      btnClose.Enabled = True 'allow closing
      If rdoLines.Checked Then
        MyDrawing.DrawLines(Drawing.Pens.Black,
DrawingPoint)
      Else
        MyDrawing.DrawCurve(Drawing.Pens.Black,
DrawingPoint)
      End If
      Drawn = True
    End If
  End Sub
```

This code copies the clicked points to the point structure for drawing and connects those points.

7. Code for the **btnClose** Click procedure:

```
Private Sub BtnClose_Click(ByVal sender As Object, ByVal e
As System.EventArgs) Handles btnClose.Click
    'close polygon/curve
    btnClose.Enabled = False
    btnFill.Enabled = True 'allow filling
    If rdoLines.Checked Then
        MyDrawing.DrawPolygon(Drawing.Pens.Black,
DrawingPoint)
    Else
        MyDrawing.DrawClosedCurve(Drawing.Pens.Black,
DrawingPoint)
    End If
End Sub
```

This code closes the line segments or curve drawn.

8. Use this code in the **btnFill Click** event procedure:

```
Private Sub BtnFill_Click(ByVal sender As System.Object,
ByVal e As System.EventArgs) Handles btnFill.Click
    Dim MyBrush As Drawing.Brush
    'fill
    btnFill.Enabled = False
    MyBrush = New
Drawing.SolidBrush(Drawing.Color.FromArgb(MyRandom.Next(255)
, MyRandom.Next(255), MyRandom.Next(255)))
    If rdoLines.Checked Then
        MyDrawing.FillPolygon(MyBrush, DrawingPoint)
        MyDrawing.DrawPolygon(Drawing.Pens.Black,
DrawingPoint)
    Else
        MyDrawing.FillClosedCurve(MyBrush, DrawingPoint)
        MyDrawing.DrawClosedCurve(Drawing.Pens.Black,
DrawingPoint)
    End If
    MyBrush.Dispose()
End Sub
```

The closed polygon or curve is filled with a random color.

9. Use this code in the **frmDrawing FormClosing** event:

```
Private Sub FrmDrawing_Closing(ByVal sender As Object,
ByVal e As System.ComponentModel.CancelEventArgs) Handles
MyBase.Closing
    MyDrawing.Dispose()
End Sub
```

10. Save and run the application (saved in **Example 9-3** folder in **LearnVB\VB Code\Class 9** folder). Try drawing points (just click the form with any button of the mouse), lines, polygons, curves and closed curves. Fill the polygons and curves. Notice how the random colors work. Notice how the button controls are enabled and disabled at different points. To start a new drawing once complete, just click the form with a new starting point. Try overlapping points to see some nice effects. Here's a polygon I drew:

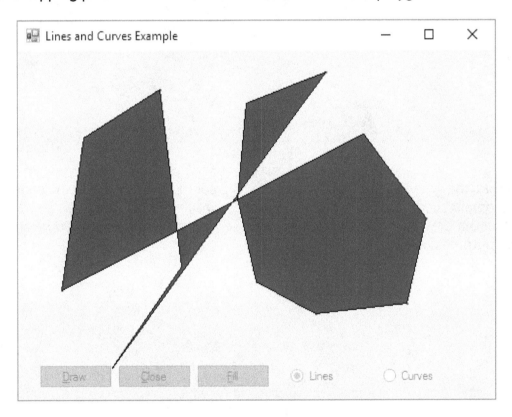

and here's a filled closed curve:

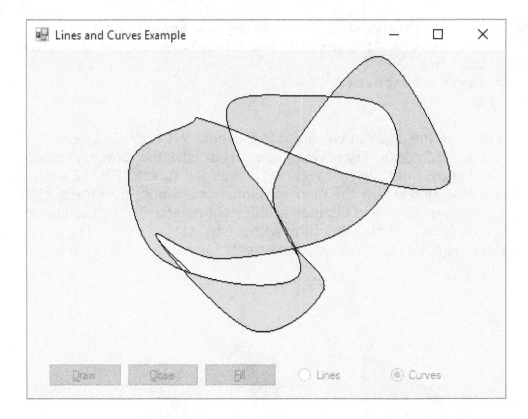

Note that the graphics are <u>not</u> persistent. We could have used a **Paint** event to insure persistence. In this example, however, we have not used such an event to make the drawing code a little clearer. Try the next example if you want to see something cool!!

Example 9-4

Drawing Animated Lines and Curves

1. In this example, we will modify the program just built to draw lines and curves. In this modification, when the user fills the shape, the shape will change itself over time! Load **Example 9-3**.

2. Add a timer control to do the animation. Set these properties:

   Timer1:
   ```
   Name          timDraw
   Interval      100
   ```

3. Make **MyBrush** a form level object. Remove its declaration from the **btnFill Click** event and place it in the general declarations area (this allows us to fill the polygon or curve from another procedure):

   ```
   Dim MyBrush As Drawing.Brush
   ```

   Also, remove line disposing of **MyBrush** object.

4. We want to start the timer when the user clicks **Fill Curve**. This is done in the **btnFill Click** event (new code is shaded):

```
Private Sub BtnFill_Click(ByVal sender As System.Object,
ByVal e As System.EventArgs) Handles btnFill.Click
    ' MyBrush declaration used to be here
    'fill
    btnFill.Enabled = False
    MyBrush = New
Drawing.SolidBrush(Drawing.Color.FromArgb(MyRandom.Next(255)
, MyRandom.Next(255), MyRandom.Next(255)))
    If rdoLines.Checked Then
        MyDrawing.FillPolygon(MyBrush, DrawingPoint)
        MyDrawing.DrawPolygon(Drawing.Pens.Black,
DrawingPoint)
    Else
        MyDrawing.FillClosedCurve(MyBrush, DrawingPoint)
        MyDrawing.DrawClosedCurve(Drawing.Pens.Black,
DrawingPoint)
    End If
    ' MyBrush disposal used to be here
    timDraw.Enabled = True
End Sub
```

5. We turn off the timer when a new curve is started in the **frmDrawing MouseDown** event (new code is shaded):

```
Private Sub FrmDrawing_MouseDown(ByVal sender As Object,
ByVal e As System.Windows.Forms.MouseEventArgs) Handles
MyBase.MouseDown
    If Drawn Then
        'starting over with new drawing
        timDraw.Enabled = False
        btnDraw.Enabled = True
        btnClose.Enabled = False
        btnFill.Enabled = False
        rdoLines.Enabled = True
        rdoCurves.Enabled = True
        Drawn = False
        MaximumPoint = 0
        MyDrawing.Clear(Me.BackColor)
    ElseIf MaximumPoint > 30 Then
        MessageBox.Show("Maximum points exceeded.", "Error",
MessageBoxButtons.OK, MessageBoxIcon.Information)
        Exit Sub
    End If
    'Save clicked point and mark with red dot
    ClickedPoint(MaximumPoint).X = e.X
    ClickedPoint(MaximumPoint).Y = e.Y
    MyDrawing.FillEllipse(Drawing.Brushes.Red,
ClickedPoint(MaximumPoint).X - 1,
ClickedPoint(MaximumPoint).Y - 1, 3, 3)
    MaximumPoint += 1
End Sub
```

6. Use this code for the **timDraw Tick** event (a new procedure):

```
Private Sub TimDraw_Tick(ByVal sender As System.Object,
ByVal e As System.EventArgs) Handles timDraw.Tick
    ' Tweak all points a bit
    Dim I As Integer
    For I = 0 To MaximumPoint - 1
        DrawingPoint(I).X += MyRandom.Next(21) - 10
        DrawingPoint(I).Y += MyRandom.Next(21) - 10
    Next I
    ' clear frame and redraw
    MyDrawing.Clear(Me.BackColor)
    If rdoLines.Checked Then
        MyDrawing.FillPolygon(MyBrush, DrawingPoint)
        MyDrawing.DrawPolygon(Drawing.Pens.Black,
DrawingPoint)
    Else
        MyDrawing.FillClosedCurve(MyBrush, DrawingPoint)
        MyDrawing.DrawClosedCurve(Drawing.Pens.Black,
DrawingPoint)
    End If
End Sub
```

In this procedure, we go through the points defining the polygon/curve and randomly change them a bit. This will 'perturb' the displayed polygon/curve giving the effect of animation.

7. Save and run the application (saved in **Example 9-4** folder in **LearnVB\VB Code\Class 9** folder). Create and fill a polygon or curve. Once filled, be amazed at its animated performance. You might like to also change colors as the animation is going on.

HatchBrush Object

The filled polygons and filled curves are pretty, but it would be nice to have them filled with something other than a solid color. Visual Basic provides other brush objects that provide interesting fill effects. These brushes are part of the **Drawing.Drawing2D** namespace. Here, we look at the **HatchBrush** object. Hatch brushes fill a region with a specific style of line. You can specify the color of the line and the background color of the fill.

To create your own **HatchBrush** object, you first declare the brush using:

```
Dim MyBrush As Drawing.Drawing2D.HatchBrush
```

The brush is then created using the **HatchBrush** constructor:

```
MyBrush = New Drawing.Drawing2D.HatchBrush(HatchStyle,
ForegroundColor, BackgroundColor)
```

where **HatchStyle** defines the line 'hatch' style, **ForegroundColor** is the line color and **BackgroundColor** the fill color. The color arguments can be one of the built-in colors or one generated with the **FromArgb** function.

There are numerous **HatchStyle** values (**Drawing.Drawing2D** namespace) to choose from. Here are some of the values; consult on-line help for a complete list (each value describes the hatch appearance):

```
BackwardDiagonal              Plaid
Cross                         Shingle
DiagonalBrick                 SolidDiamond
DiagonalCross                 Sphere
Divot                         Trellis
ForwardDiagonal               Vertical
Horizontal                    Wave
HorizontalBrick               Weave
LargeCheckerBoard             ZigZag
LargeConfetti
LargeGrid
OutlinedDiamond
```

Once created, you can change the hatch style or either color of a hatch brush in code using the respective properties of the hatch brush object. The syntax is:

```
MyBrush.HatchStyle = NewStyle
MyBrush.ForegroundColor = NewForegroundColor
MyBrush.BackgroundColor = NewBackgroundColor
```

where **NewStyle, NewForegroundColor** and **NewBackgroundColor** are newly specified values.

When done painting with a hatch brush object, it should be disposed using the Dispose method:

```
MyBrush.Dispose()
```

Example 9-5

Hatch Brush

In the **LearnVB\VB Code\Class 9** folder is a project named **Example 9-5**. We will not build this project (not much would be gained in the way of learning), but will use it to demonstrate the different effects provided by a hatch brush. If desired, you can look through the code to see how things are done.

Open and run that project. You should see:

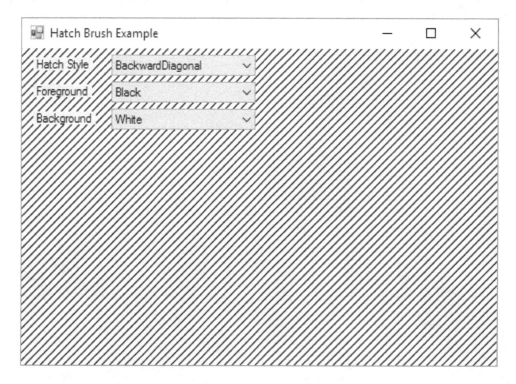

There are three combo boxes that let you select different hatch styles, foreground colors and background colors. The form is painted with the selected brush. Try different choices to see how the hatch brush works.

Here's a diagonal brick pattern:

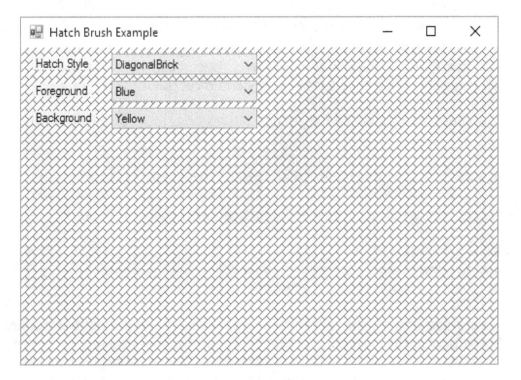

Once a combo box is active, you can use the cursor arrows on the keyboard to 'scroll' through the list. Notice you can resize the form and it's still painted correctly.

LinearGradientBrush Object

Another brush in the **Drawing.Drawing2D** namespace is the **LinearGradientBrush**. This brush fills a graphics object with a blending of two colors. It starts with one color and gradually 'becomes' the other color in a specified direction. You specify the colors and direction of the 'gradient.'

To create your own **LinearGradientBrush** object, you first declare the brush using:

```
Dim MyBrush As Drawing.Drawing2D.LinearGradientBrush
```

The brush is then created using the **LinearGradientBrush** constructor:

```
MyBrush = New
Drawing.Drawing2D.LinearGradientBrush(Rectangle,
StartColor, EndColor, LinearGradientMode)
```

where **Rectangle** defines the rectangular region where the gradient starts and ends, **StartColor** is the gradient start color, **EndColor** the gradient end color, and **LinearGradientMode**, the gradient direction. The color arguments can be one of the built-in colors or one generated with the **FromArgb** function.

You can achieve interesting effects by changing the size of the rectangularregion (**Rectangle** argument) assigned to the brush. Small regions give 'tight' gradients, while large rectangles yield gradients spread over long distances.

There are four **LinearGradientMode** values (**Drawing.Drawing2D** namespace) to choose from:

```
BackwardDiagonal        ForwardDiagonal
Horizontal              Vertical
```

Once created, you can the brush in code using the respective properties. The syntax is:

```
MyBrush.LinearColors(0) = NewStartColor
MyBrush.LinearColors(1) = NewEndColor
MyBrush.LinearGradientMode = NewLinearGradientMode
```

where **NewStartColor, NewEndColor** and **NewLinearGradientMode** are newly specified values.

When done painting with a linear gradient brush object, it should be disposed using the Dispose method:

```
MyBrush.Dispose()
```

Example 9-6

Linear Gradient Brush

In the **LearnVB\VB Code\Class 9** folder is a project named **Example 9-6**. We will not build this project (not much would be gained in the way of learning), but will use it to demonstrate the different effects provided by a linear gradient brush. If desired, you can look through the code to see how things are done.

Open and run that project. You should see:

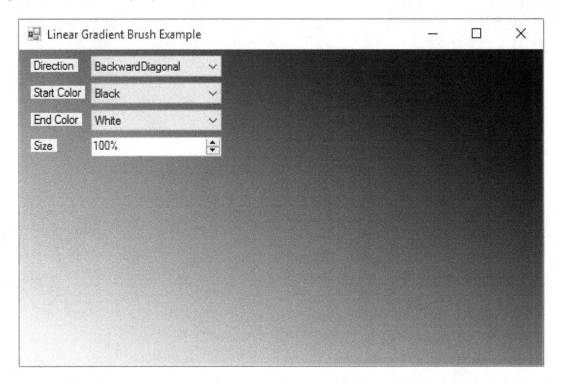

There are three combo boxes and an updown control that let you select different gradient directions, colors and sizes. The form is painted with the selected brush. Try different choices to see how the linear gradient brush works.

Here's a pretty effect:

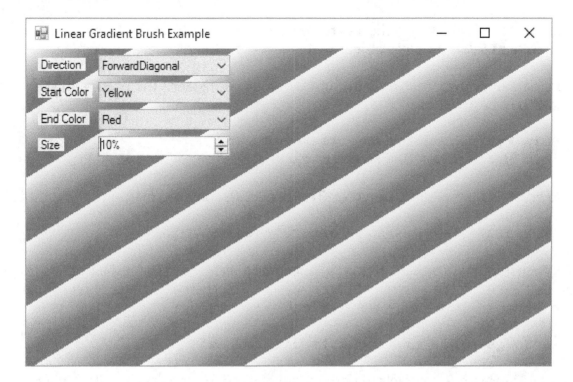

Once any control is active, you can use the cursor arrows on the keyboard to 'scroll' through the list. Notice you can resize the form and it's still painted correctly. .

TextureBrush Object

The last brush we study is the **TextureBrush**. This brush (in the **Drawing** namespace) fills a graphics object with an image – fun effects are possible.

To create your own **TextureBrush** object, you first declare the brush and the **Image** object it will use:

```
Dim MyBrush As Drawing.TextureBrush
Dim MyImage As Drawing.Image
```

The brush is then created using the **TextureBrush** constructor:

```
MyBrush = New Drawing.TextureBrush(MyImage)
```

The **Image** object can be a bitmap, an icon or a metafile. The object needs to be defined using the appropriate constructor. To create an **Image** object using the **Bitmap** constructor (seen earlier in this chapter), use:

```
MyImage = New Drawing.Bitmap(FileName)
```

where **FileName** is a complete path to the desired bitmap graphic file. Icons and metafile objects are created with their respective constructors (**Drawing.Icon, Drawing.Metafile**).

When done painting with a texture brush object, it should be disposed using the Dispose method:

```
MyBrush.Dispose()
```

We've only introduced the **Texture** brush. There are many other properties that can be used to obtain interesting effects. Study the on-line help for further details.

Example 9-7

Texture Brush

In the **LearnVB\VB Code\Class 9** folder is a project named **Example 9-7**. Like the previous two projects, we will not build this project, but will use it to demonstrate the different effects provided by a texture brush. If desired, you can look through the code to see how things are done.

Open and run that project. You should see:

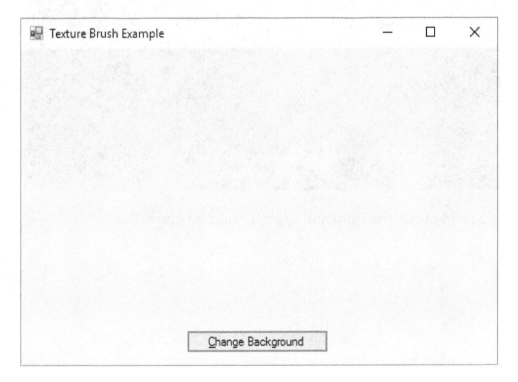

There is a single button (**Change Background**) on the form. Click that button and an open file dialog will appear. Select different bitmaps (a few are in the project folder) for painting the form. Try different choices to see how the texture brush works.

Here's a denim background:

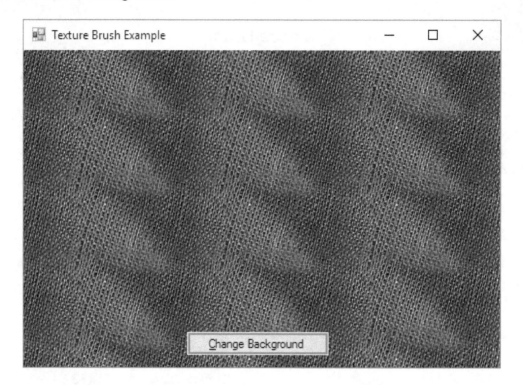

Notice you can resize the form and it's still painted correctly.

DrawString Method

The last drawing method we study 'draws' text information on a graphics object using a brush object. Text adds useful information to graphics objects, especially for plots. The line, bar and pie chart examples built in Chapter 8 are rather boring without the usual titles, labels and legends. The **DrawString** method will let us add text to any graphic object.

The **DrawString** method is easy to use. You need to know what text you want to draw, what font object you want to use, what brush object to use and where you want to locate the text. The method operates on a previously created graphics object (use **CreateGraphics** method with a control). The syntax is:

```
MyGraphics.DrawString(MyString, MyFont, MyBrush, x, y)
```

where **MyGraphics** is the graphics object, **MyString** is the text to display (a **String** type), **MyFont** is the font to use (**Font** object), **MyBrush** is the selected brush (**Brush** object) and (**x, y**) is the Cartesian coordinate (**Integer** type) specifying location of the upper left corner of the text string

Let's look at an example. Can you see what this line of code will produce?

```
MyGraphics.DrawString("Hello World!", New Font("Arial",
24), Brushes.Red, 0, 0)
```

This says print the string **"Hello World!"** using an **Arial**, Size **24**, font and a **red solid brush** in the upper left hand corner (**x = 0, y = 0**) of the graphics object MyGraphics. Using this code with the form as the graphics object, we would see:

Simple, huh? This example is saved in the **DrawString Demo** folder in the **LearnVB\VB Code\Class 9** folder.

A key decision in using **DrawString** is placement. That is, what **x** and **y** values should you use? To help in this decision, it is helpful to know what size a particular text string is. If we know how wide and how tall (in pixels) a string is, we can perform precise placements, including left, center and right justifications.

If you are only interested in obtaining the height of a string for correct vertical placement, you can use the Visual Basic GetHeight method. This method operates on the font object. If you have a font object named MyFont, the height is given by:

```
MyHeight = MyFont.GetHeight()
```

The returned MyHeight value (Single data type) is in pixels.

If you need both width and height, the Visual Basic method **MeasureString** gives us this information. The size (**MySize**) of a string **MyString** written using **MyFont** is computed using:

```
MySize = MyGraphics.MeasureString(MyString, MyFont)
```

The returned value **MySize** is a **SizeF** structure with two properties, **Width** and **Height**. This is the information we want. **SizeF** is another Visual Basic structure similar to the **Rectangle** and **Point** structures. To determine string size, we need such a structure.

There are two steps involved in creating a **SizeF** structure. We first declare the structure (in the **Drawing** namespace) using the standard **Dim** statement:

```
Dim MySize as Drawing.SizeF
```

Placement of this statement depends on scope. Place it in a procedure for procedure level scope. Place it with other form level declarations for form level scope. Once declared, the structure is created using the **SizeF** constructor:

```
MySize = New Drawing.SizeF()
```

No arguments are needed. You can assign width and height arguments, but we don't need to. We are just using **MySize** to determine such properties.

If we use this **SizeF** structure with our previous example:

```
MySize = MyGraphics.MeasureString("Hello World!", New
Font("Arial", 24))
```

We would see (you could use the debugger to get these values):

```
MySize.Width = 190.151
MySize.Height = 39.75
```

These measurements are floating point representations (type **Double**) of pixels. The 'F' in **SizeF** implies a floating point, rather than integer, number. There is also a **Size** structure in Visual Basic that provides integer information. This structure, though, can't be used with **MeasureString**.

The height of a string lets us know how much to increment the desired vertical position after printing each line in multiple lines of text. Or, it can be used to 'vertically justify' a string within the client rectangle of a graphics object. For example, assume we have found the height of a string (**MySize.Height**). To vertically justify this string in the host control (**MyObject**) for a graphics object, the **y** coordinate (converted to an **Integer** type needed by **DrawString**) would be:

```
y = CInt(0.5 * (MyObject.ClientSize.Height -
MySize.Height))
```

This assumes the string is 'shorter' than the graphics object client rectangle.

Similarly, the width of a string lets us define margins and left, right or center justify a string within the client rectangle of a graphics object. For left justification, establish a left margin and set the x coordinate to this value in the **DrawString** method. If we know the width of a string (**MySize.Width**), it is centered justified in the client area of a graphics object's host control **MyObject** using an **x** value of (again converted to **Integer**):

```
x = CInt(0.5 * (MyObject.ClientSize.Width - MySize.Width))
```

To right justify the same string, use:

```
x = CInt(MyObject.ClientSize.Width - MySize.Width)
```

Both of the above equations, of course, assume the string is 'narrower' than the graphics object.

Let's go back and apply these relations to our "Hello World!" example. The text **vertically** and **center** justified looks like this:

Vertically and **right** justified, the text appears like this:

Even more interesting effects can be obtained using other brushes. Try drawing strings with hatch, linear gradient and texture brushes. Here's the "Hello World!" example with a larger font and a 'denim' textured brush:

Modify the **DrawString Demo** project to see if you can achieve the above effect. A 'denim' bitmap is included in the Example 9-7 folder.

We won't do much more with the **DrawString** function here. You will, however, see the **DrawString** method again in Chapter 10. This method is integral in obtaining printed information from a Visual Basic application. And, you will see its use is identical. You need to determine what to print, in what font, with what brush and where on the page it needs to be.

Multimedia Effects

Everywhere you look in the world of computers today, you see **multimedia effects**. Computer games, web sites and meeting presentations are filled with animated graphics and fun sounds. It is relatively easy to add such effects to our Visual Basic applications.

In Chapter 8, we achieved simple animation effects by changing the image in a picture box control and, if desired, moving the control by modifying **Left** and **Top** properties. Sophisticated animation relies on the ability to move several changing objects over a changing background. The simple techniques we learned cannot be used here. To achieve more sophisticated animation, we will use the Visual Basic **DrawImage** method.

Animation requires the moving of rectangular regions. We need ways to move these rectangular regions. The mouse (using mouse events) is one option. Another option considered is movement using **keyboard events**. And, many times we want to know if these rectangular regions overlap to detect things like files reaching trash cans, balls hitting paddles or little creatures eating power pellets. We will learn how to detect if two **rectangles intersect**.

And, multimedia presentations also use **sounds**. Visual Basic uses the **SoundPlayer** class to play sound files.

Animation with DrawImage Method

To achieve animation in a Visual Basic application, whether it is background scrolling, sprite animation, or other special effects, we use the **DrawImage** graphics method. In its simplest form, this method draws an **Image** object at a particular position in a graphics object. Changing and/or moving the image within the graphics object achieves animation. And, multiple images can be moved/changed within the graphics object. There are many overloaded versions of **DrawImage**. We will look a few of them in this chapter. We encourage you to study the other forms, as you need them.

Before using **DrawImage**, you need two things: a **graphics** object to draw to and an **image** object to draw. The graphics and image objects are declared in the usual manner:

```
Dim MyGraphics As Drawing.Graphics
Dim MyImage As Drawing.Image
```

We create the graphics object (assume **MyObject** is the host object):

```
MyGraphics = MyObject.CreateGraphics()
```

The **Image** object is usually created from a graphics file:

```
MyImage = Drawing.Image.FromFile(FileName)
```

where **FileName** is a complete path to the graphics file describing the image to draw. At this point, we can draw **MyImage** in **MyGraphics**.

In its simplest form, the **DrawImage** method is:

```
MyGraphics.DrawImage(MyImage, MyRectangle)
```

where **MyRectangle** is a rectangle structure that positions **MyImage** within **MyGraphics**. **MyRectangle** is specified by **X** the horizontal position, **Y** the vertical position, the width **W** and height **H**:

```
MyRectangle = New Drawing.Rectangle(X, Y, W, H)
```

The width and height can be the original image size or scaled up or down. It's your choice.

A picture illustrates what's going on with **DrawImage**:

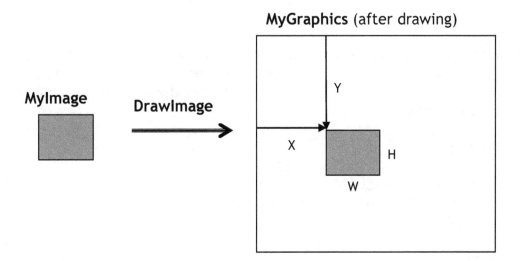

Note how the transfer of the rectangular region occurs. Successive bitmap transfers gives the impression of motion, or animation. Recall **W** and **H** in the graphics object do not have to necessarily match the width and height of the **Image** object. Scaling (up or down) is possible.

Example 9-8

Bouncing Ball

1. We'll build an application with a ball bouncing from the top to the bottom (and back) as an illustration of the use of **DrawImage**. Start a new application. Add a panel control (will display the animation), a timer control, and a button. Set these properties:

Form1:

Name	frmBall
FormBorderStyle	FixedSingle
StartPosition	CenterScreen
Text	Bouncing Balls

Timer1:

Name	timBall
Interval	100

Panel1:

Name	pnlDisplay
BackColor	Light Blue
BorderStyle	Fixed3D

Button1:

Name	btnStart
Text	&Start

When done, my form looks like this:

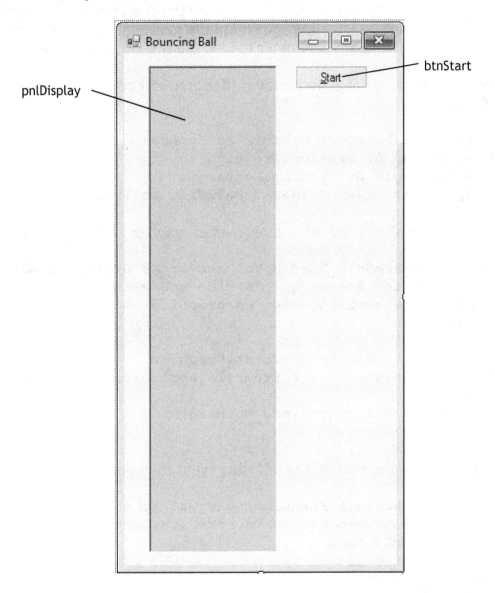

Other controls in tray:

⏱ timBall

2. In the **LearnVB\VB Code\Class 9\Example 9-8** folder is a graphics file named **ball.gif**. This will be our bouncing ball. Copy this file into the application **Bin\Debug** folder (you may have to create the folder first). We will use the **Application.StartupPath** parameter to load the file into the **Image** object.

3. Form level scope variable declarations (declares objects and movement variables):

```
Dim BallY As Integer, BallDir As Integer
Dim MyDisplay As Drawing.Graphics
Dim MyRectangle As Drawing.Rectangle
Dim MyBall As Drawing.Image, BallSize As Integer = 50
```

4. Add code to **frmBall Load** procedure (creates graphics and image objects):

```
Private Sub FrmBall_Load(ByVal sender As System.Object,
ByVal e As System.EventArgs) Handles MyBase.Load
    'initialize variables/set up graphics objects
    BallY = 0
    BallDir = 1
    MyDisplay = pnlDisplay.CreateGraphics
    MyBall = Drawing.Image.FromFile(Application.StartupPath
+ "\ball.gif")
    pnlDisplay_Paint(Nothing, Nothing)
End Sub
```

5. Use this code in the **frmBall FormClosing** event to dispose of objects:

```
Private Sub FrmBall_FormClosing(ByVal sender As Object,
ByVal e As System.Windows.Forms.FormClosingEventArgs)
Handles Me.FormClosing
    'dispose of objects
    MyDisplay.Dispose()
    MyBall.Dispose()
End Sub
```

6. Write a **btnStart Click** event procedure to toggle the timer:

```
Private Sub BtnStart_Click(ByVal sender As System.Object,
ByVal e As System.EventArgs) Handles btnStart.Click
    'toggle timer
    If timBall.Enabled Then
      timBall.Enabled = False
      btnStart.Text = "&Start"
    Else
      timBall.Enabled = True
      btnStart.Text = "&Stop"
    End If
  End Sub
```

7. The **timBall Tick** event controls the bouncing ball position:

```
Private Sub TimBall_Tick(ByVal sender As System.Object,
ByVal e As System.EventArgs) Handles timBall.Tick
    'determine ball position and draw it
    BallY = CInt(BallY + BallDir *
pnlDisplay.ClientSize.Height / 50)
    'check for bounce
    If BallY < 0 Then
      BallY = 0
      BallDir = 1
    ElseIf BallY + BallSize > pnlDisplay.ClientSize.Height
Then
      BallY = pnlDisplay.ClientSize.Height - BallSize
      BallDir = -1
    End If
    pnlDisplay_Paint(Nothing, Nothing)
  End Sub
```

8. And, the **pnlDisplay Paint** event does the actual image drawing:

```
Private Sub PnlDisplay_Paint(ByVal sender As Object, ByVal
e As System.Windows.Forms.PaintEventArgs) Handles
pnlDisplay.Paint
    'horizontally center ball in display rectangle
    MyRectangle = New Rectangle(CInt(0.5 *
(pnlDisplay.ClientSize.Width - BallSize)), BallY, 50, 50)
    MyDisplay.Clear(pnlDisplay.BackColor)
    MyDisplay.DrawImage(MyBall, MyRectangle)
End Sub
```

9. Once everything is together, save it (saved in **Example 9-8** folder in the **LearnVB\VB Code\Class 9** folder), run it and follow the bouncing ball!

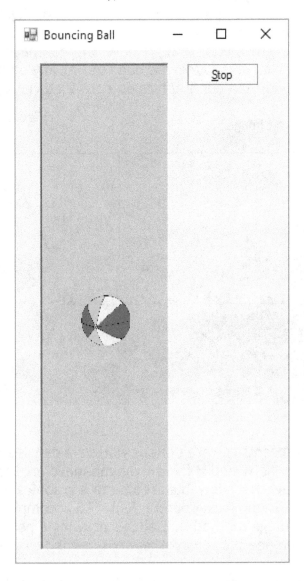

Note we have added a **Paint** event to make the graphics (ball position) persistent.

Scrolling Backgrounds

Most action arcade games employ scrolling or moving backgrounds. What looks like a very sophisticated effect is really just a simple application of the **DrawImage** method. The idea is that we have a large image representing the background "world" we want to move around in. At any point, we can view a small region of that world in our graphics object. Pictorially, we have:

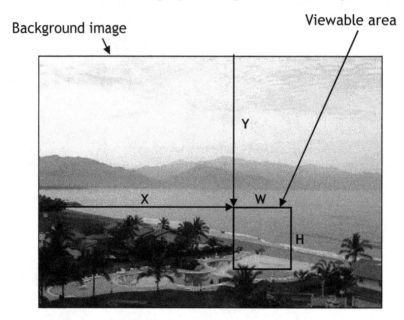

The boxed area represents the area of our world we can see at any one time. By varying **X** and **Y** (leaving **W** and **H** fixed), we can move around in this world. As X and Y vary, if we draw the "viewable area" into a graphics object of the same size, we obtain the moving background effect. To accomplish this task, we need a form of the **DrawImage** method that allows drawing a portion of a source image. But, first, we need to review the steps needed to use **DrawImage**.

Before using **DrawImage**, we need: a **graphics** object to draw to and an **image** object to draw from. The graphics and image objects are declared in the usual manner:

```
Dim MyGraphics As Drawing.Graphics
Dim MyImage As Drawing.Image
```

Create the graphics object (assume **MyObject** is the host object) and **Image** object:

```
MyGraphics = MyObject.CreateGraphics()
MyImage = Drawing.Image.FromFile(FileName)
```

where **FileName** is a complete path to the graphics file describing the background image to draw.

To draw a portion of the source image (**MyImage**) in the graphics object (**MyGraphics**), we use an overloaded version of the **DrawImage** method:

```
MyGraphics.DrawImage(MyImage, RectangleDest, RectangleSrc,
Drawing.GraphicsUnit.Pixel)
```

where:

RectangleDest	A rectangle structure within the graphics object (the destination location) where the image will be drawn.
RectangleSrc	A rectangle structure within the image object (the source location) defining the portion of the image to draw in the graphics object.

The last argument is the physical unit used in measuring the graphics. We use **pixels.**

For scrolling backgrounds, the 'destination' rectangle (**RectangleDest**) encompasses the entire control (**MyObject**) hosting the graphics object used as the viewing area:

```
RectangleDest = New Rectangle(0, 0,
MyObject.ClientSize.Width, MyObject.ClientSize.Height)
```

The 'source' rectangle (**RectangleSrc**) contains the portion of the image we want to copy into the graphics object. This rectangle has the same dimensions (width and height) as the destination rectangle, with the upper left corner described by a desired position (x, y) within the source image:

```
RectangleSrc = New Rectangle(X, Y,
MyObject.ClientSize.Width, MyObject.ClientSize.Height)
```

An example using our beach photo should clear things up (hopefully). Applying the **DrawImage** using **MyImage** will result in the following display in **MyGraphics:**

MyImage

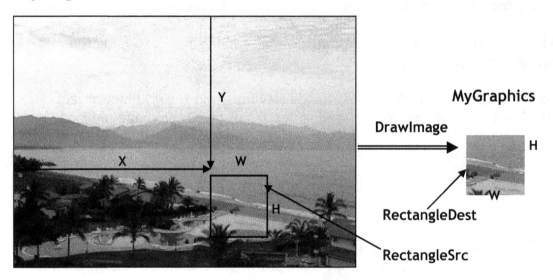

In this picture, **W** is the width of the client rectangle (**ClientSize.Width**) of the graphics object host control and **H** is the height of that rectangle (**ClientSize.Height**).

Hence, the process for moving (or scrolling) backgrounds is simple (once the image is available):

> ➤ Decide on the desired viewing area (set width **W** and height **H**).
> ➤ Choose a mechanism for varying **X** and **Y**. Scroll bars and cursor control keys are often used, or they can be varied using Timer controls.
> ➤ As X and Y vary, use **DrawImage** to draw the current "viewable area" of the source image into the viewer (graphics object).

Example 9-9

Horizontally Scrolling Background

1. Start a new application. In this project, we'll view a horizontally scrolling seascape. Add a horizontal scroll bar, a panel control, and a timer control. Set these properties:

Form1:

Name	frmScroll
FormBorderStyle	FixedSingle
StartPosition	CenterScreen
Text	Scrolling Background

HScrollBar1:

Name	hsbScroll
LargeChange	2
Maximum	20
Minimum	0
SmallChange	1
Value	0

Panel1:

Name	pnlViewer
BorderStyle	FixedSingle

Timer1:

Name	timScroll
Interval	50
Enabled	True

When done, my form looks like this:

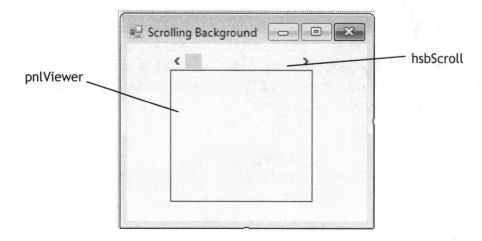

Other controls in tray:

⏱ timScroll

2. In the **LearnVB\VB Code\Class 9\Example 9-9** folder is a graphics file named **undrsea1.bmp**. This will be our background. Copy this file into the application **Bin\Debug** folder (you may have to create the folder first). Here is the graphic:

As X increases, the background appears to scroll to the left. Note as X reaches the end of this source image, we need to copy a little of both ends to the destination graphics object. We will use our **Application.StartupPath** parameter to load this file into the **Image** object.

3. Form level scope variable declarations (declares objects and movement variables):

```
Dim Viewer As Drawing.Graphics, Background As
Drawing.Image
Dim ScrollX As Integer = 0
```

4. Add code to **frmScroll Load** procedure (creates graphics and image objects):

```
Private Sub FrmScroll_Load(ByVal sender As System.Object,
ByVal e As System.EventArgs) Handles MyBase.Load
    Background =
Drawing.Image.FromFile(Application.StartupPath +
"\undrsea1.bmp")
    'make sure viewer is same height as background image
    pnlViewer.Height = Background.Height
    Viewer = pnlViewer.CreateGraphics
End Sub
```

5. Use this code in the **frmScroll FormClosing** event to dispose of objects:

```
Private Sub FrmScroll_FormClosing(ByVal sender As Object,
ByVal e As System.Windows.Forms.FormClosingEventArgs)
Handles Me.FormClosing
    'dispose of objects
    Viewer.Dispose()
    Background.Dispose()
End Sub
```

6. The **timScroll Tick** event controls scrolling. At each program cycle, we update the position on the background image and draw the result.

```
Private Sub TimScroll_Tick(ByVal sender As System.Object,
ByVal e As System.EventArgs) Handles timScroll.Tick
    Dim AddedWidth As Integer
    Dim RectangleDest As Drawing.Rectangle, RectangleSrc As
Drawing.Rectangle
    'Find next location on background
    ScrollX += hsbScroll.Value
    If ScrollX > Background.Width Then
      ScrollX = 0
    End If
    'When x is near right edge, we need to copy
    'two segments of the background into viewer
    If ScrollX > (Background.Width -
pnlViewer.ClientSize.Width) Then
        AddedWidth = Background.Width - ScrollX
```

```
          RectangleDest = New Rectangle(0, 0, AddedWidth,
      pnlViewer.ClientSize.Height)
          RectangleSrc = New Rectangle(ScrollX, 0, AddedWidth,
      Background.Height)
          Viewer.DrawImage(Background, RectangleDest,
      RectangleSrc, Drawing.GraphicsUnit.Pixel)
          RectangleDest = New Rectangle(AddedWidth, 0,
      pnlViewer.ClientSize.Width - AddedWidth,
      pnlViewer.ClientSize.Height)
          RectangleSrc = New Rectangle(0, 0,
      pnlViewer.ClientSize.Width - AddedWidth, Background.Height)
          Viewer.DrawImage(Background, RectangleDest,
      RectangleSrc, Drawing.GraphicsUnit.Pixel)
      Else
          RectangleDest = New Rectangle(0, 0,
      pnlViewer.ClientSize.Width, pnlViewer.ClientSize.Height)
          RectangleSrc = New Rectangle(ScrollX, 0,
      pnlViewer.ClientSize.Width, Background.Height)
          Viewer.DrawImage(Background, RectangleDest,
      RectangleSrc, Drawing.GraphicsUnit.Pixel)
      End If
    End Sub
```

7. Save the application (saved in **Example 9-9** folder in the **LearnVB\VB Code\Class 9** folder) and run it. Watch the sea go by. The scroll bar is used to control the speed of the scrolling (the amount X increases each time a tick event occurs). Here's my sea scrolling:

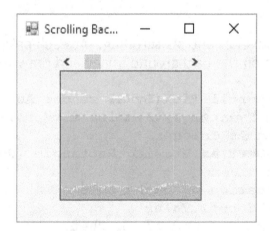

Notice the graphics are persistent, even though there is no **Paint** event. The reason this occurs is because the timer control **Tick** event is automatically updating the displayed picture 20 times each second.

Sprite Animation

Using the **DrawImage** method to draw a scrolling background leads us to an obvious question. Can we make an object move across the background – the kind of effect you see in video games? Yes we can – it just takes a little more effort. The moving picture is called a **sprite**. Working with the previous example, say we want a fish to bob up and down through the moving waters. The first thing we need is a bitmap picture of a fish – draw one with a painting program or borrow one from somewhere and convert it to bitmap format (**bmp** extension). Here's one (**fish.bmp**) I came up with:

If you copy this picture onto the background using the **DrawImage** method, the fish will be there, but the background will be gray. We could paint the background the same color as the water and things would look OK, but what if the fish jumps out of the water or swims near the rocks? The background is obliterated. We want whatever background the fish is swimming in to "come through." We accomplish this via **sprite animation**.

Sprite animation is done by invoking a different version of the DrawImage method using an **ImageAttributes** object. Such an object will allow us to declare one color within the bitmap to be transparent. Then, when the bitmap is drawn over a background, that background will show through. Let's go through the necessary steps for sprite animation.

The **ImageAttributes** object is part of the **Imaging** namespace. The ImageAttributes object (**MyImageAttributes**) is declared using:

```
Dim MyImageAttributes As Drawing.Imaging.ImageAttributes
```

and constructed using:

```
MyImageAttributes = New Drawing.Imaging.ImageAttributes()
```

The desired transparent color (**ClearColor**) is established using the **SetColorKey** method:

```
MyImageAttributes.SetColorKey(ClearColor, ClearColor)
```

You may wonder why the color argument is repeated. The **SetColorKey** method actually allows specification of a range of colors that can be considered transparent. The two arguments specify a **Low** color and a **High** color. In our example, we only want a single color; hence both arguments are the same.

Finally, to draw the entire source image (**MyImage**) using the ImageAttributes object in a graphics object (**MyGraphics**), we use this version of the **DrawImage** method:

```
MyGraphics.DrawImage(MyImage, RectangleDest, 0, 0,
MyImage.Width, MyImage.Height, GraphicsUnit.Pixel,
MyImageAttributes);
```

where **RectangleDest** is the rectangle structure within the graphics object (the destination location) where the image will be drawn. Arguments 3 (**0**), 4 (**0**), 5 (**MyImage.Width**), and 6 (**MyImage.Height**) specify the source rectangle. These are respectively, the desired **x** within the source image, **y** within the source image, **Width** from the source image, and **Height** from source image. The values used will copy the entire source image. If you only want to copy a portion of the source, you would adjust these arguments. With this method (now including the ImageAttributes object), **MyImage** will be drawn in **MyGraphics** with the desired transparent color.

One question is lingering – how do you determine the desired transparent color? In our fish example, it is a gray, but that's not a real definite specification. The **ClearColor** argument must be a Visual Basic **Color** object, usually using the **FromArgb** method with values for the red, green and blue contributions. How do you come up with such values? I'll give you one approach using the little fish bitmap as an example.

Here's a snippet of code to identify the background color in the fish bitmap:

```
Dim Fish As Drawing.Image
Fish = Image.FromFile(Application.StartupPath +
"\fish.bmp")
Dim FishBitmap As New Bitmap(Fish)
Console.WriteLine(FishBitmap.GetPixel(0, 0))
```

First, the fish image is loaded from its file. Next, the **Image** object is converted to a **Bitmap** object. We can determine the color of individual pixels in such objects. That is what is done in the final line of code – we read the color, using **GetPixel**, of the pixel in the upper left corner of **FishBitmap** (part of the background) and print it to the output window. Doing this results in:

This tells us the red contribution is 192 (R=192), the green contribution is 192 (G=192) and the blue contribution is 192 (B=192). Hence, the background color can be represented by:

```
Color.FromArgb(192, 192, 192)
```

This is the color argument we would use in the **ImageAttributes** object to make the background of the fish transparent.

We'll place the fish in our scrolling background soon, but first let's look at ways to move the fish once it's in the picture.

Keyboard Events

In multimedia applications, particularly games, you often need to move objects around. This movement can be automatic (using the **Timer** control) for animation effects. But then there are times you want the user to have the ability to move objects. One possibility (studied earlier in this chapter) is using the mouse and the corresponding mouse events. Here, we consider an alternate movement technique: **keyboard events**. We learn how to detect both the pressing of keys and the releasing of keys. These events can be used to trigger desired effects (such as object movement) in your application.

In applications using text box controls, we've already seen one keyboard event, the **KeyPress** event. In that event, we were able to examine user keystrokes and determine if they were acceptable in the context of the current control. The **KeyPress** event is useful for detecting keys with ASCII representations. It cannot detect keys without such representations. Examples of keys without ASCII values are the Alt, Ctrl, Shift, cursor control and other control keys. To detect pressing such keys (and ASCII keys) and combinations of such keys, we use the **KeyDown** event procedure. The form of this procedure is:

```
Private Sub ControlName_KeyDown(ByVal sender As Object,
ByVal e As System.Windows.Forms.KeyEventArgs) Handles
ControlName.KeyDown
   .
   .
End Sub
```

The arguments are:

sender	Control active when key pressed to invoke procedure
e	Event handler revealing which key was pressed and status of certain control keys when key was pressed

We are interested in several properties of the event handler **e**:

e.Alt	Boolean property that indicates if Alt key is pressed
e.Control	Boolean property that indicates if Ctrl key is pressed
e.KeyCode	Gives the key code for the key pressed
e.Shift	Boolean property that indicates if either Shift key is pressed

The **KeyCode** property is a member of the **Keys** class. There are values for every key that can be pressed (see on-line help). The Intellisense feature of the Visual Basic IDE will provide **KeyCode** values when needed. The **KeyDown** event usually has a **Select Case** structure with a **Case** clause for each possible key (or key combination) expected.

You may also want to detect the release of a previously pressed key. This can be done by the **KeyUp** event. The procedure outline is:

```
Private Sub ControlName_KeyUp(ByVal sender As Object,
ByVal e As System.Windows.Forms.KeyEventArgs) Handles
ControlName.KeyUp
    .
    .
    .
End Sub
```

The arguments are:

sender	Control active when key released to invoke procedure
e	Event handler revealing which key was released and status of certain control keys when key was released

We are interested in several properties of the event handler **e**:

e.Alt	Boolean property that indicates if Alt key is pressed
e.Control	Boolean property that indicates if Ctrl key is pressed
e.KeyCode	Gives the key code for the key released
e.Shift	Boolean property that indicates if either Shift key is pressed

The **KeyCode** property is used as it is in the **KeyDown** event.

Example 9-10

Sprite Animation

1. In this application, we will add a swimming fish to the scrolling background implemented in Example 9-9. And, we use cursor control keys to move the fish up and down. We just need to make a couple of changes to the code. Open **Example 9-9.**

2. In the **LearnVB\VB Code\Class 9\Example 9-10** folder is a graphics file named **fish.bmp.** This is the fish graphics. Copy this file into the application **Bin\Debug** folder (you may have to create the folder first).

3. Set the **frmScroll KeyPreview** property to **True**.

4. Add these 'fish' variables to the form level declarations:

```
Dim Fish As Drawing.Image
Dim FishAttributes As Drawing.Imaging.ImageAttributes
Dim FishX As Integer, FishY As Integer
```

5. Add the shaded code to the **frmScroll Load** event procedure to initialize the 'fish' variables:

```
Private Sub FrmScroll_Load(ByVal sender As System.Object,
ByVal e As System.EventArgs) Handles MyBase.Load
    Background =
Drawing.Image.FromFile(Application.StartupPath +
"\undrsea1.bmp")
    'make sure viewer is same height as background image
    pnlViewer.Height = Background.Height
    Viewer = pnlViewer.CreateGraphics
    FishAttributes = New Drawing.Imaging.ImageAttributes
    FishAttributes.SetColorKey(Color.FromArgb(192, 192,
192), Color.FromArgb(192, 192, 192))
    Fish = Image.FromFile(Application.StartupPath +
"\\fish.bmp")
    ' draw fish in middle of viewer
    FishX = CInt(0.5 * (pnlViewer.ClientSize.Width -
Fish.Width))
    FishY = CInt(0.5 * (pnlViewer.ClientSize.Height -
Fish.Height))
End Sub
```

6. Add the shaded code to the **timScroll Tick** procedure to draw the fish on the background:

```
Private Sub TimScroll_Tick(ByVal sender As System.Object,
ByVal e As System.EventArgs) Handles timScroll.Tick
    Dim AddedWidth As Integer
    Dim RectangleDest As Drawing.Rectangle, RectangleSrc As
Drawing.Rectangle
    'Find next location on background
    ScrollX += hsbScroll.Value
    If ScrollX > Background.Width Then
      ScrollX = 0
    End If
    'When x is near right edge, we need to copy
    'two segments of the background into viewer
    If ScrollX > (Background.Width -
pnlViewer.ClientSize.Width) Then
        AddedWidth = Background.Width - ScrollX
        RectangleDest = New Rectangle(0, 0, AddedWidth,
pnlViewer.ClientSize.Height)
        RectangleSrc = New Rectangle(ScrollX, 0, AddedWidth,
Background.Height)
        Viewer.DrawImage(Background, RectangleDest,
RectangleSrc, Drawing.GraphicsUnit.Pixel)
```

```
        RectangleDest = New Rectangle(AddedWidth, 0,
pnlViewer.ClientSize.Width - AddedWidth,
pnlViewer.ClientSize.Height)
        RectangleSrc = New Rectangle(0, 0,
pnlViewer.ClientSize.Width - AddedWidth, Background.Height)
        Viewer.DrawImage(Background, RectangleDest,
RectangleSrc, Drawing.GraphicsUnit.Pixel)
      Else
        RectangleDest = New Rectangle(0, 0,
pnlViewer.ClientSize.Width, pnlViewer.ClientSize.Height)
        RectangleSrc = New Rectangle(ScrollX, 0,
pnlViewer.ClientSize.Width, Background.Height)
        Viewer.DrawImage(Background, RectangleDest,
RectangleSrc, Drawing.GraphicsUnit.Pixel)
      End If
      'draw fish
      Dim FishDest As Drawing.Rectangle
      FishDest = New Rectangle(FishX, FishY, Fish.Width,
Fish.Height)
        Viewer.DrawImage(Fish, FishDest, 0, 0, Fish.Width,
Fish.Height, GraphicsUnit.Pixel, FishAttributes)
    End Sub
```

7. Use this code in the **frmScroll KeyDown** method (new code):

```
    Private Sub FrmScroll_KeyDown(ByVal sender As Object,
ByVal e As System.Windows.Forms.KeyEventArgs) Handles
Me.KeyDown
      If (e.KeyCode = Keys.U) Then
        FishY -= 5
      ElseIf e.KeyCode = Keys.D Then
        FishY += 5
      End If
    End Sub
```

This moves the fish up (U key) and down (D key).

8. Run the application and save it (saved in **Example 9-10** folder in **LearnVB\VB Code\Class 9** folder). Use the U key to move the fish up and the D key to move the fish down. Notice that, no matter where the fish is, the background shows through. Here's the fish in the middle of the water:

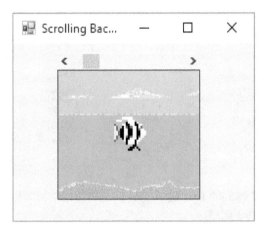

Here's the fish down by the rocks:

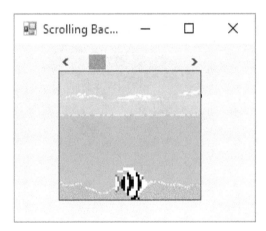

And, here's a fabulous flying fish:

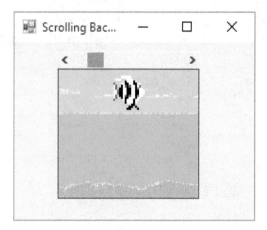

You now know the secrets of doing animations in video games – scrolling backgrounds and the use of sprites.

Collision Detection

As objects move in a multimedia presentation or video game, we need some way to see if two items collide or overlap. For example, in a basketball game, you need to see if the ball goes in the hoop. In a solitaire card game, you need to see if a card is placed on another card properly. In a file disposal application, you want to know when the file reaches the trashcan. Rectangular regions describe all the moving objects in a multimedia application. Hence, we want to know if two rectangles intersect. In Visual Basic, this test can be accomplished using the **IntersectsWith** method of the **Rectangle** structure (from the **Drawing** namespace) we've seen before.

To use the **IntersectsWith** method, we need two **Rectangle** structures. If **Rectangle1** and **Rectangle2** describe the rectangles being checked for intersection, this expression:

```
Rectangle1.IntersectsWith(Rectangle2)
```

will return one of two Boolean values. It returns **True** if Rectangle1 and Rectangle2 intersect. It returns **False** if there is no intersection between Rectangle1 and Rectangle2.

Just because two rectangles intersect, you may not want to declare a collision. There are other methods (look at the **Intersect** method) that actually determine not only if there is an intersection, but also determine the size of the overlap between the two rectangles. With these alternates, you can detect an intersection and, once detected, see how large the intersection area is. If this intersection area is small compared to the size of the compared rectangles, you might not allow the collision. Or, you might want different response depending on location of the intersection region. For example, if a ball hits (collides with) a paddle on one side, the ball will go in one direction. If the ball hits the paddle on the other side, a different rebound direction is assumed.

Example 9-11

Collision Detection

1. In this application, we will add a paddle (a **Rectangle** object) at the bottom of the bouncing ball application built in Example 9-8. If the ball collides with the paddle, we allow it to bounce back up. If it misses the paddle, we let it drop off the bottom of the form. The paddle will be moved to the **left** using the **F** key and to the **right** using the **J** key. These keys were selected because they are in a natural typing position. Open **Example 9-8**.

2. First, widen the panel control to give the paddle room to move. My modified form looks like this:

3. Set the **frmBall KeyPreview** property to **True**.

4. Add these variables to the form level declarations:

```
Dim MyPaddle As Drawing.Rectangle
Dim PaddleX As Integer = 100
```

5. Add the shaded code to the **frmBall Load** method. This creates the paddle rectangle structure:

```
Private Sub FrmBall_Load(ByVal sender As System.Object,
ByVal e As System.EventArgs) Handles MyBase.Load
    'initialize variables/set up graphics objects
    BallY = 0
    BallDir = 1
    MyDisplay = pnlDisplay.CreateGraphics
    MyBall = Drawing.Image.FromFile(Application.StartupPath
+ "\ball.gif")
    MyPaddle = New Drawing.Rectangle(PaddleX,
pnlDisplay.Height - 20, BallSize, 10)
    pnlDisplay_Paint(Nothing, Nothing)
End Sub
```

6. Modify the **timBall Tick** method to add checking for a collision between the paddle and the ball (changes are shaded):

```
Private Sub TimBall_Tick(ByVal sender As System.Object,
ByVal e As System.EventArgs) Handles timBall.Tick
    'determine ball position and draw it
    BallY = CInt(BallY + BallDir *
pnlDisplay.ClientSize.Height / 50)
    'check for bounce
    If BallY < 0 Then
      BallY = 0
      BallDir = 1
    Else
      ' check for collision with paddle
      If (MyRectangle.IntersectsWith(MyPaddle)) Then
        BallY = MyPaddle.Y - BallSize
        BallDir = -1
      End If
    End If
    ' check to see if ball went off bottom - if so,
reposition at top
    If (BallY > pnlDisplay.ClientSize.Height) Then
      BallY = -BallSize
    End If
    pnlDisplay_Paint(Nothing, Nothing)
  End Sub
```

7. Add the shaded code to the **pnlDisplay Paint** method. This draws the paddle:

```
Private Sub PnlDisplay_Paint(ByVal sender As Object, ByVal
e As System.Windows.Forms.PaintEventArgs) Handles
pnlDisplay.Paint
    'horizontally center ball in display rectangle
    MyRectangle = New Rectangle(CInt(0.5 *
(pnlDisplay.ClientSize.Width - BallSize)), BallY, 50, 50)
    MyDisplay.Clear(pnlDisplay.BackColor)
    MyDisplay.DrawImage(MyBall, MyRectangle)
    'draw paddle
    MyDisplay.FillRectangle(Brushes.Red, MyPaddle)
End Sub
```

8. Add a **frmBall KeyDown** method to move the paddle (new code):

```
Private Sub FrmBall_KeyDown(ByVal sender As Object, ByVal
e As System.Windows.Forms.KeyEventArgs) Handles Me.KeyDown
    If (e.KeyCode = Keys.F) Then
      PaddleX -= 5
    ElseIf (e.KeyCode = Keys.J) Then
      PaddleX += 5
    End If
    MyPaddle.X = PaddleX
End Sub
```

9. Save and run the application (saved in **Example 9-11** in the **LearnVB\VB Code\Class 9** folder). Use the keyboard **F** key to move the paddle to the left and the **J** key to move it to the right. Make sure it can bounce off the paddle. Make sure it goes off the screen if it misses the paddle (note the code to make it reappear if this happens). Here's a run I made:

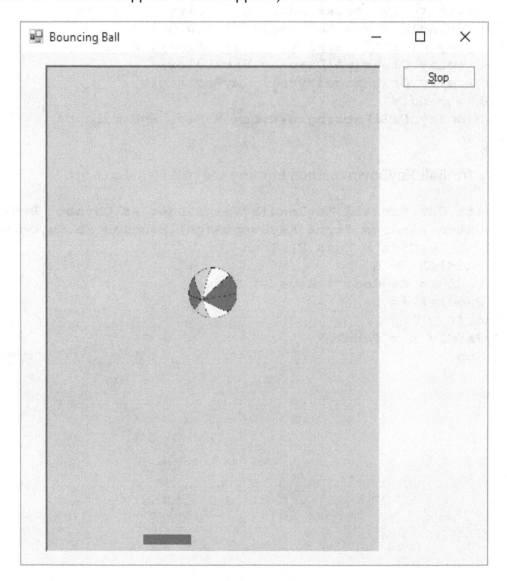

Playing Sounds

There is only one sound available with the BASIC language, a simple beep (the **Beep** function). This unexciting sound plays through the computer's built-in speaker, if there is one. Games feature elaborate sounds that take advantage of stereo sound cards. By using the Visual Basic **SoundPlayer** class (located in the **System.Media** namespace), we can add such sounds to our projects.

The **SoundPlayer** class is used to play one particular type of sound, those represented by **wav** files (files with wav extensions). Most sounds you hear played in Windows applications are saved as **wav** files. These are the files formed when you record using one of the many sound recorder programs available

Prior to playing a sound, a **SoundPlayer** object (**MySound**) must be declared using the usual **Dim** statement.

```
Dim MySound As System.Media.SoundPlayer
```

The object is then constructed using:

```
MySound = New System.Media.SoundPlayer(SoundFile)
```

where **SoundFile** is a complete path to the **wav** file to be played.

A sound is loaded into memory using the **Load** method of the **SoundPlayer** class:

```
MySound.Load()
```

This is an <u>optional</u> step that should be done for sounds that will be played often – it allows them to be played quickly.

There are two methods available to play a sound, the **Play** method and the **PlaySync** method:

```
MySound.Play()
MySound.PlaySync()
```

With the **Play** method, a sound is played **asynchronously**. This means that execution of code continues as the sound is played. With **PlaySync**, the sound is played **synchronously**. In this case, the sound is played to completion, and then code execution continues. With either method, if the sound is not loaded into memory, it will be loaded first. This will slow down your program depending on how big the file is. This is why we preload sounds (using the **Load** method) that are played often.

It is normal practice to include any sound files an application uses in the same directory as the application executable file (the **Bin\Debug folder**). This makes them easily accessible (use the **Application.StartupPath** parameter). As such, when building a deployment package for an application, you must remember to include the sound files in the package. And, you must insure these files are installed in the proper directory.

Example 9-12

Bouncing Ball with Sound!

1. Open **Example 9-11**, the bouncing ball example. We will play one sound when the ball bounces and another sound when the ball leaves the bottom of the panel. In the **Learn VB\VB Code\Class 9\Example 9-12** is a bouncing sound (**bong.wav**) and a miss sound (**missed.wav**). Copy these files to the application's **Bin\Debug** folder (you may have to create the folder first). Also copy the **ball.gif** file (the bouncing ball) to the same folder.

2. Add these variables to the form level declarations:

```
Dim BounceSound As System.Media.SoundPlayer
Dim MissSound As System.Media.SoundPlayer
```

3. Modify the **frmBall Load** procedure to create the sound variables (new code is shaded):

```
Private Sub frmBall_Load(ByVal sender As System.Object,
ByVal e As System.EventArgs) Handles MyBase.Load
    'initialize variables/set up graphics objects
    BallY = 0
    BallDir = 1
    MyDisplay = pnlDisplay.CreateGraphics
    MyBall = Drawing.Image.FromFile(Application.StartupPath
+ "\ball.gif")
    MyPaddle = New Drawing.Rectangle(PaddleX,
pnlDisplay.Height - 20, BallSize, 10)
    pnlDisplay_Paint(Nothing, Nothing)
    BounceSound = New
System.Media.SoundPlayer(Application.StartupPath +
"\bong.wav")
    MissSound = New
System.Media.SoundPlayer(Application.StartupPath +
"\missed.wav")
  End Sub
```

4. Add code to the **timBall Tick** procedure to play the 'bounce' and 'missed' sounds when needed (added code is shaded):

```
Private Sub timBall_Tick(ByVal sender As System.Object,
ByVal e As System.EventArgs) Handles timBall.Tick
    'determine ball position and draw it
    BallY = CInt(BallY + BallDir *
pnlDisplay.ClientSize.Height / 50)
    'check for bounce
    If BallY < 0 Then
      BallY = 0
      BallDir = 1
      BounceSound.Play()
    Else
      ' check for collision with paddle
      If (MyRectangle.IntersectsWith(MyPaddle)) Then
        BallY = MyPaddle.Y - BallSize
        BallDir = -1
        BounceSound.Play()
      End If
    End If
    ' check to see if ball went off bottom - if so,
reposition at top
    If (BallY > pnlDisplay.ClientSize.Height) Then
      BallY = -BallSize
      MissSound.PlaySync()
    End If
    pnlDisplay_Paint(Nothing, Nothing)
  End Sub
```

The bounce sound is played asynchronously, while the miss sound is played synchronously.

5. Save the application and run it (saved in **Example 9-12** in the **LearnVB\VB Code\Class 9** folder). Each time the ball bounces, you should hear a bonk! When it misses the paddle and falls off the bottom, you hear another sound.

Class Review

After completing this class, you should understand:

> ➢ How to detect and use mouse events
> ➢ How to add persistence to graphics objects without a Paint event
> ➢ How to draw lines, polygons and filled polygons
> ➢ How to draw curves, closed curves and filled closed curves
> ➢ How to use hatch, gradient and texture brushes
> ➢ How to add text to a graphics object
> ➢ How to do animation using DrawImage
> ➢ How to work with scrolling backgrounds
> ➢ How to do sprite animation
> ➢ How to use keyboard events and detect collision of two rectangular regions
> ➢ How to play sound files

Practice Problems 9

Problem 9-1. Blackboard Problem. Modify the **Blackboard** application (Example 9-2) to allow adjustable line width while drawing. Also, allow saving and opening of drawing files.

Problem 9-2. Rubber Band Problem. Build an application where the user draws a 'rubber band' rectangle on the form. Let a left-click start drawing (defining upper left corner). Then move the mouse until the rectangle is as desired and release the mouse button. When the 'rubber band' is complete, draw an ellipse in the defined region.

Problem 9-3. Shape Guessing Game. Build a game where the user is presented with three different shapes. Give the user one shape name and have them identify the matching shape.

Problem 9-4. Plot Labels Problem. In Problem 8-4, we built an application that plotted the win streak for the Seattle Mariners 1995 season. Use the DrawString method to add any labeling information desired.

Problem 9-5. Bouncing Balls Problem. Build an application with two bouncing balls. When they collide make them disappear with some kind of sound. Add any other effects you might like.

Problem 9-6. Moon Problem. In the **LearnVB\VB Code\Class 9\Problem 9-6** folder is a bitmap file named **THEMOON.BMP.** It is a large (450 pixels high, 640 pixels wide) lunar landscape. Build an application that lets you traverse this landscape in a small viewing window. Use cursor control keys to move horizontally and vertically.

Problem 9-7. Sound Files Problem. Build an application that lets you look through your computer directories for sound files (.wav extension). When you select a file, play it using the **SoundPlayer** object. The image viewer (Example 5-4) built in Class 5 is a good starting point.

Exercise 9

The Original Video Game - Pong!

In the early 1970's, Nolan Bushnell began the video game revolution with Atari's Pong game -- a very simple Ping-Pong kind of game. Try to replicate this game using Visual Basic. In the game, a ball bounces from one end of a court to another, bouncing off sidewalls. Players try to deflect the ball at each end using a controllable paddle. Use sounds where appropriate.

10. Other Windows Application Topics

Review and Preview

In this class, we conclude our discussion of general Visual Basic Windows applications. We look at some other controls, how to add and use controls at run-time, how to print from an application, how to use the Windows API (Application Programming Interface) and how to add help systems to our applications.

 In the final chapter (Chapter 11), we look at how to use Visual Basic for database management and another exciting feature of Visual Basic - the Web form. This form lets us build applications that work on the Internet.

Other Controls

In the past several chapters, we've looked at many of the controls in the Visual Basic toolbox. But, there are still others. We will look at several of these **other controls** in this chapter. For each control, we will build a short example to demonstrate its use. With your programming skills, you should be able to expand these examples to fit your particular needs.

What if you can't find the exact control you need for a particular task? Another skill you can develop, using the knowledge gained in this course, is the ability to build and deploy your own Visual Basic controls. You can modify an existing control (we did that way back in Chapter 3), build a control made up of several existing controls or create an entirely new control. Building your own controls is beyond the scope of this course. There are several excellent texts and websites that address this topic.

LinkLabel Control

In Toolbox:

On Form (Default Properties):

A **LinkLabel** control is like the **Label** control we've used many times before, with one important additional feature. The LinkLabel control allows you to put web style URL (Universal Resource Locator; a web page address) links in a Visual Basic application. This lets your user visit relevant web sites from within an application.

LinkLabel **Properties:**

Name	Gets or sets the name of the link label (three letter prefix for label name is **lkl**).
ActiveLinkColor	Gets or sets the color used to display an active link.
AutoSize	Gets or sets a value indicating whether the link label is automatically resized to display its entire contents.
BackColor	Get or sets the link label background color.
BorderStyle	Gets or sets the border style for the link label.
DisabledLinkColor	Gets or sets the color used when displaying a disabled link.
Font	Gets or sets font name, style, size.
ForeColor	Gets or sets color of text or graphics.
LinkArea	Gets or sets the range in the text to treat as a link.
LinkBehavior	Gets or sets a value that represents the behavior of a link.
LinkColor	Gets or sets the color used when displaying a normal link.
LinkVisited	Gets or sets a value indicating whether a link should be displayed as though it were visited.
Text	Gets or sets string displayed on link label.
TextAlign	Gets or sets the alignment of text in the link label.
VisitedLinkColor	Gets or sets the color used when displaying a link that that has been previously visited.

LinkLabel **Methods:**

    Refresh   Forces an update of the link label control contents.

LinkLabel **Events:**

    LinkClicked   Occurs when a link is clicked within the control.

Once a link is clicked in the link label control, we need to know how to display the specified web page. Knowing a URL (the **Text** property of the link label control), the web page is displayed using the **Process.Start** method in the Visual Basic **Diagnostics** namespace. In code, this line would be for a control named **lklExample:**

```
Diagnostics.Process.Start(lklExample.Text)
```

Typical use of **LinkLabel** control:

> ➤ Set the **Name** and **Text** property (the URL for the web page).
> ➤ You may also want to change the **Font** and various **link colors.**
> ➤ Write code in the link label's **LinkClicked** event. This code should access the web page (using **Process.Start**) and set the **LinkVisited** property to **True.**

Example 10-1

Link Label Control

1. Start a new project. In this project, you'll use the link label control to visit some web site (we've selected ours; you can use any one you want). This is a popular feature of many commercial applications. Place a link label control on the form.

2. Set the properties of the form and each object.

   Form1:
Name	frmLinkLabel
FormBorderStyle	FixedSingle
StartPosition	CenterScreen
Text	Link Label Example

   LinkLabel1:
Name	lklURL
FontSize	12
Text	http://www.kidwaresoftware.com

Your form should look like this:

4. Use the following code in the **lklURL LinkClicked** event.

```
    Private Sub LklURL_LinkClicked(ByVal sender As
System.Object, ByVal e As
System.Windows.Forms.LinkLabelLinkClickedEventArgs) Handles
lklURL.LinkClicked
    ' Call the Process.Start method to open the default
browser
    ' with a URL:
    lklURL.LinkVisited = True

Diagnostics.Process.Start("http://www.kidwaresoftware.com")
    End Sub
```

5. Save your project (saved in **Example 10-1** folder in the **LearnVB\VB Code\Class 10** folder). Run the application. Click the link. What happens next depends on the state of your computer. Here's the running project after I clicked the link (notice the change in text color):

So what happens after clicking the link? If you're already logged on to the Internet and your browser is running, program control will switch to the browser and you'll see our web site's home page. If you're logged in, but your browser is not running, the browser will start and then you'll see the web page. If not logged in, your browser will start and your default login procedure will begin. If you successfully log in, our web site will appear. All of this performance comes with no extra code!

TabControl Control

In Toolbox:

On Form (Default Properties):

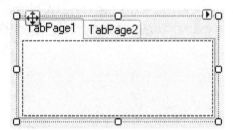

The **TabControl** control provides an easy way to present several dialogs or screens of information on a single form. This is the same interface seen in many commercial Windows applications. The tab control provides a group of tabs, each of which acts as a container (works just like a group box or panel) for other controls. In particular, groups of radio buttons within a tab 'page' operate as an independent group. Only one tab can be active at a time. Using this control is easy. Just build each tab container as a separate group: add controls, set properties, and write code like you do for any application. Navigation from one tab to the next is simple: just click on the corresponding tab.

TabControl **Properties:**

Name	Gets or sets the name of the tab control (three letter prefix for control name is **tab**).
BackColor	Get or sets the tab control background color.
BorderStyle	Gets or sets the border style for the tab control.
Font	Gets or sets font name, style, size.
ForeColor	Gets or sets color of text or graphics.
ItemSize	Size structure determining tab size.
SelectedIndex	Gets or sets the currently displayed tab index.
SizeMode	Determines how tabs are sized.
TabPages	Collection describing each tab page.

TabControl **Events**:

    SelectedIndexChanged   Occurs when the **SelectedIndex** property changes.

The most important property for the tab control is **TabPages**. It is used to design each tab (known as a **TabPage**). Choosing the **TabPages** property in the Properties window and clicking the ellipsis that appears will display the **TabPage Collection Editor**. With this editor, you can add, delete, insert and move tab pages. To add a tab page, click the **Add** button. A name and index will be assigned to a tab. There are two tabs added initially so the editor appears like this:

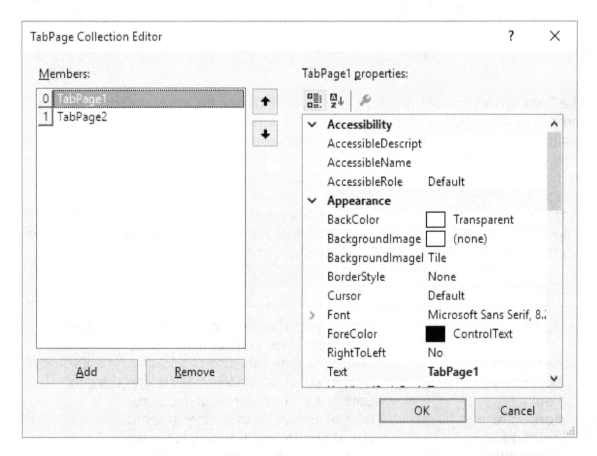

Add as many tab pages as you like. The tab page 'array' is zero-based; hence, if you have N tabs, the first is index 0, the last index N – 1. You can change any property you desire in the **Properties** area.

TabPage **Properties:**

Name	Gets or sets the name of the tab page (three letter prefix for control name is **tab**).
BackColor	Get or sets the tab page background color.
BorderStyle	Gets or sets the border style for the tab page.
Font	Gets or sets font name, style, size.
ForeColor	Gets or sets color of text or graphics.
Text	Titling information appearing on tab.

When done, click **OK** to leave the TabPage Collection Editor.

The next step is to add controls to each 'page' of the tab control. This is straightforward. Simply display the desired tab page by clicking on the tab. Then place controls on the tab page, treating the page like a group box or panel control. Make sure your controls become 'attached' to the tab page. You can still place controls on the form that are not associated with any tab. As the programmer, you need to know which tab is active (**SelectedIndex** property). And, you need to keep track of which controls are available with each tab page.

Typical use of **TabControl** control:

> ➢ Set the **Name** property and size appropriately.
> ➢ Establish each tab page using the **TabPage Collection Editor**.
> ➢ Add controls to tabs and form.
> ➢ Write code for the various events associated with controls on the tab control and form.

Example 10-2

Tab Control

1. Start a new project. In this project, we'll build a simple three tab application to demonstrate the grouping ability of the tab control. The first two tabs will allow background color selection for the respective tab. The third tab will allow the viewing of graphics files. Place a tab control and button control on the form. Set the properties of the form and each object.

Form1:

Name	frmTabControl
FormBorderStyle	FixedSingle
StartPosition	CenterScreen
Text	Tab Control Example

Button1:

Name	btnExit
Text	E&xit

TabControl1:

Name	tabExample
Size	80,20
SizeMode	Fixed
TabPages	[Create three pages, name them tabPage1, tabPage2, tabPage3]

2. Click on the first tab page (**TabPage1**). Set the **Text** property to **First Tab**. Add four radio button controls to this page. Set these properties:

RadioButton1:
     Name   rdoRed1
     Text   Red

RadioButton2:
     Name   rdoBlue1
     Text   Blue

RadioButton3:
     Name   rdoGreen1
     Text   Green

RadioButton4:
     Name   rdoYellow1
     Text   Yellow

At this point, you should see:

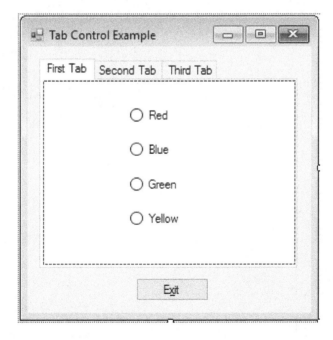

3. Click on the second tab page (**TabPage2**). Set the **Text** property to **Second Tab**. Add four radio button controls to this page (the same as we did for the first tab). Set these properties:

RadioButton1:
     Name   rdoRed2
     Text   Red

RadioButton2:
     Name   rdoBlue2
     Text   Blue

RadioButton3:
     Name   rdoGreen2
     Text   Green

RadioButton4:
     Name   rdoYellow2
     Text   Yellow

At this point, the form with the second tab active shows:

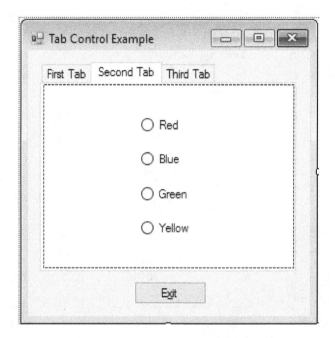

4. Click on the third tab page (**TabPage3**). Set the **Text** property to **Third Tab**. Add a picture box and button control. Also add an open dialog control – this is not associated with a particular page; it is associated with the form. Set these properties:

PictureBox1:
      Name   picExample
      BackColor   White
      SizeMode   StretchImage

Button1:
      Name   btnPicture
      Text   &Show Picture

OpenFileDialog1:
      Name   dlgOpen

The form with the third tab active shows:

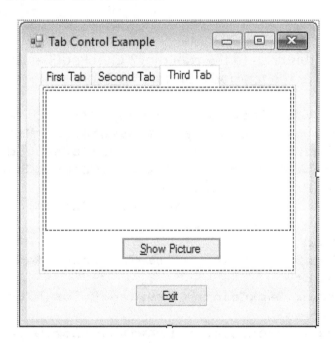

And now, in the tray area, we have:

      dlgOpen

5. Add this code to the **rdoColor1 CheckedChanged** event (handles clicking on any of the four radio buttons on **TabPage1**):

```
Private Sub RdoColor1_CheckedChanged(ByVal sender As
System.Object, ByVal e As System.EventArgs) Handles
rdoRed1.CheckedChanged, rdoBlue1.CheckedChanged,
rdoGreen1.CheckedChanged, rdoYellow1.CheckedChanged
    Dim ButtonPicked As RadioButton
    ButtonPicked = CType(sender, RadioButton)
    Select Case ButtonPicked.Text
      Case "Red"
        TabPage1.BackColor = Drawing.Color.Red
      Case "Blue"
        TabPage1.BackColor = Drawing.Color.Blue
      Case "Green"
        TabPage1.BackColor = Drawing.Color.Green
      Case "Yellow"
        TabPage1.BackColor = Drawing.Color.Yellow
    End Select
End Sub
```

6. Similarly, add this code to the **rdoColor2 CheckedChanged** event (handles clicking on any of the four radio buttons on **TabPage2**):

```
Private Sub RdoColor2_CheckedChanged(ByVal sender As
System.Object, ByVal e As System.EventArgs) Handles
rdoRed2.CheckedChanged, rdoBlue2.CheckedChanged,
rdoGreen2.CheckedChanged, rdoYellow2.CheckedChanged
    Dim ButtonPicked As RadioButton
    ButtonPicked = CType(sender, RadioButton)
    Select Case ButtonPicked.Text
      Case "Red"
        TabPage2.BackColor = Drawing.Color.Red
      Case "Blue"
        TabPage2.BackColor = Drawing.Color.Blue
      Case "Green"
        TabPage2.BackColor = Drawing.Color.Green
      Case "Yellow"
        TabPage2.BackColor = Drawing.Color.Yellow
    End Select
End Sub
```

7. Use this code in the **btnPicture Click** event (handles button click on tabPage3):

```
Private Sub BtnPicture_Click(ByVal sender As
System.Object, ByVal e As System.EventArgs) Handles
btnPicture.Click
    dlgOpen.Filter = "Bitmaps (*.bmp)|*.bmp|JPEG
(*.jpg)|*.jpg|GIF (*.gif)|*.gif"""
    If dlgOpen.ShowDialog = Windows.Forms.DialogResult.OK
Then
        picExample.Image =
Drawing.Image.FromFile(dlgOpen.FileName)
    End If
End Sub
```

8. Use the following code in the **btnExit Click** event.

```
Private Sub BtnExit_Click(ByVal sender As System.Object,
ByVal e As System.EventArgs) Handles btnExit.Click
    Me.Close()
End Sub
```

9. Save your project (saved in **Example 10-2** folder in the **LearnVB\VB Code\Class 10** folder). Run the application. Navigate from tab to tab by just clicking the tabs. Notice how you can change the colors of the first two tab pages independently. Notice how the third tab is another independent group of controls. And, notice the **Exit** button is always displayed (since it is on the form, not the tab control). Here, I've changed the color of the second tab:

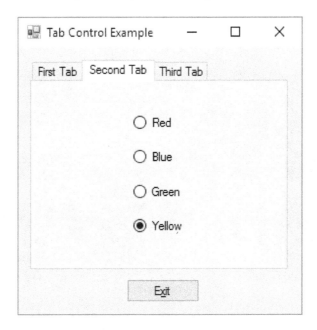

and here's a picture on the third tab:

MonthCalendar Control

In Toolbox:

 MonthCalendar

On Form (Default Properties):

The **MonthCalendar** control allows a user to select a date. It is a very easy to use interface - just point and click. This control is useful for ordering information, making reservations or choosing the current date. It can be used to select a single date or a range of dates.

MonthCalendar **Properties:**

Name	Gets or sets the name of the month calendar (three letter prefix for label name is **cal**).
BackColor	Get or sets the month calendar background color.
CalendarDimensions	Gets or sets the number of columns and rows of months displayed.
FirstDayOfWeek	Gets or sets the first day of the week as displayed in the month calendar.
Font	Gets or sets font name, style, size.
ForeColor	Gets or sets color of text or graphics.
MaxDate	Gets or sets the maximum allowable date.
MaxSelectionCount	The maximum number of days that can be selected in a month calendar control.
MinDate	Gets or sets the minimum allowable date.
SelectionEnd	Gets or sets the end date of the selected range of dates.

MonthCalendar **Properties** (continued):

SelectionRange	Retrieves the selected range of dates for a month calendar control.
SelectionStart	Gets or sets the start date of the selected range of dates.
ShowToday	Gets or sets a value indicating whether the date represent by the TodayDate property is shown at the bottom of the control.
ShowTodayCircle	Gets or sets a value indicating whether today's date is circled.
TodayDate	Gets or sets the value that is used by MonthCalendar as today's date.

MonthCalendar **Methods:**

SetDate	Sets date as the current selected date.

MonthCalendar **Events:**

DateChanged	Occurs when the date in the MonthCalendar changes.
DateSelected	Occurs when a date is selected.

Typical use of **MonthCalendar** control:

> ➢ Set the **Name** property. Set **MaxSelection** Count (set to 1 if just picking a single date).
> ➢ Monitor **DateChanged** and/or **DateSelected** events to determine date value(s). Values are between **SelectionStart** and **SelectionEnd** properties.

DateTimePicker Control

In Toolbox:

 DateTimePicker

On Form (Default Properties):

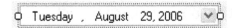 Tuesday , August 29, 2006

The **DateTimePicker** control works like the MonthCalendar control with a different interface and formatting options. It allows the user to select a single date. The selected date appears in a combo box. The calendar portion is available as a 'drop down.' This control can also be used to select a time; we won't look at that option.

DateTimePicker **Properties:**

Name	Gets or sets the name of the date/time picker control (three letter prefix for label name is **dtp**).
BackColor	Get or sets the control background color.
Font	Gets or sets font name, style, size.
ForeColor	Gets or sets color of text or graphics.
Format	Gets or sets the format of the date displayed in the control.
MaxDate	Gets or sets the maximum allowable date.
MinDate	Gets or sets the minimum allowable date.
Value	Gets or sets the date value assigned to the control.

DateTimePicker **Events:**

ValueChanged	Occurs when the **Value** property changes.

Typical use of **DateTimePicker** control:

➢ Set the **Name** and Format properties.
➢ When needed, read **Value** property for selected date.

Example 10-3

Date Selections

Start a new project. In this project, we'll look at single date selection using the **MonthCalendar** and **DateTimePicker** controls. Add one of each of these controls to the form.

1. Set the properties of the form and each object.

Form1:

Name	frmMonth
FormBorderStyle	FixedSingle
StartPosition	CenterScreen
Text	Calendar Examples

MonthCalendar1:

Name	calExample
MaxSelectionCount	1

DateTimePicker1:

Name	dtpExample
Format	Long

Your form should look like this:

2. Use this code in the **calExample DateSelected** event:

```
Private Sub CalExample_DateSelected(ByVal sender As
Object, ByVal e As System.Windows.Forms.DateRangeEventArgs)
Handles calExample.DateSelected
    MessageBox.Show("You selected " +
CStr(calExample.SelectionStart), "Date Selected in Month
Calendar Control")
    End Sub
```

3. Save your project (saved in **Example 10-3** folder in the **LearnVB\VB Code\Class 10** folder). Run the application. Notice how easy it is to select dates for your applications. Here's my birthday (yes, I'm getting old) in the top calendar and today's in the lower control:

When I clicked this date, this message box appeared:

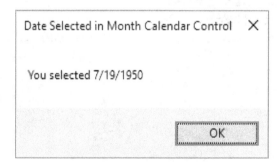

Play with the date time picker control too – can you write code to display its selection in a message box.

RichTextbox Control

In Toolbox:

On Form (Default Properties):

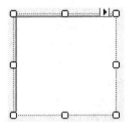

The **RichTextBox** control allows the user to enter and edit text, providing more advanced formatting features than the conventional textbox control. You can use different fonts and font styles for different text sections (see the '**Selection**' properties). You can even control indents, hanging indents, and bulleted paragraphs. Possible uses for this control include: reading and viewing large text files or implementing a full-featured text editor into any applications.

RichTextBox **Properties**:

Name	Gets or sets the name of the rich text box (three letter prefix for text box name is **rtb**).
AutoSize	Gets or sets a value indicating whether the height of the text box automatically adjusts when the font assigned to the control is changed.
BackColor	Get or sets the text box background color.
BorderStyle	Gets or sets the border style for the text box.
Font	Gets or sets font name, style, size.
ForeColor	Gets or sets color of text or graphics.
HideSelection	Gets or sets a value indicating whether the selected text in the text box control remains highlighted when the control loses focus.
Lines	Gets or sets the lines of text in a text box control.

RichTextBox **Properties** (continued):

MaxLength	Gets or sets the maximum number of characters the user can type into the text box control.
MultiLine	Gets or sets a value indicating whether this is a multiline text box control.
ReadOnly	Gets or sets a value indicating whether text in the text box is read-only.
ScrollBars	Gets or sets which scroll bars should appear in a multiline TextBox control.
SelectedText	Gets or sets a value indicating the currently selected text in the control.
SelectionColor	Gets or sets the text color of the current text selection or insertion point.
SelectionFont	Gets or sets the font of the current text selection or insertion point.
SelectionLength	Gets or sets the number of characters selected in the text box.
SelectionStart	Gets or sets the starting point of text selected in the text box.
Tag	Stores a string expression.
Text	Gets or sets the current text in the text box.
TextAlign	Gets or sets the alignment of text in the text box.
TextLength	Gets length of text in text box.

RichTextBox **Methods:**

AppendText	Appends text to the current text of text box.
Clear	Clears all text in text box.
Copy	Copies selected text to clipboard.
Cut	Moves selected text to clipboard.
Focus	Places the cursor in a specified text box.
LoadFile	Loads the contents of a file into the RichTextBox control.
Paste	Replaces the current selection in the text box with the contents of the Clipboard.
SaveFile	Saves the contents (including all formatting) of the RichTextBox to a file.
Undo	Undoes the last edit operation in the text box.

RichTextBox **Events:**

Click	Occurs when the user clicks the text box.
Focused	Occurs when the control receives focus.
KeyDown	Occurs when a key is pressed down while the control has focus.
KeyPress	Occurs when a key is pressed while the control has focus – used for key trapping.
Leave	Triggered when the user leaves the text box. This is a good place to examine the contents of a text box after editing.
TextChanged	Occurs when the Text property value has changed.

Note particularly the **LoadFile** and **SaveFile** methods. **SaveFile** will save the contents of the rich text box control as an **rtf** (rich text format) file. Almost all word processing programs can open such a document. The format for a rich text box control named **rtbExample** is:

```
rtbExample.SaveFile(FileName)
```

where **FileName** is a complete path to the file. To open a previously saved file, the format is:

```
rtbExample.LoadFile(FileName)
```

Typical use of **RichTextBox** control as display control:

➢ Set the **Name** property. Initialize **Text** property to desired string.
➢ If displaying more than one line, set **MultiLine** property to **True**.
➢ Assign **Text** property in code where needed.
➢ If desired, write code to selectively format displayed text.

Typical use of **RichTextBox** control as input device:

➢ Set the **Name** property. Initialize **Text** property to desired string.
➢ If it is possible to input multiple lines, set **MultiLine** property to **True**.
➢ In code, give **Focus** to control when needed. Provide key trapping code in **KeyPress** event. Read **Text** property when **LostFocus** event occurs.
➢ If desired, write code to selectively format displayed text.

<u>**Example 10-4**</u>

Rich Text Box Example

1. Start a new project. In this project, we'll change the font of selected text using the rich text box control. Add a rich text box control, a button control and a font dialog control to the project.

2. Set the properties of the form and each object.

> **Form1:**
>> Name   frmRichTextBox
>> FormBorderStyle   FixedSingle
>> StartPosition   CenterScreen
>> Text   Rich Text Box Example
>
> **RichTextBox1:**
>> Name   rtbExample
>> MultiLine   True
>> ScrollBars   ForcedVertical
>
> **Button1:**
>> Name   btnFont
>> Text   &Change Font
>
> **FontDialog1:**
>> Name   dlgFont

Your form should look like this:

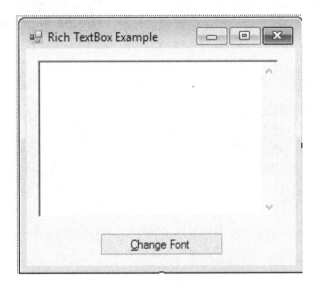

Other controls in tray:

dlgFont

3. Use this code in the **btnFont Click** event:

```
Private Sub BtnFont_Click(ByVal sender As System.Object,
ByVal e As System.EventArgs) Handles btnFont.Click
    If dlgFont.ShowDialog = Windows.Forms.DialogResult.OK
Then
        rtbExample.SelectionFont = dlgFont.Font
    End If
End Sub
```

4. Save your project (saved in **Example 10-4** folder in the **LearnVB\VB Code\Class 10** folder). Run the application. Type some text in the text box. Select a section of text and change the font. Notice you can format as many text selections as your desire. Here's some text with various formats:

ToolStrip (Toolbar) Control

In Toolbox:

On Form (Default Properties):

Below Form (Default Properties):

Almost all Windows applications these days use toolbars. A toolbar provides quick access to the most frequently used menu commands in an application. The **ToolStrip** control (also referred to as the **Toolbar** control) is a mini-application in itself. It provides everything you need to design and implement a toolbar into your application. Possible uses for this control include: provide a consistent interface between applications with matching toolbars, place commonly used functions in an easily-accessed space and provide an intuitive, graphical interface for your application.

ToolStrip **Properties:**

Name	Gets or sets the name of the toolstrip (toolbar) control (three letter prefix for label name is **tlb**).
BackColor	Background color of toolstrip.
Items	Gets the collection of controls assigned to the toolstrip control.
LayoutStyle	Establishes whether toolbar is vertical or horizontal.
Dock	Establishes location of toolbar on form.

The primary property of concern is the **Items** collection. This establishes each item in the toolbar. Choosing the **Items** property in the Properties window and clicking the ellipsis that appears will display the **Items Collection Editor**. With this editor, you can add, delete, insert and move items. We will look at adding just two types of items: **ToolStripButton** and **ToolStripSeparator** (used to separate tool bar buttons). To add a button, make sure **Button** appears in the drop-down box and click the **Add** button. A name will be assigned to a button. After adding one button, the editor will look like this:

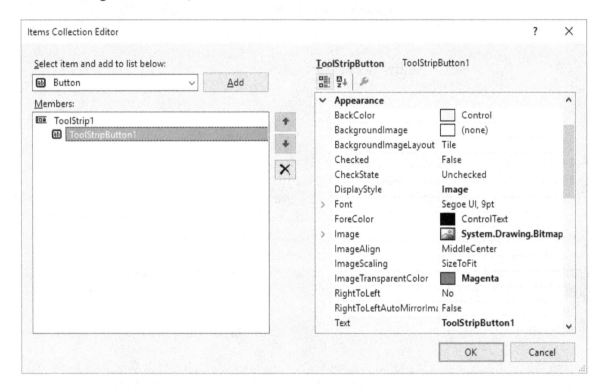

Add as many buttons as you like. You can change any property you desire in the **Properties** area.

ToolStripButton **Properties:**

Name	Gets or sets the name of the button (three letter prefix for control name is **tlb**).
DisplayStyle	Sets whether image, text or both are displayed on button.
Image	Image to display on button.
Text	Caption information on the button, often blank.
TextImageRelation	Where text appears relative to image.
ToolTipText	Text to display in button tool tip.

To add a separator, make sure **ToolStripSeparator** appears in drop-down box and click **Add**. When done editing buttons, click **OK** to leave the Items Collection Editor.

Setting the **Image** property requires a few steps (a process similar to that used for the picture box control). First, click the ellipsis next to the **Image** property in the property window. This **Select Resource** window will appear:

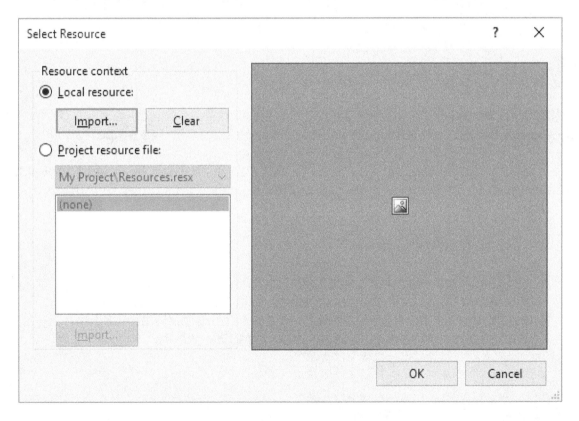

The images will be a local resource, so select the **Local resource** radio button and click the **Import** button.

An **Open** window will display graphics files (if you want to see an **ico** file, you must change **Files of type** to **All Files**). In the **LearnVB\VB Code\Class 10** folder is a folder named **Toolbar Graphics**. In this folder, there are many bitmap files for toolbar use:

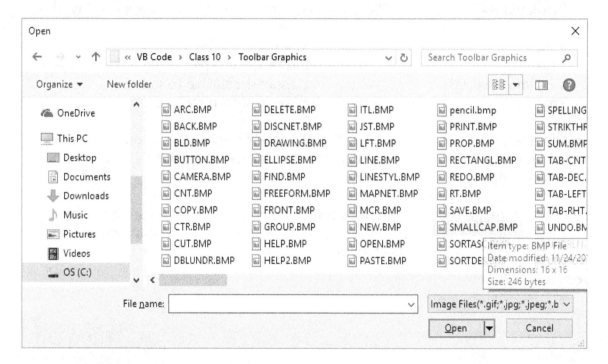

Select the desired file and click **Open**. Once an image is selected, click **OK** in the **Select Resource** window. It will be assigned to the **Image** property

After setting up the toolbar, you need to write code for the **Click** event for each toolbar button. This event is the same **Click** event we encounter for button controls.

Typical use of **ToolStrip** control:

> ➢ Set the **Name** property and desired location.
> ➢ Decide on image, text, and tooltip text for each button.
> ➢ Establish each button/separator using the **Items Collection Editor**.
> ➢ Write code for the each toolbar button's **Click** event.

Example 10-5

Note Editor Toolbar

1. Back in Chapters 6 and 7, we built and modified a **Note Editor** application. In the application, we could type and format text in a text box control. In this example, we'll add a toolbar to that application. Load **Example 7-7** (the last incarnation of the Note Editor). You will probably have to resize the form and move the text box to make room for the toolbar. Name the toolbar **tlbNoteEditor**. The form should look like this:

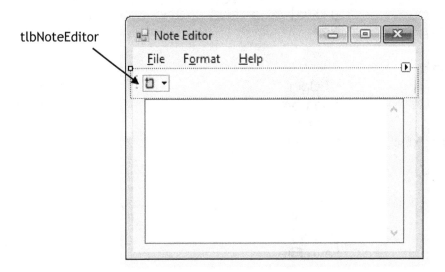

Added control in tray:

tlbNoteEditor

2. The toolbar will have six buttons: one to create a **new** file, one to **open** a file, one to **save** a file, one to **bold** text, one to **italicize** text and one to **underline** text. Click on the **Items** property of the toolbar control. The **Items Collection Editor** will appear. We use this editor to sequentially add seven buttons to the toolbar: the six mentioned above plus one button as a space holder between file functions (New, Open, Save) and edit functions (Bold, Italicize, Underline). So, **Add** seven buttons with these properties:

ToolBarButton1:
Name	tlbNew
Image	new.bmp
Text	[Blank]
ToolTipText	New File

ToolBarButton2:
Name	tlbOpen
Image	open.bmp
Text	[Blank]
ToolTipText	Open File

ToolBarButton3:
Name	tlbSave
Image	save.bmp
Text	[Blank]
ToolTipText	Save File

ToolBarButton4:
Name	tlbSpace
Style	Separator

ToolBarButton5:
Name	tlbBold
Image	bld.bmp
Text	[Blank]
ToolTipText	Bold Text

ToolBarButton6:
Name	tlbItalic
Image	itl.bmp
Text	[Blank]
ToolTipText	Italicize Text

ToolBarButton7:

Name	tlbUnderline
Image	undrln.bmp
Text	[Blank]
ToolTipText	Underline Text

Note six images are needed with the buttons. Recall these are added using the **Select Resource** window (click the **Image** property for one of the buttons). All the graphics files are included in the **LearnVB\VB Code\Class 10\Toolbar Graphics** folder.

Also, note (as desired) **tlbSpace** is a placeholder button (choose **Separator** as the type before adding) that puts some space between the file and formatting buttons.

The finished **Items Collection Editor** window appears as:

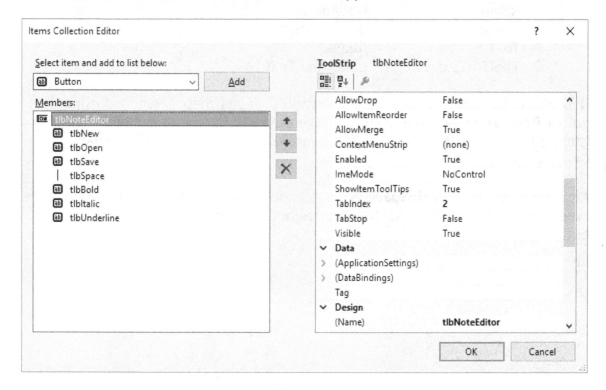

Click **OK** to close this box.

The top of my form now looks like this:

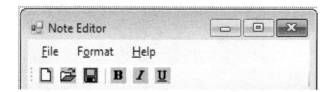

Notice the separator 'button.'

3. Lastly, add this code to the **tlbNoteEditor Click** event (handles the **Click** event for each toolbar button). Each toolbar button replicates an existing menu item, so the code is simply a 'click' on the corresponding menu option (using the **PerformClick** method):

```
Private Sub tlbNoteEditor_Click(ByVal sender As
System.Object, ByVal e As System.EventArgs) Handles
tlbNew.Click, tlbUnderline.Click, tlbSave.Click,
tlbOpen.Click, tlbItalic.Click, tlbBold.Click
    Dim ToolButton As ToolStripButton
    ToolButton = CType(sender, ToolStripButton)
    Select Case ToolButton.Name
      Case "tlbNew"
        mnuFileNew.PerformClick()
      Case "tlbOpen"
        mnuFileOpen.PerformClick()
      Case "tlbSave"
        mnuFileSave.PerformClick()
      Case "tlbBold"
        mnuFmtBold.PerformClick()
      Case "tlbItalic"
        mnuFmtItalic.PerformClick()
      Case "tlbUnderline"
        mnuFmtUnderline.PerformClick()
    End Select
  End Sub
```

4. Save (saved in **Example 10-5** folder in the **LearnVB\VB Code\Class 10** folder) and run the application. Make sure all the toolbar buttons work properly. Check out how the tool tips work. Here's the Note Editor with toolbar added:

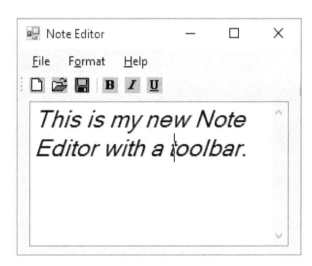

ToolTip Control

In Toolbox:

Below Form (Default Properties):

In the last example, we saw that tool tips are useful for indicating what a particular toolbar button does. Using the **ToolTip** control, we can add tool tips to any control in an application. This can be used to help explain a control's use and purpose.

ToolTip **Properties:**

Name	Gets or sets the name of the tooltip control (three letter prefix for label name is **tlt**).
AutomaticDelay	Sets the length of time that the ToolTip string is shown, how long the user must point at the control for the ToolTip to appear, and how long it takes for subsequent ToolTip windows to appear. Usually, the default values are quite adequate.

Once added to an application, all controls in the application will have an additional property: **ToolTip.** Just set a value of this property for each control you want to have a tool tip. It's that easy!

Example 10-6

Tool Tip Control

1. Start a new project. In this project, you'll use the tool tip control to add tool tips to a few controls. Place two button controls and two text box controls on the form. Add a tool tip control to the application. Set these properties:

Form1:
          Name   frmToolTip
          FormBorderStyle   FixedSingle
          StartPosition   CenterScreen
          Text   ToolTip Example

Button1:
          ToolTip   This is Button 1

Button2:
          ToolTip   This is Button 2

TextBox1:
          ToolTip   Type some stuff here

TextBox2:
          ToolTip   Need more stuff here!

Your form should now look like this:

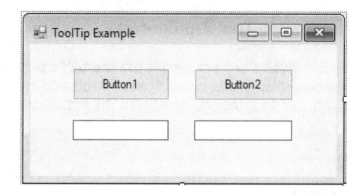

Other controls in tray:

tltExample

2. Save your project (saved in **Example 10-6** folder in the **LearnVB\VB Code\Class 10** folder). Run the application. Move the cursor over each control and see how the tool tips work. If you like, try changing the various delay properties to see how these affect the tool tip behavior. Here's a couple of the tool tips for this project:

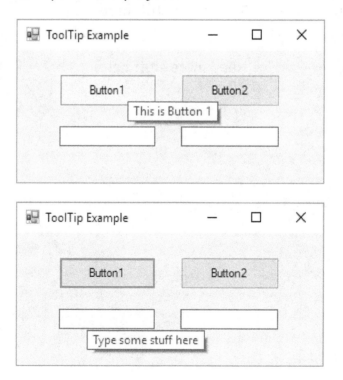

Adding Controls at Run-Time

In building Visual Basic applications, the process of adding controls and setting properties at design time is straightforward and simple. There are times, however, when it might be advantageous to add controls at run-time. For example, what if the number of radio button controls displayed for a certain choice depended on some user input. Or, perhaps the task of adding many similar controls is a lot of tedious work. With just a bit of code, we can automate the task of **adding controls** to a form at **run-time**. We can also remove controls if desired. This is a review of some material seen back in Chapter 3, where we introduced object-oriented programming.

To add a control at run-time, we need to follow five steps: (1) declare the control, (2) create the control, (3) set control properties, (4) add control to form and (5) connect event handlers. We look at each step separately for a generic control named **MyControl** of type **ControlType**.

The first step is to declare a control using the usual **Dim** statement:

```
Dim MyControl As ControlType
```

Quite often we declare an array of controls. Then, the control is created using the respective constructor:

```
MyControl = New ControlType()
```

At this point, **MyControl** is established with a default set of properties. You can overwrite any properties you choose. In particular, you must set values for the **Left** and **Top** properties. If you don't, all your new controls will be stacked in the upper left corner of the form (Left = 0, Top = 0). You probably also want to change the **Width** and **Height** properties. Once the properties are set, the control is added to the form using the **Add** method of the **Controls** object:

```
Me.Controls.Add(MyControl)
```

If you are adding the control to a group box or panel control, you would replace **Me** (referring to the form) in the above statement with the container control's name.

So, now the control is created and on the form, but recognizes no events. Decide what events you want your control to respond to. For each event **MyEvent**, an event handler is created using:

```
AddHandler MyControl.MyEvent, AddressOf Me.MyProcedure
```

Before using this statement, the procedure **MyProcedure** must exist in the code window. It could be a procedure corresponding to an existing control or a new procedure you create. If you create it, the format is:

```
Private Sub MyProcedure(ByVal sender As Object, ByVal e As
System.EventArgs)
    .
    .
End Sub
```

You would write code in this procedure, assuming event handlers are added at run-time.

As an aside, you can use the **AddHandler** statement for existing controls also. This sometimes saves a little typing at design time. For example, say you have a procedure that handles clicking on 20 button controls. Rather than append the **Handles** clause in the code window, you could add it in code.

You can also remove controls from your application. To remove a control (named **MyControl**) from the form, use:

```
Me.Controls.Remove(MyControl)
```

If you are removing a control from a group box or panel control, replace the keyword **Me** with the container control's name. When the control is removed, all event handlers for this control are modified to no longer include the removed control. This also happens when a control is deleted at design time.

Example 10-7

Rolodex - Adding Controls at Run-Time

1. Start a new project. In this project, we'll build a computer rolodex index. We will neatly format 26 button controls in two rows across a form. Each button will have a letter of the alphabet. Such a 'control array' could be used for searching a database for information, looking for a last name, or finding a word in a dictionary. Set these properties (all we have is a form):

    Form1:
Name	frmControls
FormBorderStyle	FixedSingle
StartPosition	CenterScreen
Text	Adding Controls

    Make your form fairly wide (it needs to hold 2 rows of 13 buttons):

    The trickiest part is determining the width of each button. It's essentially the form width divided by 13, since there are 13 buttons in each row. In the code, we add a little space for margins. For each button, we need to establish **Left**, **Top**, **Width** and **Height** properties. We also set the **ForeColor**, **BackColor** and **Text** properties. See the code for our solution.

2. All the buttons are created in the **Form Load** event (you should be able to follow the commented code):

```
Private Sub FrmControls_Load(ByVal sender As Object, ByVal
e As System.EventArgs) Handles MyBase.Load
    Dim W As Integer, LStart As Integer, L As Integer, T As
Integer
    Dim ButtonHeight As Integer = 35
    Dim I As Integer
    Dim Rolodex(26) As Button
    'search buttons
    'determine button width (don't round up) - 13 on a row
    W = CInt(Me.ClientSize.Width / 14 - 0.5)
    'center buttons on form
    LStart = CInt(0.5 * (Me.ClientSize.Width - 13 * W))
    L = LStart
    T = CInt(0.5 * (Me.ClientSize.Height - 2 *
ButtonHeight))
    'create and position 26 buttons
    For I = 1 To 26
      'create new pushbutton
      Rolodex(I) = New Button()
      Rolodex(I).TabStop = False
      'set text property
      Rolodex(I).Text = Chr(64 + I)
      'position
      Rolodex(I).Width = W
      Rolodex(I).Height = ButtonHeight
      Rolodex(I).Left = L
      Rolodex(I).Top = T
      'give cool colors
      Rolodex(I).BackColor = Color.Red
      Rolodex(I).ForeColor = Color.Yellow
      'add button to form
      Me.Controls.Add(Rolodex(I))
      'add event handler
      AddHandler Rolodex(I).Click, AddressOf
Me.Rolodex_Click
      'next left
      L += W
      If I = 13 Then
        'move to next row
        L = LStart
        T = T + ButtonHeight
      End If
    Next I
  End Sub
```

3. Add this code to the **Rolodex Click** event (handles clicks on all buttons –
   handlers added in code):

```
Private Sub Rolodex_Click(ByVal sender As System.Object,
ByVal e As System.EventArgs)
    Dim ButtonClicked As Button
    ButtonClicked = CType(sender, Button)
    MessageBox.Show("You clicked the " + ButtonClicked.Text
+ " button.", "", MessageBoxButtons.OK)
    End Sub
```

4. Save your project (saved in **Example 10-7** folder in the **LearnVB\VB
   Code\Class 10** folder). Run the application. Notice the nicely spaced
   buttons.

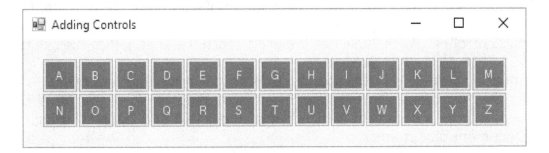

Click on a button and a message box appears telling you what you clicked. Stop
the application and resize the form. See how the new buttons adapt to the new
size. This is another nice feature of adding controls at run-time – it adapts to
any changes in form size you might make.

Printing with Visual Basic

Any serious Visual Basic application will use a **printer** to provide the user with a hard copy of any results (text or graphics) they might need. Printing is one of the more tedious programming tasks within Visual Basic. But, fortunately, it is straightforward and there are several dialog controls that help with the tasks. We will introduce lots of new topics here. All steps will be reviewed.

To perform printing in Visual Basic, we use the **PrintDocument** object (in the **Drawing.Printing** namespace). This object controls the printing process and has four important properties:

Property	Description
DefaultPageSettings	Indicates default page settings for the document.
DocumentName	Indicates the name displayed while the document is printing.
PrintController	Indicates the print controller that guides the printing process.
PrinterSettings	Indicates the printer that prints the document.

The steps to print a document (which may includes text and graphics) using the **PrintDocument** object are:

> ➤ Declare a **PrintDocument** object
> ➤ Create a **PrintDocument** object
> ➤ Set any properties desired.
> ➤ Print the document using the **Print** method of the **PrintDocument** object.

The first three steps are straightforward. To declare and create a **PrintDocument** object named **MyDocument**, use:

```
Dim MyDocument As Drawing.Printing.PrintDocument
   .

   .
MyDocument = New Drawing.Printing.PrintDocument()
```

Any properties needed usually come from print dialog boxes we'll examine in a bit.

The last step poses the question: how does the **PrintDocument** object print with the **Print** method? Printing is done in a general Visual Basic procedure associated with the **PrintDocument.PrintPage** event. This is a procedure you must create and write. The procedure tells the **PrintDocument** object what goes on each page of your document. Once the procedure is written, you need to add the event handler in code (we just learned how to do that) so the **PrintDocument** object knows where to go when it's ready to print a page. It may sound confusing now, but once you've done a little printing, it's very straightforward.

The general Visual Basic procedure for printing your pages (**PrintPage** in this case) must be of the form:

```
Private Sub PrintPage(ByVal sender As Object, ByVal e As
Drawing.Printing.PrintPageEventArgs)
    .
    .
End Sub
```

In this procedure, you 'construct' each page that the **PrintDocument** object is to print. And, you'll see the code in this procedure is familiar.

In the **PrintPage** procedure, the argument **e** (of type **Drawing.Printing.PrintPageEventArgs**) has many properties with information about the printing process. The most important property is the **graphics object**:

```
e.Graphics
```

Something familiar! **PrintDocument** provides us with a graphics object to 'draw' each page we want to print. This is the same graphics object we used in Chapters 8 and 9 to draw lines, curves, rectangles, ellipses, text and images. And, all the methods we learned there apply here! We'll look at how to do this in detail next. But, first, let's review how to establish and use the **PrintDocument** object.

A diagram summarizes the printing process:

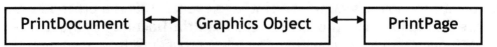

The **PrintDocument** object provides a **Graphics Object** to 'draw' each page. Each page is created in the **PrintPage** event handler (called by the PrintDocument **Print** method).

Here is an annotated code segment that establishes a **PrintDocument** object (**MyDocument**) and connects it to a procedure named **PrintPage** that provides the pages to print via the graphics object:

```
'Declare the document
Dim MyDocument As Drawing.Printing.PrintDocument
    .
    .

'Create the document and name it
MyDocument = New Drawing.Printing.PrintDocument()
MyDocument.DocumentName = "My Document"
    .
    .
'You could set other properties here
    .
    .
'Add code handler
AddHandler MyDocument.PrintPage, AddressOf Me.PrintPage
'Print document
MyDocument.Print()
'Dispose of document when done printing
MyDocument.Dispose()
```

This code assumes the procedure **PrintPage** is available. Let's see how to build such a procedure.

Printing Pages of a Document

The **PrintDocument** object provides (in its **PrintPage** event) a graphics object (**e.Graphics**) for 'drawing' our pages. And, that's just what we do using familiar graphics methods. For each page in our printed document, we draw the desired text information (**DrawString** method), any lines (**DrawLine** method), rectangles (**DrawRectangle** method) or images (**DrawImage** method).

Once a page is completely drawn to the graphics object, we 'tell' the **PrintDocument** object to print it. We repeat this process for each page we want to print. This does require a little bit of work on your part. You must know how many pages your document has and what goes on each page. I usually define a page number variable to help keep track of the current page being drawn.

Once a page is complete, there are two possibilities: there are more pages to print or there are no more pages to print. The **e.HasMorePages** property (Boolean) is used specify which possibility exists. If a page is complete and there are still more pages to print, use:

```
e.HasMorePages = True
```

In this case, the **PrintDocument** object will return to the **PrintPages** event for the next page. If the page is complete and printing is complete (no more pages), use:

```
e.HasMorePages = False
```

This tells the **PrintDocument** object its job is done. At this point, you should dispose of the **PrintDocument** object.

Let's look at the graphics object for a single page. The boundaries of the printed page are defined by the **e.MarginBounds** properties (these are established by the **PrinterSettings** property):

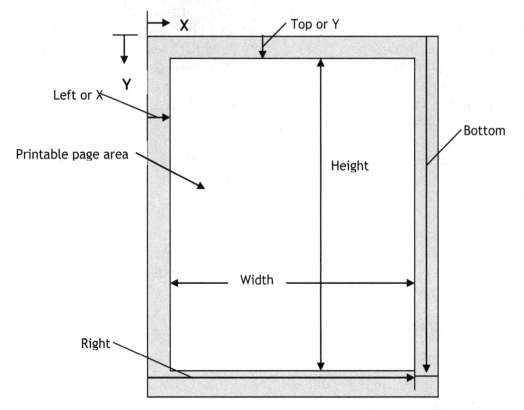

This becomes our palette for positioning items on a page. All values are in units of 1/100th of an inch. Horizontal position is governed by **X** (increases from 0 to the right) and vertical position is governed by **Y** (increases from 0 to the bottom).

The process for each page is to decide "what goes where" and then position the desired information using the appropriate graphics method. Any of the graphics methods we have learned can be used to put information on the graphic object. Here, we limit the discussion to printing text, lines, rectangles and images.

To place text on the graphics object (**e.Graphics**), use the **DrawString** method introduced in Chapter 9. To place the string **MyString** at position (**X, Y**), using the font object **MyFont** and brush object **MyBrush**, the syntax is:

```
e.Graphics.DrawString(MyString, MyFont, MyBrush, X, Y)
```

With this statement, you can place any text, anywhere you like, with any font, any color and any brush style. You just need to make the desired specifications. Each line of text on a printed page will require a **DrawString** statement.

Also in Chapter 9, we saw two methods for determining the size of strings. This is helpful for both vertical and horizontal placement of text on a page. To determine the height (in pixels) of a particular font, use:

```
MyFont.GetHeight()
```

If you need width and height of a string use:

```
e.Graphics.MeasureString(MyString, MyFont)
```

This method returns a **SizeF** structure with two properties: **Width** and **Height** (both in 1/100th of an inch). These two properties are useful for justifying (left, right, center, vertical) text strings.

Many times, you use lines in a document to delineate various sections. To draw a line on the graphics object, use the **DrawLine** method (from Chapter 8):

```
e.Graphics.DrawLine(MyPen, x1, y1, x2, y2)
```

This statement will draw a line from (**x1, y1**) to (**x2, y2**) using the pen object **MyPen**.

To draw a rectangle (used with tables or graphics regions), use the **DrawRectangle** method (from Chapter 8):

```
e.Graphics.DrawRectangle(MyPen, x1, y1, x2, y2)
```

This statement will draw a rectangle with upper left corner at (**x1, y1**) and lower right corner at (**x2, y2**) using the pen object **MyPen**.

Finally, the **DrawImage** method (from Chapter 9) is used to position an image (**MyImage**) object on a page. The syntax is:

```
e.Graphics.DrawImage(MyImage, X, Y, Width, Height)
```

The upper left corner of **MyImage** will be at (**X, Y**) with the specified **Width** and **Height**. Any image will be scaled to fit the specified region.

If **DrawImage** is to be used to print the contents of a panel control hosting a graphics object, you must insure the graphics are persistent as discussed in Chapter 9. We review those steps. For a panel named **pnlExample**, establish the **BackgroundImage** as an empty bitmap:

```
pnlExample.BackgroundImage = New
Drawing.Bitmap(pnlExample.ClientSize.Width,
pnlExample.ClientSize.Height,
Drawing.Imaging.PixelFormat.Format24bppRgb)
```

Then, establish the drawing object **MyObject** using:

```
MyObject =
Drawing.Graphics.FromImage(pnlExample.BackgroundImage)
```

Now, any graphics methods applied to this object will be persistent. To maintain this persistence, after each drawing operation to this object, use:

```
MyObject.Refresh()
```

The image in this object can then be printed with the **DrawImage** method:

```
e.Graphics.DrawImage(pnlExample.BackgroundImage, X, Y,
Width, Height)
```

The upper left corner of the image will be at (**X, Y**) with the specified **Width** and **Height**. The image will be scaled to fit the specified region.

We've seen all of these graphics methods before, so their use should be familiar. You should note that each item on a printed page requires at least one line of code. That results in lots of coding for printing. So, if you're writing lots of code in your print routines, you're probably doing it right. Look at this little code snippet (this assumes we have a picture box control named **picMap** with a persistent **Image** property):

```
'Draw map
e.Graphics.DrawImage(picMap.Image, e.MarginBounds.Left +
20, e.MarginBounds.Top + 20, e.MarginBounds.Width - 40,
CInt(0.5 * e.MarginBounds.Height - 40))

'Draw rectangle around map
e.Graphics.DrawRectangle(Pens.Black, e.MarginBounds.Left +
20, e.MarginBounds.Top + 20, e.MarginBounds.Width - 40,
CInt(0.5 * e.MarginBounds.Height - 40))

'Draw line near middle of page
e.Graphics.DrawLine(Pens.Black, e.MarginBounds.Left,
e.MarginBounds.Top + CInt(0.5 * e.MarginBounds.Height),
e.MarginBounds.Right, e.MarginBounds.Top + CInt(0.5 *
e.MarginBounds.Height))

'Draw string under line
e.Graphics.DrawString("This is my map!!", New
Drawing.Font("Arial", 48, FontStyle.Bold),
Drawing.Brushes.Black, e.MarginBounds.Left,
e.MarginBounds.Top + CInt(0.5 * e.MarginBounds.Height +
50))
```

Can you see this code will produce this printed page?

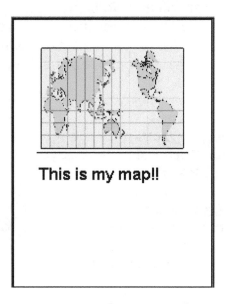

The image (**picMap**) is drawn with a rectangle surrounding it. Then, a line near mid page, then the string "This is my map!!" Of course, this assumes that the PrintDocument object is created and connected to the PrintPage event.

The best way to learn how to print in Visual Basic is to do lots of it. You'll develop your own approaches and techniques as you gain familiarity. You might want to see how some of the other graphics methods (**DrawEllipse**, **DrawLines**, **DrawCurves**) might work with printing. Or, look at different brush and pen objects.

Many print jobs just involve the user clicking a button marked '**Print**' and the results appear on printed page with no further interaction. If more interaction is desired, there are three dialog controls that help specify desired printing job properties: **PageSetupDialog**, **PrintDialog**, and **PrintPreviewDialog**. Using these controls adds more code to your application. You must take any user inputs and implement these values in your program. We'll show what each control can do and let you decide if you want to use them in your work. The **PrintPreviewDialog** control is especially cool!!

PageSetupDialog Control

In Toolbox:

 PageSetupDialog

Below Form (Default Properties):

 PageSetupDialog1

The **PageSetupDialog** control allows the user to set various parameters regarding a printing task. This is the same dialog box that appears in most Windows applications. Users can set border and margin adjustments, headers and footers, and portrait vs. landscape orientation.

PageSetupDialog **Properties:**

Name	Gets or sets the name of the page setup dialog (I usually name this control **dlgSetup**).
AllowMargins	Gets or sets a value indicating whether the margins section of the dialog box is enabled.
AllowOrientation	Gets or sets a value indicating whether the orientation section of the dialog box (landscape vs. portrait) is enabled.
AllowPaper	Gets or sets a value indicating whether the paper section of the dialog box (paper size and paper source) is enabled.
AllowPrinter	Gets or sets a value indicating whether the Printer button is enabled.
Document	Gets or sets a value indicating the PrintDocument to get page settings from.
MinMargins	Gets or sets a value indicating the minimum margins the user is allowed to select, in hundredths of an inch.
PageSettings	Gets or sets a value indicating the page settings to modify.
PrinterSettings	Gets or sets the printer settings the dialog box is to modify when the user clicks the Printer button

FontDialog **Methods:**

> **ShowDialog**   Displays the dialog box. Returned value indicates which button was clicked by user (**OK** or **Cancel**).

To use the **PageSetupDialog** control, we add it to our application the same as any control. It will appear in the tray below the form. Once added, we set a few properties. Then, we write code to make the dialog box appear when desired. The user then makes selections and closes the dialog box. At this point, we use the provided information for our tasks.

The **ShowDialog** method is used to display the **PageSetupDialog** control. For a control named **dlgSetup**, the appropriate code is:

```
dlgSetup.ShowDialog()
```

And the displayed dialog box is:

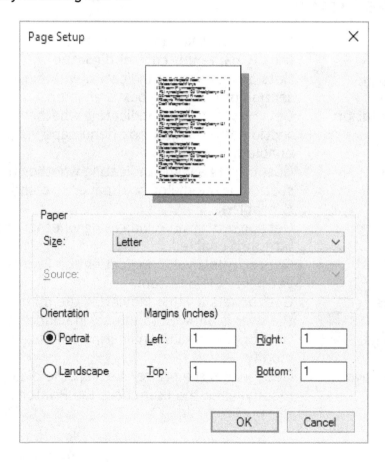

The user makes any desired choices. Once complete, the **OK** button is clicked.
At this point, various properties are available for use (namely **PageSettings** and
PrinterSettings).   **Cancel** can be clicked to cancel the changes. The
ShowDialog method returns the clicked button. It returns **DialogResult.OK** if OK
is clicked and returns **DialogResult.Cancel** if Cancel is clicked.

Typical use of **PageSetupDialog** control:

> ➢ Set the **Name** property. Decide what options should be available.
> ➢ Use **ShowDialog** method to display dialog box, prior to printing.
> ➢ Use **PageSettings** and **PrinterSetting** properties to change printed output.

PrintDialog Control

In Toolbox:

Below Form (Default Properties):

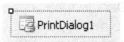

The **PrintDialog** control allows the user to select which printer to use, choose page orientation, printed page range and number of copies. This is the same dialog box that appears in many Windows applications.

PrintDialog **Properties:**

Name	Gets or sets the name of the print dialog (I usually name this control **dlgPrint**).
AllowPrintToFile	Gets or sets a value indicating whether the Print to file check box is enabled.
AllowSelection	Gets or sets a value indicating whether the From... To... Page option button is enabled.
AllowSomePages	Gets or sets a value indicating whether the Pages option button is enabled.
Document	Gets or sets a value indicating the PrintDocument used to obtain PrinterSettings.
PrinterSettings	Gets or sets the PrinterSettings the dialog box is to modify.
PrintToFile	Gets or sets a value indicating whether the Print to file check box is checked

PrintDialog **Methods:**

ShowDialog	Displays the dialog box. Returned value indicates which button was clicked by user (**OK** or **Cancel**).

To use the **PrintDialog** control, we add it to our application the same as any control. It will appear in the tray below the form. Once added, we set a few properties. Then, we write code to make the dialog box appear when desired. The user then makes selections and closes the dialog box. At this point, we use the provided information for our tasks.

The **ShowDialog** method is used to display the **PrintDialog** control. For a control named **dlgPrint**, the appropriate code is:

```
dlgPrint.ShowDialog()
```

And the displayed dialog box is:

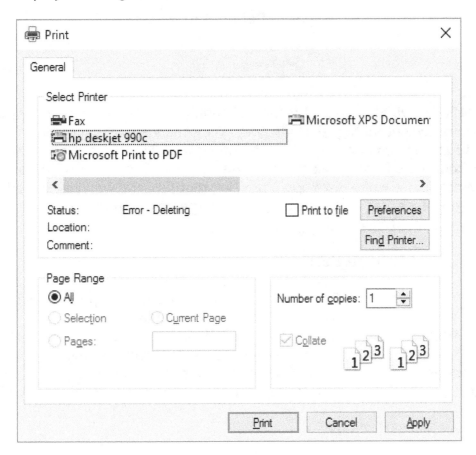

The user makes any desired choices. Once complete, the **OK** button is clicked. At this point, various properties are available for use (namely **PrinterSettings**). **Cancel** can be clicked to cancel the changes. The ShowDialog method returns the clicked button. It returns **DialogResult.OK** if OK is clicked and returns **DialogResult.Cancel** if Cancel is clicked.

Typical use of **PrintDialog** control:

 ➤ Set the **Name** property. Decide what options should be available.
 ➤ Use **ShowDialog** method to display dialog box, prior to printing with the PrintDocument object.
 ➤ Use **PrinterSettings** properties to change printed output.

PrintPreviewDialog Control

In Toolbox:

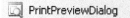

Below Form (Default Properties):

The **PrintPreviewDialog** control is a great addition to Visual Basic. It lets the user see printed output in preview mode. They can view all pages, format page views and zoom in on or out of any. The previewed document can also be printed from this control. This is also a useful "temporary" control for a programmer to use while developing printing routines. By viewing printed pages in a preview mode, rather than on a printed page, many trees are saved as you fine tune your printing code.

PrintPreviewDialog **Properties:**

Name	Gets or sets the name of the print preview dialog (I usually name this control **dlgPreview**)
AcceptButton	Gets or sets the button on the form that is clicked when the user presses the <Enter> key.
Document	Gets or sets the document to preview.
Text	Gets or sets the text associated with this control.

PrintPreviewDialog **Methods:**

ShowDialog	Displays the dialog box. Returned value indicates which button was clicked by user (**OK** or **Cancel**).

To use the **PrintDialog** control, we add it to our application the same as any control. It will appear in the tray below the form. Once added, we set a few properties, primarily **Document**. Make sure the **PrintPage** event Is properly coded for the selected **Document**. Add code to make the dialog box appear when desired. The document pages will be generated and the user can see it in the preview window.

The **ShowDialog** method is used to display the **PrintPreviewDialog** control. For a control named **dlgPreview**, the appropriate code is:

```
dlgPreview.ShowDialog()
```

And the displayed dialog box (with no document) is:

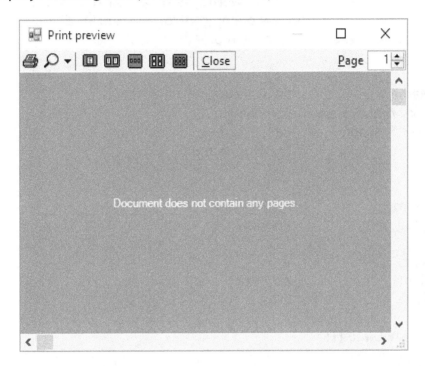

The user can use the various layout, zoom and print options in previewing the displayed document. When done, the user closes the dialog control.

Typical use of **PrintPreviewDialog** control:

> ➤ Set the **Name** property. Set the **Document** property.
> ➤ Use **ShowDialog** method to display dialog box and see the previewed document.

Example 10-8

Printing

1. Start a new project. In this project, you'll print out a list of countries and capitals, along with a map of the world. Add two button controls to the form. Also add a print preview dialog control and a print dialog control. Set the properties of the form and each object.

Form1:

Name	frmPrinting
FormBorderStyle	FixedSingle
StartPosition	CenterScreen
Text	Printing Example

Button1:

Name	btnPreview
Text	Preview

Button2:

Name	btnPrint
Text	Print

PrintPreviewDialog1:

Name	dlgPreview

PrintDialog1:

Name	dlgPrint
AllowPrintToFile	False

Your form should now look like this:

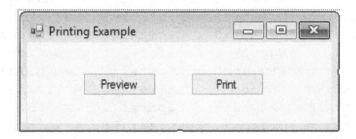

Other controls in tray:

2. In the **LearnVB\VB Code\Class 10\Example 10-8** folder is a map graphic named **world.wmf**. Copy this graphic into your application's **Bin\Debug** folder (you may have to create the folder first). The code below assumes the map graphic is in the application folder. We use the **Application.StartupPath** parameter to identify this folder.

3. Form Level Scope Declarations:

```
Dim PageNumber As Integer
Dim MyDocument As Drawing.Printing.PrintDocument
Dim MyImage As Drawing.Image
Dim Country(100) As String, Capital(100) As String
Const NumberCountries As Integer = 62
Const CountriesPerPage As Integer = 25
Dim LastPage As Boolean
```

4. Use the following code in the **Form Load** event (loads country/capital arrays and map image):

```
Private Sub FrmPrinting_Load(ByVal sender As
System.Object, ByVal e As System.EventArgs) Handles
MyBase.Load
    'Load country/capital arrays
    Country(1) = "Afghanistan" : Capital(1) = "Kabul"
    Country(2) = "Albania" : Capital(2) = "Tirane"
    Country(3) = "Australia" : Capital(3) = "Canberra"
    Country(4) = "Austria" : Capital(4) = "Vienna"
    Country(5) = "Bangladesh" : Capital(5) = "Dacca"
    Country(6) = "Barbados" : Capital(6) = "Bridgetown"
    Country(7) = "Belgium" : Capital(7) = "Brussels"
    Country(8) = "Bulgaria" : Capital(8) = "Sofia"
    Country(9) = "Burma" : Capital(9) = "Rangoon"
```

```
Country(10) = "Cambodia" : Capital(10) = "Phnom Penh"
Country(11) = "China" : Capital(11) = "Peking"
Country(12) = "Czechoslovakia" : Capital(12) = "Prague"
Country(13) = "Denmark" : Capital(13) = "Copenhagen"
Country(14) = "Egypt" : Capital(14) = "Cairo"
Country(15) = "Finland" : Capital(15) = "Helsinki"
Country(16) = "France" : Capital(16) = "Paris"
Country(17) = "Germany" : Capital(17) = " Berlin"
Country(18) = "Greece" : Capital(18) = "Athens"
Country(19) = "Hungary" : Capital(19) = "Budapest"
Country(20) = "Iceland" : Capital(20) = "Reykjavik"
Country(21) = "India" : Capital(21) = "New Delhi"
Country(22) = "Indonesia" : Capital(22) = "Jakarta"
Country(23) = "Iran" : Capital(23) = "Tehran"
Country(24) = "Iraq" : Capital(24) = "Baghdad"
Country(25) = "Ireland" : Capital(25) = "Dublin"
Country(26) = "Israel" : Capital(26) = "Jerusalem"
Country(27) = "Italy" : Capital(27) = "Rome"
Country(28) = "Japan" : Capital(28) = "Tokyo"
Country(29) = "Jordan" : Capital(29) = "Amman"
Country(30) = "Kuwait" : Capital(30) = "Kuwait"
Country(31) = "Laos" : Capital(31) = "Vientiane"
Country(32) = "Lebanon" : Capital(32) = "Beirut"
Country(33) = "Luxembourg" : Capital(33) = "Luxembourg"
Country(34) = "Malaysia" : Capital(34) = "Kuala Lumpur"
Country(35) = "Mongolia" : Capital(35) = "Ulaanbaatar"
Country(36) = "Nepal" : Capital(36) = "Katmandu"
Country(37) = "Netherlands" : Capital(37) = "Amsterdam"
Country(38) = "New Zealand" : Capital(38) = "Wellington"
Country(39) = "North Korea" : Capital(39) = "Pyongyang"
Country(40) = "Norway" : Capital(40) = "Oslo"
Country(41) = "Oman" : Capital(41) = "Muscat"
Country(42) = "Pakistan" : Capital(42) = "Islamabad"
Country(43) = "Philippines" : Capital(43) = "Manila"
Country(44) = "Poland" : Capital(44) = "Warsaw"
Country(45) = "Portugal" : Capital(45) = "Lisbon"
Country(46) = "Romania" : Capital(46) = "Bucharest"
Country(47) = "Russia" : Capital(47) = "Moscow"
Country(48) = "Saudi Arabia" : Capital(48) = "Riyadh"
Country(49) = "Singapore" : Capital(49) = "Singapore"
Country(50) = "South Korea" : Capital(50) = "Seoul"
Country(51) = "Spain" : Capital(51) = "Madrid"
Country(52) = "Sri Lanka" : Capital(52) = "Colombo"
Country(53) = "Sweden" : Capital(53) = "Stockholm"
Country(54) = "Switzerland" : Capital(54) = "Bern"
Country(55) = "Syria" : Capital(55) = "Damascus"
Country(56) = "Taiwan" : Capital(56) = "Taipei"
```

```
    Country(57) = "Thailand" : Capital(57) = "Bangkok"
    Country(58) = "Turkey" : Capital(58) = "Ankara"
    Country(59) = "United Kingdom" : Capital(59) = "London"
    Country(60) = "Vietnam" : Capital(60) = "Hanoi"
    Country(61) = "Yemen" : Capital(61) = "Sana"
    Country(62) = "Yugoslavia" : Capital(62) = "Belgrade"
    MyImage = Image.FromFile(Application.StartupPath +
"\world.wmf")
  End Sub
```

5. Add this code to the **btnPreview Click** event (sets up document for preview):

```
    Private Sub BtnPreview_Click(ByVal sender As
System.Object, ByVal e As System.EventArgs) Handles
btnPreview.Click
      'preview printing
      PageNumber = 1 : LastPage = False
      'create document
      MyDocument = New Drawing.Printing.PrintDocument()
      MyDocument.DocumentName = "World Capitals"
      AddHandler MyDocument.PrintPage, AddressOf Me.PrintPage
      'preview dialog
      dlgPreview.Document = MyDocument
      dlgPreview.Text = "Countries and Capitals"
      dlgPreview.ShowDialog()
      MyDocument.Dispose()
    End Sub
```

6. Add this code to the **btnPrint Click** event (sets up document for printing):

```
Private Sub BtnPrint_Click(ByVal sender As System.Object,
ByVal e As System.EventArgs) Handles btnPrint.Click
    'do printing
    Dim I As Integer
    PageNumber = 1 : LastPage = False
    'create document
    MyDocument = New Drawing.Printing.PrintDocument()
    MyDocument.DocumentName = "World Capitals"
    AddHandler MyDocument.PrintPage, AddressOf Me.PrintPage
      'print dialog
      dlgPrint.Document = MyDocument
    If dlgPrint.ShowDialog = Windows.Forms.DialogResult.OK
Then
        For I = 1 To dlgPrint.PrinterSettings.Copies
          MyDocument.Print()
      Next I
    End If
    MyDocument.Dispose()
  End Sub
```

7. Create this **PrintPage** general procedure. This code establishes what is printed on each page:

```
Private Sub PrintPage(ByVal sender As Object, ByVal e As
Drawing.Printing.PrintPageEventArgs)
    Dim PrintFont As Drawing.Font, SSize As New
Drawing.SizeF()
    Dim Y As Integer, I As Integer, IEnd As Integer
    Dim Ratio As Single
    'here you decide what goes on each page and draw it
there
    'print countries/capitals and map on different pages
    If Not (LastPage) Then
      'on firstpages, put titles and countries/capitals
      PrintFont = New Font("Arial", 20, FontStyle.Bold)
      SSize = e.Graphics.MeasureString("Countries and
Capitals - Page" + Str(PageNumber), PrintFont)
      e.Graphics.DrawString("Countries and Capitals - Page"
+ Str(PageNumber), PrintFont, Brushes.Black,
e.MarginBounds.Left + CInt(0.5 * (e.MarginBounds.Width -
SSize.Width)), e.MarginBounds.Top)
      'starting y position
      PrintFont = New Font("Arial", 14, FontStyle.Underline)
      Y = CInt(e.MarginBounds.Top + 4 * PrintFont.GetHeight)
```

```vb
        e.Graphics.DrawString("Country", PrintFont,
Brushes.Black, e.MarginBounds.X, Y)
        e.Graphics.DrawString("Capital", PrintFont,
Brushes.Black, CInt(e.MarginBounds.X + 0.5 *
e.MarginBounds.Width), Y)
      Y += CInt(2 * PrintFont.GetHeight)
      PrintFont = New Font("Arial", 14, FontStyle.Regular)
      IEnd = CountriesPerPage * PageNumber
      If IEnd > NumberCountries Then
        IEnd = NumberCountries
        LastPage = True
      End If
      For I = 1 + CountriesPerPage * (PageNumber - 1) To
IEnd
        e.Graphics.DrawString(Country(I), PrintFont,
Brushes.Black, e.MarginBounds.X, Y)
        e.Graphics.DrawString(Capital(I), PrintFont,
Brushes.Black, CInt(e.MarginBounds.X + 0.5 *
e.MarginBounds.Width), Y)
        Y += CInt(PrintFont.GetHeight)
      Next I
      PageNumber += 1
      e.HasMorePages = True
    Else
      'on last page draw map and  a rectangle around map
region
      'maintain original width/height ratio
      Ratio = CSng(MyImage.Width / MyImage.Height)
      e.Graphics.DrawImage(MyImage, e.MarginBounds.Left,
e.MarginBounds.Top, e.MarginBounds.Width,
CInt(e.MarginBounds.Height / Ratio))
      e.Graphics.DrawRectangle(Pens.Black,
e.MarginBounds.Left, e.MarginBounds.Top,
e.MarginBounds.Width, CInt(e.MarginBounds.Height / Ratio))
      e.HasMorePages = False
      PageNumber = 1
      LastPage = False
    End If
  End Sub
```

8. Save your project (saved in **Example 10-8** folder in the **LearnVB\VB Code\Class 10** folder). Run the application. Try the preview function (click **Preview**) and see how nicely it displays the printed document:

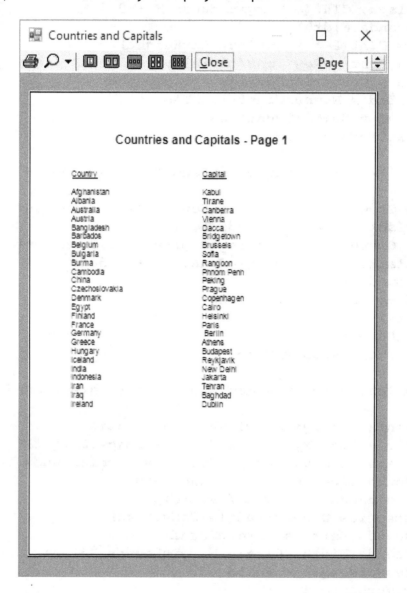

And the map is on the last page:

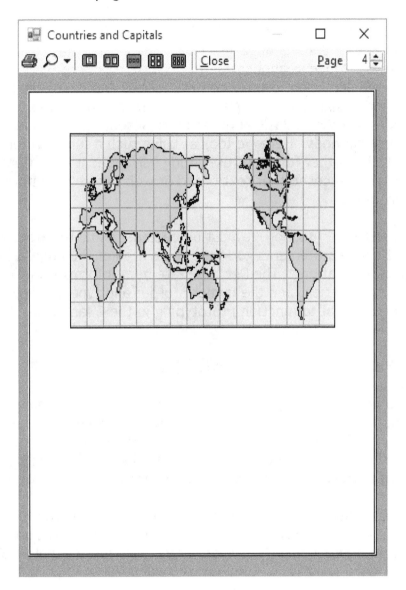

If you want, print out the document on your printer by clicking **Print**.

Using the Windows API

The Windows **Application Programming Interface** (**API**) consists of hundreds of functions (usually written in languages like C and C++). These functions are used by virtually every Windows application to perform functions like displaying windows, file manipulation, printer control, menus and dialog boxes, multimedia, string manipulation, graphics, and managing memory. We can use these functions in a Visual Basic application to accomplish tasks not possible using any other methods. Here we look at using such a function for timing. You may choose to find other functions useful in your applications. Consult one of the many API references (either text based or web based) for information on available functions.

Before you use an API function, it must be declared using the **Declare** statement. Declare statements go in the same area of the code window as form level variable declarations. The Declare statement informs your program about the name of the function, and the number, order and type of arguments it takes. This is nearly identical to function prototyping in the C language. For an API function (**APIFcn**), the syntax is:

Declare Function APIFcn **Lib** *DLLname* [(argument list)] **As** *Type*

where **DLLname** is a string specifying the name of the DLL (dynamic link library) file that contains the procedure and **Type** is the returned value type. In modules, you need to preface the Declare statements with the keywords **Public** or **Private** to indicate the function scope. In forms, preface the Declare statement with **Private**, the default scope in a form.

Once declared, using an API function is not much different from using a general function in Visual Basic. Just make sure you pass it the correct number and correct type of arguments in the correct order. For our example (**APIFcn**), proper syntax is:

```
ReturnValue = APIFcn(Arguments)
```

All arguments for API functions are passed by value (use the **ByVal** keyword), so the argument list has the syntax:

    ByVal *Argname1* **As** *Type*, **ByVal** *Argname2* **As** *Type*, ...

It is very important, when using API functions, that argument lists be correct, both regarding number, type and order. If the list is not correct, very bad things can happen. We need to show this same care using built-in and general functions in Visual Basic; the consequences of an error are usually not as severe, however.

And, it is critical that the **Declare** statement be correct. Older versions of Visual Basic (prior to Visual Basic) included a program called the **API Text Viewer**. This program was used to construct any Declare statement you might need. At this writing, no such program is included with Visual Basic. This is not a problem. We will only use one API function - we will provide the correct Declare statement. You can then use it any code you develop. The documentation for any other API function you may use should also include the proper Declare statement.

There is a price to pay for using the Windows API. Once you leave the protective surroundings of the Visual Basic environment, as you must to use the API, you get to taunt and tease the dreaded general protection fault (**GPF**) monster, which can bring your entire computer system to a screeching halt! So, be careful. And, if you don't have to use API functions, don't.

Lastly, **always, always, always save** your Visual Basic application before testing any API calls. More good code has gone down the tubes with GPF's - they are very difficult to recover from. Sometimes, the trusty on-off switch is the only recovery mechanism.

Timing with the Windows API

Often you need some method of **timing** within an application. You may want to know how long a certain routine takes to execute for performance evaluation. You may need to time a student as they take an on-line quiz. You might want to perform "real-time" simulation where the computer produces real-life results. Sports simulations and racing games are examples of such simulations. Or, you might want to build an on-screen clock. Each of these examples requires the ability to compute an elapsed time. Depending on the accuracy you need, there are different methods to compute elapsed time in a Visual Basic application.

Visual Basic provides two methods of computing times. We looked at one method in the very first chapter – the **Now** function. The **Now** function returns the current date and time as a **Date** data type. The time is given in hours, minutes and seconds. Hence, elapsed times can be computed with **one second resolution**. Such resolution is adequate for an on-screen clock, but not very useful for timing a swimmer doing a 50 meter freestyle.

A second Visual Basic function used for timing is the **Timer** function (**Microsoft.VisualBasic.Timer**). Do not confuse this with the Timer control. The **Timer** function returns a **Single** data type representing the number of seconds that has elapsed since midnight. Experience has shown that elapsed times computed with this function are accurate within about **0.1 to 0.2 seconds resolution**.

Many computations require **millisecond** (1/1000th of a second) **resolution**. To obtain this level of resolution, we turn to the Windows API and the **GetTickCount** function. This function returns an **Integer** data type that represents the number of milliseconds that have elapsed since you turned your computer on. The **Declare** statement for **GetTickCount** is:

```
Private Declare Function GetTickCount Lib "kernel32" () As
Integer
```

Note there are no arguments.

GetTickCount (as well as the Visual Basic **Now** and **Timer** functions) is almost always used to compute an elapsed time (or difference between two times). The actual value returned by **GetTickCount** is not interesting by itself. The only time you might use it is if you had some need to know how long your computer has been on. The usage syntax to compute an elapsed time (in milliseconds) is:

```
Dim StartTime As Integer
Dim ElapsedTime As Integer
    .
StartTime = GetTickCount()
    .
  [Do some stuff here]
    .
ElapsedTime = GetTickCount() - StartTime
```

Example 10-9

Stopwatch Application (Revisited)

1. Remember way back in Class 1 where we built our first Visual Basic application, a stopwatch. That stopwatch provided timing with one second of resolution. We'll modify that example here, using **GetTickCount** to do our timing. This will give us resolution to within 1/1000th of a second. Load **Example 1-3** from long, long ago (saved in **Example 1-3** folder of **LearnVB\VB Code\Class 1** folder).

2. Copy the **GetTickCount** Declare statement from these notes and paste it into the code window. Recall this declaration goes in the same area as the form level variables. Also change all times to **Double** data types (times will printed as decimal numbers). This code is (new and/or modified code is shaded):

```
Dim StartTime As Double
Dim EndTime As Double
Dim ElapsedTime As Double
Private Declare Function GetTickCount Lib "kernel32" () As
Integer
```

3. Modify the **btnStart Click** procedure where shaded:

```
Private Sub BtnStart_Click(ByVal sender As Object, ByVal e
As System.EventArgs) Handles btnStart.Click
    'Establish and print starting time
    StartTime = GetTickCount() / 1000
    txtStart.Text = Format(StartTime, "0.000")
    txtEnd.Text = ""
    txtElapsed.Text = ""
End Sub
```

4. Modify the **btnEnd Click** procedure as shaded:

```
Private Sub BtnEnd_Click(ByVal sender As System.Object,
ByVal e As System.EventArgs) Handles btnEnd.Click
    'Find the ending time, compute the elapsed time
    'Put both values in text boxes
    EndTime = GetTickCount() / 1000
    ElapsedTime = EndTime - StartTime
    txtEnd.Text = Format(EndTime, "0.000")
    txtElapsed.Text = Format(ElapsedTime, "0.000")
End Sub
```

5. Run the application and save it (saved in **Example 10-9** folder in the **LearnVB\VB Code\Class 10** folder). Note we now have timing with millisecond (as opposed to one second) accuracy. Here's a run I made:

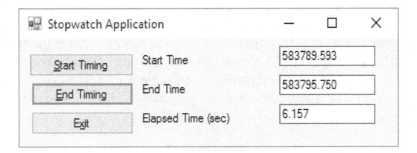

Also note the values in the start and end time label controls are not of much use. There's even a chance they'll be negative numbers! How's that, you ask? The value returned by GetTickCount is an **Integer** data type. The maximum value that can be represented by this data type is 2,147,483,647. Once that number of milliseconds has elapsed (a little less than 25 days), the value can't increase anymore or an overflow error will result. At this point, the returned value switches to -2,147,483,648, the smallest value possible and starts increasing again. So, if your computer has been on for over 25 days, you may see negative values for **GetTickCount**. The returned value always increases, though. Hence, elapsed times will always be positive. But, think about what happens if you're trying to compute an elapsed time when this switch from a very large positive number to a very large negative number occurs.

Adding a Help System to Your Application

When someone is using a Windows application and gets stumped about what to do next, instinct tells the user to press the **<F1>** function key. Long ago, someone in the old DOS world decided this would be the magic "Help Me!" key. Users expect help when pressing <F1> (I'm sure you rely on it a lot when using Visual Basic). If nothing appears after pressing <F1>, user frustration sets in – not a good thing.

All Visual Basic applications written for other than your personal use should include some form of an **on-line help system**. It doesn't have to be elegant, but it should be there. Adding a **help file** to your Visual Basic application will give it real polish, as well as making it easier to use. In this section, we will show you how to build a very basic on-line help system for your applications. This system will simply have a list of help topics the user can choose from.

We create what is known as an **HTML help** system. HTML stands for **hypertext markup language** and is the 'programming' language of choice for generating web pages. This language will be used to generate and display the topics displayed in the help system. Fortunately, we won't need to learn much (if any) HTML. Building an HTML help system involves several files and several steps. In diagram form, we have:

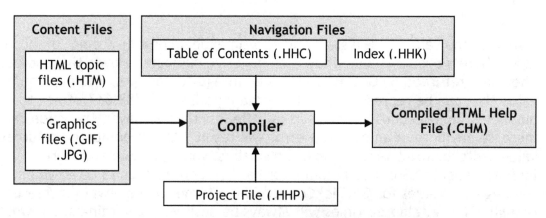

We need to create topic files (**.HTM** files) for each topic in our help system. (We could also add graphics.) These topics are organized by a Table of Contents file (**.HHC**) and Index file (**.HHK**). The Project File (**.HHP**) specifies the components of a help project. All of these files are 'compiled' to create the finished help file (**.CHM**). This file is the file that can be opened for viewing the finished help system.

The developed help system is similar to help systems used by all Windows applications. As an example, here is a help system (.CHM file) that explains how to add or remove programs from your computer:

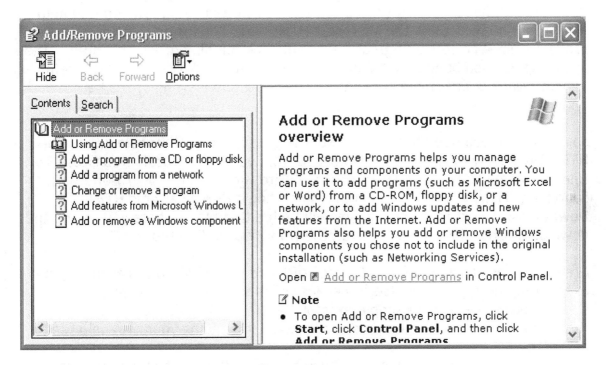

The left frame is a hierarchical structure (**Contents**) of clickable topics. The right frame displays the currently selected topic information. Other tabs in the left frame allow a user to browse an **Index** (none shown here) and **Search** the help file. The file also features several navigation features and print options. The key point here is that this help system is familiar to your user. No new instruction is needed in how to use on-line help.

We will build an HTML help system similar to the one displayed above, but with minimal features. Learning how to build a full-featured help system would be a course in itself. In this chapter, we will learn how to create text-only topics, add a contents file, create a project file and see how to compile the entire package into a useful (if simple) help system.

Creating a Help File

We could create a help system using only text editors if we knew the required structure for the various files. We won't take that approach. The on-line help system will be built using the **Microsoft HTML Help Workshop**. This is a free product from Microsoft that greatly simplifies the building of a help system. The workshop lets you build and organize all the files needed for building the help system. Once built, simple clicks allow compiling and viewing of the help system.

So, obviously, you need to have the workshop installed on your computer. The **HTML Help Workshop** can be downloaded from various Microsoft web sites. To find a download link, go to Microsoft's web site (http://www.microsoft.com). Search on "**HTML Help**" – the search results should display a topic **HTML Downloads**. Select that link and you will be led to a place where you can do the download. Once downloaded, install the workshop as directed.

Creating a complete help file is a major task and sometimes takes as much time as creating the application itself! Because of this, we will only skim over the steps involved, generate a simple example, and provide guidance for further reference. There are five major steps involved in building your own help file:

1. Create your application and develop a hierarchical list of help system topics. This list would consist of headings and topics under specific headings.
2. Create the **topic files** (**HTM** extensions). Please make sure you spell and grammar check your topic files. If there are mistakes in your help system, your user base may not have much confidence in the care you showed in developing your application.
3. Create a **Table of Contents** (**HHC** extension).
4. Create the **Help Project File** (**HHP** extension).
5. Compile the help file to create your finished help system (**CHM** extension).

Step 1 is application-dependent. Here, we'll look at how to use the HTML Help Workshop to complete the last four steps.

Starting the HTML Help Workshop

We will demonstrate the use of the **HTML Help Workshop** to build a very basic help system. The help file will have two headings. Each heading will have three sub-topics:

Heading 1
    Topic 1
    Topic 2
    Topic 3
Heading 2
    Topic 1
    Topic 2
    Topic 3

Though simple, the steps followed here can be used to build an adequate help system. All of the files created while building this help system can be found in the **LearnVB\VB Code\Class 10\Sample Help** folder.

If properly installed, there will be an entry for the help workshop on your computer's **Programs** menu. Click **Start**, then **All apps**. Select **HTML Help Workshop**, then **HTML Help Workshop** again. This dialog box should appear:

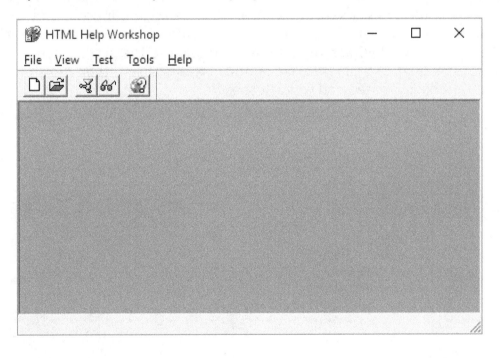

We want to start a new project. Select **New** under the **File** menu. In the selection box that appears, choose **Project** and click **OK**. A cute little **New Project Wizard** appears:

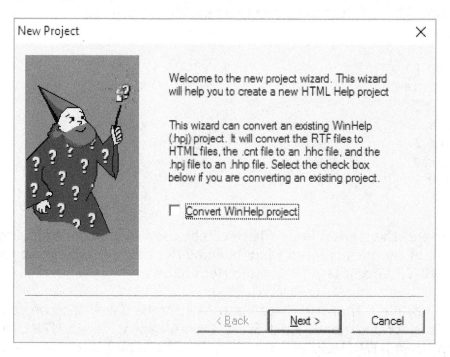

All we need to tell the wizard at this point is the name of our project file. Click **Next**. On the next screen, find (or create) the folder to hold your files (again, I used **LearnVB\VB Code\Class 10\Sample Help**) and use the project name **Sample**. Click **Next** two times (make no further selections), then **Finish**. The file **Sample.hhp** is created and you will see:

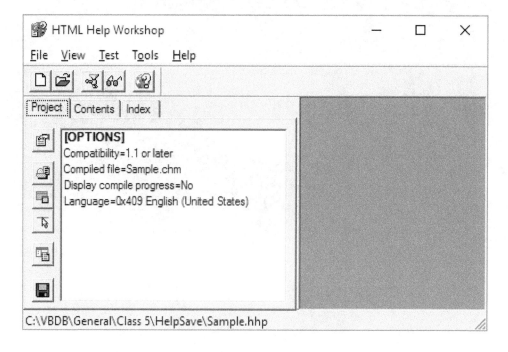

Creating Topic Files

At this point, we are ready to create our topic files. These are the files your user can view for help on topics listed in the contents region of the help system. We will have eight such files in our example (one for each of the two headings and one for each of the two sets of three topics).

Each file is individually created and saved as an HTM file. To create the first file (for Heading 1), choose **New** under the **File** menu. Select **HTML File** and click **OK**. Enter a name for the file (**Heading 1**) and click **OK**. A topic file HTML framework will appear:

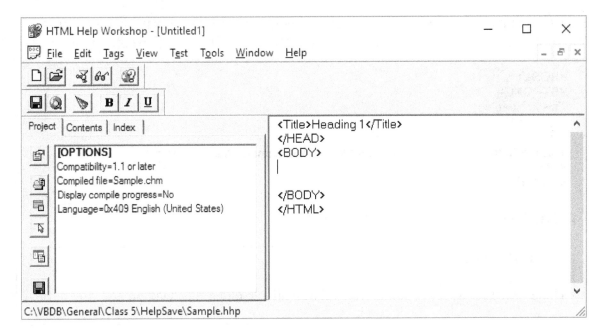

The window on the right is where you type your topic information. The file has some HTML code there already. If you've never seen HTML before, don't panic. We will make it easy. We are only concerned with what goes between the **<BODY>** and **</BODY>** 'tags'. These tags mark the beginning and end of the text displayed when a user selects this particular heading topic.

Most HTML tags work in pairs. The first tag says start something, then the second tag with the slash preface **</>** says stop something. Hence, **<BODY>** says the body of the text starts here. The **</BODY>** tag says the body stops here. It's really pretty easy to understand HTML.

It would help to know just a little more HTML to make your text have a nice appearance. To change the font, use the **FONT** tag:

    <FONT FACE="FontName**" SIZE="**FontSize**">**

where **FontName** is the name of the desired font and **FontSize** the desired size. Notice this is very similar to the **Font** constructor in Visual Basic. When you are done with one font and want to specify a new one, you must use a **</FONT>** tag before specifying the new font. To bold text, use the **<STRONG>** and **</STRONG>** tags. To delineate a paragraph in HTML, use the **<P>** and **</P>** tags. To cause a line break, use **
.** There is no corresponding </BR> tag.

So, using our minimal HTML knowledge (if you know more, use it), we can create our first topic file. The HTML I used to create the first topic (**Heading1**) is:

```
<BODY>
<STRONG>
This is Heading 1
</STRONG>
<P>
This is where I explain what the subtopics available under this heading are.
</P>
</BODY>
```

This HTML will create this finished topic:

> **This is Heading 1**
>
> This is where I explain what the subtopics available under this heading are.

When done typing this first topic, choose **Close File** under the **File** menu. Select a file name (I used **Heading1.HTM**) to use and save the topic file. Of course, at any time, you can reopen, modify and resave any topic file.

You repeat the above process for every topic in your help system. That is, create a new file, type your topic and save it. You will have an HTM file for every topic in your help system. For our example, create seven more HTM files using whatever text and formatting you desire. The files I created are saved as: **Heading1.HTM, Topic11.HTM, Topic12.HTM, Topic13.HTM, Heading2.HTM, Topic21.HTM, Topic22.HTM, Topic23.HTM.**

Creating HTML topic files using the Help Workshop is a bit tedious. You need to use HTML tags and don't really know what your topic file will look like until you've completed the help system. Using a **WYSIWYG** (what you see is what you get) editor is a better choice. Such editors allow you to create HTML files without knowing any HTML. You just type the file in a normal word processing-type environment, then save it in HTML format. There are several WYSIWYG HTML editors available. Check Internet download sites for other options. Also, most word processors offer an option to save a document as an HTML file. I always use a WYSIWYG editor for topic files. I simply save each topic file in the same folder as my help system files, just as if I was using the built-in editor.

Next, we create a **Table of Contents** file. But, before leaving your topic files, make sure they are as complete and accurate as possible. And, again, please check for misspellings – nothing scares a user more than a poorly prepared help file. They quickly draw the conclusion that if the help system is not built with care, the application must also be sloppily built.

Creating Table of Contents File

The **Table of Contents** file specifies the hierarchy of topics to display when the help system's **Contents** tab is selected. In the **HTML Help Workshop**, choose the **New** option under the **File** menu. Choose **Table of Contents**, then click **OK**. The following window appears:

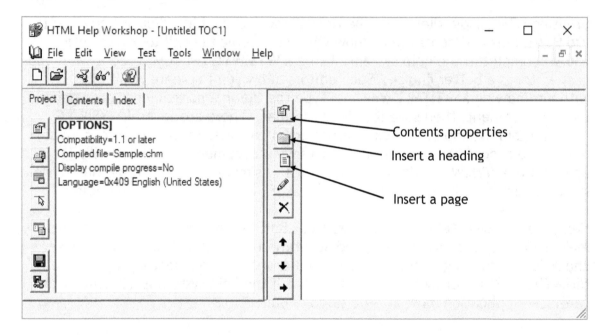

We want to add two headings with three topics under each. To insert a heading, in the right frame, click the toolbar button with a folder (**Insert a heading**). This window appears:

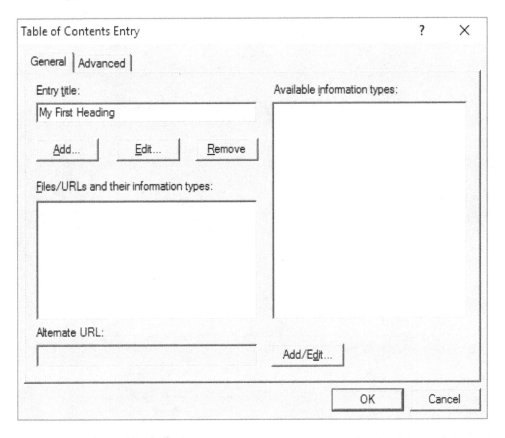

Type a title for the entry in **Entry title** (this is what will appear in the **Contents** – I used **My First Heading**).

You also need to link this topic to its topic file (HTM file). To do this, click **Add** and this appears:

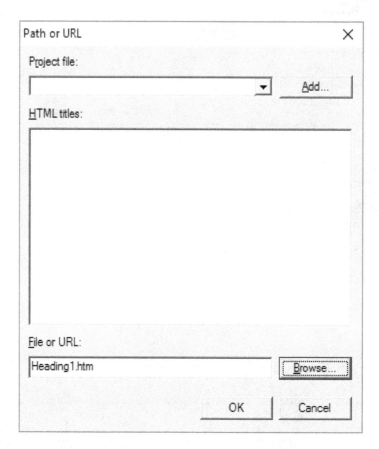

Click the Browse button and 'point' to the corresponding topic file (**Heading1.HTM** in this case). Click **OK** to close this window.

Click **OK** to close the Table of Contents entry window and you'll now see:

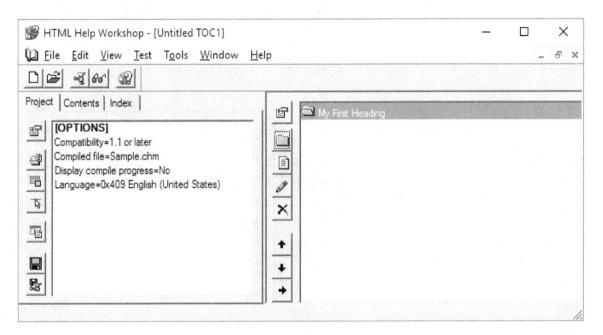

You've created your first entry in the Table of Contents. Notice the icon next to the heading is an 'open folder.' To change this to the more familiar 'open book,' click the top toolbar button (**Contents properties**). In the window that appears, remove the check mark next to '**Use Folders Instead of Books**,' and click **OK**.

Now, we need to enter our first topic under this first heading. Click the toolbar button (**Insert a page**) under the heading button. This dialog will appear:

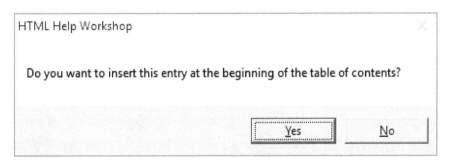

Answer **No** – we want the entry after the heading topic. At this point, you follow the same steps followed for the heading: enter a title and add a link to the topic file.

Add Table of Contents entries for all topic files in our little example. Use whatever titling information you choose. When you enter the second heading, it will be listed under the third topic in the first heading. To move it to the left (making it a major heading), right-click the heading and choose **Move Left**, the left arrow button on the toolbar). When done, I have this:

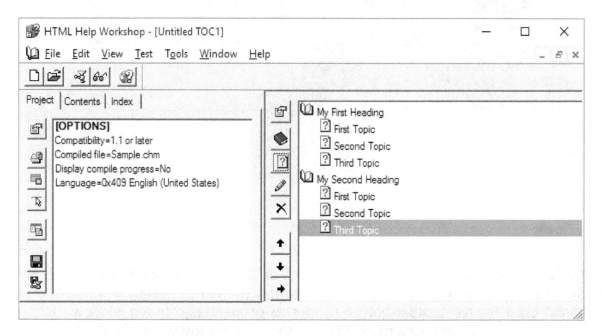

Save the contents file. Choose **Close File** under the **File** menu and assign a name of **Sample.HHC** to this contents file.

Compiling the Help File

We're almost ready to compile and create our help system. Before doing this, we need to add entries to the **Project** file. The project file at this point appears as:

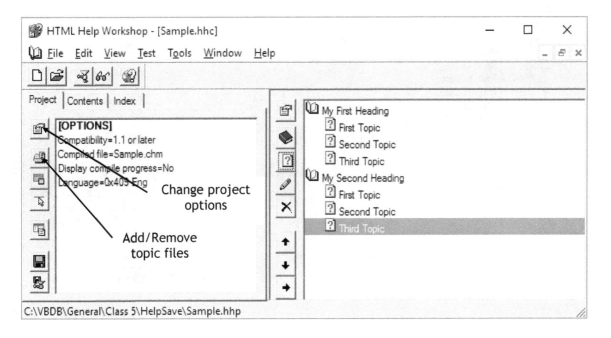

We first need to add our topic files. To do this, choose the **Add/remove topic files** toolbar button. In the window that appears, click **Add**, then select all topics files. You should see:

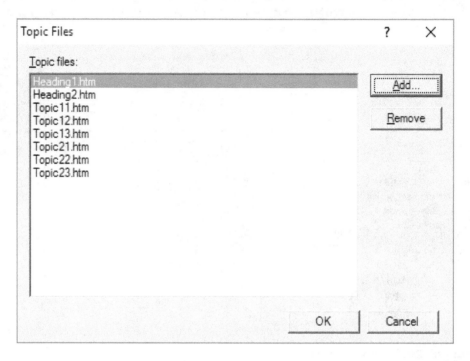

Click **OK.**

Now, the project file has the topic files added:

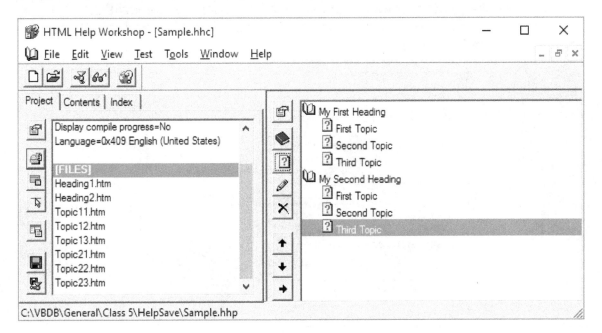

Now, we specify the **Table of Contents** file and set a few other properties. Click the **Change project options** toolbar button. Click the **General** tab and type a title for your help system (I used **My Sample Help File**) and specify the default file (**Heading1.htm**):

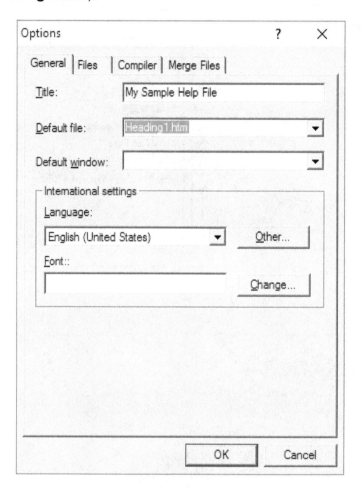

Click on the **Files** tab and select **Sample.hhc** as your contents file. Click **OK** to complete specification of your project file. At this point, save all files by choosing **Save Project** under the **File** menu.

We can now compile our project into the finished product – a complete HTML help system. To do this, click the **Compile HTML file** button (resembles a meat grinder) on the workshop toolbar. **Browse** so your project file (**Sample.hhp**) is selected. Choose **Compile** in the resulting window and things start 'grinding.' If no errors are reported, you should now have a **CHM** file in your directory. If errors did occur, you need to fix any reported problems.

At long last, we can view our finished product. Click on the **View compiled file** button (a pair of sunglasses) on the workshop toolbar. **Browse** so your help file (**Sample.chm**) is selected. Choose **View**, and this will appear (I've expanded the headings to show the topics):

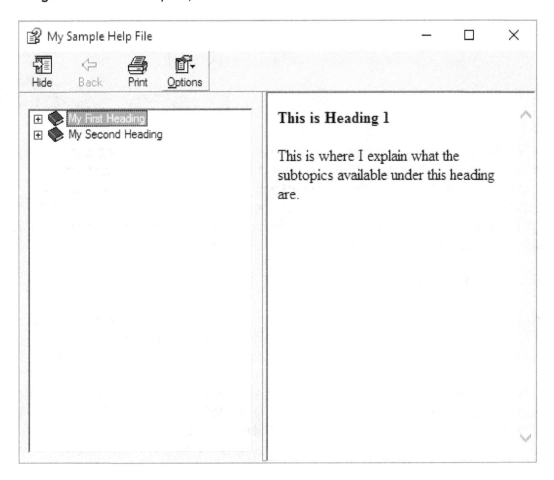

Click to see the various topics and headings displayed.

After all this work, you still only have a simple help file, nothing that rivals those seen in most applications. But, it is a very adequate help system. To improve your help system, you need to add more features. Investigate the HTML Help Workshop for information on tasks such as adding an index file, using context-sensitive help, adding search capabilities and adding graphics to the help system.

HelpProvider Control

In Toolbox:

Below Form (Default Properties):

Once we have a completed HTML help system, we need to connect our Visual Basic application to the help file. You need to decide how you want your application to interact with the help system. We will demonstrate a simple approach. We will have the help system appear when the user presses **<F1>** or clicks some control related to obtaining help (menu item, button control). The Visual Basic **HelpProvider** control provides this connection.

HelpProvider **Properties**:

Name	Gets or sets the name of the help provider control (three letter prefix for label name is **hlp**).
HelpNamespace	Complete path to compiled help file (**CHM** file)

The **HelpNamespace** property is usually established at run-time. The help file is often installed in the application directory (**Bin\Debug** folder). If this is the case, we can use the **Application.StartupPath** parameter to establish **HelpNamespace**. You also must include the help file in any deployment package you build for your application.

To have the help file appear when a user presses **<F1>**, we set the **HelpNavigator** property of the application form to **TableofContents**. With this setting, the help file will appear displaying the **Table of Contents**, set to the default form.

To have the help file appear in a **Click** event, we use the **ShowHelp** method of the **Help** object. The Visual Basic **Help** object allows us to display HTML help files. To replicate the **<F1>** functionality above, we use the syntax:

```
Help.ShowHelp(Me, HelpProvider.HelpNamespace)
```

This line of code will display the specified help file.

Typical use of **HelpProvider** control:

> ➢ Set the **Name** property.
> ➢ Set **HelpNameSpace** property in code (file is usually in **Bin** folder of application).
> ➢ Set **HelpNavigator** property for form to **TableofContents**.
> ➢ Write code for events meant to display the help file (use **Help.ShowHelp**).

The steps above provide minimal, but sufficient, access to an HTML help system. If you need more functionality (context-sensitive help, help on individual controls, pop-up help, adding help to dialog boxes), consult the Visual Basic documentation on the **Help Provider** control.

Example 10-10

Help System Display

1. Start a new application. In this simple project, we will show how to display our example help system using <F1> and programmatic control. Add a button control and help provider control to the form. Set these properties:

Form1:
Name	frmHelp
HelpNavigator	Table of Contents
Text	Help Example

Button1:
Name	btnHelp
Text	&Help!!

HelpProvider1:
Name	hlpExample

My form now looks like this:

Other controls in tray:

2. Copy the example help file (**Sample.chm** in **LearnVB\VB Code\Class 10\Sample Help** folder into the **Bin\Debug** folder of this application (you may have to create the folder first). We will use the **Application.StartupPath** parameter to load the file.

3. Use this code in the **Form Load** event to establish help file path:

```
Private Sub FrmHelp_Load(ByVal sender As Object, ByVal e
As System.EventArgs) Handles MyBase.Load
    hlpExample.HelpNamespace = Application.StartupPath +
"\sample.chm"
End Sub
```

4. Use this code in the **btnHelp Click** event to programmatically display the help file:

```
Private Sub BtnHelp_Click(ByVal sender As System.Object,
ByVal e As System.EventArgs) Handles btnHelp.Click
    Help.ShowHelp(Me, hlpExample.HelpNamespace)
End Sub
```

5. Save (saved in **Example 10-10** folder in the **LearnVB\VB Code\Class 10** folder) and run the application. Click the button and the help system will appear. Press **<F1>** and the help system will appear:

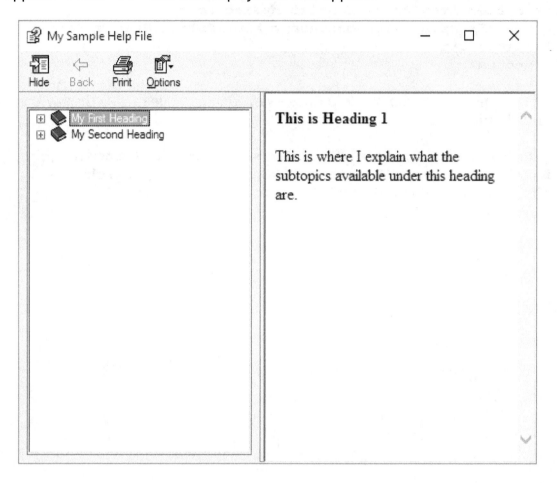

We did it!

Class Review

After completing this class, you should understand:

- ➢ How to use several new controls: link label, tab control, date selection controls, rich textbox control
- ➢ How to add a toolbar control and tooltips to a Visual Basic application
- ➢ How to add controls at run-time
- ➢ The concepts of printing from a Visual Basic application, including use of dialog controls
- ➢ How to use the Windows API (Application Programming Interface) for precise timing
- ➢ How to use the HTML Help Workshop to develop a simple on-line help system
- ➢ How to attach a help file to a Visual Basic application, both via function keys and via code

Practice Problems 10

Problem 10-1. Biorhythm Problem. Some people think our lives are guided by biorhythm cycles that begin on the day we are born. There are three cycles: **physical, emotional** and **intellectual.** Each cycle can range in value from a low of -100 to a high of +100. If **NumberDays** is the number of days since birth, the three cycles are described by these Visual Basic equations:

```
Physical = 100 * Math.Sin(2 * Math.PI * NumberDays / 23)
Emotional = 100 * Math.Sin(2 * Math.PI * NumberDays / 28)
Intellectual = 100 * Math.Sin(2 * Math.PI * NumberDays / 33)
```

(For the mathematically inclined, each cycle is a sine wave with different periods.) Build an application that computes these values knowing someone's birth date.

Problem 10-2. Rich Textbox Note Editor Problem. Load the Note Editor example we have been building throughout this course. The last incarnation is in this class where we added a toolbar control (saved as **Example 10-5** in the **LearnVB\VB Code\Class 10** folder). Replace the text box control with a rich textbox control. Modify the code to allow selective formatting of text (bold, italics, underline, font size). You will also need to modify the code that opens and saves files (use the **LoadFile** and **SaveFile** methods) to insure saving of the formatting.

Problem 10-3. Loan Printing Problem. The two lines of Visual Basic code that compute the monthly payment on an installment loan are:

```
Multiplier = (1 + Interest / 1200) ^ Months
Payment = Loan * Interest * Multiplier / (1200 *
(Multiplier - 1))
```

where:

Interest	Yearly interest percentage
Months	Number of months of payments
Loan	Loan amount
Multiplier	Interest multiplier
Payment	Computed monthly payment

(The 1200 value in these equations converts yearly interest to a monthly rate.) Use this code to build a general function that computes **Payment**, given the other three variables.

Now, use this function in an application that computes the payment after the user inputs loan amount, yearly interest and number of months. Allow the user to print out a repayment schedule for the loan. The printed report should include the inputs, computed payments, total of payments and total interest paid. Then, a month-by-month accounting of the declining balance, as the loan is paid, should be printed. In this accounting, include how much of each payment goes toward principal and how much toward interest.

Problem 10-4. Plot Printing Problem. In Problem 9-4, we built an application that displayed a labeled plot of the win streaks for the Seattle Mariners 1995 season. Build an application that prints this plot and its labeling information.

Problem 10-5. Sound Timing Problem. Modify Problem 9-7 (where we played sound files) to include a feature to compute and display the time elapsed (using the Windows API) while the sound plays.

Problem 10-6. Note Editor Help Problem. Develop a help file for the **Note Editor** application (use Problem 10-2 above as a starting point). Explain whatever topics you feel are important. Allow access to this help file via a menu item, a toolbar button and by pressing <F1>.

Exercise 10

Phone Directory

Develop an application that tracks people and phone numbers (include home, work and cell phones). Allow sorting, editing, adding, deleting and saving of entries. Add search capabilities. Allow printing of listings. Develop an on-line help system. In summary, build a full-featured Visual Basic phone directory application.

11. Visual Basic Database and Web Applications

Review and Preview

Many Visual Basic Windows applications are built and deployed as 'front-ends' for databases. That is, they provide the interface between a user and a database. A database is a well-organized system of information. Visual Basic offers a suite of tools that allows viewing, editing, adding, deleting and printing data from a database. We take a brief look at these tools in this last class.

Prior to Visual Basic, building and deploying applications that run on the Internet was a major headache. Visual Basic includes the web form that makes the process of building a web application nearly as simple as the process for building a Windows application. We conclude **Learn Visual Basic** by introducing the steps involved in building a web application.

Database Applications

In this course, we've presented an in-depth study in the development and deployment of Visual Basic Windows applications. A very powerful, and popular, use for such applications is to work as an interface to an existing **database**. Databases are everywhere in today's world: e-commerce sites use databases to track sales and inventories; airlines use databases to schedule flights; doctors use databases to schedule patients; and even sports announcers use databases to provide useless trivial statistics about players.

Products such as Microsoft Access, Microsoft SQL Server, Oracle or Sybase can be used to create databases. Visual Basic offers a variety of tools and objects for connecting to, retrieving, viewing and updating data in such databases.

In this class, we look at a few of the tools used for database access. And, we will limit our study to viewing databases created using Microsoft Access. In this class, we will study:

> ➢ Database structure and terminology
> ➢ How to connect to a Microsoft Access database
> ➢ Ways to view data in the database
> ➢ How to navigate within a database

Database Structure and Terminology

Database management has a language all its own. Here, we introduce some of that terminology. In simplest terms, a **database** is a collection of information. This collection is stored in well-defined **tables**, or matrices.

The **rows** in a database table are used to describe similar items. The rows are referred to as database **records**. In general, no two rows in a database table will be alike.

The **columns** in a database table provide characteristics of the records. These characteristics are called database **fields**. Each field contains one specific piece of information. In defining a database field, you specify the data type, assign a length, and describe other attributes.

Here is a simple database example:

Field

ID No	Name	Date of Birth	Height	Weight
1	Bob Jones	01/04/58	72	170
2	Mary Rodgers	11/22/61	65	125
3	Sue Williams	06/11/57	68	130

} **Record**

Table

In this database **table**, each **record** represents a single individual. The **fields** (descriptors of the individuals) include an identification number (ID No), Name, Date of Birth, Height, and Weight.

Most databases use **indexes** to allow faster access to the information in the database. Indexes are sorted lists that point to a particular row in a table. In the example just seen, the **ID No** field could be used as an index.

A database using a single table is called a **flat database**. Most databases are made up of many tables. When using multiple tables within a database, these tables must have some common fields to allow cross-referencing of the tables. The referral of one table to another via a common field is called a **relation**. Such groupings of database tables are called **relational databases**.

In our examples, we will use a sample multi-table database containing information on books about computers. This Microsoft Access database (**books.accdb**) is found in the **LearnVB\VB Code\Class 11** folder. Let's look at its relational structure. The **books.accdb** database is made up of four tables:

Authors Table (6246 Records, 3 Fields)

Au_ID	Author	Year Born

Publishers Table (727 Records, 10 Fields)

PubID	Name	Company		Fax	Comments

Title Author Table (16056 Records, 2 Fields)

ISBN	Au_ID

Titles Table (8569 Records, 8 Fields)

Title	Year Pub	ISBN	PubID		Comments

The **Authors** table consists of author identification numbers, the author's name, and the year born. The **Publishers** table has information regarding book publishers. Some of the fields include an identification number, the publisher name, and pertinent phone numbers. The **Title Author** table correlates a book's ISBN (a universal number assigned to books) with an author's identification number. And, the **Titles** table has several fields describing each individual book, including title, ISBN, and publisher identification.

Note each table has two types of information: **source** data and **relational** data. Source data is actual information, such as titles and author names. Relational data are references to data in other tables, such as Au_ID and PubID. In the Authors, Publishers and Title Author tables, the first column is used as the table **index**. In the Titles table, the ISBN value is the **index**.

Using the relational data in the four tables, we should be able to obtain a complete description of any book title in the database. Let's look at one example:

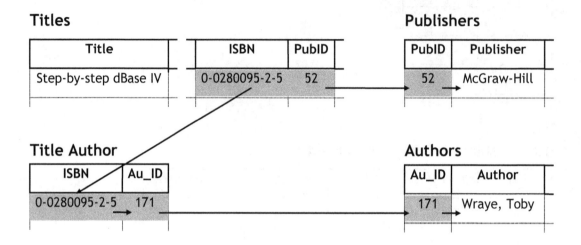

Here, the book in the **Titles** table, entitled "Step-by-step dBase IV," has an ISBN of 0-0280095-2-5 and a PubID of 52. Taking the PubID into the **Publishers** table, determines the book is published by McGraw-Hill and also allows us to access all other information concerning the publisher. Using the ISBN in the **Title Author** table provides us with the author identification (Au_ID) of 171, which, when used in the **Authors** table, tells us the book's author is Toby Wraye.

We can form alternate tables from a database's inherent tables. Such **virtual tables**, or **logical views**, are made using queries of the database. A **query** is simply a request for information from the database tables. As an example with the **books.accdb** database, using pre-defined query languages, we could 'ask' the database to form a table of all authors and books published after 1992, or provide all author names starting with B. We'll look briefly at queries.

Keeping track of all the information in a database is handled by a **database management system** (DBMS). Visual Basic provides several tools to help in these management tasks, using what is known as **ADO .NET**. ADO **(ActiveX Data Object)** .NET is the latest incarnation in a series of Visual Basic data access technologies.   In this class, we will see how to use Visual Basic (and ADO .NET) to perform two tasks: accessing data and displaying data.

DataSet Objects

The **DataSet** object is the heart of ADO .NET. With this object, we can connect to a database and then generate a table (or tables) of data (the **DataSet**) to view. Making **queries** of the database generates tables. The language used to make a query is **SQL** (pronounced 'ess-cue-ell' meaning structured query language). SQL is an English-like language that has evolved into the most widely used database query language. You use SQL to formulate a question to ask of the database. The database 'answers' that question with a new table of records and fields that match your criteria. Sometimes, like in our first example, you don't need any SQL at all – a wizard handles the work for you!

To get data into a **DataSet**, you first establish a connection to the database. The **Connection** object lets you specify the database you will be working with. Communication between the database and **DataSet** is accomplished via the **DataAdapter** object. Connection to the database is done using the **Data Source Configuration Wizard**. The best way to learn to use this wizard and others is by example and that's what we'll do. We will use the wizards to connect to our example database (**books.accdb** in the **LearnVB\VB Code\Class 11** folder) and form a table with two fields (**Title**, **ISBN**) from the **Titles** table. Let's go.

But, first, the Access database used here only works with 32-bit operating systems. If you are using a 64-bit version of Visual Studio, you need to make one change to each project you build.

Follow these steps:

> ➢ Once your project is built, choose the **Project** menu item, and select your project's **Properties** entry.
> ➢ In the window that appears, choose the **Compile** tab.
> ➢ Under **Target CPU**, make sure the selection is **x86**, not **AnyCPU**. The changed window should look like this:

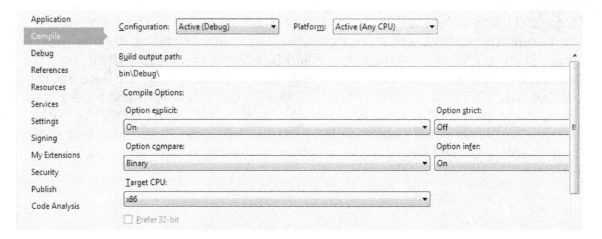

> ➢ Close the window to finalize the change.

How will you know if you have an operating system problem? The first symptom is that your application will have no data displayed, indicating the database did not open correctly. Secondly, the **Immediate Window** will have this error message:

An unhandled exception of type 'System.InvalidOperationException' occurred in System.Data.dll

Or, when opening the database, you may see a window similar to this:

Exception Unhandled   ♯ ✕

System.InvalidOperationException: 'The 'Microsoft.ACE.OLEDB.12.0'
provider is not registered on the local machine.'

View Details | Copy Details | Start Live Share session...
▷ Exception Settings

If you see such symptoms, make the above noted correction to your project's properties.

Start a new application in Visual Basic. Select the **Project** menu option and choose **Add New Data Source**. This window will appear:

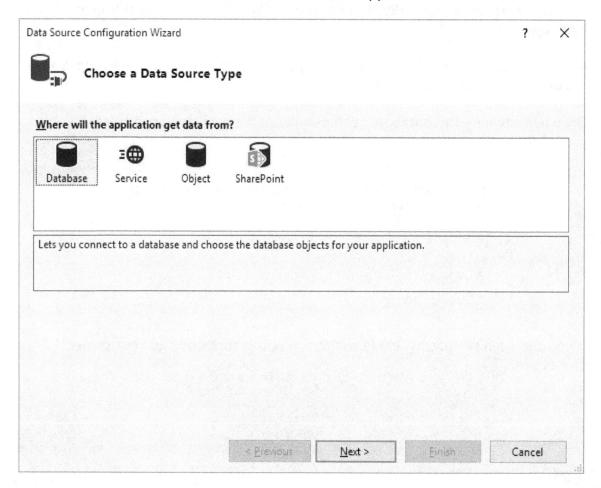

Choose the **Database** application and click **Next**.

You will next see a screen asking what **database model** you want to use. Choose **Dataset** and click **Next**.

You next specify where the database is located:

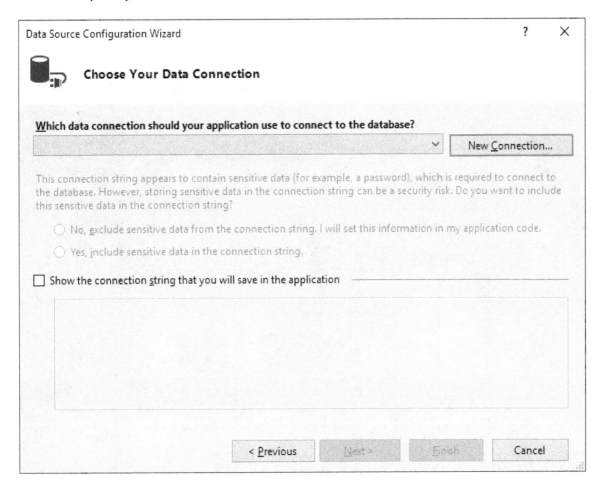

There may or may not be a connection listed in the drop down box. Here is where we will form a needed **Connection string** to connect to the database. Click **New Connection.**

In the next screen, you may or may not see:

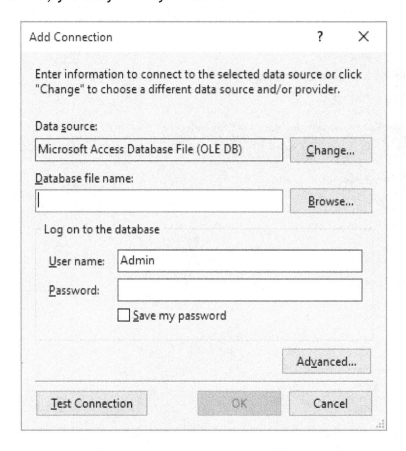

Make sure the **Data source** shows **Microsoft Access Database File**. If not, click **Change** to see:

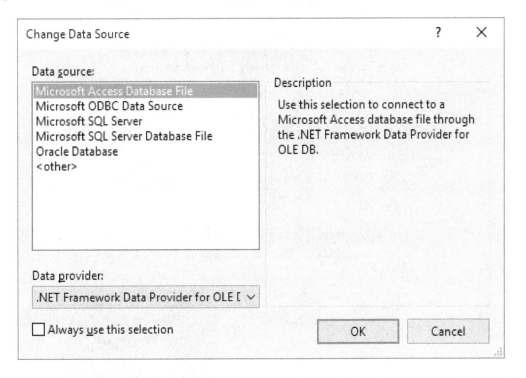

As shown, choose **Microsoft Access Database File**. This is the proper choice for a Microsoft Access database. Click **OK**.

You will return to the **Add Connection** window:

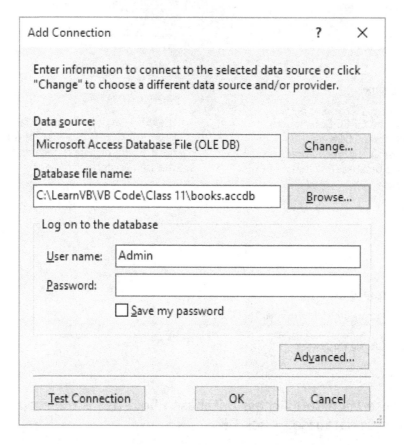

Click the **Browse** button and point to the **books.accdb** database (in **LearnVB\VB Code\Class 11** folder). Once selected, click **Test Connection** to insure a proper connection.

When testing the connection, you may see:

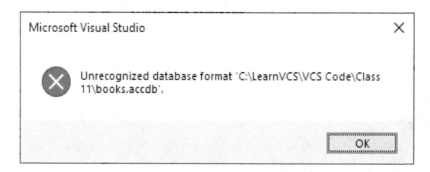

This indicates you are missing the proper driver for the Access Database. To fix this problem, download and install the driver from

Download Driver

Once installed, restart Visual Studio and retry connecting to the database. When you get to this screen

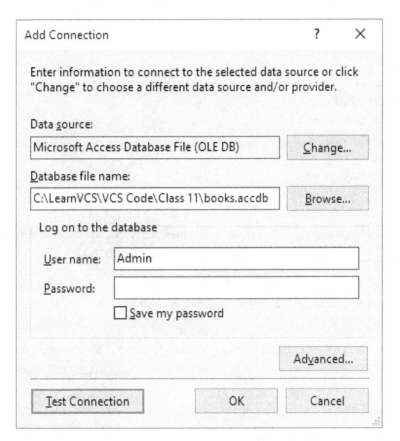

Click the **Advanced** button.

Select the **Provider** property as shown:

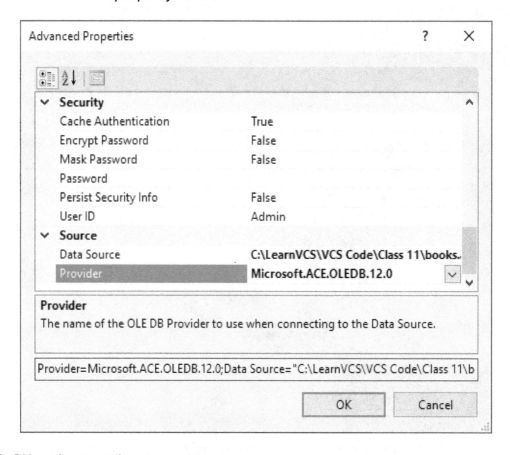

Click **OK** and retest the connection.

Once the connection is verified, click **OK** and you will be returned to the **Data Source Configuration Wizard** main screen. Click **Next** and you will be asked if you want to copy the database to your project:

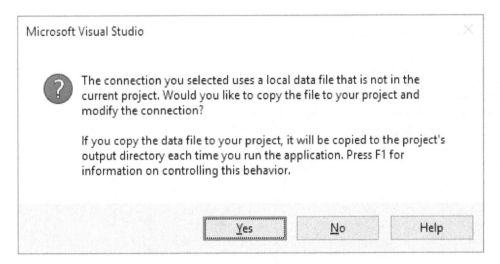

For our example, answer **No**. When you build applications that actually distribute the database, you would want a copy in your project.

The next screen shows:

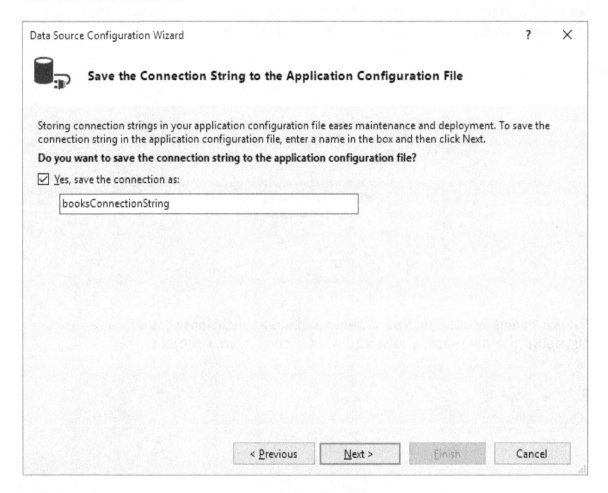

The **connection string** specifies what database fields are used to form the dataset. Choose the default connection string and click **Next**.

The connection is complete; we now need to specify the **DataSet** or table of data we want to generate. We want to choose the **Title** and **ISBN** fields in the **Titles** table. Expand the **Tables** object, then choose the **Titles** table and place checks next to the **Title** and **ISBN** fields:

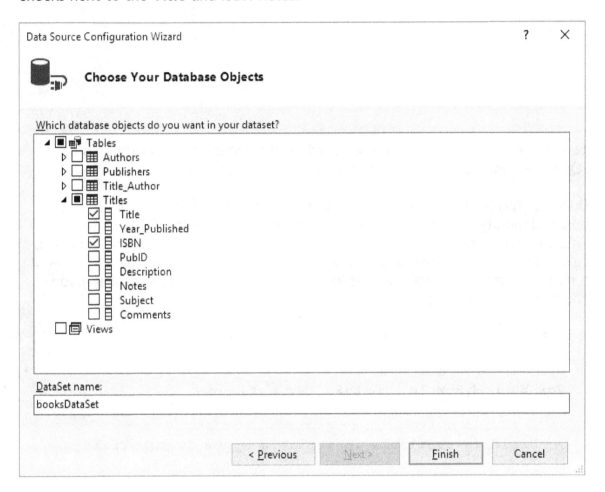

Once these selections are done, click **Finish** to complete specification of the **DataSet**.

Look in the **Data Sources** window in your project and you should see the newly created **DataSet** object (**booksDataSet**):

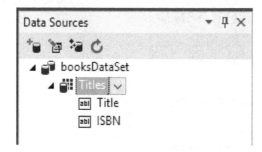

To form this **DataSet**, Visual Basic 'queried' the database (generating its own SQL statement) to pull the **Title** and **ISBN** fields out of the database.

Once generated, there are many properties and methods that allow us to view, edit and modify the dataset. One very useful property is the **Rows** collection. This collection contains all rows in the data set. The **DataRow** object allows us to examine (or establish) fields in each row of the data set. To see all values of a field (**MyField**) in a table (**MyTable**) existing in a DataSet (**MyDataSet**), you could use this code snippet:

```
Dim MyRow As DataRow
   .
   .
   .
For Each MyRow In MyDataSet.MyTable.Rows
   .
   .
   'Field is available in variable MyRow.Item(MyField)
   .
   .
Next
```

In this snippet, **MyField** is a string data type. The snippet uses a special form of the **For/Next** loop that goes through all elements of the **Rows** collection. Such code could be used to make bulk changes to a database. For example, you could use it to add area codes to all your phone numbers or change the case of particular fields.

In summary, the relationship between the **ConnectionString** property (set using the wizard), the **SQL** query (formed automatically in this example) and the **DataSet** is:

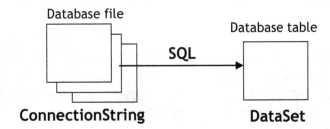

We now need a mechanism to view the information in the database table. This is done using a process known as **data binding**.

Simple Data Binding

Data binding allows us to take data from a data set object and bind it to a particular Visual Basic control. This means some property is automatically established by the database.

Most of the Visual Basic tools we've studied can be used as **bound** controls. The process of 'connecting' a particular property to a particular database field is known as **simple binding**. Simple binding is best illustrated by example. Add a label control to the form of the example we've been working on – set **AutoSize** to **False** and make it fairly large:

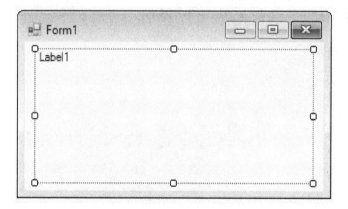

In the properties window for the label control, find the **DataBindings** entry (usually near the top). Expand the entry by clicking the enclosed plus (+) sign. Choose the **Text** property and click the drop-down arrow that appears. Expand the selections until you see this:

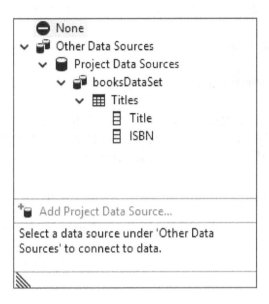

Choose **Title**.

We have now 'bound' the **Text** property of the label control to the **Title** field of our dataset. You should also note that three objects have been added to the project (in the tray area under the form):

We recognize the **BooksDBDataSet** object. The **TitlesTableAdapter** object is a **DataAdapter** that controls communication between the books database and the dataset. The **TitlesBindingSource** controls navigation through the dataset. Important: For proper navigation, all subsequent data bindings for this dataset should connect to this **BindingSource** object, not the original dataset.

One other change has been made to your project. Open the code window. You should see two lines of code have been added to the **Form Load** procedure:

```
'TODO: This line of code loads data into the
'BooksDataSet.Titles' table. You can move, or remove it,
as needed.
Me.TitlesTableAdapter.Fill(Me.BooksDBDataSet.Titles)
```

As mentioned in the comment, this is needed to load the data into the dataset.

Guess what? We're finally about to see data! **Run** the sample project. If the database is successfully connected, the data set correctly generated and the label is correctly bound, you will see this on your form:

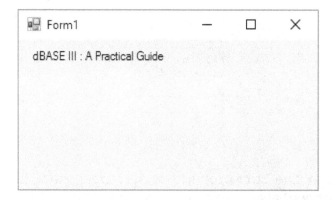

The label control is displaying the **Title** of the first book in the **books.accdb** database! The **Text** property of the control is bound to that field. This is nice, but kind of boring. How can we see the other titles in the database? We need some way to navigate among the rows (records) of the data set table.

Database Navigation

To navigate the rows of a database table, we use the **BindingSource** object associated with the dataset. Recall this object is added to the project once the first data binding is assigned. With just a few properties and methods, we can do quite a few navigation tasks.

For a **BindingSource** named **MyBindingSource**, the number of records in the corresponding dataset (table) is given by:

```
MyBindingSource.Count
```

The 'record number' for the same binding source is given by:

```
MyBindingSource.Position
```

This **Position** property is modified using one of four **BindingSource** methods: **MoveFirst** (move to the first record), **MoveNext** (increment Position by one), **MovePrevious** (decrement Position by one), **MoveLast** (move to the last record). When changed, all controls bound to the dataset will be updated with the current values. The relationship between a data bound control and the Position property is:

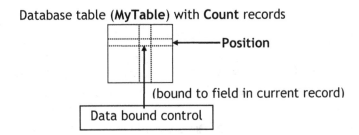

Database table (**MyTable**) with **Count** records

Position

(bound to field in current record)

Data bound control

The records are a 'zero-based' array, ranging from a low **Position** value of **0** to a high value of **Count - 1**

To help clarify everything, we summarize all the steps for connecting to a database, establishing a dataset, binding controls and database navigation in Example 11-1.

Example 11-1

Accessing the Books Database

1. Start a new application. We'll develop a form where we can skim through the books database, examining **Titles** and **ISBN** values. Place four label controls and four buttons on the form. It should look something like this:

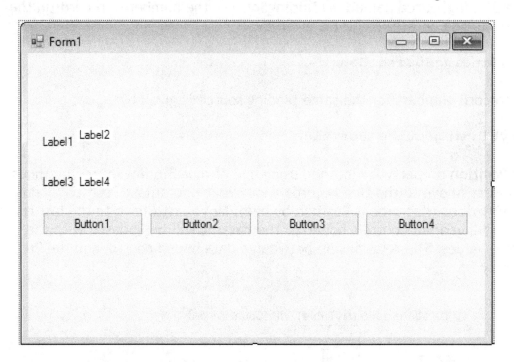

2. Use the **Data Source Configuration Wizard** to connect to the **books.accdb** database and form a DataSet (**BooksDBDataSet**) that contains the **Title** and **ISBN** fields from the **Titles** table. Here, you simply repeat the steps just covered in the course notes. We use the default names for all components – you may change them if you like.

3. Set the following properties the form and each control

Form1:

Name	frmBooks
FormBorderStyle	FixedSingle
StartPosition	CenterScreen
Text	Books Database

Label1:

AutoSize	False
Text	Title
TextAlign	MiddleLeft

Label2:

Name	lblTitle
AutoSize	False
BackColor	White
BorderStyle	Fixed3D
DataBindings	Text: BooksDataSet – Titles.Title
Text	[Blank]
TextAlign	MiddleLeft

Label3:

AutoSize	False
Text	ISBN
TextAlign	MiddleLeft

Label4:

Name	lblISBN
AutoSize	False
BackColor	White
BorderStyle	Fixed3D
DataBindings	Text: TitlesBindingSource.ISBN (this object will be added following binding of lblTitle)
Text	[Blank]
TextAlign	MiddleLeft

Button1:
    Name   btnFirst
    Text   First Record

Button2:
    Name   btnPrevious
    Text   Previous Record

Button3:
    Name   btnNext
    Text   Next Record

Button4:
    Name   btnLast
    Text   Last Record

When done, the form will look something like this (try to space your controls as shown; we'll use all the blank space as we continue with this example):

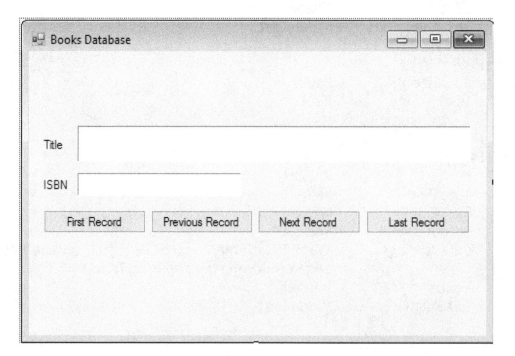

Other controls in tray:

4. Add the shaded line to the **frmBooks Load** procedure:

```
Private Sub FrmBooks_Load(ByVal sender As System.Object,
ByVal e As System.EventArgs) Handles MyBase.Load
    'TODO: This line of code loads data into the
'BooksDataSet.Titles' table. You can move, or remove it, as
needed.
    Me.TitlesTableAdapter.Fill(Me.BooksDataSet.Titles)
    btnFirst.PerformClick()
End Sub
```

5. Add this general procedure (**UpdateTitle**) to display the **Text** property of the Form:

```
Private Sub UpdateTitle()
    Me.Text = "Books Database - Record" +
Str(TitlesBindingSource.Position + 1) + " of" +
Str(TitlesBindingSource.Count)
End Sub
```

6. Use these four procedures for the navigation buttons:

```
Private Sub BtnFirst_Click(ByVal sender As System.Object,
ByVal e As System.EventArgs) Handles btnFirst.Click
    btnFirst.Enabled = False
    btnPrevious.Enabled = False
    btnNext.Enabled = True
    btnLast.Enabled = True
    TitlesBindingSource.MoveFirst()
    UpdateTitle()
End Sub
```

```
    Private Sub BtnPrevious_Click(ByVal sender As
System.Object, ByVal e As System.EventArgs) Handles
btnPrevious.Click
        btnNext.Enabled = True
        btnLast.Enabled = True
        TitlesBindingSource.MovePrevious()
        If TitlesBindingSource.Position = 0 Then
          btnFirst.Enabled = False
          btnPrevious.Enabled = False
        Else
          btnFirst.Enabled = True
          btnPrevious.Enabled = True
        End If
        UpdateTitle()
    End Sub

    Private Sub BtnNext_Click(ByVal sender As System.Object,
ByVal e As System.EventArgs) Handles btnNext.Click
        btnFirst.Enabled = True
        btnPrevious.Enabled = True
        TitlesBindingSource.MoveNext()
        If TitlesBindingSource.Position =
TitlesBindingSource.Count - 1 Then
          btnNext.Enabled = False
          btnLast.Enabled = False
        Else
          btnNext.Enabled = True
          btnLast.Enabled = True
        End If
        UpdateTitle()
    End Sub

    Private Sub BtnLast_Click(ByVal sender As System.Object,
ByVal e As System.EventArgs) Handles btnLast.Click
        btnFirst.Enabled = True
        btnPrevious.Enabled = True
        btnNext.Enabled = False
        btnLast.Enabled = False
        TitlesBindingSource.MoveLast()
        UpdateTitle()
    End Sub
```

These procedures increment/decrement the Position value, keeping track of beginning and end of records and enabling/disabling buttons when needed.

7. Save the application. (This application is saved in the **Example 11-1** folder in the **LearnVB\VB Code\Class 11** folder.) Run the application. You should see the first record:

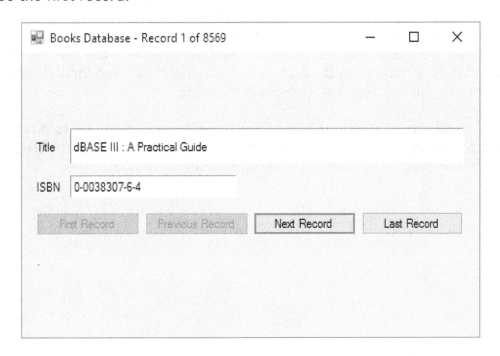

If you load and try to execute this project from the class notes, the books database must be located in the **LearnVB\VB Code\Class 11** folder or the application will not run. This will also be the case for other database examples and problems in this class. If you have the database in another folder, you need to go through the steps to configure the data source to point to your database's location. You may have to delete the **DataSet**, **DataAdapter** and **BindingSource** objects first. And, you might have to rebind the controls.

Cycle through the various book titles using the navigation buttons. Notice how the different buttons are enabled and disabled as you reach the beginning and end of the data table. This is part of good interface design.

Creating a Virtual Table

Many times, a database table has more information than we want to display. Or, perhaps a table does not have all the information we want to display. For instance, in Example 11-1, seeing the Title and ISBN of a book is not real informative - we would also like to see the Author, but the Titles table does not provide that information. In these cases, we can build our own **virtual table**, displaying only the information we want the user to see.

We need to form a SQL statement for the data adapter component to process. This will form a new data set containing the desired information. The steps to do this for our books database are covered in Example 11-2.

Example 11-2

Creating a Virtual Table

1. We will modify Example 11-1 so it will display an Author listing along with the Title and ISBN. To do this, we need to form a virtual table with three fields: Author (from the Authors table), Title and ISBN (from the Titles table). This will require a new dataset, a new data adapter and a SQL statement. Let's create the new dataset. Open Example 11-1. Choose the **Project** menu item, then **Add New Data Source**. Click **Next** until you see:

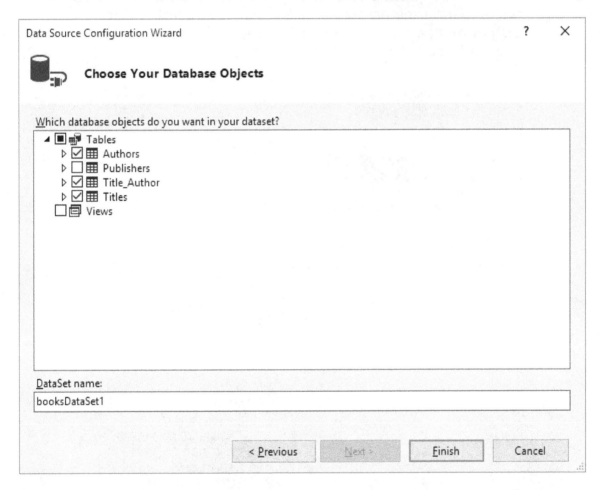

We need three tables in our dataset. Check **Authors**, **Title Author** and **Titles**. Then, click **Finish**.

A new dataset (**booksDataSet1**) will appear in the Data Sources window:

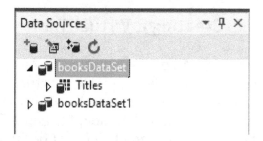

2. We now need to add a table adapter to generate the needed fields from the three tables to form another table. Right-click the **booksDataSet1** in the **Data Sources** window and choose **Edit DataSet with Designer**. This window, displaying the three individual tables, will appear:

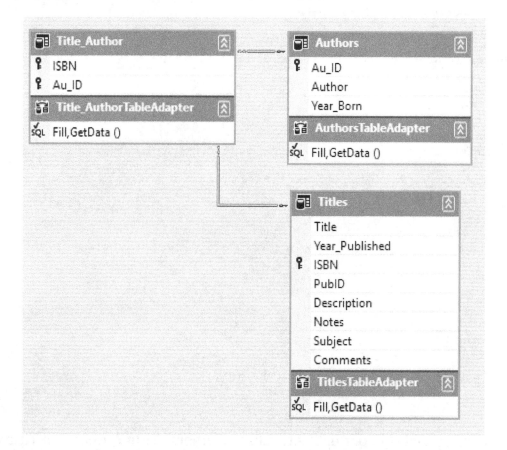

Our virtual table will include the **Author**, **Title**, and **ISBN** fields. To build this table, we need a new **TableAdapter**. Right-click the display window, and choose **Add**, then **TableAdapter**.

A new adapter will added and the **TableAdapter Configuration Wizard** will start up. Click **Next** on the **Choose Your Data Connection** window and the subsequent **Choose a Command Type Window** (where we tell the adapter we are using **SQL**). The **Enter a SQL Statement** window will appear:

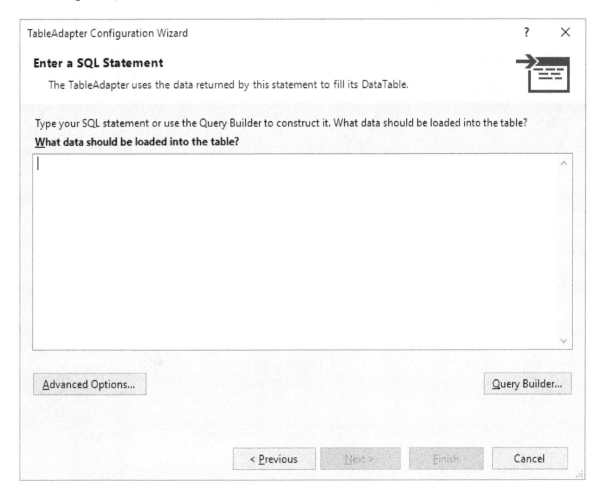

We can enter the SQL statement to build the table here or have Visual Basic build it for us. We'll let Visual Basic do the work.

Click **Query Builder** to see:

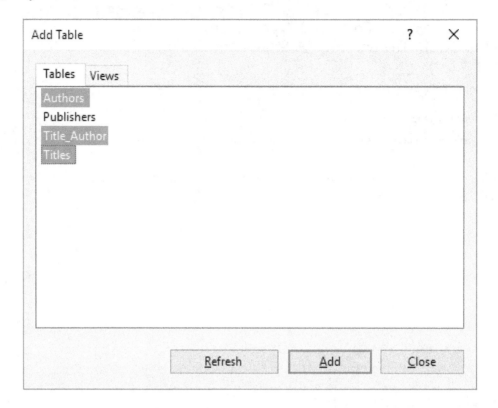

Select the **Authors**, **Title Author** and **Titles** tables and click **Add.**

Click **Close**. You will see:

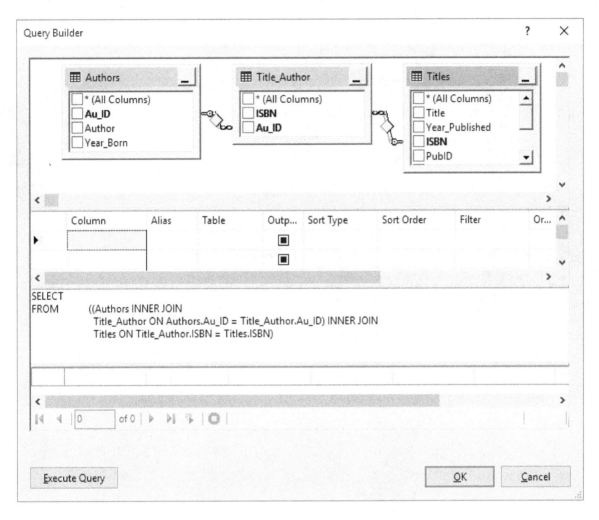

The Query Builder is showing the relationships among the three tables (i.e. how the **ISBN** value connects **Titles** with **Title Author** and how **Au_ID** connects **Title Author** with **Authors**). Select **Title** and **ISBN** in the **Titles** table. Then, select **Author** in the **Authors** table. Once added, select a sort type of **Ascending** in the table below. This will sort the table according to Author name.

Once your selections are complete, click **OK** and the window will appear as:

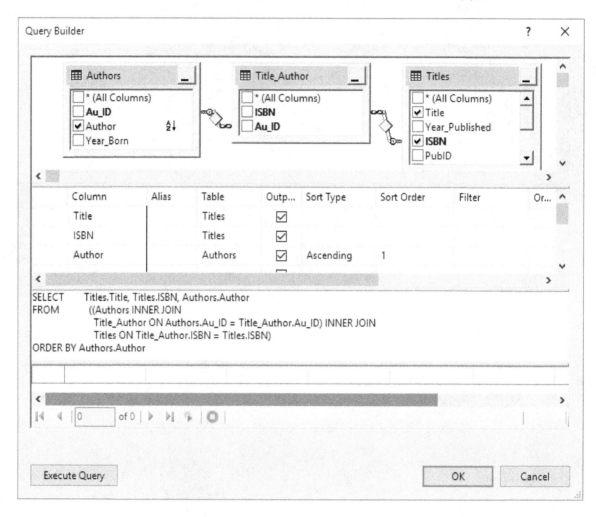

The following SQL statement is generated:

```
SELECT Titles.Title, Titles.ISBN, Authors.Author
FROM ((Authors INNER JOIN
  [Title Author] ON Authors.Au_ID = [Title Author].Au_ID)
INNER JOIN
  Titles ON [Title Author].ISBN = Titles.ISBN)
ORDER BY Authors.Author
```

Even without knowing SQL, you should be able to see what's going on here. The three desired fields are selected by 'joining' the Titles, Title Author and Authors tables using rules that match ISBN and Au_ID values. The results are ordered by the Author field. Click **OK**. Then, click **Finish** to complete specification of the table adapter.

A new data table (**DataTable1**, if you used the default name) will appear in the designer window and in the **Data Sources** window under **booksDataSet1**:

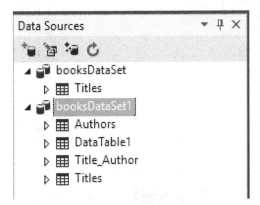

This table holds the virtual table including the Author, Title, and ISBN files for the books database. Admittedly, there were lots of steps needed to form this table. Once you've built a few tables though, these steps become second nature. Now, let's continue the example.

3. Add two new label controls to the form. Set these properties:

    Label5:

Text	Author

    Label6:

Name	lblAuthor
BackColor	White
BorderStyle	Fixed3D
DataBindings	Text: booksDataSet1 – DataTable1.Author
Text	[Blank]
TextAlign	MiddleLeft

The modified form looks like this:

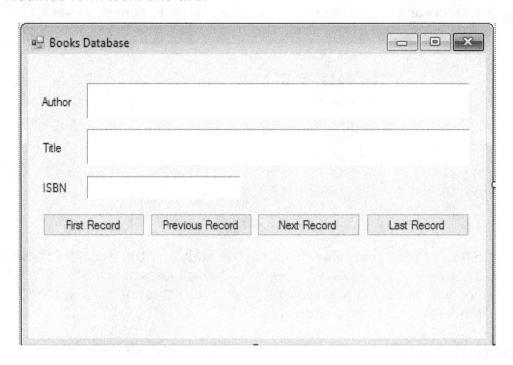

with three new objects added associated with the new virtual table:

4. Modify the data bindings on **lblTitle** and **lblISBN** so they are bound to the correct fields in the newly added **DataTable1BindingSource**. This will insure matching sets of Author, Title and ISBN as we move through the rows of the table. Correspondingly, change all references to the **TitlesBindingSource** in code to refer to the new **DataTable1BindingSource**. I made such 9 such changes.

5. Save your work (saved in **Example 11-2** folder in **LearnVB\VB Code\Class 11** folder). Run the application and now you'll see the author information has been added:

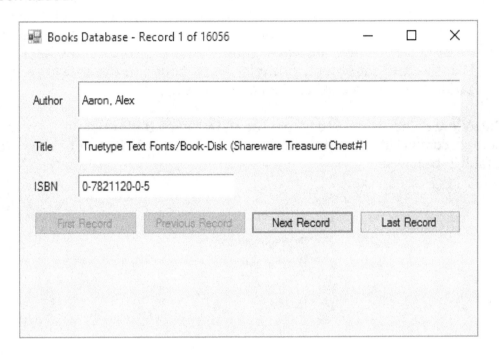

Notice how the books are now ordered based on an alphabetical listing of authors' last names.

DataView Objects

In many cases, we would like to see an alternate view of tables established by the data set object. Perhaps, we want the data sorted in a different manner or filtered based on some criteria. The **DataView** object allows us to do just that. The data view object is used to form a 'subset' of the records in the data set object. Like the data set object, controls can be bound to the data view object and navigation from one record to the next is possible.

The **DataView** object is selected from the **Data** tab of the Visual Basic toolbox. The default configuration for this tab may not have this object. For example, my default tab shows:

To add the **DataView** object to the toolbox, right-click the toolbox and select **Choose Items**. When the **Choose Toolbox Items** window appears, click the **.NET Framework Components** tab and place a check next to **DataView**, then click **OK**:

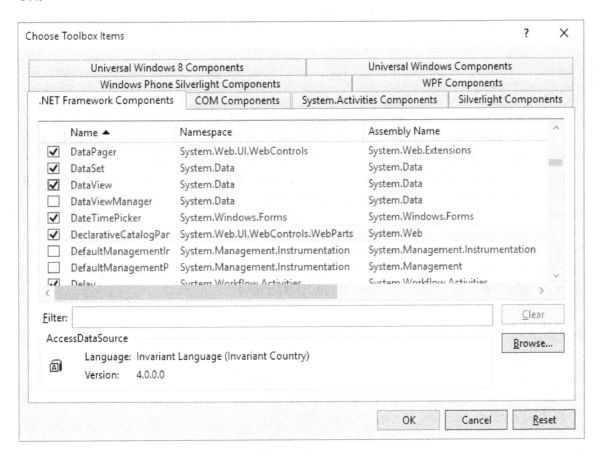

The **DataView** object should now be in the toolbox (it may be in the **General** tab):

```
⊿ Data
    ▶   Pointer
    ⊞   BindingNavigator
    ⊡   BindingSource
    ⊞   DataGridView
    ⊟   DataSet
    ⊞   DataView
```

Once in the toolbox, the **DataView** object is added to a project like any other object. To use the **DataView** object, you first must have established a table in a data set. Once added, the **Table** property should be set to the table it will "view."

Once the **DataView** object is connected with a table, you can do many things to that table. We will look at how to sort and how to filter the table. To sort the records in a DataView object (named **MyDataView**):

```
MyDataView.Sort("FieldName")
```

This will resort the table in ascending order using the specified **FieldName** as key. If you wish to sort in descending order, use:

```
MyDataView.Sort("FieldName DESC")
```

To filter the data (obtain an alternate view of the table), use:

```
MyDataView.RowFilter = Criteria
```

where **Criteria** is a string data type indicating the 'rule' to use in filtering. The criteria is much like a WHERE clause in SQL. To form a criteria, specify the name of a column (field) followed by an operator and a value to filter on. The value must be in single quotes. For example:

```
"LastName = 'Smith'"
```

would return all rows (records) where the **LastName** field was **Smith**. The number of records returned by the **RowFilter** property is provided by the **Count** property of the data view object.

The **DataRowView** object allows us to examine (or establish) fields in each row of a data view. To see all values of a field (**MyField**) in a DataView (**MyDataView**), you could use this code snippet:

```
Dim MyRow As DataRowView
   .
   .
For Each MyRow In MyDataView
   .
   .
   'Field is available in variable MyRow.Item(MyField)
   .
   .
Next
```

In this snippet, **MyField** is a string data type. The snippet uses a special form of the **For/Next** loop that goes through all rows in the data view.

Navigation among records in a **DataView** object is analogous to navigation within a data set object. Add a **BindingSource** object to the project and set its **DataSource** property to the **DataView** object (unlike the data set, a binding source is <u>not</u> automatically added for us). Then, for a **BindingSource** named **MyBindingSource**, the number of records in the corresponding dataview (table) is given by:

```
MyBindingSource.Count
```

The 'record number' for the same binding source is given by:

```
MyBindingSource.Position
```

This **Position** property is modified using one of four **BindingSource** methods: **MoveFirst** (move to the first record), **MoveNext** (increment Position by one), **MovePrevious** (decrement Position by one), **MoveLast** (move to the last record). When changed, all controls bound to the data view will be updated with the current values.

To see values generated in a **DataView** object, controls should be bound to fields in the data view's **BindingSource**. Simple binding is done using a method analogous to that of binding to a data set object. For the control to be bound, select the **DataBindings** property and point to the desired field in the listed **BindingSource** object.

Example 11-3

'Rolodex' Searching of the Books Database

1. We will modify Example 11-2 to allow searching for author names that begin with a selected letter of the alphabet. To implement the search, we'll use a 'rolodex' approach (borrowing code from Example 10-7). A **DataView** object will contain the resulting records. Open Example 11-2. Add a **DataView** object and set the **Table** property to **BooksDataSet1.DataTable1** (the DataTable1 table of the data set). We leave the default name set to **DataView1**; you may change it if you like.

2. Add a **BindingSource** (default name **BindingSource1**) object and set the **DataSource** property to **DataView1** (look under **Other Data Sources**, then **frmBooks List Instances**) This will give us navigation capabilities for the data view.

3. Since the displayed data will now be taken from the binding source for the data view object (rather than the data set object), we need to change the data bindings on the label controls:

   lblAuthor:
   > DataBindings   Text: BindingSource1.Author

   lblTitle:
   > DataBindings   Text: BindingSource1.Title

   lblISBN:
   > DataBindings   Text: BindingSource1.ISBN

4. In the code window, change all instances of **DataTable1BindingSource** to the new binding source, **BindingSource1**. I found 9 places where this change needs to be made.

5. Modify the code in the **frmBooks Load** procedure (new and/or modified code is shaded). The new code sets up the rolodex buttons (two rows with 13 buttons each - see Example 8-7:

```
Private Sub FrmBooks_Load(ByVal sender As System.Object,
ByVal e As System.EventArgs) Handles MyBase.Load
    Dim W As Integer, LStart As Integer, L As Integer, T As
Integer
    Dim ButtonHeight As Integer = 35
    Dim I As Integer
    Dim Rolodex(26) As Button
    'search buttons
    'determine button width (don't round up) - 13 on a row
    W = CInt(Me.ClientSize.Width / 14 - 0.5)
    'center buttons on form
    LStart = CInt(0.5 * (Me.ClientSize.Width - 13 * W))
    L = LStart
    T = Me.ClientSize.Height - 3 * ButtonHeight
    'create and position 26 buttons
    For I = 1 To 26
       'create new pushbutton
       Rolodex(I) = New Button()
       Rolodex(I).TabStop = False
       'set text property
       Rolodex(I).Text = Chr(64 + I)
       'position (button height set to 35 pixels)
       Rolodex(I).Width = W
       Rolodex(I).Height = ButtonHeight
       Rolodex(I).Left = L
       Rolodex(I).Top = T
       'give cool colors
       Rolodex(I).BackColor = Color.Blue
       Rolodex(I).ForeColor = Color.Yellow
       'add button to form
       Me.Controls.Add(Rolodex(I))
       'add event handler
       AddHandler Rolodex(I).Click, AddressOf
Me.Rolodex_Click
       'next left
       L += W
       If I = 13 Then
          'move to next row
          L = LStart
          T = T + ButtonHeight
       End If
    Next I
```

```
      'TODO: This line of code loads data into the
'BooksDataSet1.DataTable1' table. You can move, or remove
it, as needed.

Me.DataTable1TableAdapter.Fill(Me.BooksDataSet1.DataTable1)
      'TODO: This line of code loads data into the
'BooksDataSet.Titles' table. You can move, or remove it, as
needed.
      Me.TitlesTableAdapter.Fill(Me.BooksDataSet.Titles)
      btnFirst.PerformClick()
   End Sub
```

6. Use this code in the **Rolodex_Click** procedure (all new code). In this procedure, we use a **RowFilter** criteria that finds the first occurrence of an author name that begins with the selected letter button

```
   Private Sub Rolodex_Click(ByVal sender As System.Object,
ByVal e As System.EventArgs)
      Dim ButtonClicked As Button
      ButtonClicked = CType(sender, Button)
      If ButtonClicked.Text <> "Z" Then
         DataView1.RowFilter = "Author >= '" +
ButtonClicked.Text + "' and Author < '" +
Chr(Asc(ButtonClicked.Text) + 1) + "'"
      Else
         DataView1.RowFilter = "Author >= 'Z'"
      End If
      BindingSource1.MoveFirst()
      UpdateTitle()
   End Sub
```

Let's look at this code a little closer. The **ButtonClicked** is determined, then a **RowFilter** value established based on that button's **Text** property (notice all letters are surrounded by single quotes). As an example, if B is pressed, the **RowFilter** is:

```
DataView1.RowFilter = "Author >= 'B' And Author < 'C'"
```

The resulting data view will only have books with authors whose last name begins with the letter B. Notice the letter Z requires its own filter value since there is no letter after Z.

7. Save your application (saved in **Example 11-3** folder in the **LearnVB\VB Code\Class 11** folder). Test its operation. It appears as:

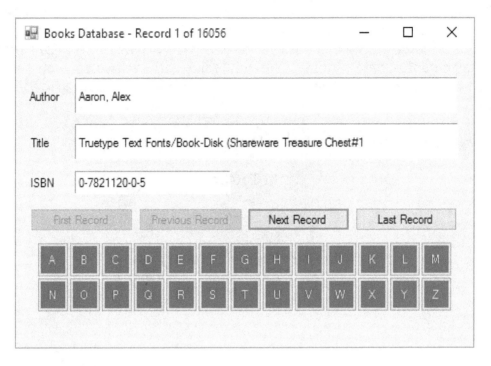

Note once the program finds the first occurrence of an author name beginning with a selected letter, you can use the navigation buttons to move among the filtered records in the data view. If I click on 'L', I see:

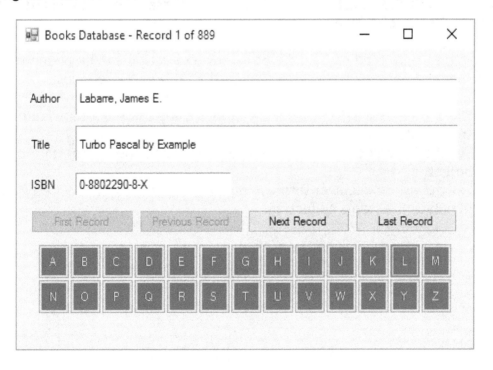

Complex Data Binding

In previous examples, we have bound a single field value to a single property in a control. This process is known as simple data binding. We can also bind an entire data source (table in a data set or data view) to a control. This process is known as **complex data binding**. We will look briefly at two controls that support complex data binding: the **list box** control and the **data grid view** control.

We have seen the **list box** control before:

In Toolbox:

On Form (Default Properties):

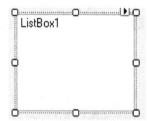

This control provides a list of items a user can choose from. The listed items are part of an **Items** collection.

With complex data binding, the list box **Items** collection can be bound to a particular field in a database table. To do this, follow these steps:

> ➤ Establish a data set or data view object using the procedures outlined in this chapter.
> ➤ Set the list box control **DataSource** property to the appropriate data object.
> ➤ Set the list box control **DisplayMember** property to the desired field to populate the **Items** collection.

As an example, say we have a **DataSet** object (**MyDataSet**) for the **Titles** table in **books.accdb**. By setting a list box control's **DataSource** property to **MyDataSet** and the **DisplayMember** property to **Titles.Title** (the **Title** field), the list box would the title of every book in the database. Here's what you would see:

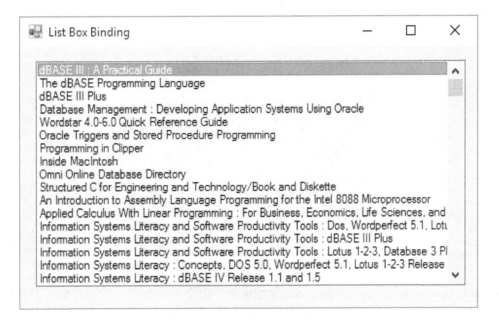

The **data grid view** control is even more powerful. It is found on the **Data** tab in the toolbox:

In Toolbox:

On Form (Default Properties):

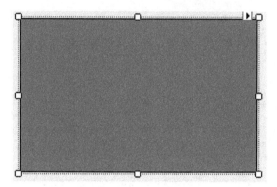

This control can display an entire database table (or even a data set generated in code). The table can then be edited as desired.

The **DataGridView** control is in a class by itself, when considering its capabilities. It is essentially a separate, highly functional program. We'll just look at how to use it to display data. Refer to the Visual Basic reference material and other sources for complete details on using the **DataGridView** control. To display data in the grid view control, follow these steps:

> ➤ Establish a data set or data view object using the procedures outlined in this chapter.
> ➤ Set the data grid control **DataSource** property to the appropriate data object.
> ➤ Set the data grid control **DataMember** property to the desired table to display.

As an example, say we have a **DataSet** object (**MyDataSet**) for the **Titles** table in **books.accdb**. By setting a data grid control's **DataSource** property to **MyDataSet** and the **DataMember** property to **Titles**, the data grid will show the entire **Titles** table! Here's what you would see:

Title	Year_Published	ISBN	PubID	Description
dBASE III : A Pra...	1985	0-0038307-6-4	469	22.5
The dBASE Prog...	1986	0-0038326-7-8	469	29.5
dBASE III Plus	1987	0-0038337-8-X	469	29.5
Database Manag...	1989	0-0131985-2-1	715	54
Wordstar 4.0-6.0 ...	1990	0-0133656-1-4	460	14.95
Oracle Triggers a...	1996	0-0134436-3-1	715	0
Programming in C...	1988	0-0201145-8-3	9	0
Inside MacIntosh	1994	0-0201406-7-3	9	99.01
Omni Online Data...	1983	0-0207992-0-9	156	0
Structured C for ...	1995	0-0230081-2-1	715	54

Web Applications

We all know the Internet has become part of everyday life. A great feature of Visual Basic is the idea of web forms. With web forms, we can build applications that run on the Internet – **web applications**. Web applications differ from the Windows applications we have been building. A user (**client**) makes a request of a **server** computer. The server generates a web page (in HTML) and returns it to the client computer so it can be viewed with browser software.

Web applications are built in Visual Basic using something called **ASP .NET** (**Active Server Pages .NET**). ASP .NET is an improved version of previous technologies used to build web applications. In the past, to build a dynamic web application, you needed to use a mishmash of programming technologies. Web pages were generated with HTML (yes, the same HTML used in Chapter 10 to write help files) and programming was done with ASP (Active Server Pages) and VB Script (a Visual Basic scripting language).

With ASP .NET, the process for building **web applications** is the same process used to build Windows applications. To build a web application, we start with a form, add web controls and write code for web control events. There is a visual project component that shows the controls and a code component with event procedures and general procedures and functions.

Like database applications studied earlier, learning about web applications is a course in itself. In these notes, we introduce the idea of web applications. You can use your new programming skills to delve into more advanced references on ASP .NET and web applications. Here, we cover a few web applications topics:

➢ Address the approaches used to build web applications using **web forms**.
➢ Discuss the **web form controls** and how they differ from their Windows counterparts.
➢ Demonstrate the process of building web applications with some examples.

Before beginning, you may be asking yourself is: if it's so easy to build a Visual Basic Windows application and it is easily deployed to a user base, why would I need web applications? That's a good question and the answer is you may never need to build web applications. Let's briefly compare **web applications** and **Windows applications**.

The biggest advantage to a web application is related to deployment and maintenance. A web application can be used by thousands (even millions) of users at once. They merely access your application via their web browser and use it to perform the programmed tasks. When you need to modify or change your application, you only need to change the application on your server and your entire user base will immediately be using the upgraded version. E-commerce systems, on-line reservation systems and on-line data retrieval systems are obvious web applications.

Some browsers limit the performance of web applications. Some web pages may appear differently to different users. This can cause user confusion. Web application performance can be slow depending on network connections. Web applications are not amenable to power graphical programs such as games or CAD (computer-aided design).

If you use Windows applications and need to upgrade your software, a new copy must be sent to each individual user. This means you need to know where all your users are. If you are selling your software as an individual product or need to control who uses your application, this is the route you must take. Fortunately, though, the upgrade procedure can usually be done on the Internet via e-mail or software downloads.

Windows applications will run faster because there is no network connection. Windows applications are great for games. Windows applications can integrate easily with other applications such as word processors, spreadsheets and database management systems.

You need to decide if your planned application is better suited for desktop (Windows) or web deployment. Now, let's look at how to build a web application using Visual Basic.

Starting a New Web Application

To start the process of building a web application, you select the **File** menu option in Visual Basic. Then, click **New**, then **Project**. This window appears:

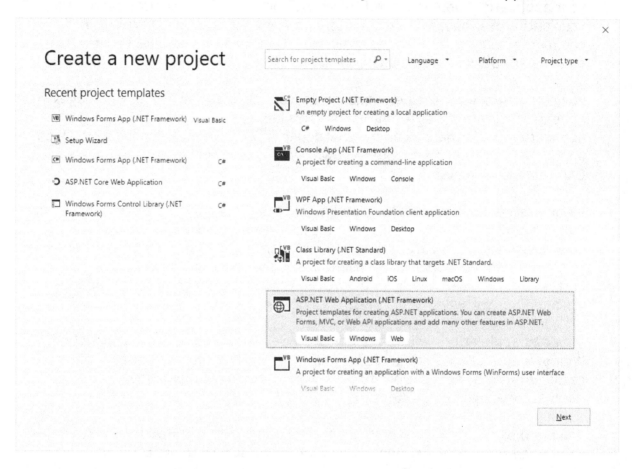

Select **ASP .NET Web Application**. Click **Next**.

This window appears:

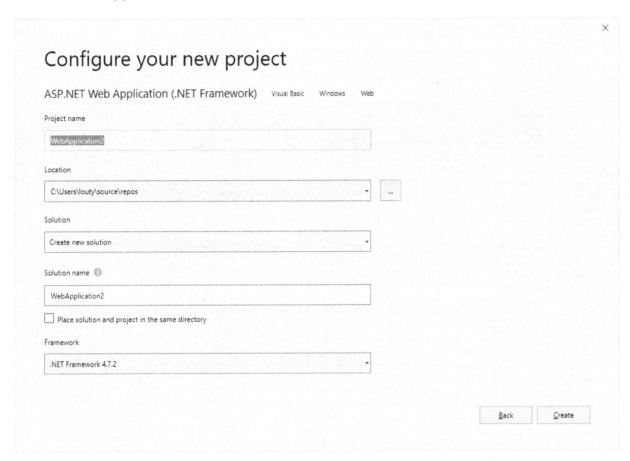

In the drop-down box to the left of the **Browse** button, either select or type the name of a folder to hold your new web site. Make sure the selected **Language** is **Visual Basic**. Click **Create** to create the application.

This window appears:

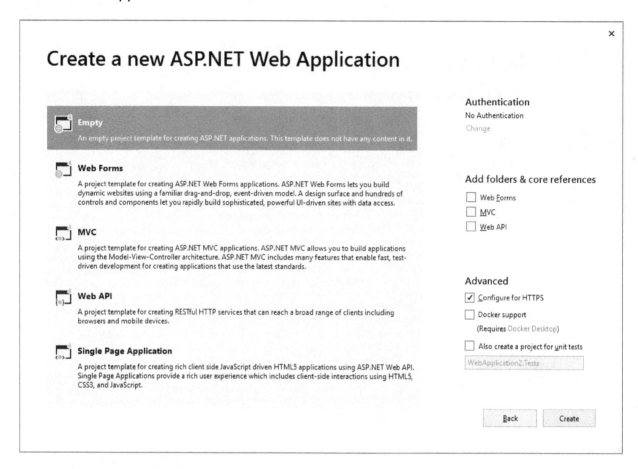

Choose **Empty** and click **Create**.

Once created, right-click the web site name in the **Solution Explorer** window and select **Add**, then **New Item**. Choose **Web**, then **Web Forms** and choose **Web Form**. Click **OK**.

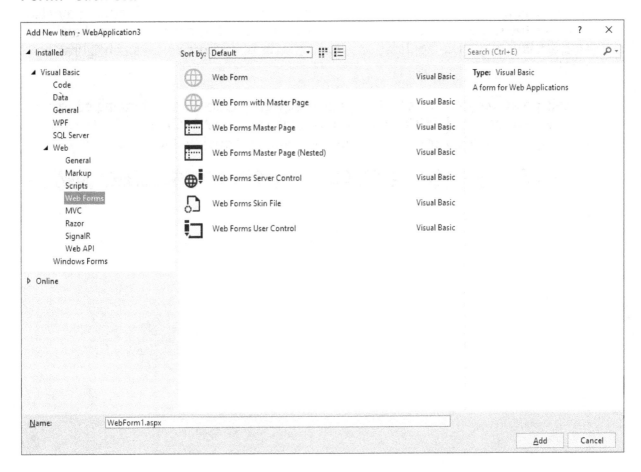

A blank web form appears (with extension **aspx**).

Let's look at some of the files associated with the web site. Your web application is in the **.aspx** file. This is the file your user requests. When a browser requests a **.aspx** file, ASP .NET executes code and presents the web form. The code for a **.aspx** file is in a **.aspx.vb** file. A web application may also have a **Global.asax** and a **Web.config** file. The first has code for event handlers to start and begin the application. The **.config** file stores various configuration settings.

At this point, we can start building our first web application by placing controls on the web form and writing code for various events. A blank form will appear in the design window (right click the file name and click **View Designer**):

There are two views of the form: **Design** (the graphical display) and **Source** (the HTML code behind the form). Let's look at the controls available and how to place them on the form.

Web Form Controls

When a web form is being edited, the controls available for placing on a web form are found in the Visual Basic toolbox. A view showing some of the resulting controls is:

The names in this menu should be familiar. The controls are similar to the Windows form controls we've used throughout this course. There are differences, however. The major differences are in the names of some properties (for example, the **ID** property is used in place of a **Name** property) and web form controls usually have far fewer events than their Windows counterparts. Let's look at some of the controls - feel free to study other controls for your particular needs.

Label Control:

A Label

The label control allows placement of formatted text information on a form (**Text** property). Font is established with the **Font** property.

TextBox Control:

abl TextBox

The text box controls allows placement of text information on a form (**Text** property). This is probably the most commonly used web form control. There is no **KeyPress** event for key trapping. Validation with web controls can be done using **validator** controls.

Button Control:

ab Button

The button control is nearly identical to the Windows counterpart. Code is written in the **Click** event.

LinkButton Control:

ab LinkButton

The link button control is clicked to follow a web page hyperlink (set with **Text** property). This is usually used to move to another web page. Code is added to the **Click** event.

ImageButton Control:

ImageButton

This control works like a button control – the user clicks it and code in the **Click** event is executed. The difference is the button displays an image (**ImageURL** property) rather than text.

HyperLink Control:

A HyperLink

The control works like the link button control except there is no Click event. Clicking this control moves the user to the link in the **Text** property.

DropDownList Control:

DropDownList

Drop down list controls are very common in web applications. Users can choose from a list of items (states, countries, product). The listed items are established using an **Items** collection and code is usually written in the **SelectedIndexChanged** event (like the Windows counterpart).

ListBox Control:

ListBox

A list box control is like a drop down list with the list portion always visible. Multiple selections can be made with a list box control.

GridView Control:

GridView

The grid view control is used to list a table of data (whether a data set from a database or data generated in your web application).

CheckBox Control:

CheckBox

The check box control is used to provide a yes or no answer to a question. The **Checked** property indicates its state. Code is usually added to the **CheckedChanged** event.

CheckBoxList Control:

The check box list control contains a series of independent check box controls. It is a useful control for quickly adding a number of check boxes to a form. It can be used in place of a list box control for a small (less than 10) number of items. The individual controls are defined in an **Items** collection (**Text** property specifies the caption, **Selected** specifies its status).

RadioButton Control:

The radio button control is identical to the Windows radio button control. It is used to select from a mutually exclusive group of options. The **Checked** property indicates its state. Code is usually added to the **CheckedChanged** event.

RadioButtonList Control:

The radio button list control provides an easy way to place a group of dependent radio buttons in a web application. The individual controls are defined in an **Items** collection (**Text** property specifies the caption, **Selected** specifies its status).

Image Control:

Images are useful in web applications. They give your application a polished look. The image control holds graphics. The image (set with **ImageURL** property) is usually a gif or jpg file.

By default, web controls are placed on the form in **flow mode**. This means each element is placed to the right of the previous element. This is different than the technique used in building Windows forms. We want to mimic the Windows forms behavior. To do this, choose the **Tools** menu option in the development environment and choose **Options.**

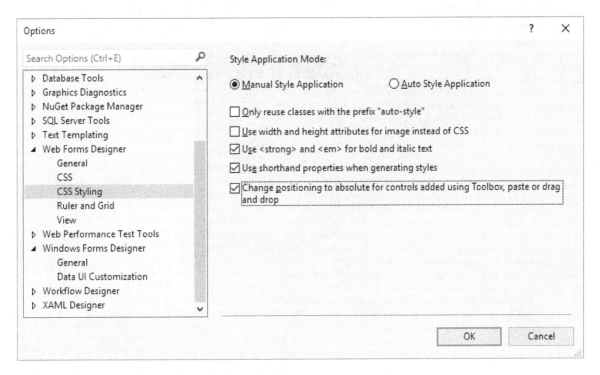

Choose the **Web Forms Designer** and **CSS Styling**. Place check next to "**Change positioning to absolute for controls ...**". Then click **OK**.

With this change, there are two ways to move a web control from the toolbox to the web form:

Click the tool in the toolbox and hold the mouse button down. Drag the selected tool over the form. When the mouse button is released, the default size control will appear in the upper left corner of the form. This is the classic "drag and drop" operation. For a button control, we would see:

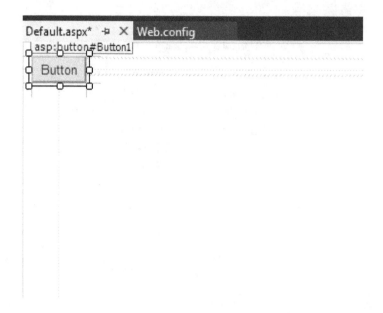

Double-click the tool in the toolbox and it is created with a default size on the form. It will be in the upper left corner of the form. You can then move it or resize it. Here is a button control placed on the form using this method:

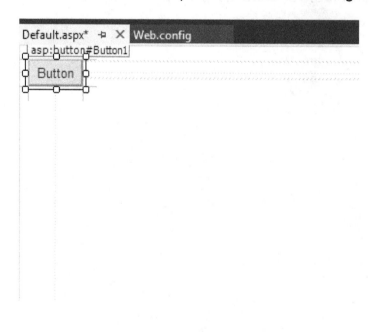

To **move** a control you have drawn, click the object in the form (a cross with arrows will appear). Now, drag the control to the new location. Release the mouse button.

To **resize** a control, click the control so that it is selected (active) and sizing handles appear. Use these handles to resize the object.

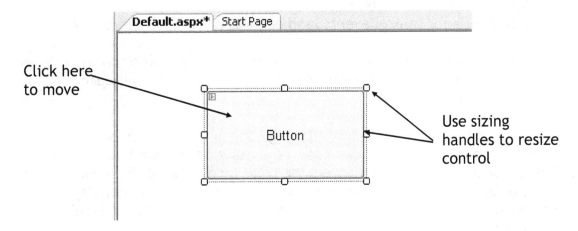

Click here to move

Use sizing handles to resize control

To delete a control, select that control so it is active (sizing handles will appear). Then, press **<Delete>** on the keyboard. Or, right-click the control. A menu will appear. Choose the **Delete** option. You can change your mind immediately after deleting a control by choosing the **Undo** option under the **Edit** menu.

Building a Web Application

To build a web application, we follow the same three steps used in building a Windows application:

1. **Draw** the user **interface** by placing controls on a web form
2. **Assign properties** to controls
3. **Write code** for control events (and perhaps write other procedures)

We've seen the web controls and how to place them on the web form. Let's see how to write code. You'll see the process is analogous to the approach we use for Windows applications.

Code is placed in the **Code Window.** Typing code in the code window is just like using any word processor. You can cut, copy, paste and delete text (use the **Edit** menu or the toolbar). You access the code window using the menu (**View**), toolbar, or by pressing <**F7**> (and there are still other ways – try double clicking a control) while the form is active. Here is the Code window for a 'blank' web application:

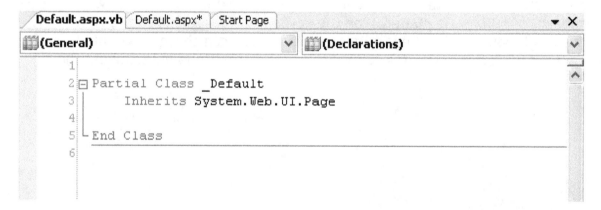

The header begins with **Partial Class.** Any web form scope level declarations are placed after this line. There is a **Page_Load** event. This is similar to the Windows form **Load** event where any needed initializations are placed.

At the top of the code window are two boxes, the **object** (or control) **list** on the left and the **procedure list** on the right. Select an object and the corresponding event procedure. A blank procedure will appear in the window where you write BASIC code. Again, this is just like we do for Windows applications. That's the beauty of web forms – there is nothing new to learn about building an application.

Once your controls are in place and code is written, you can run your web application. Before running, it is a good idea to make sure your browser is up and running. Click the **Start** button in the Visual Basic toolbar and your browser should display your application (the **aspx** file). You may see this window once started:

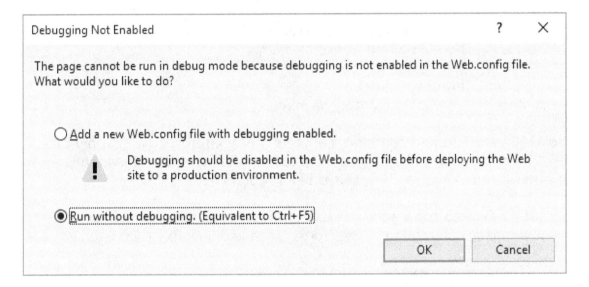

Special steps need to be taken to use the debugger with web applications. We will not take these steps. So, if this window appears, just select **Run without debugging** and click **OK**. Once running in the browser, select the **View** menu and choose **View Source** to see the actual HTML code used to produce the displayed web page.

We conclude this brief examination of web applications with a couple of examples. Study the examples for further tips on using the new ASP .NET paradigm.

Example 11-4

Loan Payments

1. The two lines of Visual Basic code that compute the monthly payment on an installment loan are:

```
Multiplier = (1 + Interest / 1200) ^ Months
Payment = Loan * Interest * Multiplier / (1200 *
(Multiplier - 1))
```

where:

Interest	Yearly interest percentage
Months	Number of months of payments
Loan	Loan amount
Multiplier	Interest multiplier
Payment	Computed monthly payment

(The 1200 value in these equations converts yearly interest to a monthly rate.) We will use this code to build a web application that computes **Payment**, given the other three variables. Yes, this is like **Problem 10-3**!

2. Start a new web application. Place four label controls, four text box controls and a button control on the web form. It should look like this:

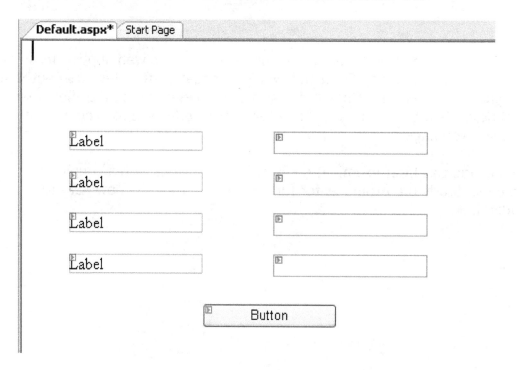

3. Set the following properties:

Label1:

Font Name	Arial
Font Size	Small
Text	Loan Amount

Label2:

Font Name	Arial
Font Size	Small
Text	Yearly Interest

Label3:

Font Name	Arial
Font Size	Small
Text	Number of Months

Label4:

Font Name	Arial
Font Size	Small
Text	Monthly Payment

TextBox1:

ID	txtLoan
Font Name	Arial
Font Size	Small

TextBox2:

ID	txtInterest
Font Name	Arial
Font Size	Small

TextBox3:

ID	txtMonths
Font Name	Arial
Font Size	Small

TextBox4:
      ID   txtPayment
      Font Name   Arial
      Font Size   Small
      ReadOnly   True

Button1:
      ID   btnCompute
      Text   Compute Payment

My finished web form looks like this:

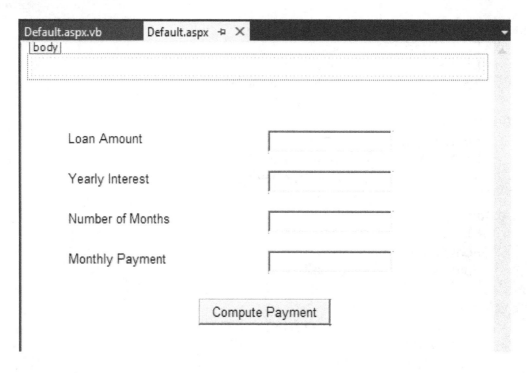

4. Use this code in the **btnCompute Click** event:

```
Private Sub BtnCompute_Click(ByVal sender As
System.Object, ByVal e As System.EventArgs) Handles
btnCompute.Click
    'Define 4 major variables
    Dim LoanAmount As Single
    Dim Interest As Single
    Dim Months As Integer
    Dim PaymentAmount As Single
    'Read text box inputs
    LoanAmount = CSng(Val(txtLoan.Text))
    Interest = CSng(Val(txtInterest.Text))
    Months = CInt(Val(txtMonths.Text))
    PaymentAmount = Payment(LoanAmount, Interest, Months)
    If PaymentAmount < 0 Then
        Exit Sub
    End If
    'Display payment
    txtPayment.Text = Format(PaymentAmount, "0.00")
    'Redefine payment to two decimals
    PaymentAmount = CSng(Val(txtPayment.Text))
End Sub
```

5. Add this **Payment** general function to compute the payment given the other parameters:

```
Private Function Payment(ByVal Loan As Single, ByVal
Interest As Single, ByVal Months As Integer) As Single
    'Compute loan payment function
    Dim Multiplier As Single
    If Months = 0 Then
        Payment = -1 ' set negative value for error flag
        Exit Function
    End If
    If Interest <> 0 Then
        Multiplier = CSng((1 + Interest / 1200) ^ Months)
        Return (Loan * Interest * Multiplier / (1200 *
(Multiplier - 1)))
    Else
        Return (Loan / Months)
    End If
End Function
```

6. Save your web application. (This application is saved in the **Example 11-4** folder in the **LearnVB\VB Code\Class 11** folder.) At this point, if things all work well, you can click the **Start** button (remember to run without debugging) and see your first web application appear in your default browser. Input some values and click **Compute Payment**. Here's a sample from my browser:

Pretty neat, huh?

Example 11-5

Loan Repayment Schedule

1. In this example, we will modify the **Loan Payment** example. After a payment is computed, we will display a repayment schedule for the loan. The display will show a month-by-month accounting of the declining balance, as the loan is paid. We will show how much of each payment goes toward principal and how much toward interest. The repayment schedule will be displayed in a data grid control (briefly mentioned when discussing database applications). Open **Example 11-4** and add a GridView control at the bottom of the form. Set these properties:

GridView1:

ID	grdPayment
Visible	False

My finished web form now looks like this:

2. Modify the **btnCompute Click** procedure to fill the grid (new code is shaded):

```
Private Sub BtnCompute_Click(ByVal sender As
System.Object, ByVal e As System.EventArgs) Handles
btnCompute.Click
    Dim LoanAmount As Single
    Dim Interest As Single
    Dim Months As Integer
    Dim PaymentAmount As Single    'Read text box inputs
    LoanAmount = CSng(Val(txtLoan.Text))
    Interest = CSng(Val(txtInterest.Text))
    Months = CInt(Val(txtMonths.Text))
    PaymentAmount = Payment(LoanAmount, Interest, Months)
    If PaymentAmount < 0 Then
      Exit Sub
    End If
    'Display payment
    txtPayment.Text = Format(PaymentAmount, "0.00")
    'Redefine payment to two decimals
    PaymentAmount = CSng(Val(txtPayment.Text))
    FillGrid(LoanAmount, Interest, Months, PaymentAmount)
  End Sub
```

3. Create a general procedure named **FillGrid** to place data in the grid control.
   Use this code:

```
Private Sub FillGrid(ByVal LoanAmount As Single, ByVal
Interest As Single, ByVal Months As Integer, ByVal
PaymentAmount As Single)
    Dim MonthNumber As Integer
    Dim Balance As Single
    Dim P As Single, I As Single
    'create data table and row objects
    Dim MyPayments As Data.DataTable
    Dim MyRow As Data.DataRow
    'Create  data table
    MyPayments = New Data.DataTable()
    'create columns
    MyPayments.Columns.Add(New Data.DataColumn("Month",
GetType(String)))
    MyPayments.Columns.Add(New Data.DataColumn("Payment",
GetType(String)))
    MyPayments.Columns.Add(New Data.DataColumn("Principal",
GetType(String)))
    MyPayments.Columns.Add(New Data.DataColumn("Interest",
GetType(String)))
```

```
      MyPayments.Columns.Add(New Data.DataColumn("Balance",
GetType(String)))
      'This assumes payment has been computed
      MonthNumber = 1 ' month number
      Balance = LoanAmount
      Do
        'Find interest
        I = Interest * Balance / 1200
        'Round to two decimals
        I = CSng(Val(Format(I, "0.00")))
        'Compute principal and balance
        If MonthNumber <> Months Then
          P = PaymentAmount - I
          Balance -= P
        Else
          'Adjust last payment to payoff balance
          PaymentAmount = Balance + I
          P = Balance
          Balance = 0
        End If
        'Create new row
        MyRow = MyPayments.NewRow
        MyRow(0) = MonthNumber
        MyRow(1) = Format(PaymentAmount, "0.00")
        MyRow(2) = Format(P, "0.00")
        MyRow(3) = Format(I, "0.00")
        MyRow(4) = Format(Balance, "0.00")
        MyPayments.Rows.Add(MyRow)
        MonthNumber += 1
      Loop Until MonthNumber > Months
      'bind data table to grid
      grdPayment.Visible = True
      grdPayment.DataSource = New Data.DataView(MyPayments)
      grdPayment.DataBind()
    End Sub
```

4. Save and run the application. (This application is saved in the **Example 11-5** folder in the **LearnVB\VB Code\Class 11** folder.) Input some values and click **Compute Payment**. The data grid should be filled with the repayment information. With the example numbers from before, my browser shows:

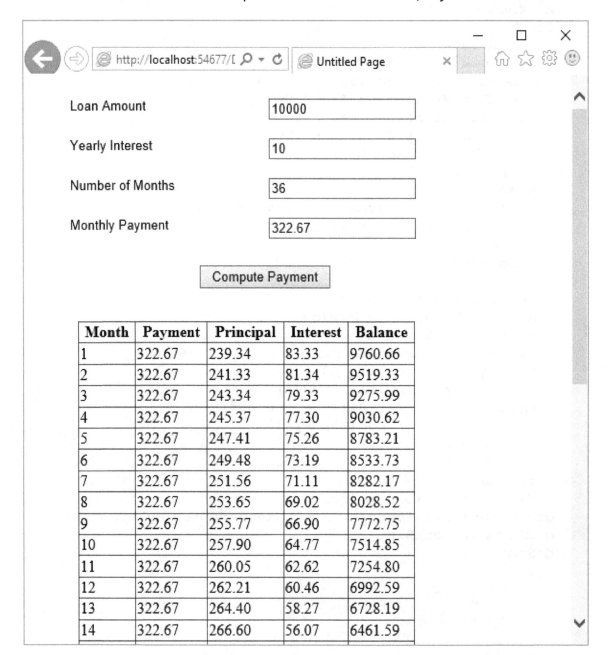

Month	Payment	Principal	Interest	Balance
1	322.67	239.34	83.33	9760.66
2	322.67	241.33	81.34	9519.33
3	322.67	243.34	79.33	9275.99
4	322.67	245.37	77.30	9030.62
5	322.67	247.41	75.26	8783.21
6	322.67	249.48	73.19	8533.73
7	322.67	251.56	71.11	8282.17
8	322.67	253.65	69.02	8028.52
9	322.67	255.77	66.90	7772.75
10	322.67	257.90	64.77	7514.85
11	322.67	260.05	62.62	7254.80
12	322.67	262.21	60.46	6992.59
13	322.67	264.40	58.27	6728.19
14	322.67	266.60	56.07	6461.59

Class Review

After completing this class, you should understand:

> - The basic structure of a relational database
> - How to use the DataSet object to connect to an Access type database
> - How to form simple SQL statements to view database tables
> - The concepts of simple and complex data binding
> - How to use the DataView object to obtain a filtered view of a DataSet object
> - The basics of Web applications
> - The three steps to build a web application using a web form
> - How to use the web form controls

Course Summary

That's all I know about Visual Basic. But, I'm still learning, as is every Visual Basic programmer out there. The new environment is vast! You should now have a good breadth of knowledge concerning the Visual Basic environment and language, especially regarding Windows applications. This breadth should serve as a springboard into learning more as you develop your own applications. Feel free to contact me, if you think I can answer any questions you might have.

Where do you go from here? In this course, we only took brief glimpses at web applications and database applications. If the Internet is your world, you should definitely extend your knowledge regarding Web applications. And, if you're into databases, study more on how to build database management systems (look at our **Visual Basic and Databases** course).

Other suggestions for further study (note that each of these topics could be a complete book by itself):

> ➤ Advanced graphics methods (including game type graphics)
> ➤ Creating and deployment of your own Windows form controls
> ➤ Creating and deployment of your own objects
> ➤ Understanding and using object-oriented concepts of overloading, inheritance, multithreading
> ➤ Advanced data access concepts, including XML (extended markup language) usage
> ➤ Creating and deployment of your own web form controls
> ➤ Database access with web applications

And, the last example:

Practice Problems 11

Problem 11-1. New DataView Problem. Modify the books database example (Example 11-3) to allow searching by title (you'll need to resort the data view object on title, as well as author).

Problem 11-2. Multiple Authors Problem. Modify the books database example (Example 11-3) such that when an author search is performed, all authors with names beginning with the searched letter are placed in a separate list box control. When the user clicks on a listed author, have the corresponding record appear.

Problem 11-3. Stopwatch Problem. Build a web application that functions as a stopwatch. Use the Visual Basic Timer function (which returns the number of seconds elapsed since midnight) to provide timing.

Exercise 11

The Ultimate Application

Design a Windows application using Visual Basic that everyone on the planet wants to buy. Place controls, assign properties, and write code. Thoroughly debug and test your application. Create a distribution and deployment package. Find a distributor or distribute it yourself through your newly created company. Become fabulously wealthy. Remember those who made it all possible by rewarding them with jobs and stock options.

More Self-Study or Instructor-Led Computer Programming Tutorials by Kidware Software

ORACLE JAVA PROGRAMMING TUTORIALS

Java™ For Kids is a beginning programming tutorial consisting of 10 chapters explaining (in simple, easy-to-follow terms) how to build a Java application. Students learn about project design, object-oriented programming, console applications, graphics applications and many elements of the Java language. Numerous examples are used to demonstrate every step in the building process. The projects include a number guessing game, a card game, an allowance calculator, a state capitals game, Tic-Tac-Toe, a simple drawing program, and even a basic video game. Designed for kids ages 12 and up.

Beginning Java™ is a semester long "beginning" programming tutorial consisting of 10 chapters explaining (in simple, easy-to-follow terms) how to build a Java application. The tutorial includes several detailed computer projects for students to build and try. These projects include a number guessing game, card game, allowance calculator, drawing program, state capitals game, and a couple of video games like Pong. We also include several college prep bonus projects including a loan calculator, portfolio manager, and checkbook balancer. Designed for students age 15 and up.

Learn Java™ GUI Applications is a 9 lesson Tutorial covering object-oriented programming concepts, using an integrated development environment to create and test Java projects, building and distributing GUI applications, understanding and using the Swing control library, exception handling, sequential file access, graphics, multimedia, advanced topics such as printing, and help system authoring. Our Beginning Java or Java For Kids tutorial is a pre-requisite for this tutorial

Programming Games with Java™ is a semester long "intermediate" programming tutorial consisting of 10 chapters explaining (in simple, easy-to-follow terms) how to build a Visual C# Video Games. The games built are non-violent, family-friendly and teach logical thinking skills. Students will learn how to program the following Visual C# video games: Safecracker, Tic Tac Toe, Match Game, Pizza Delivery, and Moon Landing. This intermediate level self-paced tutorial can be used at home or school. The tutorial is simple enough for kids yet engaging enough for beginning adults. Our Learn Java GUI Applications tutorial is a required pre-requisite for this tutorial.

Java™ Homework Projects is a Java GUI Swing tutorial covering object-oriented programming concepts. It explains (in simple, easy-to-follow terms) how to build Java GUI project to use around the home. Students learn about project design, the Java Swing controls, many elements of the Java language, and how to distribute finished projects. The projects built include a Dual-Mode Stopwatch, Flash Card Math Quiz, Multiple Choice Exam, Blackjack Card Game, Weight Monitor, Home Inventory Manager and a Snowball Toss Game. Our Learn Java GUI Applications tutorial is a pre-requisite for this tutorial

MICROSOFT SMALL BASIC PROGRAMMING TUTORIALS

Small Basic For Kids is an illustrated introduction to computer programming that provides an interactive, self-paced tutorial to the new Small Basic programming environment. The book consists of 30 short lessons that explain how to create and run a Small Basic program. Elementary students learn about program design and many elements of the Small Basic language. Numerous examples are used to demonstrate every step in the building process. The tutorial also includes two complete games (Hangman and Pizza Zapper) for students to build and try. Designed for kids ages 8+.

The Beginning Microsoft Small Basic Programming Tutorial is a self-study first semester "beginner" programming tutorial consisting of 11 chapters explaining (in simple, easy-to-follow terms) how to write Microsoft Small Basic programs. Numerous examples are used to demonstrate every step in the building process. The last chapter of this tutorial shows you how four different Small Basic games could port to Visual Basic, Visual C# and Java. This beginning level self-paced tutorial can be used at home or at school. The tutorial is simple enough for kids ages 10+ yet engaging enough for adults.

Basic Computer Games - Small Basic Edition is a re-make of the classic BASIC COMPUTER GAMES book originally edited by David H. Ahl. It contains 100 of the original text based BASIC games that inspired a whole generation of programmers. Now these classic BASIC games have been re-written in Microsoft Small Basic for a new generation to enjoy! The new Small Basic games look and act like the original text based games. The book includes all the original spaghetti code and GOTO commands!

Programming Home Projects with Microsoft Small Basic is a self-paced programming tutorial explains (in simple, easy-to-follow terms) how to build Small Basic Windows applications. Students learn about program design, Small Basic objects, many elements of the Small Basic language, and how to debug and distribute finished programs. Sequential file input and output is also introduced. The projects built include a Dual-Mode Stopwatch, Flash Card Math Quiz, Multiple Choice Exam, Blackjack Card Game, Weight Monitor, Home Inventory Manager and a Snowball Toss Game.

The Developer's Reference Guide to Microsoft Small Basic While developing all the different Microsoft Small Basic tutorials we found it necessary to write The Developer's Reference Guide to Microsoft Small Basic. The Developer's Reference Guide to Microsoft Small Basic is over 500 pages long and includes over 100 Small Basic programming examples for you to learn from and include in your own Microsoft Small Basic programs. It is a detailed reference guide for new developers.

David Ahl's Small Basic Computer Adventures is a Microsoft Small Basic re-make of the classic *Basic Computer Games* programming *book* originally written by David H. Ahl. This new book includes the following classic adventure simulations; Marco Polo, Westward Ho!, The Longest Automobile Race, The Orient Express, Amelia Earhart: Around the World Flight, Tour de France, Subway Scavenger, Hong Kong Hustle, and Voyage to Neptune. Learn how to program these classic computer simulations in Microsoft Small Basic.

MICROSOFT VISUAL BASIC & VISUAL C# PROGRAMMING TUTORIALS

LEARN VISUAL BASIC is a comprehensive college level programming tutorial covering object-oriented programming, the Visual Basic integrated development environment, building and distributing Windows applications using the Windows Installer, exception handling, sequential file access, graphics, multimedia, advanced topics such as web access, printing, and HTML help system authoring. The tutorial also introduces database applications (using ADO .NET) and web applications (using ASP.NET).

VISUAL BASIC AND DATABASES is a tutorial that provides a detailed introduction to using Visual Basic for accessing and maintaining databases for desktop applications. Topics covered include: database structure, database design, Visual Basic project building, ADO .NET data objects (connection, data adapter, command, data table), data bound controls, proper interface design, structured query language (SQL), creating databases using Access, SQL Server and ADOX, and database reports. Actual projects developed include a book tracking system, a sales invoicing program, a home inventory system and a daily weather monitor.

LEARN VISUAL C# is a comprehensive college level computer programming tutorial covering object-oriented programming, the Visual C# integrated development environment and toolbox, building and distributing Windows applications (using the Windows Installer), exception handling, sequential file input and output, graphics, multimedia effects (animation and sounds), advanced topics such as web access, printing, and HTML help system authoring. The tutorial also introduces database applications (using ADO .NET) and web applications (using ASP.NET).

VISUAL C# AND DATABASES is a tutorial that provides a detailed introduction to using Visual C# for accessing and maintaining databases for desktop applications. Topics covered include: database structure, database design, Visual C# project building, ADO .NET data objects (connection, data adapter, command, data table), data bound controls, proper interface design, structured query language (SQL), creating databases using Access, SQL Server and ADOX, and database reports. Actual projects developed include a book tracking system, a sales invoicing program, a home inventory system and a daily weather monitor.

CPSIA information can be obtained
at www.ICGtesting.com
Printed in the USA
LVHW010705150421
684482LV00006B/193